READINGS ON CHURCH AND STATE

READINGS ON CHURCH AND STATE

EDITED BY
James E. Wood, Jr.

J. M. DAWSON INSTITUTE OF CHURCH-STATE STUDIES
Baylor University • Waco, Texas 76798-7308

Published by J.M. Dawson Institute of Church-State Studies
At Baylor University
On Lake Brazos at
Waco, Texas
76798
USA

READINGS ON CHURCH AND STATE: SELECTIONS FROM
JOURNAL OF CHURCH AND STATE

© Copyright 1989 J.M. Dawson Institute of Church-State Studies
Printed in the United States of America
No part of this book may be used or reproduced
In any manner whatsoever without permission
Except in the case of brief quotations embodied
In critical articles and reviews.
For information address
J.M. Dawson Institute of Church-State Studies
Box 7308, Baylor University, Waco, Texas 76798-7308

FIRST EDITION 1989

International Standard Book Number:
Cloth ISBN 0-929182-00-6
Paper ISBN 0-929182-01-4

Contents

Preface

Religious Conscience in Colonial New England
ROBERT T. MILLER   9

A Disestablished Society: Origins of the First Amendment
EDWIN SCOTT GAUSTAD   25

Neither Church nor State: Reflections on James Madison's "Line of Separation"
SIDNEY E. MEAD   41

Living with Establishment and Disestablishment in Nineteenth-Century Anglo-America
MARTIN E. MARTY   55

American Missionary Efforts to Influence Government Indian Policy
R. PIERCE BEAVER   71

This Most Favored Nation: Reflections on the Vocation of America
WINTHROP S. HUDSON   87

Nation, Church, and Private Religion: The Emergence of an American Pattern
CONRAD CHERRY   99

The Status of the First Amendment's Religion Clauses: Some Reflections on Lines and Limits
HENRY J. ABRAHAM   109

What Hath God Wrought to Caesar: The Church as a Self-Interest Interest Group
LEO PFEFFER   127

Does Church-State Separation Necessarily Mean the
Privatization of Religion?
JAMES LEO GARRETT, JR. 141

A New Meaning for Tax Exemption?
DEAN M. KELLEY 149

The Advancement of Religion versus Teaching About
Religion in the Public Schools
NIELS C. NIELSEN, JR. 161

Religion and Americanism
WILLIAM LEE MILLER 173

A Historian's Response to the Concept of American
Civil Religion
HENRY WARNER BOWDEN 185

Colonialism and Missions: Progressive Separation
KENNETH SCOTT LATOURETTE 195

Christianity and Other Religions in a Changing World
Situation
ERNST BENZ 213

Ecumenical Perspectives of the Vatican Declaration on
Religious Liberty
A. F. CARRILLO DE ALBORNOZ 227

Embracing a Socialist Vision: The Evolution of Catholic
Social Thought, Leo XIII to John Paul II
JOHN J. MITCHELL, JR. 237

The Orthodox Churches on Church-State Relations and
Religious Liberty
JOHN S. ROMANIDES 255

The Nemesis of Christian Antisemitism
A. ROY ECKARDT 265

From Barmen (1934) to Stuttgart (1945): The Path of the
Confessing Church in Germany
FRANKLIN HAMLIN LITTELL 281

Catholic Opposition to Hitler: The Perils of Ambiguity
GORDON C. ZAHN   291

The Formulation of Religious Policy in the Soviet Union
BOHDAN R. BOCIURKIW   303

The Status of Christianity in Albania
JANICE A. BROUN   319

Religion and the State in China: Winter Is Past
JAMES E. WOOD, JR.   337

Religion and the State in Japan
NOBUHIKO TAKIZAWA   353

The Ideal Social Order in the Arab World, 1800-1968
ISMA'IL R. AL FARUQI   373

State and Religion: Religious Conflict Among Jews in Israel
EPHRAIM TABORY   385

Revolution and the Church in Nicaragua and El Salvador
BAHMAN BAKHTIARI   395

Human Rights: The Role of the State and the Church
KENNETH W. THOMPSON   423

Notes on Contributors   435

PREFACE

The subject of church and state is forever timely, but perhaps never more so than in the present period because of the phenomenal growth of nationalism, often allied with a resurgence of religion, the growing role of religion in national and international affairs, the rise of religious pluralism through out much of the modern world, the increasing encounters of world faiths with one another, the spread of authoritarian and totalitarian governments, and the growing recognition of religious liberty as an axiomatic principle basic to all human rights. Since all of these trends may be expected to continue for some time to come, tensions and even conflicts between church and state are, of course, inevitable. The widely varied, informative, and provocative essays in this volume address all of these issues and more. They are presented in this collection as an aid to inquiry and understanding.

The appearance of this volume comes upon the completion of thirty years of publication of *Journal of Church and State*. While the occasion of this publication is a commemorative one, its has a far more substantive reason for being since the essays in this volume represent three decades of scholarly reflection and research on the subject of church and state. Quite appropriately, these essays also reflect the ecumenical, interdisciplinary, and international dimensions of *JCS*, to which the journal has been committed from its founding in 1959.

The distinguished authors of these essays represent a wide variety of academic disciplines and religious traditions. While particular attention is given to the American experience of church-state relations, more than half of the essays focus on other parts of the world and on subjects of special importance in today's world. All of these essays are original works that were first published in *Journal of Church and State*. The thirty essays included in this volume constitute only a small portion of the almost six hundred essays that have been published in *JCS* during the past three decades. Nonetheless, the essays cover a wide range of topics on a subject that remains an enduring problem both for communities of faith and nation states throughout the world.

Profound appreciation is acknowledged here to the contributors of the essays in this volume and for all of those who have contributed to and have been associated with *Journal of Church and State* through the years. Particular recognition is given to Robert T. Miller, for his long and distinguished service as Associate Editor of *JCS* throughout its thirty years of publication. To all members of the Editorial Board and the Editorial Council, both past and present, a special word of gratitude is expressed. Finally, Marion Travis deserves personal mention for her able editorial assistance in the preparation of this volume for publication.

James E. Wood, Jr.

Religious Conscience in Colonial New England

ROBERT T. MILLER

Religious freedom, unlike so many other American liberties, is largely an indigenous product. It is not an inheritance transplanted from Europe by the founding fathers, but is rather the outcome of peculiarly American circumstances and problems and is the end result of a slow and oftentimes painful experience. It is perhaps not an overstatement to assert that religious liberty is "the great gift of America to civilization and to the world."[1]

The Europe on which the colonists turned their backs did not believe even in religious toleration, much less in religious liberty. "Nowhere on earth prior to 1640, unless it were in Holland, was toleration in any effective form whatsoever anything more than the dream of a few persecuted sectaries or deep private thinkers."[2] For over a thousand years previous to the settlement of America the Old World had developed the concept of a close union of church and state which had become axiomatic. The church was the mentor of the state, and the state the protector of the church. The failure properly to appreciate the mutual importance and necessity could but end in civil disorder. The civil authorities legislated for the benefit of a system of church

---

1. Sanford H. Cobb, *The Rise of Religious Liberty in America* (New York: The Macmillan Company, 1902). This is perhaps the most thorough, widely cited, and helpful single work on the history of religious liberty in this country from the earliest colonial period to the first state constitutions adopted during and immediately after the Revolution. Other beneficial historical studies concerned either primarily or incidentally with the question are: Willam W. Sweet, *Religion in Colonial America* (New York: C. Scribner's Sons, 1942); James T. Adams, *The Founding of New England* (Boston: The Atlantic Monthly Press, 1921); Robert Baird, *Religion in America; or an Account of the Origin, Progress, Relation to the State, and Present Condition of the Evangelical Churches in the United States* (New York: Harper and Brothers, 1844); and Leon Whipple, *Our Ancient Liberties, The Story of the Origin and Meaning of Civil and Religious Liberty in the United States* (New York: The H. W. Wilson Company, 1927).
2. David Masson, *The Life of Milton* (7 vols., London: Macmillan and Company, 1859-94), 3:108.

beliefs and established a particular church as the advocate of the only legally approved set of religious tenets. Uniformity, at least in the outward manifestation, was regarded as essential to national unity.

In order to enforce this uniformity, Europe of the sixteenth and seventeenth centuries was rent by both religious wars and religious persecution. Protestant dissenters were harassed in Catholic Spain and France, while Catholics received like treatment in Protestant countries. In England the particular group to be mistreated depended upon the religion of the sovereign in power at the time.

Religious persecution and the religious wars which swept France, Germany, and the Low Countries were of a particularly bloody nature because of the certainty of the persecutors and of those waging war that God was at their right hand. An outstanding church historian has commented: "Of all forms of persecution, religious persecution is the worst because it is enacted in the name of God. It violates the sacred rights of conscience, and it arouses the strongest passions."[3]

Lord Bryce, in lauding the United States upon the religious liberty and separation of church and state which he found present, wrote:

Of all the differences between the Old World and the New this is perhaps the most salient. Half the wars of Europe, half the internal troubles that have vexed European states, from the Monophysite controversies in the Roman Empire of the fifth century down to the Kulturkampf in the German Empire of the nineteenth, have arisen from theological differences or from rival claims of church and state.[4]

THE RELIGIOUS MOTIVE IN THE ENGLISH COLONIZATION OF AMERICA

The English colonization movement in North America was too complex to be attributed to any one motivating factor. Imperialism, economic and social pressures, humanitarianism, and the spirit of adventure played their part in varying degrees in the colonization effort. Too often in the early historical writings in this country these mundane elements were overlooked in stressing the spiritual urges presented by the desire either to escape the scourge of religious persecution or to respond to a missionary fervor to Christianize the natives. As a result of this undue emphasis on the religious motive for colonization, a reaction appeared which caused certain later historians to tend to minimize religion as a driving factor.[5]

---

3. Philip Schaff, *History of the Christian Church* (3rd ed.; 7 vols.; New York: C. Scribner's Sons, 1882-1910), 7:693.
4. James Bryce, *The American Commonwealth* (3rd ed.; 2 vols.; New York: The Macmillan Company, 1904), 2:695.
5. For example, Henry K. Rowe wrote in 1924, "Religion had a part in the colonization of America, but it was not the dominant factor." *The History of Religion in the United States* (New York: The Macmillan Company, 1924), 8; James T. Adams, in *The Founding of New England, advances and defends the thesis that even in theocratic Massachusetts, four out of*

Recent writers strike a balance in their analyses. Recognizing the complexity of motives behind the colonization movements, they refuse to oversimplify the issue by undue emphasis on religion. While so doing, however, they are also unwilling to deny or delete the part played by religion, and they reserve for it an important role.

If there exists any doubt as to the importance of the religious motive, one has but to examine the documents of the day to understand the significance attached to this cause for colonization by those who actually journeyed toward the unknown wilderness. In practically every statement of purpose or plan drawn up and in every charter issued, as well as in the statements of those who participated in the migration to the New World, the missionary and religious purposes are obvious.

Though the settlement of Virginia and the other southern colonies is generally assumed to have been primarily prompted by economic considerations, the laymen who set the movement afoot and the clergy who encourage it were deeply sensitive to the religious aspects. The first Charter for Virginia of 1606 emphasized the desire for:

Propagating of Christian Religion to such People, as yet live in Darkness and miserable Ignorance of the true Knowledge and Worship of God, and may in time bring the Infidels and Savages, living in those parts to human Civility, and to a settled and quiet government.[6]

Likewise, in "A True and Sincere Declaration of the purposes and ends of the Plantation begun in Virginia" set forth by the Governors and Councilors for the Plantation on 14 December 1609, it is proclaimed that:

The Principall and Maine Ends . . . we are first to preach, and baptize into Christian Religion, and by propogation of the Gospell, to recover out of the armes of the Divell, a number of poore and miserable soules, wrapt up into death, in almost invincible ignorance.[7]

Whatever private economic motives may have been present in the minds of the business men issuing these statements which sought to influence public opinion, it is significant that the religious arguments were placed first.

The Charter of New England granted in 1620 by James I to the Plymouth Company, after having noted that within "late Yeares there hath by God's Visitation raigned a wonderfull Plague, together with many horrible Slaughters, and Murthers" which had greatly reduced the native population of the area to be settled, continued:

---

five of the colonists had no sympathy for the Puritan Church but rather were primarily interested in adventure and economic advancement.

6. Benjamin P. Poore, ed., *The Federal and State Constitutions. Colonial Charters, and Other Organic Laws of the United States* (2 vols.; Washington: Government Printing Office, 1878), 2:1888.

7. Alexander Brown, *The Genesis of the United States* (2 vols.; Boston: Houghton Mifflin and Company, 1890), 1:339.

and as We trust to His Glory, Wee may with Boldness goe on to the settling of soe hopeful a Work, which tendeth to the reducing and Conversion of such Savages as remaine wandering in Desolacion and Distress, to Civil Socitie and Christian Religion. . .[8]

The Charter of Rhode Island and Providence Plantations, granted belatedly by Charles II in 1663, stated the original purpose of those petitioning for the charter as follows:

. . . that they pursueing, with peaceable and loyall mindes, their sober, serious and religious intentions, of godlie edifieing themselves, and one another, in the holie Christian ffaith and worshipp as they were peswaded; together with the gaineing over and conversione of the poore ignorant Indian natives, in those partes of America, to the sincere professione and obedienc of same faith and worship . . .[9]

The first governor of the Massachusetts Bay Colony, John Winthrop, in his *Modell of Christian Charity*, which he wrote during the voyage from England, expressed the ideal of at least a large portion of the settlers. He emphasized that instead of attempting to found a colony for profit or for the glory of the English crown the voyagers were seeking a place where they could sojourn together under a "due forme of Government both civil and ecclesiasticall" in order that they might attend to the "comforte and encrease of the body of Christe whereof we are members."[10]

In addition to the missionary spirit, a closely associated purpose drove thousands of men and women to the New World. These were they who sought for the sake of conscience and of conviction to worship God in their own way. Pilgrims, Puritans, Roman Catholics, Quakers, Huguenots, Moravians, Mennonites, and various other sects participated in the settlement of America. Each group was primarily interested in escape from a land, be it England, France, or Germany, in which they could not practice their religious tenets because of opposition or actual persecution.

The Pilgrims first left England and sought refuge from the persecution of James I in Leyden, Holland, from which city they migrated to America in 1620. The Puritans departed from England ten years later to establish a City of God in the wilderness, avowing their love for the "dear mother Church" but regarding themselves as having been subjected to penalty and persecution because of their objections to certain harmful and unscriptural exactions in its discipline and ceremony to which they could not subscribe. Pennsylvania and Delaware were instituted by William Penn chiefly as havens for the Quakers. The Roman Catholic Lord Baltimore desired Maryland as a refuge for his

---

8. Poore, 1:922.
9. Ibid., 2:1596.
10. *Collections of the Massachusetts Historical Society* (79 vols.; Cambridge: The Society, 1792-1941), 7:33.

co-religionists. Many French Huguenots migrated to South Carolina. Members of German Pietist sects such as the Moravians came to various parts of America because of opposition to their religious practices in the homeland. Thus the memory of religious persecution was vivid in the minds of many of the colonists who made the long voyage to America.

Religious Intolerance From Old to New England

It is a mistake, however, to assume that all of these early settlers so vitally interested in the advancement of religion believed in freedom of religion. The phrase "liberty of conscience" which was frequently used by the founding fathers did not mean then what it means today. Those who claimed and sought religious freedom for themselves all too often did not perceive that others of unlike beliefs were also entitled to that same liberty.

One of the paradoxes of early American colonial history was the extreme intolerance of many of those, particularly the settlers of New England, who had only recently fled to this country to escape persecution. Freedon of religion meant freedom only for their own peculiar concepts and practices. Theirs was the true and only "Way," and they were not concerned with the consciences of those who disagreed. Those who dissented must remain quiet or withdraw. "It is strange indeed," says John C. Ridpath, the historian,

that the very men who had so recently, through perils by sea and land, escaped with only their lives to find religious freedom in another continent, should have begun their career with intolerance and persecution. The only excuse that can be found for the gross inconsistency and injustice . . . is that bigotry was the vice of the age rather than of the Puritans.[11]

The sermons and general writings of the founding fathers make it clear that, far from being the champions of toleration, they opposed it bitterly. " 'Tis Satan's policy, to plead for an indefinite and boundless toleration," said Thomas Shepard,[12] As late as 1673, Uriah Oakes, President of Harvard, denounced religious freedom as the "first-born of all Abominations," while Increase Mather struck out at the "hideous clamours for liberty of Conscience."[13] In 1677, Mather declared, "I believe that antichrist hath not at this day a more probable way to ad-

---

11. John C. Ridpath, *A Popular History of the United States of America, from the Aboriginal Times to the Present Day* (Cincinnati: Jones Brothers and Company, 1877), 128.
12. Lindsay Swift, "The Massachusetts Election Sermons," *Colonial Society of Massachusetts, Publications*, I, 400, as cited in Thomas J. Wertenbaker, *The First Americans, 1607-1690* (New York: The Macmillan Co., 1927), 91.
13. Ibid.

vance his kingdom of darkness, than by a toleration of all religions and persuasions."[14]

Perhaps the most widely quoted statement regarding the opinion of the New England Puritans toward their non-conforming brethren is found in a 1645 pamphlet by Nathaniel Ward in which he wrote:

> I dare take it upon me, to bee the Herauld of *New-England* so farre, as to proclaime to the world, in the name of our Colony, that all Familists, Antinomians, Anabaptists, and other Enthusiasts, shall have free Liberty to keep away from us, and such as will come to be gone as fast as they can, the sooner the better.
>
> Secondly, I dare averre, that God doth no where in his world tolerate Christian States, to give Tolerations to such adversaries of his Truth, if they have power in their hands to suppresse them.[15]

That these were not simply idle expressions of opinion is evidenced by the many laws passed and the acts of intolerance and persecution which dot the early records of virtually every colony. Ironic as it may seem, the mother country on several occasions found it necessary to admonish the colonial governments for their illiberal actions. In 1679, Charles II wrote to the governor of Massachusetts criticizing that government for the persecution of those who did "not agree in the Congregational way." In 1651, Sir Richard Saltonstall wrote to John Cotton and John Wilson, leaders of the Massachusetts Puritans, in the same vein:

> It doth not a little grieve my spirit what sadd things are reported dayly of your tyranny and persecution in New England . . . . These rigid wayse have layd you very lowe in the hearts of the saynts. I doe assure I have heard them pray in the publique assemblies that the Lord would give you meeke and humble spirits, not to stryve soe much for uniformity as to keepe the unity of the Spirit in the bond of peace.[16]

New World Establishments — Massachusetts Bay

The leaders of the Massachusetts Bay Colony were Church of England men who made it clear from the outset that they did not separate from the Church of England, nor from the ordinances of God, but only from the corruptions and disorders of that Church: that they came away from the Common-Prayer and Ceremonies.[17] They had no basic objection to a state church. They were intent on perpetuating their own tenets and their form of worship, and in order to do so they

---

14. *Sermons*, 106, as cited in Isaac Backus, *Church History of New England from 1620 to 1804* (Philadelphia: American Baptist Society, 1853), 119.
15. Nathaniel Ward, *The Simple Cobbler of Aggawam in America*, (Boston: James Munroe and Company, 1843), 3.
16. Isaac Backus, *A Church History of New England* (3 vols.; Boston: Edward Draper, 1777), 1:246.
17. Cotton Mather, *Magnalia Christi Americana; or the Ecclesiastical History of New England from its first planting in the year 1620 into the year of our Lord, 1698* (London: T. Parkhurst, 1702), Book 1:13.

established a Puritan state-church, Congregationalism, which gradually took the place of the Anglican state-church to which they were accustomed in England.

Having established their Bible Commonwealth, they were fully prepared to further it and protect it from invocation by the authority of the civil law. They expected the state to support public worship and suppress heresy.[18] The theocratic state had its chief interest centered in the church, and there always existed the closest possible degree of co-operation between the officials of the community and the ministers of the church. Not only the religious interests, but the social and political life as well centered around the church. The ministers, who were regarded as "chosen men of God," were also leaders in public affairs and their opinions carried great weight though they might hold no public office.

Theocracy was the form of government recommended in Holy Writ; democracy was government unfit for pious men. "Democracy, I do not conceyve that ever God did orderyn as a fitt government eyther for church or commonwealth," said the Reverend John Cotton of Boston. "If the people be governors who shall be governed? As for monarchy, and aristocracy, they are both of them clearly approved, and directed in scripture ... and setteth up Theocracy ... as the best forme of government in the commonwealth, as well as in the church."[19]

Governor Winthrop agreed wholeheartedly as to the lack of scriptural warrant for democracy, "the meanest and worst of all forms of government." He held that power should be kept "in the hands of those whose Christian calling is to govern and that their number should remain as small as possible."[20] The franchise was soon limited to church membership in 1631,

---

18. Although it is customary to refer to the Puritan colonies, and especially to Massachusetts, as theocracies, the aptness of the term has been challenged by various authorities in the field. Charles M. Andrews, for example, says that "Massachusetts was not a theocracy, as it has too often been called, for the influence of the clergy was entirely unofficial and without the sanction of law." *The Colonial Period of American History* (4 vols.; New Haven: Yale University Press, 1934-38), 1:448. Other historians have made the same point, but commenting upon this distinction, Ernest S. Bates says, "This argument seems to the present writer a legalistic splitting of hairs." *American Faith: Its Religious, Political and Economic Foundations* (New York: W. W. Norton and Co., 1940), 124. Andrews, himself agrees that "there are times when, in some respects, the functions of church and state would seem to have been interchangeable." Andrews, 450.
19. Thomas Hutchinson, *The History of the Colony and Province of Massachusetts-Bay* (3 vols.; Cambridge: Harvard University Press, 1936), 1:415. Cotton Mather, *Magnalia Christi*, Book III, 21, states the opinion of the Reverend John Cotton in this fashion: "Mr. Cotton effectually recommended it unto them, that none should be Electors, nor Elected therein, except such as were visible subjects of our Lord Jesus Christ, personally confederated in our Churches. In these, and many other ways, he propounded unto them, an Endeavour after a Theocracy, as near as might be, to that which was the Glory of Israel, the peculiar People."
20. *Collections of the Mass. Hist. Soc.*, "Winthrop Papers," 1:5.

to the end that the body of the comons may be pserved of honest & good men, it was likewise ordered and agreed that for time to come noe man shalbe admitted to the freedome of this body polliticke, but such as are members of some of the churches within the lymitts of the same.[21]

A resident of the colony, whether a citizen or not, was under obligation to support both the state and the church. In 1638 the General Court declared:

> Every inhabitant of any towne is lyable to contribute to all charges, both in church & comon welth, whereof hee doth or may receive benefit; & withall it is also ordered, that every such inhabitant who shall not volentarily contribute, pportionably to his ability, with other freemen of the same towne, to all comon charges, as well for upholding the ordinances in the churches as otherwise shalbe compelled thereto by assessment & distress to bee levied by the cunstable, or other officer of the towne.[22]

The inhabitants were also required to attend preaching on the Sabbath, and absence from church without legitimate cause rendered the offender liable to a fine of five shillings. In 1658 the General Court was given power as to the ordination or continued ministries of any preacher, since it was declared to be the "duty of the Christian magistrate to take care the people be fed with wholesome & sound doctrine . . . "[23] State control was made complete in 1679 when the building of meeting-houses was prohibited without permission from the freemen of the town or the General Court.

The Word of God and the ministers of the Word alike were to be free from criticism or contempt, and punishment for such contempt for a second offender was either to pay a fine of five pounds or to "stand two hours openly upon a block 4 foote high, on a lecture day, with a pap fixed on his breast, with this, A WANTON GOSPELLER, written in capitall letters, yt othrs may fear & be ashamed of breaking out into the like wickedness."[24] There was no place for heretics and blasphemers. In addition to fines for numerous types of "heresy," the law set forth the fate of the blasphemer as death.

Although there were undoubtedly those who failed to comply with the many religious laws and who yet escaped any official punishment,

---

21. Nathaniel B. Shurtleff, ed., *Records of the Governor and Company of the Massachusetts Bay in New England* (5 vols.; Boston: William White, 1853-54), 1:87.
22. Ibid., 1:240-41.
23. Ibid., 2:4, Part 1, 328. In order to see that the law concerning church attendance was enforced as well as to preserve order and guarantee attention within the meeting place, the quaint office of tithingman was created. In 1644, for example, in Salem two men were "appointed every Lord's day to walke forth in the time of God's worshippe, to take notice of such as either lye about the meeting-howse without attending to the word or ordinances, or that lye at home or in the fields, w'thout giving good account thereof, and to take the names of such persons & to present them to the Magistrate, whereby they may be accordinglie proceeded against." Town Records of Salem, 131, Part 1, 1634-1659, published in the *Historical Collections of the Essex Institute* (35 vols.; Salem, Mass.: Published for the Essex Institute, 1859-1919), Second Series, Vol. 1.
24. Act of 4 November 1646, *Records of Massachusetts*, 2:179.

that the civil authorities were not lax in their punishment of reported breaches is evidenced by the many notations in the records of the day. One Hugh Buet, being found guilty of "heresy," was ordered to leave the colony within three weeks or be hanged. Two others were imprisoned for criticizing the clergy; and for a like offense, Katherine Finch was condemned to be whipped.

With the clergy and the magistracy in agreement as to the religious doctrine and discipline, no small amount of courage was required to stand up against them openly. Fine, imprisonment, or banishment would surely follow. As a result, most dissidents outwardly complied though privately rebelling against the system. However, from time to time there appeared on the scene stubborn "troublers of Israel" who refused to be silent. Perhaps the most famous instance of dissent and discipline was the Antinomian controversy in the years 1636-1638. This struggle within the church resulted in the sentencing and banishment of a number of those who openly refused to conform and who spoke against certain practices of the established Congregational Church which were deemed essential to salvation. The best known figures to be purged from the colony at this time were Roger Williams, Mrs. Anne Hutchinson, and the Reverend John Wheelwright.[25]

If little sympathy were shown to protesting members of the recognized church, even less could be expected by members of other religious faiths. For those outside the confines of the established churches who dared disturb the religious peace of the community, an even more arbitrary and cruel treatment was prescribed. Roman Catholics were not allowed to live in the colony, and in 1647 Jesuits were forbidden to enter under penalty of banishment for the first offense, and death if they returned. Few if any accounts of Catholic persecution exist, but only because the Catholics did not attempt to enter.

Baptists and Quakers bore the brunt of the persecutions. In 1644 the General Court ordered the banishment of all Anabaptists,[26] and persecutions were numerous. The most notable case occurred in 1651 near Lynn when John Clarke and Obadiah Holmes were arrested while holding a meeting in a friend's home, haled before the court, and sentenced to pay a fine or, in default, to be whipped. Clarke's fine was

---

25. The literature on the Antinomian controversy is extensive. The classic account is that of Charles F. Adams, *Three Episodes in Massachusetts History* (2 vols.; Boston: Houghton Mifflin and Company, 1893), 1:363-532; 2:533-578. See also the work edited by the same author, *Antinomianism in the Colony of Massachusetts Bay, 1636-1638* (Boston: The Prince Society, 1894.)
26. James K. Hosmer, ed. *Records of Massachusetts*, Vol. 2; John Winthrop, *Winthrop's Journal, History of New England, 1630-1649*, (2 vols.; New York: C. Scribner's Sons, 1900), 2:177.

paid for him, but Holmes was "whipped unmercifully" on the streets of Boston.[27]

The treatment of the Quakers was even harsher. Ship captains were forbidden under penalty of fine to bring them to the colony. Persons found in a Quaker meeting were to be imprisoned for three days on bread and water, and in October, 1647, the General Court provided:

> If any Quaker or Quakers shall presume, after they have once suffered whate the lawe requireth, to come into this jurisdiction every such male Quaker shall for the first offenc have one of his eares cutt off, and be kept as at worke in the howse of correction till he cann be sent away at his own charge, and for the second offenc shall have his other eare cutt off . . . and every woman Quaker . . . shall be severely whipt, and kept at the howse of correction at worke till she shall be sent away . . . and for every Quaker, he or she, that shall a third time herein againe offend, they shall have theire tongues bored through with a hot iron . . . .[28]

If all these measures failed, the persistent Quakers were to be put to death. Under these severe enactments, Marmaduke Stevenson, William Robinson, William Leddra, and one woman, Mary Dyer, were hanged. Several were mutilated or branded; at least two were known to have died from starvation and whipping, and several hundred were imprisoned.

The most disgraceful episode of all, perhaps, was that of the witchcraft craze which sprang up and passed almost in the span of the year 1692. During this brief period the jails were filled with unfortunates, usually old women, accused of witchcraft. Twenty-two of these victims were condemned in a Salem court; two died while in jail; and nineteen were hanged. It should be said to their honor that the men of Massachusetts soon repented of this shameful work. The twelve jurors in the case published a declaration of sorrow, and Samuel Sewall made public confession of his sense of guilt in South Church in 1697, "asking pardon of men, And especially desiring prayers that God . . . would pardon that sin and all others of his sins . . . ."[29] The general revulsion and penance arising from the witchcraft incidents undoubtedly

---

27. Backus, *A Church History of New England*, 1:207-72, gives a detailed account of this instance and many other illustrations of persecution and discrimination against the Baptists. President Dunster of Harvard was forced to resign his position because he refused to allow his child to be baptized. Stephen Winthrop, while serving in Cromwell's army, wrote his father in 1645 that "here is great complaine agt us for or severetye agt Aanabaptists." *Collections of the Mass. Hist. Soc.*, Series 5, 9:200.
28. *Records of Massachusetts*, 4, Part I, 308, 345-46, 349, 367, 383. The trials and tribulations of the mistreated Quakers are chronicled in Rufus M. Jones, *The Quakers in the American Colonies* (London: The Macmillan Company, 1911).
29. Samuel Sewall, *Diary*, 1:445, as found in *Collections of the Mass. Hist. Soc.*, Vols. 5 and 6. Many accounts of the witchcraft delusion have been recorded, and perhaps it has been exaggerated beyond its true scope. The most lengthy account on the general subject of "witchcraft" is George L. Kittredge, *"Witchcraft in Old and New England"* (Cambridge: Harvard University Press, 1929).

had a most desirable ultimate effect as they hastened the removal of the theocratic hold upon the colony. Barrett Wendell, in his account of the life of Cotton Mather, in commenting upon the effect, says, "It was the great tragedy of witchcraft, I think, that finally broke the power of theocracy."[30]

OTHER NEW ENGLAND ESTABLISHMENTS

The punishment of dissenters was never as prominent in the other Congregational colonies as in Massachusetts. A more liberal policy prevailed in Plymouth, though its records are not without blemish. As early as 1645 a majority of the House of Delegates was in favor of a resolution for a "full and free toleration of religion of all men," without "exception against Turk, Jew, Papist, Arian, Socinian, Familist, or any other," but the governor would not put the question to a vote, so it failed to become law.[31] In 1650, to protect the established church, it was forbidden to organize any churches or public meetings diverse from those already set up, without approval of the government; and in 1651 church attendance was encouraged by a ten shilling penalty for those neglecting such attendance. At first, the ministers were maintained by voluntary contributions, but in 1657 taxes were levied in each township for the support of "an able Godly Teaching Minnester which is approved by this Government."[32] The records of the Court of the colony show that the collection of these ministerial fees was strictly enforced. Plymouth also joined in the hue and cry against the Quakers by legislation in 1657 and 1658. Quaker literature was banned, their meetings were prohibited, and their presence was to be followed by fine, imprisonment, and banishment; but they were not made subject to death or injury to life or limb.

The founding of Connecticut, under the leadership of Thomas Hooker, was in large degree a protest against the theocracy of Massachusetts. Yet, the Fundamental Orders of Connecticut drawn up in 1639 was a thoroughly Puritan document in that its declared purpose was not only to establish "an orderly and decent Government," but also to "mayntayne and prseave the liberty and purity of the gospell of our Lord Jesus wch we now prfesse, as also the disciplyne of the Churches . . . ."[33] There was no formal church membership qualifica-

---

30. Barrett Wendell, *Cotton Mather, the Puritan Priest* (Cambridge: Harvard University Press, 1926), 88.
31. George Bancroft, *History of the United States, From the Discovery of the American Continent* (6 vols.; New York: D. Appleton and Company, 1891-1892), 1:214.
32. *Records of the Colony of New Plymouth in New England* (12 vols.; Boston: William White, 1855-1861), 11:67.
33. Poore, 1:249.

tion for the suffrage, but the governor was required to be a member of some "approved congregation." In 1717 an act provided for the election of the town minister by the voters and the town was authorized to levy taxes for his support. Connecticut enacted legislation against the Quakers in 1657 and 1658, but the laws were far less harshly applied than in the Massachusetts Bay colony.[34]

The short-lived New Haven colony undertook to establish a theocracy even more strict than that of Massachusetts. The entire organization was religious. The "seven pillars" of the New Haven Church were the magistrates of the town and they also chose the colonial governor. They also served as judges, and disposed of trial by jury because no authority could be found for it in the laws of Moses. None but church members could vote, the churches were supported by taxes, and church absence was punishable by fine. Although the famous "Blue Laws" of New Haven, published in 1781 by the Reverend Samuel Peters of London, were no more than figments of the satirical imagination of that worthy, the fictitious laws did not much exceed in severity the actual laws of the colony.[35] The rumor of Quakers awoke the usual frenzy in New Haven, and in 1658 an elaborate act against that group was passed. Both the Quakers and their writings were prohibited. Though the death penalty was not provided, hard labor, branding and banishment were all included as punishments for those holders of diabolical doctrines.

New Hampshire, as did Rhode Island and Connecticut, owed its origin in large part to the intolerance of the Bay Colony. John Wheelwright, upon his banishment from the commonwealth in 1638, departed with a number of friends for the Piscataqua. They were joined later in the year by others; and in 1639 the three settlements of Exeter, Hampton, and Dover associated themselves in an "Agreement" in which the religious foundation of the colony was evident, but which failed to provide for a theocratic system. The franchise was not dependent upon a profession of religious faith. However, the church was established and tithes were assessed and collected under the civil law.

From 1641 to 1679 New Hampshire was under the control of Massachusetts and hence under its laws. However, in the latter year this union was dissolved by royal order, and the instructions to the

---

34. Cobb, 261, states that there was no persecution under these acts. Paul E. Lauer, "Church and State in New England," *John Hopkins University Studies*, vol. 10, Nos. 2, 3, Baltimore: 1892, 136, says simply, "They were imprisoned until they could be sent out of the colony." Lauer's work presents a fine study of the colonial church-state situation in the New England Colonies.
35. For an account of these forgeries of Peters as well as the actual blue laws, see J. Hammond Trumbull, *The True-Blue Laws of Connecticut and New Haven and the False Blue-Laws Invented by Rev. Samuel Peters* (Hartford: American Publishing Company, 1876). A very readable account of the various Sunday observance laws throughout New England is found in Alice M. Earle, *The Sabbath in Puritan New England* (New York: Charles Scribner's Sons, 1892).

commissioners commanded that "liberty of conscience shall be allowed unto all protestants" although those conforming to the rites of the Church of England were to be "particularly countenanced and encouraged."[36] Governor Cranfield, who arrived in 1682, even in the face of these instructions attempted to force the Church of England on the colony, but after a flurry of harassment of Congregational ministers for refusal to conform, the governor was recalled and no further effort was made to convert the churches to Episcopacy.

An Experiment in Liberty

The shining exception to the general New England pattern of religious intolerance and establishment was the little colony of Rhode Island. In point of religious liberty, Rhode Island unquestionably holds the foremost rank among the colonies. It never had an established church, and from the beginning it was free from the taint of religious persecution. Driven out of Massachusetts in 1636 because of his denial of the jurisdiction of the State over the consciences of men, the factious but fearless Roger Williams established a settlement at Providence. There, joined by exiles and dissenters from the other colonies, he put into operation the principles of religious and civil liberty for which he had contended in vain in the Bay Colony. Rhode Island was raised up as a standing, conscious protest against the religious intolerance of the day, and dedicated "to hold forth a livilie experiment, that a most flourishing civill state may stand and best bee maintained . . . with a full libertie of religious concernements."[37]

In his best known work, Williams propounded his ideas respecting religious freedom and complete separation of church and state, after having tested them empirically for eight years. They represented a belief advanced beyond the times and clearly foreshadowed the doctrines of a much later American age. They are milestones of religious liberty worthy of repetition:

All civil states, with their officers of justice, in their respective constitutions and administrations are proved essentially civil, and therefore not judges, governors, or defenders of the spiritual or Christian state and worship.

It is the will and command of God that (since the coming of his Son the Lord Jesus) a permission of the most Paganish, Jewish, Turkish, or anti-christian consciences and worships be granted to all men in all nations and countries: and they are only to be fought against with that sword which is only (in soul matters) able to conquer: to wit, the sword of God's Spirit, the word of God.

. . . God requireth not an uniformity of religion to be enacted and enforced in any civil state; which enforced uniformity (sooner or later) is the greatest occasion of civil

---

36. Nathaniel Boutan, et al., eds., Provincial and State Papers of New Hampshire (33 vols.; Concord: 1867-1915), 1:378.
37. The Charter of Rhode Island and Providence Plantations, 1663, Poore, 2:1596.

war, ravishing of conscience, persecution of Christ Jesus in his servants, and of the hypocrisy and destruction of million of souls.

... An enforced uniformity of religion throughout a nation or civil state, confounds the civil and religious, denies the principles of Christianity and civility, and that Jesus Christ is come in the flesh.[38]

Rhode Island's practices were consistent with her founder's theories. In a "Plantation Agreement" at Providence in 1640 it was agreed "as formerly hath bin the liberties of the town, so still, to hould forth liberty of Conscience."[39] In 1641, the General Court of Election ordered further that "none bee accounted a Delinquent for *Doctrine*: Provided, it be not directly repugnant to ye Government or Lawes established." The same body elaborated in its 1647 acts by decreeing:

All men may walk as their consciences perswade them, every one in the name of his God. And lett the Saints of the Most High walk in this Colonie without Molestation in the name of Jehovah, their God for Ever and Ever ...[40]

From the spirit of these liberal pronouncements Rhode Island never varied. In 1663 a charter was issued by the king which recognized and further guaranteed religious liberty. No Sabbath-observance legislation was enacted, and though the offense of witchcraft appears on the statute books, no prosecutions were ever had under the witchcraft law. To the great consternation of neighboring colonies, Quakers were admitted to Rhode Island although their doctrines and activities were personally objectionable to the founder. When a bill of outlawry of Quakers was proposed in 1665, the people protested to such a degree that it failed of enactment. The only doubtful laws ever to mar the Rhode Island statutes appeared about the beginning of the eighteenth century. These acts seem to have denied the full right of citizenship to Catholics and Jews. However, the authenticity of the law concerning the Catholics has been generally questioned by historians, and both Catholics and Jews at later dates freely settled in Rhode Island, and members of both faiths were on numerous occasions granted citizenship upon application to the Assembly.[41] The record of Rhode Island

---

38. Roger Williams, "The Bloudy Tenent, of Persecution, for cause of Conscience, discussed, in A conference betweene Truth and Peace" (1664) in Samuel L. Caldwell, ed., *Publications of the Narragansett Club* (First Series, Providence, 1867), 3:3-4. Two competent biographies of Williams in which his ideas concerning religious liberty are carefully discussed are: James E. Ernst, *Roger Williams, New England Firebrand* (New York: The Macmillan Company, 1932), and Samuel H. Brockunier, *The Irrepressible Democrat, Roger Williams* (New York: The Ronald Press Company, 1940).
39. John R. Bartlett, ed., *Records of the Colony of Rhode Island and Providence Plantations in New England,* (10 vols.; Providence: 1856-1865), 1:28.
40. Ibid., 113, 190.
41. Samuel G. Arnold, *History of the State of Rhode Island and Providence Plantations* (2 vols.; New York: D. Appleton and Company, 1859-1860), 1:493; Lauer, 175. *The Records of Rhode Island*, conclude, (2:36-37), that "It cannot, therefore, be believed that any sect was excluded from their civil rights for their religious opinions." In 1738 the Rhode Island Assembly took note of the "interpolations" by extending all rights to Catholics. Ibid., 9:674-5.

with respect to religious liberty was a unique and happy one on the colonial stage and subsequent generations are heavily indebted to the convictions and tenacity of its founder, Roger Williams.

Religious Liberty and Disestablishment

At the end of the seventeenth century the old Puritan order was still firmly entrenched in the New England colonies, but the handwriting was on the wall. Except in Rhode Island, the Congregational Church was still supported by public taxes paid by dissenters as well as communicants. However, after Charles II had felt called upon to rebuke the Massachusetts authorities for their persecutions and high-handed methods, and after their charter had been revoked in 1685, the new charter of 1691, which united Plymouth and Massachusetts Bay, granted "liberty of conscience to all Christians, except Papists." The church membership qualification was superseded by property qualification. Persecutions of Baptists and Quakers gradually died out, and in 1729 an act was passed exempting these two groups from taxation for the support of ministers.[42] Other extenuating acts were passed in the years that followed, but it was not until 1818 that Connecticut in its new constitution completely destroyed the establishment. The church died even harder in Massachusetts, in which the year 1833 finally saw its disestablishment. In New Hampshire separate legislative acts of 1792, 1804, 1805, and 1817 gave exemptions to Episcopalians, Baptists, Universalists, and Methodists. In 1819 an act gave freedom to all Christian sects. As usual, the spirit of the times was ahead of the laws, and state persecution for religious conscience's sake had ceased to plague New England long before the enactment of these formal liberalizing statutes.

It is difficult to judge the leaders of New England with any degree of fairness. By our standards, their concepts of the proper relationship of church and state, with some notable exceptions, were not oppressive, unreasonable, and unwise. Their extreme intolerance in word and deed is most unworthy of their many unquestioned Christian virtues. Nonetheless, the harshness of our judgment must be tempered by the knowledge of the character of the times in which they lived. They were intolerant men. However, they were, after all, but products of their age, and just as they largely transferred their social and political customs to the new land, so they sought to transplant the Old-World

---

42. The Baptists, in order to secure exemption, were required to furnish certificates signed by "two principal members of the persuasion." A complete account of the final struggle for religious liberty and disestablishment in New England is found in Joseph E. Thorning, *Religious Liberty in Transition* (Washington, D. C.: The Catholic University of America, 1931).

patterns of church-state relations and intolerance to the New. The transplantation flourished in the new soil for too long a time; but long before Europe had shaken loose her shackles of coerced religious conformity, the development of a fresh and more wholesome conscience brought forth by the end of the colonial period a wider freedom of religion, even in reluctant New England, than had been achieved anywhere in the Old World.

A Disestablished Society: Origins of the First Amendment

EDWIN SCOTT GAUSTAD

As the American Revolution was being won and its blessings of liberty were being secured, another revolution was taking place. A deliberate, peaceful, voluntary separation of church and state was revolution enough to distinguish the modern from the medieval world. That separation was also revolution enough to close a long, turbulent, bloody chapter of Christian history that had begun some 1400 years before in the fourth century A.D. It is this fundamental alteration in the institutions of politics and religion that is examined here.

How did disestablishment come about? Far from the commonplace thing to do, it was an almost unthinkable thing to do. Far from the proven and safe course of action, it was widely condemned and deeply feared. Far from a path of least resistance, it was a path filled with obstacle, accusation, imprecation, and threat. Yet, it happened. And our immediate task is to attempt to explain why. Four sources of sentiment for disestablishment, not equal in strength, will be considered: the principles of radical religion; the pragmatism of conservative religion; the position of natural religion; and the indifference to and hostility toward religion.

I

Radical religion requires some definition, but none will be wholly satisfactory. In general, as used here, radical religion refers to those Protestant bodies steadily opposed to alliances of church and state, those withdrawing sectarians more concerned in personal than in social redemption. The Anabaptists of the sixteenth century, sometimes called the Left-Wing of the Reformation, comprise the continental fountainhead for this deep river of religion which finds authority in direct encounter with God. The less mediation the better, whether that mediation be by state, by society, by school, or even by church. In America, Quakers and Baptists represent this stream most conspicuously but other groups in the eighteenth century, e.g., Presbyterians, Separate Congregationalists, Mennonites, Jews, and the like, often swam in the same current. The convictions of William Penn and Roger Williams are well known; partly for that reason, but also partly because of their historical proximity, consideration will be given to later men actively engaged in constitutional deliberations.

It is a commonplace that men are not to be understood apart from their times, but of no persons is this more conspicuously true than Isaac Backus (1724-1806) and John Leland (1754-1841).[1] Born in Norwich, Connecticut, in 1724, Backus grew up in the fold of established Congregationalism. But within his home there was strong opposition to the Saybrook Platform, and when the Norwich Church adopted that "presbyterianizing" plan, the Backus family voiced its objections. Under the sway of the Great Awakening, Backus was converted in June of 1741, joining the Norwich church with much misgiving the following year. In 1746 he withdrew from this church along with twelve others to form a New Light church. After a stormy eight-year pastorate, during which time Backus gradually adopted Baptist views, he participated in the organization of the First Baptist Church of nearby Middleborough. On June 23, 1756, he was ordained pastor of this flock, a relationship which was continued for the remaining fifty-two years of his life.

John Leland was born in Grafton, Massachusetts, in 1754, also of Congregational parents. At the age of twenty, John was baptized, and soon found that he possessed some talent in exhorting and preaching. In September of 1776 he was married, and went to Virginia for fifteen years of effective and popular ministry. In March 1791 Leland with his family (wife and eight children), left Virginia for New England, settling (if that word may every be accurately applied to Leland) ultimately in Cheshire, Massachusetts. From this position, Leland itinerated widely and almost unceasingly, preaching with vigor and effect up to his very last days.

Both Backus and Leland spent much time in seeking to make the distinction between civil and ecclesiastical government unmistakably clear. A casual survey of the titles of their published works is one convenient and convincing evidence of this. As agent for the Warren

---

1. On Backus, see the superior biography by William McLoughlin, *Isaac Backus and the American Pietistic Tradition* (Boston: Little, Brown & Co., 1967) as well as his edition of major Backus pamphlets: *Isaac Backus on Church, State and Calvinism* (Cambridge, Mass.: Harvard University Press, 1968). On Leland, see Lyman Butterfield, *Elder John Leland, Jeffersonian Itinerant,* (Worcester, Mass.: American Antiquarian Society, 1953) and L. F. Greene, ed., *The Writings of the Late Elder John Leland....*, (New York: G. W. Wood, 1845; reprint, Arno Press, 1970).

Association in Rhode Island and environs, Backus was charged with the responsibility of obtaining relief from the meddling of civil government in religious affairs. Leland not only labored for adequate protection of freedoms on a national level but also, unlike Backus, lived to participate in the battle for disestablishment both in Connecticut (1818) and in Masschusetts (1832).

In 1774 Backus was sent by the Warren Association to the Continental Congress with a memorial seeking redress of grievances long endured by the New England Baptists. The document which Backus carried to Philadelphia reviewed the history of intolerance in New England, the several temporary laws granting measures of relief when honestly administered, and the continuing assumption by the state that noble concessions were being made rather than inalienable rights being recognized. Backus sought freedom, not toleration. In his own church, he had fought through a great many of the involved, interminable, and usually unsatisfying litigations. He ultimately refused even to issue a certificate to civil authorities, indicating who were members of his church—for this was a tacit acknowledgment of the right of the state to interfere. Backus' mother and brother had both been imprisoned in 1752 for refusal to pay the tax to support a minister whom they did not hear. Thus the matter was far from academic, though John Adams protested that the Massachusetts establishment was a "slender thing," hardly deserving the name. The Memorial presented by Backus concluded:

It may now be asked—What is the liberty desired? The answer is: as the kingdom of Christ is not of this world, and religion is a concern between God and the soul with which no human authority can intermeddle; consistently with the principles of Christianity, and according to the dictates of Protestantism, we claim and expect the liberty of worshipping God according to our consciences, not being obliged to support a ministry we cannot attend .... These we have an undoubted right to, as men, as Christians, and by charter as inhabitants of Massachusetts Bay.[2]

Later in the same year Backus again represented the cause of his co-religionists, this time before the Massachusetts legislature. The principle of "taxation without representation" seemed like a timely one to draw upon in an area where a tea party had recently been held. Backus argued:

That which has made the greatest noise, is a tax of three pence a pound upon tea; but your law of last June laid a tax of the same sum every year upon the Baptists in each parish, as they would expect to defend themselves against a greater one. And only because the Baptists in Middleboro' have refused to pay that little tax, we hear that the first parish in said town have this fall voted to lay a greater tax upon us. All America are alarmed at the tea tax; though, if they please, they can avoid it by not

---

2. Alvah Hovey, *A Memoir of the Life and Times of the Rev. Isaac Backus* (Boston: Gould & Lincoln, 1859), 210.

buying the tea; but we have not such liberty. We must either pay the little tax, or else your people appear even in this time of extremity, determined to lay the great one upon us. But these lines are to let you know, that we are determined not to pay either of them; not only upon your principle of not being taxed where we are not represented, but also because we dare not render that homage to any earthly power, which I and many of my brethren are fully convinced belongs only to God. Here, therefore, we claim charter rights, liberty of conscience.[3]

For John Leland, it was not enough to say that the state should not impede or obstruct the progress of any religion; neither should it show any official recognition to religion as such. On the one hand no special tax should be levied against ministers, but just as surely, on the other, they were not to be exempt from taxation, or military service, or any thing else required of citizens at large. "The law should be silent about them; protect them as citizens, not as sacred officers, for the civil law knows no sacred officers." Religion is not in any direct way the concern of the state.

Government has no more to do with the religious opinions of men, than is has with the principles of mathematics. Let every man speak freely without fear, maintain the principles that he believes, worship according to his own faith, either one God, three Gods, no God, or twenty Gods; and let government protect him in so doing, i.e., see that he meets with no personal abuse, or loss of property, for his religious opinions.[4]

Leland many times defended the right of the state to punish behavior that is contrary to good law, no matter how "religious" the motivation of such behavior might be. But the state can only punish for untoward action, not for opinion or belief. If a man in any way disturbs "the peace and good order of the civil police, he should be punished according to his crime, let his religion be what it will." But when there has been no violation of the civil order, then that same man should be unmolested, even protected, in his peaceable worship of God in accordance with the dictates of his own conscience.

Leland's laissez faire views caused him to question the propriety of military and legislative chaplains, particularly if they were paid for out of the public treasury. (And he was not reassured when on the occasion of Thomas Jefferson's showing him around the senate he espied the official chaplain *reading* his prayers from a book. He remarked to the President that the minister needed the eyes of a goose, so that with one eye he could look up to heaven, while with the other he could read his prayer.) If there must be such chaplains, Leland pleaded that they be supported by private and voluntary contribution. By the same principle, the government (either state or federal) should have nothing to do with sabbatarian legislation. It is even questionable whether Sun-

---

3. Ibid., 220f.
4. Green, *The Writings of John Leland*, 184.

day has the same divine command behind it that the Jewish Sabbath did, but if Jesus did appoint the day to be observed, "he did as the head of the church, and not as the king of nations." Leland points out that he is not "an enemy of holy days," as such, but that whatever fixed times are established for religious duties they are to be set "by the mutual agreement of religious societies, according to the word of God, and not by civil authority."

Leland and Backus strove for this degree of religious freedom neither for their own sakes nor for that of the communion of which they were members. It was for Christ's sake. Churches founded on civil law, Leland wrote, may "call themselves churches of Christ, but in reality, they are creatures of the state." In this he may have been unduly influenced by Jefferson and later by Jackson, but that he sincerely believed this to be the way of highest loyalty both to the church and the state can hardly be gainsaid. "Experience . . . has informed us, that the fondness of magistrates to foster Christianity, has done it more harm than all the persecutions ever did. Persecution, like a lion, tears the saints to death, but leaves Christianity pure: state establishment of religion, like a bear, hugs the saints, but corrupts Christianity . . . ."[5]

II

Turning now from the left to the right, that is, to the pragmatism of conservative religion, again some attempt at definition must be made. In general, this designation is applied to those institutions which either historically or theoretically favored some alliance between church and state. This took in *most* Christian groups, of course, both in this country and abroad. But in America two of these had developed special strength and prominence: Congregationalism in New England and Anglicanism in the Southern Colonies. While Lutherans, Dutch Reformed, Roman Catholics, and Scottish Presbyterians all enjoyed establishment in the Old World, they did not in the New. Thus prudence and principle were unevenly mixed, unsurely affirmed.

The two colonial heavyweights constituted, then, the only real contenders for federal establishment in the new nation. But neither had a monopoly, and both had enemies. The hostilities lined up against Anglicanism were especially severe. Colonists warring against the nation of England were hardly in a mood to favor or establish the Church of that England. Prejudices were high and passions inflamed against anything that might appear in the name of English authority or as an extension of King George's Crown.

Even more deeply rooted, however, were antagonisms that antedated

---

5. Ibid., 278.

the military clash. Throughout much of the eighteenth century, colonists were haunted by a fear of *episcopacy* — i.e., a fear that Anglican bishops would sail to America, there to exercise spiritual *and* temporal powers — powers made the more fearful because no proper distinction between them was made.

The spiritual overseers of the Church of England were always more than just that; they were wielders of great power in parliament and out. About four-fifths of the American population at the time of the Revolution were of British background; and in their memories, sacred or seared, England's civil and ecclesiastical jurisdictions were wondrously or woefully mixed. Whether it was wonder or woe depended upon which church one called his own.

Congregationalists, Presbyterians, Baptists, and Quakers had, in varying degrees, a personal knowledge of "the bloudy tenant of persecution for cause of conscience." In the turbulence of seventeenth century England, thousands had been tossed about: jailed, exiled, or put to death. The merest possibility of such Anglican power being imposed upon the dissenting churches raised immediate fears and resolute resistance.

But even among many Anglicans themselves, especially in the Southern Colonies, enthusiasm for a resident bishop was weak or wholly absent. In Virginia, vestries which controlled their clergy were reluctant to yield that authority to bishops. And those clergy who hardly missed an overzealous overseer supported the status quo. There was honest recognition, moreover, that the arrival of bishops would destroy any hope of amiable relations with dissenters. In 1771 Virginia's House of Burgesses voted unanimously against "the expediency of an American Episcopate." Richard Bland, one of that body's members and himself an Anglican, noted that the colony's "whole ecclesiastical constitution . . . must be altered if a bishop is appointed in America." Obviously reluctant to surrender legislative powers to an appointed bishop, Bland also warned of the divisive effort such a move would have. "For let me tell you, a religious dispute is the most fierce and destructive of all others to the peace and happiness of government." Bland concluded with a sentiment typical of many Southern Anglicans: "I profess myself a sincere son of the established church, but I can embrace her doctrines without approving of her hierarchy. . . ."[6]

In the Middle Colonies, William Livingston continued to be a painful thorn in the Anglicans' side. With his newspaper dedicated to "Opposing oppression and vindicating the liberty of man," Livingston let no spark of suspicion grow cool. Denying that he was against the Church of England as such, he acknowledged his unwavering resistance

---

6. Carl Bridenbaugh, *Mitre and Sceptre* (New York: Oxford University Press, 1962), 319.

to "her unreasonable encroachments" and to "all tyrants civil or ecclesiastic." Every exercise of Anglican authority in New York, every case of church-state manipulation was fully reported in his press and reported in such a way as to aggravate all dissenters' fears of what the future, under England or England's Church, might bring.[7]

Yale's Ezra Stiles also joined in the battle against episcopacy, recognizing that objections raised before a bishop had even arrived were "much founded in the anticipation of futurity." But, he warned, "I have so thoroughly studied the views and ultimate designs of American Episcopalians that I know I am not deceived." Dissenters confidently expected that an episcopate meant at least (1) the loss of their colonial charters, (2) the imposition of taxes for the support of the Anglican Church, clergy, and "bishop's palace," and (3) a restriction of all public offices to members of the Church of England. A convention of delegates assembled at Yale's commencement in 1769, having "reason to dread the establishment of bishops' courts among us," observed: "We have so long tasted the sweets of civil and religious liberty that we cannot be easily prevailed upon to submit to a yoke of bondage, which neither we nor our fathers were able to bear."[8]

"The Great Fear," as Carl Bridenbaugh calls it in *Mitre and Sceptre*, bound the colonies together in a mutual anxiety which helped create that unity of spirit manifest in 1776. Anglican clergymen, predominantly Tory in the Middle and New England Colonies, aggravated those fears as the moment of military clash approached. "The revolution," John Adams wrote, "was in the mind and hearts of the people, and in the union of the colonies." This revolution was accomplished, he observes, before the War for Independence ever began.

Congregationalism, on the other hand, by maintaining greater restrictions on religious freedom than obtained anywhere else in the colonies, had likewise made enemies and aroused fears. Quakers hanged in Boston, Roger Williams and Anne Hutchinson driven into exile, dissenters by the dozen jailed in Connecticut, itinerant and unauthorized preachers handed over from sheriff to sheriff until the wastelands of New York or the badlands of Rhode Island had been reached—all this somehow failed to win wide sympathy for an establishment of New England's religion! Throughout the eighteenth century, greater religious toleration was fought for inch by inch, and was conceded in a series of painful, bitterly resisted retreats. Consider Connecticut, for example.

In the same act which established the Saybrook Platform, an Act of Toleration was included. By the terms of this proviso, the right to

---

7. Ibid., chap. 6. See also Edwin S. Gaustad, *Religious Issues in American History* (New York: Harper & Row, 1968), chap. 4.
8. Bridenbaugh, *Mitre and Sceptre*, 288, 281 and, indeed, all of chap. 10.

worship and exercise discipline in their own way was granted to "any Society of Church that is or shall be allowed by the laws of this government, who soberly differ or dissent from the United Churches hereby established . . . ." This measure of toleration was primarily an attempt to court the favor of disaffected Congregational churches which did not wish to subscribe to the Saybrook Platform. It did not come, as later toleration acts did, largely through pressure exerted by other religious bodies. The right to worship according to conscience, here granted, did not annul the requirement to continue to support the "United Churches" by taxation.

There, the problem of toleration and religious liberty became more acute as the oppressed religious groups became more numerous. As long as dissenters were a voiceless minority, lacking social respectability and political influence—lacking even the ability to be much of a nuisance—officials of church and state could well ignore the principles or complaints that the former faintly articulated. The Anglicans were the first to make effective protest against the narrowness of the Toleration Act of 1708. This group had only scattered adherents in Connecticut in the seventeenth century, but as the Church continued to grow in influence and members its agitation for full recognition of its religious rights increased. Its voice was strengthened by the fact that it made frequent appeals to the English government to bring pressure to bear on the colony for a complete toleration of its worship and exemption from support of any other. In 1727 they were rewarded for their efforts by the General Court's passing of an act "providing how taxes levied upon members of the Church of England for the support of the Gospel should be disposed of."[9]

Baptists and Quakers received similar concessions. In May 1729 the Quakers appealed to the General Court for exemption from compulsory support of the established ministry and from paying any tax levied for building its meeting houses. Like the Anglicans, they had to live "near" a Society of their own faith, certify their support of it, and regularly attend it. This petition was granted. In October of the same year, exemption on equivalent terms was granted to the Baptists, the influence of Rhode Island's Baptist governor being employed to this end. These groups, sharing a common cause, were in no way united; yet together they spelled mutiny for the "good old ship Connecticut."

The Great Awakening further weakened the structure of establishment by producing divisiveness within Congregationalism itself. The supporters of this revival reacted against the compromising Half-Way Covenant and the formalizing, authoritarian Saybrook Platform. Many

---

9. See M. L. Greene, *The Development of Religious Liberty in Connecticut* (Boston: Houghton Mifflin & Co., 1905), chap. 7.

returned to the earlier Congregationalism which held that only those persons who had had a definite experience of grace were properly members of the church. Churches adopting this position were called Separate churches (or "New Light"). In an effort to halt a widespread movement away from the Saybrook Platform, the General Assembly ruled "that those commonly called Presbyterians or Congregationalists should *not* take the benefit of that Toleration Act." Repeated attempts on the part of the Separatists to claim tax exemptions as "sober dissenters," or to come under the protection of the Act by changing the name of their church to Baptist led, in 1743, to the repeal of the Toleration Act. A year earlier the General Assembly had declared that no college, seminary, or public school could be established without the permission of the legislature, and that "no one should take the benefits of the law regarding the settlement and support of ministers, unless he were a graduate of Yale or Harvard, or some other approved Protestant university."[10] Yale expelled students contaminated with New Light teaching, tightening its discipline and its orthodoxy. Itinerant ministers were treated under laws of vagrancy; New Light civil officials were deprived of their office. The Great Awakening had retarded for the moment the drive which the dissenting groups were making for a recognition of their equal religious rights. These intolerant acts of 1742-43 were never formally repealed, but later they were quietly omitted.

Neither Anglicans nor Congregationalists, therefore, had enough strength or support to win establishment for themselves. And if this was true of the two heavyweights, it was even more obviously true of the several bantam weights in colonial America—those smaller churches which historically supported the notion of establishment but which now, prudently, saw it as either impossible or unwise. Thus the pragmatism of the conservative churches—a pragmatism that declared in effect: If we cannot attain federal patronage for ourselves, we do not want it for anyone else. Or, in another form, pragmatism dictated these words: If patronage be granted to any other, then we, small in size and devoid of political power, stand to lose and lose most heavily. In circumstances such as these, therefore, religious freedom proved more attractive than religious favor. These churches, as Perry Miller notes, did not "contribute to religious liberty, they stumbled into it." But in another sense, disestablishment first seen as desirable on pragmatic grounds could and did become defensible on ideological grounds.

III

---

10. Ibid., 255; also, Edwin S. Gaustad, *The Great Awakening in New England* (New York: Harper & Brothers, 1957), 108f.

Third, natural religion, or deism, or rationalism, contributed directly to the move for disestablishment. Natural religion was, at best, indifferent to institutional structures, to denominational loyalties. Like the pietists, the rationalists found the institutions, the priestcraft, and the creedal complexities to be superfluous if not obstructive to true faith. Thus disestablishment would be no blow to real religion; it would only discourage that officious externalism that society, in any case, was better off without.

The growing confidence in reason as a capable, dependable, and perhaps all-sufficient human instrument was usually achieved at the expense of revelation. And in the eighteenth century, any weakening of revelation was a weakening of institutional religion; a disestablishment, if you will, of *its* prestige and authority in the minds of men. Reason, after all, is our only revelation, as John Adams wrote Jefferson, "a revelation from its makers, which can never be disputed or doubted." He added:

> No prophecies, no miracles are necessary to prove this celestial communication. This revelation has made it certain that two and one make three, and that one is not three nor can three be one. We can never be so certain of any prophecy, or the fulfillment of any prophecy, or of any miracle, or the design of any miracle, as we are from the revelation of nature, that is nature's God, that two and two are equal to four.[11]

In this discussion of rationalism it will be useful to distinguish between stages or degrees (and sometimes it was both) of the new loyalty to and confidence in reason. An attempt will be made to differentiate three phases: reason and revelation, reason above revelation, and reason instead of revelation.

In the first of these, reason and revelation were treated as equal courts of appeal. Each had its own jurisdiction and bounds. This was a subtle and sometimes merely a tactical movement within eighteenth century New England. The great willingness to appeal to reason's court was invariably accompanied by a great confidence that revelation would never be overruled. Reason's judgment could be sought unashamedly and unhesitatingly as long as there was little question that it would issue in a powerful endorsement of the Westminster Confession, the Synod of 1682, and the Saybrook Platform. Revelation and mystery, said James Dana in 1767, are incompatible. That is, revelation must be the ally of reason and vice versa. There are many things, he added, "declared in the holy scriptures, of which we should otherwise have had no tho't or idea; which yet contradict no principle of reason, but are admitted as soon as proposed — admitted [and note the order] on account of their reasonableness and excellence and upon the authority of God confirming His word by incontestable miracles."[12]

---

11. John Adams, *The Works of John Adams* (Boston: Little, Brown & Co., 1850-56), 10:66; the letter is dated 14 September 1813.
12. James Dana, *Two Discourses Delivered at Cambridge* (Boston: Edes & Gill, 1767), 31, 41.

The second phase in the historic juggle between reason and revelation involved an uneasy shifting away from this equal basis toward a greater reliance upon reason. The colonies had their own latitudinarianism. Revelation was not despised, only ignored; reason was not glorified, only obeyed. This shift was, amazingly enough, sometimes made under the guise of a greater allegiance to revelation. It was soon noted that reason did not always come out in perfect congruence with Christian creeds. And to many this was just as well. So, the attempt to have one's cake and eat it too (i.e., to give greater prominence to reason and at the same time to refrain from attacking revelation) took the form of an appeal directly to the Bible. Let us get back to the Scriptures, which men are well able to interpret for themselves, with their own intellect. There is no need for anyone to tell us, in so many propositions, that this is what the Bible really says. Early Christian creeds sometimes had the virtue of ambiguity, but the sixteenth and seventeenth centuries had whittled away much of that advantage. Thus it became necessary, in order to recapture a more comfortable latitude, to appeal directly to the New Testament, or perhaps to the teachings of Jesus. Hence, rationalist is aligned with pietist as both resist the rigid requirements of doctrine. In the question of John Tucker of Newbury: Are divine truths "some how better or more important cloathed in human expressions than when uttered in the words of the *Holy Ghost?*"[13]

The last stage in the sparring between reason and revelation is the most clearly seen and the most severely damaging to the churches' authority. This was the acceptance of reason instead of revelation. Here, of course, the force of all Western Europe comes into play, as one reckons with the names of Clarke, Tillotson, Butler, Paine, Diderot, and Voltaire. In Paris, with ultimate logic, Reason was crowned. All the ways of man and society were to be judged by their approach to or violation of the "natural"—that most capacious of sematic booby traps. And the church, when so judged by this somewhat elusive Procrustean bed, proved to be artificial, unnecessary, and quite possibly evil.

The church was artificial sociologically and intellectually. With reference to the first, churchmen made the fundamental mistake of looking upon their institution as having some prior and metaphysical right. They bound people by a covenant and then acted as though the association were divinely ordained. The fact is, however, that in the state of nature no such institution is to be found. On the contrary, the individual is prior and all important. Noble savages, it appears, never congregate; they stand bold and alone. Curiously the same is

---

13. Quoted in Conrad Wright, *The Beginnings of Unitarianism in America* (Boston: Starr King Press, 1955), 235.

true of noble prophets; they stand naked before God. Once more the fortuitous conjunction of pietist and rationalist presents itself; both could view the church, the visible and established church at any rate, as the corrupt work of scheming men. Jefferson, in his famous letter to the Danbury Baptists, declared that "religion is a matter which lies solely between man and his God . . . ." Such deism was not the enemy of religion but only of the church—that artificial creation which obtrusively and detrimentally shoved its way into what was properly a pure, natural, private entente.

Not only was the gathering within the church artificial, but its intellectual pretensions were equally artificial and vain. Theology was so much mental mischief, or as Emerson was later to say, most of its puzzles are "the soul's mumps and measles and whooping cough . . . A simple mind will not know these enemies."[14] Thus rationalism, perverse as it must sound, could be every bit as anti-intellectual as pietism; and with respect to their effect upon the church, again, these two forces were complementary rather than opposing. In the name of common sense, all uncommon speculation was dismissed. In Rousseau's words, "a state of reflection is a state against nature." Indeed, the rationalist could outdo the pietist and his impatience with mystery and theory, and the unlikely alliance between the two can account in no small part for Emerson's renowned exaggeration that in Massachusetts from 1790 to 1820 "there was not a book, a speech, a conversation, or a thought in the State."[15]

The church, furthermore, was unnecessary—unnecessary because man was good, God was good, and society, if not already good, was assuredly and steadily getting better. If man was a rational animal, it was no less true that he was a moral animal. The goodness of man, moreover, came about naturally and not sacramentally. "I agree perfectly with you," Adams wrote Jefferson, "that 'the moral sense is as much a part of our condition as that of feeling.' "[16] Man was disposed to the love of others just as much as to self-love, and conscience, Joseph Butler had argued in England, is that faculty which umpires between the two. And when the good bishop got through explaining what love to neighbor really meant, hardly any self-respecting citizen could fail to volunteer for that pleasant assignment, or more likely he would find that he was already "loving his neighbor" without knowing it. To be sure, there is hardly a more dramatic contrast to be found in the history of Western thought than in the meaning of the phrase "natural man"

---

14. Ralph Waldo Emerson, "Spiritual Laws," *Essays, First Series* (New York: Lovell Bros. & Co., n.d.), 112.
15. *The Journals of Ralph Waldo Emerson* (Boston: Houghton Mifflin & Co., 1912), 8:339.
16. Adams, *The Works of John Adams*, 10:229.

in seventeenth century Puritanism and its meaning in eighteenth century deism.

But if man was good, God was magnificent. His benevolence staggered the imagination. Men vied with one another to demonstrate how all the universe had been created with the convenience and welfare of a man in mind. Natural religion (which could so easily become a religion of nature) found no evil that required explaining away, and the naive Christian optimism which Voltaire easily ridiculed came home to roost. The universe was orderly and predictable; therefore, the God of the universe was orderly and predictable. As such, He is far more likely to reveal himself in geology and geometry than in theology and litany.

The ultimate in divine benevolence was not that God loved those who loved Him, but that He loved all and would redeem all. Universalism, while honoring the munificence of God, made the church more nearly superfluous. "I believe with Justin Martyr," Adams wrote, "that all good men are Christians, and I believe there have been, and are good men in all nations, sincere and conscientious."[17] Amid such circumstances, a discussion of the merits of the Half-Way Covenant could appear a trifle academic.

To some deists, more radical than any yet considered, the church was more than merely artificial or innocently unnecessary; it was evil. Through trickery and superstition ecclesiasticism has enslaved mankind. Here was a chain that free men should strike off; crush the infamy!

Thomas Jefferson wrote in 1816: "My opinion is that there would never have been an infidel, if there had never been a priest. The artificial structure they have built on the purest of all moral systems for the purpose of deriving from it pence and power revolt those who think for themselves, and who read in that system only what is really there."[18] Or Thomas Paine in his *Age of Reason*: "All national institutions of churches, whether Jewish, Christian or Turkish, appear to me no other than human inventions, set up to terrify and enslave mankind, and monopolize power and profit."[19] And Joseph Priestly, in 1782, published a two-volume work entitled *History of the Corruption of Christianity*, explaining that the spirit of Jesus had been debased and virtually destroyed by the encrustations of institutions, professionals, and dogmas. Establish that? Never!! Reason, as Ethan Allen explained in the title of his book, is "the only oracle of man" (1784). If anything be patronized by government, let it be the freedom of men's minds.[20]

---

17. Ibid., 10:390.
18. Quoted in Sidney E. Mead, *The Lively Experiment* (New York: Harper & Row, 1963), 46.
19. Quoted *ibid.*, 47.
20. Ibid.; all of chaps. 3 and 4 herein are pointedly relevant to my argument.

IV

Finally, hostility not only to priestcraft but to religion itself contributed to disestablishment. While anticlericalism never reached the heights in America that it did in France, that movement here as well as there could become an opposition to the substance of all religion. In America, the horror of Jacobinism and infidelity was partly but not wholly an irrational fear. Most of America's population at this time, it must be remembered, was *not* aligned with either synagogue or church. The 80-90% outside of the institutions of religion were, of course, not thereby against all religion, but some were, and many more were merely indifferent.

Connecticut's Lyman Beecher in his Toleration Dream voiced the fears of many a churchman when he argued that religious toleration was only a subtle strategem for religion's annihilation. Toleration, he said, is just another name for license, just another name for selling rum and making merry — what crimes, injustices, and immoralities are committed in its name! The Republicans (Jeffersonians, that is), he declared, ally themselves with the Baptists merely to destroy the Congregationalists. When the latter have gone, then the politicians will ally themselves with the Methodists to destroy the Baptists, and so on. "And when we have got things in a sure train, we shall permit this or that sect to have the ascendancy, as will best promote our own power and their mutual jealousies. In this way we intend to make them destroy each other, and the way will then be prepared for the universal reign for reason and philosophy."[21] It was, to repeat, partly but not wholly an irrational fear. James Madison's affection for factions lay in his confidence that factions would tend to nullify each other, to cancel each other out.

These are the four factors, then, which in sometimes discordant harmony led to the disestablishment of religion. Partly by design, partly by accident, partly by faith and hope, partly by doubt and despair, the state was freed from a narrow sectarianism. But even more significantly, the church was freed from a restraining, corrupting, and corroding entanglement with government. The great legal milestones were three: (1) Jefferson's Bill for Establishing Religious Freedom, passed by the Virginia assempfly in 1779. In this Bill, Jefferson noted that the political pressure in religion is "a departure from the plan of the Holy Author of our religion, who being Lord both of body and mind, yet chose not to propagate it by coercions on either, as was in his Almighty power to do." (2) Ten years later, the adoption of the Constitution which in Article VI stated with remarkable brevity that "No

---

21. Lyman Beecher, *Autobiography, Correspondence* ... (New York: Harper & Brothers, 1864), 1:392-406.

religious test shall ever be required as a qualification to any office or public trust under the United States." That is the only reference to religion in the Constitution proper. (3) Then, two years after that, the adoption of the Bill of Rigths, the First Amendment affirming that "Congress shall make no law respecting an establishment of religion, or prohibiting the free exercise thereof" — sixteen words to be wrestled with, interpreted, explained, tested, and judged.

Neither Church nor State: Reflections on James Madison's "Line of Separation"

SIDNEY E. MEAD

It is common these days to use the term "church-state" to embrace all questions that arise under our Constitution respecting religious freedom, the relation of law and religion, and the relation of churches and governments. Although this terminology has its usefulness as a shortcut and as a symbol of current problems, it suffers from weaknesses and inadequacies. Church-state terminology comes to us from Europe and recalls a background which is quite unlike the American scene. It had its origin in a time when the church was indeed a single monolithic Church and governmental power was centered in a single ruler. It is inadequate to describe the American situation because of both the multitude of churches in this country and the dispersion of governmental power among the federal government, the states, and the local communities.[1]

In 1832 James Madison, after surveying the consequences in America of rejecting the long standing dogma that "religion could not be preserved without the support of Government nor Government be supported without an established religion," wrote that he had to

admit ... that it may not be easy, in every possible case, to trace the line of separation between the rights of religion and the Civil authority with such distinctness as to avoid collisions & doubts on unessential points. The tendency to a usurpation on one side or the other, or to a corrupting coalition or alliance between them, will be best guarded against by an entire abstinance of the Government from interference in any way whatever, beyond the necessity of preserving public order, & protecting each sect against trespasses on its legal rights by others.[2]

It is unfortunate that the phrase Thomas Jefferson had used thirty years before in his letter to the Danbury (Connecticut) Baptist Association — "a wall of separation between church and state" — became almost universally known and used while Madison's more accurate terminology was forgotten. For Jefferson's words have been the source

---

1. Paul G. Kauper, *Religion and the Constitution* (Baton Rouge: Louisiana State University Press, 1964), 3.
2. From a letter to the Rev. Jasper Adams, in John F. Wilson, *Church & State in American History* (Boston: D. C. Heath and Co., 1965), 77, 78.

of much confusion and conflict because they have helped to perpetuate thinking about the situation in the United States with the traditional concepts of "church" and "state" which are really not applicable to the experienced order of Americans. And the reference to a "wall" conjures up the image of something quite tangible and solid, which was built once for all in the beginning.

Madison's words—"the line of separation between the rights of religion and the Civil authority"—are much more precisely descriptive. For while there are religions, or "sects" as he called them, in the United States, there is no "church" in the traditional institutional sense. And while there is "Civil authority," there is no "state" in the meaning of the word during the centuries when national religious uniformity was the ideal and Establishments existed. And Madison's word, "line," unlike Jefferson's "wall," does not conjure up the image of a solid and unchanging structure built by the founders, but rather "the path of a moving point, thought of as having length but not breadth," as my dictionary explains it. Further, the concept of a "line," unlike that of a "wall," permits one to think of a point constantly moving, and even zig-zagging, and therefore, as Madison noted, not always easy to trace "with such distinctness as to avoid collisions & doubts . . . ."

If we think of the American situation with Jefferson's concepts of "church," "state," and a "wall," the image conjured up is of two distinct and settled institutions in the society once and for all time separated by a clearly defined and impregnable barrier which has solid foundations in the Constitution. It is in this context that "ignorant armies clash by night," and also by day.

But if we think of the American situation with Madison's concepts of religious "sects," "Civil authority," and a "line" between them, the image is fluid, its elements constantly changing shape and moving into different relationships with each other. Religious "sects" may and have appeared in hundreds of different forms, and "Civil authority" under our Constitutional Federalism may wear hundreds of different masks. In the beginning no one knew, or could know, just where the line between them was or would be because no one could anticipate the multitudinous insitutional forms of religion or the numerous masks of civil authority that would appear and because there were practically no precedents to serve as guidelines.

If we think with Jefferson's concepts, the image is of two antagonistic parties in the society, the one defending, the other attacking and attempting to tear down a "wall." Each might take his slogan from Robert Frost's "Mending Wall." The defender of the wall with his father image of Jefferson

> . . . will not go behind his father's sayings,
> And he likes having thought of it so well
> He says again, "Good fences make good neighbors."

The attacker of the wall, commonly unreflectively accepting the concepts developed in his religious tradition in the good old days before freedom and pluralism were permitted, stubbornly reiterates,

> "Something there is that doesn't love a wall,
> That wants it down"....

If we think with Madison's concepts, we are launched, all together as Americans, on a common quest to find out where the line or lines may be between ecclesiastical bodies and between one or more of the forms of ecclesiastical bodies and one or more of the current masks of "Civil authority."

The Constitution is the fundamental law of the land. But, as Lincoln said in his first Inaugural Address, "No organic law can ever be framed with a provision specifically applicable to every question which may occur in practical administration. No foresight can anticipate nor any document of reasonable length contain express provisions for all possible questions."

The Constitution and First Amendment laid down as guidelines very general, abstract principles in terms of no religious test for national office, no "establishment of religion," and no prohibition of the "free exercise thereof." But what these abstract principles would mean in practice no one could anticipate. That was left to be determined only as specific questions arose—justiciable issues under the rules of the game. Some of the questions have been: Do they mean that a state may not finance through taxation bus transportation to parochial schools, or textbooks, or lunches for children in such schools? Do they mean that a state may not appropriate money raised by taxation for the construction of buildings for a denominational college? Do they mean that I may not handle poisonous snakes as an act of worship although I think God commands it? Do they mean that I may not refuse a blood transfusion for my child when the men in white deem it necessary to save his life although I believe it is forbidden by God? Do they mean that a majority in a school district may institute its forms of religious exercises in the public schools? Do they mean that a child may refrain from participation in the salute to the flag because to him it is an act of idol worship forbidden by God?

All of these specific questions have been raised by persons with "standing," and dealt with one way or another in court decisions arrived at through the observance of elaborately defined legal procedures, which are part of the rules of the game we are playing for the high stakes of freedom.

I suppose that to most of us who are without legal training the word "decision" has connotations of definiteness and finality. At least it took some time for me to realize that a court decision in the United States is never the last word on the point at issue. But if we think of a particular Supreme Court decision with Jefferson's concept of a "wall" in mind, the decision is likely to be imaged as another large stone well-mortared into a solid barrier. However, if we think of a particular decision with Madison's concept of a "line" in mind, it is apt to be imaged as only a temporary point where the line appeared to a majority of the Justices to be at the moment.

A decision is never absolutely final. "The Federal constitution," as Mr. Justice Douglas once put it, "is not a code, but a rule of action — a statement of philosophy and point of view, a summation of general principles, a delineation of the broad outlines of a regime which the Fathers designed for us."[3] The work of the Court is the translation of these general principles "into concrete constitutional commands"[4] — "the application of universal principles to the endless and infinitely varied concrete instances that occur in the real world."[5] Further, almost every specific issue can be looked at from the perspective of "more than one so-called principle."[6] This means that every case involves "arguable controversies, problems of judgment and choice on which reasonable men can disagree and reasonable Justices of the Supreme Court of the United States divide five to four, or six to three, or in some other ratio."[7]

Again, unlike the practice in most other nations, the dissenting as well as the majority opinions are published. The dissenter, of course, "strives to undermine the Court's reasoning and discredit its results," and, compared to the spokesman of the court, he is "irresponsible" and can be freer and more vivid in expression. Consequently even careful study of a decision may leave one puzzled about "whether the majority opinion meant what it seemed to say or what the minority said it meant."[8] For this reason a decision where there are dissenting opinions may provide no sound basis for predicting where the next point in the line will be located.

A case always involves a conflict of interests between two parties in the society. Because of the way the Supreme Court operates, the issues that it takes up are commonly those on which parties in the society are hotly divided. The Justices, quite aware of the practical consequences and in the midst of all the ambiguities, must within a reasonable time come to a definite decision respecting which party wins and which

---

3. Willaim O. Douglas, "In Defense of Dissent" in Alan F. Westin, ed., *The Supreme Court: Views from Inside* (New York: W. W. Norton & Co., 1965), 52.
4. Robert H. Jackson, *The Supreme Court in the American System of Government* (New York: Harper Torchbook, 1963), 23.
5. Harry W. Jones, "Church-State Relations: Our Constitutional Heritage," in Harold Stahmer, ed., *Religion & Contemporary Society* (New York: The Macmillan Company, 1963), 168.
6. Felix Frankfurter, "The Process of Judging in the Supreme Court," in Westin, 43.
7. Jones, *Church-State Relations*, 168-69.
8. Jackson, *The Supreme Court*, 17-19.

loses. This, as Mr. Justice Frankfurter said, is "for any conscientious judge . . . the agony of his duty."[9]

So we return to Madison's concept of the "line" which Chief Justice Hughes once used in summarizing the situation:

All rights tend to declare themselves absolute to their logical extreme. Yet all in fact are limited by the neighborhood of principles of policy which are other than those on which the particular right is founded, and which become strong enough to hold their own when a certain point is reached . . . . The boundary at which the conflicting interests balance cannot be determined by any general formula in advance, *but points in the line, or helping to establish it, or fixed by decisions that this or that concrete case falls on the nearer or farther side.*[10]

A decision, then, is never absolutely final but, rather, as Chief Justice Hughes said of dissenting opinions, ". . . an appeal to the brooding spirit of the law, to the intelligence of a future day"[11] when future decisions will perchance correct the error of the present one in the light of much discussion of the issues, more experience in living with the results, and, hopefully, of greater wisdom in the people. This system, if really working, would prevent the hardening of any and all particular forms. As Christians now speak of "religionless' Christianity, so one might say that the American system was designed to perpetuate "stateless" government.

To be sure the Court has declared in the Schempp-Murray decision that some points on the line have been "decisively settled":

First, this Court has decisively settled that the First Amendment's mandate that "Congress shall make no law respecting an establishment of religion, or prohibiting the free exercise thereof" has been made wholly applicable to the states by the Fourteenth Amendment . . . Second, this Court has rejected unequivocally the contention that the establishment clause forbids only governmental preference of one religion over another . . . . the Court said that "[n]either a state nor the Federal government can set up a church. Neither can pass laws which aid one religion, aid all religions, or prefer one religion over another.". . . "The [First] Amendment's purpose . . . was to create a complete and permanent separation of the spheres of religious activity and civil authority by comprehensively forbidding every form of public aid or support for religion."[12]

Perhaps this was merely a temporary lapse into undue optimism or into wishful thinking induced by fatigue.

I noted above that in the United States there is no "church" in the traditional institutional sense. What, then, is there? At most we may say that the catholic or universal church, the body of Christ, is here

---

9. Frankfurter, "The Process of Judging in the Supreme Court," 44.
10. Ibid., 43-44. Emphasis added.
11. Douglas, "In Defense of Dissent," 55.
12. Authur Frommer, ed., *The Bible and the Public Schools* (New York: Liberal Press Books, 1963), 68-69. Full text of *Abington School District* v. *Schempp* and *Murray* v. *Curlett*, 374, U.S. 203 (1963) to be found in ibid., 57-79 and *Journal of Church and State, 5* (November 1963); 280-90.

divided visibly into hundreds of institutions. It is important to have a clear idea of the nature of these institutions in the American system.

Madison's "sect," now commonly called a "church," is a tangible voluntary association for the pursuit of religious or spiritual ends. As "an ecclesiastical body . . . [it is] a law unto itself, [and] self-governing . . . in the discharge of its religious functions."[13] This means that the civil courts if called upon to adjudicate a conflict between factions within this body will do so on the basis of the polity of that particular body.[14]

But "an ecclesiastical body" as such has no recognized legal being. Its temporal interests are cared for and its responsibilities discharged by a corporation which is the creation of the civil authority and has recognized legal being. As such the corporation has justiciable rights and responsibilities. The corporation "is formed [primarily] for the acquisition and taking care of the property of the church, and is in no sense ecclesiastical [or spiritual] in its functions."[15] Because the ecclesiastical body can define the qualifications for membership in its corporation and censure or remove members for causes defined by its laws, the two are inextricably bound together.

Now then, when in Madison's words the civil authority in the interests of "preserving public order" protects a "sect" or church "against trespasses on its legal rights by others," the reference is to the corporation. This is why, as Supreme Court Justices have declared, it is not necessary for them in order to adjudicate conflicts between "sects" to understand or know what the particular "sects" involved, or scholars in general, mean by "religion." As Mr. Justice Jackson put it, the duty of the Court "to apply the Bill of Rights to assertions of official authority" does not "depend upon our possession of marked competence in the field where the invasion of rights occurs."[16] They do not have to know what "religion" is in the abstract, to know when one sect, or group of sects, is infringing upon the rights of other sects, or of unbelievers, to "free exercise" and/or equal protection of the laws.

This is a point that religionists have sometimes greatly misunderstood. For example, in an article in *The Christian Century* of 4 September 1963, Clyde A. Holbrook argued that because scholars are not agreed on the "criteria for religious activity" the Court can have no "competence to distinguish religious acts from nonreligious acts" and

---

13. *Hundley* v. *Collins*, 131 Ala. 234, 32 S. 575 (1902), in John J. McGrath, ed., *Church and State in American Law: Cases and Materials* (Milwaukee: Bruce Publishing Co., 1962), 9.
14. *Kedroff* v. *St. Nicholas Cathedral*, 344 U.S. 94 (1952), in Joseph Tussman, ed., *The Supreme Court on Church and State* (New York: Oxford University Press, 1962), 298ff.
15. McGrath, *Church and State in American Law*, 6.
16. *West Virginia State Board of Education* v. *Barnette*, 319 U.S. 624 (1943), in Tussman, *The Supreme Court in Church and State*, 149.

therefore ought to "leave this area alone" at least "until such time as . . . [it] has done its homework on the nature of religion in American society."[17] Aside from the stop-the-world-we-want-to-get-off-for-the-time-being" attitude implied by this stance, if Mr. Holbrook's position were imposed on the American situation it would mean that the civil authority would define for the "sects" what "religion" is — one of the precise things the founders with their knowledge of English Erastianism sought to avoid. As it is, the civil authority will protect the right of each "ecclesiastical body" to define "religion" as it chooses. And if, through its corporation, a "sect" attempts to trespass upon the similar right of other "sects" the civil Courts may be appealed to, to prevent this.

Granted the traditional usage in Christendom, just as Jefferson's concept of the "church" conjures up the image of one monolithic ecclesiastical body in the society whose authority is vested in certain persons, so the concept of the "state" induces the image of one monolithic concentration of supreme civil authority vested in certain persons. But this image of the "state" is no more applicable to the American system than is that image of the "church." This nation never created such a "state." We should all be properly shocked if, reminiscent of Louis XIV, our elected national executive officers, senators, and congressmen should some day stand up in a body and declare, "We are the state!"

In the Anglo-American tradition since time immemorial an accepted premise has been that sovereignty resides in the people, and therefore government must be by the consent of the governed. In this context emerged the various forms of the myth of the contractual origins of society, of government, and of the state. Commonly there were three steps. In the first, individuals entered into reciprocal engagements with others to manage their common interests and secure their common happiness. This formed "society."

In the second step, having agreed to form society, they took measures to form the kind of government they wanted as the locus of supreme power in the commonwealth. In the third step this supreme power was vested in one or more persons. These persons, I take it, constituted "the state," or John Locke's "Legislative."

In one line of interpretation the people in these successive steps passed the sovereignty (supreme power) resident in them on to Locke's "Legislative." In this line Sir William Blackstone held that "Sovereignty and legislature are . . . convertible terms; one cannot subsist without the other." It followed in Blackstone's view, "the supreme and absolute authority of the state is vested . . . in the British Parliament." And "so

---

17. Clyde A. Holbrook, "Religious Scholarship and the Court," *The Christian Century,* 4 September 1963), 1076-1078. And see reply in ibid., 80 (October 30, 1963), 1342-1343.

long as the English constitution lasts" in which the people indicated their choice of government, "the power of parliament is absolute and without control" and what it does "no authority upon earth can undo."[18]

As I understood Locke's view, sovereignty is not thus completely and finally passed in this fashion to the legislative. In the second step the legislative is made "the *supream power* of the Commonwealth" and as such it is "sacred and unalterable in the hands where the Community have once placed it . . . ." But it is the *"supream power"* only in the sense that its edicts alone "have the force and obligation of a *Law*" of the Commonwealth.[19] But always "there remains still *in the people a Supream Power* to remove or alter the *Legislative*, when they find the *Legislative* act contrary to the trust reposed in them . . . ."[20] This is a government of law, and it seems clear that sovereignty (the *"supream power"*) always remains in the people.

But Locke, in keeping with the English pattern, conceived the Legislative as "placed in the Concurrence of three distinct Persons," "An Assembly of Representatives chosen *pro tempore*, by the People," "An Assembly of Hereditary Nobility," and a hereditary monarch "having the constant, supream, executive Power, and with it the Power of Convoking and Dissolving the other two within certain Periods of Time."[21] When the Legislative or any part of it acts contrary to the trust reposed in it, they "put themselves into a state of War with the People, who are thereupon absolved from any further Obedience, and are left to the common Refuge, which God hath provided for all Men against Force and Violence,"[22] namely, contrary force. For in all States and Conditions the true remedy of *Force* without Authority is to oppose Force to it. The use of *force* without Authority, always puts him that uses it into a *state of War*, as the Aggressor, and renders him liable to be treated accordingly.[23] It would appear, then, that to Locke, because there were hereditary elements in the Legislative, the *only* recourse of the people against tyranny on the part of the State was revolution.

The United States by eliminating hereditary elements from its Legislative, and (symbolically at least) completely returning *all* executive and legislative power to the people periodically in free elections, eliminated the elements most likely to become tyrannous because not

---

18. For the ideas and quotations from Blackstone in the paragraph I am indebted to Robert Green McCloskey, ed., *The Works of James Wilson* (2 vols.; Cambridge: The Belknap Press of Harvard University Press, 1967), 1, 168-69.
19. John Locke, *Second Treatise of Government*, chap. 11, sect. 134, in Peter Laslett, ed., *Locke's Two Treatises of Government*, (New York: Mentor Books, 1965), 401.
20. Ibid., chap 13, sec. 149, 413.
21. Ibid., chap. 19, sect. 213, 456.
22. Ibid., chap. 19, sect. 222, 460-61.
23. Ibid., chap. 12, sect. 155, 417.

subject to election. And these were the elements which, because of their permanency, carried the image of "the State" separate from the people. From Locke's point of view the American system might seem a government of continual and perpetual, albeit peaceful, revolution, in which the only possible tyranny was that of a majority. Hence the Constitutional checks on the power of the majority, rooted primarily in the Bill of Rights.

This was the feature that so impressed Alexis de Tocqueville, who said that "any discussion of the political laws of the United States must always begin with the dogma of the sovereignty of the people." This principle, he continued, seems to be found "at the bottom of almost all human institutions" and it is commonly invoked and "abused [even] by intriguers and despots of every age." But usually, if publicly appealed to, "it is hastily thrust back into the gloom of the sanctuary"—that is, it is professed but not actualized in practice. However, Tocqueville argued, it was "the creative principle of most of the English colonies in America" exemplified in the practices of the townships. In the Revolution "the dogma of the sovereignty of the people came out from the township and took possession of the [national] government; every class enlisted in its cause; the war was fought and victory obtained in its name; it became the law of laws." Hence in the United States the principle "is neither hidden nor sterile as with some other nations; mores recognize it, and the laws proclaim it; it spreads with freedom and attains unimpeded its ultimate consequences." It swept away the traditional "voting qualifications," for once the principle was accepted there was no "halting place until universal suffrage" was attained.

Consequently, in America, Tocqueville concluded, unlike most other countries, there is no "authority, in a sense outside the body social [which] influences it and forces it to progress in a certain direction" (e.g., a church), and not even a divided power which is "at the same time within the society and outside it" (e.g., a hereditary monarch and/or Lords). For in the United States

society acts by and for itself. There are no authorities except within itself; one can hardly meet anybody who would dare to conceive, much less to suggest, seeking power elsewhere. The people take part in the making of the laws by choosing the lawgivers, and they share in their application by electing the agents of the executive power; one might say that they govern themselves, so feeble and restricted is the part left to the administration, so vividly is that administration aware of its popular origin, and so obedient is it to the fount of power. The people reign over the American political world as God rules over the universe. It is the cause and the end of all things; everything rises out of it and is absorbed back into it.[24]

---

24. Alexis de Tocqueville, *Democracy in America*, edited by J. P. Mayer and Max Lerner, trans. by George Laurence (2 vols.; New York: Harper & Row, 1966), 1, chap. 4.

In this context regular elections on all levels symbolize the continual return of sovereignty to the people who in Locke's phrase "shall be judge" of whether or not their representatives are fulfilling the trust temporarily placed in them. Seen in this perspective, our Constitutional Federalism and all the elaborate mechanisms or procedures observed in the practice of our Republic are merely means devised to actualize government by the immediate consent of the governed. There is no "State" in the traditional sense.

In 1837 Senator Asher Robbins of Rhode Island interpreted James Madison's vision very much in Tocqueville's terms. It was, he said, that "this scattered and countless multitude were to be ruled in freedom as one people and by the popular will—that will was to be uncontrolled in itself, and controlling everything." Robbins thought that Madison realized that "such an achievement the most enlightened friends of freedom and human rights, in all countries, and in all ages, had deemed to be morally and physically impossible." In the face of this almost universal negative, the task confronted by Madison and his co-workers was to institute "one simple [over-all] government, with all the purposes of peace and war" without completely absorbing and thus destroying "as States" the original "thirteen States, and all the other States to be formed out of that vast territory . . . ." Here the traditional concept of the unitary state, if clung to, would make the job impossible by definition, and the alternative of a Confederation of sovereign States had already been tried and found wanting. Senator Robbins located Madison's and the Americans' genius, first, in their concept of "federalism"—a novel principle "unexplored and unknown before . . . our confederate and national republic"; and, second, in the astute political ability they displayed "in engineering this system from idea to reality."[25]

It seems, then, that the Americans departed from Locke in this very important respect. To Locke, apparently, sovereignty was indivisible, and he could not conceive of distributing the sovereignty resident in the people between several "legislatives."[26] He held that "there can be but *one Supream Power*, which is the *Legislative*, to which all the rest

---

25. The ideas and quotations in this paragraph are taken from Adrienne Koch, *Madison's "Advice to My Country"* (Princeton: Princeton University Press, 1966), 93-95.
26. Lyman Beecher (1775-1863) was clear that what Tocqueville called "the dogma of the sovereignty of the people" meant that there was no longer a "state" in the traditional sense, and therefore that "public opinion" was the real ruler or "executive" in the Republic. Therefore, he argued, the churches must rethink their relationship to this new situation, and much of his thought, speaking, and publication was devoted to this task. He suggests a theologically oriented view of the role of the churches in this new kind of Republic which, I think, still suggests viable guidelines.

are and must be subordinate . . . "[27] This, I suppose, is the common conception of the unitary "State."

The Americans created, not this, but a federalism which in Felix Frankfurter's words "presupposes the distribution of governmental powers between national and local authority. Between these two authorities there is shared the power entirely possessed by a unitary state."[28] This means that there could be no American "State" in the traditional sense. And the situation is further complicated by the fact that "In addition to the provisions of our Constitution making this distribution of authority between the two governments, there is also in the United States Constitution a withdrawal of power from both governments, or, at least, the exercise of governmental power is subject to limitations protective of the rights of the individual."[28] Because and insofar as the areas of authority of the national and local governments are defined, the latter are not "subordinate" in Locke's sense to the former. Each is in its defined area a locus of the supreme power. In addition, the individual has both enumerated (The Bill of Rights) and unenumerated (Ninth Amendment) rights, recognition of which limits the power of both national and local authorities.

In this situation "the Supreme Court," as Mr. Justice Brennan put it, "has been assigned the unique responsibility for umpiring our federal system."[30] Its work was described by Mr. Justice Jackson as that of "arbitrating the allocation of powers between different branches of the Federal Government, between state and nation, between state and state, and between majority government and minority rights."[31]

Once one grasps the tremendous complexity of the possible relationships between the hundreds of religious bodies and between one or more of them and one or more of the many institutionalized foci of the civil authority, he sees the complete inadequacy of Jefferson's simple concepts of a wall, a church, and a State to encompass and promote understanding of the actualities of the American situation. In America both the "church," as such, and the "State" in the traditional sense are conceptual abstractions not applicable to the realities experienced in the United States.

---

27. Locke, *Second Treatise*, chap. 13, sect. 149, in Laslett, 412-413. Locke was very clear on this point: "Though, as I said, the *Executive* and *Federative* Power of every Community be really distinct in themselves, yet they are hardly to be separated, and placed, at the same time, in the hands of distinct Persons. For both of them requiring the force of the Society for their exercise, it is almost impracticable to place the Force of the Commonwealth in distinct, and not subordinate hands; or that the *Executive* and *Federative Power* should be placed in Persons that might act separately, whereby the Force of the Publick would be under different Commands: which would be apt sometime or other to cause disorder and ruine" (chap. 12, sect. 148, 412).
28. Frankfurter, *The Process of Judging in the Supreme Court*, 35.
29. Ibid.
30. William J. Brennan, Jr., "State Court Decisions and the Supreme Court," in Westin, *The Supreme Court*, 103.
31. Jackson, *The Supreme Court*, 9.

Even the Supreme Court cannot adjudicate differences between two abstractions, at least not when the names for them are not found in the Constitution which it is the Justices' job to interpret. It can only adjudicate practical differences between entities in the society with legal being and standing. It is specifically precluded from "rendering . . . every form of pronouncement on abstract, contingent, or hypothetical issues."[32] This is why if we think with Jefferson's concepts of "church" and "state" we tend not to discuss the actual problems and legal issues before us but rather the differences between two abstractions which can be dealt with only hypothetically and resolved only in the realm of ideas. It is this that seems to me to give an air of unreality to many of the discussions of "church and state" in the United States and serves to distract attention from notice and discussion of one of the chief sources of conflicts over matters pertaining to religion—namely, the clashes between the religious "sects" themselves.

We should be mindful of the fact that from the viewpoint of those responsible for the civil order in the nations of Christendom during the past four hundred years "religion" organized in many "sects" has not been a unifying force but a divisive element in the body politic. And the clashes between the religious "sects" are periodically still threats to "the domestic tranquility" if not to the political society itself.

For centuries some ecclesiastical bodies were armed, either directly or indirectly, with coercive power in the defense of their "orthodox" beliefs and practices. And they often used every weapon in the arsenal of physical violence against the heretic, dissenter, or schismatic person. It was the civil authority that deprived them of these weapons. If now we admit that Christians were wrong in using such weapons in defense of the Gospel of Jesus Christ, it seems to me that credit is due the religiously "neutral" civil authority that took the Sword of the Steel from them and left them dependent upon the Sword of the Spirit alone. If our theology permits, we may even suppose that God was using the civil authority to force Christians to act overtly in accordance with what they professed. And this might suggest an area in which to begin to look for a theological justification of our form of civil government. But instead of probing in this direction, some religionists continue to speak pejoratively of the "secular" or "Godless" state.

Madison's "sects" are the only religious institutions that have legal being, rights, and standing in the United States. Their corporate differences can, and often have, resulted in justiciable issues subject to adjudication in the civil courts and having far reaching consequences. For example, the progressive elimination of religious exercises in the

---

32. Ibid., 12.

public schools in the forms of Bible reading and prayers was not the result of initiative on the part of the civil authorities, but rather the result of the initiative of religious groups that rightly questioned the legality of using the civil power to impose the forms of a particular "sect" or group of "sects" on all the persons in a public institution of the pluralistic society.[33]

The civil authorities, indeed, have little opportunity to take the initiative in religious matters. Acceptance of the idea of a commonwealth with religious pluralism and conflicting "ecclesiastical bodies" forced the civil authority to assume an attitude of neutrality toward their conflicting claims, neither helping nor hindering any religious institution while protecting the rights of each and all. For when all the religious groups are equal before the law, the authority which must adjudicate the differences between them that threaten the civil order cannot be a party in the conflicts—as was the case in Christendom for centuries.

Of course it may be assumed that the civil authorities in adjudicating the differences between "ecclesiastical bodies" must have some guidelines, presumably rooted in some conception of the nature of man and his relation to the cosmos in which he finds himself. The philosophical and/or theological context implied here I call "the religion of the Republic." What is it? I find it at least adumbrated in the "enlightened" thought of the eighteenth century and the Protestant evangelical thought of the nineteenth. I have argued, therefore, that at the heart of the matter for religionists is, in no traditional sense, an issue between "church" and "state," but the theological issue between the particularistic theologies of the "sects" and the cosmopolitan theology of the Republic. But I cannot claim competence in this area, and wish that more of our professional theologians would take up the question.

---

33. Frommer, *The Bible and the Public Schools*, 27.

Living with Establishment and Disestablishment in Nineteenth-Century Anglo-America

MARTIN E. MARTY

The Problem of Law and Ethos in Secularization

The problem of secularization preoccupies most historians of modern religion. In its context, the stories of legal issues and adjustments are most attractive. While it is difficult to chronicle changes in the ideas, mores, ethos, customs, and behavioral nuances of a people, changes in laws are tangible and readily documentable. Yet the passage of laws or acceptance of amendments, treaties, charters, and constitutions can often draw a variety of responses, including citizens' creative foot-dragging or widespread ignoring of the new resolutions.

Seldom has the drama of legal change or the confusion of behavioral and ideological correlates been more focused than in nineteenth-century England and America. In England, the religious establishment continued to receive support from spokesmen who wanted to be tolerant and even encompassing in their outlook. In America, disestablishment was virtually universally accepted by people who actually desired to see religion "established" no longer by law but by favor in the habits and ideas of a nation.

Both sides produced impressive apologetic literature which advocated opposite courses on the two shores of the Atlantic, yet without much polemic against the course taken by their transatlantic counterparts. The British worried in general about disestablishment without making much negative reference to America. Broad Churchman Thomas Arnold, a prime defender of the national church, superficially seemed to be an exception. Speaking to his countrymen, he stated a fear that "if we do not mind, we shall come to the American fashion, and have no provision made for the teaching of Christianity at all."

As Arnold thought about it, America fitted into his argument well:

"We are told to look at America; the United States have no national religion; but yet we are assured that they are as religious a people as ourselves." Such a statement, he thought, shrouded a confusion. "We forget that 'America' is, in the first place, a very vague word, and that in those parts of the union in which religion is in the healthiest state, *there is what is almost equivalent to an Establishment* . . . ." In New York and in New England, where the people were more religious, *"there is an Establishment, or what amounts to nearly the same thing*, in these parts of the United States" [Emphasis added]. The southern and western states, where religion was less established, were not so moral or religious, he decided, as northeastern America or the places in England where the Church of England was well-established with clerics and support.[1]

If the British largely ignored America's legal disestablishment while tending to praise church life there, Americans took their negative models of establishment from the longer Christian past or the Roman Catholic present and rarely referred to England's situation. Perhaps both sides were gentle out of ignorance, myopia, or a sense that it was unwise to advertise an alternative that was effective elsewhere. Yet Christians in both nations also felt a common destiny. An American Episcopalian noted that modern commerce, along with responsibility for Christian mission and talent for enterprise and colonization, had "fallen mainly into the hands of two of the most Christian nations in earth."[2] British Congregationalists Andrew Reed and James Matheson, in a famous passage reporting on their trip to America, spiritualized this vision: "Unite Britain and America in energetic and resolved co-operation for the world's salvation, and the world is saved"[3] On such a scale, differing legal patterns meant little, while for domestic consumption significant leaders on both sides could stress the importance of the course their nation had taken.

A Comparative Approach: On Privilege and Service

The problem addressed in this article can be summarized in a hypothesis about the interaction of spokesmen on both sides. Both were getting what they wanted and wanted more of what they had.

---

1. Thomas Arnold, *Principles of Church Reform* (1833), ed. M. J. Jackson and J. Rogan (London: Society for Promoting Christian Knowledge, 1962), 143-44.
2. John S. Stone, "The Bearings of Modern Commerce on the Progress of Modern Missions," quoted by Samuel Miller in *The Missionary Enterprise* (Boston, 1846), 257. Stone's words date from 1839.
3. Andrew Reed and James Matheson, *A Narrative of the Visit to the American Churches, by the Deputation from the Congregational Union of England and Wales*, 2 vols. (London: Harper and Brothers, 1835), 2:300.

"What they wanted" turned out to be similar in England and America, even though the legal paths in both instances differed drastically. The spokesmen of the established Church of England wanted legal establishment retained so that they could better enjoy privileges and serve the nation. In making their claims they gradually shifted from arguments based on the philosophical or theological "truth" behind establishment to one based on utility.

The American spokesmen for similar reasons wanted to see the refinement and development of the new pattern of legal disestablishment. The British worked toward their goals by supporting the concept of the national church. The Americans found themselves speaking of "national churches," established de facto because they reposed in the hearts of the citizens without benefit of law. Their argument sometimes shifted slightly from one of utility to the claim that privilege for these churches and their service to the nation was based on the very nature of things, on truth.

The reality of the American situation, that "there is what is almost equivalent to an Establishment," can, of course, be discerned without reference to comparative instances, but comparison with England helps to isolate and to define the issue substantively. Without the British reference it is easy to fall into the trap of making the legal resolution serve as the be-all and end-all indicator of modernity in religious life. Without reference to America, historians of British establishment and nationhood in the nineteenth century could easily overlook the virtual voluntaryism which forced Church of England leaders to plead for continued refinement and development of the concept of the national church.

The choice of periods for comparative study is relatively simple. The late eighteenth and early nineteenth centuries in America would be too early, since the legal resolution was being worked out between the 1770s and the early 1830s, while the issue of "living with disestablishment" was still waiting to be located. Between final disestablishment (in Massachusetts) in 1833 and the passage of the Fourteenth Amendment (1868), which guaranteed that the Bill of Rights, whose First Amendment enjoined Congress from passing laws effecting the establishment of religion, would be applicable in all states, the voluntary churches proved that they could live very well indeed with disestablishment. They expanded into the West, sent missionaries into the world, formed benevolent and reform societies, experienced major revivals (as in 1857-58), and survived the Civil War. "Infidels" lost ground, dissent disappeared into tolerant denominationalism, and the Roman Catholic immigrants—who actually also advocated the evangelicals' kind of resolutions on church and state—were not yet displacing the white Protestant churches, which could still speak for the American majority.

The same years were full of tumult in the British establishment, which was yielding ground and forced to change its rationales. The repeal of the Test and Corporation acts in 1828, the similar repeal of the Indemnity Act in the same year, Catholic Emancipation in 1829, the Reform Bill of 1832 (which had seen most Church of England bishops on the unpopular antireform side), and John Keble's "Oxfordian" sermon on "National Apostasy" all signalled a new era. Toward the end of this period a reform of the divorce law in 1857 worked against establishment; the Reform Bill of 1867 is marked as the time after which the preoccupying question was disestablishment and not internal reform of the Church of England, while in 1871 the Church of Ireland became a precedent for disestablishment.

More difficult in this history of comparative advocacies is the choice of advocates. Paradoxically, the American case is simpler, despite the denominational pluralism and competition. For reasons already stated, white Protestants occupied the field. Most of the best remembered spokesmen were Congregationalists or Presbyterians at a time (around 1855) when Baptists and Methodists must have constituted more than 70 percent of the evangelical Protestant church membership. But there were few differences among the evangelicals. A French pastor, puzzled over American half-heartedness about a proto-ecumenical organization, concluded after a visit "why our American brethren have shown so little forwardness to unite with us in the Evangelical Alliance. It is because they have its reality at home."[4]

In Presbyterian Robert Baird's review, these "Evangelicals," "when viewed in relation to the great doctrines which are universally conceded by Protestants to be fundamental, and necessary to salvation, . . . all form but one body, recognising Christ as their common head."[5] They were even more united when viewed in relation to the public realm.

The choice of representatives in England is more complicated because of partisanship within the Church of England. Secularists, Roman Catholics, and Dissenters, of course, are out of the running since this is a story of establishment expression. "The Church of England by law established" (Canons of 1604 terminology) might by mid-century have been called "the Church of privilege," for its leaders sought not a state church but privileged status. Thus the bishop of Oxford, Charles Lloyd, observed in parliamentary debate in 1828 that many powers had already

---

4. The French pastor was J. H. Grand Pièrre, *A Parisian Pastor's Glance at America* (Boston: n.p., 1854), quoted in Timothy L. Smith, *Revivalism and Social Reform in Mid-Nineteenth-Century America* (Nashville: Abingdon Press, 1957), 19.
5. Robert Baird, *Religion in America, or an Account of the Origin, Progress, Relation to the State, and Present Condition of the Evangelical Churches in the United States with Notices of Unevangelical Denominations* (Glasgow, Edinburgh: Blackie and Son, 1844), 449.

been taken away from the Church of England or were being shared with Dissenters. That left only "certain *civil* privileges, which, according to this definition of the Establishment are necessary to its existence—Take then away these civil Privileges, and where will be the Establishment?"[6]

The Religious Census of 1851, the only one ever conducted in Great Britain, devastated those who claimed privilege by right, since it revealed that about half the people at worship on March 30 were not members of the Church of England. An "arithmetical war" resulted, while the census "finally established the impossibility of treating the establishment as privileged on the ground that it was the church of the immense majority of the country."[7] By this time the Anglican Evangelicals were going about their business without much reference to the debate over legal privilege. Oxford Tractarians, when they saw the Church of England subordinated to the state, often even attacked the bond. The center of the support for establishment came from what was to be called the Broad Church or from people of no party who could identify with Broad Churchmen on this one issue. Theirs was a minority party at the time it received its name in 1853. Its formal apologists were generally moderate-to-liberal theological types who favored toleration of religious differences, allowed for mild biblical criticism, supported lay involvement and church reform, and were ready to include Dissenters in the national church. No claim can be made that they spoke for all Anglicans, but only that their defense of establishment was most inclusive and most strenuous and that they best illumine the present case.

The leaders were no minor figures; at some stage or other people as prominent as Samuel Taylor Coleridge, Thomas Arnold, Frederick Denison Maurice, A. P. Stanley, and successive bishops of London Charles James Blomfield and Archibald Campbell Tait can be seen in the shadow of this broad tent.

Defense of an Established National Church in England

Defense of a broadly established national church which implied privilege was argued on the ground that it would best serve the nation and its citizens and moved from defense based on the inherent "truth" in such a relation to one of its general utility.

---

6. British Museum, Additional Ms. 40343, 234ff., quoted in Olive J. Brose, *Church and Parliament: The Reshaping of the Church of England, 1826-1860* (Stanford, Calif.: Stanford University Press, 1959), 17.
7. Owen Chadwick, *The Victorian Church*, 2 vols. (New York: Oxford University Press, 1970), 1:369.

These two traditions derive sometimes explicitly and at other times only symbolically from Richard Hooker (c. 1554-1600) and William Warburton (1698-1779). One of the most passionate and eloquent partisans of Hooker's view that the establishment of a national church belonged to the nature of things itself was the young William E. Gladstone. While Gladstone later moved toward more tolerant views and even repudiated his early writings, the latter writings demonstrate how "Hookerism" was able to survive in the Anglican spectrum well into the nineteenth century. For Hooker, "The Church and the Commonweal . . . are . . . personally one society, which society being termed a Commonweal as it liveth under whatsoever form of secular law and regiment, a Church as it hath the spiritual law of Christ."[8] Gladstone praised Hooker as the source of "the great doctrine that the state is a person, having a conscience, cognisant of matter of religion, and bound by all constitutional and natural means to advance it."[9]

On the other hand, the future prime minister criticized Warburton's theory that "civil society, being defective in the controul [sic] of motives and in the sanction of reward, had in all ages called in the aid of religion to supply and want,"[10] and that therefore merely pragmatic alliances were valid between church and state. How then could the state move beyond utilitarian arrangements to recognize truth, as Gladstone thought it should?

Gladstone, a dedicated High Church layman, in *The State in Its Relations with the Church* (1838) and *Church Principles Considered in Their Results* (1840) claimed that the church was grounded in divine revelation and had its security apart from the state. But the state needed to be united to the church. The church's "condition would be anything rather than pitiable, should she once more occupy the position which she held before the reign of Constantine. But the State, in rejecting her, would actively violate its most solemn duty."[11] "Take the Church of England out of the history of England, and the history of England becomes a chaos, without order, without life, and without meaning."[12]

While the state should support the church on the basis of truth, it "ought not to use coercion for the propagation of religious truth, or for the repression of erroneous opinion, because the employment of

---

8. Richard Hooker, *The Works of That Learned and Judicious Divine Mr. Richard Hooker containing Eight Books of the Laws of Ecclesiastical Polity . . .*, 3 vols. (Oxford: Clarendon Press, 1820), 3:269.
9. William E. Gladstone, *The State in Its Relations with the Church*, 2 vols. (London, 1838), 1:14.
10. Ibid., 16-20.
11. Ibid., 5.
12. Hansard, 3rd series (216) (1873), 47-48, quoted in Peter T. Marsh, *The Victorian Church in Decline: Archbishop Tait and the Church of England, 1868-1882* (Pittsburgh: University of Pittsburgh Press, 1969), 144.

force by man upon man is essentially inappropriate for such a purpose."[13] "The State and the Church have both of them moral agencies. But the State aims at character through conduct; the Church at conduct through character; in harmony with which, the State forbids more than enjoins, the Church enjoins more than forbids."[14]

Gladstone seemed to know that the practical arrangement was on borrowed time. To John Henry Newman he wrote, "My language has always been, 'Here is the genuine and proper theory of government as to religion; hold it as long as you can, and as far as you can.' Government must subsist; and if not as (in strictness) it ought, then as it may."[15] Gladstone (and Thomas Arnold) propagated the concept of the state as a "moral personality." There is "generally in societies a real and substantial personality."[16] He was to back away from the application of his concepts. In 1847 he admitted that "it is now impossible to regulate the connection between Church and State in this country by reference to an abstract principle."[17]

Rather than make the case on the basis of tracts by young Gladstone, it is more profitable to turn to representative churchmen. Frederick Denison Maurice, perhaps the most notable Anglican thinker at mid-century, continued the Hookerian lineage. He supported establishment because of his prior views of the nature of government and civil society as extensions of God's reign and would have felt thoroughly at home with Gladstone's view of the state as having "a real and substantial personality." In his major work he argued that church and state were "a union which has cemented itself by no human contrivances, and which exists *in the very nature of things.*"[18] [Emphasis added] The ethos of the nation represented "contiguity in place." "Never for a moment let us try to separate, or dream that we can separate, our individual life from our national."[19] This life was religiously expressed through the national church. Gladstone's High Church and Maurice's Broad Church argument about a bond based on "the very nature of things" was to lose out to the utilitarian advocates of a national church.

---

13. Gladstone, *The State in Its Relations with the Church*, 310.
14. Ibid., 115-16.
15. Gladstone to John Henry Newman, 19 April 1845, *Correspondence on Church and Religion of William Edward Gladstone*, ed. D. C. Lathbury, 2 vols. (London: John Murray; New York: Macmillan Co., 1910), 1:72.
16. Gladstone, *The State in Its Relations with the Church*, 65-66.
17. Gladstone to R. J. Phillimore, 15 February 1847, *Correspondence on Church and Religion of William Edward Gladstone*, 2:7.
18. Frederick Denison Maurice, *The Kingdom of Christ: or, Hints to a Quaker, Respecting the Principles, Constitution and Ordinances of the Catholic Church*, 2d ed., 2 vols. (London: J. G. F. and J. Rivington, 1842), 2:298.
19. Frederick Denison Maurice, *The Doctrine of Sacrifice, Deduced from the Scriptures: A Series of Sermons* (Cambridge: Macmillan and Co., 1854), 64.

Behind the latter was the figure of William Warburton, whose tract title in 1736 summarized his case: *The Alliance of Church and State, and the Necessity and Equity of Established Religion and a Test Law demonstrated, from the Essence and End of Civil Society, upon the Fundamental Principles of the Law of Nature and Nations.* He believed that his views could be applicable to any religious force in any society. In the Christian world, the alliance would mean that the state would protect the church while the church would minister to the state, receiving benefits in return while it surrendered its independence to the supreme civil magistrate. In a sense, the state would go shopping for the most representative church and grant it privileges.

The nineteenth century was a good time for the Warburtonian utilitarian case. Bishop Richard Watson saw the establishment to be an instrument of social control.[20] In 1833 the *Quarterly Review* placed its cards on the Table. The Church of England's great virtue: "It *maintains order.*"[21] Roman Catholic convert W. G. Ward was eventually to complain that the national church's burden of responsibility was distracting. "Your church so desired to be a National Church, that it failed to take any security that it should be an orthodox one."[22] Truth claims slipped away, especially when Thomas Arnold and others would embrace virtually all dissent in the privileged national church.

Samuel Taylor Coleridge was a distinguished representative of the case based on utility. In *The Constitution of Church and State* he spoke of a universal ideal church and a relative and imperfect church in human society. The latter would be organized along differing national lines. Within each nation, the church was to preserve culture and inspire the society. For this task there would have to be a "clerisy" of learned men who would educate the society, to produce a better religious spirit.[23]

Coleridge was never specific as to how the English national church and the ideal church were to be connected. His significance lies more in the way he informed other notables such as Thomas Arnold, Maurice, historian Julius Charles Hare, and the bishops of London. Archibald Tait, for one, thought that the Church of England could be called "an endowment for the teaching of the Christian religion to

---

20. Richard Watson, *Anecdotes of the Life of Richard Watson, Written by Himself at Different Intervals and Revised in 1814* . . ., 2 vols. (London: R. Watson, 1818), 2:127.
21. W. Dealtry, "The Church and Its Endowments: A Charge," *Quarterly Review* 49 (1833) :211.
22. William G. Ward, *Anglican Establishment Contrasted with the Catholic Church of Every Age: Being a Second Letter to the Editor of the "Guardian," with Strictures on the Articles in That Journal Entitled "Anglo-Romanism"* (London: Burns and Lambert, 1850), 35.
23. Samuel Taylor Coleridge, *On the Constitution of the Church and State according to the Idea of Each: With Aids-Towards a Right Judgment on the Late Catholic Bill*, 2d ed. (London: Hurst, Chance, and Co., 1830), 50.

the nation."[24] His predecessor, Charles Blomfield, sided with the Warburtonians, as his title makes clear: *On the Uses of an Established Church*. "The strongest of arguments for an Established Church is this: that it is the only, or at any rate the most efficient, instrument of instructing the people in the doctrines of religion, and of habituating them to its decencies and restraints."[25] "The established Church must be 'efficient' to show forth 'the beauty of its holy usefulness.' "[26]

> Many and powerful are the arguments by which we may prove our right to the attention and respect of individual Christians and our claims upon the support and protection of the State. But they will fail to produce conviction in the minds of the greater part of mankind, if unaccompanied by the more conclusive proof of *usefulness*. In spite of all the reasons which are to be urged in behalf of our excellent Church, — the purity of her doctrines; the wisdom of her discipline; her legitimate authority; the unbroken succession and right ordination of her ministry; the excellence of her constitution and formularies; — yet if there be a failure in activity and zeal on the part of the clergy, the Establishment must sink beneath them. But it will never cease to be respected and maintained, while it is *useful* . . . .[27]

The most dogged defender of the concept of an inclusive, useful national church was Thomas Arnold, who set forth a complete theory and practice for such an institution in his semi-secular and increasingly pluralistic age. He could not "understand what is the good of a national Church if it be not to Christianize the Nation, and introduce the principles of Christianity into men's social and civil relations, and expose . . . wickedness."[28] "The clergy of a national Church are directly called upon to Christianize the nation; not only to inculcate the private virtues of the Gospel but its pure and holy principles in their full extent; those divine laws of which it may indeed be said that their voice is the harmony of the world."[29]

However else people would remember the headmaster of Rugby, "The 'Idea' of my life, to which I think every thought of my mind more or less tends, is the perfecting the 'idea' of the Edward the Sixth Reformers, — constructing a truly National and Christian Church."[30] For his lay-oriented, almost anticlerical and sometimes nonclerical

---

24. Archibald Campbell Tait, *The Present Position of the Church of England: Seven Addresses Delivered to the Clergy and Churchwardens of His Diocese as His Primary Visitation* (London: Macmillan and Co., 1873), 41.
25. Quoted in G. E. Biber, *Bishop Blomfield and His Times: An Historical Sketch* (London: Harrison, 1857), 149.
26. Quoted in Alfred Blomfield, *A Memoir of Charles James Blomfield, D. D., Bishop of London, with Selections from His Correspondence* (London: John Murray, 1864), 140.
27. Quoted in Biber, *Bishop Blomfield and His Times*, 60.
28. Arthur P. Stanley, *Life and Correspondence of Dr. Arnold* (London: John Murray, 1901), 293.
29. Thomas Arnold, *The Miscellaneous Works of Thomas Arnold*, ed. Arthur P. Stanley (London: B. Fellowes, 1845), Appendix 1: see the introduction to Arnold, *Principles of Church Reform*, ed. Jackson and Rogan, 30-31.
30. Stanley, *Life and Correspondence of Dr. Arnold*, 386.

model of churchmanship, whose major outlet would be social reform, Arnold feared that a disestablished set of churches would lose the nation's ear. For this model, "Nothing, as it seems to me, can save the Church but an union with the Dissenters."[31] This did not imply their conversion, especially since theological niceties concerned him little. Arnold intended to stress the differences between Christians and non-Christians and to deemphasize differences among the Christian denominations.

Scores of examples paralleling the testimonies of Gladstone and Maurice or, more frequently, Coleridge, Arnold, Blomfield, and Tait could be adduced, but it is time to draw up the totals on one side of the balance sheet. These are the arguments of those who most supported establishment and least took it for granted. From the angle of comparative Anglo-American history, the American who would have cared to could have asked in the middle of the century, "What is left, then, of establishment?" A legal arrangement, guaranteeing some privileges; but that the Church of England more privileged than American evangelicalism? Cynics might say that fiscal support was decisive. But American churches have always been tax-exempt; in the course of time financial privileges in America were to amount to as much as financial subsidy meant in England. Was establishment exclusivistic? No, it was to be as broad as the concept and reality of interactive evangelicalism in America. Should it survive because of theological truth, "the nature of things"? The argument was made on the basis of utility, as the Victorian years went on.

Defense of Disestablished National Churches in America

The American case began more in practical adjustments than in claims of theological truth. More Presbyterians, Episcopalians, and Congregationalists had not led the legal separationist battles in the late eighteenth century. They clung to moderate and relatively inclusive establishment until they drifted or were dragged into disestablishment by "Enlightened" statesmen, the dissenting churches (Baptist and the like), and, most of all, by the practical situation of nation-building in the face of religious pluralism. It was useful to give up legal privilege in order to retain other kinds of privilege and in order to serve the state in a new way.

Once disestablishment was destined to prevail, it found virtually unanimous support even from church people who earlier had opposed

---

31. Quoted in William Law Mathieson, *English Church Reform, 1815-1840* (London: Longmans, Green, 1923), 71.

it. From Philip Schaff and Robert Baird at the beginning in the middle of that century to the historians active today, religious freedom based on some sort of separation of religious and civil realms and accompanied by voluntaryism has been the center of the plot of American Christianity in the period. Schaff in 1857 wrote that "the glory of America is a free Christianity, independent of the secular government, and supported by the voluntary contributions of a free people. This is one of the greatest facts in modern history."[32]

Almost never challenged was visitor James Lord Bryce's conclusion after a lengthy visit in America (1888) that it was "accepted as an axiom by all Americans that the civil power ought to be not only neutral and impartial as between different forms of faith, but ought to leave these matters entirely on one side.... There seem to be no two opinions on this subject in the United States." "All religious bodies are absolutely equal before the law and unrecognized by law, except as voluntary associations of private citizens." "No established church looks down scornfully upon dissenters from the height of its titles and endowments, and talks of them as hindrances in the way of its work. No dissenters pursue an established church in a spirit of watchful jealousy, nor agitate for its overthrow," he wrote in obvious reference to his own English context.[33]

Bryce properly detected a nominalist strain in American life, one which distanced it from Hooker's understanding or from Gladstone's or Maurice's view about the state as a corporate personality:

Americans conceive that the religious character of a government consists in nothing but the religious belief of individual citizens, and the conformity of their conduct to that belief.... They deem the general acceptance of Christianity to be one of the main sources of their national prosperity, and their nation a special object of the Divine favour.[34]

Did the argument of pro-voluntaryist evangelicals make them sound as if they were "disestablished"? By law, yes. As far as privilege or service to the nation is concerned? Hardly. Legal disestablishment meant instant reestablishment in the national ethos. Years before, they had given up the idea of receiving much financial support of privilege, even when vestigial establishment remained. They now had little more to lose. They had much to gain: parity, prestige, privilege, the absence of anticlericalism and of public resentment. They could achieve what the contenders for the national church wanted in England, but they needed no legal support.

---

32. Philip Schaff, *Germany: Its Universities, Theology, and Religion* . . . (Philadelphia: Lindsay and Blakiston, 1857), 105.
33. James Bryce, *The American Commonwealth* (New York: Macmillan, 1910), 2:766, 763, 874.
34. Ibid., 768-70.

To achieve this status, these Protestant "national churches" did not dare to wallow in *mere* pluralism. They were less varied than they thought they were. Blacks had no voice; Jews were few; Catholics were unacceptable. The Protestant "unevangelicals" on Robert Baird's list were a small minority on the scene: Unitarians, Universalists, Christian Connectionists, Swedenborgians, Dunkers, Rappists, Shakers, Mormons, Atheists, Deists, Socialists, Fourierists, and the like. These all have to be tolerated, but not affirmed.

Meanwhile, evangelicals could tolerate differences for the sake of de facto establishment, but a premium was placed on the convergences and similarities. Charles Hodge of Princeton saw the citizens becoming one people, "having one language, one literature, essentially one religion, and one common soul." With less than befitting humility he added that America would exert thus "a greater influence on the human family than any other nation that has ever existed."[35]

Lyman Beecher, fighting against the Sunday mails, had to face the issue of whether the interest of churches in laws to halt such mails might not contradict the Bill of Rights. Beecher showed how little legal disestablishment meant in the technical sense: "Let God be praised that there is at length one nation . . . where church and state are not united and where reason and conscience are free. But the petitions are, not that Congress will do anything *for* religion, but, simply, that by legislation they will do nothing *against* religion . . . . We asked for no union of church and state; but simply, that the moral influence of the Sabbath may not be thus bartered away for secular gain."[36]

The old dream of a Dutch Reformed minister, Edward Livingston, expressed in 1788, was coming true: the American churches, once appendanges of England's national churches, have "now become national Churches themselves in this new Empire." When disestablishment did come and many feared consequent spiritual disintegration, Andover Seminary's Leonard Woods thought that God would provide a homogenizing force. Men seek community. "The idea of *national churches* seems thus to be deeply founded in the very nature of religious development." Left to themselves, Christians in their piety would lead "to the formation of Christian communities, at least as extensive as the civil bodies with which they are connected."[37]

Here was the germ of the argument that national churches belonged to the nature of things and could be advocated on the basis of philosophical and theological truth. After all the arguments for the

---

35. Charles Hodge, "Anniversary Address," *The Home Missionary* 2 (1829) :18.
36. Lyman Beecher, *Sermons Delivered on Various Occasions* (Boston, 1828), 159-60.
37. Edward Livingston and Leonard Woods are quoted in Perry Miller, *The Life of the Mind in America* (New York: Harcourt, Brace and World, 1965), 40, 44.

utility of the arrangement—claims that were, of course, never to be left behind in America, the truth claims came ever more to the fore. Horace Bushnell thought that he was arguing against the crowd, but support for the views on church and state of this moderately liberal Congregationalist can be found across the spectrum from Southern Baptists to Roman Catholic bishops in his day. So his complaint came without complete accuracy. "We have taken up, in this country, almost universally, theories of government which totally forbid the entrance of moral considerations. Government, we think, is a social compact or agreement—a mere human creation, having as little connection with God, as little of a moral quality, as a ship of war or a public road,"[38] Yet government and church-in-nation were divinely instituted.

So effective was the unofficial establishment that those who could not accept the truth claims could at least passively agree with those based on utility. Alexis de Tocqueville pointed to the presence of the unbeliever who, while he "does not admit religion to be true, . . . still considers it useful. Regarding religious institutions in a human point of view, he acknowledges their influences upon manners and legislation . . . . He regrets the faith that he has lost; and as he is deprived of a treasure of which he knows the value, he fears to take it away from those who still possess it."[39] The citizens did not generally oppose the calling of days of thanksgiving or prayer, the provisions for chaplaincies, the showing of decent respect, support, and granting of a privileged position to the inoffensive churches. Nathaniel William Taylor, a well-known Congregationalist cleric, said, "We only ask for those provisions of law . . . in behalf of a common Christianity, which are its due as a nation's strength and a nation's glory."[40]

The program of the disestablished national churches in America was almost identical with that proposed by leaders of the established national church in England. They would serve as educators, providers of a moral foundation, preservers of order, and inculcators of virtue and piety and would provide a network of voluntary associations which became, said critic-from-within Calvin Colton, "so numerous, so great, so active and influential, that, as a whole, they now constitute the great school of public education, in the formation of those practical opinions, religious, social, and political, which lead the public mind and govern the country."[41] Colton in *Protestant Jesuitism* detected early

---

38. Horace Bushnell, *Politics under the Law of God: A Discourse, Delivered in the North Congregational Church on the Annual Fast of 1844* (Hartford: E. Hunt, 1844), 10.
39. Alexis de Tocqueville, *Democracy in America*, 2 vols. (New York: Vantage Books, 1954), 1:324.
40. Nathaniel William Taylor, *A Sermon Addressed to the Legislature of the State of Connecticut, etc.*, 2d ed. (New Haven: A. H. Maltby and Co., 1823), 12-13.
41. Calvin Colton, *A Voice from America to England: By an American Gentleman* (London: Colborn, 1839), 97.

the extent of the new kind of establishment in his criticism of people like Lyman Beecher, who acted "Catholically," by trying to make an "attempt to establish a spiritual supremacy over the mind of this country."

> It is a remarkable fact that in less than the period that belongs to a single generation, the economy of society in this country, in all that pertains to moral reform and religious enterprise, has been formed on a model entirely new to ourselves, but not without type in history. It is the assumption of a controlling influence by a few, who stand at the head of moral and religious organizations of various names. The public ... do not understand when and how the whole frame of society is getting a new structure .... [42]

To historians who agree, as this writer does, that Colton is thus accurately reporting, he provides a Q.E.D. for the latter half of this present comparative article. A new structure, bewildering to but accepted by the public, "not without type in history" (viz., in religious establishments), had immediately emerged.

The parallel question to that posed for hypothetical mid-nineteenth century Englishmen can now be turned on America: What is left of disestablishment? The legal arrangement allowed for privilege to mainstream churches and to religion in general. Implicit fiscal support followed. The national churches aspired to the kind of unity a national church might have implied but, in England, could no longer know. Advocacy on the basis of truth accompanied the majority support on grounds of utility.

Indications: Comparative Studies and Society's Structure

What has become clear in this mid-nineteenth century comparative study is that, while partisans of the two polities staked everything on establishment or disestablishment by law, the legal situation was relatively unimportant. What the law took in the American instance, ethos gave back. What ethos did not provide in England, law was hardly able to produce. Operating on contradictory policies and programs, accompanied by an impressive variety of rationales which were contended for with eloquence and passion, church leaders contended for opposite kinds of approaches. What each received and what each lost in that century had little to do with legal provisions for religion or its removal. What mattered in both cases was the effectiveness of persuasion by leaders and the loyalty of the adherents.

In the future it will be profitable to contrast American or British instances with both northwest European continental situations (Pro-

---

42. Calvin Colton, *Protestant Jesuitism: By a Protestant* ... (New York: Harper and Bros, 1836), preface and 107.

testant establishments, or Protestant-Catholic coexistences) and southern Eurpoean (Roman Catholic) establishments, just as it would be valid to see the nineteenth-century Christian examples compared with the secularization of modern constitutions in the non-Western world, as, for example, in India. Each of these studies would illumine a different aspect of the way religion lives in nation and nation lives in religion.

Historians in general tend to eschew fashionable philosophical or sociological presuppositions, at least explicitly. But this study of mid-nineteenth century Anglo-America would probably be satisfying to and give support for those who are at home with structural-functional models. In these, the structure of a whole society is studied along with the functional relations of its parts, much as a biologist studies the structures and functions of the whole organismic system and its parts. Such analyses assume that social units interact to form a more or less organic system. American "exceptionalism" inevitably suffers if historical events confirm what the hypothesis suggests.

Modern Anglo-American society, seen from such a point of view, seems to have had room for a religion which would fulfill certain functions. In England one fitted into the structure on a formal legal basis, while in America, bereft of many legal props, another found a different set of means by which to relate to its whole. Law and the legal resolutions, about which apologists then and historians since have made such a point, were of a secondary character. Modern pluralistic societies, which England and the United States had become in the past century, evidently allow certain slots for religion in national life.

Legislation, in the instances compared here, altered circumstances less than one might have supposed. Leonard Woods seems to have been correct when he said that "the idea of *national churches* seems . . . to be deeply founded in the very nature of religious development."

American Missionary Efforts to Influence Government Indian Policy

R. PIERCE BEAVER

Three centuries of partnership between church and state in the Indian missions came to a climax in President U. S. Grant's "Peace Policy." The churches under that scheme accepted definite responsibilities in administration, education, and evangelism. If that program were to succeed, two other services appeared to the mission boards to be required of them. One was to champion the cause of Indian rights in order that public opinion might better support the plan. The other was to defend the Peace Policy before the nation and to criticize it before government so as to shape and guide it more effectively towards achieving peace, civilization, and eventually citizenship for the Indian.

The first task of the churches appeared to be convincing the public and frontier church members that the policy of civilization was a valid and practical alternative to the popular demand for extermination of the Indian. The new policy must have a chance to prove itself. Extermination was inhuman and unchristian. Every Indian uprising, every account of a massacre, every instance of resistance to aggression and injustice brought new demands for repression, even for extermination, from a large part of the Western populace. The average frontier church member was likely to hold the same views as his unchurched neighbor. Both the Christian conscience and the national conscience had to be awakened. One editor lamented: "It is still an open question with Christian people whether the bullet or the Gospel is to settle the fate of the Indian — whether extermination or redemption is our duty towards him." One heard such remarks as "The rule for the Indian is six feet and a bullet." "Give them the Gospel, but begin with power and ball." It was the common feeling that Indians were outlaws, savages without rights which white men need respect. The missionary forces tried to convert exterminationists and arouse the friends of truth by presenting evidence that more Indians were murdered by whites than whites by Indians, that tales of massacres were often fabrications, and that Indian wars were due either to aggression by white settlers or broken promises by government.

The mission boards endeavored also to enlighten those who believed that the Indian was doomed to destruction by natural circumstances and that government policy ought to speed that end. The American Board, for example, rebuked those who expected God to solve the Indian question by sending disease upon them. Another Congregationalist agency feared destruction from another source, and said: "It is still a question whether the Indian tribes can be delivered from border ruffians, whiskey, and violence, and brought thoroughly under the influence of Christian agents and Christian missionaries, and thus be saved from final extinction." The boards sent out a call to those who feared the inevitability of extinction to support the Peace Policy and missionary expansion, since: "These Indian missions are the sole refuge of the heathen tribes, so long neglected and cruelly oppressed, against foes that seek to destroy both body and soul. . . . time is short." The Baptists even asserted that "the wild Indian is deteriorating and dying out, while the Christianized Indian is improving and increasing."

The missionary circles had little hope of awakening either the "border ruffians" or the corrupt Indian rings of Washington and the frontier to qualms of conscience, but they hoped so to stir up the good people of the West that they would restrain the ruffians, while public opinion throughout the nation could force Congress to enact desirable legislation. They were concerned, however, not only with justice for the Indian, but equally for the redemption of the honor of the American people in the eyes of the world. The United States was about to be judged at the bar of history. But as Lincoln had the honor of giving liberty to the Negro, so Grant was now to be credited with devising a plan of honest dealing with the Indian and of attempting his moral and material elevation. Therefore, let the nation back the Peace Policy with prayer, with pressure on Congressmen, and with contributions to mission boards.

However, there were many persons who would not respond to arguments about justice and national honor. These might possibly be reached by arguments showing that repression was extremely costly to the taxpayer. Indians were certainly expensive. Even feeding them on reservations cost $5,000,000 each year, but that was cheap compared with military operations. It cost the federal government one million dollars and twenty-five white lives for each single warrior killed in the Sioux and Florida Wars of 1852 and 1854. Fifteen or twenty Indians had been killed in the Cheyenne War of 1864-1865 at a total cost of $35,000,000 plus the destruction of lives and property in the frontier settlements. The military repression of the wild Apaches cost

$100,000,000 during the twenty years from 1846 to 1866. It was currently costing the government $12,500,000 for military operations. Let all that expense be contrasted with the fact that not one cent for military purposes was needed to keep in order the civilized Cherokees, Choctaws, Chickasaws, Creeks, and Seminoles.

The mission boards tried by such arguments as these to gain support for the Peace Policy and for their schools and evangelistic work. They cried: "The churches of the land must arouse the consciences of the American people more and more, until it shall be impossible to return to the old ways of Indian fraud and cruelty." They regularly commended the President on the success of his plan and urged its continuance and further development. The church press in general echoed the missionary magazines.

There was also recourse to that favorite ecclesiastical device, the resolution. The mission boards individually, and jointly at the annual conference with the Indian Commissioners, made resolutions with respect to every aspect of program and policy. Sometimes even a national denominational body would act, such as the General Assembly of the Presbyterian Church in the U. S. A., print its resolutions in the church and public press, and forward them to the President and to Congress. Such resolutions eased the consciences of the resolvers, but it was hoped that they would stir up churchmen and bring pressure to bear on Congress. However, as one writer put it: "If resolutions and memorials could have saved the American Indian, he would long ago have been lifted into blessedness. But, unfortunately, reports of committees and expressions of favor from benevolent societies, are but a poor substitute for either manly justice or Christian beneficence."

Therefore, given the uncertain power of resolutions, local groups which would be zealous in community education and organize representation to Congress were greatly to be desired. Consequently some interdenominational Indian rights associations under various names were organized in New York, Boston, Philadelphia, and a few other places. The Friends organized many associations across the country among their own people, which not only supplied agents and schools with material but also gained the public ear. The Episcopal Church sponsored similar aid societies doing the same work. There was one large scale effort by churchwomen to make an impact on Congress. Bishop Hare referred to a strange scene in the Senate in the spring of 1882 when several Western Senators were "lashed almost to fury by the simple reading of a petition of one hundred thousand church women praying that the Government would keep its promises to the Indians and extend to them the protection of the law."

No other denomination in this period was so well organized to work for Indian rights as the Protestant Episcopal Church. Immediately upon accepting responsibility for the nomination and supervision of agents, the General Convention of 1871 created a Standing Committee on Indian Affairs, chaired by William Welsh. It was charged with supervising the agents, supplying them, and gaining the assistance of the government and the courts in protecting Indian rights. This Committee soon became the Commission on Indian Missions. It had a director residing in Washington, who watched over politics, visited the reservations, and promoted missions in the churches. It had a subcommittee headed by Senator Stevenson of Kentucky which lobbied in Congress. That Commission, of the Domestic and Foreign Missionary Society, did excellent work, but it seemed as if a more official organ concerned solely with the question of rights could be more effective. Therefore, the General Convention of 1877 established a committee of three bishops and three deputies "On Securing for the Indians the Protection of the Law." This committee reported in 1880 that the matter was highly complicated, and that it was necessary to secure parallel legislation by the federal government and the states. Bishops Whipple and Hare were constantly promoting Indian rights and welfare in their dioceses, throughout the Episcopal Church, and in Washington. They wrote letters, interviewed the President, and used the press.

The missionary societies placed the greatest hope for sound policy and effective legislation in the Board of Indian Commissioners when it was established by Congress and the President in 1869 and composed of wealthy philanthropists who were regarded as representing the churches. However, the original members of that Board resigned in 1874 because they had no power and neither the Indian Service, the administration, nor Congress paid heed to their reasonable recommendations. The second group of appointees supposedly also represented the churches, but those persons were not so able and influential. After 1875 the fiction of church representation was abandoned. The Board steadily declined in influence, and churchmen turned more hopefully to the voluntary Indian Rights Association after 1882.

It is difficult to say what effect the efforts of the churches achieved in shaping government policy and winning recognition of Indian rights during this period. Certainly the mission boards succeeded in increasing public interest considerably. The churches were not again to be so loudly vocal about justice for the Indian until the decade of the 1950s.

Civilization, the Alternative to War and Extermination

The Indians were an obstacle to white settlement. Even where their lands were poor, whites were certain that they wanted them. The Indians had lost their game lands and were being segregated on reservations where the government had to feed them in idleness. Unable to adjust to such a life, resentful at broken treaties and repeated removals, provoked by atrocities and wrongs inflicted by "the border ruffians," the Indians could be expected to break out in frequent rebellion. Then there would be bloody reprisals. The government was faced with two practical questions, according to General Francis A. Walker, while he was Commissioner of Indian Affairs: What shall be done with the Indian as an obstacle to the progress of settlement and industry; what shall be done with him as a pensioner on our civilization, when, and so far as, he ceases to oppose or obstruct the extension of railroads and of settlement? Walker's answer to the first was to strike the Indian down with the army; to the second, confine him to reservations and somehow keep him there. The Indian's only hope in either case was submission. President Grant's Peace Policy was built upon the assumption that there was another possibility than extermination or sullen submission in degrading idleness. It was the Indian's voluntary acceptance of civilization and his emulation of the white man in living by his own labor. Secretary Schurz later under Hayes said: "If the Indians are to live at all, they must learn to live as white men." But could the Indians be civilized? The arguments were the same as at the beginning, but now there were abundant contemporary illustrations. Every annual report of the Commissioner of Indian Affairs, the Board of Indian Commissioners, and of each mission board offered ample proof. The condition of the Five Civilized Tribes in the South and the Dakotas of Sisseton, Santee, and elsewhere in the North were the prize exhibits.

The government and the missionary societies were at one, at least in the beginning, in agreement that the churches must add the indispensable ingredient which could not be given by government if the Indians were to become civilized. This was the Christian religion. The assumption which had been current for nearly three hundred years was still held: the Gospel brings about civilization. Moses N. Adams, agent for the Sisseton and Wahpeton Sioux was voicing the general opinion when he wrote in 1872: "There seems to be no obstacle in the way of their civilization, except such as are common to all Indian tribes, and which the gospel of Christ and Bible civilization can meet and remove." Not all would have agreed with every item on his list. He mentioned ignorance, idleness, prodigality, hunting, fishing, smoking, babbling, tattling, love of spirituous liquors, riding horseback from house to house, and polygamy. Christianity would replace these characteristics and pursuits with others more desirable. Most important, the gospel would awaken individualism and the desire for a home and sanctified family life. E. P. Smith, missionary and Indian agent, and then Commissioner of Indian Affairs, asserted that the incentive to Christian faith and life had to be caught by contagion from a fellow man, wiser than the Indian, coming personally to extend a hand of sympathy and truth. Therefore, send missionaries, and then "every year will witness a steady decrease of barbarism."

The chief question connected with the policy of civilization which agitated the churches was whether or not the Bureau of Indian Affairs should be transferred from the Department of the Interior to the War Department. Frontier society was always pressing for such a move, and it was repeatedly proposed in Congress. There was general agreement among missionaries, even those who testified to the high quality of the majority of officers, that the presence of a military post inevitably brought demoralization and degradation to neighboring Indians. The Army was not a fit teacher of civilization. Bishop Hare's desire to use troops as a police force to assist agents to keep order and expell obnoxious whites brought him much criticism. It was common knowledge that the Roman Catholic Church favored such a transfer, and that further strengthened opposition by Protestants who were convinced that the Catholics were working against the whole Peace Policy.

The anticipated transfer was opposed in 1873 by all the boards, and again in 1874. The American Board protested: "If they are the children—the wards—of the government, it should be careful not to answer a cry for bread with *lead*, or when they ask for fish to give them scorpions." The question was apparently being decided in favor of the War Department in 1878, and the Baptists objected that such a transfer would be "a mistake alike in morals and economy, and unworthy of the character of the American people." There was great rejoicing in defeat of the proposal.

While they were opposing the transfer to the War Department, the missionary organizations were appealing for establishment of an independent Indian Department with cabinet rank. However, they never undertook a vigorous campaign on behalf of that proposal.

RESERVATIONS, REMOVAL, INDIAN TERRITORY

The missions, with the exception of the American Board and some Episcopalians, were heartily in favor of the official policy of concentrating and segregating Indians upon reservations. There was a nostalgic remembrance of the seventeenth, eighteenth, and early nineteenth century Christian Indian towns and of the prosperous stations among the Five Civilized Tribes. Not the voluntary wandering of the Indians, but white aggression had destroyed them. The wandering tribes of the prairies and plains, however, had baffled the missions. They refused to stay put, and made expensive stations obsolete in short order. Therefore, most societies deemed "schools and missions impracticable until the Indians are collected on reservations"; and they welcomed this policy of the government. Immobilized, the Indians could be "reached." There they could also be protected against white aggression and be taught to work. The editor of the *American Missionary*, commenting approvingly on General Walker's suggestion of concentration, stated: "The true policy is, we believe, to provide a suitable number of reservations, where the efforts of the Government, seconded by the Christian sentiment of the country, may create oases in the sight of cognate tribes, who shall be drawn towards them by affinity, and the opportunity of bettering their condition. The blessing of God on earnest Christian labor must do the rest."

Bishop Hare was an example of those who, on the contrary, could regard a reservation only as a necessary evil or temporary expedient. The American Board missionaries held a similar view. They urged that any reservation be terminated before it interfered with attainment of citizenship. Bishop Hare called the reservation "a gravel-stone in the machinery of our political and social life." Segregation thwarted attainment of civilization. He denounced the system in these strong terms:

The present system, by which, too often, reservations of thousands upon thousands of acres are a vast common, in which any man scratches a piece of land where he will, and where beef, flour, sugar, coffee, etc., are doled out to vicious and virtuous, indolent and industrious alike, is a monstrous evil, which should be tolerated not a day longer than is absolutely necessary. Even were our taxpayers willing to endure it, we have no right to inflict it upon the Indians, who ought to receive from us a useful and not a pernicious training; nor have we any right to rear a race of paupers to be a curse to our whole Western country; nor any right to fight God's good law that man shall labor, and that if any man will not work neither should he eat.

Repeated removals were held clearly to be bad for Indian morale, injurious to progress in civilization, and acts of bad faith as well. Treaty stipulations should be faithfully met so long as treaties existed, it was asserted. Provisions issued under those treaties ought also to be promptly dispensed in such manner as would cause the Indians the least inconvenience and interruption of labor. The Baptists protested in 1882 that at that moment thousands of Indians were in danger of starving because Congress had failed to make appropriations for supplies. The Indians were becoming frantic, and government officials were calling upon the Army to keep the Indians on the reservations and make them "starve quietly."

Nearly all of the mission boards favored concentration of the tribes within Indian Territory as far as possible. There the Indians must be protected against contact with the whites. There were already far too many white persons there for the kind of isolation desired, but the majority held to the view that Indian Territory could still be purely an Indian land. Bishop Hare and the American Board missionaries alone objected to the plan, saying that it would prevent Indian contact with the right kind of white men and would delay absorption into the national society. The others thought that isolation from the white people was a requirement for progress in civilation so that the Indian might eventually come out of seclusion into citizenship. The Quakers fought every effort to open the Territory, to organize it as a regular United States territory, or to admit it to the Union as a state. Title had been legally conveyed to the Indians by the United States, the Friends said, and there must be no intrusion upon it. Speaking for the churches, the Board of Indian Commissioners stated that any law passed for the organization of the country must be agreeable to the Indians. Individual societies also stressed the requirement of consent. As late as 1883 the Board of Foreign Missions of the Presbyterian Church was protesting the incursion of 100,000 settlers each year.

INDIVIDUALISM, HOMES, LAND IN SEVERALTY

Congregationalists and Episcopalians among the missions people deplored the concept behind the treaties, which required that the Indians be treated as sovereign powers and ward of the nation at one and the same time. Yet while treaties existed, stipulations should be faithfully kept. They thought that treaties maintained tribal unity which ought to give way to individualism. Therefore, these people applauded the act of Congress repudiating further treaty making.

Individual responsibility was thought to be prerequisite to progress in civilization and towards citizenship, and it invariably began with the desire for a real, settled home—so these missionaries said. And the primary condition for a home, they asserted, "is an exclusive title to the land upon which it stands and from which its support can be drawn." There was a conviction common to all the mission boards that homemaking depended upon granting of homesteading rights and title to land in severalty to individual Indians. The progress of the Indians connected with the Episcopal and American Board Sioux or Dakota Missions in agricultural homemaking despite all obstacles, including those imposed by government policy, was cited and praised. The missionaries asked that these Indians be given equal rights with the homesteading immigrants from Europe, as well as aid in acquiring initial livestock and implements equal in value to rations that they would have received had they remained reservation Indians. Some thought that government should provide a market and buy part of its supplies from Indians in order to stimulate their farming activities.

CIVIL LAW AND CITIZENSHIP

The missionaries and their friends were convinced that civil law could protect the Indians far better than segregation on a reservation could do. The law would be both protector and educator. Non-taxpaying Indians, who had no status before the law, were not permitted to testify against white men who had wronged them. Neither did the law follow white lawbreakers onto the reservations because the agents had no police to assist them. Bishop Hare warned: "Civilization has loosened, in some places broken, the bonds which regulate and hold together Indian society and its wild state, and has failed to give the people law and officers of justice in their place." Dr. Thomas S. Williamson, missionary to the Dakotas, said that the two great hindrances to progress were the Indian religion and the absence of law. The chiefs did not have the function of punishment of evil doers, and good Indians, who suffered much from white men, suffered still more injury from their own people. The Board of Indian Commissioners in 1871 observed: "We owe it to them, and to ourselves, to teach them the majesty of civilized law, and extend to them its protection against the lawless among themselves." The Protestant Episcopal Church established a special committee to seek to obtain the extension of the law over the Indians. The American Board, remembering the Cherokee and Choctaw republican governments, encouraged the Dakotas to adopt such voluntary systems, beginning with the Hazelwood Republic of 1856. The other mission boards all repeatedly recommended the application of the common law of the country to the Indians.

The mission boards decried the government's "theory that you can only treat the Indian as a member of a clan." Consequently the idea that the Indian is an Indian and must always be treated as an Indian was the root of much of the lack of success and the failures. Let there be no more Indians raised, only men. Disintegrate the clan and elevate the individual. "And then nothing should bar them from all the rights and responsibilities of American manhood, as fast as they are able to assume them." And the chief of these rights and responsibilities, in the view of the churches, was citizenship, the crown of the whole process of civilization.

EDUCATION

Effective education was quite generally believed to be the method and means to civilization, citizenship, and Christianization alike. As long as the Indians were not citizens, the several states of the Union had no obligation to provide them with schools. The mission boards believed that until the states should make such provision, equivalent schooling ought to be furnished by the federal government. If the government were not inclined to bear the expense, it might take the expense from Indian trust funds which it held. The extensive school systems of the Cherokees and Choctaws gave such a precedent. The

Presbyterians early supplemented from their own funds the low salaries of teachers until the government should do better. The Friends openly worked entirely through agency schools, to which they appointed teachers who were paid by government, and stated: "When a school is opened it is for the purpose of imparting to the pupils a knowledge of Christianity, as well as of the ordinary rudiments of education," since they must be "led to a higher life than that to which they have been accustomed in their wild condition." The Baptists said that education added permanence and power to Christian influences.

The proper missionary supplement to the government agency day school was thought to be the mission boarding school. A few of the boards appear to have expected to follow the old rule of providing one-third the expense of the buildings and all the salary of teachers, but the Methodists seem to have expected merely to supplement government appropriations in their school at Ft. Peck, and the Baptists to do the same at Tahlequah with respect to the college that was later moved to Muskogee. The general practice of the boards soon was to provide buildings, teachers, and supplies from mission funds and to receive rations of food and clothing from the government for the scholars. The boarding school was regarded as the effective instrument for removing the pupils from their home associations for periods long enough to wean them from tribal customs, to teach them civilized ways, and introduce them to Christian life and doctrine. "Book learning" was always joined with crafts and agriculture.

The boarding school was generally thought to be more effective than the day schools in teaching English. Ability to use English was a great objective of the government and most of the missions, and they used only that language in instruction. However, the three missions working with the Dakotas insisted that pupils taught only in English learned that language by rote and did not really comprehend it. Even Secretary Lowrie of the Presbyterians was converted to that view after his Board took over half of the American Board Dakota Mission. Experience had taught the American Board and Episcopal missionaries that genuine progress in education and in Christian knowledge depended upon instruction in the Indian vernacular. Once literate in the vernacular students could then easily learn and comprehend English. Even though English might be the goal, the vernacular was the indepensable means to it. English was, indeed, necessary to citizenship.

The American Missionary Association was enthusiastic about sending students to Carlisle, especially to Hampton, and to its schools for freemen in the South, but recognized that adequate schools on reservations were necessary. Bishop Hare was pleased with Hampton Institute and sent advanced students there. The American Board wanted the country to realize that Carlisle and Hampton could never educate many Indian children, and that school houses by the thousands would have to be built throughout the Indian country. Its missionaries also believed that Indian education must be self-propagating. Therefore, they trained native teachers for the work, and regarded the mission as being only "the energizing power."

GENERAL STATEMENTS OF POLICY

The pronouncements and statements of the missionary organizations were usually on specific points, and general statements of policy were infrequent. The Hicksite Friends gave the government a simple seven-point statement in 1869. It advocated faithful and liberal keeping of treaty stipulations, no more removals of Nebraska tribes, no more sale of reservation lands for the present and later only under strict control, hospitals for each reservation, industrial schools with English instruction for all children, and competent instruction of adults in agriculture and lumbering with provision of teams and tools. The Dakota Mission of the American Board adopted a document in 1877 which the Board endorsed. It affirmed that Indians were men with the same wants and impulses as others; demanded civil law; asked compulsory education in books, agriculture, and mechanic arts, so that "no more Indians be raised"; accepted the reservation system only as a temporary expedient; asked the right of Indians to land titles; advocated the establishment of a "true Indian civil service"; and affirmed that the teaching of Christianity is indispensable to civilization, enlightenment, and education. Bishop Whipple made frequent pronouncements along the same lines, and also on the matters covered in the statement of the annual conference of the mission boards in 1879. That conference statement asked retention of the Indian Bureau under the Department of the Interior, the granting of land in severalty, provision of civil law, and a common school system. The General Assembly of the Presbyterian Church in the U. S. A. addressed a memorial to the President and Congress in 1880, which was adopted by the annual conference of mission representatives in 1881 and taken personally to the President. It called for American education, American homes, American rights, and American citizenship for the Indians.

Most of the religious societies seem never to have made specific statements as to what they expected as the final result of the Peace Policy, but some degree of integration appeared to be implicit in citizenship. The most vocal ones, however, especially Episcopalians, Congregationalists, and Presbyterians, clearly looked forward to the integration and absorption of the civilized Indian citizen into the general American society and economy. Bishop Hare spoke for many when he deprecated any policy of program which, "if permanently maintained, would tend to make Indian life something separate from the common life of our country: a solid foreign mass indigestible by our common civilization."

THE ATTITUDE OF THE CHURCHES IN LATER YEARS

The active partnership of the mission boards with the United States government in the administration of the agencies until 1882 and in education until the middle of the last decade of the century had stimulated the churches to far greater concern and action with respect to the Indians than had ever before been the case. After the dissolution of the partnership there was a very evident slump in interest in the Indians. A few of the major boards continued and enlarged their work, and a few additional churches began Indian missions; but neither the Indians nor the Indian missions were in the foreground of the churches' interest. During the early years of the twentieth century the American Baptist Home Mission Society passed resolutions noting that the government was doing well in Indian education and expressing satisfaction. There were no critical notes on policy at the time. It was much the same in other churches. The mission boards no longer stimulated one another to interest and action. The discontinuance of the annual conference of the secretaries with the Board of Commissioners for Indian Affairs had removed an hitherto potent source of mutual sharing of information, consultation, and consensus. Some of the secretaries and workers attended the annual Lake Mohonk Conference on Indian Affairs, and it was a help to them, but it was not an agency or instrument of the missions. There was a tendency for some years to rely upon the Indian Rights Association to perform the functions of criticism of policy and quest for justice which the boards had jointly exercised.

The transfer of all Indian mission work from foreign mission boards to home mission agencies tended to reinforce individualism among the Indian missions also over against the recent tradition of concerted policy and action. The home mission boards were at the turn of the century still competitive and opportunistic. Then the usual course of retirements and deaths brought a change in personnel in the management, and the tradition of sharing in a common cause was to a considerable extent forgotten. Consequently, Indian missions became largely a housekeeping affair concerned mostly with the maintenance, rather than expansion, of existing operations. The old methods were followed with little change. Then after the founding of the Home Missions Council of North America, the fourteen members boards which carried on Indian mission work established the Committee on Indian Affairs in 1909. Its very name indicated that it intended to be concerned with more than the internal matters of mission work. It included in addition to the denominational boards such allied organizations as the American Bible Society, the Y.M.C.A., and the Indian Rights Association. Association in the common cause created a sense of unity among the people associated with the committee and through the fellowship and consultation which it provided, once again consensus on most matters relating to missions and general Indian affairs was attained. The Council of Women for Home Missions also had an Indian Committee, and it produced an occasional study book on the Indians in the annual series which the Women's Council put out. The first conference of Indian mission workers was held in 1919, and in 1935 there was organized under the auspices of the Home Missions Council a professional society called the National Fellowship of Indian Workers, comprising missionaries, mission board members, and government employees. The cooperating denominations and their missionaries henceforth had ample means for consultation, study, speaking to the churches and the nation, and for action, should they so desire.

There appears to have been little fundamental change in attitudes and viewpoints during the first third of the twentieth century. Instead of partnership, there had developed close collaboration between the missions and the churches. Some government schools were actually staffed by Roman Catholic sisters. It was claimed that in many schools Protestant and Roman Catholic missionaries actually controlled the institution. One finds complaints that children were forced to take part in worship and take religious instruction, and thus were denied religious liberty. At any rate there was a fairly warm cooperation between mission workers and government employees on most of the reservations. Closer relations at headquarters in Washington were fostered by the appointment from 1912 to 1916 of H. B. F. MacFarland as legal counsel to the Committee on Indian Affairs. Congress in 1922 gave the missions title to the land which they were occupying on the reservations.

Despite the often close collaboration of the missionaries and government officers on the reservations, the churches were still committed to their position on separation of church and state which they had assumed during the last decade of the previous century. The ground of it appeared still to lie more in fear of, and opposition to, Roman Catholic aims and strategy, than in fundamental theory. The earliest instances of concerted action by the churches after the creation of the Committee on Indian Affairs were directed towards Roman Catholic actions and practices. The Home Missions Council in 1911 vigorously opposed a government grant of three hundred thousand acres of land in New Mexico to a Roman Catholic training school. The Council was consistent, and at the same time opposed a grant of $20,000 to a Protestant society in California. The next year the Council threw the weight of its support to Commissioner Valentine's effort to eliminate the wearing of religious garb by teachers in government schools. About 1915 the organization joined forces with those who were fighting to protect the interest of the Mescalero Apache and Papago tribes of Arizona in their lands.

The churches were in general agreement with the government's policy of working towards the termination of wardship and the integration of the Indians into the general American society. This was in line with the position of the missions on Indian civilization and citizenship at the beginning of the century, but with the passage of time and the failure of segregation to produce the expected blessings, the churches began to ask the abandonment of segregated schools. They also became concerned about the migration of the Indians from the reservations to the cities with all the consequent problems encountered by the transplanted people. A special Home Missions Congress in 1930, therefore, asked vigorous efforts to combat the exploitation and commercialism of the Indian, disavowed a permanent policy of segregation, recommended the gradual abandonment of segregated schools and the educating of Indian children in the public schools. The two Councils voted jointly to provide directors of religious education in all government schools both on and off the reservations; and apparently there was no feeling that this measure might infringe upon the proper separation of church and state.

There was little conflict between the missions and the Indian Service over government policy towards the Indians until the appointment of John Collier as Commissioner of Indian Affairs by President Franklin D. Roosevelt. Up to that time the churches had usually approved the government policy in the main. Then the Indian Reorganization Act of 1934 encouraged return to the tribal control and the limitation of giving of allotments of land to individuals because of the ease with which so many were then separated from their land. Collier also set out vigorously to rescue and foster the traditional tribal culture. The missions thought that the land and cultural policies of the Indian Service now meant a return to wardship and paternalism by the government, the making of the reservations a kind of human zoo, and the end of official effort to integrate the Indians into society. They clashed with Collier over the Peyote cult and in general aligned themselves against him. The order of the Commissioner which prohibited any interference with Indian religious life or ceremonial expression was resented. Collier was on firm ground when he sought to end compulsory attendance of Indian children at Christian classes of instruction and worship. He did offer continued use of school facilities for both worship and instruction of children whose parents approved and of youths over eighteen years of age who voluntarily consented. The Council's pamphlet on *Indian Wardship* set forth the consensus of most of the churches and missions on wardship and citizenship. Its general tone is expressed in the words that halting the Indian's "modern adaptation and imprisoning him in his yesterday's culture is futility itself."

However, in the decade of the 1940s the churches began to awaken to the understanding that neither the government nor white voluntary agencies had the right to make unilateral decisions about the Indian's present and future and that his consent was needed. There came to be also a more realistic acknowledgment that speedy termination of wardship often just made it easier for white men to exploit the Indian and deprive him of his possessions. And there was joined with both of these the insight that much more was needed in inducing state and local governments to acknowledge concern for Indian welfare and to participate in the processes of adjustment. All of this was preparatory for a considerable shift of position in the decade of the 1950s. The Eisenhower administration reversed the principles on which the Indian Service had operated under Commissioner Collier and promoted a policy of rapid termination of federal responsibility for the Indians. The eagerness of business interests to deprive the Indians of their resources regardless of any questions of justice and some grave acts of injustice by governments, both national and state, alarmed the churches. Therefore, the past decade or so has seen the churches increasingly insisting on the consent of the Indians to all legislation which affects them, and a growth of tension between them and the government on matters of fundamental policy. One can probably say with truth that in the decade of the 1950s the churches and their mission boards once more showed a range of concern about Indian affairs comparable to that of the twenty years following the end of the Civil War, but that neither the causes of Indian missions nor Indian rights drew a very large percentage of church members into passionate participation. The dissolution of the partnership of missions and government in Indian civilization and education was certainly required by the evolution of the interpretation of the doctrine of the separation of church and state. However, the American people have always been reluctant to face squarely their responsibility for, and obligation to, the Indians. The record of the churches is little better than that of the general populace. However, as long as the partnership in civilization and evangelization endured, there was more incentive for the churches to face and acknowledge their responsibility.

A Note on Bibliography

The major primary sources for this article are: Annual Reports of the Commissioner of Indian Affairs; Annual Reports of the Secretary of the Interior; Annual Reports of the Board of Indian Commissioners;

The Congressional Record; the Annual Reports and the periodicals of each of the mission boards involved in missions to the Indians; denominational journals; general newspaper and magazines; correspondence of the Indian agents with the Boards and with the Indian Office; autobiographical works such as H. B. Whipple, *Lights and Shadows of a Long Episcopate*; and for the later years the publications of the Indian Rights' Association and similar organizations. The Roman Catholic viewpoint on the "Peace Policy" period will be found in Peter J. Rahill, *The Catholic Indian Missions and Grant's Peace Policy, 1870-1884*. The most important secondary work is Anson P. Stokes, *Church and State in the United States* (3 vols.).

This Most Favored Nation: Reflections on the Vocation of America

WINTHROP S. HUDSON

"Oh, somewhere in this favored land the sun is shining bright,"[1] Ernest Thayer wrote in 1888, but then he added sadly that there was no joy in Mudville for the mighty Casey had struck out.

As this line from "Casey at the Bat" indicates, the notion of the United States as a favored land was commonplace among Americans, widely believed and widely accepted. From the very beginning of its national life, it was repeatedly noted that the new nation was favored by geography, by the vastness of the land it encompassed, by its temperate climate, by the fertility of its soil, by the richness of its untapped resources, by its isolation from the quarrels and corruptions of Europe. But these were only incidental aspects of the United States as a most favored nation.

Geographical location, with all the advantages it provided, was only part of what most nineteenth-century Americans had in mind when they spoke of "this most favored nation." Even when they recounted the blessings of nature, they did not attribute them to any mindless smile of heaven. If the American people, even taking into account the vicissitudes through which they had passed, had been blessed beyond measure by the Supreme Architect of the universe by whose hand all nations rise and fall, it was because he had a larger end in view for them than their own ease, peace, and prosperity. What the phrase "this most favored nation" primarily called to mind was the remembrance of a nation supported, sustained, protected, and preserved by the dictates of God's own providential government for the furtherance of his own designs. This was the theme rehearsed in Fourth of July orations and Thanksgiving Day sermons. This was the theme set forth

---

1. Martin Gardner, *The Annotated Casey at the Bat: A Collection of Ballads about Mighty Casey* (New York: Clarkson N. Potter, Inc., 1976), 23.

throughout the nineteenth century by the most celebrated historians and the most widely acclaimed poets. This was the theme acknowledged by both politicians and preachers.

The Divine Purpose and a Sacred Trust

Few Americans believed that their status as a most favored nation was derived from the whims of a capricious Deity. The United States was not the darling of a fickle Providence, the passing fancy of a heedless favoritism. Quite the contrary! The favor was bestowed because God had designed the new nation to be an instrument for effecting his purposes for all people everywhere. It was God's deliberate choice to fashion a new people, a new Israel, to accomplish his ancient intention.[2]

John Adams anticipated what he believed to be God's design for America a full decade before the Declaration of Independence, when he wrote in his diary: "I always consider the settlement of America with reverence and wonder as the opening of a grand design of Providence for the illumination of the ignorant and the emancipation of the slavish part of mankind all over the earth."[3] Tom Paine was equally certain that the American colonists in their struggle for independence were acting out the purposes of God. In *Common Sense*, Paine wrote:

> The distance at which the Almighty hath placed England and America is a strong and natural proof that the authority of the one over the other was never the design of Heaven. The time, likewise, at which the continent was discovered adds to the weight of the argument, and the manner in which the continent was peopled increases the force of it. The Reformation was preceded by the discovery of America, as if the Almighty graciously meant to open a sanctuary to the persecuted in future years when home could afford neither friendship nor safety.

Hither to this new world "the persecuted lovers of civil and religious liberty in every part of Europe" have fled. Now, even as "the same tyran-

---

2. John Foxe, in the sixteenth century, had popularized the conviction in England that the island kingdom had long harbored a people chosen by God for unusual service in the advancement of his providential design for the world. Ezra Stiles, *The United States Elevated to Glory and Honor* (Worcester, Mass.: Isaiah Thomas, 1785), provided one of the most familiar statements of the transference of this role to the people of the United States when Stiles had the Lord declare: "Oh England! how did I once love thee? how did I once glory in thee? . . . In the rapturous anticipation of thine enlargement and reflourishing in this western world, how have I been wont to glory . . . . But now farewell—a long farewell—to all this greatness!" (p. 53). This transference of a "chosen" role to the American shore had long been adumbrated in seminal form by John Winthrop in his "city set on a hill" metaphor and by Edward Johnson in his *Wonder-Working Providence of Sion's Saviour in New England* (Andover, Mass: W. F. Draper, 1867), 1-3. The same view was later represented by Jonathan Edwards's conviction that the latter-day glory of the Lord was probably to begin in America. See Conrad Cherry, ed., *God's New Israel: Religious Interpretations of American Destiny* (Englewood Cliffs, N.J.: Prentice-Hall, Inc., 1971), 43, 55-58.
3. Charles F. Adams, ed., *The Works of John Adams*, 10 vols. (Boston: Little, Brown and Co., 1850-56), 1:66.

ny which drove the first emigrants from home pursues their descendants," God is providing a new dispensation. "We have every opportunity and every encouragement before us to form the purest constitution on the face of the earth. We have it in our power to begin the world over again. A situation similar to the present has not happened since the days of Noah till now. The birthday of a new world is at hand." Shortly thereafter, *The American Crisis*, Paine wrote that he was as confident that God would not give up the American people to "military destruction nor leave them unsupported to perish" as he was that "God governs the world." There are many tokens, he continued, that God Almighty is "visibly on our side."[4]

This was the common rhetoric of the American Revolution and of the new nation. Accordingly, the American people were the recipients of divine favor because they were custodians of a sacred trust.[5] No one stated this more vividly and more concisely than Andrew Jackson when he admonished the nation concerning its duty in his Farewell Address.

You have the highest of human trusts committed to your care. Providence has showered on this favored land blessings without number, and has chosen you as the guardians of freedom to preserve it for the benefit of the human race. May He who holds in His hands the destinies of nations make you worthy of the favors He has bestowed, and enable you . . . to guard and defend to the end of time the great charge He has committed to your keeping.[6]

Earlier, in his Second Inaugural Address, Jackson had pressed home the heavy obligation resting upon the American people. "Great is the stake placed in our hands; great is the responsibility which must rest upon the people of the United States." This is true because "the eyes of all nations are fixed on our Republic," and its success or failure will be "decisive in the opinion of mankind."[7]

The New Israel and Its Holy Days: Observed and Obscured

The major feature of the United States as a most favored nation was the equation of the United States with ancient Israel. At almost every point, the most familiar archetypes were Hebraic: exodus, chosen

---

4. Thomas Paine, "Common Sense," in *The Complete Writings of Thomas Paine*, ed. Philip Foner, 2 vols. (New York: Citadel Press, 1945), 1:21, 29, 39; and "The American Crisis," in ibid, 50, 54, 66, 72.
5. The rhetoric of Americans as custodians of a "sacred trust" has been traced in detail by Paul C. Nagel, *This Sacred Trust: American Nationality, 1798-1898* (New York: Oxford University Press, 1971).
6. J. D. Richardson, *A Compilation of the Messages and Papers of the Presidents*, 20 vols. (Washington, D.C.: Bureau of National Literature, 1897-1917), 2:1527.
7. Ibid., 3:1223.

people, promised land. The central theme was that of a people in covenant with God escaping from Egyptian bondage to a new Canaan and then being led to establish in America political arrangements, pleasing to God and appropriate to a free society, that would serve as a haven of liberty, as a light and example to all nations, and, by the very contagion of its example, as God's instrument for the emancipation of people everywhere.

The equation of the United States with Israel was made clear at the outset by proposals of both Benjamin Franklin and Thomas Jefferson for the great seal of the new nation. Appointed on 4 July 1776 as members of a committee of three to fashion the device, Franklin proposed that Moses be depicted dividing the Red Sea with his wand and Pharaoh and his forces be shown being overwhelmed as the waters converged again, while Jefferson suggested that the seal should picture the children of Israel being led through the wilderness by a cloud by day and a pillar of fire by night.[8] This equation of the United States with Israel was to be a refrain throughout most of the nineteenth century in tracts, treatises, sermons, and addresses, as well as in writings of the nation's leading literary figures.[9] In similar fashion, the chief public observances of the republic were interpreted within a biblical context. The Fourth of July, for example was commonly referred to as the American Passover. Provision was also made in customary practice for days of atonement and days of thanksgiving patterned after Hebrew precedent and observed according to Hebrew precepts.

By the middle of the twentieth century, however, the fundamental assumptions embedded in the notion of the United States as a most favored nation had become obscured. For one thing, as part of the shift to a more pluralistic, sophisticated, and secular society, the Hebraic metaphors tended to disappear from political rhetoric. More important in obscuring the context of the long tradition of national self-understanding was the way in which public observances of the national faith were transformed into private rather than communal affairs after World War I.

---

8. Anson Phelps Stokes, *Church and State in the United States*, 3 vols. (New York: Harper and Row, 1950), 1:467-68.
9. Abiel Abbot's Thanksgiving sermon of 1799 in Haverhill, Mass., "Traits of the Resemblance in the People of the United States of America to Ancient Israel" (cf. Charles Evans, *American Bibliography*, 14 vols. [Chicago: Columbia Press, 1903-55], 12:248, entry no. 35071), was not untypical of the prevailing imagery in discussions of the nation's millennial role. See also Nicholas Street "The American States Acting Over the Part of the Children of Israel," and Samuel Langdon, "The Republic of the Israelites an Example of the American States," in Cherry, ed., *God's New Israel*, 67-81, 93-105. For a general discussion of the millennialism which underlay the comparison, see J. F. Maclear, "The Republic and the Millennium," in Elwyn A. Smith, ed., *The Religion of the Republic* (Philadelphia: Fortress Press, 1971), 183-216.

The birth of the nation had been ritually celebrated each year by a day of remembrance, the Fourth of July. The day began with a parade and ended with fireworks, but the central act of the ritual was the assembling of the people in each community throughout the land to listen both to the reading of the Declaration of Independence and to an oration interpreting the Declaration and the nation's vocation within the scope of God's design for the world. Even before the third decade of the twentieth century, the parades were beginning to dwindle, the fireworks were beginning to be banned, and the day of remembrance with its reading of the Declaration and its oration was being turned into an occasion to go to one's summer cottage, to visit friends, to have a family outing, or at least to have a cookout in the backyard.

Memorial Day suffered a like fate. By 1950 few remembered that Memorial Day had been designed to recapitulate the rebirth of the nation through a bloody sacrifice, that is, a war that had continued as an expiation for sin "until every drop of blood drawn with the lash shall be paid by another drawn with the sword." The day was seldom observed in the South, but elsewhere in the nation the ritual, while more somber, was not unlike the observance of the anniversary of the initial birthday of the nation. During the second quarter of the twentieth century, however, Memorial Day was becoming little more than a welcome release from the ordinary routine of work. Some had begun to think of the day as a time to put flowers on their parents' graves while the more patriotically inclined utilized Memorial Day and Armistice Day (renamed Veterans Day) as dual opportunities to honor quite indiscriminately all who had participated in the nation's wars.

Washington's Birthday and Lincoln's Birthday, as days of remembrance, paralleled Independence Day and Memorial Day, but they were not occasions for public ritual. The significant role of these two birthdays was the use to which they were put for instructional purposes in the public schools, that is, to elucidate the birth and rebirth of the nation. Ultimately this function was abandoned when the two birthdays were collapsed into a single "Presidents' Day." This was a clear indication that the original purpose of the two observances had been forgotten.

Thanksgiving Day also was in process of being altered and transformed as the twentieth century advanced. Thanksgiving began as a movable feast, a day set aside by presidential proclamation to express gratitude to God for some signal display of divine mercy to the nation. After the Civil War, Thanksgiving became an annual ritual for the nation to review the year and humbly to acknowledge the blessings, and sometimes as well the judgments, of God upon the land and the people. While Thanksgiving Day proclamations continued to be cast within the themes of national identity, purpose, and mission well into the twentieth century, the day itself was in process of being both denationalized and secularized. Few would argue with John F. Wilson's verdict that the modern version of Thanksgiving "celebrates, not national dependence upon a divinely ordained destiny, but family fellowship and enjoyment of the bounties of the land and society."[10] This stress on family fellowship represented a drastic denationalization at a time when the day was steadily being commercialized and secularized. The final secularization of the day, a Bicentennial first, came with President Gerald R. Ford's proclamation that 27 November 1975 be observed as the annual day of national thanksgiving. The previous year, in his first Thanksgiving Day proclamation, President Ford had noted that the United States had become the "mightiest" nation in human history and had summoned all Americans to "join in giving thanks to God." But in 1975 President Ford forgot even to mention that Thanksgiving was an occasion for expressing gratitude to God. In place of any reference to God, the proclamation called upon the American people to indulge in congratulating themselves for "this great nation" which was of their own making. The specific blessings enumerated were viewed, not as derived from God, but as the product of the "dynamic spirit" of the American people.

Fast Days in Colonial America

Because of the secularization of the surviving national observances, it is difficult to view them apart from their twentieth-century dilutions, accretions, and transformations. One can escape this problem and achieve greater clarity as to America's past self-understanding by centering attention upon a public observance which has not survived but which once was commonly and customarily observed. Such an observance is more easily viewed within its earlier context and thus more adapted to discerning the fundamental assumptions which, for the greater part of the American national life, were embedded in the notion of the United States as a most favored nation.

The fast days, which may be reckoned as the American Days of Atonement, are admirably suited for analyzing America's past understanding of divine favor. The fast days were a prominent feature of colonial life in America and were observed with periodic regularity throughout the American Revolution. Typical of the repeated resolutions of the Continental Congress that fast days be observed was the resolution of 12 June 1775. Taking cognizance of "the present critical,

---

10. John F. Wilson, "A Historian's Approach to Civil Religion," in Russell E. Richey and Donald G. Jones, eds., *American Civil Religion* (New York: Harper and Row, 1974), 134.

alarming, and calamitous state of these colonies," the Continental Congress resolved that 20 July 1775 be observed as a day of "public humiliation, fasting, and prayer" by "the inhabitants of all the English colonies on this continent" to the end that "we may, with united hearts and voices, unfeignedly confess and deplore our many sins and offer up our joint supplications to the all-wise, omnipotent, and merciful Disposer of All Events, humbly beseeching him to forgive our iniquities, to remove our present calamities, and to avert those desolating judgments with which we are threatened."[11]

Confession of sin rather than a claim to righteousness, or a pointing to one's own iniquity rather than to the iniquity of the enemy, may seem a curious way to solicit divine aid and nerve people for battle. But strange as it may seem to twentieth-century Americans, the ritual of humiliation and fasting did not seem strange to members of the Continental Congress. This had long been the use to which national fasts had been put in Great Britain and America. They were utilized as a means of awakening faith and repentance, of effecting amendment of life and reconciliation with God, and thus of averting divine wrath and impending judgment.

The self-abnegation of fast days implied no fatalistic resignation to a predetermined course of events. Quite the contrary! Since God uses individuals and nations as instruments to serve the purposes of his providential government, the summons to repentance was also a summons to renewed obedience and vigorous action. Divine favor could be expected only as a people acknowledge themselves to be unworthy and unprofitable servants and resolutely set themselves to mend their ways. Strictly speaking, God's mercy was not conditional. Still it was not without qualification. "Covenant mercies," John Higginson declared, presuppose "covenant duties,"[12] As it was phrased in an oft-quoted text, "The Lord is with you, while ye be with him" (2 Chron. 15:2c, KJV).

Both in Britain and America, fast day sermons usually were based on Old Testament texts which were used to illustrate God's claim on a nation and the consequent duties and obligations which it imposed. Even when a sermon was based on a New Testament text, it was a text which served as a convenient handle to direct attention back to the Old Testament.[13] Quite obviously what was involved in these days of

---

11. Several of the Fast Day resolutions of the Continental Congress are reprinted in Winthrop S. Hudson, ed., *Nationalism and Religion in America: Concepts of American Identity and Mission* (New York: Harper and Row, 1970), 26-31.
12. John Higginson, "An Attestation to This Church-History of New England," in Cotton Mather, *Magnalia Christi Americana*, 2 vols. (Hartford: Silas Andrus and Son, 1853-55), 1:14.
13. For an analysis of the texts of the sermons, see Winthrop S. Hudson, "Fast Days and Civil Religion," In *Theology in Sixteenth- and Seventeenth-Century England* (Los Angeles: William Andrews Clark Library, University of California at Los Angeles, 1971), 12-13.

repentance, and in days of remembrance and thanksgiving as well, was an Hebraic understanding of history. The basic structure of this understanding can be summarized as follows: (1) God governs the destinies of nations. (2) He singled out Israel as a chosen people and instrument of his purpose, receiving Israel into covenant with himself. (3) So long as God was served with singleness of heart, Israel prospered. (4) When Israel became proud and self-willed, forgetting God's past mercies, God afflicted the Israelites with the rod of correction, measured out judgment in proportion to their offenses, and threatened them with desolation and destruction. (5) In despair, the people were led to humble themselves before God with fasting and prayer, repenting of their sins, mending their ways, and crying to God for mercy. (6) The Lord, being "gracious and merciful, slow to anger, and of great kindness," would then hear their cries, take pity upon them, repent of the evils he had sent, and look upon them once again with favor (Joel 2:13, KJV). The covenant did not offer protection from God's wrath, but it did make explicit the basis on which God's anger would be turned aside and his favor regained.

The new element introduced in England, making use of the comment of John the Baptist that "God is able of these stones to raise up children unto Abraham" (Matthew 3:9, KJV), was the conviction that England had inherited the Hebrews' ancient role as God's chosen instrument for the redemption of mankind. John Foxe, in his *Acts and Monuments* (the "Book of Martyrs"), picked up this theme and wrote a universal history to document England's central role in God's providential dealings with people and nations. The "Book of Martyrs" was a sequel to the Scriptures which brought the story of God's people down to date. In America the story was extended still farther by the chroniclers of New England; e.g., by William Bradford's *Of Plymouth Plantation,* Nathaniel Morton's *New England's Memorial*, Edward Johnson's *Wonder-Working Providence of Sion's Saviour in New England*, and Cotton Mather's *Magnalia Christi Americana.*[14]

This was no exclusive or narrow nationalism that was represented by Foxe and the preachers of fast-day sermons. As Hans Kohn has noted, it was a peculiarly open-ended nationalism since the community or nation was "a community decided not by blood but by faith."[15] England was a nation by adoption and by grace after the manner of the Old Testament, and the faith from which it derived its vocation was a faith destined for all mankind. It was a nationalism that could

---

14. It is interesting to note how each of the chroniclers made it explicit that he regarded himself as continuing Foxe's narrative.
15. Hans Kohn, *The Idea of Nationalism: A Study in Its Origins and Background* (New York: Macmillan Company, 1944), 167, 168.

run easily and naturally into internationalism. In the words of Ernest Barker, "The chosen people of one nation, and the whole of that people through them, have a community and fellowship with the chosen people of other nations, and with other nations through them."

This was, to be sure, a national piety. It was a piety that was not antithetical to, yet clearly differentiated from, the religion of the churches. A. S. P. Woodhouse detailed how a "principle of segregation" between the realm of nature and the realm of grace was developed after 1642 during the course of the English Civil War. The realm of nature was God's "great kingdom, the world." The realm of grace was "his special or peculiar kingdom, the kingdom of grace." In the first kingdom, God rules "every natural man" by "the light of nature to a civil outward good and end." In the second kingdom, in the life of grace, God rules the Christian by his special revelation in Christ to an inward end, one's own eternal salvation. In the first, God's government pertained to the state. In the second, God's government pertained to the church.[16] Natural religion was the religion available to all persons through "natural reason," i.e., through the lessons of history, including the history of the Hebrew people, which made plain the manner of God's providential dealings with peoples and nations. This distinction between the religion of nature and the religion of grace was basic to the thinking of Roger Williams and a significant number of English Independents. By the end of the seventeenth century, it received its most influential expression in John Locke's famous *Letter Concerning Toleration* (1689).[17]

No Fast Days but the Double Vision

A significant shift took place in the time of the American Revolution. The colonists believed that England by her tyrannical proceedings and by her denial of God-given freedoms had forfeited her role as God's chosen instrument and had been replaced by an American Israel, or a new most favored nation destined to display before the world the blessings accruing to a society fully committed to God and to the principles of liberty, both civil and ecclesiastical. Since the national piety transferred from England to the United States was basically Hebraic as well as "natural" in its formulations, neither Roman Catholics nor Jews found it unduly divisive or offensive. The basic Old Testament categories and understandings sped the process of accommodation,

---

16. A. S. P. Woodhouse, *Puritanism and Liberty* (Chicago: University of Chicago Press, 1951), 57-60, 84-86, 247-48. For a more extended discussion on this point see Winthrop S. Hudson, "John Locke: Heir of Puritan Political Theorists," in George Laird Hunt, ed., *Calvinism and the Political Order* (Philadelphia: Westminster Press, 1965), 115-16, 118-24.
17. Hudson, "John Locke," passim.

and Roman Catholics and Jews, as well as Protestants, were able to assimilate this "religion of the republic" within the context of their own distinctive religious views.

Both national fasts and thanksgivings were observed intermittently after the American Revolution as expressions of national piety. Thanksgiving was ultimately institutionalized on an annual basis and took on some of the characteristics of a harvest festival, but national days of fasting, humiliation, and prayer were observed only when some signal event or crisis was interpreted as a sign of God's displeasure. Fast days were proclaimed by John Adams, James Madison, John Tyler, Zachary Taylor, and James Buchanan, and on three separate occasions by Abraham Lincoln. The last president to summon the nation to a day of national humiliation, fasting, and prayer was Andrew Johnson, on the occasion of Abraham Lincoln's assassination.[18]

It is true that on 23 December 1973, with the unsavory aspects of the Vietnam debacle fully revealed and the Watergate crisis beginning to unfold, Senator Mark O. Hatfield persuaded the U. S. Senate, and subsequently the House of Representatives to concur in a joint resolution of Congress proclaiming 30 April 1974 a "national day for humiliation, fasting, and prayer." The resolution, patterned after one of Abraham Lincoln's fast day proclamations, affirmed as its basic postulate "the duty of nations, as well as of men, . . . to confess their sins and transgressions." Having forgotten God by whose gracious hand Americans "have been the recipients of the choicest bounties of Heaven," the resolution noted, "we have vainly imagined, in the deceitfulness of our hearts, that all these blessings were produced by some superior wisdom and virtue of our own." Furthermore, "intoxicated with unbroken success, we have become . . . too proud to pray to the God that made us;" "we have made such an idol out of our pursuit of 'national security' " and "have become so absorbed with the selfish pursuits of pleasure and profit that we have blinded ourselves to God's standard of justice and righteousness." The resolution, closing with a summons to the American people to humble themselves before Almighty God and to seek "clemency and forgiveness" through acknowledgment and repentance of the manifold sins, corruptions, and waywardness of the nation, was adopted without objection. In terms of any widespread response, however, the resolution proved abortive, for by 1974 few Americans knew what to make of such a day of na-

---

18. Annual state fast days lingered on in New England for several decades, with Massachusetts substituting Patriots' Day for the annual fast day in 1894. Maine, New Hampshire, and Vermont followed the example of Massachusetts some years later. W. D. Love, *The Fast and Thanksgiving Days of New England* (Boston: Houghton, Mifflin and Company, 1895), 373-75, 392-93, 406, 408, 448.

tional humiliation, fasting, and prayer and how it should be and could be observed.[19]

The Hebraic interpretation of national vocation, so clearly delineated in the fast days, provided the basis for what Robert Bellah has called the double vision of American self-understanding.[20] There was "chosenness," but there was also "accountability." Bellah lists the polarities of this double vision: conversion and covenant; liberation and constitutionalism (i.e., the institutionalization of liberty); emancipation and discipline; an emphasis on both the individual and the community. Social psychologists, Bellah notes, describe this double vision in terms of "impulse" and "control." Political scientists, using other terms, on the one hand, speak of the impelling power of an ideology, and, on the other, stress and constraint that often are imposed by myths, beliefs, and convictions. The danger, Bellah observes, takes place when the double vision is reduced to a single vision—a vision without qualifications, conditions, accountability. Without the double vision the emphasis on "chosenness," for example, easily slips into pride, self-righteousness, and arrogance. In similar fashion, a single-minded stress on conversion, liberation, emancipation, and impulse breeds anarchy and despotism.

It is unfortunate that fast days were allowed to disappear. It is unfortunate because at the center of the fast day observance was a dual emphasis, or a double vision, that never was so clearly articulated in other national rituals and observances. It was this dual emphasis of fast days that served as a bridle to undue national pretensions and arrogance. The basic theme for most fast day sermons was expressed by Edmund Calamy on 22 December 1641, when he reminded the English House of Commons of the warning voiced in Jeremiah 18:7-10 that God can both " 'build and plant' a nation, and he can 'pluck up, pull down, and destroy' a nation." If a nation grows proud and presumptuous, " 'then will God repent of the good wherewith he would have benefitted them,' and pull down what he hath built and pluck up what he hath planted and of a fruitful Paradise, make it a barren wilderness."[21]

The surprising feature of American life is that, even without the reminder of fast days, the sense of national vocation and the parallel sense of impending divine judgment remained relatively strong in the

---

19. It is interesting that many Americans quite spontaneously acted out such an observance by repairing to their churches in shock, horror, and sorrow when President John F. Kennedy and then Martin Luther King, Jr., were assassinated.
20. See Robert N. Bellah, *The Broken Covenant: American Civil Religion in a Time of Trial* (New York: Seabury Press, 1975), 9-21, 32-35, 36-86.
21. A portion of Calamy's sermon, "England's Looking-Glasse" (London, 1642), is reprinted in Hudson, ed., *Nationalism and Religion in America*, 174-76.

American consciousness. An awareness of a sacred trust, of obligation and constraint, of the conditional character of God's favor persisted. During the 1880s and 1890s this sense of vocation served as a powerful ideological restraint inhibiting the nation for a considerable period of time from embarking on a career of imperialist adventure.[22] The sense of judgment, to be sure, was not as lively as it had been in 1857-1858 when, in the midst of a financial panic, businessmen across the land gathered spontaneously in noonday prayer meetings for self-examination, asking what they had done wrong to displease God and cause him to punish the nation.[23]

The sense of judgment was weakened in later years because God's providence seemed less directly and immediately related to specific events. Still, warnings continued to be voiced which echoed Lincoln's observation that "sometimes it seems necessary that we should be confronted with perils which threaten us with disaster in order that we may not get puffed up and forget Him who has much work for us yet to do."[24] It was in this sense of threatening disaster that Walter Rauschenbusch in 1899 was able to call Czar Nicholas, the Russian despot, "God's gift to humanity."[25] A restatement of the basic principle was provided by H. Richard Niebuhr in 1935 when he commented that the church should know "the ways of God too well not to understand that he can and will raise up another people" if those entrusted with his mission should fail him.[26] Although Senator Hatfield's resolution setting aside 30 April 1974 as a national fast day proved abortive in the sense that few knew how to respond to its summons, the point which the senator was seeking to make had been perceptively and sensitively emphasized in the inaugural address of Lyndon B. Johnson, perhaps by speechwriter and erstwhile Baptist clergyman Bill D. Moyers, with the reminder that "the judgment of God is harshest on those who are most favored" and that the United States has "no promise" from God that its "greatness will endure."

---

22. See Winthrop S. Hudson, "Protestant Clergy Debate the Nation's Vocation, 1898-99," *Church History 42* (March 1973): 110-18. See also Ernest May, *American Imperialism: A Speculative Essay* (New York: Atheneum, 1968).
23. See Timothy L. Smith, *Revivalism and Social Reform in Mid-Nineteenth Century America* (New York: Abingdon Press, 1957), 63-79.
24. Carl Sandburg, *Abraham Lincoln: The War Years*, 4 vols. (New York: Harcourt, Brace and Co., 1936-39), 3:381.
25. Rochester, New York, *Democrat and Chronicle*, 13 February 1899.
26. H. Richard Niebuhr, et al., *The Church Against the World* (New York: Willett, Clark and Co., 1935), 9.

Nation, Church, and Private Religion: The Emergence of an American Pattern

CONRAD CHERRY

An Approach to the Contemporary Religious Situation

If anything utterly defies definitive explanation, it is the current religious scene in America. Not only does the contemporary observer face the perennial problem of attaining a relatively unbiased perspective on events in which he is a participant; his task is further complicated by a rapidly changing society that catches up religious life in its change. Yet the American religious scene calls for understanding, even if the most illumination that we can hope for is to cast some light on its complexity and confusion. Certainly a portion of that understanding must derive from an historical awareness of the road Americans have traveled up to the present. This study will propose that certain key features of our religious situation represent the culmination of a pattern of values that is deeply rooted in the national experience. The pattern has developed according to the interplay among three factors: nation, church, and private faith.

The contours of the picture of current religious life are blurred, but they do form a rough shape. It is a picture of the traditional churches in apparent slow decline, while the religious impulse itself is far from dead—in fact, it seems diffused throughout our culture. On the one hand, surveys and public opinion polls report a drop in church membership, attendance, and giving, together with a majority of laymen voicing their opinion that religion is losing its influence on American life. And recent sociological analyses have described a growing sense of alienation from the church on the part of middle-class members because of their disagreement with the liberal stand of their clergy on such issues as civil rights and American foreign policy. On the other hand, a majority of Americans polled insisted that they adhere to traditional religious beliefs. Religious books, especially those on personal and self-help themes, continue to fare quite well on the market. Zen, the sects of the occult, and a variety of forms of meditation arouse interest and participation from Americans of all ages. Religious symbols, myths, and rituals pervade civic ceremonies, right wing rallies, and peace marches.[1]

Such random data can, of course, like the Bible, be quoted to most any effect. By themselves they constitute "proof" of nothing and only skim the surface of our situation. They are worth noting, however, because on balance they offer some confirmation of what we can observe first-hand, viz. an American society in which the larger churches, if not clearly declining in appeal and support, are scarcely surging ahead. Yet at the same time there is an almost frantic, impulsive quest for religion throughout the society. Robert Lifton's "Protean Man" is an eminently apt description of the religious dimension of contemporary America. Increasingly religion is characterized by "an interminable series of experiments and explorations—some shallow, some profound—each of which may be readily abandoned in favor of still new . . . quests."[2] The diagnosis for American religion, as for so much of our culture, is most probably a form of "identity diffusion."

It is more than a little incautious to say, as one sociologist has done, that the present shape of things prefigures the end of religion as a large-scale social institution and that we can expect the religion of the twenty-first century to be confined to small, closely-knit sect groups.[3] In this country the sect group has always shown a marked tendency to develop into a fully socialized, acculturated denomination. And since the large religious institution has weathered other crises in the past, the prophet of its doom is obligated not only to reveal his crystal ball but also to delineate the special character of the church's present crises that would lead inevitably to its demise. Nevertheless, it is equally

---

1. For reports on the poll see *New York Times*, 25 May 1968 and 24 and 25 December 1970. Regarding the alienation of the layman see Jeffrey Hadden, *The Gathering Storm in the Churches* (New York & Garden City: Doubleday, 1969) and *New York Times*, 12 April 1968. For a discussion of the religious book market see Martin E. Marty, "Religious Publishing: A Decline but not a Demise," *Christian Century 88 (28 April 1971): 524-28.* For an unusually perceptive analysis of American interests in Eastern religions see Winston L. King, "Eastern Religions: A New Interest and Influence," *Annals of the American Academy of Political and Social Science* 387 (January 1970) : 66-76. For a description of sacred ceremonies in American civic life see Conrad Cherry, "American Sacred Ceremonies," in *American Mosaic: Social Patterns of Religion in the United States*, ed. P. E. Hammond and Benton Johnson (New York: Random House, 1970), 303-16.
2. Robert Jay Lifton, "Protean Man," in *Religious Situation 1968,* ed. Donald R. Cutler (Boston: Beacon Press, 1968), 319.
3. Peter Berger as quoted in *New York Times*, 25 February 1968.

foolhardy either to underestimate the decline in the church's appeal or to dismiss the religious diffusion and experimentation today as phenomena of no importance. To be sure, many of the current forms of religious interest and expression are quickly-abandoned experiments, even fads, but in a rapidly changing technological society longevity no longer is an adequate measure of cultural value for many social forms.

Clues to the emergence of the present religious ferment are to be found in the church's contribution to American nationalism and individualism. Beginning at least as soon as the early nineteenth century, Americans more and more valued their churches for their instrumental rather than for their symbolic roles. The churches were turned to principally because of their performance of one of two—sometimes both—functions: agents of Americanization and nationalism, or instruments serving a privatized, highly individualistic religious piety. The churches were prized less and less for the symbols which they traditionally housed and were valued chiefly for the way they served national ideology on the one hand and individualistic religion on the other. As a consequence, sustaining religious symbols were more often sought in the national or individual experience, rather than in church experience as such. The eventual loss of power in national and individual symbolism, as well as the church's abandonment of its symbolic role, accounts for much of the identity diffusion so characteristic of American religion today.[4]

The Emerging Pattern

In his *Democratic Vistas* Walt Whitman identified the major features of this emerging pattern of American values and specified one possible response to it. Whitman claimed that in his own day there was a conflict between individualism and patriotism. But he was confident that eventually the conflict would be transcended and individualism and love of country would "merge and . . . mutually profit and brace each other."[5] The factor that would bring about this synthesis was religion. Whitman predicted that both individualism and patriotism would be "vitalized by religion (sole worthiest elevator of man or state),

---

4. By way of definition it should be noted here that by "religious symbol" I mean that language, ritual, and mythology which convey a sense of the presence of the sacred. By "symbolic function" I mean the role of putting a community of persons in touch with this sacred reality. Although the symbolic function of the religious institution need not exclude or conflict with other functions it performs, when the churches subordinate the symbol to ends other than conveyance of the sacred or neglect the symbolic for other roles, we have the appearance of religious utilitarianism.
5. Walt Whitman, "Democratic Vistas," *Leaves of Grass and Selected Prose*, ed. J. Kouwenhoven (New York: Modern Library, 1950), 470.

breathing into the proud, material tissues, the breath of life. For I say at the core of democracy, finally, is the religious element."[6] It is important, however, that this religion which Whitman believed would quicken and merge individualism and patriotism was not church religion. "Religion," he said, "although casually arrested, and after a fashion, preserved in the churches and creeds, does not depend at all upon them, but is part of the identified soul . . . which can really confront Religion when it extricates itself entirely from the churches, and not before . . . . Bibles may convey, the priests expound, but it is exclusively for the noiseless operation of one's isolated Self, to enter the pure ether of veneration, reach the divine levels, and commune with the unutterable."[7]

Whitman's anti-institutional religion, joined with a fervid commitment to the "religion of democracy," was of course nothing new on the American scene. It can be traced directly to the Deism of the American Founding Fathers and had full flower in New England transcendentalism. Though this perspective has survived until our own day, it has by no means represented a widespread option in American history. The more common response to the equally inviting sirens of patriotism and individualism has involved the retention of the religious institution as the means of reaching both. This was particularly the case in Whitman's own century, for it was then that Americans earned their reputation as a "nation of joiners." No small number of the organizations that Americans were busy joining were churches and the societies affiliated with or growing out of church religion. Thrown thoroughly upon their own resources by the laws of disestablishment, the denominations confidently assumed the role of the voluntary organization, relying totally upon the tactics of persuasion for the winning and holding of members.

Within Protestantism the tactic of persuasion frequently and most effectively resorted to was revivalism. Modern American revivalism furnishes a clear instance of the church and its functions—especially preaching—serving as avenues to individualism and nationalism. In his classic study of modern revivalism, William McLoughlin has demonstrated how revivalists from Charles Finney to Billy Graham have directed their preaching toward both the winning of the individual to a private faith and the cultivation of "one hundred per cent Americanism."[8] The implications of the former function merit special consideration.

---

6. Ibid., 477.
7. Ibid., 491.
8. William McLoughlin, Jr., *Modern Revivalism: Charles Grandison Finney to Billy Graham* (New York: Ronald Press, 1959).

The church as an agent of an individualized faith was candidly advocated by the father of modern revivalism, Charles Finney. In his immensely influential handbook of revivalism, *Lectures on Revivals of Religion*, Finney proposed a series of techniques carefully designed to win the individual to a heart-felt religious experience. Convinced that the very essence of the church's life was its preaching, Finney argued that preaching is most properly a form of human engineering. In his words, a revival "is a purely philosophical result of the right use of the constituted means — as much so as any other effect produced by the application of means."[9] The spontaneity and abandon of early American evangelical preaching gave way to revivalism as a carefully planned technique. As McLoughlin has said, beginning with Finney revivalism became "as much a science as bridge building."[10]

Finney certainly did not conceive of the individual piety worked up by revivals as existing apart from the church as an institution. In his lecture on "Instructions to Converts" he proposed that those who had been converted by his techniques should offer themselves for admission to some church at their first opportunity, and he warned against discouraging young converts by examining them too closely on doctrinal points — the only important question was whether they had experienced a change of heart.[11] Finney understood his revivalist techniques as instruments in the service of the church. Yet it is also clear that he understood the church chiefly as a bulwark for protecting the individual's piety and morality from the snares of the world. As he put it, "Sometimes persons professing to be converts will make an excuse for not joining the church, that they can enjoy religion just as well without it. This is always suspicious . . . . Ordinarily, if a person does not desire to be associated with the people of God, he is rotten at the bottom . . . . He has a feeling within him that he had rather be free, so that he can by and by go back to the world again if he likes, without the reproach of instability or hypocrisy."[12] For Finney and the tradition of revivalistic Protestantism which followed him, the church as celebrant and interpreter of sacred symbolic meanings has been replaced by a church bent on cultivating and protecting the individual's faith and morality. It was precisely this change in the conception of the church that led two of nineteenth century America's most distinguished theologians, Horace Bushnell and John Nevin, to bring the utilitarianism and individualism of the revivalist movement under

---

9. Charles G. Finney, *Lectures on Revivals of Religion,* rev. ed. (Oberlin: E. J. Goodrich, 1868), 12.
10. McLoughlin, *Modern Revivalism,* 84.
11. Finney, *Lectures,* 371, 375.
12. Ibid., 377.

criticism. But their criticism was unable to stem the rising tide of the movement.

The utilitarianism of a Christianity influenced by revivalism is nowhere more apparent than in its attitude toward music. Susanne Langer has written that the power of great music resides in its action as an unconsummated symbol—that is, a symbol which resists utilitarian exploitation for the sake of specific human emotions. For, according to Langer, "Music can have not only a content, but a transient play of contents. It can articulate feelings without becoming wedded to them."[13] The music employed by modern evangelical Protestantism has been notoriously lacking it this kind of symbolic richness and variety, for it has been intentionally wedded to specific affections. Finney and his successors looked upon music as a technique for putting the congregation in the proper frame of mind for repentance and conversion. The choirs, gospel singers and revivalist song books were utilized for the purpose of arousing the specific feelings that could serve as antecedents to the conversion experience.

The revivalist tradition was not something confined to the frontier camp meeting. It penetrated all regions of the country and found a home in American Protestantism's largest denominations. And many of those contemporary Protestant churches which no longer hold special revival meetings have been shaped by the outlook of the tradition. The church in the service of an individualized, heart-felt religion remains a hallmark of evangelical Protestantism.

Catholicism in America, despite its resilient tradition of communal religious experience, did not totally escape the seductions of American individualism. But Catholicism in this country contributed more to the development of nationalism than to individualism. Dorothy Dohen has documented the manner in which American Catholic leadership has often felt compelled to prove both "How Catholic America Is" and "How American the Catholic Church Is."[14] Especially during times of national crises, when the old nativist suspicion of Catholics as representatives of a "foreign power" has sounded its alarm, Catholic spokesmen have responded with arguments for the close correlation between their faith and the national spirit. Such influential leaders as Archbishop John Hughes, Cardinal James Gibbons, Archbishop John Ireland, and Cardinal Francis Spellman have bent their mightiest efforts to this correlation.

---

13. Susanne K. Langer, *Philosophy in a New Key: A Study in the Symbolism of Reason, Rite and Art* (New York: Mentor Books, 1942, 1951), 204, 206.
14. Dorothy Dohen, *Nationalism and American Catholicism* (New York: Sheed & Ward, 1967), chaps. 4, 5.

John Ireland must suffice as an example. Ireland, who once expressed the opinion that the non-voter deserved exile,[15] defended in numerous speeches the widely held conviction that the American nation was ordained by God for a special task in the world. In the following quotation from one of these speeches we hear his claim that the Catholic Church's mission is assured success when it is aligned with the national mission:

> We cannot but believe that a singular mission is assigned to America, glorious for itself and beneficent to the whole race, the mission of bringing about a new social and political order, based more than any other upon the common brotherhood of man, and more than any other securing to the multitude of the people social happiness and the equality of rights. With our hopes are bound up the hopes of the millions of the earth. The Church triumphing in America, Catholic truth will travel on the wings of American influence, and encircle the universe.[16]

Here the distinctive mythos of Catholic Christianity is submerged in the mythos of the "elect American nation," and the appeal of Catholic truth is made dependent on the success of American influence abroad.

Throughout the late nineteenth and early twentieth centuries, American Catholics increasingly measured their religion according to its proximity to national ideals and institutions. One indication of the prevalence of the measurement is found in a dissenting voice, that of Bishop John Spalding. Critical of the growing tendency among Catholics to value their religion according to its social and political utility, Spalding declared in the early part of this century: "Our religion and our education are cherished for the practical ends which they serve; for the support they give to our political institutions, while these institutions themselves are made a kind of fetish."[17] Yet as Miss Dohen has said, "The Spalding influence in the development of American Catholicism remained negligible, and it was the patriotic declamations of Cardinal Gibbons and Archbishop Ireland that . . . set the pattern."[18]

Occasionally, in its most extreme forms, the pattern of Catholic accommodation to national ideologies led not only to the subordination of Catholic mythos to national mythos but also the transformation of the very essence of the Church's symbolic life—the mass—into a nationalistic ritual. Shortly after U.S. entrance into World War I, for example, American Catholic clergy across the land contributed to a widely circulated collection called *War Addresses from Catholic Pulpit and Platform*.[19] Although most of the addresses refreshingly avoided the narrowest forms of jingoism and xenophobia so

---

15. Ibid., 107-08.
16. Ibid., 109.
17. Ibid., 120.
18. Ibid., 121.
19. *War Addresses from Catholic Pulpit and Platform* (New York: Joseph F. Wagner, n.d.).

characteristic of the time, they did convey their intended message to a suspicious Protestant majority, viz. that the American Catholic pulpit was definitely engaged in defending U.S. war aims. What was particularly striking was the way in which many of these addresses delivered during masses for the Knights of Columbus and on patriotic holidays construed the ritual of the mass as an occasion for appropriating the benefits both of the crucified Christ and sacrificed American war dead! For these Catholic clergy the American soldier who gave his life on the battlefield, as well as Jesus the Christ, possessed salvific significance.

The churches' contribution to American nationalism and individualism can be documented in vast amounts of Protestant, Catholic, and sectarian literature in the nineteenth and twentieth centuries. It was a phenomenon that did not escape the notice of the foreign observers of American life. Alexis de Tocqueville remarked that religious zeal was "perpetually warmed in the United States by the fires of patriotism" and that when conversing with "missionaries of Christian civilization" one frequently met "a politician where you expected to find a priest."[20] And in the early nineteenth century the Jesuit Father Giovanni Grassi recorded with considerable horror how American shifted from denomination to denomination, depending on how well each church served a member's individual interests of the moment.[21]

The Culmination of the Pattern

The interactions of religion, nationalism, and individualism yielded a situation in which Americans were prompted to seek their religious frameworks within the nation and a privatized faith. Surely underlying the identity diffusion so characteristic of the present is the churches' handing over to the nation and to the individual the greater portion of the symbolic task. Ironically the churches' very success in their service to nationalism and individualism accounts for much of their loss of appeal. If the integrity of an institution attaches primarily to its utilitarian functions, that institution is subject to abandonment when it has served its purpose; or else it is retained, but it remains largely empty of meaning for the human condition until its symbolic function is restored. Yet nation and individual have scarcely proved to be unambiguously satisfactory forms for the symbolic order of human experience. In terms of Whitman's vision for America, there has not arisen a secure, healthy synthesis of individualism and patriotism, wrought by an elevating, mystical faith. Rather, the terms of that dialec-

---

20. Alexis de Tocqueville, *Democracy in America*, 2 vols. (New York: Vintage Books, 1945), 1:317.
21. G. A. Grassi, "The Jesuit Scholar," in *This Was America*, ed. O. Handlin (Cambridge: Harvard University Press, 1949), 147-48.

tic have spun off into separate directions and are in critical states of their own.

On the one hand, the privatization of religion has contributed to that crisis in American individualism which Philip Slater has called "the pursuit of loneliness." "When a value is as strongly held as individualism in America," Slater has said, "the illnesses it produces tend to be treated by increasing the dosage, in the same way an alcoholic treats a hangover . . . . We seek a private house, a private means of transportation, a private garden, a private laundry, self-service stores, and do-it-yourself skills of every kind."[22] Slater could have added to his list: a private faith. The quest for privacy which increases contemporary loneliness and alienation bridges the generation gap. It is as apparent in the "Do your own thing" motto of the youth as in the gadgetry of privacy among their parents. It is no wonder that Americans of all ages are engaged in a search for new forms of community and different types of religious expression. Unfortunately, this search is often plagued by the same ideology of individualism that led to the dilemma in the first place.[23]

On the other hand, the religious dimension of the nation—the American civil religion—is undergoing such a crisis of its own that it offers little prospect of overcoming the consequences of individualism. Robert Bellah has ably demonstrated that the civil religion cannot be reduced to anything so vague as the "American way of life" or anything so trivial as "cookie prayers" recited by American school children.[24] The American civil religion or national faith is a distinctive collection of powerful symbols, myths, rituals, and sacred scriptures created by the unfolding American experience, and it is subject to the same opportunities for parochialism and cosmopolitanism as any other religion. At present, however, the civil religion reveals a greater capacity to divide the American people than to unite them. Especially since the end of World War II, struggles over domestic and international issues have augured a loss of national identity and an end to what Emile Durkheim called "collective religious sentiments." War groups and peace groups, hardhats and longhairs struggle for possession of the symbols and rituals of the civil religion. Furthermore, disadvantaged minority groups are living proof of the way in which the documents, heroes, and

---

22. Philip E. Slater, *The Pursuit of Loneliness: American Culture at the Breaking Point* (Boston: Beacon Press, 1970), 7.
23. Those portions of the youth culture which are engaged in a quest for new forms and bases of community are often thoroughly in the grip of American versions of individualism. For a discussion of the dilemma this creates for American youth and how this dilemma is reflected in their music see Lawrence Chenoweth, "The Rhetoric of Hope and Despair: A Study of the Jimi Hendrix Experience and the Jefferson Airplane," *American Quarterly* 23 (Spring 1971) : 25-45.
24. Robert N. Bellah, "Civil Religion in America," *Daedalus* 96 (Winter 1967) : 1-19.

paradigmatic events of the civil religion have been drawn almost exclusively from the history of white, affluent America. By no stretch of the imagination is the nation presently a locus of widely shared religious symbols.

Anthropologist Clifford Geertz has defined the sacred symbol as an image of reality which synthesizes a people's ethos and their world view. Symbolic activity, he adds, is *sui generis*. Man's "drive to make sense out of experience, to give it form and order is as real and as pressing as the more familiar biological needs."[25] Americans today require a sacred symbolism that meets this basic human need for giving some form and order to experience by synthesizing our ethos and our religious perspectives. Finally it does not matter whether the symbols are articulated within the churches, the civil religion, or some other part of our culture. But to be constructive and appropriate they must transcend atomistic individualism without deprecating the worth of the individual, they must unite Americans beyond their destructive conflicts without obscuring the real advantages of a cooperative pluralism, and they must move beyond narrow nationalism without losing touch with the national ethos. That, of course, is only one way of describing a very old American dream. But dreams, like ideas, may still have consequences, particularly when they are joined with lively symbols.

---

25. Clifford Geertz, "Ethos, World-View and the Analysis of Sacred Symbols," *Antioch Review*, December 1957, 422, 436.

The Status of the First Amendment's Religion Clauses: Some Reflections on Lines and Limits

HENRY J. ABRAHAM

I

Those among us who are students of government and politics in general, and of the Constitution and its theory, history, and law in particular, indubitably rejoice in being able to stipulate that at least some aspects of our fundamental document are evidently complied with more or less felicitously, even freely, and more or less readily, both in spirit and in letter, by both the private and the governmental sector, if not necessarily always evenly or equally. Although some may disagree, I, for one, am persuaded that, by and large, the basic guarantees of our Bill of Rights—the one hundred ninetieth anniversary of whose adoption we shall honor and observe next year—are in sound health, notwithstanding sporadic and no doubt continuing assaults upon sundry of its provisions. I am also persuaded that for its specific language and psychological entity a good many among our fellow citizens would still willingly lay down their lives—indeed they have done so throughout periods of crisis in our history—while ironically denying the invocation and application of certain individual components of the Bill of Rights with equal fervor. Hence I fear that Chief Justice Earl Warren may have been quite realistic when he would observe with sadness that he was convinced that the Bill of Rights could not pass a contemporary Congress in its entirety. Nonetheless, we may well take heart and pride in the recognition that, at least in the realm of those among the circa twenty-five articulated rights in the four-hundred-sixty-two-word Bill of Rights that Justice Benjamin N. Cardozo so felicitously termed as being "of the very essence of a scheme of ordered liberty," and as constituting freedoms that are—again employing his uniquely beautiful language—"the matrix, the indispensable condition, of nearly every other form of freedom," such as the quintet of guarantees of the First Amendment, the record is a good, a solid, and often even a comforting one, *pace* a plethora of vocal detractors to the contrary. That, I submit, is emphatically true of the first two clauses of that justly hallowed amendment, authored by that determined trio of Virginians, Thomas Jefferson, James Madison, and George Mason, which reads: "Congress shall make no law respecting an establishment of religion, or prohibiting the free exercise thereof . . . ."

Let it be stated at once that, unquestionably, there exist differences in the degree of observance of a commitment to these two arguably separately identifiably yet interrelated rights, e.g., the Court's 1979 opinion by Chief Justice Warren Burger in *National Labor Relations Board* v. *Bishop of Chicago*,[1] in which he referred to the two components consistently simply as "the religion clauses." Thus, if one were to award grades to the body politic and its government—not at all inappropriate at this time of the year in an academic setting—the second clause, "or prohibiting the free exercise thereof," should receive an "A," and the first, "no law respecting an establishment of religion," perhaps no more than a "B"; but that depends upon the grader and the eye of the beholder. The history of the U.S. Supreme Court's incorporation or absorption or application of the language and mandates of the Bill of Rights, which had originally been designed to apply to the national government only, bears out that distinction in terms of the judicio-legal process: the free exercise guarantee was "incorporated" or, to

---

1. *National Labor Relations Board* v. *Bishop of Chicago*, 440 U.S. 490 (1979). It ought to be noted, however, that the Court ducked the constitutional issue here.

use a more mundane term, "nationalized," in 1934 in the interesting and important case of *Hamilton v. Regents of the University of California*,[2] whereas the establishment clause was not similarly incorporated or nationalized until thirteen years later in the seminal 1947 New Jersey bus subsidies case of *Everson v. Board of Education of Ewing Township*.[3] Also of pertinent interest here is the fact that the vote on the merits in *Hamilton* was unanimous, although Justice Cardozo deemed it prudent to pen a separate concurring opinion which was joined by his colleagues Louis D. Brandeis and Harlan F. Stone, while the vote in *Everson* was a close five-to-four. There, a saddened and angry Justice Wiley Rutledge appended Madison's entire "Memorial and Remonstrance against Religious Assessment" to his stirring dissenting opinion; it was joined by his colleagues Felix Frankfurter, Harold Burton, and Robert H. Jackson, with the latter issuing a separate dissent in which Frankfurter concurred.

II

Indeed, I am persuaded that the record of both state and society vis-à-vis the free exercise of religion guarantee is probably better in civil libertarian terms than that of any other provision of the Bill of Rights, with the possible exception of freedom of the press notwithstanding the not infrequently exaggerated special pleading wails of the latter. To be sure, certainty in constitutional law is often elusive. Nothing is perfect in our imperfect constitutional world or any other world and there is no gainsaying the basic dilemma which the free exercise of religion language has posed sporadically. Yet the guarantee clearly militates against any governmental action prohibiting that free exercise, the clause having been designed to mean what it says, namely that neither Congress nor, by the aforementioned subsequent interpretation cum extension, the states may interfere with the sacred rights of freedom of religious "belief" and religious "exercise." Obviously, however, as Justice Owen J. Roberts took pains to point out in his opinion for a unanimous Court in the crucial 1940 *Cantwell* case,[4] while "freedom of exercise" embraces both the freedom to believe and the freedom to act, "the first is absolute, but, in the nature of things, the second cannot be. Conduct remains subject to [governmental] regulation for the

---

2. *Hamilton v. Regents of the University of California*, 293 U.S. 245 (1934).
3. *Everson v. Board of Education of Ewing Township*, 330 U.S. 1 (1947).
4. *Cantwell v. Connecticut*, 310 U.S. 296 (1940).

protection of society. The freedom to act must have appropriate definition to preserve the enforcement of that protection." In every case, Roberts continued, "the power to regulate must be so exercised as not, in attaining a permissible end, unduly to infringe the protected freedom."[5]

This, of course, raises as many practical questions as it settles. Yet the now four decades since Roberts penned his landmark opinion bear witness to a commendably ascending commitment to a maximum regard for free exercise, even when, as has been so true of the practices of such evangelistic sects as the Jehovah's Witnesses and Seventh-Day Adventists, that exercise cum action does not readily sit very well with a majority of the body politic, e.g., refusal to salute the flag; refusal to mount license plates with superpatriotic inscriptions; public playing of the offensive phonograph record "Enemies"; refusal to provide necessary medical care for minor children; insistence upon observing a day of rest other than Sunday; conscientious objection to military service generally, or specifically, to refuse to bear arms; and rejection of compulsory educational requirements beyond the eighth grade. There are limits, of course, although, with one or two exceptions, they are hardly controversial. Thus, few would regard as a valid free exercise claim such unsuccessfully mounted ones as the practice of polygamy, the alleged right to hold parades on major public highways without obtaining a permit, the refusal to pay taxes in the absence of statutory exemption, the handling of poisonous snakes in church, the claim that prohibitions against growing marijuana in one's garden and the growing of wheat in excess of federal acreage allotment regulations constitute interference with God's Will as manifested by the fruits of the soil, and that the failure of electrodes to function on an electric chair manifested an act of God superior to otherwise constitutional procedures at the bar of criminal justice.

The one aspect of the free exercise syndrome that has continued to be broadly controversial is the realm of conscientious objection to military service, but that has been neutralized, at least for the time being, by the abolition of the draft. Even prior thereto, the Court had so generously interpreted the so-called C.O. rule that the only judicial stricture that remained when compulsory military service was abandoned in 1971 was the Court's eight-to-one decision two years earlier—to me, entirely rational and fair—against "selective" conscientious objection, i.e., the claimed prerogative of distinguishing, on free exercise grounds, between "just" and "unjust" wars.[6]

---

5. Ibid., p. 306.
6. *Gillette* v. *United States* and *Negre* v. *Larsen,* 401 U.S. 437 (1971).

Only Justice William O. Douglas, then in his thirty-third year on the Court, dissented, observing wistfully: "I had assumed that the welfare of a single human soul was the ultimate test of the vitality of the First Amendment."[7]

That Douglas dissent not only raises the tantalizing question of what would happen to America's ability to constitute and field armed forces in a "controversial" war, but it is also symptomatic of the already alluded to, sometimes rather generous, claims or assertions raised by litigants under the religion clauses. A handful of rather novel ones, just advanced during the past year, albeit without success, are the following: a challenge by members of the Yhwhhoshua religion to Colorado's requirement that all drivers have photographs on their licenses because the sect believes the taking of photographs to be sinful;[8] a charge by the National Bible Association and the National Foundation for Fairness in Education that the failure of the Smithsonian Institution to depict the biblical version of the universe's creation in an exhibit, which showed only the evolutionary theory of the world's beginning, unconstitutionally established a "religion of secular humanism";[9] a contention that the United Methodist church could not be sued for alleged fraud and securities law violations in connection with seven retirement homes it operated on the West Coast because the church "lacked central management";[10] a claim by a "fanatically devout" public elementary school teacher that the school's celebration of Halloween constituted a "pagan observance of every evil and wicked thing in the world" and was hence impermissibly violative of his religious conscience;[11] the always controversial and busy Madalyn Murray O'Hair's suit to remove the phrase "In God We Trust" from U.S. coins and currency;[12] on the other hand, Mrs. O'Hair garnered a considerable amount of support for her also unsuccessful federal law suit to restrain the celebration of what she termed a "stupid, archaic" Mass by Pope John Paul II on the national mall during his Washington, D.C., visit on Sunday, 7 October 1979;[13] and a final example of an abortive effort to render the religion clauses' preroga-

---

7. Ibid., p. 469. For a discussion of the problem, see Henry J. Abraham, *Freedom and the Court; Civil Rights and Liberties in the United States*, 3d ed. (New York: Oxford University Press, 1977), pp. 252-63.
8. *Johnson* v. *Motor Vehicle Division*, 48 L.W. 3222 (1979), certiorari denied.
9. *Crowley* v. *Smithsonian Institution*, 462 F. Supp. 725 (1978).
10. *Milhouse* v. *District Court*, 100 S.Ct. 466, *United Methodist Church* v. *Barr*, 100 S.Ct. 468, decided 26 November 1979.
11. *Daily Progress* (Charlottesville, Va.), 22 December 1979.
12. *O'Hair* v. *Blumenthal*, 588 F. 2d, 1144 (1979).
13. *Daily Progress* (Charlottesville, Va.), 18 September 1979.

tives beyond the pale of their basic constitutional guarantees, the appeal by a Chicago public kindergarten school teacher, a Jehovah's Witness who had been fired by the city's superintendent of schools for "deliberate nonconformity with curriculum" because she frankly refused to teach the legally required instruction of the pledge of allegiance and patriotic songs,[14] her contention being that under her religious beliefs, the described activities constituted "forms of idolatry, the worship of man-made images, banned by the Bible," thus allegedly violative of her First Amendment rights.

The mere fact that these intriguing challenges would be litigated at all is living testimony to the high value the American body politic and its governmental organs bring to and place upon our religious prerogatives. That there are limits neither violates the spirit nor the letter of the religion clauses, for lines must be drawn under the Constitution. Its law cements our society.

III

If, on the whole and on balance, the state of affairs in the free exercise segment of the religion guarantees vis-à-vis state interference is really quite clear, safe, and comfortably satisfactory in the civil libertarian perspective under our Constitution, we come to a rather different situation as we turn to the establishment clause, the volatile issue of the separation of church and state. For if that clause, "Congress shall make no law respecting an establishment of religion," is commanding in tone and clear in syntax, it is inexorably unclear in its intention. What does it mean? Just what does it forbid? References to history would seem only to intensify the riddle, and because the establishment and free exercise clauses are closely related, the complexities of establishment simply cannot be understood if they are treated in isolation from the central problem of religion, of liberty itself. Hence it is hardly astonishing that the establishment clause has proved to be a "riddle within an enigma," a Pandora's box, and an emotion-charged issue of public policy and public law.

At least to a degree this is astonishing, for the intent of those American revolutionary and postrevolutionary leaders for religious freedom and a nonestablishment church, or more precisely churches—headed by that trio of great Virginians, Jefferson, Madison, and Mason, and during an earlier day and on a somewhat different level, by Rhode Island's Roger Williams—would seem to be very clear

---

14. *Palmer* v. *Board*, 100 S.Ct. 689, decided 7 January 1980.

indeed; to wit, that there must not be an established church, such as Virginia's Anglican church used to be ante Jefferson's seminal Disestablishment Statute, and that there should never be "the preferred position of a favored Church." One could hardly impute any doubt, whatsoever, to the intentions of the reigning manifesto of Jefferson's great Disestablishment Bill of 1786. Looking back at the end of a life filled with achievement for his beloved republic and commonwealth, he regarded that bill's authorship as second in significance only to that of the Declaration of Independence, and he requested that it be so listed and ranked on his tombstone under the stately trees of the family graveyard at the foot of his beloved Monticello.[15] Nor is there doubt about Madison's widely circulated and highly influential "Memorial and Remonstrance" of 1785 against the Virginia House of Delegates' proposal to provide, through assessment, for teachers of the Christian religion. In fifteen eloquently stated points, that famed, Jefferson-backed document argued persuasively that the state as the secular authority must have jurisdiction over temporal matters and that such authority does not extend over spiritual matters, "which lie in the domain of private belief and the churches." One ought again to note that the term used is "churches," not "church." To these leading Virginians and their devoted followers, the principle of separation was absolutely indispensable to the basic freedoms of belief, conscience, and dissent. They were in no sense hostile to religion; far from it, they simply regarded it as an entirely private matter. Overridingly determined to keep religion out of the domain of public affairs—a point made with remarkable consistency on the present Court by its devout Roman Catholic member, Justice William J. Brennan—they were as much concerned with "freedom *from* religion as freedom *of* religion." It is a live concern, a concern still reflected in the Virginia Constitution and indeed reconfirmed by its revisionist 1971 model. The latter's tough prohibitory language (Article I, Section 16) thus bars "any appropriation of public funds, or personal property, or any real estate to any church, or sectarian society, association or institution of *any kind whatever*, which is entirely or partly, directly or indirectly, controlled by any church or sectarian society."

Yet, as we look about us and reflect on the contemporary status of the relationship between state and church or churches, something obviously must have happened to alter the tenor and the intent of

---

15. "And not a word more," were his instructions for the epitaph he composed: "Here was buried Thomas Jefferson . . . author of the Declaration of Independence, [of the] Statute of Virginia for Religious Freedom [and] Father of the University of Virginia."

those noble principles. One would not be terribly far from the mark if one were to sum matters up, somewhat cynically perhaps, but not really far-fetched, by concluding that once again that omnipresent and omnipotent alliance of lawyers and politicians has done us in. However, such a conclusion depends, of course, upon one's point of view, and, be it stipulated at once, that point of view differs both dramatically and drastically. Indeed, it runs the veritable gamut: from an on-its-face all but utter lack of alarm or even concern, e.g., the observation by Professor Richard Funston, a sophisticated scholar of Court and Constitution, that the establishment clause cases boil down to "much ado about nothing" and that the Court might be well advised to "abandon the field";[16] through that by the distinguished, long-time separation watchdog, First Amendment attorney specialist Leo Pfeffer, that "compared to the state of law construing other provisions of [that Amendment] such as freedom of the press, or of the right of persons charged with crimes—the Court's interpretation of [the separation clause] is a model of clarity";[17] through that by U.S. Senator Daniel Patrick Moynihan (D-N.Y.) who contends that "in the years since 1947 [the year of the New Jersey bus case[18]] the Court's decisions have become ever more confused and contradictory,"[19] resulting in "an intellectual shambles: one confused and convoluted decision, requiring a yet more confused and convoluted explanation or modification";[20] through the thoughtful but deceptively facile question by the wise veteran columnist James Reston of the *New York Times*, whether the United States, "in this secular and permissive age, is somehow threatened by helping to finance the instruction and practice of religion or whether it is in trouble for lack of religion";[21] through the intriguingly controversial position by a knowledgeable civil rights and liberties scholar-author, Professor Richard Morgan, who is not at all worried by financial aid to "specialized and independent parochial schools" but very much so by even "modest prayers in the common public schools";[22] to Mrs. O'Hair's ubiquitous assaults upon

---

16. Richard Y. Funston, *Constitutional Counterrevolution?* (Cambridge, Mass.: Schenkman, 1977), p. 235.
17. Leo Pfeffer, "The Current State of the Law in the United States and the Separationist Agenda," *Annals of the American Academy of Political and Social Science* 446 (November 1979):5.
18. *Everson*, 330 U.S. 1 (1947).
19. As quoted by James Reston in "Moynihan and the Court," *New York Times*, 3 June 1979, from a speech Senator Moynihan had delivered in Staten Island a few days earlier.
20. "What Do You Do When the Supreme Court is Wrong?" 57 *Public Interest* (Fall 1979):11.
21. *New York Times*, 3 June 1979.
22. Richard E. Morgan, *The Supreme Court and Religion* (New York: Free Press, 1972), p. 207.

STATUS OF THE FIRST AMENDMENT'S RELIGION CLAUSES 117

anything she regards as establishment, including her Supreme Court-dismissed contention that the astronauts' memorable reading of the Bible from outer space violated the separation clause.[23]

Yet it is assuredly fair to propound the central questions of where in fact we do stand contemporarily on the separation issue in constitutional terms? We ask quite naturally, especially in the face of such a priori head shaking, invoking Supreme Court decisional distinctions between, for example, the following: the providing of "books" to nonpublic school pupils, the "loaning" of which has consistently been upheld by the Court since it approved it eight-to-zero on due process grounds in the 1930 *Cochran* case,[24] and, more pointedly, six-to-three in 1968, there against a potent First Amendment challenge,[25] with the author of the key bus-subvention-approving ruling in *Everson*,[26] Justice Hugo L. Black, angrily exclaiming that "a book is not a bus," and the Court's repeated disallowal on grounds of violation of the separation clause of the providing of certain "instructional materials and equipment," as it did more or less recently in the 1973 New York,[27] 1975 Pennsylvania,[28] and 1977 Ohio[29] litigations, in each instance by a six-to-three vote. A cynic might quickly ask what books are since they do not seem to be "instructional materials" in the Court's eyes. Fairness, however, dictates the repeated and indeed realistic acknowledgment by the Court that the wall of separation that must unquestionably, or so I would contend, be maintained between church and state is, in its frequently reiterated words, "a blurred, indistinct, and variable barrier depending on all the circumstances of a particular relationship."[30] Few students of the issue would disagree with that wistful observation. More, however, would question the Court's collateral contention, with which Justice Harry A. Blackmun followed his just aforementioned confessional, namely, that "[n]one the less, the Court's numerous precedents have become firmly rooted, and now provide substantial guidance."[31]

---

23. *O'Hair* v. *Payne*, 397 U.S. 531 (1970), appeal dismissed.
24. *Cochran* v. *Louisiana State Board of Education*, 281 U.S. 370 (1930).
25. *Board of Education* v. *Allen*, 392 U.S. 236 (1968).
26. 330 U.S. 1.
27. *Committee for Public Education and Religious Liberty* v. *Nyquist*, 413 U.S. 476 (1973).
28. *Meek* v. *Pittenger*, 421 U.S. 349 (1975).
29. *Wolman* v. *Walter*, 433 U.S. 229 (1977).
30. For example, Chief Justice Burger's opinion for the Court in *Lemon* v. *Kurtzman*, 403 U.S. 614 (1971) and Justice Blackmun's in *Wolman*, 433 U.S. 233 (1977).
31. *Wolman*, 433 U.S. 233, opinion for the Court.

IV

Since these "reflections" endeavor to address themselves to the inherent lines and limits of the religion clauses, fairness now accordingly dictates at least a brief, if necessarily sketchy, examination of what has happened to the separation concept during the two centuries since the Virginia statesmen penned their concerns.

What has happened beyond any shadow of a doubt is that Jefferson's concept of the "wall of separation between Church and State" has been demonstrably eroded. Whether that is "good" or "bad" depends again, of course, upon one's point of view, both on philosophical and pragmatic grounds. Be that as it may, in responding to the ongoing fact of life of continuing demands for involvement by the state in terms of financial aid to churches, church facilities, and most markedly, to parochial elementary and secondary schools and church-affiliated institutions of higher learning, the judiciary, in its role as ultimate constitutional interpreter cum arbiter, has based its sundry decisions on what may be identified as roughly three principal theories of separation that have come to be advanced as more or less compatible with the exhortations of the establishment clause of the First Amendment. I have outlined these in considerable details in my *Freedom and the Court*,[32] but I should like to reencapsulate them here.

One is the "Strict Separation" or "No Aid" theory which, presumably incorporating the Jeffersonian-Madisonian "wall of separation" approach to the problem, holds that its requirements of strict separation forbid any and all governmental support of religion and religious interests. This theory was judicially applied, for example, by Justice Black in his eight-to-one opinion for the Court in the 1948 case of *McCollum* v. *Board of Education*,[33] striking down Champaign, Illinois's practice of "released time" that featured classes in religious instruction to public school children on public school premises. Yet that same Justice Black—my judicial hero—had, alas, found no violation in upholding five-to-four just one year earlier the aforementioned New Jersey practice of authorizing treasury subventions for the busing of parochial and other private as well as public school children. Actually, in the locality at issue, Ewing Township, they were confined to four Roman Catholic schools. Enunciating the troublesome "child benefit" theory, he could write there:

---

32. See Abraham, pp. 297-320.
33. *McCollum* v. *Board of Education*, 333 U.S. 203 (1948).

The "establishment of religion" clause of the First Amendment means at least this: Neither a state nor the Federal Government can set up a church. Neither can pass laws which aid one religion, aid all religions, or prefer one religion over another. Neither can force or influence a person to go or remain away from church against his will or force him to profess a belief or disbelief in any religion. No person can be punished for entertaining or professing religious beliefs or disbeliefs, for church attendance or nonattendance. No tax in any amount, large or small, can be levied to support any religious activities or institution, whatever they may be called, or whatever form they may adopt to teach or practice religion. Neither a state nor the Federal Government can, openly or secretly, participate in the affairs of any religious organizations or groups and vice-versa. In the words of Jefferson, the clause against establishment of religion by law was intended to erect a "wall of separation between Church and State."[34]

In the light of the above manifesto, Black's concluding passage in his opinion must have come as a bit of a surprise to some of his readers as well as his colleagues: "The First Amendment," he warned, "has erected a wall between church and state. The wall must be kept high and impregnable. We could not approve the slightest breach. New Jersey has not breached it here."[35] Had it not? Four of his colleagues thought so emphatically, yet the principle of *Everson* has been, and is, the law of the land to this day, notwithstanding Justice Douglas's 1962 from-the-bench announcement that he had erred in joining the *Everson* majority.[36] On the other hand, it was again Justice Black, now invoking the "strict separation" theory, who spoke for another eight-to-one majority in the New York prayer case,[37] striking down New York State's practice of permitting the recitation in public schools of a twenty-two word, nondenominational daily prayer drafted by state agency officials, concluding eloquently: "It is neither sacrilegious nor antireligious to say that each separate government in this country should stay out of the business of writing or sanctioning official prayers and leave that purely religious function to the people themselves and to those the people look to for religious guidance."[38]

The second theory is the so-called Government Neutrality theory, which requires the government to be resolutely "neutral" in matters religious, so neutral, in fact, that government cannot do anything that either aids or hampers religion; that there must be, in the Court's own words, "a secular legislative purpose and a primary effect that neither advances nor inhibits religion; that there can be no government action that would either confer a benefit or impose a

---

34. *Everson*, 330 U.S. 15-16 (1947).
35. Ibid., p. 16.
36. *Engel* v. *Vitale*, 370 U.S. 421 (1963), concurring opinion, p. 443.
37. Ibid., majority opinion.
38. Ibid., p. 435.

burden."³⁹ Less categorical than the first theory, the "neutrality" approach leaves us with the delicate need not only to interpret "secular," "burden," and "benefit," but also "religion" itself. Under that theory or doctrine, the Court, again in two back-to-back eight-to-one opinions totalling one hundred forty-four pages and featuring five opinions with each of the "representatives" of the three major domestic religious faiths writing a lengthy concurring one, declared unconstitutional a Pennsylvania law requiring daily reading, sans comment, of ten verses from the King James Version of the Bible, and the city of Baltimore's similar requirement of a Bible chapter and/or the Lord's Prayer. Authoring the controlling opinion, Justice Thomas C. Clark, a devout Presbyterian, wrote with feeling:

The place of religion in our society is an exalted one, achieved through a long tradition of reliance on the home, the church and the inviolable citadel of the individual heart and mind. We have come to recognize through bitter experience that it is not within the power of government to invade that citadel, whether its purpose or effect be to aid or oppose, to advance or retard. In the relationship between man and religion, the state is firmly committed to a position of neutrality.⁴⁰

And he explained:

[T]o withstand the strictures of the Establishment Clause there must be a secular legislative purpose and a primary effect, that neither advances nor inhibits religion . . . [and] the fact [advanced by the Pennsylvania and Maryland laws] that individual students may absent themselves upon parental request . . . furnishes no defense to a claim of constitutionality under the Establishment Clause.⁴¹

He concluded with the reminder that the Court:

cannot accept that the concept of neutrality, which does not permit a state to require a religious exercise even with the consent of the majority of those affected, collides with the majority's right to free exercise of religion. While the Free Exercise Clause clearly prohibits the use of state action to deny the right of free exercise to anyone, it has never meant that a majority could use the machinery of the State to practice its beliefs.⁴²

We now come to the third theory, which, I suggest, is very likely the controlling one today, although it is not the sole one utilized. I term it the "Governmental Accommodation" theory, for it has featured a now fairly consistent judicial willingness to reconcile the natural clash between the free exercise and separation clauses by accepting some accommodations between the diverse claims of government and religion, and *a fortiori* between state and church.

---

39. *Abington Township School District* v. *Schempp* and *Murray* v. *Curlett*, 374 U.S. 203 (1963), 222, 224.
40. Ibid., p. 226.
41. Ibid., pp. 222, 224.
42. Ibid., pp. 225-26.

This accommodation is often, but not necessarily always, grounded in the controversial "child benefit" concept, which lends itself to rather ready attack in both logical and constitutional terms. The genesis of the accommodation theory lies in a six-to-three opinion written by, of all people, Justice Douglas in 1952.[43] It upheld New York's released time program, which differed from the one struck down in Illinois only in the sense that those New York public school children who were to be given religious instruction were released from classes while the "heathens" had to stay in class, attendance being taken, covertly and overtly, respectively. A livid Justice Black, joined by his colleagues Frankfurter and Jackson, thundered in dissent: "State help to religion injects political and party prejudices into a holy field. It too often substitutes force for prayer, hate for love, and persecution for persuasion. Government should not be allowed; under cover of the soft euphemism of 'co-operation', to steal into the sacred area of religious choice."[44]

The "accommodation" theory received further impetus with another six-to-three "child benefit" philosophy ruling in 1968, this one by Justice Byron R. White,[45] upholding the so-called lending of textbooks to students in parochial as well as public schools, a program under which the parochial schools could request the books they wanted, books that might be different than those used by the public school students. Again, Justice Black dissented, this time joined by Justices Douglas and Fortas, contending with passion that:

it requires no prophet to foresee that on the argument used to support this law others could be upheld providing for state or federal government funds to buy property on which to erect religious school buildings or to erect the buildings themselves, to pay the salaries of the religious school teachers, and finally to have the sectarian religious groups cease to rely on voluntary contributions of members of their sects while waiting for the Government to pick up all the bills for the religious schools.[46]

As already pointed out, the textbook loan approach of accommodation has been repeatedly upheld since that time, falling only once in the instance of Mississippi's law which had included as beneficiaries pupils in all schools, even in those which practiced racial segregation.[47]

Given the evidently solid, and conceivably increasing, number of votes on the Court in favor of certain kinds of "accommodation," it

---

43. *Zorach v. Clauson*, 343 U.S. 306 (1952).
44. Ibid., p. 32.
45. *Board of Education v. Allen*, 392 U.S. 236 (1968).
46. Ibid., p. 253.
47. *Norwood v. Harrison*, 413 U.S. 455 (1973).

came as no surprise that, utilizing the "child benefit" loophole to the fullest, both the federal legislature and a good many state legislatures began to do their utmost to find ways to provide funds for the activities of parochial schools. A host of statutes was enacted, e.g., the Federal Aid to Elementary and Secondary Education Act of 1965, severally amended and extended since; the Federal Educational Facilities Acts of 1963 and 1973; and a plethora of state laws, such as those in Pennsylvania, New York, Rhode Island, Ohio, and New Jersey in the 1960s and 1970s, all designed to provide public funds for direct instructional aid in "non-religious subjects" to Roman Catholic and other church-related primary and secondary schools, including such intriguing devices as the "purchasing" of "secular services" for the teaching of "secular subjects" by parochial school teachers. The cascading number of challenges to the cascading number of laws prompted the Court, through the chief justice, to come up with a collateral umbrella test, namely, that no accommodation may constitute an "excessive entanglement" between government and religion—a nonexcessive entanglement evidently being acceptable constitutionally.[48]

Under that additional doctrine, which was joined to the precedential "secular legislative purpose" and "primary effect of neither advancing nor inhibiting religion" requirements, and which now constitutes the judicial test of the establishment clause, the Burger Court has since 1971 handed down a series of rulings under the accommodation approach, upholding some and striking down other attempts and devices to fund nonpublic school activities. A sketchy summary, cataloguing some of the more important decisions and examples, renders the following dichotomous tableau for the last decade of Court-decisional activity.

Case	Year	Upheld	Struck Down
Walz	1970	(7:1) Tax exemption of property used exclusively for religious purposes	
Lemon [I]	1971		(0:8) Partial payment of salaries of parochial school teachers
Early	1971		(1:8) Purchases of secular services for sectarian schools
Tilton	1971	(5:4) Construction funds for religiously affiliated colleges and universities	

---

48. Articulated initially by him in *Walz* v. *Tax Commission of the City of New York*, 397 U.S. 664 (1970), although the Court found no such "entanglement" there.

Essex	1972		(1:8) Direct tuition rebates per child of $90.00
Nyquist	1973	(6:3) Lending of textbooks	(3:6 to 1:8) Maintenance, repair, tuition, equipment, and record keeping and tuition reimbursement
Meek	1975	(6:3) Lending of textbooks	(3:6) Counseling, testing, remedial classes, instructional materials and equipment, speech and hearing therapy, psychological services
Roemer	1976	(5:4) Noncategorical financial (Maryland) aid to church-related colleges, if not used for sectarian purposes (first time in history Court approved general purpose subsidies)	
Blanton	1976	(9:0) Tuition grants to college students, no matter where enrolled	
Wolman	1977	(7:2) Therapeutic, remedial, and guidance counseling on "neutral" sites off-grounds; (6:3) Lending of textbooks; (8:1) Diagnostic services on grounds; (6:3) Standardized texts and test scoring (provided by public schools)	(4:5) Field trip financing; (3:6) Providing to parents or pupils (loan) classroom paraphernalia, e.g., wall charts, maps, projectors, tape recorders
Cathedral	1977		(3:6) Direct financial aid for testing and record keeping
Byrne	1979		(3:6) Income tax deductions for parents of parochial school students
Regan	1980	(5:4) Reimbursement for expenses incurred by nonpublic schools in connection with keeping official attendance and other records, for administering three state-prepared tests, and for grading two of these	

The five 1977 *Wolman* opinions, ranging from eight-to-one to three-to-six, that were billed as lodestar decisions on the accommodation front, were hardly models of clarity. They constituted a veritable mishmash of interpretations that were not precisely elucidated, indeed they were compounded, by the December 1977 New York *Cathedral* holding. Consequently it was not surprising that, building upon aspects of *Wolman*, the Court, in a five-to-four White opinion that contained numerous caveats and acknowledged a course that "sacrifices clarity and predictability for flexibility,"[49] would thus uphold in early 1980 New York's revised 1974 version of the 1970 law that the justices had struck down six-to-three in the 1973 *Nyquist* decision. The 1980 ruling in what became known as the *Regan* case, distinguished the latter decision by pointing to the fact that the 1974 revision mandated that the tests and supporting procedures were to be prepared by the state rather than by teachers as had been the case under the 1970 law. The four dissenters, Blackmun, Brennan, Marshall, and Stevens, however, saw a demonstrable primary effect of advancing religion and entanglement violative of the First Amendment.

Yet in forbidding New Jersey's attempt to provide special income tax deductions for parents who send their offspring to nonpublic schools, the Court made clear that neither tax credits nor tax deductions nor exemptions nor rebates, nor any form of direct financial aid to parents or teachers, will now pass constitutional muster with six of the current nine members of the Court, at least not in the absence of some permissible type of federal statutory sanction. Chief Justice Burger and Justices White and Rehnquist, on the other hand, appear to be firmly on record as finding constitutional support for almost any type of "accommodation," provided they can detect some kind of secular purpose. In the instance of Chief Justice Burger, this posture obtains only so long as he does not perceive an entanglement that is "excessive," but Justices White and Rehnquist, especially the former, do not seem to be concerned at all about either the "primary effect" of the state involvement or the attendant "entanglement." If they see a viable secular purpose, they will vote to uphold the measure or action. For them, in fine, the three-pronged test has essentially been reduced to the single one of the presence of a secular purpose as perceived by them.

V

Where, then, do we stand? In my judgment, although the Court has avowedly retained and perhaps loosely cemented its purpose-effect-entanglement line with respect to such realms of state support as on-premises prayers, religious observances, religious instruction, employee salaries, direct tuition grants to below college and university level students (as contrasted with those at that higher educational level), or any grants to parents (although this may well be

---

49. *Committee for Public Education and Religious Liberty* v. *Regan*, 100 S.Ct. 851 (1980).

changing for the federal level if the repeatedly but still not enacted $250.00 tax deduction for parents of college and university students passes Congress), there is but little doubt that a distinct erosion has taken place. This relaxed vigilance appears to have become Court policy in a host of areas broadly describable as financial support for auxiliary educational services in parochial schools. For those who, like Senator Moynihan, see this as mere harmless accommodation or as a matter of fundamental fairness or equity, this poses few, if any, problems. For those who, like myself, are committed to what they embrace and regard as the Jeffersonian-Madisonian imperative of separation under the First Amendment, it represents an alarming development. I, for one, thus prefer to take my stand with Justice Rutledge's dissenting pronouncement in the New Jersey bus case of 1947 when he warned that: "Like St. Paul's freedom, religious liberty with a great price must be bought. And for those who exercise it most fully, but insisting upon religious education for their children mixed with secular, by the terms of our Constitution the price is greater than for others."[50] It is, I submit, a price tag well worth paying for the hallowed imperative of liberty.

---

50. *Everson*, 330 U.S. 1 (1947), dissenting opinion, p. 28.

What Hath God Wrought to Caesar: The Church as a Self-Interest Interest Group

LEO PFEFFER

INTEREST GROUPS

In 1940 Congress took the church out of religion. In 1965 the Supreme Court took God out of religion and in 1970 it took religion out of religion. The first universal draft law, the Selective Service Act of 1917, exempted religious objectors provided they were members of some recognized denomination or sect, such as the Quakers or Mennonites, whose doctrine or discipline forbids participation in military service. In 1940 Congress amended the law to remove this requirement and substituted for it the requirement that the applicant individually "by reason of religious training and belief" possess conscientious scruples against participation in war. To make clear that it was defining religion in this conventional way, it expressly excluded (in 1948) objection based on "essentially political, sociological or philosophical views or a merely personal code" and required the applicant to profess a belief in a "Supreme Being."

The Supreme Court in 1965 said this does not necessarily mean belief in the God of Abraham, Jesus, or Mohammed or in any supernatural being. In upholding the right to exemption of an applicant who rejected a relationship "vertically towards Godness directly" but accepted one "horizontally towards Godness through Mankind and the World," the Court held that exemption must be accorded to anyone who possesses "a sincere and meaningful belief which occupies in the life of its possessor a place parallel to that filled by the God of those who admittedly qualify for the exemption."[1]

This decision was not entirely surprising, for a few years earlier the Court had noted in another case that there were beliefs that were

---

1. *United States* v. *Seeger*, 380 U.S. 163 (1965).

generally considered religious faiths which were not based on theism, such as Buddhism, Taoism, and Ethical Culture.[2] Congress accepted the Court's decision and later changed the law to eliminate the requirement of belief in a Supreme Being, but retained the requirement that objection to military service be based upon religious training and belief. But the Supreme Court countered by defining religion to encompass a strongly and sincerely held belief that war is immoral, thus according to exemption to an applicant who denied that there was anything religious about his belief.[3]

If religion, then, is to be equated with sincerely and strongly held views on morality, it becomes so all-encompassing as practically to be meaningless. Even the more restricted definitions of the 1965 decision and the 1940 Congressional amendment which view religion in individualistic terms would not be helpful. In exploring the effects upon the state of religious intervention in state affairs, as a practical matter, religion must be considered in the context of political science, that is as a structured, institutional interest group.

An interest group may be defined as a collection of individuals who share some common attitude, seek recognition or advancement either of their own position in and claims on society or of the attitude they share or of both and engage in repeated and patterned activity to achieve these objectives.[4] With some groups, such as the National Association of Manufacturers, the traditional bread-and-butter trade unions, the NAACP, the Women's Liberation Movement, the major focus is upon the recognition or advancement of their own claims upon society; these may be called self-interest interest groups. With others, such as the league to abolish capital punishment or the Women's Christian Temperance Union, self-interest is a secondary or even negligible factor; these are called ideological interest groups.

All religions groups are both self-interest and ideological (often resulting in internal tensions), although in varying degrees. Some such as the Hasidim of Brooklyn, concentrate their activity primarily towards preventing discrimination against themselves or to obtaining governmental funds for their institutions. Others, such as the Unitarians and Ethical Culturists, expend their energies on reforming society. However, most engage in considerable continued and patterned activity to achieve both self-interest and ideological objectives. Finally, it should be noted that not all interest groups seek to achieve their objectives through

---

2. *Torcaso* v. *Watkins*, 367 U.S. 488 (1961).
3. *Welsh* v. *United States*, 90 S. Ct. 1792 (1970).
4. Adapted from E. S. Redford, et. al. *Politics and Government in the United States* (New York: Harcourt, Brace & World, 1968), 118; D. Truman, *The Government Process* (New York: Alfred A. Knopf, 1951), 33; V. O. Key, Jr., *Politics, Parties and Pressure Groups* (New York: Crowell & Co., 1964), 103.

political action (a term used to encompass judicial as well as legislative action; "hippies" and Old Order Amish (the latter will not even defend themselves in court) are examples; but most religious groups do and the concern here is with them.

It would be impossible to treat with any meaningful adequacy both roles of church activity within the limits of this article. I have discussed elsewhere the church as an ideological interest group and the effect of its activities on the body politic. I have suggested that religious groups, "avowedly or not, seek to translate their own particular hierarchy of values into categorical imperatives for the community at large, including those members of the community outside of their own respective folds. Each religious group, consciously or unconsciously, attempts to shape the culture of the community according to its own concept of the good life. Since government and law are a highly potent and effective means of translating particular values into universal rules of conduct, each competing religious group will seek to prevail upon the government to accept its particular values as the best."[5] Here I propose to limit myself to a few instances of the role of the church as a self-interest interest group and what effect this has upon the state.

Military Chaplaincy

The beginning of this paper considered the subject of religious exemption from military service; now consideration needs to be given this in terms of the church as a self-interest group. The Deuteronomist informs us that when the Children of Israel went out to war an announcement was made by the officers that whoever had built a house and had not dedicated it or planted a vineyard and not eaten of its fruit or betrothed a wife and had not taken her or was fearful or fainthearted[6] should leave and return home.[7] No mention of priests was made in this announcement, but it was quite clear that throughout the history of Israel priests were not required to serve as combatants in the armed forces.[8]

It may be assumed that the immunity of the priestly class from obligatory combatant service was not limited to the Aaronites of Israel.

---

5. Leo Pfeffer, *Creeds in Competition* (New York: Harper and Row, 1958), 153.
6. According to at least one Rabbinic view in the Talmud, the word "faintheartedly" referred to those who were too compassionate to take human life, which may therefore be the earliest instance of exemption from military service for conscientious objection, and non-religious objection at that. *Sotah* 44a, *Tosefta*.
7. Deut. 20:1-8.
8. The Levites were not numbered in the census of those "able to go forth to war." Num. 1:3, 47. Levi is not mentioned in Judges 5 among the tribes who are either praised for joining in the battle against the Canaanites or condemned for not doing so, quite obviously because their participation was not expected.

It is and probably always has been a universal concomitant of compulsory military service.[9] Unlike immunity from secular criminal law jurisdiction,[10] immunity from military service may not have required rigorous affirmative political action on the part of the priesthood. Yet, though ostensibly a unilateral act of grace on the part of the state, it is quite likely that a *quid pro quo* has always been implicitly expected by the state and always received from the church.[11]

Before the Israelite officers announced the exemption of the housebuilders, vineyard planters, and wife-takers, the priests also addressed the troops, saying: "Hear, O Israel, ye approach this day unto battle against your enemies; let not your hearts be faint, fear not and do not tremble, neither be ye terrified because of them; for the Lord your God is he that goeth with you, to fight against your enemies, to save you."[12]

Such morale building is taken for granted as a proper function of military chaplains. The chaplain is expected to urge the soldiers not merely to praise the Lord but also to pass the ammunition. The military establishment is not uncognizant of the usefulness of religion in effectuating military purposes.[13] The regulations of the academies of all three branches of our armed forces require all cadets to attend church or synagogue every Sunday (a mosque apparently will not do). A lawsuit was brought by a number of cadets challenging the constitutionality of the regulation but a federal judge dismissed their complaint. Under the First Amendment of the Constitution, as interpreted by the Supreme Court, government action in the sphere of religion is valid only if it

---

9. Exemption of clergymen from military service has been included in every American conscription statute.
10. The martyrdom and ultimate sainthood of Thomas á Becket had its origin in his refusal to recognize the state's jurisdiction to try and to punish priests charged with the commission of secular crimes.
11. The American statutes exempting clergymen from compulsory combatant service have never required them to participate as military chaplains. However, among the Jews (and undoubtedly other religious groups) the major theological seminaries, Orthodox, Conservative and Reform, have until recently exacted a pledge of all registrants to serve as chaplains for at least two years after ordination. See generally, A. Ray Applequist, ed. *Church, State and Chaplaincy* (Washington, D.C.: General Commission on Chaplains and Armed Forces Personnel, 1969).
12. Deut. 20:2-3.
13. The 1 March 1967 issue of the Jewist Telegraphic Agency *Daily News Bulletin* reports the following:

A U.S. Army private who embarked on a "death fast" because he claimed his religious conviction as an Orthodox Jew prevented him from serving "an army practicing violence" in Viet Nam has been taken into custody and confined in a mental ward at Madigan General Hospital, Tacoma, Wash., military authorities revealed today.

The soldier, Pvt. Robert Levy, 22, of Kansas City, Mo., started a hunger strike two weeks ago at Fort Lewis, Wash. For 14 days he ate only milk and honey. Yesterday, he stopped eating altogether, stating that "as an expression of my religious conviction as an Orthodox Jew, I break the law of the United States and refuse to remain a soldier."

Defense Department officials disclosed that the Army is trying to get rabbis to convince Levy that the war is righteous and his fast unjustified.

serves a secular purpose.[14] The judge held that this requirement was satisfied because attendance at regular services makes one a better military officer.[15] Testifying at the hearing, Admiral Thomas H. Moorer, newly appointed chairman of the Joint Chiefs of Staff, said, "I don't think you will find an atheist who has reached the peak in the Armed Forces."

The role of the chaplain as an arm of the military leads to anomalous results. A Christian chaplain serving in the American army in World War I could assure his troops that "God is with us," while his German counterpart, invoking the same deity and the same faith, could tell his troops with equal confidence, "Gott mit uns."[16] Individual clerical pacifists can and do assert that neither is correct, but the church, as a self-interest interest group, cannot. (Of course, this is so not only because the state exempts its priests from combatant service, but for many other favors the church receives from the state as well.) This not only compromises God's claim to judge Caesar, but deprives society of an authoritative and disinterested arbiter of moral values in an area where one is sorely needed.

Americans have reluctantly accepted the correctness of our involvement in Vietnam because of their reliance upon the judgment of their President and the absence of any comparatively authoritative institution challenging that judgment. It is not unreasonable to suggest that because the challenge has come not from the church but from the university (which occupies a much lower status in the eyes of middle America) that the war drags on. (And it may also be because of this default that the Supreme Court has accorded secular objection to war parity with religious objection.)

There is, however, another side to the matter. Military chaplains, besides morale building, fill a need which civilian chaplains without official rank, status, and pay could not fill, or not as effectively. A young man of eighteen or nineteen, away from home and family perhaps for the first time, who finds himself in some kind of trouble

---

14. *Abington School Board* v. *Schempp*, 374 U.S. 203 (1963); *Board of Education* v. *Allen*, 392 U.S. 236 (1968).
15. *Anderson* v. *Laird*, U.S. D.C., D.C., decided 31 July 1970. The crux of the decision was that if an officer, through attendance at worship, becomes familiar with "the manner and the extent to which they [the soldiers] draw upon God as a supernatural being in the conduct of their lives" he can use that knowledge to make them more effective in battlefield combat.
16. In a Memorial and Remonstrance written by James Madison in 1786 in opposition to a bill introduced in the Virginia legislature to assess taxes on all citizens for the support of the churches, one of the fifteen reasons for opposition was that "the bill implies either that the Civil Magistrate is a competent Judge of Religious truth; or that he may employ Religion as an engine of Civil policy. The first is an arrogant pretension falisfied by the contradictory opinions of Rulers of all ages, and throughout the world: The second an unhallowed perversion of the means of salvation." Cf. *Writings of James Madison*, ed. by G. Hunt, 2:183-91.

with the terrifyingly large, disciplined, and impersonal institution known as the army may need an ombudsman and need him desperately. In such a situation, a chaplain who has the same military rank and wears the same uniform as the commanders, who eats with them and calls them by first name, can be far more valuable than either of the Berrigan brothers with all their idealism and self-sacrifice.

Tax Exemption[17]

Like priestly exemption from military service, tax exemption for churches is not new. Scripture relates that when Joseph bought the Egyptians' land for the food he had stored during the seven years of plenty, he turned back to each Egyptian his land and "made it a law over the land of Egypt unto this day that Pharaoh should have the fifth part [of the produce]; except the land of the priests only, which became not Pharaoh's."[18] Later, when Artaxerxes, king of Persia, authorized Ezra to levy a tax for the rebuilding of the Temple, he specifically directed that "touching any of the priests and Levites, singers, porters, Nethinim, or ministers of the house of God, it shall not be lawful to impose toll, tribute or custom upon them."[19]

In the United States, churches enjoy many benefits under the tax laws, but three are of major importance. The first and most important is the deductibility from gross income of contributions made by taxpayers to churches. It is most important because, even among the churches engaged in profit-making enterprises (of which, in proportion to membership the Mormon Church is probably the first), the major part of church income comes not from business profits but from voluntary contributions, and the most important nonspiritual incentive to contributions is tax deductibility. This form of church benefit is also the least controversial because, unlike for example oil-depletion allowances, it is a game any number can play and almost any taxpayer takes advantage of.

A second major tax benefit enjoyed by churches is exemption from taxation of the income of businesses and other commercial enterprises owned by them. This benefit has but another four years of life, but it is worth noting for it illustrates well the effectiveness of the church as a self-interest interest group.

In the 1940s, a professor of law at New York University advised the institution that under the federal tax law as it then read it could ac-

---

17. On tax exemption for churches, see generally, D. B. Robertson, *Should Churches Be Taxed?* (Philadelphia: Westminster Press, 1968).
18. Genesis 47:26.
19. Ezra 7:24.

quire the stock of the Mueller Spaghetti Company and pay no tax on the profits earned by the sale of spaghetti so long as they were all used for educational purposes. The University accepted the advice and found itself in the spaghetti business and in a position to undersell its non-tax-exempt competitors. It was not long before other tax-exempt organizations followed suit.

The ensuing hue and cry raised by non-exempt corporations forced Congress in 1950 to change the law so as to limit the exemption to income earned from enterprises directly related to the purpose of the exempt organization. The change might continue the exemption on the profits of university presses (if university presses make profits) but not on spaghetti factories, for there is no visible direct religion between spaghetti and scholarship. The church lobbies, however, proved more powerful than educational and charitable lobbies and the Treasury Department, for at the last moment the bill was amended to continue the exemption on unrelated business activities of churches.[20] The result is that today a church can operate a girdle business (which one church does) or an apartment house or a department store without paying a federal tax on the profits, but nobody else can. However, within the past year Congress, responding to widespread protests, changed the law and put churches in the same category as other tax-exempt institutions, except that they receive a five-year grace period during which they will still be exempt on the unrelated businesses they owned when the amendment was passed.[21]

The third, and today most controversial, tax benefit enjoyed by churches is the exemption from real estate taxes of property used for religious purposes. The constitutionality of the exemption under the First Amendment's guaranty of the separation of church and state has long been a subject of dispute, but all doubts were laid to rest last May [1970] when the Supreme Court, with only Justice Douglas dissenting, held it to be constitutional. The importance to the churches of continuation of the exemption was manifested by the fact that the three major religious organizations, the National Council of Churches of Christ, the United States Catholic Conference, and the Synagogue Council of America, together with a number of denominational groups, filed briefs with the Court urging it to uphold its constitutionality. Briefs on the other side were presented only by the American Civil Liberties

---

20. An analogous situation occurred in 1964. In that year, Congress passed the historic Civil Rights Law. One section (Title VI) of the bill provided that no Federal funds were to be paid to any institution which discriminates on grounds of race, color, religion, or national origin. At the last moment, the bill was amended to eliminate the word "religion" thus permitting sectarian welfare institutuions such as homes for the aged, the infirm or the orphaned to receive Federal grants even though they bar admission to all but members of a particular denomination.
21. Tax Reform Act of 1969.

Union and the dauntless Madalyn Murray O'Hair, she who petitioned the Court to stop astronauts from praying on the moon.

When Americans United for Separation of Church and State and the United States Catholic Conference file briefs on the same side in a church-state case, it is hardly surprising that the Court should decide in their direction rather than in Mrs. O'Hair's. But the victory of the churches as an interest group was far from complete. They sought a decision from the Court not merely that states may constitutionally grant exemption to churches without violating the principle of church-state separation, but that the states must accord such exemption else it would violate the guaranty of the free exercise of religion. They contended that a tax upon land and buildings used for worship is an interference with freedom of worship and hence a violation of the First Amendment.

In their briefs, some of the church groups asserted that a tax on churches would fall most heavily upon the poor, particularly those who attend store-front churches in the urban ghettoes.[22] At first glance this would seem to be valid, yet it merits closer examination. Earlier it was suggested that the lack of opposition to deductibility for church contributions is explainable by the fact that almost any taxpayer can take advantage of it. More accurately, it should be said almost any middle- or upper-income taxpayer; the very poor, the welfare recipients, pay no taxes; the moderately poor, who do, do not itemize their deductions but take the flat 10 percent allowed by the law. Neither gain anything from the deductibility privilege.

Similarly, those who worship in storefront churches do not own real estate, yet ironically they are the ones who at least indirectly pay real estate taxes on church property. This is so because they pay rent to the owner of the building who is required to pay real estate taxes and fixes the rents of the tenants, including the storefront church, to absorb the tax.

In her brief in the Supreme Court, Mrs. O'Hair noted rather irreverently that while there may be no atheists in foxholes, neither are there any temples, and that the founder of America's major religion preached and prayed in the open fields. But even if buildings are required for worship, there are those who assert that the use and the exemption are often greatly disproportionate. Early last year in Spanish Harlem in New York City, a group of militant Puerto Ricans called the Young Lords took over a Methodist church to use as a place for

---

22. Justice Brennan seemed to be impressed by this argument, "Taxation," he said in his concurring opinion, "would bear unequally on different churches, having its most disruptive effect on those with the least ability to meet the annual levies against them."

feeding and caring for children while their mothers were at work and as a rehabilitation center for drug addicts.[23] They justified the takeover on the ground, among others, that while the church enjoyed tax exemption for 365 days a year, actually it was used for worship only three hours a week, remaining closed and idle the rest of the time. Others have suggested that each congregation be allowed a specified exemption measured by the value of a modest church structure sufficient to accommodate the members of the congregation. The congregation could, if it wished, build a more costly church structure on a larger or higher priced parcel of land, but the value above the specified exemption would be subject to taxation as non-exempt property.

In any event, the Supreme Court refused to hold that churches are entitled to exemption as a matter of right, but are given it by the state only as a matter of grace. The unavoidable implication is that what the state gives the state can take away, and it may not be long before the state begins taking away unlimited exemption for church property. Although every test of public opinion shows that by an overwhelming majority Americans favor tax exemption for churches, there is an increasing discontent with the practice. In February of last year, a state legislator representing the New York suburban area of Long Island polled his constituents and found that of the 3,000 who responded, fully 55 percent favored the abolition of exemption for church property. A recent poll taken in Minnesota showed that 72 percent of those responding favored giving the legislature power to limit the exemption of church property.[24] State legislatures in various parts of the country are subjecting to serious scrutiny the effects of church exemption upon the general tax structure and the economy.

If, as I believe, the years if not the days of unlimited exemption are numbered, it is because the church as a self-interest interest group is coming in conflict with its own clientele — its clientele, not its constituency. The constituency of the church are its faithful; its clientele is and perhaps always has been the institutions of power in the society. The military chaplain serves his clientele when he builds morale among the soldiers, he serves his constituency when he acts as their ombudsman.

In pre-capitalist Europe (and its Latin American colonies) the dominant possesors of power were the royalty, aristocracy, and military, and they were the clientele of the church. In America today it is Middle America which is the possessor of that power and has become the clientele of the church.

---

23. Dean Kelley, "The Young Lords and the Spanish Congregation" *Christian Century*, 18 February 1970, 208.
24. *Religious News Service* 10 August 1970.

Tax exemption for city churches does not visibly affect urban middle-income Americans, but more and more of them are moving to the suburbs and becoming owners of heavily mortgaged homes. In the suburbs, often large estates are bought and converted to churches, thus taking them off the tax rolls while at the same time requiring the community to provide additional services. Since in the suburbs real estate taxes are almost the sole source of local finances, the increased burden on the homeowner can become quite heavy.[25] This concern with the burden upon suburban homeowners resulting from the tax exemption of church property is manifested not only by the polls in Long Island and Minnesota but also by the action of many town authorities in refusing zoning permits for the establishment of new or expansion of old churches.[26]

Private Schools and the Public Purse

While tax exemption for church property reflects a tension between the self-interest of the church and of its clientele, state support for denominational welfare and educational systems reflects a harmonious relationship between them. Church hospitals originated as charity institutions for the poor; today the poor go to state and municipal hospitals; middle income patients to hospitals which, though non-profit, are not charity institutions, and most of these are denominational hospitals receiving substantial governmental funds. Formerly, old age homes were for the poor; today heavily federally financed apartments for senior citizens operated by religious groups cater almost exclusively to the middle income class; the aged poor, if they are fortunate, live in public housing projects. But it is in the field of education that the church may be on the verge of playing its most significant role as an interest group of and for the middle classes.[27]

An institution which develops to meet a specific need or needs will, after the need or needs disappear, atrophy and in time disappear unless it finds some new need which it is able to satisfy. The Catholic parochial school system developed in the United States to meet two principal

---

25. A number of years ago as a suburb on the Eastern Seaboard grew in size and population, the Catholic Church authorities found it necessary to split if off from the central-city diocese and establish a new independent diocese with its own center in one of the towns within the suburban area. This in turn necessitated the acquisition of considerable additional land for administration and other buildings. This land accretion reached such a point that a group of the most loyal and prestigious Catholics in the community paid a quiet visit to the bishop and pleaded with him not to buy up any more land.
26. This is not the sole motivation for denial of zoning permits, but it is a substanitial one, and in many cases the decisive one.
27. See James Graham's interesting though polemical *The Enemies of the Poor* (New York: Random House, 1970), especially Part Three, "The Churches."

needs. When in the second quarter of the nineteenth century Catholics began emigrating here in great numbers, the recently established public schools were still under the influence and control of Protestant administrators and teachers, many of whom retained the evangelism that was a major motivation of the church school system which public education displaced. Moreover, the United States was then entering upon a period of substantial anti-Catholic nativism, an influence which permeated the public schools as it did other social institutions.

The Catholic child in a Protestant oriented public school thus faced two threats: to his faith from evangelism, and to his security from nativism. The parochial school served to meet both threats and therefore took root and flourished.

Today, after the Supreme Court decisions barring religions instruction, prayer, and Bible reading in the schools, the election of a Catholic president, and the ecumenicism flowing from Vatican II, neither of those threats is sufficiently meaningful to justify in the eyes of increasing numbers in the Catholic community the substantial and ever-increasing financial burden of maintaining the parochial school system. It is perhaps not too much to suggest that the parochial school system is an institution in search of a rationale.

There is considerable evidence that church schools which provide a secular education (and this is by no means limited to Catholic parochial schools) are in large measure fulfilling a function which cannot remotely be characterized as spiritual. In the South, where such schools are comparatively rare, increasingly large numbers of private "academies" (some of which are Protestant church affiliated) are springing up with the avowed purpose of evading the judicial decisions requiring racial integration of public schools.[28] In the North, there are long-established and communally accepted schools which to many parents serve the same purpose. An influx of a large number of black children into a public school leads in a large number of cases to an exodus of whites either to the suburbs or to nonpublic schools. When for a variety of reasons they find it necessary to choose the latter alternative, they are fleeing not to God but from Caesar.

Occasionally, the situation becomes so flagrant that Caesar, by no means insensitive to God's political power, nevertheless finds intervention unavoidable. In October of 1969, the United States Department of Justice brought suit against the Board of Education in Waterbury, Connecticut, charging, among other things, that "white children who

---

28. In those areas in the South where there are parochial schools, e.g., Louisiana, they too are used by many parents to avoid desegregation. See Ferrell Guillory, "Louisiana Desegregation and Catholic Schools," *America*, 5 September 1970, 119.

reside in public school districts where substantial numbers of Negro and Puerto Rican children also reside have been transported by the City of Waterbury from such public school districts to all white or predominantly white independent nonpublic schools, wherein to a substantial extent, facilities of public schools which commonly are located adjacent to or near the respective independent non-public schools are shared. This practice has resulted in certain public elementary schools becoming and remaining predominantly Negro and Puerto Rican."[29]

Two months later, the *New York Times* of 7 December 1969 reported that Dr. Nathan Brown, Acting Superintendent of Schools in New York City, in an address delivered at an Orthodox Jewish theological seminary, called upon Jewish leaders to keep middle-class youngsters in the school system by de-emphasizing and, in some instances, discouraging enrollment in Jewish day schools. "I deplore," he said, "any action on the part of Jewish parents who escape the city school system for the sole purpose of avoiding racially integrated schools." He referred to what he called the increasing Jewish enrollment in religious and "pseudo-religious" schools in the light of social, ethnic, and class conflicts arising from school reorganization, and expressed the fear that alienation of the Jewish middle-class from the system could result in a city of "ghettos surrounded by police protecting one group from another."

The fact of the matter is that the church-school is an institution of and for white middle-class America. The 1967 Report of the United States Commission on Civil Rights, *Racial Integration in the Public Schools*, indicated that in the 15 large cities which the Commission studied, 39 percent of the white and only 6 percent of the nonwhite pupils attended nonpublic schools. In the suburbs of the same cities, 24 percent of the white and 3 percent of the nonwhite attended nonpublic schools.

A compilation by the Catholic Archdiocese of Hartford for the year 1968-1969 showed that 2.6 percent of the student population of Connecticut parochial schools was black, and 1.2 percent Spanish speaking (Puerto Rican). The comparative figures for the public schools were respectively 8.3 percent and 2.8 percent.[30] The disparity in respect to black pupils is of course explainable by the fact that the parochial

---

29. Complaint in *United States* v. *Board of Education of Waterbury*, U.S.D.C., Connecticut Civil Action No. 13465. The complaint was signed by Attorney General John N. Mitchell.
30. The parochial school compilation is on file in the United States District Court for Connecticut in the case of *Johnson* v. *Sanders*, Civil Action No. 13432. The public school figures are from Research Bulletin No. 1, Volume 1, Series 1969-1970, Connecticut State Department of Education, Bureau of Research, Statistics and Finance.

schools are an institution of white Americans. That they are also an institution of middle and upper class Americans appears from a comparison of the percentages of poor children, i.e., those receiving benefits under the Federal Aid to Families with Dependent Children (AFDC), in public and nonpublic schools in Connecticut as of 1970.[31] This shows that while 6.3 percent of children attending the public schools in that state are AFDC children, only 1.4 percent of the children in nonpublic schools are of that category.[32]

A report by the Connecticut State Department of Education issued in April 1970 showed that in September 1967 7.8 percent of the enrollment in the public schools of that state was black; one year later, it had risen to 8.3 percent; one year after that, in October 1969, it had again risen and was now 8.6 percent. The percentages of Spanish-surnamed pupils increased from 2.5 percent of the total enrollment in 1968-1969 to 2.8 percent in 1969-1970.[33] I do not have comparable figures for the nonpublic schools, and it may be that these increases in percentages can be explained by a higher birth rate for blacks and Puerto Ricans or higher rate of migration into the state. Yet, it is not unreasonable to suggest that at least in part they can be explained by the exodus of middle-class white children from the public schools. Nor is it unreasonable to predict that increase in allocation of tax-raised funds to nonpublic schools will accelerate the exodus.

In the completion for public funds between public and private institutions, it is the latter who are more likely to come out ahead. In 1946 Congress enacted the Hill-Burton Act to provide funds for hospital expansion. It was assumed that the major funds would go to public hospitals and in the original appropriation the public hospitals received considerably more than did the private ones. But each year the ratio changed and it was not long before the private hospitals were receiving more than the public ones, and this disparity continues to increase. A consequence of the disparity is indicated by the following statement of Senator Abraham Ribicoff, who chaired a Senatorial investigation committee on public health: "The scandal of publicly owned hospitals

---

31. The figures are taken from App. I, entitled "Table Two; Distribution of Economically Deprived Students in the Public and Private Schools in the State of Connecticut," on file in the United States District Court for Connecticut in the case of *Johnson* v. *Sanders*. The gross figures are:

Total Enrollment	Public School Enrollment	Private School Enrollment	AFDC	Public	Private
575,003	462,252	112,751	39,792	29,222	1,570

32. The Table does not separate religious from nonreligious private schools. If it be assumed that all AFDC children attend the religious schools, the percentage of AFDC children in religious schools would be 1.5.
33. Research Bulletin No. 1, Volume 1, Series 1969-1970, pp. 1, 2. It should be noted that these percentages are not merely of inner city schools but of all public schools in the state. It may be assumed that the increase in percentages would be substantially higher in inner city schools.

has been well documented by young interns and residents, forcing the Joint Commission on the Accreditation of Hospitals to strip some large city hospitals of their already minimal levels of accreditation and to threaten others with similar action."[34]

If public funding of public and private education follows the same pattern as that of hospitals, and there is no reason to believe that it will not, we may have another realization of Jesus' prediction that "for whosoever hath, to him shall be given, and he shall have more abundance; but whosoever hath not, from him shall be taken away even that he hath."[35]

That the Negro community—at least that part of it which strives for integration rather than separationism—is aware of and concerned about this development is manifested by the presence, along with organizations committed to the separation of church and state such as the American Civil Liberties Union and the American Jewish Congress, of branches and officers of the NAACP as sponsors and occasionally as plaintiffs in lawsuits challenging grants of governmental funds of parochial schools, as well as in legislative campaigns against such grants.

No one can predict the future, but it is difficult to close our eyes to the real possibility that unlimited or even greatly expanded governmental financing of nonpublic schools may lead to an America in which blacks, Puerto Ricans, Mexican Americans, and poor whites attend public schools (as they live in public housing developments and are treated for illness in public hospitals) while upper and middle class whites attend nonpublic schools whose continued existence is made possible only by reason of the governmental financing. This may well turn out to be what God hath wrought to Caesar.

---

34. "The 'Healthiest Nation' Myth," *Saturday Review*, 22 August 1970, 19.
35. Matt. 12:12.

Does Church-State Separation Necessarily Mean the Privatization of Religion?

JAMES LEO GARRETT, JR.

The action of the United States Internal Revenue Service in revoking the tax-exempt status of certain religious organizations, especially on the ground that such had engaged in "substantial" efforts to influence legislation, has helped to focus anew the question as to the distinction and the relation between the "public" and the "private."

Widely accepted as an implication of the separation of church and state that is guaranteed by the "no . . . establishment" clause of the First Amendment to the United States Constitution and defined by decisions of the United States Supreme Court has been the concept that religion, the special sphere of concern of churches and synagogues, is essentially a "private" matter. Leo Pfeffer, for example, has recently cited as the epitome of "the American consensus in the arena of church-state relations" the statement of Thomas Paine in *Common Sense*, "As for religion, I hold it to be the indispensable duty of government to protect all conscientious professors thereof, and I know of no other business which government hath to do therewith," and has interpreted Paine's statement to mean that " 'religion is a private affair.' "[1] Far less clear, however, is the exact meaning of the term "private" when so employed—whether "nonpublic" or "noncorporate" or "exterasocietal" or a combination of these.

I

---

1. *God, Caesar, and the Constitution: The Court as Referee of Church-State Confrontation* (Boston: Beacon Press, 1975), 348, 349. Neither in his chapter on the "meaning" of "the American experiment of freedom and separation" nor in his own "ten theses" had Pfeffer in *Church, State and Freedom*, rev. ed. (Boston: Beacom Press, 1967), 128-80, 727-28, put such stress on the "private" character of religion.

Perhaps Thomas Jefferson (1743-1826), even more than Thomas Paine, fathered, introduced, or fostered in the American context the concept of the essentially private character of religion. Robert M. Healey, while explicating Jefferson's religious beliefs, has noted: "Some biographers of Jefferson [notably Gilbert Chinard] have expressed reluctance to deal with the religion of Thomas Jefferson because he himself insisted so often that it was a private matter."[2] The influence of Jefferson's religious beliefs has been clearly recognized, as in Sydney E. Ahlstrom's recent assessment that Jefferson's "philosophy of religion and his political theory form such a thoughtfully united whole" and that he "was also so important an architect of the United States' solution of the church and state problem that some have seen this 'solution' as the virtual establishment of his own theology."[3]

Did Jefferson actually desire that his religious beliefs not be the subject of public attention? His letters indicate that such was true, at least during his later years. In writing to Mathew Carey in 1816 Jefferson said:

> You ask me if I mean to publish anything on the subject of a letter of mine to my friend Charles Thompson? certainly not. I write nothing for publication, and last of all things should it be on . . . religion. On the dogmas of religion as distinguished from moral principles, all mankind, from the beginning of the world to this day, has been quarrelling, fighting, burning and torturing one another, for abstractions unintelligible to themselves and to all others . . . . Were I to enter on that arena, I should only add an unit to the number of Bedlamites.[4]

Then early in 1817 in a letter to Charles Thomson [sic] Jefferson referred to a letter from Joseph Delaplaine that asked "me questions which I answer only to one Being." To Delaplaine, Jefferson had replied: "Say nothing of my Religion: it is known to my God and myself alone; its evidence before the world is to be sought in my life; if that has been honest and dutiful to society the Religion which has regulated it cannot be a bad one." To Thompson he also argued the desirability of a variety of thoughts in religion.[5] To George Thacher in 1824 he responded: "You press me to consent to the publication of my sentiments and suppose they might have effect even on Sectarian bigotry . . . . I must pray permission . . . to continue in quiet during the short time remaining to me . . . ."[6]

To what extent, one should ask, was Jefferson's reluctance due to his circumstances and to what extent to his views as to the essentially

---

2. *Jefferson on Religion in Public Education* (New Haven, London: Yale University Press, 1962), 25.
3. *A Religious History of the American People* (New Haven, London: Yale University Press, 1972), 367-68.
4. Thomas Jefferson to Mathew Carey, 11 November 1816, in *The Writings of Thomas Jefferson*, comp. and ed. Paul Leicester Ford, 10 vols. (New York: G. P. Putnam's Sons, 1892-99), 10:67-68. Hereafter cited as "Ford."
5. Thomas Jefferson to Charles Thomson, 29 January 1817, Ford, 10:75-76.
6. Thomas Jefferson to George Thacher, 26 January 1824, Ford, 10:289.

private nature of religion? If in his later years Jefferson was indeed a Unitarian in belief, as the evidence seems to corroborate, then the strong and widespread criticism by leaders ("priests") of various Trinitarian churches may be sufficient to explain the Jeffersonian reluctance. But in writing to Mrs. M. Harrison Smith in 1816 Jefferson not only acknowledged such criticisms but also declared: "But I have ever thought religion a concern purely between our God and our consciences, for which we were accountable to Him, and not to the priests. I never told my own religion, nor scrutinized that of another. I never attempted to make a convert, nor wished to change another's creed."[7]

Once the Jeffersonian reluctance has been noted, one may ask the further question: What was the religion of Jefferson which he desired to be reckoned as a "private" matter? Saul K. Padover has suggested that Jefferson's "true religious position" "is perhaps best viewed from three angles": (1) "his personal faith, or credo"; (2) "his critical opinion of organized religion," especially historic Christianity; and (3) "his public policy, which involved the unalterable maintenance of a 'wall of separation' between Church and State."[8] Admittedly such "angles" are interpenetrating; however, for the present discussion the first angle is paramount. Although reared by his parents in the Church of England, Jefferson "as an adult . . . was not an active church member." His own faith was that of "a Deist" or "a believer in . . . 'natural religion,' " and such faith could be described as that of "a rationalist and moralist" who greatly admired Jesus as the greatest moral teacher of history,[9] but without deity, miracles, or resurrection. Jefferson wrote in 1820 to William Short: "Of this band of dupes and imposters, Paul was the great Coryphaeus, and first corruptor of the doctrines of Jesus."[10] Furthermore, Jefferson espoused a Unitarian position, or what he called belief in "one only God."[11] Henry Wilder Foote has contended that be the time of the writing of his *Syllabus of an Estimate of the Merit of the Doctrines of Jesus, Compared with Those of Others* (1803) Jefferson "had become a Unitarian in his beliefs, largely through the influence of Dr. Joseph Priestley, the English Unitarian."[12]

---

7. Thomas Jefferson to Mrs. M. Harrison Smith, 6 August 1816, in *The Writings of Thomas Jefferson*, ed. Andrew A. Lipscomb and Albert Ellery Bergh, 20 vols. (Washington, D.C.: Thomas Jefferson Memorial Association, 1903-4), 15:60. Hereafter cited as "Lipscomb-Bergh."
8. *Thomas Jefferson and the Foundations of American Freedom* (Princeton, N.J.: D. Van Nostrand Co., Inc., 1965), 65.
9. Ibid., 66, 65, 66, 67.
10. Thomas Jefferson to William Short, 13 April 1820, Ford, 15:245. Ironically, Saul K. Padover, ed., *Democracy by Thomas Jefferson*, reprinted ed. (New York: Greenwood Press, 1969), p. 1, has referred to Jefferson as "the St. Paul of American democracy."
11. Thomas Jefferson to Doctor Benjamin Waterhouse, 26 June 1822, Ford 10:219, 220.
12. *Thomas Jefferson: Champion of Religious Freedom, Advocate of Christian Morals* (Boston: Beacon Press, 1947), 57. Cf. Thomas Jefferson to Doctor Benjamin Waterhouse, 19 July 1822, Lipscomb-Bergh, 15:391.

At least the later letters frequently embody affirmations of Unitarianism and negations of Calvinism. "The metaphysical insanities of Athanasius, of Loyola, and of Calvin, are to my understanding, mere relapses into polytheism, differing from paganism only by being more unintelligible"[13] "When we shall have done away the incomprehensible jargon of the Trinitarian arithmetic, that three are one, and one is three; . . . we shall then be truly and worthily His disciples . . . . I have little doubt that the whole of our country will soon be rallied to the unity of the Creator, and, I hope, to the pure doctrines of Jesus also."[14] Jefferson rejected the teachings of "Platonizing Christians," including "the demoralizing dogmas of Calvin." "I trust that there is not a *young man* now living in the United States who will not die an Unitarian."[15] "No historical fact is better established, than that the doctrine of one God, pure and uncompounded, was that of the early ages of Christianity . . . . [It] is now all but ascendant to the Eastern States; it is dawning in the West, and advancing towards the South; and I confidently expect that the present generation will see Unitarianism become the general religion of the United States"[16] "I can never join Calvin in addressing *his God*. He was indeed an atheist, which I can never be; or rather his religion was daemonism. If ever man worshipped a false God, he did."[17] Jefferson "never became a member of a Unitarian church" because there was none in the vicinity of Charlottesville, the "nearest" being "those in Baltimore (organized 1817) and in Washington (organized 1821)."[18]

That Jefferson did not find need for active participation in a religious congregation or community seems to be indicated by his own statements of aversion to parties or sects. As early as 1789 he wrote from Paris to Francis Hopkinson: "I am not a Federalist, because I never submitted the whole system of my opinions to the creed of any party of men whatsoever in religion, in philosophy, in politics, or in anything else where I was capable of thinking for myself. Such an addiction is the last degradation of a free and moral agent. If I could not go to heaven but with a party, I would not go there at all."[19] In an anticlerical vein he wrote to John Adams in 1813: "We should all then, like Quakers, live without an order of priests, moralize for ourselves, follow the oracle of conscience, and say nothing about what no man can understand,

---

13. Thomas Jefferson to the Reverend Jared Sparks, 4 November 1820, Lipscomb-Bergh, 15:288.
14. Thomas Jefferson to Timothy Pickering, 27 November 1821, Lipscomb-Bergh, 15:323, 324.
15. Thomas Jefferson to Doctor Benjamin Waterhouse, 26 July 1822, Lipscomb-Bergh, 15:383, 384, 385. See also Thomas Jefferson to John Adams, 5 July 1814, Ford, 9:462-64.
16. Thomas Jefferson to James Smith, 8 December 1822, Lipscomb-Bergh, 15:408, 409.
17. Thomas Jefferson to John Adams, 11 April 1823, Lipscomb-Bergh, 15:425.
18. Foote, *Thomas Jefferson*, 63.
19. Thomas Jefferson to Francis Hopkinson, 13 March 1789, Ford, 5:76.

nor therefore believe; for I suppose belief to be the assent of the mind to an intelligible proposition."[20] To Ezra Styles he wrote in 1819: "You say you are a Calvinist, I am not. I am a sect by myself, as far as I know. I am not a Jew, and therefore do not adopt their theology. . . . I am, therefore, of His [Jesus'] theology, believing that we have neither words nor ideas adequate to that definition."[21]

In summary, Jefferson in the correspondence of his later years indicated his reluctance to have his religious beliefs made public or published, though in letters he clearly identified these beliefs as Deistic and Unitarian, and his unwillingness to identify with parties or sects. Whether and to what extent Jefferson sought deliberately to impose his views as to the nature and role of religion upon the new republic and its citizens is not so clear.

II

The extent to which Jefferson could be accurately identified as the fountainhead of American thinking about the essentially private character of religion may be a question that calls for much more extensive investigation. Prior to and along with such investigation, however, contemporary Americans ought to ask what is meant by the term "private" in statements concerning the "private" nature of religion.

Whenever the term "private" is used as the antonym of "public" and hence means "nonpublic," its application to religion and/or to religious bodies (i.e., churches, synagogues) clearly denotes the institutional separation of religious bodies and governments. However, if and when the term "private" should be used to mean either "noncorporate" or "extrasocietal," such usages would convey very different meaning. The current dictionary definition of the new word "privatization" suggests that the expansion of the usage of "private" has already begun: "the tendency for an individual to withdraw from participation in social and especially political life into a world of personal concerns usually as a result of a feeling of insignificance and lack of understanding of complex social processes."[22]

III

If the "private" character of religion is to mean that religion is essentially individualistic and noncorporate, then such terminology poses a genuine issue for those who stand within one of the great monotheistic

---

20. Thomas Jefferson to John Adams, 22 August 1813, Ford, 9:413-14.
21. Thomas Jefferson to Ezra Styles, 25 June 1819, Lipscomb-Bergh, 15:203.
22. *Webster's Third New International Dictionary*, s.v. "privatization."

religions: Judaism, Christianity, or Islam. Admittedly these monotheistic faiths have had their mystics who have espoused an intuitive apprehension of God apart from close relationships with fellow believers: the hermits, the Sufis, the *Spiritualisten*. Yet, a prevailing characteristic of these religions has been the existence of and normal participation in religious communities: the synagogues, the congregations, the brotherhoods. Within Christianity the *ecclesia* has been a common element even among the widely divergent traditions: Eastern Orthodox, Roman Catholic, and Protestant. Not only among the Eastern Orthodox and Roman Catholics, who have confessed that the church is "one, holy, catholic, and apostolic," but also among the various Protestants or Evangelicals, who have experienced the gathered and scattered fellowship of believers, to be a Christian has been to be, in some sense, *in the church*. Nor should the free church Protestant emphasis on voluntaryism in churchmanship be wrongly equated with purely individualistic religion. Rather voluntaryism means to be free and responsible in willing to believe or not to believe and, having believed, to be free and responsible in one's expected decision to seek membership in some particular body of believers. The secularization of modern life, including religion, the individualism which is idealized, if not always practiced, in Western culture, and the increasing mobility of populations have contributed to a decline in the sense of the importance of the church in the lives of Christians,[23] and Jews in rapidly increasing numbers are found to be without any meaningful relation to any synagogue.

Sociologists of religion differ in interpreting the data as to whether ecclesial religion now has an effective or significant role in contemporary society. Thomas Luckmann, for example, has concluded that "church-oriented religion has become a marginal phenomenon in modern society." In Europe it has been "pushed to the periphery of modern life," whereas in the United States it has become "more 'modern' . . . by undergoing a process of internal secularization," that is, by "adoption of the *secular* version of the Protestant ethos."[24] Andrew M. Greeley, on the other hand, has contended that "[t]he achievement-oriented gesellschaft society does not replace gemeinschaft relationships" and that there is a "manic 'quest for community' which is manifested in so many different ways in contemporary society."[25]

---

23. At the same time, however, new ecclesial communities which, according to their members, have great significance have come into existence, especially as a consequence of the Jesus and the charismatic movements.
24. *The Invisible Religion: The Problem of Religion in Modern Society* (New York: Macmillan Company, 1967), 35, 37, 36.
25. *Unsecular Man: The Persistence of Religion* (New York: Shocken Books, 1972), 143, 144.

Those who profess to belong to the people of Abraham or to the body of Jesus Christ would amid the individualistic and secularizing tendencies of the present do well to consider seriously whether they ought to accept the description of their religion as "private" if the term is to be synonymous with "noncorporate."

IV

Furthermore, if the "private" nature of religion is to mean that religion is essentially extrasocietal, then such terminology poses a genuine issue for Christians and others who believe that they both individually and corporately, have a responsibly prophetic role in and for their societies. The history of Christianity does include monastic communities and pietistic *ecclesiolae in ecclesia*, both of which have represented, at least to an extent, withdrawals from society. Even so, the Western monk was often the transmitter of literary treasures, the Russian *starets* the sought-after counselor of princes, and the Pietist the pioneer in diaconal ministries later taken up by civil governments. Indeed the history of Christianity also includes the pattern of passive accommodation to the existent society with its evils, oppression, injustice, and dehumanization, whether medieval feudalism, Byzantine caesaropapism, inquisitorial Spain, German Lutheran Erastianism, or African slavery and the racism of the American South. Culture-religion, by no means a new phenomenon, has long existed in many forms. Yet between the movements of withdrawal and the patterns of accommodation many Christians have sought as "salt" and "light" (Matt. 5:13, 14) to be "in the world" but "not of the world" (John 17:11, 14, 16). As changed persons they have attempted to change the society in which they have lived, whether to monogamous marriage, to the sacredness of human life, to the breakdown of class and caste, to the healing of bodily infirmities, to emancipation from slavery, or to political self-determination. From Tertullian's ethic of the "third race" to Walter Rauschenbusch's Social Gospel and the nonviolent resistance of Martin Luther King, Jr., Christian leaders have been in the vanguard of social change.

Now, therefore, the very implication that religion as "private" is to be detached or disengaged from society seems to deny the prophetic, society-changing role of the churches. The National Council of the Churches of Christ in the U.S.A. through its office of civil and religious liberty rightly discerned a basic issue at stake in the revocation by the Internal Revenue Service of the tax-exempt status of Billy James Hargis's anticommunist Christian Echoes National Ministry for its "substantial" efforts to influence legislation and indeed also its endorsement of a presidential candidate.[26] Moreover, Leo Pfeffer has declared: "Sooner or later the [U. S. Supreme] Court will have to decide definitely whether the state can demand political silence of the church in exchange for the privilege of tax exemption"[27] To put the issue in another form, can prophetic mission be distinguished from illegitimate lobbying?

The question as to the varied possible meanings of the term "private" when applied to religion seems to be a major consideration with implications probably unanticipated by Thomas Jefferson and his fellow architects of the new republic. Furthermore, the answers now to be given to this question may help to shape both the religion and the government of the future.

---

26. *United States* v. *Christian Echoes National Ministry*, 470 F 2d 849, certiorari denied, 404 U.S. 561 (1972).
27. *God, Caesar, and the Constitution*, 74.

A New Meaning for Tax Exemption?

DEAN M. KELLEY

On two successive days in May 1983, the Supreme Court of the United States made some sweeping changes in the legal meaning of tax exemption that will have far-reaching, though as yet little-understood, results. Up to this point there have been at least two very different understandings of what tax exemption of nonprofit organizations is, and the Supreme Court had not previously adopted one in clear preference to the other.

One understanding of tax exemption is that it is, in effect, a subsidy granted by legislative grace to those organizations performing services that the government would otherwise have to perform, and that such a subsidy relieves the exempt organization of tax obligations that other taxpayers are then obliged to assume. This view is clearly expressed in such lower court decisions as *Christian Echoes National Ministry* v. *U.S.* (470 F.2d 849, 10th Circuit, 1972), and has been referred to as the *quid pro quo* or "tax expenditure" theory.

The other understanding is that nonprofit organizations are simply not part of the tax base to begin with, since their members already pay their (presumably fair) share of the costs of the commonwealth in their capacity as private citizens and should not be taxed again for activities they undertake out of motives of public service and from which they derive no personal monetary gain. This view has been advanced by Boris Bittker of the Yale Law School, author of the definitive five-volume *Federal Taxation of Income, Estates and Gifts* (1982); Peter Swords, assistant dean of the Columbia Law School, author of *Charitable Real Property Tax Exemptions in New York State* (1981); and the present author in *Why Churches Should Not Pay Taxes* (1977).

The United States Supreme Court seemed to have sided with the latter view when the tax exemption of churches was challenged on the ground that taxes not paid by churches were then loaded on other taxpayers, who thus were obliged to contribute to a governmental subsidy of churches. The Court rejected that view in an important opinion written by Chief Justice Warren E. Burger, for an 8-1 majority upholding the tax exemption of churches, in which he announced: "Obviously a direct money subsidy would be a relationship pregnant with involvement . . ., but that is not the case . . . . The government does not transfer part of its revenue to churches but simply abstains from demanding that the church support the state" (*Walz* v. *Tax Commission*, 397 U.S. 664, 1970).

In *Walz*, Justice Burger also rejected the *quid pro quo* rationale in refusing to assess the social services rendered by churches as the basis of their exemption:

We find it unnecessary to justify the tax exemption on the social welfare services or "good works" that some churches perform for parishioners and others . . . . Churches vary substantially in the scope of such services . . . . To give emphasis to so variable an aspect of the work of religious bodies would introduce an element of governmental evaluation and standards as to the worth of particular social welfare programs, thus producing a kind of continuing day-to-day relationship which the policy of neutrality seeks to minimize.

The tenth circuit, however, in deciding two years later to approve the revocation of Christian Echoes' tax exemption for alleged substantial lobbying and electioneering, resorted to the *quid pro quo* rationale without ever citing or referring to the Supreme Court's *Walz* decision, notwithstanding which, the Supreme Court declined to review that case (414 U.S. 864, 1973). Congress, however, in an unusual step, included in the Tax Reform Act of 1976 a disclaimer that it was not approving or disapproving the decisions *in that case*, thus avoiding "re-enacting" the tenth circuit's interpretation into the Internal Revenue Code when it added Section 501(h) to permit certain exempt organizations to do a limited amount of direct-interest lobbying.

These two views of tax exemption were still in lively competition until 23 and 24 May 1983, when the U.S. Supreme Court delivered two significant decisions that seemed to tip the scales in favor of the *quid pro quo* rationale.

On 23 May, the Court announced its unanimous decision in *Regan* v. *Taxation with Representation* (TWR), reversing the District of Columbia circuit, which had voided the restrictions on lobbying by organizations exempt from federal income taxation under Section 501(c)(3). That section provides the most advantageous category of exemption—limited to organizations whose purposes are "religious, charitable, scientific, testing for public safety, literary, educational," and so on—because donors to those organizations are entitled to deduct contributions to them from their taxable income (under Section 170, pertaining to "charitable deductions"). Organizations exempt under Section 501(c)(3), however, are prohibited from engaging in any "substantial" attempts to influence legislation.

As an organization, *Taxation with Representation* had been denied exemption by the IRS under Section 501(c)(3) because TWR announced that it intended to seek improvements in the tax code by extensive lobbying. It went to court to obtain its 501(c)(3) exemption, insisting that the limitation on lobbying in that section was unconstitutional, since it conditioned a public benefit (deductibility) on abandoning the exercise of rights guaranteed by the Constitution (freedom of speech, press, assembly and petition of Congress for redress of grievances).

The circuit court held that Congress could so condition exemption and deductibility if it chose, but struck down the section for another reason: veterans organizations — exempt under Section 501(c)(19) — are permitted to engage in lobbying without losing deductibility of contributions, and the circuit court held that that was an unfair arrangement, since it did not treat similarly situated parties alike, as required by the Fifth Amendment.

The Supreme Court unanimously reversed in an opinion written by Justice William H. Rehnquist, holding that Congress could make a specially advantageous provision for veterans because of their special services to the nation. In reaching this not unreasonable conclusion, however, Justice Rehnquist went out of his way to embrace the *quid pro quo* theory of tax exemption:

Both tax exemptions and tax-deductibility are a form of *subsidy* that is administered through the tax system. A tax exemption has much the same effect as a *cash grant* to the organization of the amount of the tax it would have to pay on its income. Deductible contributions are similar to *cash grants* of the amount of a portion of the individual's contributions. The system Congress has enacted provides this kind of *subsidy* to non profit civil welfare organizations generally, and an additional *subsidy* to those charitable organizations that do not engage in substantial lobbying. In short, Congress chose not to *subsidize* lobbying as extensively as it chose to *subsidize* other activities that non profit organizations undertake to promote the public welfare (*Regan v. Taxation with Representation*, emphasis added).

Justice Rehnquist, in a brief ten-page opinion, employed the term "subsidy" — or synonyms like "largesse" or "grants" no less than thirty-one times! And no member of the Court demurred at this characterization, nor at the assumption that Congress could grant exemption and/or deductibility pretty much as it pleased, and could do so on the basis of supposed benefit to the nation. In other words, the Court seems to have endorsed the main lines of the *quid pro quo* rationale without weighing other alternatives or examining the possible implications of its choice.

Justice Harry Blackmun entered a valuable concurring opinion (joined by Justices William J. Brennan and Thurgood Marshall), pointing out that the lobbying restriction in Section 501(c)(3), "if viewed in isolation," would violate the principle, reaffirmed in the Court's opinion, "that the Government may not deny a benefit to a person because he exercises a constitutional right." The only thing that saves the legislative scheme is the provision in Section 501(c)(4), under which an "action organization" *can* lobby without losing its exemptions. Of course, an "action organization" cannot receive deductible contributions. A Section 501(c)(3) organization, however, can set up a Section 501(c)(4) subsidiary to do its lobbying, using nondeductible contributions.

That is exactly what has been done by several organizations, including the American Civil Liberties Union and the National Association for the Advancement of Colored People. A constant problem, however, has been the degree of control the one organization could exert over the other, and in the case of the NAACP, its 501(c)(3) part, the NAACP Legal Defense Fund, drifted away and became independent of the other! In addressing this issue, Justice Blackmun declared:

A § 501(c)(3) organization's right to speak is not infringed, because it is free to make known its views on legislation through its § 501(c)(4) affiliate without losing tax benefits for its nonlobbying activities . . . . Should the IRS attempt to limit the control these organizations exercise over the lobbying of their § 501(c)(4) affiliates, the First Amendment problems would be insurmountable. It hardly answers one person's objection to a restriction on his speech that another person, outside his control, may speak for him. Similarly, an attempt to prevent § 501(c)(4) organizations from lobbying explicitly on behalf of their § 501(c)(3) affiliates would perpetuate § 501(c)(3) organizations' inability to make known their views on legislation without incurring the unconstitutional penalty. Such restrictions would extend far beyond Congress' mere refusal to subsidize lobbying . . . . In my view, any such restriction would render the statutory scheme unconstitutional.

The day following the *Regan* decision, the Supreme Court "dropped the other shoe" in ruling on the combined cases of *Bob Jones University* v. *U.S.* and *Goldsboro Christian Schools* v. *U.S.*, in which it started from the assumption that tax exemption is a subsidy—so reiteratively declared the day before—and drew some further implications of portentous significance for all exempt organizations, particularly religious ones.

The *Bob Jones University* decision had been awaited with intense attention ever since the Reagan Administration had raised it to a *cause célèbre* by attempting to render the case moot on 8 January 1982. Already controversial because it appeared to pit the important principles of religious liberty and racial nondiscrimination against each other, it suddenly became a political "hot potato" overnight as well. The two schools had had their tax exemptions revoked because they discriminated against black students and faculty. That question had apparently been decided as to *non*religious private schools in the 1971 case of *Green* v. *Connally*, which explicitly reserved the question of racial discrimination carried on by *religious* private schools in obedience to tenets of their faith, and that was the precise question posed by the *Bob Jones University* cases. Both Bob Jones University and Goldsboro Christian Schools maintained that they were primarily religious rather than educational institutions, and that racial discrimination was required by their religious beliefs. The lower courts had not questioned their sincerity in this respect; the trial court held (in *Bob Jones University*) that denial of tax exemption would infringe the school's religious liberty; the circuit court reversed, holding that an overriding national interest justified that infringement.

The Supreme Court had received briefs on that issue when the United States government suddenly reversed its position and requested the court to vacate both cases as moot because it had decided that Congress had not authorized the IRS to deny tax exemption for racial discrimination, and it was therefore ordering tax exemption restored to all private schools, religious and *non*religious. The uproar was immediate and intense. The administration introduced legislation in Congress to give such authorization to the IRS, which was resisted by many legislators — some because they contended that the courts had already settled the matter as to nonreligious schools, some because they supported the autonomy of private schools (witness the Dornan-Ashbrook amendments to Treasury appropriations denying the IRS funds to enforce its regulations requiring private schools to give evidence of nondiscrimination to qualify for tax exemption), and some because they enjoyed the administration's discomfiture. Meanwhile, the administration, assisted by a lower court order forbidding it to restore any exemptions, consented to maintain the status quo until Congress or the Supreme Court acted.

In the face of this by-play, the Supreme Court took an unusual action. Although one of the parties (the government) had in effect conceded the case, the court reinstated it and invited a "friend of the court," a black attorney, William T. Coleman, Jr., to argue the position the government had abandoned. On 12 October 1982, the case was argued before a packed courtroom. William B. Ball, a Roman Catholic attorney from Harrisburg, Pennsylvania, who has long been a champion of religious liberty causes, argued for Bob Jones University that no one should have to choose between tax exemption and obedience to conscience.

On 24 May 1983, the Court announced its decision in an opinion written by the chief justice, with only Justice Rehnquist in dissent, which resoundingly rejected the administration's course and declared that educational institutions engaging in racial discrimination are not entitled to federal income tax exemption. Thus the Court checked what many viewed as a gradual erosion of the nation's determination to eliminate racial discrimination. In so doing, however, the Court may have made some important (and perhaps unnecessary) trade-offs that will affect other vital interests of the nation in the future.

Criteria of charitable trusts. The Supreme Court began by ratifying the full force of *Green* v. *Connally* (which it had affirmed in 1971 by a mere *per curiam* memorandum opinion, and had later slighted in 1974 by saying it lacked "the precedential weight of a case involving a truly adversary controversy" — the government having abandoned its position on the way to the Supreme Court and joined its opponents' camp — the same as in the instant case, only in the opposite direction).

It was *Green* v. *Connally* that first linked "public policy" to tax exemption, and the Supreme Court in *Bob Jones University* cemented that linkage with further explication. It explained at great length that the law of charities has always required that charitable trusts must (1) serve a public purpose, and (2) not violate public policy (quoting from its opinions on charitable trusts of 1861 and 1878) — a contention no one has doubted. The troublesome step is linking the law of charitable trusts to the basic statute of exempt organizations Section 501(c)(3) of the Internal Revenue Code, which does not require all exempt entities to be "charities" that meet the criteria of the Elizabethan Statute of Charitable Uses. "Charitable" is one of the purposes listed as eligible for exemption, but so is "educational," and so is "religious." Does a "religious" organization also have to be "charitable" in the sense of fitting those criteria? The Court now says they do. But did Congress ever say so? If so, when and where?

At this point, the Court came under some strain, and the chief justice labored valiantly to persuade his colleagues and the public that Congress really intended organizations exempt under Section 501(c)(3) to serve a public purpose and not violate public policy. Justice Burger strove to do that in several ways: (1) Contributions to such organizations are deductible under Section 170 as "charitable contributions," which the Court insisted, "explains" the charitable character of all Section 501(c)(3) organizations. (2) Congress has had a dozen years in which to correct the logic of *Green* v. *Connally* and the IRS policy resulting from it, but has not done so. This "failure of Congress to modify the IRS rulings . . . make[s] out an unusually strong case of legislature acquiescence in and ratification by implication of the 1970 and 1971 rulings." (3) Section 501(i) was added to the Internal Revenue Code by Congress in 1976 to bar tax exemption for social clubs that discriminate on the basis of race, and the exports of the House and Senate accompanying the amendment cited *Green* v. *Connally* and explained that "discrimination on account of race is inconsistent with an educational institution's tax exempt status."

These arguments, however, did not persuade the Court's lone dissenter, Justice Rehnquist, who replied to them as follows:

In approaching this statutory construction question the Court quite adeptly avoids the statute it is construing. This I am sure is no accident, for there is nothing in the language of § 501(c)(3) that supports the result obtained by the Court.

Perhaps recognizing the lack of support in the statute itself, or in its history, for the IRS change in interpretation, . . . the Court relies first on several bills introduced to overturn the IRS interpretation of § 501(c)(3) . . . . But we have said before, and it is equally applicable here, that this type of congressional inaction is of virtually no weight in determining legislative intent.

The Court continuously has been hesitant to find ratification through inaction . . . . this Court has no business finding that Congress had adopted the new IRS position by failing to enact legislation to reverse it.

The Court seizes the words "charitable contribution" and with little discussion concludes that "[o]n its face, therefore § 170 reveals that Congress' intention was to provide tax benefits to organizations serving charitable purposes," intimating that this implies some unspecified common law charitable trust requirement . . . . Plainly § 170 simply tracks the requirements set forth in § 501(c)(3). Since § 170 is no more than a mirror of § 501(c)(3) and, as the Court points out, § 170 followed § 501(c)(3) by more than two decades . . . ., it is at best of little usefulness in finding the meaning of § 501(c)(3).

The Court next asserts [that Congress acted to ratify the IRS policy] "when it enacted the present § 501(i) of the Code . . . ." Quite to the contrary, it seems to me that in § 501(i) Congress showed that when it wants to add a requirement prohibiting racial discrimination to one of the tax-benefit provisions, it is fully aware of how to do it.

Some of the implications of this trade-off will be noted later.

Slippage in the doctrine of "unconstitutional conditions." In his concurrence in *Taxation with Representation*, Justice Blackmun noted the Court's reaffirmation of the principle "that the government may not deny a benefit to a person because he exercises a constitutional right." The Court has previously held that, even though no one has a constitutional right to welfare benefits or unemployment compensation or a government job or tax exemption, the government — once having offered such benefits — cannot withhold or withdraw them from persons who exercise a right that the Constitution does guarantee. For example, states may not set minimum-length-of-residence requirements for public assistance because that would burden the right to travel protected by the federal Constitution (*Shapiro* v. *Thompson*, 1969). Neither may a state deny unemployment compensation to a woman whose religion prohibits her from accepting jobs that would require her to work on her Sabbath, Saturday (*Sherbert* v. *Verner*, 1963).

The Court, however, would require Bob Jones University to choose between tax exemption and the free exercise of religion. The Court recognized that "denial of tax benefits will inevitably have a substantial impact on the operation of private religious schools," and then went on to reassure religious schools that this "will not prevent those schools from observing their religious tenets." Perhaps it will not absolutely *prevent* them, but it will certainly *burden* them — to an extent far greater than Mrs. Sherbert would have been burdened for her Seventh-Day Adventist tenets if the Court had permitted the state of South Carolina to impose such a Hobson's choice on her.

This point has been much muddied by bringing in extreme cases: Is an organization to retain tax exemption if its religious tenets call for snake-handling or ritual murder? The circuit court in *Bob Jones University* had posed as an unthinkable consequence of deciding *for* Bob Jones University the possibility that exemption would then have to be extended to "Fagin's School for pick-pockets"! Of course, snake-handling, murder, and pocket-picking are *crimes*, and are prohibited whether religiously motivated or not. Racial discrimination is not (as yet) a crime, and Bob Jones University had done nothing *illegal* in pursuance of its long-proclaimed religious doctrines on racial "purity," however obnoxious they may appear to others (including this author). To invoke loss of tax exemption for conduct that is religiously motivated and not illegal is to start down a long and dubious road that may lead to many unexpected places—including possibly the doorsteps of some who most vociferously urged the Court to punish Bob Jones University for its heinous conduct.

If, however, tax exemption is not construed to be a government grant or subsidy, then it would not be necessary to think of giving it as an incentive or withholding it as punishment for conduct the legislature wishes from time to time to encourage or discourage. There are, however, already some tax exemptions that *are* clearly intended as incentives (as for industrial development, housing renovation, environmental protection, etc.), and it is probably too much to hope that the tax code will not increasingly be used as a carrot or a stick to reward or punish conduct not otherwise reachable by law. That will lend additional pressure toward conformity of the kind that Justice Lewis F. Powell viewed with alarm in his (partly) concurring opinon.

Pressures to conformity. Justice Powell concurred in the Court's judgment and in part of its opinion, but he was troubled by the idea that tax exemption was to be tied to public policy. He wrote:

With all respect, I am unconvinced that the critical question in determining tax-exempt status is whether an organization provides a clear "public benefit" as defined by the Court. Over 106,000 organizations filed § 501(c)(3) returns in 1981 . . . I find it impossible to believe that all or even most of those organizations could prove that they "demonstrably serve and [are] in harmony with the public interest," or that they are "beneficial and stabilizing influences in community life . . . ."

Even more troubling to me is the element of conformity that appears to inform the Court's analysis . . . . Taken together these passages suggest that the primary function of a tax-exempt organization is to act on behalf of the Government in carrying out governmentally approved policies. In my opinion, such a view . . . ignores the important role played by tax exemptions in encouraging diverse, indeed often sharply conflicting, activities and viewpoints . . . . Far from representing an effort to reinforce any perceived "common community conscience," the provision of tax exemptions to nonprofit groups is one indispensable means of limiting the influence of governmental orthodoxy on important areas of community life . . . .

I am unwilling to join any suggestion that the Internal Revenue Service is invested with authority to decide which public policies are sufficiently "fundamental" to require denials of tax exemptions.

Justice Powell's concern did evoke from the majority a concession in footnote 23, denying that the IRS will be permitted to make such determinations. But who else—in the first instance—is to make them? How many people adversely affected thereby will have the determination and resources to fight back through the courts to gain the protection offered by that footnote?

Some would contend that it is the role of voluntary citizens' organizations in a democratic society continuously to help form and determine "public policy" and the meaning and effect of "public benefit," not to be bound by earlier formulations thereof and punished by loss of tax exemption if they depart therefrom in efforts to explore and embody alternative formulations. Tax exemption has provided a valuable sort of fiscal extraterritoriality where nonprofit groups of like-minded people could work together to advance shared ideas and objectives without falling under governmental scrutiny, regulation, and supervision. Will that still be possible under the Court's new formulation? Was it already being eroded by onerous and officious requirements of application, qualification, and reportage that were rapidly turning what had been protections of freedom of speech and association into curtailments and oppressions?

Consequences for churches. It is distressing that none of the justices seemed unduly troubled by the Court's treatment of the free exercise of religion. (Justice Powell and Justice Rehnquist both indicated their agreement with that part of the Court's analysis.) The Court rather casually disposed of the claims of the petitioners to the free exercise of religion by (1) treating them as educational rather than religious institutions (without even debating the matter or evaluating the extensive treatment of the question by the lower courts in the case), (2) assuring them that they could still practice their "religious tenets"—albeit without a tax exemption, and (3) pointing out that the free exercise of religion can be burdened by government if it is "essential to accomplish an overriding governmental interest."

The Court explained that the governmental interest in eliminating racial discrimination is indeed compelling—with which many would agree—and "no less restrictive means . . . are available to achieve the governmental interest," with which perhaps many might disagree. There are not many intensely religious schools like Bob Jones University, and not too many people of black (or any other) race are clamoring to attend them. There is, however, the countervailing consideration that a decision allowing such schools to continue on their perverse way might generate a proliferation of "segregation academies" professing to be for whites only in fulfillment of (newly-discovered) religious convictions, and the Court may have feared that having to sort out real from spurious religious commitments would be a greater peril to religious freedom than simply disregarding them and saying that discriminatory conduct will be penalized whatever its motivation.

There is some reason to think that the Court may be moving toward a separate category of tax exemption for churches (*sub silentio*), reflected in its characterization of such exemption in *Walz* (quoted above) and in its footnote 29 in *Bob Jones Univesity*, which reads as follows: "We deal here only with religious *schools*—not with churches or other purely religious institutions; here, the governmental interest is in denying public support to racial discrimination in education." Perhaps the Court is unconsciously entertaining the possibility that within Section 501(c)(3) there are exempt entities to which the *Bob Jones University* and *Taxation with Representation* decisions apply more than to others. After all, the *quid pro quo* rationale—that tax exemption is given by governments or organizations that perform functions the government would otherwise have to perform—cannot under the First Amendment apply to *churches*, since the government cannot ordinarily set up or supply churches if the citizenry does not do so. Therefore, tax exemption of churches may be a constitutionally different character from that of other Section 501(c)(3) organizations. That, however, is thus far only conjecture.

Even if this were the case, would churches be free of the requirements that the Court says Section 501(c)(3) entities must meet—particularly not violating public policy? In the aftermath of *Bob Jones University*, how many churches will be prepared to risk their tax exemptions by (1) engaging in secondary boycotts against firms doing business in South Africa, (2) offering sanctuary to refuge-seekers from Central America, or (3) counseling young people to refuse to register for the draft, or otherwise dissenting from what an incumbent administration views as proper conduct?

A prominent member of the present administration was heard to remark after *Bob Jones University* that "now we can lift the tax exemption of those nuclear freeze groups"! The IRS will be under some pressure to proceed against the tax exemptions of churches that discriminate against women in ordination to the clergy. If, as all the justices of the U.S. Supreme Court seen uncritically to conclude, tax exemption *is* a subsidy, then is the Court not likely to conclude eventually that churches are not entitled to such a government subsidy at all?

These are some of the trade-offs explicit or implicit in these two important decisions, and they promise troubling dilemmas and lively controversies in the years ahead. We should keep in mind, however, that churches have survived under the most hostile—as well as the most friendly—governments, with and without tax exemptions, and some of them will persevere in doing their duty as they see it at whatever cost. So our concern is not so much for them as for the rest of the nation, which may have missed a chance to keep open some opportunities for organizational diversity and citizen initiative that would have been of benefit to the citizenry at large.

The Advancement of Religion versus Teaching About Religion in the Public Schools

NIELS C. NIELSEN, JR.

CONTINUING ISSUES

It is now two decades since the United States Supreme Court's decisions, forbidding prayers and devotions in public school classrooms, but encouraging what the Court called "teaching about religion."[1] One can say fairly that many of the basic issues have not been clarified and settled, either in the public mind or practically. The Supreme Court's necessary distinction between "advancement of religion" and "teaching about religion" in the public schools has not been accepted as widely as might have been hoped, and confusion about it still exists among many educational professionals as well as parents. This author was among the hopeful, twenty years ago, when he wrote a book for general reading entitled, *God in Education, A New Opportunity for American Public Schools*. It appeared in print shortly after the Supreme Court's decisions. Although the author is a Protestant, the book was published by a Roman Catholic firm, Sheed and Ward. Its editor, Philip Scharfer, recognized the importance of the Court's decisions.

There was an evident optimism following the Court's ruling. A number of universities have sponsored workshops for teachers in cooperation with departments of education. The effect has been positive and they have succeeded in encouraging teaching about religion in public education. Some fairly ambitious projects have been undertaken in various parts of the United States.

A number of other trends, however, hold the field today: con-

---

1. Niels C. Nielsen, Jr., *God in Education, A New Opportunity for American Public Schools* (New York: Sheed and Ward, 1966), Chapter 1.

tinuing pressure for prayers and devotions in the classroom, political controversy about scientific creationism as well as fundamentalist censorship of textbook adoptions. More is not being accomplished positively because of a confrontation between two extremes—sectarianism and secularism. The sectarians, be they fundamentalist or not, want to teach their own point of view. Secularists (the term is used in an omnibus way for identification) believe that religion has no legitimate place in public education. The continuing theological issue, of course, is the relation between religion and culture.

Three Positions

Three categories may be helpful by way of an historical analysis of religion and culture. They are general, to be sure, but they nonetheless may be helpful: pre-Enlightenment, Enlightenment, and post-Enlightenment secular. The thesis set forth here is that the United States was founded primarily on an Enlightenment ideology.[2] Moreover, this nation came into being without the acute tension between institutional religion and Enlightenment beliefs present on the continent of Europe. It began without the bitter anticlericalism of the French Revolution, for example, one that continued in a long struggle between church and state throughout the nineteenth century. Culture and faith seemed to support each other more easily in the civil religion of the new North American nation. Some critics have argued that such an outlook was simplistic, but this was not the case.

Can one not say fairly that leaders like Thomas Jefferson and James Madison were rejecting what might be called a pre-Enlightenment stance? They recognized that there had been a millennium and a half of intolerance and persecution in Christendom. Of course, it was not the Reformation that ended persecution and brought tolerance. Both Roman Catholics and Protestants hunted down and killed Anabaptists. Michael Servetus probably would have been executed by the Roman Catholic authorities if they could have found him before Protestant Geneva burned him at the stake.

Today, most informed persons would agree that restraint of conscience is contrary to the spirit of Christianity as well as to the teaching of Jesus, but the facts of religious history remain. One need not eulogize tolerance uncritically. Nonetheless, here

---

2. Ibid., Chapter 3.

it is taken for granted that Americans generally would oppose the pre-Enlightenment political means which were so long used to support religious establishment in the union of throne and altar. Enlightenment thinkers like Jefferson and Madison fought such a pattern of theocracy while recognizing the cultural importance of religion. As Enlightenment leaders, they reflected on the problems of the relation of science to religion, philosophy of religion, and even comparative religions.

World Religions

Historically, by and large, the major religions have lived in separation from each other throughout most of their respective lives. No doubt, there have been exceptions: the Crusades, Jewish-Christian relations, and Buddhism's rise and decline in various parts of Asia. In general, however, it can be said that contact between major faith traditions took place very slowly. Christianity did not become a worldwide religion until the nineteenth century, although there were important missionary efforts in the Counter Reformation period. China remained Confucian, India remained Hindu, and Africa, south of the Sahara, lived largely in tribal isolation. Europe was divided confessionally more or less south and north, between Roman Catholics and Protestants. Even with establishment, secularism increased under the influence of the Enlightenment and modern science, and today, the cultural situation has become a very different one with the advent of modern communication and transportation.

The world has grown small—suddenly and dramatically—and religions are no longer isolated. The Enlightenment ethos has diminished for many reasons—not the least was the rise of Darwinism. It was no longer easy to believe in the Enlightenment World Orderer in the face of evolutionary biology based on the survival of the fittest. There were other factors that contributed, often positively, to a changed ethos. In the later nineteenth century, the impact of biblical higher criticism as well as research in comparative religions began to be felt. A vast expansion of archaeological information, along with new anthropological research, added knowledge about what religion has been and is.

Modernism was an attempt to accommodate to this new knowledge in a post-Enlightenment world. Fundamentalism, by contrast, reacted defensively to its insights as well as against secularism. How were these developments related to the earlier Enlightenment convictions on which the American nation was founded?

The Meaning of Enlightenment

Enlightenment ideology contributed in a major way to the demise of religious establishments and their exclusivistic theologies. This could not help but have implications for education. Most important, teaching was freed from ecclesiastical sponsorship. Disregarding the profundity of Roman Catholic and Protestant scholasticisms, it seems fair to label Fundamentalism "pre-Enlightenment." Fundamentalists refuse to raise critical questions about the history of religions, about the Bible, and about science and religion—questions that were being asked at least in a general way when this nation was founded.

Such a manner of speaking renders much of human history—most of human history, in fact—pre-Enlightenment. Enlightenment thinkers like the German philosopher, Immanuel Kant, for example, recognized that this was the case. In a less philosophical, less critical form, the Enlightenment was the dominant ethos in the United States as the leaders of the new nation appraised and attempted to appropriate the earlier cultural heritage. The situation on the continent of Europe, to be sure, was more many-sided and complex.

Kant asked in principle about the new situation when he wrote his short treatise, *What Is Enlightenment?*.[3] In earlier eras, he argued, moral and religious opinions had been imposed from above—by authorities, ecclesiastical, political, and academic. A stage had been reached in human history in which persons were to be free to choose for themselves, he believed. One forgets all too quickly what Kant was against; how long monarchy had been in control—how long the religion of the prince was required to be the religion of the realm even following the Reformation. The leaders of the American Revolution could never forget.

The argument here is that the problem of religion in public education takes the form that it does because our nation was founded on Enlightenment premises. "In God we trust" was a national motto, but this God was not to be a sectarian deity. Historically, Enlightenment ideology arose in Western Europe as a protest against the post-Reformation wars of religion. Decent men were tired of Roman Catholics and Protestants killing each other for more than a century and a half—all in the name of Christianity. Tolerance and republicanism were better ways of

---

3. Immanuel Kant, *What Is Enlightenment?*, 6 vols. (Frankfurt am Main: Insel Verlag, 1964), 1:53-61.

life. As against the older theologies, this development assuredly raised faith and reason questions as well as science and religion questions in a way that contemporary Fundamentalism does not.

Many, indeed most, of the parties trying to get prayer back into the schools or advocating the teaching of scientific creationism are pre-Enlightenment. In this setting, critical questions are not asked about the history of religions, and until they are basic issues will remain unresolved in this pluralistic society. At times, there is a convergence of the sectarians and the secularists. To cite an extreme case, Madalyn Murray O'Hair, in a radio discussion-debate which this author had with her, advocated teaching about religion in the public schools—on her terms. One day the Methodists would come in, another day—the Presbyterians, another day—the Church of Christ, the Roman Catholics, the Baptists, and the Mormons, and then one day Madalyn Murray O'Hair. The end could be only confusion in what, to say the least, would be an abuse of the public school classroom.

The plain fact is, of course, that if the American religious community or communities could agree on an agenda for teaching about religion in public education—it could be effected. Institutionally, the religious communities are concerned primarily with their own self-interest in agencies that are by and large not too effective in relation to the public at large. To say the least, they could have given more support to "teaching about religion" following the Supreme Court's decisions. It was for good reason that Jefferson and Madison found themselves in opposition to the religious establishment in Virginia, similarly concerned for its own self-interest. Even as the American Revolution was being fought, they carried on the battle for freedom of conscience and religious tolerance in their own state.

United States Polity

Against the dire predictions of the defenders of ecclesiastical establishment, the pattern of separation of church and state had positive results for religion. It enabled a growing nineteenth-century popular piety in the United States to have a vital life without the deadening effects of government interference or clericalism. The polity incorporated into the constitution by amendment was not one of freedom from religion but freedom for religion. To the present, amid changing circumstances, competition and pluralism have contributed to the health of religion in the country. In time, Jews and Roman Catholics found their place of acceptance in the three-religion pattern identified by Will Herberg.[4] Muslims, Buddhists, and Hindus worship uncontested by any counter-establishment. Their history and contemporary expression cannot remain unrecognized if teaching about religion is to have a legitimate place in American public education.

A polity of Enlightenment origin today must find expression in a post-Enlightenment time. Assuredly, there is a greater pluralism. The religious common sense is more diverse. There is no major and overt antireligious pressure. This is the milieu in which the Supreme Court issued the 1963 decisions that have had, in turn, very little success in changing it.

NATURALISM

The exclusion of teaching about religion from most public school classrooms continues to the present. Assuredly, it is often the result of sectarian strife joined at times to a naturalistic conviction. The latter was expressed succinctly in John Dewey's volume, *Common Faith*. Dewey praised the "religious attitude" but denied it any cognitive value.[5] Enlightenment deism, unlike later evolutionary naturalism, had a place for God—albeit a sometimes precarious one. At least, it did not propose a simply reductionistic view of religion. By contrast, evolutionary naturalism often was presupposed in the writings of the early researchers in the history of religions. Sir James Frazer, for example, author of *The Golden Bough*, argued that science and not religion is the key to reality.[6] There are echoes of this outlook in the classroom to the present. Its premises are often as uncritical as religious Fundamentalism. Very different from Enlightenment rationalism, it shows itself, for example, in the present controversy about evolution.

To be specific, the controversy about scientific creationism has received major public attention. Unfortunate in most respects, whether unrecognized or not, it has nonetheless raised the issue of scientism. John A. Moore, a biologist who wrote for the new textbook series which in part engendered the controversy, has described the situation accurately.[7] As a scientist, Moore would

---

4. Will Herberg, *Protestant, Catholic, Jew: An Essay on American Sociology* (New York: Doubleday, 1955).
5. John Dewey, *A Common Faith* (New Haven, Conn.: Yale University Press, 1934).
6. James Frazer, *The Golden Bough*, 12 vols., 3rd ed. (London: Macmillan, 1911-1915).
7. Cf., Dorothy Nelkin, *The Creation Controversy, Science or Scripture in the Schools* (New York: W. W. Norton, 1982), 156.

like to believe "that there has been steady progress toward the acceptance of naturalistic explanations for the phenomena of nature." He finds, however, no hard evidence to support this view. Rather, as a result of his textbook writing, he has received not only letters but petitions from whole classes, asking him to change his outlook. He concludes that the public is less willing than before to accept naturalistic explanations.

Moore cites as a model the French Nobel Prize winning microbiologist, Jacques Monod, whose views Moore thinks should be accepted. Monod believes that man is like a gypsy on the edge of the universe, a universe that is blind to his hopes and fears. This, allegedly, is science and therefore true. Monod is explicit that all philosophy and religion are meaningless:

> The great religions are of similar form, resting on the story of the life of an inspired prophet, who, if not himself the founder of all things, represents that founder, speaks for him, and recounts the history of mankind as well as its destiny. Of all the great religions, Judeo-Christianity is probably the most "primitive," since its strictly historicist structure is directly plotted upon the saga of a bedouin tribe before being enriched by a divine prophet.
>
> ....
>
> [Science] wrote an end to the ancient animist covenant between man and nature, leaving nothing in place of that previous bond but an anxious quest in a frozen universe of solitude.[8]

Against such scientism as well as an uncritical confessionalism or Fundamentalism (the two are not the same), the American Enlightenment with all its limitations seems a better way. As against Monod and Dewey—two very different thinkers who agree in their reductionism—it allows that there are negotiable philosophical and religious as well as scientific models. The Supreme Court decision called for teaching about religion in American public schools in recognition that without it education is truncated and incomplete. Such teaching was to be historical and nonsectarian. Probably this is the only effective pattern in a pluralistic society.

One may contrast this stance with the confessional teaching that is still going on in a number of European countries—by and large not too effectively. In Great Britain, the pattern of teaching has shifted significantly to world religions and away from apologetics and doctrine. In short, the curriculum has adapted to the modern world as teachers working with it readily acknowledge. The question remains as to why religion cannot be more widely included in a responsible way in the United States.

---

8. Jacques Monod, *Chance and Necessity* (New York: Knopf, 1971), 168, 170.

Practical Considerations

Political questions remain, however. With respect to the United States, in present circumstances, is it not simply utopian to talk about teaching religion on any interconfessional model? Does the community situation allow it? One can argue easily enough that culture, politics, history, literature, music, and the arts cannot be understood without reference to religion. Furthermore, the history of Europe and the United States, like the history of Asia and Africa, has undeniable religious aspects. Some of the material, however, is thought to be so controversial that many public school teachers fear to mention it under the threat of sectarian or antireligious protest. Majority religious sentiments in many parts of the country might resolve the matter by common school prayers and Bible reading. Still, the constitutional principle should prevail: majorities ought not to be allowed to impose their will on minorities. Positively, however, an open educational ethos is very hard to achieve.

History of Religions

In the court of public opinion as well as for the educational profession, there are substantial arguments that too often have been overlooked. Academically, the field of the history of religions has become so advanced as to merit a legitimate place in the curriculum. Mircea Eliade, professor of the history of religions at the University of Chicago, once made a very provocative remark at a professional meeting. We have now reached the stage, he said, that we know what mankind's religious life has been in every era of human history, virtually in all times and places.[9] This has become possible not primarily through the work of theologians, but that of philologists, anthropologists, archeologists, and historians of culture. In short, there is a wealth of factual material about religion that needs to be included in the curriculum.

Wilfred Cantwell Smith has written one of the most impressive recent books in the field of the history of religions, *Towards a World Theology*.[10] Smith is a professor at Harvard and formerly headed the Center for the Study of World Religions in Cam-

---

9. Cf., Mircea Eliade, *A History of Religious Ideas*, vol. 1 (Chicago: University of Chicago Press, 1979).
10. Wilfred Cantwell Smith, *Towards a World Theology: Faith and the Comparative History of Religion* (Philadelphia: Westminster Press, 1981).

bridge, Massachusetts, where persons from different major religious traditions live together and study in conversation with each other. A Presbyterian and specialist in Islam, he expresses the firm conviction that major religions are and must be in dialogue with each other. The historian simply cannot describe past cultures authentically or the anthropologist say what it means to be human, apart from religion. Modern attempts to naturalize and secularize the history of religion, Smith believes, have not been successful in the end. Today, religions are in positive dialogue with each other in spite of all fundamentalism and sectarianism.

As illustration, one may cite the address of Archbishop Jean Jadot, formerly Apostolic Delegate to the United States and now head of the Secretariat for Non-Christian Religions at the Vatican, who was recently a guest speaker at Rice University. His topic was the commitment of the Roman Catholic Church to the dialogue between world religions.[11] The archbishop's stance was anything but apologetic in the traditional sense, even as the materials published by the Secretariat that he heads are not polemical, but written with good scholarship in the understanding that major religions will have to live with each other throughout the forseeable future. All religions, of course, face opposition from Marxism. Under such pressure, the dialogue between world religions is necessary and often creative. A member of one religion who comes to understand something about another, may learn more about his own faith at the same time. At any rate, the history of religions cannot be ignored in education for the modern world.

CRITICISM

Sometimes it is easier to get support for teaching about Islam, Hinduism, or Judaism than Christianity in the public schools. There is no reason, however, why students should not come to know their own religious heritage intellectually. Religion never has been an exclusively private matter, and fears that it will dissolve if it is approached historically or intellectually are unfounded. Of course, there are obscurantist pressures against religion in public education, and it would be utopian to suppose that they will disappear overnight. One finds it singularly diffi-

---

11. "The Growth in Roman Catholic Commitment to Interreligious Dialogue Since Vatican II," *Journal of Ecumenical Studies* 20 (Summer 1983):365-78.

cult to get breadth as well as depth in the discussion of religion. The notion that human beings can or do live, however, in a merely secular world is probably mistaken and ought not to be nurtured in public education. When it is, an intellectual vacuum develops and one ought not to be surprised that Fundamentalists seek to fill it in a pre-Enlightenment manner.

This is not to be uncritical about the meaning of the late eighteenth-century Enlightenment ideology that was dominant at the time of the founding of the United States. Nonetheless, it is inevident antithesis to a post-Enlightenment reductionistic naturalism. To give a simply naturalistic account of world origins without raising philosophical and religious questions seems unfair educationally. Already in the last century, Chauncey Wright offered a responsible criticism of the overuse of evolutionary categories in the United States.[12] In retrospect, Auguste Comte's analysis of the progressive displacement of religion and philosophy by science—often used to justify it—is simplistic. Positivism in the end is without understanding for metaphysical as well as theological questions. Scientific creationism, singularly uncritical of the nature and meaning of science, ought to give more time to its refutation rather than trying to prove the "factual" character of Genesis in its spirit.

Today, neither religion nor science is in the same situation that it was in 1859 at the time of the publication of the *Origin of Species*. The modern revolution in physics—relativity theory and quantum mechanics—has given a very different picture of the world than at Darwin's time. The Enlightenment view of the universe, emphasizing reason and mind, is in many respects closer to that of modern physics than post-Enlightenment reductionism and naturalism. One need not react defensively to modern science in the name of religion. Practically, what is needed most of all, is to affirm that religion can be studied objectively, historically, without destruction of faith. Indeed, the project can be exciting intellectually. Fortunately, there are teachers and parents who are willing to cooperate in supporting interfaith study, at times even over religion-secularist lines. One way to do religion real harm is to make the school a place for pre-Enlightenment prayers or cosmology. To leave out all mention of religion in post-Enlightenment reductionism, however, is to foster an evident intellectual void that invites abuse by the very

---

12. Cf., Philip P. Weiner, *Evolution and the Founders of Pragmatism* (Cambridge: Harvard University Press, 1949), Chapter III.

presence of ignorance. A middle way needs to be found between pre-Enlightenment intolerance and post-Enlightenment secularism. It is not an easy way, but it is not unmarked.

Conclusion

Michael Polanyi's writing and reflection offer support for the outlook of this essay. One of the more profound thinkers of the post-war era, Polanyi wrote on science, philosophy, and even religion. Hungarian and Jewish, he felt deeply the crisis of two world wars. In his book entitled, *Meaning*, edited by Harry Prosch, Polanyi speaks of the unhappy antithesis between left and right in the history of Central Europe.[13] More than in the United States, he argues, the Enlightenment was often anticlerical. Its skeptical, negative implications were carried full length in Central Europe, with tragic results, he believes. By contrast, in the Anglo-Saxon world, a kind of pragmatic moralism remained and was often reflected in education. In the end, a view of life and behavior that really required religious bases was set forth in practical, even scientific terms.

Polanyi argues that the Enlightenment, in this context, was a kind of half-way house, a stance that has great risks and remains precarious. This outlook seems to be confirmed by the historian, Carl Becker who, while not a Christian, argued that without the medieval vision of a heavenly city, the heavenly city of eighteenth-century philosophers would not have been possible.[14] This background relates to the present situation in the United States. Today, a religious common sense continues to be widespread and secularity has not become completely dominant in the American cultural ethos. Individual faith may be left to the churches and synagogues. There remains, however, a responsibility for an informed common life in a pluralistic democracy. The educational problem is one of filling a present vacuum in knowledge, historically and intellectually, and not just caring for personal faith. Cultural factors can be recognized in what the sociologist, Robert Bellah, has designated as "civil religion."[15] The Enlightenment model recognized their presence even as it

---

13. Michael Polanyi and Harry Prosch, *Meaning* (Chicago: University of Chicago Press, 1977).
14. Carl L. Becker, *The Heavenly City of Eighteenth Century Philosophers* (New Haven, Conn.: Yale University Press, 1932).
15. Robert N. Bellah, *The Broken Covenant, American Civil Religion in a Time of Trial* (New York: Seabury Press, 1976).

supported freedom of conscience; and this model remains exemplary.

At present, the vacuum in teaching about religion needs to be filled—a difficult task indeed in the face of sectarianism and fundamentalism which are often without social responsibility, as well as secularity. Although "secularism as a religion" was disavowed by the Supreme Court, these alternatives continue to confuse the educational scene. Even when public opinion is irresponsible in calling for change—for example, reinstatement of school prayers—the Enlightenment tradition of a middle way ought not to be ignored. Basic questions continue to be raised about the goals of education: who human beings are and what values should be fostered in public education. Religion ought not to be excluded from the public schools, as both its problematic nature and history offer a dimension apart from which—to say the least—education is incomplete.

Religion and Americanism

WILLIAM LEE MILLER

Among the arguments against strict separation of church and state, the one with the greatest popular appeal is patriotic: religion, it is said, is at the foundation of our institutions, is in our people, is central to our heritage. Therefore, say many, do not interpret separation of church and state in such a way as to remove the many expressions of our *national*, our *American*, religious heritage.

This linking of patriotism and religion echoed and re-echoed through the protests against the Supreme Court's decision in the Regent's Prayer case. The arguments of the defenders of the Lord's prayer and Bible reading in the schools, in the cases now before the Court, echo it once more.

The other themes appealed to by those opposing the most strict position on separation—that of rights of the majority, that of hallowed traditions and customs of the people, that of social benefits of religion, that of allowable incidental help to religion—all are given fire by their association with this one. The majority that claims its rights, for example, is the *national religious* majority, and the hallowed traditions are those of a "religious" nation and people.

This theme, combined with conservative religion's feeling that it must have state-expression of religion to combat "secularism," gives the force to most of the arguments against strict separation. This theme seems to be the *least* tenable ground for qualifying the separation tradition, at the same time that it is the *most* powerful in the public forum. Therefore, singling it out, let us examine it.

The American people—or a central segment of them—are caught in the conflict between two claims, that they held simultaneously before, without any strain: separation of church and state and the religious foundation of our nation. Now they find these two themes, both warmly held, arrayed in opposition to each other in the controversies of the day: for and against released time religious instruction; for and against prayer and religious instruction; for and against prayer and religious observance in the public schools; for and against religious symbols in public life; for and against state aid to religious schools.

In this new situation each of the traditional themes must be critically re-examined. This is especially true of this patriotic-religious theme, which has taken on a new life in the Cold War period.

Americans have long believed that religion furnished the moral foundation their democracy required; and that they were a religious people, and that their institutions presupposed a Supreme Being. They have long believed this, in fact, even in the face of considerable evidence to the contrary. Franklin H. Littell has recently shown again how overblown the popular, orthodox picture of the Christian foundations of the nation, and of the religiousness of the people, have been; actually at some periods in the nation's past—crucially in the period of the revolution and the constitution—the spread of religion was very thin.[1]

There may be more truth in the picture of the religious past than some critics grant—some secular critics, and some neo-orthodox opponents of our religiosity. True, the period of the founding of the nation was one of a low ebb of religion; however, earlier in that century that great awakening ("our national conversion," as Richard Niebuhr called it) had a profound effect, and after that period, beginning around 1800, the wave of revivals sometimes called the second great awakening swept across the country, bringing in their wake the great increase in the denominations of the free church that have done much to set the character of the American. Underneath the ups and downs of the religious awakenings and sleepenings there flows a stream beginning with Puritan sources turning into evangelical Protestantism, turning into liberal Protestantism and conservative and fundamentalist branches that has been a central strand of our culture. It has been of *great* importance in making us what we are. Moreover, as one looks at the future, one may have doubts about what will happen if the substance bred into men by a religious faith is evaporated. Do not think of just one person or one generation but of many, of a whole generation after generation of a whole culture through a whole future: that a humane and democratic substance, and a goodness in life even deeper than that can maintain itself if the roots in biblical tradition are entirely cut, one may well doubt.

However, whatever one's picture of the past and whatever one's picture fears of the future, one should not connect these to state-enforced religion. One should not carry these to the point of desiring some *of-*

---

1. Cf. Franklin H. Littell, *From State Church to Pluralism: A Protestant Interpretation of Religion in American History* (New York: Doubleday and Co., 1962).

ficial commitment to a religious position. We are not a religious people in any way that binds the irreligious among us to a commitment they do not freely make. Our institutions do not presuppose a Supreme Being in any way that makes those who do not so believe foreign to our institutions. Our institutions are such, rather, that men *may* have, and men *do* have, *differing* understandings of what they presuppose. The struggle over the religious substance of the people takes place on a different plane from the argument about a policy in school or in public office or in other public life. The home ground of religious argument is within the faithful communities, and between and among believers and non-believers in their moments of confession. "Secularism," or various nonreligious views, did not come into our world as the result of some state policy or some state neglect but arose from much deeper sources in the nature of our age. Similarly, such views will not be defeated, nor even significantly impeded, by any state enforced public recognition of God or act of worship. Indeed, it has been the faith of the voluntary tradition that such state religion, *far* from *helping* to preserve the religious substance in a people, works rather to decay it. There are three reasons why we should not actively defend *state* religious services, like the New York Regent's Prayer, the Lord's prayer and Bible readings in the schools: compulsion; empty ritual; civic religiosity.

We "should not actively defend," rather than that we should oppose, because the matter requires a heavy dose of prudence, of toleration of ambiguity and even of minor violation of "deliberation" rather than "speed." We should not be—we believers in separation of church and state—or believers in any other social idea, for that matter—seekers after tidiness, after neat and complete realizations of our idea. Human society, real, complicated, filled with habit and custom and irrationality, does not allow for the neat consistency the mind can picture. Perhaps it would have been better if the Supreme Court had not taken these cases—had not, as the lawyers say, granted certiorari. Why? Because the infringement of the Constitution may not have been weighty enough to have been worth the furor; because the cases were bound to have been misunderstood, as they have been, and therefore to complicate the Court's role when it is involved in many other deep matters in our society; and because ambiguity, or an unsettled constitutional state, might have been the only available way to allow the local variety on such a question that prudence might suggest for the time (the Long Island problem is quite different from that of an Oklahoma or South Carolina small town).

But the Court did take the cases, and, having taken them, had to decide them—in my view—as it did. To have positively decided the other way, allowing state-written school-imposed prayer, would have been a departure that would have been severe.

The first reason for supporting the decision is the one that is decisive for all Americans—religious or not—under the Constitution: prayer is an act of worship; public school prayer coerces the non-believing and minority religious groups, and involves compulsion in the religious act of all.

Here is a case in which the state directly imposes a religious observance upon the public, under conditions of compulsion. The Court, as it seems to me rightly, rejected the argument that the prayer was voluntary, in that students technically could stand silent or be excused; under conditions of the fifth grade this possibility seems merely academic. In effect, all students are included; to pull out of such a thing would require more than most grade school children can be expected to do—they should not be required to do that, to be free of it.

This is direct imposition of a religious service on those who may not believe. One is made uncomfortable by references to the smallness of the number of such persons. One wonders whether the number really is so small, if we include along with unequivocal non-believers, the penumbra of semi-believing and nominally believing multitude. But, anyway, if we deal in direct compulsion in religious belief, then do we ask about *numbers*?

Moreover, even many who have a religious belief, may find the content or—as in this case—absence of content—of any prayer, objectionable. Imagine yourself in a Moslem country, with even such a superficial observance as this prayer; doubts about one's feeling of propriety in participating in it, assail one. Minorities feel the dubiety of such an observance in a way that self-confident—not to say arrogant—majorities do not do.

There is a very large group that tends to be underestimated as to its size for reasons that are obvious, that is outside any religious tradition; some of these are negative and hostile, others are simply indifferent. Their freedom with respect to ultimate belief must of course be respected. Although we cannot carry their argument to the point of removal of every vestige of religious observance from public life—we can resist those observances that directly impose a worship act contrary to belief upon them and their children. Freedom of religion includes freedom *from* religion, freedom of *ir*religion, at least with respect to one's own personal participation.

This essay argues against the prayers on the grounds of compulsion, especially but not exclusively that of the nonbeliever. That ground seems to be the decisive one both in constitutional law and in principles of the free society. It is soundly arguable to say the Supreme Court would have been on more solid ground at least to have put its decision against the prayer not on grounds of nonestablishment but on grounds of free exercise. The extended version of the nonestablishment doctrine reaches out finally into controverted territory — rightly controverted, in my view. The free exercise ground, on the other hand, is narrower and less subject to legitimate challenge. When the objection is put upon grounds of establishment — that any state-financed or officially-prescribed observance is an establishment and therefore unconstitutional — we are led out into the far reaching negative of the strange concurrence that Justice Douglas wrote in the Regent's Prayer case, a concurrence suggesting that nonestablishment should strike down all that list of state religious practices we regularly cite including even the appeal to God with which the Supreme Court itself opens. Earlier Justice Douglas, whose changing career on these matters is confusing, had observed with a wry and humorous dig, that a "fastidious atheist" might even object to the phrase with which this court itself begins: God save this honorable court. Now it appears that that is no joke. It seems now, apparently, to Justice Douglas that the nonestablishment clause might follow that fastidious fellow to that extreme point.

Better to stay with the Free Exercise Clause, where more substantial goods and evils are involved. My objection to the constitutionality of the prayer is not that the state should never be caught under any circumstances underwriting any religious activity; rather it is that in this case the state is imposing a religious act, implying commitment, on those who may hold no such belief.

In the course of the opinion Justice Black said no showing of compulsion is required in finding such an act unconstitutional on the establishment ground. Better to rest the case on the ground that showing of compulsion in this case can be clearly made, that of a denial of free exercise to the non-believer, and also to the believer, in that his "exercise" here is not free.

But, one may say, does this mean granting full freedom to atheists and unbelievers? Of course it does. Why do not all the arguments for religious liberty — all the arguments Roger Williams made to John Cotton — apply to the irreligious man and his conscience? Actually, it would be better if we would use again the phrase that Madison regularly used — freedom of conscience — instead of the more ambiguous phrase — religious liberty or religious freedom; sometimes these later phrases are interpreted to mean freedom only for the distinct thing religion, or, a distinct people in the religionists, to exercise their liberty of religious worship, belief, action, evangelism, etc. Now those are important freedoms, and our society respects them, but they do not exhaust the meaning of our freedom in this matter — freedom to doubt and disbelieve being included.

An untenable notion appeared in the campaign in 1960 that it was all right to elect a man of any religion, so long as he had one. Ideally we should not make even this minimal religious test for office in this land. Socially of course the fact is we will do so, as in effect many minority groups are excluded from the presidency by the dynamics of politics. Still in both cases we should resist the social inclination, looking toward a future free of such disqualifications.

But can the society exist coherently and in order with such a breadth of view of freedom of conscience? Yes, it can. It was the faith of the founding fathers that we could and the experience of the country at its best that we can. To deny to candidates for president or men who will be teachers or public officials of any kind these posts on grounds of any religious test does not protect anything real in our country, but damages what is real, its freedom.

This is not an argument that every "acknowledgment of God," as it is called, should be removed from our public life; both on grounds of prudence, and on grounds of sound purpose, such a thorough-going position does not appear to be necessary. To try to do it would create a furor unjustified by the results. Moreover, at some point we would be unfair to the religious communities — to the religious believer who brings his faith into the public arena all innocently and with no intent to impose, nor to require state confession, but only as an expression of his own ultimate loyalty. The religious community should and must insist that they and theirs have full room to nurture their young and express their faith; this does not however require any imposition by official stating of religious acts on the nonbeliever.

The other two reasons for opposing public school religious observances are not consitituional, but have to do with the kinds of religion and patriotism that result.

Such religion tends toward — in the language of the Presbyterian statement on church and state — "empty ritual." A prayer is an act of worship, implying commitment, and a common commitment on the part of the community that participates in it. In the public school children of many faiths and none join together under the leadership of a teacher of any faith or none in the civic setting to make this religious act. The inclination is toward emptiness and toward mere form. Ritual given content by no particular tradition, with no symbols that have depth, nor any common religious experience that can be presumed, nor any community that interprets what the words said, is religiously undesirable. Words written by civic bodies like a Board of Regents of New York, necessarily are stripped of particular references and necessarily reflect a kind of lowest common denominator of religiosity, and therefore are dubious at best.

Herein lies a highly ojectionable matter: such public religion, tends toward a patriotic-religious amalgam which is dubious both as religion and as patriotism.

Think how strong is our patriotic loyalty. The symbols of the nation in fact evoke in most of us a much deeper response than those of our religious traditions; we would deny that this is so if we were asked on a poll or in a statement of faith, but in fact in introspection we can see and in observation of others (especially en masse) we can also see, that the national one, the American one, is the stronger operative pull. American national patriotic loyalty has always had a strong grip on its people, and rightly so. Nationalism is a strong force everywhere, and American nationalism, with its peculiar blend of universal ideals (the free society and democracy) and particular peoplehood and experience, is an exceptionally strong one. This nation — unlike others — seems to its people to have been founded in one conscious act by founding fathers as a distinct nation with a distinct mission; to test whether any nation so conceived and so dedicated could long endure. It has been a tremendous success as a human experiment — conceived in liberty and dedicated to the proposition that all men are created equal. Especially now in the period of world power and cold war this loyalty to the nation and the passions that go with it are increased. They tend in fact to develop a defensive edge. Because a nation is under threat — in a new experience — the patriotic loyalty tends to take on an edge of defensiveness, of suspicion, of coercion, of hardened compulsory creed. Think of how strong is our revulsion at the negative: treason, disloyalty, unAmericanism. How powerful are these as negative symbols in the national life!

Since this is a strong and passionate loyalty — the highest one in real effect for a great part of our people — it tends to reach out and gather every other loyalty to it, subordinating these to its passionate purpose. It does so with respect to religious faith and religious affirmation.

For example: the tendency to compose a creed, required of all Americans by compulsion, appears both including and excluding religious components; either way it is bad. It is bad because the nature of a free society goes against compulsory creeds.

When such a coercive Americanism excludes religion, making it a subordinate thing to a civic religion, a religion of democracy or of the American way of life, then the transcendent dimension upon which religion must insist is threatened. The religions of the Bible cannot accept the notion that national loyalty and national creed is final and superior, and subordinate loyalties to God to it. At some point they must resist, saying "We must obey God, rather than men."

When, on the other hand, a compulsory Americanism *includes* a religious element — as is now more common — mixing a faith in God with American patriotic loyalty — then there is also a dubious situation. This strong passion in us reaches out and takes over the highest symbols and loyalties as part of itself: faith in God is the first point in the American belief. Stated with any edge of requirement, that is an infringement of liberty of conscience. Even without such an edge it amalgamates what should be kept in some degree separate. The believer holds that God stands over against and in judgment upon his nation, as upon every nation, and that the loyalty he tries to make ultimate and determinative of all the others is not the one to his nation, deep and powerful though that be, but his faith in the One God behind all the nations.

Amalgamating patriotism and religious faith, obscuring this point, is bad both for national loyalty and politics, and for religion. Its effect upon religious understanding is to blur together various pieties, the various objects of reverence, which we should keep separated. It is to catch up into our belief in God, as Judge and Creator, our affection for and devotion to the institutions and people of our own land, thus making a tribal religion at worst. Religion stands constantly in danger of becoming such a thing: the worship not of One beyond ourselves, but of a projection of ourselves—Americanism in the sky. The devotion not to One who acts before we act, to whose action we respond, and whose action is never exactly what we want or expect— but rather simply an endorsement in capital letters of what we are going to do and be anyway. This is true in our individual lives and it takes on an added power in national life where the pull of everything we believe about ourselves collectively as a nation draws up powerfully toward an absolute and uncritical and unquestioning position. When we then include religion simply as a part of this national and cultural thing we have a culture religion, not the distinct religion of the biblical understanding. Though the God of the Old Testament has a chosen people the chosen people suffer his special requirement and his special chastisement. The American nation in the biblical framework should regard itself as special only in responsibility and requirement, only in the severity of the judgment upon it because of the effects of its action on all the peoples of the world—not in any self-praising, self-exalting way.

To return to that school room, what is the operative common faith of the people gathered there, and the relevant shared loyalty in that setting? Quite properly national, democratic, commitment—to the United States of America, and to liberty and justice which it extends to all. That is a deep and powerful commitment that we want to keep alive. However, it is not the same as faith in God, the Father Almighty. Contemporary theologians and preachers remind us that the chief danger of our time is this cultural religion, which is not Christian faith but a substitute and rival. It is marked by the absence of a sharp ethical demand, especially a social ethical demand in the religion; it is marked by an absence of the dimension of the Transcendence and of Judgment of God. From the point of view of the religious community this rival to faith should not be encouraged.

Three themes in the contemporary argument illustrate the danger: one the inclination to make religion a servant of national power and national ideology in the cold war; two, the insistence that religion, or faith in God, is basic to and required for our national institutions; and three, the inclination to regard religion as an instrument of, and merely of, moral training. All three collapse high religion down into a social instrument in the way that biblical faith must always resist.

Examples of the first—religion as an instrument of cold war nationalism—surround us of course on every side. One finds it even in the language of some courts, dealing with these matters. In the *Doremus* v. *Board of Education* case it was said: "Our way of life is on challenge. Organized atheistic society is making a determined drive for the supremacy by conquest as well as by infiltration . . . we are at a crucial hour in which it may behoove our people to conserve all the elements which have made our land what it is."

The objections to this theme are that it makes religion a national resource in the world battle, like coal or oil, and hurts both American politics and religion. Religion is made tribal; world politics is made into a holy war, a black-white opposition between intransigent forces. Our religious faith should have the opposite effect on our conception of the world political stage: It should make us aware of the limitedness of our own purposes, of the only relative goodness of our cause, in the eyes of the good God, of the power beyond our power that holds the whole struggle of East and West in his hand and who will bring out of it not our purposes but his, of our common humanity even with our enemies. Our religious faith should give us patience, humility, and the ability to forgive even the most intransigent and dangerous enemy, so far as his personal being is concerned, eliminating the vindictive and the demon-making impulse from our hearts. Religious faith should lend a dimension of depth to our political understanding and make our politics more subtle and wise, and more prudent and sober. Religion should not turn politics into hard, literal, radical operation, self-righteous, self-congratulatory, us against them.

Something of the same argument applies to our second example, that claim that religion or belief in God is fundamental to our institutions. This notion appears widely of course, and in the courts not only in Justice Douglas' dictum but in fiercer form, for example, in the statement of the Supreme Court of Florida in the Miami school case that will one day be coming to the Supreme Court. The Florida court said: "The concept of God has been and is so interwoven into every aspect of American institution that to attack this concept is to threaten the very fiber of our existence as a nation."

The order of thought and belief within which this may be true is not the order of thought and belief in which we operate when we deal with civic matters. It is a matter of this author's faithful understanding that democratic institutions require a belief in the dignity of the person, which in turn rests on an understanding of the person as a child of God. This affirmation, however, is in the order of faith, not in the order of our common civic requirement for all men in society. In fact it is part of the dignity of the person to be allowed not to believe in the theological foundition of that dignity. Weaving the belief in God into the fiber of our existence as a nation in the way that statement does is again no service either to those institutions, which presuppose freedom, or to God who works and moves in gracious ways above our efforts to confine him.

Third, the understanding or religion as the basis of the morality of our society fits again the same pattern. When the attorney for the state of Pennsylvania argues that Bible reading in the public schools is done simply to teach morality, without religion, he is reducing to its baldest form the argument many Americans have felt and made before. What it says about the meaning of the Bible is evident—it is a moral code book, not the scripture of faith.

Again there is truth in what the lawyer says, and in what Americans believe, but not a truth that should appear in that setting. The religious shaping of moral men is important to the operation of the kind of free society we have. However, one should not go from that belief to any notion that reading of Bible verses should be enforced in the state operated schools.

One who believes in God and in the moral substance that biblical faith creates, and who believes furthermore that such moral substance is important to the health and life of our country should exhibit that loyalty, show it forth in earnest effort after justice, preach it, practice it, try to persuade men to understand it, exhibit it, and show it forth in our own life as citizens—but not require it, not enforce it, not inflict it necessarily by the power of the state upon those who do not freely accept that conviction.

No understanding is more central to Christian faith, at least as it has been appropriated in the Protestant community, than that such faith must be freely accepted. And no understanding is more central to Americanism than that it is a society of free men. Where is it more essential that they be free than with resepct to the most fundamental matters of all—their religious faith, their final loyalty, their ultimate belief? Religion and Americanism alike want men who have freely decided that they affirm. One of the *inalienable* rights with which all men have been endowed by their Creator is: not to be forced by the state to acknowledge that Creator. Or, to put the same point in the words of Thomas Jefferson: "Almighty God hath created the mind free."

A Historian's Response to the Concept of American Civil Religion

HENRY WARNER BOWDEN

In writing about the place of religion in American life, many commentators have concluded that there exists a pattern of ideas and activities, "characteristics . . . relatively distinctive of religion in America," inclusive enough to count most citizens as supporters.[1] Some interpreters value this concept of shared ultimate convictions because it helps them to explain the stability of American society despite its divisive intermediate values. Others have denounced this "American Way of Life" as a shallow, compromising alternative to traditional faiths.[2] Still in a negative vein, other observers have concluded that American civil religion came to prominence as a cult of the state, making the nation's destiny and dominance its central affirmation.[3] But all these analysts tend to agree that a distinct body of beliefs and activities, to which their references apply, has existed from the eighteenth century to our own day.

In 1967 Robert N. Bellah brought fresh insight to this debate with the publication of his essay, "Civil Religion in America." Moving beyond conceptions of a common denominator religion or of Christianity as the tacit national faith, Bellah noted that "there actually exists alongside of and rather clearly differentiated from the churches an elaborate and

---

1. The quoted phrase is from one of the best early analysts, Robin Murphy Williams, Jr., *American Society: A Sociological Interpretation* (New York: Alfred A. Knopf, 1951), 315.
2. Will Herberg, *Protestant, Catholic, Jew: An Essay in American Religious Sociology*, new rev. ed. (Garden City, N.Y.: Doubleday and Co., 1960), 75.
3. John E. Smylie, "Editorial: National Ethos and the Church," *Theology Today* 20 (October 1963): 314-16 and 320-21; see also Stephen C. Rose, "Culture Religion: Competitor to Christian Faith," *Social Action* 37 (February 1971): 8-9.

well-institutionalized civil religion in America."[4] His perspective on the topic was substantially new, but since it used terms bearing connotations of preceding controversy, it was too quickly incorporated into the old frame of reference.[5]

I

Most discussions of American civil religion take its existence for granted, dwelling at length on descriptions and critiques of its belief structure, institutional framework, and relation to national goals. The purpose of this response, written primarily from the viewpoint of a historian, is to argue against the uncritical acceptance of "civil religion" as if it were a positive entity and then to suggest limitations within which it might be used validly. The major focus is on insufficient data and, until this state of affairs is recognized, it impedes rather than facilitates the interpretation of evidence already available. Unfortunately Bellah's language was imprecise on this matter, and it allows persons of divergent views to claim him as corroborating their ideas. It is necessary to understand the narrow limits within which he worked, what kind of observations he was making, and what kind he did not intend. Bellah's perspective is still valuable, but limitations of his usage and other possible references must be set before one can proceed to a discriminating treatment of phenomena related to this concept.

Essays on American civil religion have usually referred to a uniform set of particulars including ideology, charismatic leaders, and ceremonies of ritual significance. In most of the standard discussions two ideological themes recur as major components of this religion's belief structure. References to God, derived from biblical texts but seen as confirmed in the national experience, are couched in rhetoric which speaks of His special concern for America as the new Israel delivered from European bondage. During the Civil War a second theme, one of martyrdom and rebirth, was added to sustain the Union in its time of testing. Both of these motifs, covering American history from colonization to civil rights, tend to support a belief in America's special purpose.[6] Such ideological themes, one is told, lay behind the first attempts to establish a republican social order, and they encourage con-

---

4. Robert N. Bellah, "Civil Religion in America," *Daedalus* 96 (Winter 1967): 1. The essay has been reprinted in Donald R. Cutler, ed., *The Religious Situation: 1968* (Boston: Beacon Press, 1968), 331-56 and in Robert N. Bellah, *Beyond Belief: Essays on Religion in a Post-Traditional World* (New York: Harper and Row, 1970), 168-89.
5. Two recent examples of blending the old kind of thinking with new perspectives can be found in the "Foreword," in Elwyn Allen Smith, ed., *The Religion of the Republic* (Philadelphia: Fortress Press, 1971), viii; and the "Introduction," in Conrad Cherry, ed., *God's New Israel: Religious Interpretations of American Destiny* (Englewood Cliffs, N.J.: Prentice-Hall, Inc., 1971), 11-14.
6. Bellah, "Civil Religion in America," 9-11.

tinuing efforts to transform American life into the last, best hope of mankind. Personal virtues seem to be based somehow on this belief in America's unique role. Respect for the dignity and freedom of individuals, a commitment to social and political democracy, community responsibility,[7] and other character traits are seen as both duty and guarantor of divine favor. Americans are said to take such a yoke upon themselves as evidence of their past in a covenant that keeps alive belief in a special providential concern for the land and its people.

National leaders are seen as particular embodiments of this ideology in public life. Washington, Lincoln, the Kennedys, and King have been exalted in popular esteem as confirming our obligation to lead nations in the ways of righteousness. Monuments such as Lincoln's temple, statuary such as that commemorating the planting by the Marines of the flag on Iwo Jima, or shrines like the Tomb of the Unknown Soldier attract visitors who seem to be on pilgrimage. These memorials, including one so recently as John F. Kennedy's eternal flame, tend to foster a celebration of past sacrifices and to evoke pledges of renewed dedication. There also seems to be an aura of sacred symbolism in many national holidays which adds greater solemnity to American corporate life.[8] Thanksgiving Day, Memorial Day, Veterans Day, Independence Day, and Columbus Day among others are cited as giving cadence to what serves as a calendar for socially unitive cermonies. Such rituals tend to remind Americans of their singular status, their heritage, and their obligation to remain faithful representatives of God's purpose. Holidays, leaders, and ideas combine to form the dimensions of a civil religion which at its best is "a genuine apprehension of universal and transcendent reality as seen in or . . . revealed through the experience of the American people."[9]

In addition to themes, persons, and holidays, references are also made to the "words and acts of the founding fathers," particularly the first four presidents, because they "shaped the form and tone of the civil religion as it has been maintained ever since."[10] Invoking the name of God in inaugural addresses, congressional proclamations of thanksgiving, legislation regarding standards of social justice, Sabbath observance, or restrictions on the use of liquor are sometimes included to substantiate the existence of a common religion that undergirds national life. Many have also turned to the public school system as an institution which reinforces shared values and transmits them to succeeding generations. Pledges of allegiance to the flag, competitive sports

---

7. See, for example, those cited in Herberg, *Protestant, Catholic, Jew*, 80.
8. William Lloyd Warner, *American Life: Dream and Reality*, rev. ed. (Chicago: University of Chicago Press, 1962), 6-8.
9. Bellah, "Civil Religion in America," 12.
10. Ibid., 7.

with their ethic of teamwork and fair play, and until recently, prayers and Bible readings in the classroom have formed part of the data used to support the conception of a civil religion as a dynamic agent in the fundamentals of American life.

II

Do such phenomena constitute a specific religion that "exists alongside of and rather clearly differentiated from" the churches and synagogues of this country? In the assessment of at least this one historian, the conception of an elaborate and distinct civil religion has not been clearly established by the data made available. The common body of evidence found in many essays and presented here in condensed form is not strong enough to support the weight most writers have placed upon it. Some interesting suggestions have been made, but the few pieces of hard data accompanying them are not convincing. Theological symbols in inaugural addresses are too often contrived to gain political ends, and such rhetoric does not appear frequently enough to sustain an ideology of providential chosenness or missionary commitment. It is not clear that national holidays convey the same message to or evoke similar responses from divergent groups. One cannot ascertain that a consensus has existed on questions of foreign policy; still less has there been any degree of unanimity about the nation's domestic purpose through revolution, territorial expansion, slavery, immigration, urbanization, labor agitation, and civil rights. The evidence presented does not, in either its comprehensiveness or thoroughness, present a compelling case for the existence of a well-institutionalized civil religion in America. These elements of piety in American culture are too few, too infrequent, and too ambiguous to constitute a religion in themselves.

If previous discussions have not demonstrated how a concept of some promise could have practical utility for historical study, what kind of evidence and how much of it could a historian legitimately require? What are the components that must be identified and analyzed in a thoroughgoing treatment of institutionalized religions? John F. Wilson touched on this problem and suggested a set of categories which have yet to be improved upon through refinement or extension. He found six general conditions essential to verifying the existence of a socially differentiated religion.[11] This first is that any religion existing over a period of time must contain cultic phenomena, with a cycle of rituals

---

11. John F. Wilson, "The Status of 'Civil Religion' in America," in Smith, ed., *Religion of the Republic*, 12.

THE CONCEPT OF AMERICAN CIVIL RELIGION 189

to interpret its meaning and emphasize its importance to members. Other criteria include the need for any well-established religion to have clearly visible offices of leadership whose authority is recognized by participants. Its membership requirements, or means of participation, should be openly declared and self-consciously accepted. With a minimum of emphasis on the degree to which its creed should be normative for those who subscribe, a religion should at least maintain a coherent pattern of beliefs that constitutes its central affirmations about existence and purpose. These beliefs must be relevant enough to the daily activities of members to have a binding effect on their conduct. Most important of all, for beliefs and action to constitute and not just resemble a religion, all of these criteria must cohere in a working relationship. Loosely coordinated phenomena which either fail to encompass all these categories or fail to knit them into a coherent pattern of faith and practice cannot be accorded the identity of a religion that exists through time as a historical entity.

Looking at assertions about the existence of an American civil religion in this context, one finds that large claims for it cannot be supported. Ceremonies with cultic overtones are performed in American society, but their significance differs according to the regional, cultural, and ethnic backgrounds of those participating. There is no acknowledged spokesman for civil religion in the United States. There are no grounds for setting membership requirements; even citizenship is not an effective guideline. The problem with beliefs which Americans affirm about their identity and purpose is not that there are so few but far too many to form any intelligible configuration. That plethora of ideals probably influences the behavior of this or that individual, but American beliefs are not binding, and there is no way to ascertain the range of their normative effectiveness. Finally, even if one could make peace with each of these five critical remarks, it would still be impossible to argue seriously that these components are actually integrated or mutually supportive enough to form a socially differentiated religion. Wilson's list of criteria will inevitably undergo modification as discussions in this field become more sophisticated. But his contribution has already settled one phase of the controversy: assertions about the existence of American civil religion as a distinct entity have been based on inadequate evidence and poor logic.

Before definition of areas of discourse in which it is valid to refer to American civil religion, it might be useful to suggest some reasons why writers might have given the concept more positive status than it warrants. One reason could be a mistake in logic. Analysts from Robin Williams (1951) to Conrad Cherry (1971) have made accurate note of religious dimensions found among the various elements of American corporate life. A nation with the soul of a church, so the reasoning goes, has within it dimensions that have produced goals for the common welfare and have elicited voluntary cooperation to achieve them. Such qualities raise national life above the political level because they derive from religious affirmations of the people. These dimensions draw on the symbols and standards of major religious traditions found in the United States, but they cannot be identified with any single confession or cultural source. It is hasty and premature to argue that, since these elements exist in American culture and are traceable to no specific tradition, they must then constitute a separate one in themselves. Religious elements in American cultural life exist only be interacting with many other kinds of elements in a tremendously complex process. Since they are seen at work in relation to other activities, they have only a relative, not a discreet, identity. It is a mistake in logic to shift from describing the functions of dependent, occasional expressions of piety to giving them a separate ontological status all their own.

Such a mistake as a category commonly occurs when one fails to observe the limits of models and allows them too quickly to stand for the real thing. No one has seen an atom, but enough knowledge has been built on the observed dynamics of atomic energy so that atoms are assumed to exist. Static models are constructed, reminiscent of the solar system, but we often forget that this is overstepping the boundary between empirical and hypothetical fact. In civil religion one finds another case of over-dependence on a conceptual model. One could question whether the many attitudes and actions connected with civil religion occur with enough regularity to justify using a model at all. Multiple patterns, ambiguous connotations, and sporadic expression warn against using any model to correlate all the religious dimensions found in civil affairs.

One obvious defense of using models is that, as long as accurate predictions can be made, it makes little difference whether or not the model points to something that "really exists." Here is precisely the difficulty with using civil religion as a model. Given the ambiguity of what the concept means and whom it affects, the probabilities of making reliable predictions about the forms or force of civil religion are negligible. One cannot safely say what new religious impulses will come to bear in national life or how they will be expressed as common myths and rituals in the future. One cannot even predict which ones will be able to maintain their present effectiveness. The concept of American civil religion seems to have only restrospective, not predictive, utility, and as such its value as a model is severely restricted. In this case as in many others, when too much stress is placed on models themselves, the overload obscures the critical understanding of those phenomena which models are attempting to clarify.

Another possible reason for giving civil religion ontological status might be the need for an opponent. Institutional religions seem to have less influence than they did in contemporary Western life, and those interested in defending ecclesiastical prestige might look for a rival to blame for their decline. Those accustomed to treating religion as a positive force, yielding only to superior force, probably find it difficult to think of their persuasion as losing out to indifference. They need a rival faith not only to account for their loss but to keep a modicum of self-respect. There are more complex factors behind the general drift toward secularism, but it is understandable that some would view the process as a struggle between competing religious systems.

A variation of this need to find in civil religion something to blame is based on the conviction that religious and civil affairs must always be separate in American life. Any coalescence of these two spheres is deplored, the reverse argument of critics just mentioned who lament the isolation of religious influences. Viewing civil religion as an encroachment on the liberty found in separation of church and state, some critics censure it as a religion that is seeking "establishment" through consensus instead of legislation.[12] These arguments are opposite sides of the same coin. Those primarily interested in either the theological effectiveness or the political separateness of churches in American society tend to consider civil religion a threat to their values and viewpoint.

More detached observers have also treated civil religion as an independent system, and one could suggest additional grounds for their doing so. If the foregoing reasons do not apply, some writers might be employing an outmoded pattern of historical interpretation. During much of the nineteenth century, evangelical Protestantism was the dominant religious ideology in America and could at that time perhaps legitimately be called the national religion. But such a righteous empire has now been dismantled by religious pluralism, ethnic diversity, and secularism to such an extent that it survives only as a memory. Those who regard civil religion as an overarching pattern of shared beliefs and virtues might be writing with this former Protestant universality in mind, even though it no longer corresponds to twentieth century American experience. While not suggesting that anyone who follows this train of thought wishes to restore the monopoly of Protestant values, one can point out that such understanding of the situation is based too exclusively on an earlier and now unrealistic state of affairs.

---

12. See, for example, Leo Pfeffer, "Commentary," in Cutler, ed., *The Religious Situation: 1968*, 362, 364.

It is logical but inaccurate to conclude that, since Protestantism was the national faith for so long, its decline created a vacuum which must be filled. Once the existence of a specific civil religion became acceptable to most people, it is natural to find observers who would expect something like it to continue. Even if its content changes, the outer forms and relationships are expected to remain relatively stable. In this case the problem with such a logical expectation is that it has survived long after having any basis in fact. Indeed, there is some question about its ever having had such a basis. Contemporary discussions of an American civil religion, implying that it exists as a successor to the nineteenth century Protestant establishment-through-consent, might be founded on such an incongruity.

Using the concept of an American civil religion as a socially differentiated system creates more problems for the historian than it solves. It multiplies unnecessary categories, requires more evidence than it now has to substantiate it, and does not provide a realistic interpretation of the data already known. But it is still possible to refer to "civil religion" and make important contributions to our knowledge by so doing. Limitations must be observed, however, and one must employ the idea with self-consciously defined objectives, working within explicit methodological strictures to avoid misleading implications.

One such useful position seems to be the mode of operation which Bellah has employed all along. When he referred to civil religion, he usually employed such terms as "dimension," "theme," and "collectivity," connecting them with verbs implying function rather than existence.[13] At one point he indicated his care to avoid the ontological question by saying that the "public religious dimension is expressed in a set of beliefs, symbols and rituals *that I am calling* the American civil religion."[14] So for him the concept serves as a shorthand device, a generalization chosen to refer succinctly to those sacred themes and symbols which he sees at work in cultural life. It would add a great deal of clarity to further discussions if the noun "religion" were avoided altogether and the adjective "religious" were used in referring to those attitudes as they are expressed in corporate affairs.

Bellah made it plain that as a sociologist he was primarily interested in two questions of function: how the religious dimension was related to political activities and how it was related to private religious organizations.[15] Throughout his work the emphasis is on the role of civil religion as a vehicle for national self-understanding, as integrating

---

13. Bellah, "Civil Religion in America," 1, 3, 4, 5, 8.
14. Ibid., 4; italics supplied. Even his most capable critic (Wilson, "Status of 'Civil Religion,' " in Smith, ed., *Religion of the Republic*, 11) did not notice Bellah's restricted use of the concept.
15. Ibid., 3.

the family and local community into a larger sphere, and for mobilizing support to secure national objectives.[16] Analyzing phenomena as a behaviorist, Bellah finds it relatively unimportant to ask whether symbols and ideals come from traditional religious sources or combine to form a new one. The questions really worth asking are ones to determine how those ideals (wherever they come from and whatever they might form) function in efforts to unify a diverse people and provide them with a common ground for cooperative efforts. In subsequent debate Bellah made clear his preference to "outflank the usual definitional hassles and get a glimpse of functioning social reality."[17]

Hopefully future writers on this topic will take a moment to state explicitly the intentions they bring to it, specifying the type of goals they wish to achieve. Care must be given to define the behavioristic, functionalistic priorities within this approach because such analysis is too often taken as a study of concrete phenomena instead of relationships. Misunderstanding of purpose and focus enter easily here because it seems that the term "civil religion" is remarkably susceptible to reification. One does well to heed William of Ockham's advice and not multiply categories unnecessarily or attribute substantiality where it is not warranted.

There is also a way in which historians use the concept of civil religion in a valuable way, but it should be clearly stated that they are not referring to a socially differentiated entity. At the same time their references are not fictional, nor are they unrelated to tangible events and strands of ideas. This kind of history is often called "symbolic" history because it is founded on categories or linguistic symbols which are more the creation of the historian than a derivation from the phenomena being studied. The symbolic historian applies comparative analogies, creative insights, or personal perspectives to a wide range of disparate data and gives to such a new sense of reality. Terms such as the Hundred Years' War, the Renaissance, the Jacksonian Era, or World War I were not used at the time their corresponding events were occurring, but they still have a valid application. By means of such symbols the historian can provide a new view or a new understanding of realities that formed the American past and confront Americans in the present. It is not denigrating his work to observe that categories thus employed have no identifiable reality other than that given them by the symbolic historian. Such writers have employed this license in alluding to civil

---

16. Ibid., 8, 11, 12, 13, 18.
17. Robert N. Bellah, "Response," in Cutler, ed., *The Religious Situation: 1968*, 392; for a similar analysis, see Clifford Geertz, *Islam Observed: Religious Development in Morocco and Indonesia* (New Haven, Conn.: Yale University Press, 1968), 96-97.

religion in America, and the worth of their contributions cannot be gainsaid.[18]

While not wishing to argue the merits of "realistic, existential" history over those of "mythic, symbolic" history, the writer may make one observation. When dealing with language that offers a new construction of reality, historians as well as sociologists risk the possibility of having their references wrongly applied. In using a model to provide a new sense of reality, it is easy to overlook the limits of models and take the word as embodying the reality itself. That is not the intent of symbolic historians any more than it is of social behaviorists, but the tendency is still there. There is no solution to this problem, but at least the danger can be mitigated if symbolic historians are explicit about their perspective and its relation to empirical evidence.

One can gain a better understanding of this concept of civil religion if he views religious motivations as deriving from and still being sustained by traditional institutional faiths and at the same time views them as applying to the wider circles of civil life. Such a perspective finds it natural that Americans, as have men in all cultures, draw upon their transcivil orientation to help provide meaning and cohesiveness to all aspects of their lives. If religion is relevant to the rest of human experience, then it can be profitably studied at work there. As far as students of American history are concerned, their task is augmented by the fact that they must deal with many religious traditions and widely varying centers of culture served by a single government. It is not necessary to reify the concept of civil religion and spend time debating its existence. If there are those who still wish to employ the concept, it is the use of rather than the source of religious dimensions that constitutes the important field of inquiry.

---

18. Probably the best historical work that uses the concepts in this way has been accomplished by Sidney E. Mead. The present writer would argue that his idea of "the religion of the Republic" is significantly different from what many others mean by civil religion, but Mead does write history that falls within this classification. See *The Lively Experiment: The Shaping of Christianity in America* (New York, London: Harper and Row, 1963), 63, 68, 71: Sidney E. Mead, "The 'Nation with the Soul of a Church,' " *Church History* 36 (September 1967): 269, 274, 277-78, 281; and "The Post-Protestant Concept and America's Two Religions," in Robert L. Ferm, ed., *Issues in American Protestantism: A Documentary History from the Puritans to the Present* (Garden City, N.Y.: Doubleday & Co., 1969), 379-81.

Colonialism and Missions: Progressive Separation

KENNETH SCOTT LATOURETTE

The nineteenth and twentieth centuries have seen a progressive separation of the close association of the spread of Christianity with empire-building which began with the conversion of Constantine in the fourth century.

Although we do not know that the conversion of the Roman Empire was Constantine's purpose when he accepted the faith, and although he did not proscribe paganism, in his new capital which he built at Byzantium and named for himself Constantine erected many churches and forbade the rapair of non-Christian temples or new representations of the old gods. With one brief exception, that of Julian "the apostate," the Emperors of the Constantinian line espoused Christianity; the second ordered that pagan sacrifices in Italy cease; and the third commanded the closing of pagan temples. As a result, from constituting only about a twentieth of the population of the realm when Constantine took his momentous step, by the end of the fourth century those who called themselves Christians were in the large majority. The conversion of the northern barbarians who invaded the Empire during the fourth, fifth, and sixth centuries was part of the acculturation by which conformation to the Greco-Roman civilization of the Mediterranean world was achieved. When Christianity spread in Western Eurpoe beyond the former Roman boundaries, it was chiefly with the support of the monarchs. Thus the "conversion" of the Saxons was promoted by Charlemagne as part of his ambition to extend his rule. His successors encouraged missions among the Germans and Scandinavians for much the same reason. The Swedish monarchs who conquered Finland brought missionaries from England to consolidate their holdings. German and Greek princes sought to use missionaries to extend their political ambitions among the Slavs in the Balkans.

The association with politically minded monarchs did not mean that among the missionaries there were no heroes or great Christians. Some of the most saintly and courageous men in the church's history worked closely with kings and emperors who sought through them to promote their territorial ambitions. Among them were Boniface, the outstanding English missionary in Germany, and Anskar, who had the support of Charlemagne's successor in the latter's attempt to extend his influence into Scandinavia.

Nor was all the extension of Christianity among the peoples of Western Europe through the ambitions of princes. The conversion of Ireland seems to have been quite independent of assistance from magnates on the neighboring island of Great Britain. None of the Irish missionaries to the Continent were backed by Irish chieftains and few of them had the support of the rulers of the peoples to whom they went. Some of the greatest of them did not hesitate to denounce the morals of the nominally Christian kings and nobels in whose domains they labored. Yet in general the conversion of most of Europe was closely connected with the ambitions and programs of secular rulers.

Most of the spread of Christianity in the sixteenth, seventeenth, and eighteenth centuries was by Roman Catholic missionaries who were agents of the kings of Spain and Portugal. The Spanish conquest of much of the West Indies, Central America, the southern portions of North America from Florida to California, the larger part of South America, and the Philippines, was one of the most striking features of that stirring period. Only second to it were the Portuguese achievements in Brazil, along the coasts of Africa, in India, Ceylon, Malaya, the East Indies, Japan, and the southern fringe of China. Contemporary with the discoveries, empire-building, commerce, and colonizing was a fresh burst of life and devotion in the Roman Catholic Church, which Protestants mistakenly often call the Counter-Reformation. It began about a half-century before Luther and had its outstanding figure Ignatius Loyola, a contemporary of Luther. From it issued the territorially most extensive missionary enterprise that Christianity — or any other religion — had thus far seen. It accompanied Spanish and Portuguese expansion and in some places, notably in Paraguay, parts of India, and China, extended beyond the areas touched by the conquerors, administrators, and merchants of those nations. Yet most of it was under the aegis of the governments of Spain and Portugal. No missionary could go to any of the Spanish possessions without the consent of the Crown. The vast majority were financed from the royal coffers. All bishops were appointed by the monarch. In several regions missions were the instrument for the extension of Spanish rule. Mission stations, some protected by troops, were the means employed to carry the Spanish frontiers into the upper region of the Orinoco, California, New Mexico, Arizona, and Texas. Similarly the Portuguese Crown controlled the missionaries and named the bishops in Brazil, Ceylon, the East Indies, and its territorial holdings in India, the Malay Peninsula, and Macao, its single foothold in China. It also attempted to dominate all the missions in South and East Asia outside its possessions, whether in India or China.

Until the closing years of the eighteenth century Protestant missions were numerically small and most of them were independent of governments. That was true of the heroic Moravian enterprise and the British missions in the Thirteen Colonies. Yet through their East India Company the Dutch supported and controlled their missions in Ceylon and the East Indies quite as effectively as did the Spanish and Portuguese Crowns in their possessions.

Significantly, and in striking contrast to what we shall see in the nineteenth and twentieth centuries, most of the churches planted by the missions of the sixteenth, seventeenth, and eighteenth centuries have proved to be extremely anemic. That is true of the Roman Catholic Church in Latin America and the Philippines. Although here Christianity made impressive territorial and numerical gains, it has given rise to few new movements and has been kept alive, and then only in a weakened condition, by repeated transfusions from the Roman Catholic Church in Europe, and latterly, from the United States. In Latin America the indigenous clergy are notoriously inadequate in numbers and in moral and intellectual character to care for the existing Christian communities. Exceptions there fortunately are, but they are relatively few. Little effort has been made to carry the Gospel to other lands and even to the non-Christian Indians on the frontiers of white settlement. Such missions as exist for the thousands of pagan Indians have been and still are staffed by personnel from Europe. In the past few years Roman Catholics in the United States — clergy and laity — have been directing major efforts toward Latin America, but that has been chiefly to improve the quality of life among the nominally Christian masses. Much the same picture exists in the Philippines. Until the American occupation the bishops were entirely from Spain and such missionary endeavor as existed was by Spaniards. Soon after annexation by the United States thousands of Catholics broke with Rome because it refused to appoint Filipinos as bishops. The Filipino Independent Church which issued from the revolt had little warm Christian life. After World War II the majority of its members established a connection with the Protestant Episcopal Church of the U.S.A. and that body undertook to train clergy for the Filipino Independent Church and thus to raise its spiritual and moral level. In the meantime missionaries from Europe and the United States endeavored to pour out new vigor into the millions who remained with Rome; and eventually the pope raised to the episcopate some of the Filipinos who emerged from this effort.

The anemia of the Roman Catholic Church in Latin America and the Philippines arose from a number of factors. Prominent was the failure to produce an adequate indigenous ministry. Another, fully as potent, was the domination of the Church by the state. In Spanish America, weakness was compounded with the struggle for political independence. The mother country demanded the continuation of its authority to appoint the bishops. The fledging governments insisted on the transfer of that authority to them. They also took from the foreign clergy the administration of the missions to the Indians and transferred it to the indigenous parish clergy. The result was the disastrous thinning out of the direction and discipline of the Church by the episcopate and the insufficiency of the staff of the missions both in numbers and in quality.

The Dutch missions, through the East India Company bound hand and foot to the civil administration, also suffered. In Ceylon, when the Dutch displaced the Portuguese, they attempted to compel the Catholics to become Protestants and expropriated Catholic churches for Protestant worship. When, as an outcome of the Napoleonic Wars, the English dispossessed the Dutch and granted religious toleration, most of the Dutch Protestantism disappeared. Yet in the East Indies the state church, financed by the civil authorities, persisted and under the Republic of Indonesia still survives.

The nineteenth century was marked by a wave of Western imperialism. Almost all of Africa, a large part of Asia, and most of the islands of the Pacific were brought under the political control of Western Europeans. Great Britain led. It established control of Egypt and obtained the lion's share of Africa south of the Sahara when, in the 1880s, that vast region was partitioned among earth-hungry Western Europe powers. It acquired Cyprus and Aden, completed the conquest of India, made itself master of Burma and most of the Malay Peninsula, and led in forcing open the doors of China. It acquired undisputed possession of Australia and New Zealand and peopled them with the predominantly British immigration. It seized a large proportion of the islands of the Pacific. Even more spectacularly, British commerce and investment penetrated the entire globe, both the territories over which the Union Jack flew and areas which remained politically independent. France was a somewhat distant second, with holdings in North and Sub-Saharan Africa, Madagascar, Indo-China, and the Pacific, and without as extensive commerce as that of Great Britain. Germany was late in entering the competition, partly because it did not achieve political unity until 1870 and had its energies engrossed attaining that goal. Italy, also delayed in attaining political integration, was even tardier in imperial expansion. Spain and Portugal, long past the zenith of their imperial days, enlarged their holdings in Africa, Portugal more extensively than Spain.

Although only on the edge of Western Europe, Russia extended her holdings across the Urals and in the Trans-Caspian region, threatened British power in India, competed with Britain for spheres of influence in Persia, constructed the Trans-Siberian Railway to the Pacific, annexed a substantial part of the decadent Manchu Empire, and aspired to a commanding role in the threatened dismemberment of China.

Peopled predominantly by Western Europe stock, the United States did not join the scramble for territory outside the Western Hemisphere. However, in the course of the nineteenth century it jumped the Mississippi to the Pacific Coast, annexed Texas and as much of Mexico as it desired, and purchased the Russian holdings in North America. At the end of the century it formally annexed the Hawaiian Islands, already governed by children of its citizens, as a corollary to its war with Spain took possession of the Philippines and Puerto Rico, and from a mixture of altruism and self-interest by its Open Door policy sought to prevent the partition of China by Europeans. On its north, Canada, part of the British Empire, expanded its borders westward to the Pacific and northward into the Arctic.

This political and commercial expansion of European peoples contributed to the worldwide cultural revolution which has been the most striking feature of the twentieth century. The globe around, all phases of human life are in rapid change. That is true among European peoples and peoples of European ancestry. It is even more marked among non-Occidentals. For the first time in history all mankind is undergoing drastic transformation. Other periods have seen radical revolutions. That was witnessed, for example, in the adoption of much of Chinese civilization by the Japanese and the absorption and adaptation of Greco-Roman-Christian cultures by the peoples of Northern Europe between the fourth and fifteenth centuries. However, never before has all mankind been so on the march.

Significantly, this vast and unprecedented revolution has come from what we have been accustomed to call Christendom, chiefly Western Christendom. It has arisen from those peoples who have been longest under the influence of Christianity where Christianity has not been on the defensive against Islam. The questions inevitably arise of the possible responsibility or share of Christianity for the revolution, and whether Christianity will disappear or prevail in the world which is emerging from the revolution. The revolution is still so much in its infancy that except to the eyes of faith no definitive answer can be given. Yet, as we suggested at the outset, Christianity has been less impeded by the association with the imperialism, which has been a major factor in the revolution, than it has earlier been by affiliation with revolution. It has been associated with that imperialism but not as intimately as in former stages of empire-buliding, and it is displaying a remarkable capacity to survive the liquidation of that imperialism and in increasing measure to root itself among peoples who are throwing off the European political yoke.

Parallel with the empire-building of the nineteenth century came a quickening of religious faith which issued in a burst of missionary activity that in geographic extent was greater than any of its predecessors. It penetrated every country brought under imperial sway. Again and again it preceded political annexation. On occasion it made the excuse for annexation, but only infrequently did missionaries further that annexation.

At the outset the nineteenth century missionary enterprise was predominantly Protestant and British. It arose chiefly from Evangelicalism in the Church of England, the non-conforming churches in England, the Church of Scotland, and the Evangelical dissidents from that church. It also sprang from Pietism on the Continent mainly but not entirely in Germany. In the United States missionary interest in peoples outside that country developed slightly later than in the British Isles and the Continent. It, too, was born of Evangelicalism. In the 1880s it issued in a great surge in the Student Volunteer Movement for Foreign Missions, with its watchword "the Evangelisation of the world in this generation," and with profound repercussions in the British Isles and on the Continent of Europe. Out of it came the young men who organized the World Missionary Conference in Edinburgh in 1910. From that conference sprang the International Missionary Council in a successful attempt to coordinate Protestant missions the world around.

Roman Catholics also rose to the challenge of the expanding frontiers of the Occident. By a strange contrast France was the chief source. From that country went more missionaries in the nineteenth century than from all the rest of the Roman Catholic Church. There, too, arose the Society for the Propagation of the Faith, which has enlisted more Catholics in more countries in contributing voluntarily to the spread of their faith than any other organization of their church. The contrast becomes apparent when it is remembered that the anti-Christian secularism in Catholic lands has had its most aggressive centers in that country.

In contrast with pre-nineteenth century missions, the initiative and the financial support of the surging nineteenth century missionary movement, whether Protestant or Roman Catholic, was less from governments than at any time since Constantine. In some of their colonies and in India the British rulers gave financial aid to mission

COLONIALISM AND MISSIONS

schools, but that was because of the desire to further education and not because the schools were Christian. The Russian government aided Russian Orthodox Missions, but these were chiefly in regions within the Empire.

Some governments sought to use missions to promote their political ambitions, but that was chiefly of non-Protestant enterprises. The Russian Tsars and their ministers regarded Russian Orthodox institutions as a means of supporting Russian ambitions in the Middle East. Even their Communist successors are not averse to continuing that policy. Although in the last quarter of the nineteenth century French governments were anticlerical and their diplomatic representatives reflected that attitude, they used Roman Catholic missions in China and Indo-China as a means of reinforcing their prestige. In China, the French insisted on a protectorate over Catholic missions of all nationalities, both their own and others. They long sought to obstruct Rome in its effort to effect direct supervision through an apostolic delegate. The protection of Roman Catholic missions, both French and Spanish, against persecution gave the French government a convenient pretext for steps which led to the extension of its domination in Indo-China.

Long into the nineteenth century the English East India Company, through which British commerce with India was conducted and the conquest of the land was effected, opposed the entrance of missions on the ground that the religious antagonism provoked would cut its profits. Although the efforts of warm Evangelicals in Parliament succeeded in ending that restriction and in creating an Anglican episcopate for India, and although after the transfer of the Company's possessions to the Crown some British officials actively aided missions, in the main the attitude of the British *raj* was religious neutrality. Under the *Pax Britannica* religious freedom was supported and missionaries of all nationalities were protected; no favoritism was shown to them or their converts.

From time to time Western governments gave official support to Christian missions, but this was in the form of obtaining legal toleration and protection, and not by control or financial support. Outstanding was the situation in China. The guarantee of extraterritorial status to citizens of countries with which China had treaties applied to all regardless of occupation, but it included missionaries as well as others. At the request of the French envoy, in 1844 the Chinese government granted toleration to Roman Catholic Christianity and the following year this was extended to all branches of the church. The treaties of 1858, forced from the reluctant Chinese by European arms, among other provisions permitted residence of foreigners in specified cities and the right to travel anywhere in the Empire, privileges of which missionaries as well as merchants took advantage, and specifically promised to missionaries and to Chinese Christians the free exercise of their faith. When, as was again and again the case, missionaries and their converts were persecuted, foreign diplomatic representatives brought pressure on Chinese officials to enforce the treaties and to reimburse the sufferers for their losses. Often the British authorities were annoyed by the insistence of missionaries to travel and preach as the treaties permitted, but from conviction that all British subjects must be supported in their treaty rights, missionaries as well as non-missionaries were backed. Here, we may note, was the source of much Chinese antagonism to Christianity, an antagonism which contributed to the expulsion or imprisonment of missionaries of all nationalities by the Communists after their triumph on the mainland in 1949. When in the 1850s Japan opened her doors to the foreigners, the American and British governments attempted to have the toleration of missionary activity written into the treaties as it was in the treaties of 1858 with China. The Japanese refused. But when in the 1860s and 1870s persecution broke out against the Christians who had secretly maintained their faith against the prohibitions enforced since the closing years of the sixteenth century and the opening decades of the seventeenth century, representatives of the Occidental powers lodged protests — on the ground not of the truth of Christianity, but that such action was contrary to civilized procedure.

On some occasions missionaries were at least partly responsible for the annexation of territory by the colonial powers. Thus the early British missions in Nyasaland, the present Malawi, brought pressure on their government to extend its rule over that territory, presumably because of fear of seizure by the Portuguese in the adjacent and much larger Mozambique and the curtailment of their operations by a Roman Catholic power. To what extent, if at all, they were responsible for the incorporation of the region into the British Empire is not clear. The pressure of missionary forces in creating public opinion in England contributed to the establishment in 1894 of a British protectorate over Uganda.

Although, in general, nineteenth century missions, especially those of Protestants, were less supported and directed by governments than at any time since the fourth century, to the casual observer and to the peoples among whom they were conducted they appeared to be intimately associated with political aggression and domination. They seemed to be the ecclesiastical phase of Western imperialism and colonialism. Christianity was regarded by non-Occidentals as the Westerner's religion. Among some tribes that conviction furthered the acceptance of the faith. For example, among the Hova on Madagascar, a ruler looked with favor on the missionaries because he hoped that through them some of the European arts and crafts which he desired

COLONIALISM AND MISSIONS

would be introduced. However, in many lands missionaries and their message met sharp resistance. That was because it was regarded as alien, destructive of the ancestral religion and inherited customs and way of life. That was especially marked in the recurring persecutions in China which culminated in the Boxer outbreak in 1900, in the anti-Christian movement in the 1920s, and in the anti-missionary measures of the Communists. The chronic opposition of Islam in the Middle East has been reinforced by memories of the Crusades and by the resentment against Western European aggression of the nineteenth and twentieth centuries.

In spite of the association in the minds of non-Western peoples of missionaries with Western imperialism, and although in some instances the actions of Occidental governments and of missionaries compromised the general independence of missions from support by these governments, the generalization still holds true that not since Constantine had the spread of Christianity had so little support by the state.

We need also to note that never before the nineteenth century had so many missionaries devoted their efforts to the spread of their faith or had such large sums been voluntarily given to support them and their enterprises by the rank and file of their fellow Christians, lay and clerical. Never before in history had any religion been propagated over so much of the globe. Moreover, never, even in more limited areas, had the spread of any religion been undergirded by so many of its adherents and with so little assistance by the state.

The achievements through this outpouring of devotion were notable. The Scriptures were translated in whole or in part into hundreds of languages and were widely distributed. To make this possible scores of languages were reduced to writing. The Gospel was proclaimed to more millions than had heard it or any other religious message. Converts and their children were gathered into churches in scores of tribes and nations. These churches were still small and were mostly among peoples of animistic background and not from the "higher" religions— Islam, Buddhism, Hinduism, and Confucianism. Most of them were still depentent on the missionaries for leadership and on constituencies in Europe and America for financial assistance, but here and there from them leadership was emerging and a few were financially self-supporting and self-governing. In a variety of ways missionaries were seeking to serve the peoples among whom they labored. In the attempt to relieve suffering they were introducing Western medicine and surgery and Western methods of the prevention of disease, such as vaccination for smallpox and, by 1914, inoculation against typhoid. They opened and maintained leper asylums and institutions for the blind and insane. They began schools for physicians and nurses. They fought famine by direct relief and by methods of famine prevention, such as better forestry and improved agriculture. They introduced the kind of education that would help prepare non-Europeans for the revoluntary world into which Asia, Africa, and the islands of the sea were being hurried by Western commerce and political rule. They pioneered in the education for women and girls which would elevate the status of that sex. Roman Catholics and Portestants were not collaborating. That was partly because of historic doctrinal differences and partly because most Roman Catholic missionaries spoke French and most Protestants, English. But Protestants were beginning to cooperate across denominational barriers. In country after country, notably in India, China, and Japan, conferences of missionaries of many denominations were seeking to learn from one another and to plan for joint effort in such enterprises as did not involve compromise of their distinctive convictions. World missionary gatherings convened in England and the United States, culminating in the World Missionary Conference of 1910.

In the first half of the twentieth century the worldwide revolution which had been foreshadowed in the nineteenth century ushered Christian missions into a radically new setting and into what many glibly declared to be the "post-Christian era." Two world wars separated by less than two decades (for World War II really began with the Japanese take-over in Manchuria in 1931 and the Japanese full scale invasion of China in 1937) were centered in Europe and were fought with weapons and methods first developed in "Christendom." These wars drastically weakened the Europe that had built the colonial empires which on the eve of these wars had embraced most of the non-Occidental world. Rumbles of revolt against "white domination" had been heard on the eve of World War I. After the war the revolt swelled. Following World War II it reached major proportions and by 1965 had obtained political independence for most of Africa, all of India, Burma, Indo-China, the Philippines, and Indonesia, and had obliterated the last traces of the "unequal treaties" by which the Occident had shackled China. Could the churches which were the fruits of pre-twentieth century missions survive the erasure of the colonialism with which they had been associated?

Moreover, the world revolution issuing from "Christendom" mounted even more rapidly than emancipation from Western imperialism and colonialism. Some phases of the revolution were belligerently anti-Christian. That was especially spectacular in Communism. Communism had arisen in "Christendom," the creation of two former Protestants, Karl Marx and Friedrich Engels. By 1965 it had captured the mainland of China, a major field of Christian missions in the preceding ten decades. It was also threatening Southeast Asia and Indonesia. In Burma a form of socialism with a European background was progressively curbing Christian missions. More serious was what was usually called secularism, a movement away from all religion, and especially Christianity. It had arisen in "Christendom." It sprang from a variety of roots, among them the industrial revolution with its attendant drifting from the faith of the laborers in mines and factories, the disruption of the kind of society of which the churches had traditionally been a part, and the scepticism which had been fed by the science and philosophy which were a part of the revolution. Mankind was declared to have come of age and no longer concerned with God, and, indeed, to feel itself to have no need of any religion. A distinguished Chinese intellectual, trained under John Dewey and not a Communist, declared that the Chinese would be the first people to "outgrow religion" – as though religion is a phase of man's infancy and youth from which maturity will bring liberation.

The combination of scepticism, secularism, and the impoverishment brought by the world wars has cut down the reinforcement of missionary staffs from Europe, especially those of Protestantism. Is the wave ebbing of the missionary devotion which had seemed to make the preceding hundred years "the great century" of the expansion of Christianity?

Here and there revivals of the "higher" religions and new religions have been appearing. They are closely associated with the nationalism which has come by contagion from the Occident. They have offered enhanced resistance to Christianity as a "foreign" faith. Thus Buddhism has been reinforced by Singhalese and Burmese nationalism and Hinduism by Indian nationalism. Each of these religions has sincerely devout souls, but their loyalty has strengthened the nationalistic aspects of the revivals. In Japan, Soka Gakkai, the most flourishing of the new religious movements of that country, is an outgrowth of Nichiren Buddhism and is intensely patriotic, anti-foreign, and anti-Christian. Resurgent Islam is strengthened by Arab and Pakistani nationalism.

In spite of all these adverse factors, Christianity is stronger in Asia, Africa, the islands of the sea, and Latin America than it was on the eve of World War I. That is seen in the continuation of missions, in the mounting number of Christians, in the deepening rootage of the churches, in advances toward Christian unity, and in the effects of Christ upon culture. The vigor of Christianity is due primarily to the vitality of the Gospel from which Christianity is sprung and to which it still witnesses, and to the fact that in the heyday of European imperialism the tie between missions and governments, marked though it seemed, was more tenuous than at any time since the fourth century. Christianity has survived and grown stronger in spite of the emancipation of Asia, Africa, and the islands of the sea from political domination by Occidentals and in the face of the anti-Christian forces issuing from the former "Christendom" and which are potent in the revolution which is a feature of the impact of that pseudo-"Christendom" upon all mankind.

Missions are continuing. The churches of Europe, North America, Australia, and New Zealand maintain them in Asia, Africa, the islands of the sea, and the nominally Christian but, until lately, the progressively de-Christianized Latin America. The sources and the character of the missionaries are being altered. North America, and especially the United States, supplies a much larger proportion of the Protestant missionaries and financial support than do the British Isles and the Continent of Europe. For example, in 1960 the number of Protestant missionaries was said to be 38,606 as against 29,188 in 1925, and during that time (which embraced World War II) the total number of Protestant missionaries from Europe was reported to have fallen off by about five thousand. In 1958 Protestants in the United States contributed approximately $120,000,000 to foreign missions and the total from other countries was about $20,000,000. The Roman Catholic missionary staff increased more rapidly than did that of Protestants. In 1925 the ratio of Roman Catholic to Protestant missionaries in Asia, Africa, and non-Occidental islands was about three to four. In 1956 it was about five to three. Most of the Roman Catholic missionary force was from the Continent of Europe. It had grown rather than declined. That is the more remarkable in view of the fact that the chief sources of these missionaries—France, Belgium, and Holland—had suffered severely from German invasions, the first two countries in both world wars and the latter in the second of the wars. France was still the source of more Roman Catholic missionaries than any other country. Yet in proportion to their numerical strength late in the 1950s, the Protestants of England, France, Belgium, and Germany were sending more missionaries than were the Roman Catholics of these lands. Roman Catholics of the United States were sending an increasing number of missionaries and were contributing more than half of the total raised by the agencies for distribution among the many orders and congregations which were carrying the main load of the foreign missions of their church. But their foreign mission staff was still only about a fifth of that from Protestants in North America. An increasing proportion of Protestant missionaries from the United States are from denominations and societies which do not cooperate with the former International Missionary Council (now the Division on World Mission and Evangelism of the World Council of Churches).

Numerically, since World War II Christianity has continued to gain in lands outside the traditional "Christendom." This growth has continued in spite of the fact that on the mainland of China, where live about one-fourth of mankind, Communism has severed contact between the churches and Christians outside that country. Although

COLONIALISM AND MISSIONS 207

precise statistics are not obtainable, the totals of Christians in that area, never more than one percent of the population, have undoubtedly fallen off. But in Japan, although the churches have as members less than one-half of one percent of its people, those who in the government census declare themselves to be Christian are three out of a hundred. In the Republic of Korea the increase of those bearing the Christian name is phenomenal. When these lines were penned no news was obtainable about Christians in North Korea. In Indonesia, predominantly Moslem though it is, the Christian communities have grown surprisingly. Protestants of the Philippines continue to multiply, and in spite of the fact that that branch of Christianity had not been introduced until after the American annexation (1898). In Burma, the face of the Japanese occupation during World War II and the subsequent independence of the country and mounting restrictions on missionaries, the Christian communities have grown. Fifty years ago the Christians of India were reported to be about one out of a hundred of the population. Today, in spite of freedom from British rule and a zooming population, Christians number about three out of a hundred. Africa south of the Sahara has latterly been the scene of a kind of mass movement to Christianity, a movement which has slowed down but not ceased because of the turmoil associated with the achievement of political independence in much of the region, efforts at independence in the Portuguese possessions, and the racial tensions in Rhodesia and South Africa. In Latin America, as we have seen, the plight of Christianity has seemingly been desperate. Yet in the twentieth century, especially during latter decades, Protestantism has grown rapidly, partly by immigration but chiefly by the conversion of nominal Roman Catholics. In the 1960s here and there the Roman Catholic Church has displayed vigor in a number of ways. That has been, as heretofore, partly by infusions from other countries, recently chiefly from the United States, but it has been as well by indigenous leadership, including that of some of the episcopate.

We must note that since World War I the numerical gains in Asia, Africa, and the islands of the sea have, as in the nineteenth century, been chiefly among peoples of animistic or near-animistic religions rather than those of "high" religious antecedents. That has been true in Korea, where Buddhism and Confucianism have long been decadent and the majority of the population have held to a thinly disguised animism. The animistic aborigines in Taiwan (Formosa) are moving by the thousands into either Roman Catholicism or Protestantism. The striking gains in Indonesia are chiefly among the animists, although as an exception to what was happening elsewhere, some are from the Moslems. The growth in Burma is predominantly from former animists and only a few hundred are from the Buddhist majority. In India the striking gains are among the hill tribes, predominantly animist, and from the depressed millions who, while with a veneer of Hinduism, are not accepted socially into the Hindu communities and are not far removed from animism. Until the coming of Christianity, most Africans south of the Sahara were animists, Islam has made and is making some gains, but chiefly on the southern fringes of the Sahara, where contact with the Moslem North has long been in progress. On the East Coast are some small Moslem enclaves through Arab infiltration, but latterly African racialism and nationalism have been a barrier. In the Pacific Ocean the nineteenth century gains, mostly among Polynesians, former animists, are being followed by accessions from Melanesians and, in New Guinea, by conversions from the Papuans, also animists.

Even more striking and significant has been the deepening rootage of Christianity among non-Occidentals in Asia, Africa, and the islands of the sea. Superficially the Christian communities which sprang from nineteenth century missions would have been expected to be dwindling enclaves of a religion associated with the hated political imperialism from which emancipation is being attained. Many in these areas, indeed, call missions a form of cultural imperialism, still dependent on Christians from the Occident. Yet, in contrast, in leadership, in attempts to reach non-Christians, and in new forms of Christianity, these enclaves are not encysted minorities, but are vigorous and hopeful.

This "indigenization" — if that word is permissible — is marked in the Roman Catholic Church. Soon after World War I, stimulated by far-seeing missionaries, at first minorities, Rome began stressing the creation of a native clergy and appointed and consecrated bishops from among them. It has continued to do so in ever mounting numbers. With extensive funds from Europe and the United States, theological seminaries have been created and superbly equipped physically and with ample teaching personnel. Thirty years ago an apostolic delegate to Africa told the author that not in the foreseeable future would Africans be raised to the episcopate. He was happy to have African priests, but, from his standpoint, for an indefinite future they would continue to require supervision by Occidental bishops. At present, from a rapidly growing body of African priests, more than sixty have been appointed bishops and two Africans have been raised to the cardinalate. Much the same development is taking place elsewhere and in some countries began earlier than in Africa. In an attempt to acclimatize Christian worship to various cultural traditions, not only is the body of the mass being put into the vernacular, but indigenous adjuncts are also being employed, among them, in Africa, drums. For several decades encouragement has been given to Christian art in native dress.

Protestantism is seeing even more startling developments. Protestants, like Roman Catholics, are stressing an indigenous ministry. In the past

COLONIALISM AND MISSIONS

five or six years what is known as the Theological Educational Fund of several million dollars has been used to assist selected theological seminaries in several countries with buildings, libraries, and staff. Progress has been amazing, especially in India, Southeast Asia, Indonesia, the Philippines, Taiwan, Korea, and Japan. In sub-Saharan Africa a major problem has been encountered in enlisting promising young men for full academic preparation for the ministry. The demands by the governments of the newly independent states for officials is so urgent and the prestige and emoluments are so great that the majority of educated Christian youth are absorbed by them. Yet progress is being reported.

Fully as encouraging is the trend among the Protestants in Asia and Africa toward efforts for comprehensive planning and effort. Within the past ten years the East Asia Christian Conference has brought together the majority of the Protestants of South and East Asia in an effort to witness to the Gospel in that vast area. Although Protestants are small minorities they are seeking to win non-Christians. About a hundred missionaries are being sent by these churches to other areas. Thus a Filipino has gone to Iran, Filipinos to Idonesia, Koreans to several countries, and Japanese to Thailand. In sub-Saharan Africa in 1963 an All-Africa Christian Conference was held and out of it came a continuing body. The only foreign participation was at the invitation of the Africans. A few weeks earlier an all-African Christian Youth Conference met in Nairobi, and the only non-African speakers were asked by Africans.

A phase of the growing rootage of Christianity in non-Occidental peoples is the appearance of new movements with little or no impulse from the Occident. Almost all of them are sprung from Protestantism. Some hold fairly closely to historic Christianity. Some depart so widely from it as scarcely to be classed with Christianity. The largest proliferation is in Africa, and especially in South Africa. The total runs far into the hundreds. In the Philippines the *Iglesia ni Cristo* ("Church of Christ") was founded in 1914 by a Filipino who received no help from abroad. It claims to be strictly Biblical, has erected large church structures, and in the 1950s claimed 4,000,000 members—but critics estimate it has only about 100,000. The *Mukyokai* ("No Church") has enlisted several tens of thousands among the intelligentsia and professional circles in Japan. It has none of the sacraments, keeps no statistics, and centers in groups for the study of the Bible.

In some countries in nominally Christian Latin America, notably Brazil and Chile, the rapidly growing bodies of Protestants are Pentecostals of various kinds. Although sprung from contacts with North America and Europe, for the most part they are without foreign funds or personnel and are essentially an indigenous form of Protestantism. Their appeal is primarily to the underprivileged elements in the cities. They are loyal to the Bible, exalt Christ, nurture a warm religious life, and have high standards of personal morality.

Advance toward Christian unity is progressing, but in unequal and varied fashion. By "unity" is not necessarily meant organic union of denominations, although that is being seen, but, rather, that mutual love which Christ enjoined on His disciples and the witness to Him in cooperative ways. Some organic unions have come into being since World War II, among them the *Kyodan* or *Nihon Kirisito Kyodan* ("The Church of Christ in Japan"), which embraces the majority of the Protestants of that country; the Church of South India, composed of former Anglicans, Presbyterians, Methodists, and Congregationalists; and the Church of Christ in Thailand, with a strong Presbyterian nucleus. Other proposed unions are in the process of negotiation. More inclusive are the many national Christian councils which came into being after World War I and are members of the Division of World Mission and Evangelism of the World Council of Churches. These, however, do not embrace all the churches founded by Protestants. In some areas only a minority cooperate through them. The past few years have been seeing increasing fellowship between Roman Catholics and Protestants. That fellowship has chiefly taken the form of joint translations of the Scriptures.

The growing cooperation of the churches in the non-Occidental world, as in "Christendom," has progressed quite apart from any connection with the state. That is also true of the deepening rootage of Christianity outside the Occident. The only major exception—indeed, the only exception—is on the mainland of China. There, as we have said, the Communist regime has compelled the severing of all formal—and for the most part informal—ties between the Christians and the Christians of other lands. Increasingly that regime is placing difficulties on conversions, the nurture of the children of Christian parents, and other forms of church life. It has constrained Protestants to come together in the "Three Self Movement"—an ostensible attempt to enable Protestants to attain a long-cherished goal of missions: self-supporting, self-governing, and self-propagating churches—and has required Roman Catholics to break all connections with the Papacy and to set up a "Patriotic Catholic Church." The vitality of the faith is seen in the fact that the churches continue, train their clergy, and have conversions, although in diminishing numbers.

In spite of the wave of Communism and of secularism associated with the world-embracing revolution issuing from "Christendom," the influence of Christ on the planet is mounting. Some of it affects governments, but it has sprung from individuals who have sought through governments to help shape man's collective life. The movements and organizations are multiplying and are making their impress on mankind. We can here take the space to mention only three. One is the Red Cross. That organization, except in its symbol, now completely divorced from organized Christianity, was begun soon after the middle of the nineteenth century by Henri Dunant. Dunant was spiritually the child of a religious awakening in his home city, Geneva. He was active in the formation stages of the world organization of the Young Men's Christian Associations. A layman, in business, he chanced to be present at a battle in Italy and was horrified by the lack of care of the sick and wounded. A book in which he described what he had seen created a European sensation. To give more effective and continuing effort to remedy such conditions, Dunant and a group of his Swiss friends organized the International Red Cross. No other organization of similar purpose has ever sprung from any religion with such world-embracing service. Similarly the United Nations and its predecessor the League of Nations were created by men inspired and sustained by Christian faith. One of the major achievements of the United Nations, the Declaration of Human Rights, came out of the efforts by an official of the World Council of Churches. Gandhi, although not a Christian, was profoundly influenced by Christ. When he died at an assassin's hand thousands of Indians declared his was a Christ-like death, acknowledging Christ as a standard by which to measure their national hero. Gandhi's example has had global repercussions.

What does all this mean? Although seemingly a feature of the colonialism and imperialism of nineteenth century "Christian" Europe, as we have said, the missions of that era actually were more nearly independent of governments than the expansion of Christianity had been since the fourth century. They were born and sustained by the purpose assigned them by Christ himself. Because of the vigor inherent in the Gospel and because of the growing emancipation of missions from the state, Christianity has survived the liquidation of imperialism and colonialism and in the world outside "Christendom" is growing in numbers and in rootage. Missionaries from the erstwhile Christendom are still needed, both to help the churches which have sprung from the efforts of earlier missionaries and to carry the Gospel to millions still untouched by it. We are becoming aware that, because of the situation in what we have been wont to call Christendom, our missionary obligation must embrace all six continents and be really global. Because of the population explosion, especially in Asia, those who are called "Christian" are a smaller minority of mankind than they were a hundred or even fifty years ago. That, however, means not failure but challenge. If mankind be viewed as a whole — as, if they are true to their Master, Christians must see the world — Christ has never been as widely influential as he is today. His words do not give us warrant to expect that in this present age all men will accept Him as Lord and Savior, but His command is clear. We have His promise that as we seek to obey, He to whom all power has been given in heaven and on earth will be with us. In another account of His post-resurrection instructions, we are assured of power and are to be His witnesses "to the uttermost part of the earth." The assignment is His. The obligation to obey is ours. For the results, we must trust God who sent Him.

Christianity and Other Religions in a Changing World Situation

ERNST BENZ

The radical change in the religious life and consciousness of these times [1969] is so revolutionary in character that it seems to be useful to rethink the present relationship of Christianity to other religions. The radical change concerns not only the role of Christianity and of the Christian churches in the world, but also the quite unexpected renaissance of older non-Christian religions in Asia and Africa and the emergence of new religions all over the world, not to mention the spreading of a global process of secularization menancing all religions.

Since World War II, not only in the field of world politics and the intellectual development of mankind but also in the field of world religions, one is confronted by the beginning of a completely new epoch in the religious history of mankind.

With respect to the changes in the structure of Christianity in the last decades, one has first to consider a fact which has been frequently overlooked or altogether ignored by modern historians. The eighteenth and nineteenth centuries have generally been understood as centuries of progressive de-Christianization and secularization of a hitherto Christian Europe. One usually forgets that in the same eighteenth and nineteenth centuries the altogether unique world-expansion of Christianity was started precisely by the so-called secularized nations of the West. The result was that for the first time in the long history of mankind, one out of all the great religions of the world, the Christian religion, reached a worldwide extension by means of a mission to the world. The missions of both the Roman Catholic Church and the Protestant churches, which started two centuries later than the former, produced the astonishing and unexpected phenomenon of the Christian church extending throughout the world, although still menaced at the end of the sixteenth century by Islam in Eastern Europe, the Near East, North Africa, and Spain and in Central Europe under constant pressure from the East, South, and West. This was indeed a new and unanticipated development of Christianity. A man like Martin Luther, for example, in the sixteenth century took it for granted that the Holy Roman Empire would be conquered by the Turks and that European Christianity would come under Muslim rule.

In spite of some setbacks, as in China, the worldwide expansion and penetration of Christianity today is an indisputable, historical fact. In the entire history of world religions, so far as one can ascertain, and despite all dynamic missionary efforts by the non-Christian religions, never has any other world religion succeeded in extending its spiritual and social activity over the whole face of the earth. Indeed, Christianity has realized in practical terms its claim of universality by its universal expansion throughout the world.

With regard to this global expansion of Christianity, it is of the greatest significance for the present state of the Christian religion and for its future that it did not propagate the institutions, doctrines, and liturgy of any single Christian church, as was originally expressed through the Roman Catholic missions of the fifteenth and sixteenth centuries. Rather, the expansion of Christianity as a worldwide movement took place within a competitive atmosphere engendered by the older and newer Christian churches and sects. That meant—and this was very decisive—that nowhere in the world was one single Christian church or confession able to rule in an exclusive way. As a result of the spreading of the Christian mission and of the fluctuation of population connected with economic and political changes, there are no longer any countries in which men of different Christian churches are not obliged to live and work together and in which the coexistence of various churches are not a vital concern of the public and private life. Thus Christianity is represented the world over by the coexistence of different Christian churches along with different types of community and constitutional structures. This fact underlines the great significance of the ecumenical movement today. This most decisive event in the modern history of Christianity is a direct result of its global expansion and of the accompanying manifestations of ecclesiastical pluralism.

This global expansion of Christianity created a completely new situation in other respects, too. For the first time Christianity came in contact with all the other living religions of the world. Prior to the middle of the last century there were still large areas of the globe in which non-Christian religions dominated the spiritual, moral, and cultural life of their inhabitants and in which there was not real contact with or knowledge of the Christian religion. Since then a complete change has taken place. Today no religion can any longer exist in a state of "splendid isolation" and ignore the Christian religion. Yet, at the same time, there is no living religion which Christianity can ignore. The great

CHRISTIANITY AND OTHER RELIGIONS

encounter of religions, Christian and non-Christian, occurs today on a global scale. This situation is new and completely unique in the history of mankind, and it explains why the partners of this global encounter are not yet fully prepared to handle the new situation.

The inadequate preparation of the religions for their new tasks of encounter and discussion is grounded in still other reasons. This meeting began taking place very late and very hesitantly, at least from the Christian standpoint. The missionary expansion of Christianity which burst forth in the eighteenth and nineteenth centuries was closely connected with the colonial expansion of the European powers and the economic and industrial expansion of the United States. In all the colonies outside Europe, the missionary institutions, comprised of foreign missionaries as well as indigenous members, enjoyed all kinds of political and social privileges, including the privilege of military protection by the ruling colonial powers in case of persecution from non-Christian political or religious groups. At the same time, the expansion of Christianity was intimately related to Western civilization, technology, industrialization, economy, education, and law. Generally, the Christian missionaries were also, by the very nature of the situation, pioneers of Western civilization in the so-called underdeveloped areas of Asia and Africa. In all these countries exposed to Christian missionary activity, the Christian religion took the form of its European or American mother church or sect. As a result, Christian missions as a rule brought about an alienation of the baptized Asians and Africans from their traditional ways of life and thinking. Consequently, Christianization appeared, even externally, to be identical with westernization.

Under these circumstances, genuine discussion between Christianity and the non-Christian religions was rare and exceptional. The non-Christian religions were considered old-fashioned, behind the times, and below modern standards by the Christians. The general adjective connected with Buddhism, Hinduism, and Islam was "corrupt." Even scholars of history of religions considered modern Buddhism or Neo-Hinduism as "corrupt."

This strong connection between the Christian world mission, the political and economic expansion of the white man, and the spread of Western civilization has in this century been called into question for many reasons. First of all, the political system of traditional colonialism has been abandoned. All the countries of Asia and most of the countries of Africa, which were previously under one or another kind of colonial administration, have become independent sovereign states. In all these former colonies the situation which confronts the Christian mission has completely changed. The Christian congregations in the missionary areas of Asia and Africa have lost their privileged political and social status and find themselves, by and large, minorities in an environment of non-Christian religions. Indeed, they sometimes even have to fight for their right to exist.

Together with the political independence won by many Asian peoples, a surprising renaissance has taken place among the non-Christian religions. For more than a hundred years missionaries had argued that Buddhism, Hinduism, and Islam were "dead." Now, these "dead" religions have awakened to unexpected vitality. They were, as a matter of fact, never dead. During the period of colonial rule they were driven out of the positions and influences they had enjoyed as ruling state religions or national religions. But their spiritual power and authority were never driven out of the hearts of their respective believers.

Today, in the new independent states of Asia, these religions are re-establishing their old and pre-eminent position in the religious and social life and in the educational system of their respective countries. This has resulted, in many cases, in a mass re-conversion from Christianity back to the older religions of these countries, *i.e.*, to Hinduism and Buddhism.

There is also another very important cause for the striking change of the world religious situation today. The population explosion, which so troubles the politicians and sociologists of today, is directly connected not only with the standard of education and the social level of the different groups of population, but also with their religion. It has been statistically proved that the Christian population of the world has a much lower birth rate than the non-Christian. The main reason for this is that the program of responsible birth control has been developed via Christian social ethics and has been propagated especially by Anglo-Saxon Protestantism through a worldwide campaign. For most of the non-Christian religions, on the other hand, it is considered a religious duty of the parents to have as many children as possible. It is not only a command of the Old Testament: "Be fruitful and multiply and replenish the earth" (Gen. 1:28), but this command corresponds to the concept of most of the older religions. Indeed, high birth rate is thought of as a sign and proof of divine blessing. Antithetically, birth control, as propagated by the Christian West, is generally considered by Africans and Asians as an infamous, secret weapon of Western neo-colonialism, propagated with the special aim of decimating the African and Asian nations.

The increasing birth rate of the non-Christians could be overcome only by an enormous expansion of the educational activity of all Christian missionary institutions. But the increasing number of non-Christians is so great that even the strongest missionary bodies have neither the required number of qualified members nor the necessary financial support at their disposition. As a result, the Christian churches, even after strengthening intensively their missionary activity, are for the present not able to respond to the challenge of the increasing birth rate among the Asian and African countries or to become majorities in the newly developing countries of Asia and Africa where they are small minorities. Consequently, more members of the Christian churches in the young states of Asia and Africa have been forced to seek friendly coexistence with their non-Christian neighbors. This situation is completely new and is, therefore, still neglected and grossly misunderstood by most Europeans and Americans. Here, too, it is necessary to free oneself from traditional historical interpretations of the past.

The Vatican's decision to establish a special secretariat for non-Christian religions on the occasion of Vatican Council II reflects the vast change not only of the general religious situation, but also, and this to a marked degree, of the legal and constitutional status of the Christian churches in the Asian and African states. It also emphasizes the fact that the Christian churches of today no longer have anything to do with "poor pagans," but with neighbors of equal rights — political partners who, in many cases, have to decide the future existence of the Christian minorities themselves.

The obvious consequence of all this is that Christians, right in the midst of this changing situation, can no more ignore or look askance at the non-Christian religions, as has been the case in the past. Today, the Christian churches must enter into dialogue with the non-Christian religions and proceed with an honest attempt at discussion regarding intellectual and spiritual matters.

This task is all the more underscored, as since the middle of the last century, a general transformation in the religious consciousness of humanity has taken place. Until then knowledge of non-Christian religions was the exclusive property of a very few scholars in the field of Oriental languages. In the meantime, however, scholars of history of religions and of Oriental literature have been collecting and editing the sacred books of all the major world religions and bringing to the public at large the result of their findings with respect to this hitherto esoteric field of studies.

The field of history of religions is witnessing today a second enlightenment, which penetrates all social classes. This has been made possible through the use of the modern mass media of information. To this mass media belongs not only television, whereby everyone may witness directly the cult and liturgy of non-Christian religions, but also the cheap paperback editions of the sacred books of non-Christian religions, which belong today to the normal reading material of modern education. The plurality of world religions was made accessible to a broad public through movies, radio, and television as well as works of religious arts from Asia and Africa in museums throughout the world. It is possible now for all high school, college, and university students to obtain true information about Buddhism, Hinduism, and Islam from authentic primary sources.

A still more important fact is that the learned representatives of the non-Christian religions have, as a result of their academic training, accepted the methods and terminology of modern historical and textual criticism as developed in modern history of religions. Moreover, they employ now these methods themselves in criticizing Christian theology and Western civilization in defense of their own doctrines and religious way of life. Thus, even in the areas of methodology and terminology, a completely new basis for discussion has been reached, a basis which heretofore did not exist. Quite representative of this new intellectual situation are the writings of Sri Radhakrishnan, former President of the Republic of India who, in using modern methods of Western history of religions, makes an ingenious critique of Western philosophy and religion, thereby providing a modern type of Hindu apologetics. Similar attempts at a systematic critique of the Christian religion of Western civilization have also been presented by Buddhist and Moslem thinkers, especially by scholars from the numerous Buddhist universities in the countries of Southeast Asia and the Islamic universities and study centers in the Near and Far East.

Another decisive change took place in the general attitude of non-Christian religions: In previous times Christianity was the only religion which undertook a worldwide missionary activity among non-Christian religions, convinced that it was the only sufficient and definitive revelation of the one true God, Lord of Heaven and Earth. Now, however, the other world religions have commenced a worldwide mission of their own. This development is, at least to some extent, a reaction of the non-Christian religions to the onslaught of Christian missions — a revival provoked by the missionary activity of the Christian churches. The higher religions of Asia, like Hinduism and Buddhism, have rediscovered their own traditions of worldwide missionary activity and their earlier claims of universality. They have re-established their own missionary — work which is promoted by recently created world-organizations like the Mahabodhi Society, founded by Anagarika Dhammapala and the Buddhist World Federation. This missionary activity has penetrated the hitherto Christian countries of Europe and the United States, not so much by well-run missionary organizations as by a silent and unobtrusive way. Buddhist philosophy and meditation, or Hindu yoga, is practiced on a large scale in the midst of the homelands of Christian missionaries, especially among the educated classes which proved themselves accessible to the religious values of these Asian religions. There are today in England, France, and the United States numerous centers of the Hindu Ramakrishna Mission,

CHRISTIANITY AND OTHER RELIGIONS

the Vivekenanda Mission, and other modern Hindu movements, all using the most modern pedagogical methods. Still stronger is the influence of Buddhism, especially the numerous Zen centers in Europe and the United States, at least among the Hippies, as Kerouac's novel, *The Dharma-Bums*, proves.

This propagandistic encounter with the non-Christian religions of Europe and the United States is today no longer a merely academic problem reserved for specialists, ministers, and teachers of the Christian churches, but rather a problem posed for the educated layman and teacher of the humanities in the high schools and colleges. It is a task challenging the help of the scholars of history of religions.

A last important point of the changing religious world situation is that *all* religions, Christian and non-Christian, are confronted with a common pugnacious and sophisticated enemy—dialectical materialism. Dialectical materialism has propagated a non-Christian, a non-value, the "opium of the people" which hinders mankind in perceiving the true causes of its suffering and mastering its social future on this earth. It tries to deprive religion, including all forms of organized and established religions, of its influence on the cultural, social, moral, and political life of the state and the society. This dialectical materialism was originally a legitimate descendant of the philosophical development of a hitherto Christian Europe but has become in the meantine the state philosophy of the two largest communist states: the Soviet Union and Red China—both of which are powerfully influencing today in a most powerful way the political and spiritual future of Asia. Moreover, dialectical materialism is spreading not only in the communist countries in the East, but also among the intelligent young people of Africa. It is also spreading among the European and American intelligentsia, among people who perhaps do not yet accept and proclaim the methods of political revolution, but who accept at least the atheistic and materialistic interpretation of man and society and who approve the methods of the further abolition of religion.

As a result of the rise of communism as a world power with its claim to global universality and its missionary activity, Christianity, in spite of its emphatic assertion to represent the radical anthithesis to all other religions, has been forced to accept the same line of defense as all other religions. Christianity today can no longer make exclusive claim to the progress of modern sciences and techniques previously considered a monopoly of Christian civilization. For communism today is also offering the non-Christian nations the achievements of modern Western sciences and technology. They are, however, no longer connected with a religious creed but are based on a *Weltanschauung* of a mere scientific outlook. The validity of its scientific ideological, social, and scientific success.

Christianity has been launched by this development into an exceptionally difficult situation. If it continues its traditional, merely negative attitude towards the non-Christian religions, it weakens the position of religion in general without gaining any advantage for itself. On the other hand, Christianity can no longer use its heretofore most convincing argument, *i.e.,* that it opens the way to higher Western science and civilization, because communism vows to offer a much more direct approach without the detour of a new religious ideology.

Since the inception of the communist menace following World War I, some theologians like Karl Barth and his pupils tried to save Christianity from this crisis by a kind of Kierkegaardian "leap," declaring "Christianity is not a religion, but the 'crisis' of all religions." That means all religions are under the ultimate judgment of the divine word of the Gospel. This formula, however, does not help in the present complicated situation, and the younger churches, being obliged to live in a non-Christian environment, were the first to discover it. It was the great delusion of dialectical theology to believe that communism would accept a Christianity which declared itself as a non-religion and would exclude it from its general anti-religious campaign. To communist doctrine, Christianity, even after three decades of dialectical theology, is still a religion like all others. If Christian churches in communist countries ever enjoy more liberal treatment from communist governments, it will not be on behalf of a change of communist doctrine on religion, which excludes eventually the Christian religion from the general condemnation of religion, but only for practical momentary and political considerations with respect to Western Europe and the United States.

The aspect of the general change in the field of religion in the United States differs in some points from the situation in Europe because of both the geographical and political situation of Europe. Generally speaking, the influence of non-Christian religions in Europe is intellectual, limited to people of higher education and connected with the progress of comparative history of religions and comparative philosophy and psychology of religion. In the United States the spreading of non-Christian religions is directly connected with the immigration of Asians, especially Japanese and Chinese, to the West coast. The Asian immigrants brought with them their Asian religions and many Buddhist centers were established on the Pacific coast of the United States and spread from there to many other states, especially to the big cities in the East. Even after the Japanese and Chinese immigration had been stopped early in this century by special anti-immigration laws in California, Asian immigration continued in Hawaii, which recently became an American state. Thus Hawaii became the center of the Buddhist mission.

But the influence of Eastern religions in the United States is not only bound to the immigration of Asian people, it is much more closely related to the complete shifting of the center of world policy on the globe. Till the end of the Middle Ages the center of world policy was the Mediterranean Sea. Indeed, European civilization has been molded by the political, cultural, and religious influences of the nations around the Mediterranean Sea and was deeply influenced by the political, cultural, and religious structure of the Roman and Byzantine Empires. Since the discovery of America, the center of world policy has shifted from the Mediterranean Sea to the Atlantic, which has become the Mediterranean Sea between the new world of America and the colonial powers of the Atlantic coast, the Netherlands, England, France, and Spain. The whole political, cultural, and religious discussion was carried on between Christians on both sides of the Atlantic — between the Christians of the older European churches and Christians of European offspring on American soil. In this time of Atlantic-oriented world policy, an encounter with non-Christian religions did not exist in the United States as a vital factor.

In the meantime, the world policies have changed again, this time from the Atlantic to the Pacific. Since the parade of Admiral Perry's fleet in Yokohama in 1866, America has been more and more involved in the problems and troubles of the nations around the Pacific and has become a close neighbor of China and Japan, non-Christian civilizations shaped by their own religious values. For the first time the United States came in direct contact with Oriental non-Christian nations and became aware of the strong impact of their religions on their political, social, and ethical attitudes in their daily life and on the arts of these nations. So the encounter with non-Christian religions brought an unexpected religious, cultural, and political significance on all levels of public and private life.

The problem of coexistence of world religions is, therefore, a crucial and a concrete actuality. The daily news reports on cruel struggles between Muslims and Christians in the Sudan, between Muslims and Hindus in Pakistan and India, between Buddhists and Roman Catholics in Vietnam, between Muslim Hausas and Christian Biafrans in Nigeria all speak for themselves. These religious conflicts do not manifest themselves in the form of mere spiritual and intellectual controversies, but in the form of bloody, mass demonstrations, in which the religious groups are fighting against each other by means of terror and are denying each other the right to live. Some of the news seems to confirm the most pessimistic interpretations: The conflict between different religions seems to be unavoidable and, in a certain sense, seems to stem essentially from the self-assertion of established religions.

But fortunately in the last two decades it has been proved that it is really possible by a common effort to overcome the traditional and inveterated type of religious controversy. It is possible, after hundreds of years of religious wars, to engender a true coexistence, even a true cooperation, by a radical transformation of the spiritual attitudes of the Christian churches within the ecumenical movement, an encounter of churches which have persecuted each other by means of military warfare, expulsion, confiscation of property, removal of rights, and other kinds of persecution.

It seems to be the special task of today to prepare and to plan in a way similar to the Christian ecumenical movement the coexistence of the different world religions. To that effect the history of religions could contribute in a similar way as theological studies in the field of New Testament, Old Testament, and church history, and the comparative history of dogmatics and liturgy have effected the change of mind manifesting itself in the ecumenical movement among the Christian churches.

Of course the development in the area of the ecumenical movement cannot be simply transferred to the problems of coexistence of the world religions. Among the Christian churches there was in spite of all historical conflicts not only a common doctrinal "denominator," but the uniting faith in the historical person of Jesus Christ. On the contrary, there is no common denominator among the different worldreligions. Nevertheless, a new way of understanding approaching other religions is needed.

This approach to religion requires considerable knowledge and critical analysis. Every effort must be made to examine and re-examine the traditional judgments and prejudices of the different religions towards each other, to spread a better knowledge of the history and the present form of other religions, and to encourage a new attitude of mind and of good will which grants to other religions their own right of interpretation of ultimate reality and their own right of worship and prayer. Some special tasks of study with respect to this new situation include the following:

1. Studies in the field of the history of religions have been concentrated up to now, understandably, in the study of the classical forms of the great world religions. The study of religions of the world has followed certain fixed patterns. There exist certain classical forms or archetypes of the great world religions, which are understood best in their primordial form, in their original texts, in their earliest representatives of piety and doctrine, and in their oldest patterns of doctrine and worship.

But this limitation on the classical religions as "fixed patterns" ignores the fact that the religions are fluid and continue to develop in great variety and often do not comply at all with the fixed patterns.

CHRISTIANITY AND OTHER RELIGIONS

The great world religions have not been any more willing than Christianity to remain static in the same classical forms with which they initially began. They also have gone through an astonishingly diverse internal development in which many various forms and degrees of religious experience and theological exposition have found expression. All of the great Asian religions, in the same manner as Christianity, have brought forth new sects and new schools of thought in the course of their historical development and their adaptation to the various national and political structures. These sects and schools represent new forms of religious consciousness and religious ethics. This specific development, however, has not yet been sufficiently studied.

2. All the great religions have influenced each other through the ages to a great extent wherever they have come into contact with each other, and their new forms generally came forth as a consequence of such new mutual contact or controversy. After Islam had taken up a considerable inheritance from Christianity—its primitive gospels and its primitive piety and devotional forms—it entered the domain of Hinduism in the subcontinent of India and created new religious forms of expression. New forms have originated also in Hinduism. They appeared partly as reform movements, but also partly took on the character of new independent religions, like Jainism. Other new religions, like Sikhism, have arisen in India through the reaction of Brahmanism and the arrival of Islam, have gone through a multiplicity of variations and even up to the present have called into life new forms of religious experience, of religious consciousness, and of social structures, as, for example, the Soka Gakkai, an offspring of Nichiren Buddhism.

Christianity itself has in no small way contributed to this further development of the non-Christian religions. The missionary attack of Christianity has led to an intensification of activity on the part of the great non-Christian religions in Asia, and these religions have borrowed some of the methods for their own renewal from the Christian mission. Buddhism and Hinduism have partly adopted the practice of the Sunday service and have developed methods of religious eduction which are copies from Christianity. Likewise the modern Hindu and Buddhist layman and youth organizations and especially the various social institutions are influenced by the model of Christian organizations and institutions. Buddhism began more and more to rediscover the social aspect of its ethics and to found the corresponding social institutions.

But this changed attitude is not limited to the institutional side of the older religions. In New Hinduism one can observe the breaking through of a monotheistic understanding of religion, of a personalistic concept of God, of a new and positive approach to worldly reality, of a new interpretation of *tat tvam asi* in the sense of social responsibility towards one's neighbor.

The history of this mutual influence of coexisting religions on one another has not yet been studied precisely, because no institutionalized religion likes to admit the fact that it has been influenced by other religions. There are certainly many observations of mutual penetration of religious ideas and practices in the different fields of world religions, but the phenomenon itself and its significance as a basic element of better contact and deeper understanding and as a creative element in the religious history of mankind should be seen in a broader context and in its general significance.

3. Even more important, the fact is that throughout the entire history of religion, methods of practical coexistence between overlapping religions have been in effect and yet few valuable studies of this amiable side-by-side existence have been made. Thus, such studies should be elaborated upon and expanded to other successful cases of coexistence of religions. This would give the chance to see which possibilities of coexistence already have been proved, where the critical points of mutual understanding or misunderstanding are to be found, where in earlier periods of history of religion certain types of cooperation have been already practiced, which types of coexistence were already approved as possible models for the future. Which are the presuppositions under which they were established? Why did they fail? Where can the efforts be resumed today? What should be avoided today? It may well be that one of the results of such studies would be the finding that the praxis of religious coexistence is much more developed and penetrates much deeper into the strata of social life than the theologians of the single religions would be ready to admit.

4. It would be also recommendable to study, besides the classical archetypes of the great world religions, more intensively the modern forms and derivations of these religions, which traditionally are considered more or less as results of depravation and degeneration or even Westernization of the original type but evidently are not. The modern reform movements of the classical religions should be studied more. In most cases these modern reform movements are themselves the result of a direct or indirect encounter and coexistence with other religions; they generally also presuppose the influence of modern Western civilization. They are confronted with similar convergent tasks in the doctrinal field as well as in the field of personal and social ethics.

5. The fact that history of religion is dynamic becomes especially obvious by the fact that new religions are formed within the best organized working areas of the older religions, even of the Christian mission. This is the case above all in Japan, but also in South America and Africa. Besides such new religions based on new revelations, a series of religions have appeared which, like the Caodai religion in Vietnam and the Baha'i religion in the West, consciously take up doctrine and

ethics of different older religions and pretend to represent the "integration" of all previous historical religious forms, including Christianity.

These new religions also are the product of coexistence of different religions. They are amalgamating the various ideals and claims of the older religions which were not fulfilled practically by these older institutions and which now demand to be realized in modern types of religious life. This should be a special subject of studies of comparative history of religions today, considering not only the doctrinal, but also the practical side of these religions.

6. After all, it is not enough to study the special problems connected with the coexistence of world religions. The result of such studies should not be reserved to some few scholars of the history of the religions or of Oriental studies, but should be brought into the curriculum of higher education. In the present situation, scholars of the history of religions are still appreciated by a rather small public, but in the life of the universities they are playing the role of rare birds singing their tender songs on the trees, amidst the roaring of the lions and the tigers and the elephants of the natural sciences and other more powerful inhabitants of the academic community. The big problem is to introduce the result of the research work of the scholars of the history of religions into the general field of studies in the humanities.

One of the most important problems confronting the educational policy of the United States calls for the avoidance of a merely formal application of the constitutional principle of separation of church and state in the field of higher education, from which the teaching of religion was hitherto usually excluded, and the admittance of a nondenominational, phenomenological presentation of the history of religions in the framework of the humanities. This will contribute not only to deepening the knowledge of the religious roots of the different world civilizations, but also to a stronger connection and interrelation and collaboration between the different fields of studies in philosophy, history, art, anthropology, and even the natural sciences. These other fields could get some fresh inspirations from studies in the history of religions as well as contribute to their own inspiring suggestions to the further development of the study of religion in the field of higher education, and even the high schools. If ever religion is to be an essential part of the study of the humanities, then the study of religion must be integral to the academic programs of the high school and colleges.

Ecumenical Perspectives of the Vatican Declaration on Religious Liberty

A. F. CARRILLO DE ALBORNOZ

I. INTRODUCTION

The Central Committee of the World Council of Churches at its meeting held in Geneva in February, 1966, considering the Declaration on Religious Liberty promulgated by the Second Vatican Council, made among others the following statements:

> We welcome with satisfaction the Vatican Council's Declaration on Religious Liberty with its clear statements proclaiming full civil religious freedom, both individual and collective, for everybody, everywhere .... We are encouraged by the fact that there is now a large measure of agreement among all the churches in these matters .... We hope that on the basis of their statements on Religious Liberty, from now on all the Churches will be able to take a common stand for the full application of the principle of religious liberty in all parts of the world and in all possible action to ensure the observance of this principle.

On its part the Commission on Religious Liberty of the World Council of Churches thought that in view of this Vatican Declaration it would be useful to investigate carefully the following questions: (1) What are the specific areas in which there is substantial agreement between the Vatican Declaration and the current ecumenical insights as they have been expressed in the official statements of the World Council of Churches?; (2) Is there the possibility of establishing the text of a statement which could be accepted by both the Roman Catholic Church and the ecumenical movement and which, therefore, could be presented as the common or universal Christian insights concerning religious liberty?

In line with these suggestions the Secretariat on Religious Liberty of the World Council of Churches has tried to put together the fundamental agreements between the Vatican Declaration and the World Council's official statements and on the basis of these agreements to draft a project of common Christian insights concerning religious liberty.

II. Fundamental Agreements Between the Vatican Declaration and the WCC Official Statements Of Religious Liberty

1. GENERAL PRINCIPLE AND UNIVERSALITY OF THE RIGHT TO RELIGIOUS FREEDOM

Vatican II. "This Vatican Council declares that the human person has a right to religious freedom. This freedom means that all men are to be immune from coercion on the part of individuals or of social groups and of any human power, in such wise that no one is to be forced to act in a manner contrary to his own beliefs, nor is anyone to be restrained from acting in accordance with his own beliefs, whether privately or publicly, whether alone or in association with others, within due limits." (No. 2)

World Council of Churches. "The rights of religious freedom herein declared shall be recognized and observed for all persons without distinction as to race, colour, sex, language, or religion, and without imposition or disabilities by virtue of legal provision or administrative acts." (Amsterdam Declaration)

"We regard this right as fundamental for men everywhere . . . . The civil freedom which we claim in the name of Christ must be freely available for all men to exercise responsibility." (New Delhi Statement)

2. INDIVIDUAL RELIGIOUS FREEDOM

Vatican II. "Man is not to be forced to act in a manner contrary to his conscience. Nor, on the other hand, is he to be restrained from acting in accordance with his conscience, especially in matters religious." (No. 3)

"The right to this immunity continued to exist even in those who do not live up to their obligation of seeking the truth and adhering to it and the exercise of this right is not to be impeded . . . ." (No. 2)

"The social nature of man . . . itself requires that he should give external expression to his internal acts of religion: that he should share with others in matters religious: that he should profess his religion in community." (No. 3)

"A wrong is done when government imposes upon its people, by force or fear or other means, the profession or repudiation of any religion, or when it hinders men from joining or leaving a religious community . . . .

"Government is to see to it that equality of citizens before the law, which is itself an element of the common good, is never violated, whether openly or covertly, for religious reasons. Nor is there to be discrimination among citizens." (No. 6)

World Council of Churches. "Every person has the right to determine his own faith and creed . . . . Every person has the right to express his religious beliefs in worship, teaching and practice, and to proclaim the implications of his beliefs for relationships in a social or political community." (Amsterdam Declaration)

"Freedom to manifest one's religion or belief, in public or in private and alone or in community with others, is essential to the expression of inner freedom." (New Delhi Statement)

"Religious liberty includes freedom to change one's religion or belief without consequent social, economic, and political disabilities. Implicit in this right is the right freely to maintain one's belief or disbelief without external coercion or disability." (New Delhi Statement)

"Every person has the right to associate with others and to organize with them for religious purposes. This right includes freedom to form religious organizations, to seek membership in religious organizations, and to sever relationship with religious organizations." (Amsterdam Declaration)

3. RELIGIOUS FREEDOM OF THE FAMILY

Vatican II. "The family . . . has the right freely to live its own domestic religious life under the guidance of parents. Parents, moreover, have the right to determine, in accordance with their own religious beliefs, the kind of religious education that their children are to receive. Government, in consequence, must acknowledge the right of parents to make a genuinely free choice of schools and of other means of education . . . ." (No. 5)

World Council of Churches "The right to determine one's belief is limited by the right of parents to decide sources of information to which their children shall have access . . . . Freedom of religious expression is limited by the rights of parents to determine the religious points of view to which their children shall be exposed . . . ." (Amsterdam Declaration)

4. FREEDOM OF RELIGIOUS ASSEMBLY AND ASSOCIATION

Vatican II. "The solid nature of man and the very nature of religion afford the foundation of the right of men freely to hold meetings and to establish educational, cultural, charitable and social organizations, under the impulse of their own religious sense." (No. 4)

"A wrong is done when government imposes upon its people, by force or fear or other means, the profession or repudiation of any religion, or when it hinders men from joining or leaving a religious community . . . ." (No. 6)

World Council of Churches. "Every person has the right to associate with others and to organize with them for religious purposes.

"This right includes freedom to form religious organizations, to seek membership in religious organizations, and to sever relationship with religious organizations." (Amsterdam Declaration)

5. CORPORATE RELIGIOUS FREEDOM

Vatican II. "Religious communities rightfully claim freedom in order that they may govern themselves according to their own norms, honor the Supreme Being in public worship, assist their members in the practice of the religious life, strengthen them by instruction, and promote institutions in which they may join together for the purpose of ordering their own lives in accordance with their religious principles.

"Religious communities also have the right not to be hindered, either by legal measures or by administrative action on the part of government, in the selection, training, appointment, and transferral of their own ministers, in communicating with religious authorities and communities abroad in erecting buildings for religious purposes, and in the acquisition and use of suitable funds or properties.

"Religious communities also have the right not to be hindered in their public teaching and witness to their faith, whether by the spoken or by the written word. . . . [and] from freely undertaking to show the special value of their doctrine in what concerns the organization of society and the inspiration of the whole of human activity." (No. 4)

World Council of Churches. "Every religious organization . . . has the right to determine its policies and practices for the accomplishment of its chosem purposes . . . . including the right to determine its faith and creed; to engage in religious worship, both public and private; to teach, educate, preach and persuade; to express implications or belief for society and government.

"To these will be added corporate rights which derive from the rights of individual persons, such as the right: to determine the form or organization, its government and conditions of membership; to select and train its own officers, leaders and workers; to publish and circulate religious literature; to carry on service and missionary activities at home and abroad; to hold property and to collect funds; to co-operate and to unite with other religious bodies at home and in other lands, including freedom to invite or to send personnel beyond national frontiers and to give or to receive financial assistance; to use such facilities, open to all citizens or associations, as will make possible the accomplishment of religious ends." (Amsterdam Declaration)

"Freedom to manifest one's religion or belief . . . includes freedom to teach, whether by formal or informal instruction, as well as preaching with a view to propagating one's faith and persuading others to accept it . . . freedom to practice religion or belief, whether by performance of acts of mercy or by the expression in word or deed of the implications of belief in social, economic and political matters, both domestic and international." (New Delhi Statement)

6. UNIVERSAL DUTIES CONCERNING RELIGIOUS FREEDOM

Vatican II. "The care of the right to religious freedom devolves upon the whole citizenry, upon social groups, upon government, and upon the Church and the other religious communities, in virtue of the duty of all toward the common welfare, and in the manner proper to each." (No. 6)

World Council of Churches. "The recognition of the inherent dignity and of the equal and inalienable rights of all members of the human family requires that the general standard here declared should be given explicit expression in every aspect of society . . . . It is the corresponding obligation of governments and of society to ensure the exercise of these civil rights without discrimination. It is for the churches in their own life, and witness . . . to play their indispensable role in promoting the realization of religious liberty for all men." (New Delhi Statement)

7. PARTICULAR TASK OF THE CIVIL AUTHORITY

Vatican II. "The function of government is to make provision for the common welfare . . . religious acts . . . transcend by their very nature the order of terrestial and temporal affairs. Government . . . would clearly transgress the limits set to its power, were it to presume to command or inhibit acts that are religious." (No. 3)

"All the more is it a violation of the will of God and of the sacred rights of the person and the family of nations, when force is brought to bear in any way in order to destroy or repress religion, either in the whole of mankind or in a particular country or in a definite community.

"The protection and promotion of the inviolable rights of man ranks among the essential duties of government. Therefore government is to assume the safeguard of the religious freedom of all its citizens, in an effective manner, by just laws and by other appropriate means . . . .

"Government is to see to it that the equality of citizens before the law, which is itself an element of the common good, is never violated, whether openly or covertly, for religious reasons. Nor is there to be discrimination among citizens."

"If, in view of peculiar circumstances obtaining among peoples, special civil recognition is given to one religious community in the constitutional order of society, it is at the same time imperative that the right of all citizens and religious communities to religious freedom should be recognized and made effective in practice." (No. 6)

World Council of Churches. "We affirm that all men are equal in the sight of God and that the rights of men derive directly from their status as the children of God . . . .

"It is presumptuous for the State to assume that it can grant or deny fundamental rights. It is for the State to embody these rights in its own legal system and to ensure their observance in practice." (Amsterdam, Report on The Church and the International Disorder)

"The nature and destiny of man . . . establish limits beyond which the government cannot with impunity go . . . ." (Amsterdam Declaration)

"We hear of legislation which makes Christian evangelism virtually impossible in certain areas. We hear of discrimination against Christians and of material advantages being offered them if they will adopt the dominant religion of the country. We also are concerned about the trend in certain nations for the State to assume responsibility for the organization of religious life, which is the province of religious communities and not of the State." (The Eastern Christian Conference, Bangkok, 1949)

"The freedom essential for the Church can in fact exist both in churches organized as free associations . . . or as established churches in an organic or otherwise special connection with the State. If, however, this connection should result in impairing the Church's freedom to carry out its distinctive mission, it would then become the duty of its ministers and members to do all in their power to secure this freedom, even at the cost of disestablishment." (World Conference on Church, Community, and State, Oxford 1937, Report on The Universal Church and the World of Nations)

8. MODERATING NORMS
Vatican II. "The right to religious freedom is exercised in human society: hence its exercise is subject to certain regulatory norms . . . . In the exercise of their rights, individual men and social groups are bound by the moral law to have respect both for the rights of others and for their own duties toward others and for the common welfare of all. Men are to deal with their fellows in justice and civility.

"Furthermore, society has the right to defend itself against possible abuses committed on the pretext of freedom of religion. It is the special duty of government to provide this protection. However, government is not to act in arbitrary fashion or in an unfair spirit of partisanship. Its action is to be controlled by juridical norms which are in conformity with the objective moral order.

"These norms arise out of the need for effective safeguard of the rights of all citizens and for peaceful settlement of conflicts of rights, also out of the need for an adequate care of genuine public peace, which comes about when men live together in good order and in true justice: and finally out of the need for a proper guardianship of public morality.

"These matters constitute the basic component of the common welfare: they are what is meant by public order. For the rest, the usages of society are to be the usages of freedom in their full range: that is, the freedom of man is to be respected as far as possible and is not to be curtailed except when and insofar as necessary." (No. 7)

"However, in spreading religious faith and introducing religious practices everyone ought at all times to refrain from any manner of action which might seem to carry a hint of coercion or of a kind of persuasion that would be dishonorable or unworthy, especially when dealing with poor or uneducated people . . . ." (No. 4)

World Council of Churches. "The freedom with which Christ has set us free calls forth responsibility for the rights of others. The civil freedom which we claim in the name of Christ must be freely available for all men to exercise responsibly." (New Delhi Statement)

"Each person must recognize the rights of others . . . .

"Everyone ought to take into account his higher self-interests and the implications of his beliefs for the well-being of his fellowmen.

Social and political institutions should grant immunity from discrimination and from legal disability on grounds of expressed religious conviction, at least to the point where recognized community interests are adversely affected.

"Freedom of religious expression is . . . . subject to such limitations, prescribed by law, as are necessary to protect order and welfare, morals and the rights and freedoms of others.

"The right to associate with others . . . is subject to the same limits imposed on all associations by non-discriminatory laws.

"The community has the right to require obedience to non-discriminatory laws passed in the interest of public order and well-being. In the exercise of its rights, a religious organization must respect the rights of other religious organizations and must safeguard the corporate and individual rights of the entire community. (Amsterdam Declaration)

"Witness is corrupted when cajolery, bribery, under pressure or intimidation is used — subtly or openly — to bring about seeming conversion . . . . Churches are called to show such restraint in their exercise of religious liberty as to avoid the causing of offense, and in the fullest possible measure to respect the convictions of other churches." (New Delhi, Report on Proselytism)

III. DRAFT OF COMMON CHRISTIAN INSIGHTS CONCERNING RELIGIOUS LIBERTY

1. General Principle of the Right to Religious Liberty. The human person has the right to religious freedom. This freedom means that, in religious matters, all men, alone or in community with others in the public or private, are to be immune from coercion on the part of individuals or of social groups and of any human power.

Religious liberty is to be recognized and observed for all persons without distinction as to race, colour, sex, language or religion, and without imposition of disabilities by virtue of legal provisions or administrative acts.

This freedom remains also in favour of those who do not comply with the moral duties dictated by their conscience.

This right of the human person to religious liberty is to be recognized in the legal order of society in such a way that it is considered a real civil right. We regard this right as fundamental for men everywhere.

2. Individual Freedoms. Every person has the right not to be impeded in freely determining his own faith and creed.

Every person has the right to express his religious beliefs, in public or in private and alone or in community with others, in worship, teaching and practice; to communicate with others in religious matters; to profess his own religion in a community; to proclaim the implications of his beliefs for relationships in a social or political community.

Religious liberty includes freedom to change one's religion or belief, or to maintain one's belief or disbelief without external coercion or disability. Therefore, a wrong is done when government imposes upon its people, by force or fear or other means the profession or repudiation of any religion, or when it hinders men from joining or leaving a religious community.

The civil authority must provide that the legal equality of all citizens be never violated on grounds of religious beliefs, openly or occultly, and that no discrimination takes place among them.

3. Religious Freedom of the Family. The family has the right freely to live its own domestic religious life under the guidance of the parents.

The parents have the right to decide sources of information to which their children shall have access, and to determine the religious point of view to which their children shall be exposed.

4. Freedom of Religious Assembly and Association. Every person, moved by his own religious convictions, has the right freely to assemble with others and to organize with them for religious purposes, forming associations for furthering educational, cultural, charitable or social ends.

This right includes freedom to form religious organizations, to seek membership in religious organizations, and to sever relationship with religious organizations.

5. Corporate Religious Freedom. Every religious organization has the same religious freedom as the individual person, particularly the right to determine its faith and creed; to engage in religious worship, both public and private; to teach, educate, preach and persuade; to communicate freely beyond national frontiers; to express implications of belief for society and government; to show the special value of its own doctrine both for the ordering of society and for the guildance of all human activity.

To these will be added certain specific corporate rights, which derive from the rights of individual persons, such as the right: to govern themselves according to their own norms, and to determine its policies and practices for the accomplishment of their chosen purposes; to assist their members in the practice of the religious life, strengthen them by instruction, and promote institutions in which they may join together for the purpose of ordering their lives in accordance with their religious principles; to select, train, appoint and transfer their own ministers; to carry on service and missionary activities at home and in other lands; to communicate, co-operate and unite with other religious bodies at home and abroad; to erect religious buildings; to hold property and to collect funds.

6. Universal Observance of Religious Liberty. The recognition of religious freedom as an equal and inalienable right of all members of the human family requires that the general standard here declared should be given explicit expression in every aspect of society. Therefore, the task of taking care of this right of religious freedom belongs to the citizens, to the social bodies, to the civil authorities, and to the church and the other religious bodies, each in their own manner.

7. Particular Task of the Civil Authorities. The proper finality or task of the civil authority is to care for the temporal common good. Religious acts, by their own nature, transcend the earthly and temporal order. Therefore, the public authority must be held to be exceeding its proper limits if it presumes to direct or to impede religious activities.

It is all the more contrary to the will of God and the sacred rights of the person and of the family of nations when force is brought to bear in any way to abolish or curtail religion itself, whether throughout the world, or in a certain area or in a particular religious group.

The promotion and protection of the inviolable rights of man is a paramount duty of every civil authority. The civil power must therefore, by means of just laws and by other proper means, effectively undertake the protection of the religious freedom of all citizens. The civil authority must provide that the legal equality of all citizens be never violated on grounds of religious beliefs, openly or occultly, and that no discrimination takes place among them.

8. Moderating Norms for the Exercise of Religious Freedom. The right of liberty in religious matters is exercised in human society, and is therefore subject to certain moderating norms on the moral as well as on the legal level.

On the moral level, the moderating criterion is the moral principle of personal and social responsibility. Individuals and social groups have the moral duty to take account of the rights of others and of their duties towards others and towards the common good of all. Their conduct towards everyone must be governed by justice and humanity. In virtue of this moral duty every corruption of the religious witness should be avoided, namely every manner of action which would seem to savour coercion, or persuasion that is dishonest or that is less fair. The moderating norms dictated exclusively by moral criterion should never be coercively imposed by the civil authority.

On the civil and legal level, the moderating criterion is the need of the civil society of protecting just public order against possible abuses committed on pretext of freedom of religion. The just public order implies the effective safeguard and peaceful settlement of rights on behalf of all citizens; the adequate care of genuine public peace consisting in ordered communal life with true justice and the due responsibility for public morality. The civil authority may moderate the exercise of religious freedom only for the necessary protection of these three public goods, which constitute the just public order.

Moreover, the civil power has to provide this protection, not arbitrarily, or with any favoured treatment given to one side, but according to legal provisions which are in conformity with the objective moral order.

Besides, the habit of complete liberty must be preserved in society, in accordance with which a man's liberty should be given all possible recognition and only curtailed when and as necessary.

Embracing a Socialist Vision: The Evolution of Catholic Social Thought, Leo XIII to John Paul II

JOHN J. MITCHELL, JR.

John Paul II used the occasion of his first detailed statement on economic justice (*On Human Work*, 1981) to point the way to a new relationship between Roman Catholic social thought and socialism. While the primary intent of the encyclical was to examine the nature of human work and the rights of workers, John Paul took this opportunity to call for the transformation of the present-day economic order. In the context of this challenge, he outlined the possibility of a new collaboration between Catholic thought and socialism as a means of overcoming the serious limitations of the collectivist economies of the East and the capitalist economies of the West.[1] In light of the new directions, the pope proposed that there may be a tendency among Catholics to look upon his economic thought as a fundamental break from the teachings of his predecessors. This judgment is hasty and unfounded. Although John Paul breaks new ground, his thought must be interpreted within a papal tradition characterized by an increasing openness to humanistic socialism in recent years.

The interaction between Catholic thought and socialism has important religious, political, and economic implications. Although there has been obvious intellectual development during the past century in the Church's attitude toward socialism, this shift has often been ignored or minimized, especially in the West. As a result, many Catholics, including members of the hierarchy, have been unable to move beyond the Church's attitude toward socialism as it was articulated almost a century ago. This is unfortunate for a number of reasons. First, many members of the Church are denied an

---

1. Michael Harrington, "The Search for Transcendental Common Values," *Cross Currents* 31 (Winter 1981-82):407-22.

appreciation of the dynamic nature of Catholic social thought. Second, an outdated understanding of the Church's attitude toward socialism can frustrate collaboration between Catholics and socialists.[2] Finally, the positions espoused by John Paul are interpreted as a rejection of traditional Catholic thought when they actually represent another stage of a development long underway in the Church. These serious limitations will have to be overcome if Catholics hope to participate more fully in the developing dialogue with socialism in the world today.

One difficulty in analyzing the development of Catholic thought toward socialism is that the term "socialism" has been used in a variety of ways throughout the tradition. Leo XIII and Pius XI associated socialism with any economic program that fosters class conflict and the abolition of private property; John XXIII and Paul VI, however, distinguished between various forms of socialism. They recognized that some forms of socialism reject class conflict and the absolute abolition of private property. John Paul II distinguishes between "collectivism" and forms of socialized ownership that seek to protect the rights and dignity of the person. There is no *definition* of socialism in the Catholic tradition. There are *definitions* of socialism that have emerged as the Church has interacted with historical forces in society. In the following, various understandings/definitions of socialism that have emerged in the history of modern Catholic social thought will be noted.

Paralleling the intellectual development in the Church's attitude toward socialism, the history of the twentieth century tells the story of various historical movements that have embodied a collaboration between Catholics and socialists. This study will not address itself to these developments. These movements, however, do provide an interesting narrative of the interaction that has occurred.[3] This study will also look at the development of the Church's attitude toward socialism as reflected in the writings of Leo XIII to John Paul II. While references have been included to studies that clarify the central thesis, this essay relies primarily on the author's interpretation of papal teachings. Although this approach is limiting in one sense, it allows for a specific look at the development that has been underway for decades in the Catholic Church.

---

2. Dorothy Solle, "Christians for Socialism," *Cross Currents* 25 (Winter 1975):419-34; and Joseph Holland, "Marxism Deserves a Catholic Hearing," *New Catholic World* (September-October, 1975).
3. Gregory Baum, *The Social Imperative* (New York: Paulist Press, 1980).

Leo XIII to Paul VI

LEO XIII

In 1891, Leo XIII condemned the social program advocated by the Socialists without qualification. In *Rerum Novarum* he wrote:

> The Socialists, exciting the envy of the poor toward the rich, contend that it is necessary to do away with private possessions of goods and in its place to make the goods of individuals common to all, and that men who preside over a municipality or who direct the entire state should act as administrators of these goods. They hold that such a transfer of private goods from private individuals to the community can cure the present evil through dividing the wealth and benefits equally among citizens.[4]

Leo finds in the program of the Socialists a rejection of the Church's traditional defense of the right of private property.[5] Their advocacy of violence to achieve their social objectives is likewise unacceptable. Neither can be tolerated: "Inasmuch as the Socialists seek to transfer the goods of private persons to the community at large, they make the lot of all wage earners worse, because in abolishing the freedom to dispose of wages they take away from them by this act the hope and the opportunity of increasing their property and of securing advantages for themselves."[6]

In *Rerum Novarum*, Leo is unable to envision a socialist program founded on a commitment to protect the rights of the individual and foster the common good. History does not provide him with appropriate models. Leo associates freedom for the individual with increased property and securing personal advantages so that dependency on higher authorities will be minimized. The historical realities of his time would not allow Leo to consider the possibility that at times freedom for the individual may best be secured through a system of socialized ownership, planning, management, and distribution of economic resources. Nowhere in *Rerum Novarum* does one find evidence of Leo's willingness or ability to distinguish between those collectivist forms of ownership pledged to class conflict and violence and other socialist models known to society today.[7] Again history denied him this opportunity. He was obliged to leave this task of refining the Church's attitude toward socialism to his successors and the future.

---

4. Leo XIII, *Rerum Novarum* #6, *Two Basic Social Encyclicals* (New York: Benzinger Brothers, 1943), 7.
5. John F. Cronin, *Social Principles and Economic Life* (Milwaukee: Bruce, 1964), 243-68; and Jean-Yves Calvez and Jacques Perrin, *The Church and Social Justice* (Chicago: H. Regnery, 1961), chap. 9.
6. *Rerum Novarum* #9, *Two Basic Social Encyclicals*, 7.
7. John A. Ryan, *The Church and Socialism* (Seattle: Washington University Press, 1919), 1-34

PIUS XI

The publication of *Quadraquesimo Anno* (1931) by Pius XI, forty years after *Rerum Novarum*, did not present the occasion for any substantive developments in the Church's attitude toward socialism. Pius XI reaffirmed the teaching of Leo XIII and elaborated on it.[8] He indicated, however, that socialism has undergone some changes since 1891. As he declared, "Socialism, against which our Predecessor, Leo XIII, had especially to inweigh, has since his time changed no less profoundly than the forms of economic life."[9]

These changes, however, are not sufficient to provide the occasion for a substantive dialogue between socialism and Catholic thought. "Socialism, which could then be termed almost a single system and which maintained definite teachings reduced into one body of doctrine, has since chiefly split into two sections, often opposing each other and bitterly hostile, without either one however abandoning a position fundamentally contrary to Christian truth that was characteristic of Socialism."[10]

Pius pointed out that some of the moderate forms of socialism share some of the same goals that are of abiding interest to the Church and they may even be willing to relinquish their advocacy of class struggle and the absolute abolition of private property. Although he recognized these changes, his openness to socialism in whatever form went no further.[11] He counseled them to break "their ties with socialism" and align themselves with the Church, which offers a fuller understanding of social life. Without this change the possibility of mutual collaboration in the social project is impossible.[12] "Whether considered as a doctrine, or as historical fact, or a movement, Socialism, even after it has yielded to truth and justice on the points we have mentioned, cannot be reconciled with the teachings of the Catholic Church because its concept of society is utterly foreign to Christian truth."[13] Pius was unable to establish a dialogue with the moderate forms of socialism because he was unwilling to recognize or accept the pluralistic nature of the social project. Because the moderate forms of socialism approach the issue of private property and property rights from a perspective different from the Church, they are unacceptable. Just as Leo XIII had to

---

8. Joseph Husslein, *The Christian Social Manifesto* (Milwaukee: Bruce, 1931).
9. Pius XI, *Quadragesimo Anno* #111, *Two Basic Social Encyclicals*, 161.
10. Ibid.
11. John F. Cronin, *The Christian Social Order*, 2d rev. ed. (Milwaukee: Bruce, 1964), 95-98.
12. Jean-Yves Calvez, *The Social Thought of John XXIII* (Chicago: H. Regnery, 1964), 66-67.
13. *Quadragesimo Anno* #117, 165-67.

leave to Pius XI the task of distinguishing between the various forms of socialism, Pius XI left to his successors the task of better understanding both the reality of pluralism and its application to economic life.

PIUS XII

Pius XII did not issue a major encyclical on economic justice during his pontificate. On this basis alone one can argue that he did not make a major contribution to the dialogue between Catholic thought and socialism, nor did he suggest any new avenues of development. Pius XII confined himself to defending and clarifying the positions outlined by Leo XIII in *Rerum Novarum* and *Quadragesimo Anno* by Pius XI.[14]

Pius recognized the dangers inherent in both the laissez-faire capitalism and the collectivist economies of his day. His ability to find within socialist programs a viable option to the laissez-faire capitalism that he criticized was certainly undermined by his obligation to reject National Socialism as a state socialism of ideological virulence capable of destroying Christendom. "We must prevent the human individual as well as the family from allowing themselves to be drawn into the abyss whither the socialization of every phase of life tends to cast them into a process of socialization at the completion of which the terrifying image of Leviathan would become a horrible reality."[15] He feared that developments within Western capitalism would make various socialist movements more attractive to the masses.

> Anyone who pushes social policy further in this direction must come against a limit for there will arise a danger that the working class will in its turn make the mistake made by capital which took the disposition of the means of production away from the personal responsibility of private owners, whether individuals or companies, and transferred it to anonymous or collective managers, principally in very large enterprises. A socialist mentality fits itself well to this kind of situation which cannot but occasion disquiet in whomever knows the fundamental importance of the right of private ownership as a means of encouraging initiative and feeling responsibilities in economic matters.[16]

Here it should be noted that the socialist movements of the day took on many different faces. One only need think about the emerging socialism in Sweden, that of the suppressed Communist and Social Democratic Party in Germany, and the socializing trends evident

---

14. John F. Cronin, "The Social Economics of Pius XII," *Catholic Mind* 49 (October 1951): 674-93.
15. Calvez, *The Social Thought of John XXIII*, 2.
16. Pius XII, "Speech to the Congress of Social Studies," *AAS* 42 (3 June 1950):486.

within Roosevelt's New Deal in the United States. Pius found himself in the midst of a dilemma that he was unable to resolve. While, on the one hand, he was willing to enter into a dialogue with the socialist movement of his day, he was convinced, on the other hand, that conditions within Western capitalism would result in more and more people embracing a socialist alternative. Pius certainly was not unaware of the priests and ministers in Europe working with various socialist groups in France and elsewhere to save the Continent from Nazism. Although he refrained from detailing a plan for a new economic order, Pius saw the need for an alternative that would overcome the inadequacies of both the socialist models of his day and the abuses of capitalism. Because he was restricted by a pre-*aggiornamento* theological imagination, he was unable to go further. He left to Pope John XXIII the task of identifying the possible areas of collaboration between socialism and Catholic thought. As John XXIII and the Second Vatican Council embraced a commitment to scrutinize "the signs of the times" new directions emerged.

JOHN XXIII

What developments took place between 1931 and 1961 to occasion the possibility of a new dialogue between Catholic social thought and socialism? Three significant developments can be identified. First, John XXIII clearly recognized that the world he had been called to minister to had changed profoundly from the world of Leo XIII, Pius XI, and Pius XII. In *Mater at Magistra* (1961), he wrote: "Just as contemporary circumstances seemed to Pius XII quite dissimilar from those of an earlier period, so they have changed greatly over the past twenty years."[17] Second, John recognized the emergence of a new pluralism in addressing social, economic, and political questions.[18] Presumably, some moderate forms of socialism could be considered. Third, John was aware that local churches were engaging in dialogue with some socialist movements and collaborative programs were developing. The reader can certainly appreciate that John was surely aware of the movements that had been germinating within several "Catholic" countries in the Communist bloc including Yugoslavia, Czechoslovakia, Hungary, and Poland.

What specifically did John XXIII contribute to the Church's attitude toward socialism? In *Mater et Magistra*, he appears to endorse a traditional hard line by simply reaffirming the teaching

---

17. John XXIII, *Mater et Magistra* #46, in *The Gospel of Peace and Justice*, ed. Joseph Gremillion (Maryknoll, N.Y.: Orbis, 1976), 152.
18. John F. Cronin, *The Social Teaching of John XXIII* (Milwaukee: Bruce, 1963).

of his predecessors. He wrote: "Nor may Catholics, in any way, give approbation to the teachings of the socialists who seemingly profess more moderate views. From their basic outlook it follows that it is directed solely to temporal welfare; that since the social relationships of men pertain merely to the production of goods human liberty is excessively restricted and the true concept of social authority is overlooked."[19]

Less than two years later, however, John broke new ground in the Church's attitude toward socialism. In *Pacem in Terris* (1963), he said: "It must be borne in mind, furthermore, that neither can false philosophical teachings regarding the nature, origin and destiny of the universe and of man be identified with historical movements that have economic, social, cultural and political ends, not even when these movements have originated from those teachings and have drawn and still draw inspiration therefrom."[20] With evident caution and obvious diplomacy, John moved beyond the unqualified censure of socialism that had characterized the thought of Leo XIII, Pius XI, and Pius XII. John built a new bridge in the Church's developing dialogue with socialism. He rejected the monolithic understanding of socialism that characterized the thought of his predecessors. The "signs of the times" called for new approaches and new alternatives in the quest for economic justice. Pluralism could no longer be denied. In the end, however, he left to his successors the task of further clarifying and elaborating on the new attitudes toward socialism that he proposed.

PAUL VI

Pope Paul VI accepted the challenge extended by John XXIII.[21] In an Apostolic Letter entitled *Octogesima Adveniens* (1971), commemorating the eightieth anniversary of *Rerum Novarum,* Paul continued the Church's developing dialogue with socialism. His first concern was to affirm the distinction that John XXIII established between "false philosophical teachings" and "current historical movements." Paul quoted at length from *Pacem in Terris* and then suggested a new attitude toward socialism within the Church. "Some Christians are today attracted by socialist currents and their various developments. They try to recognize therein a certain number of aspirations which they carry within themselves in the name of faith.

---

19. John XXIII, *Mater et Magistra* #34, in *The Gospel of Peace and Justice*, 150.
20. John XXIII, *Pacem in Terris* #159, in *The Gospel of Peace and Justice*, 235-36.
21. Philip Land, "The Social Theology of Paul VI," *America* 140 (12 May 1979):392-94.

They feel that they are part of that historical movement and wish to play a part within it."²²

Paul displayed his own skills at moderation. He pointed out that some socialist movements instill the imagination of men with new hopes of building just societies. He cautioned his listeners, however, against a false and dangerous idealism. "Careful judgment is called for. Too often, Christians attracted by socialism tend to idealize it in terms which, apart from everything else, are very general: a will for justice, solidarity and equality."²³

Paul admonished Christians to proceed cautiously in making those choices and commitments that are acceptable.

Distinctions must be made to guide concrete choices between various levels of expression of socialism: a generous aspiration seeking for a more just society, historical movements with a political organization and aim, and an ideology which claims to give a complete and self-sufficient picture of man. Nevertheless, these distinctions must not lead one to consider such levels as completely separate and independent. The concrete link which, according to the circumstances, exists between them must be clearly marked out. This insight will enable Christians to see the degree of commitment possible along these lines, while safeguarding the values, especially those of liberty, responsibility and openness to the spiritual, which guarantees the integral development of man.²⁴

What specific contributions did Paul VI make in the Church's attitude toward socialism? Surely it can be said that Paul recognized new opportunities for dialogue and collaboration between Catholics and socialists. The unqualified condemnation of socialism that characterized earlier Catholic social thought was overcome. A continuing "aggiornamento" created new possibilities. Paul introduced new distinctions within socialism enabling Catholics to identify with many of the social goals of socialists. For Paul, the possibility of collaboration between Catholics and socialists was linked to those forms of socialism that seek to promote the whole development of the human person.

Actually, Paul went beyond merely suggesting collaboration between Catholics and socialists. While reluctant to carry his thoughts to their full implications, Paul's was a vision that could contemplate a Christian socialism. Although unwilling to associate the social goals of the Church with any specific socioeconomic program, a shortcoming of the Church in the past, Paul envisioned Christians who not only collaborate with socialists but Christian socialists who find in the program of socialists a means of achieving the social goals long identified by the Church. Paul made a significant

---

22. Paul VI, *Octogesima Adveniens* #31, in *The Gospel of Peace and Justice*, 499.
23. Ibid., 499-500.
24. Ibid.

contribution to the dialogue between Catholics and socialists. While building on the earlier work of John XXIII, he left to Pope John Paul II the task of identifying in greater detail the potential relationship between Catholics and socialists.

The Contribution of John Paul II

Pope John Paul II has already made a significant contribution to the dialogue between Catholic social thought and socialism. In part this contribution is linked to his call for the creation of a new international economic order capable of protecting both individuals and the common good. The present economic order characterized by a purely materialistic orientation and "a consumer attitude uncontrolled by ethics" undermines the foundations of human freedom and the dignity of the person. In the *Redeemer of Man* (1979), John Paul wrote:

So widespread is the phenomenon that it brings into question the financial, monetary, production and commercial mechanism that, resting on various political pressures, support the world economy. These are proving incapable either of remedying the unjust social situations inherited from the past or of dealing with the urgent challenges and ethical demands of the present. By submitting man to tensions created by himself, dilapidating at an accelerated pace material and energy resources, and compromising the geophysical environment, these structures unceasingly make the areas of misery spread, accompanied by anguish, frustration and bitterness.[25]

A simple adjustment of the present economic order will not be sufficient to remedy the fundamental inequities that exist. Structural and systemic changes are required. This alone will offer the hope of rooting out the social evil that exists and creating a more just economic order. He said: "This difficult road of the indispensable transformation of the structures of economic life is one on which it will not be easy to go forward without the intervention of a true conversion of mind, will and heart. The task requires resolute commitment by individuals and peoples that are free and linked in solidarity."[26]

In his recent encyclical *On Human Work* (1981), John Paul clarified the foundations of his own economic thought and contributed to the dialogue between Catholic thought and socialism. Catholic social teaching has never developed in a vacuum. Certainly this is true of papal encyclicals. John Paul II's own contributions to the relationship between Catholic thought and socialism emerged out of not only his theological vision but also the social, political,

---

25. John Paul II, *Christ, The Redeemer of Man*, #16, Origins 8 (22 March 1979):635.
26. Ibid., 636.

economic, and cultural matrix of his homeland, Poland. His lifelong attempt to come to terms with Marxist thought and its implications for a contemporary Catholic social ethic provide the foundations of his own economic thought. He established "the dignity of the worker" as the center of his analysis of the economic question today. The quality of justice accorded the worker and those affected by economic activity is the key to analyzing the moral legitimacy of economic systems and structures. John Paul focused on the human person as the "subject" of work.

> Man has to subdue the earth and dominate it, because as the "image of God" he is a person, that is to say, a subjective being capable of acting in a planned and rational way, capable of deciding about himself and with a tendency to self-realization. As a person, man is therefore the subject of work. As a person he works, he performs various actions belonging to the work process; independently of their objective content, these actions must all serve to realize his humanity, to fulfill the calling to be a person that is his by reason of his humanity. The principal truths concerning this theme were recently recalled by the Second Vatican Council in the constitution "Gaudium et Spes" especially in Chapter 1, which is devoted to man's calling.[27]

Through work, men and women participate in the unfolding of God's plan for all humanity. In addition to this, human work is designed to serve the full development—the personalization—of the worker. Human work should contribute to the well-being and dignity of the worker. It should foster the growth of fundamental human goods, such as respect for oneself, concern for others, freedom, creativity, and self-determination.

This way of understanding the nature of human work—directed primarily to the well-being of the worker—has often been frustrated. This was especially the case at the outset of the industrial age when the worker was treated as a commodity, a "thing." Conditions have changed since that time, as John Paul pointed out; however, the danger always remains that the worker will be treated as an "object." Evidence of this pattern of dehumanization is apparent today and it has found legitimation in certain economic ideologies. "The danger of treating work as a special kind of 'merchandise' or as an impersonal 'force' needed for production (the expression of 'work force' is in fact in common use) always exists, especially when the whole way of looking at the question of economics is marked by the premises of materialistic economism."[28] John Paul called into question the moral legitimacy of any economic system that results in the degradation of the worker. This is the cornerstone of his analysis.

---

27. John Paul II, *On Human Work* #6, in *Proclaiming Justice and Peace*, ed. Michael Walsh (Mystic, Conn.: Twenty-Third Publications, 1984), 280.
28. Ibid., #7, 281.

He recognized that every economic system must be evaluated on the basis of its ability to care for the dignity of the human person both as an individual and as a member of the community. This criteria takes precedence over the defense of any abstract principle.

An appreciation of John Paul's attitude toward property and property rights is essential if the reader is to understand his attitude toward socialism today. Historically, many Catholics have claimed an absolute incompatibility between Catholic thought and socialism solely on the basis of the position espoused by various socialists towards private property and property rights. This need not be the case. In speaking to the issue of property rights within the Catholic tradition, John Paul espouses a position fundamental to Catholic social thought, yet often ignored or dismissed by those who look to Catholic thought as a justification for Western capitalism. In *On Human Work*, John Paul wrote: "Christian tradition has never upheld this right [private property] as absolute and untouchable. On the contrary, it has always understood this right within the broader context of the right common to all to use the goods of the whole of creation: the right of private property is subordinated to the right to common use, to the fact that goods are meant for everyone."[29]

John Paul could not have been clearer in presenting his position on the question of private property rights. While the Catholic tradition continues to defend the right of individuals to own private property, especially to the extent it is necessary for self-determination, this right is not without limitations. Private ownership of capital must be directed to the service of the common good. If, contrary to this purpose, it frustrates the well-being of the common good, as is often the case today, private ownership is without moral justification according to Catholic teaching.

To this point, two important contributions by John Paul to a better understanding of the economic question today have been noted. These contributions, indirectly at least, provide the opportunity for his dialogue with moderate forms of socialism today. First, the moral legitimacy of any economic system must be evaluated from the perspective of its impact on the dignity of the individual and the well-being of the common good. These two goods must always be considered. Second, the moral legitimacy of private ownership is defended to the degree that such ownership serves the common good. When it fails to do this, the moral justification for private ownership is seriously eroded.

What additional contribution has John Paul made to the dialogue

---

29. Ibid., #14, 292.

between Catholic thought and socialism? Understandably, John Paul does not contend, in light of the grave deficiencies of Western capitalism or Eastern collectivism, that a moderate socialism is the only viable economic alternative today. A careful reading of *On Human Work* indicates that he believes that greater worker participation in the policy-making processes within capitalist economies can represent an important contribution to protecting the individual and nourishing the common good. To some degree, this development may reduce the danger that either impersonal or centralized bureaucracy will usurp the legitimate rights of workers and endanger the common good.

This is not the only acceptable response to the economic injustices of the present time. John Paul recognizes that at times, under specific historical conditions, even the growth of worker-controlled industries will need to be balanced by either public authorities or quasi-public authorities, which can play a crucial role in protecting the interests and rights of all the members of society. This balance—and the economic model it represents—can serve as a corrective both to the rigid individualism of Western capitalism and the impersonalism of Eastern collectivism. The former, while proclaiming to protect the rights of the individual, all too often undermines the common good, while the latter, claiming to enhance society as a whole, negates the legitimate right of the individual.

In advocating the need for greater worker participation in the management and ownership of capital, John Paul upholds the principle of subsidiarity long defended by the Catholic tradition. In advocating the need, at times, for public authorities to exercise various economic functions in the service of the common good, John Paul upholds the principle of socialization defended by the Catholic tradition.[30] To this point he says: "In consideration of human labor of common access to the goods meant for man, one cannot exclude the socialization, in suitable conditions, of certain means of production."[31] When the socialization of economic activity will best serve to protect both the individual and the common good, this course of action is acceptable. In speaking about the proper socialization of economic activity, John Paul certainly does not have in mind the collectivist economies of the Soviet bloc that deny the proper participation of the worker in the economic life of society as is evident in Poland today. He introduces important distinctions. "Merely converting the means of production into state property in

---

30. Gregory Baum, "John Paul II's Encyclical on Labor," *Ecumenist* 20 (November/December 1981):1-4.
31. John Paul II, *On Human Work* #14, in *Proclaiming Justice and Peace*, 292.

the collectivist systems is by no means equivalent to 'socializing' that property. We can speak of socializing only when the subject character of society is ensured, that is to say, when on the basis of his work each person is fully entitled to consider himself a part owner of the great workbench at which he is working with everyone else."[32] Only those forms of socialized ownership that will protect the fundamental rights of the individual could be acceptable. Every socialized model must be judged against the "personalist" argument that John Paul sets forth.

> The economic system itself and the production process benefit precisely when these personal values are fully respected. In the mind of St. Thomas Aquinas, this is the principle reason in favor of private ownership of the means of production. While we accept that for certain well-founded reasons exceptions can be made to the principle of private ownership—in our time we even see that the system of socialized ownership has been introduced—nevertheless the personalist argument still holds good both the level of principle and on the practical level. If it is to be rational and fruitful, any socialization of the means of production must take this argument into consideration. Every effort must be made to ensure that in this kind of system also the human person can preserve his awareness of working "for himself." If this is not done, uncalculable damage is inevitably done throughout the economic process, not only economic damage but first and foremost damage to man.[33]

In conclusion, the following is a summary of the economic principles articulated by John Paul II, which either directly or indirectly indicate the openness of contemporary Catholic social thought to the moderate forms of socialism emerging in the world today. John Paul's thought set the stage for even more imaginative developments in the years ahead.

First, respect for the dignity of the individual and sincere attentiveness to the common good in economic affairs are the twin measures against which the moral legitimacy of each and every economic system must be judged.

Second, the primary responsibility of Catholic economic thought is not to endorse any specific economic system but rather to defend consistently the fundamental moral principles that warrant support and implementation in economic life.

Third, the Church's defense of private property must be understood as subordinate to its teaching that the goods of the earth must serve the needs of all God's children.

Fourth, the principle of subsidiarity, applied to economic life, can enhance the rightful participation of the worker in the economic life of society.

---

32. Ibid.
33. Ibid., 15.

Fifth, the principle of socialization, as applied to economic life, accepts and recognizes the need for the socialization of the means of production when this model of economic life can best serve to protect the rights of the individual and the common good.

Finally, the "personalist" principle, the foundation of John Paul's economic thought, must be the cornerstone of economic life and activity. Preservation of this principle calls for the creation of an economic model that overcomes the grave deficiencies of the collectivist economies of the East and the capitalist economies of the West.

Implications for the Future

The development of Catholic economic thought from Leo XIII to the present is challenging indeed. While it reflects a consistent tradition in terms of the principles and values it upholds and defends, the application of these principles to concrete historical circumstances has resulted in new emphases during the past century. This is clearly evident when one examines the present-day attitude of Catholic economic thought toward socialism in its moderate form. A number of important implications flow from the ongoing dialogue between socialism and Catholic thought. The following summary is not exhaustive. It does, however, outline the premises upon which future developments will rest.

1. A commitment to protecting the dignity and rights of the worker (labor and management) in concert with nourishing the common good has moved to the center of the Church's understanding of the economic question today. Defending the rights of the worker takes precedence over the defense of any particular economic system or philosophy.

2. Today, the Church claims neither the competence nor the right to invest itself in the defense of any historically conditioned economic system or philosophy. Pledging itself to scrutinize "the signs of the times," the Church accepts the primary responsibility of proclaiming those moral principles that are fundamental to economic justice.

3. The Church recognizes today that the economic question is first and foremost international in nature. Global interdependence and the gross inequities in the distribution of economic resources create a moral imperative for the redistribution of economic goods in accordance with established moral principles.

4. Catholic economic thought, as a dimension of the Church's pledge to scrutinize "the signs of the times" in the light of the Gospel, is dynamic in nature and subject to ongoing development. While

the foundational moral principles remain constant, their application varies in accordance with historical, cultural, social, and political conditions and circumstances.

5. The Church's defense of private property cannot be equated with a defense of Western capitalism as if it represented an embodiment of Catholic economic philosophy. The recent harsh criticism of the economic philosophy of the West contradicts any such claims.

6. The traditional defense of private property, a hallmark of Catholic economic thought, must be balanced by the Church's traditional insistence that economic goods serve the needs of the common good. Accordingly, in concrete economic activity, guaranteeing the basic economic rights of the needy takes precedence over defending the economic privileges of the affluent.

7. Catholic teaching distinguishes between the right of private property in terms of fundamental human needs, i.e., food, shelter, clothing, education, and so forth, and the right of private property when the goods accumulated are far in excess of what is reasonably required to meet basic human needs according to time and circumstances. Surplus goods should be placed in the service of the common good.

8. Socialism, in principle, is no longer anathema in the mind of the Church. The Church's commitment to scrutinize the "signs of the times" has led to a new appreciation of the truth, which can be found in some forms of socialism today.

9. Today, Catholic teaching recognizes "socialism" as a pluralistic reality and rejects the legitimacy of a wholesale condemnation of this historically conditioned approach to economic life. The attitude toward socialism reflected in Catholic social thought prior to John XXIII has been overcome.

10. Catholic economic thought is not incompatible with those economic models, socialist in design, which seek to regulate the production of economic goods, so long as this activity does not violate the legitimate rights of the individual.

11. The Church's historical concern that centralized economic planning will inevitably undermine the rights of the individual has been balanced today by the Church's growing concern about the enormous power of transnational capitalism. This alarming development has increased the Church's appreciation for the legitimate role that public authorities can play in economic affairs.

12. Catholic economic thought today recognizes that the complex and varied conditions in the world may create circumstances whereby a socialized model of economic life may prove to be the best means

for protecting the rights of the individual as well as the common good.

13. The Church's historical defense of the principle of subsidiarity in economic life has been balanced today by the principle of socialization. This development has enabled the Church to adopt a more comprehensive attitude toward economic pluralism, and to reinterpret its principles of economic justice accordingly.

14. The dialogue between Catholic social thought and socialism will continue in the years ahead, creating new possibilities for collaborative action in light of the "the signs of the times" and the quest for economic justice within the world community.

Conclusion

The interaction between Catholic papal teaching and socialism from Leo XIII in 1891 to the present has been dynamic in nature. No single rubric can be used to interpret the development that has taken place during the past century. Many of the factors that have contributed to this interaction have been indicated here. Others remain to be analyzed. The Church's response to socialism throughout the past century has been shaped by a genuine fear that the socialist path in its many guises would be detrimental to the individual and by a limiting defensiveness which restricted the ability of papal teaching to embrace a more open-minded attitude toward socialism. A major consequence of this decision has been the creation of a distinct impression that the Church, not withstanding protestation to the contrary, has formed a strategic alliance with neo-capitalism. Gary MacEoin has identified the problem:

What I am saying, if I understand myself, is that the Church continues to hanker after an ahistorical role. It lives a myth, modelling attitudes and behaviors in a series of preconceptions of reality, not on the reality expressed in the signs of the times. But all of us, including the Church, are in history, and history, as I have tried to explain, imposes concrete choices to each era. Our socio-economic choices today are, I submit, limited to two: capitalism and socialism. I am aware of the spectrum into which each system is divisible, particularly the latter, but the basic option takes priority. Today, the Church verbally rejects both systems, though with different practical consequences. Vested interests and centuries of not always edifying cohabitation have created a fellow feeling for the devil it knows.[34]

If this author's interpretation of *On Human Work* is accurate, and if Pope John Paul II's third encyclical is read in concert with his other statements on economic justice, one can fairly conclude that the pontiff from Poland has brought modern papal teaching

---

34. Gary MacEoin, "Forming a Catholic Conscience on Social Questions," *Cross Currents* 25 (Summer 1975):196.

into a new arena. Pope John Paul II's openness to a credible reading of "the signs of the times" and his willingness to endorse a strategic morality for economic justice lifts papal teaching to a new height and offers new opportunities for dialogue and collaboration with those forms of socialism that struggle to nourish the well-being of the individual and the community.

Papal teaching from Pope John XXIII to Pope John Paul II does not in itself represent a singular vehicle for forming a Christian social conscience on economic questions. Nonetheless, beginning with John XXIII, a tremendous shift has been under way culminating at this time with the publication of *On Human Work*. Christians of both the First World and the Third World who seek guidance in matters pertaining to economic justice now have available to them a tradition that is willing to wrestle with the practical realities and injustices of the present world order. The "reality" level of papal teaching with respect to socialism has been enriched appreciably. One can only hope that a pilgrim Church will remain open to further developments in the years ahead.

The Orthodox Churches on Church-State Relations and Religious Liberty

JOHN S. ROMANIDES

Apart from the pre-Constantinian era of church history, the areas conquered by Islam, and the modern situation under the rule of militant atheism, the Orthodox churches show a very strong preference for church-state unity and have even been somewhat over-accused of submission to the state, especially by those who try to apply Latin problematics in dealing with this question.

Within the Roman Empire, the Latin churches were involved in the very same church-state relations as the Greek churches, until the barbarian invasions gave occasion to the papacy to revolt against the Roman Empire by accepting the status of a vassal feudal kingdom of the Frankish Empire. The actual result of this arrangement was the enslavement of the church to powerful secular interests, since the election of pope and king of Papal States became one identical event, and since the election of bishops was generally put into the hands of the kings of Europe. In order to liberate the papacy and the churches of the West from secular interests, strict clericalism and papo-caesaristic theories were evolved, which, however, proved in the long run much more successful on paper and in the imagination of pious Catholics and some Protestants than in practice. There are still [1965] alive many members of the last generation to witness the centuries-old veto power exercised over papal elections by the Emperors of the Holy Roman Empire and Austria.

Aside from the so-called radical reformers, the Reformation churches also showed strong tendencies to unite church and state. In America, pluralism and secular humanism made it necessary to follow the lead of the free churches in developing church and state separation in order to guarantee religious liberty and to make possible civic cooperation for the common good. Besides this American concern for religious liberty, there is the missionary concern for the freedom of prosyletizing activities within those countries and societies which treat such enterprises as a form of foreign aggression. Then there is the weaker concern for the religious liberty of the "other" religious minorities in general.

An historical description of Orthodox church-state relations and religious liberty is beyond the scope of this article. Rather an attempt will be made to give a general outline of those Orthodox theological, and especially ecclesiological, principles which may indicate why certain directions in Orthodox church-state relations prevailed in history, and what an ideal and consistent Orthodox position could be if it were ever really possible for principle to become the norm in such relations.

I

Within Greek patristic thought there is no room for theories concerning *natural law* in terms of physical, social, and moral laws being copies of eternal and immutable forms in the mind of God. The existence of transcendental immutable universals according to which everything is and ought to be patterned is flatly rejected by the Orthodox Patristic tradition, which is neither Platonic nor mystic. There is, according to Orthodox belief, no similarity whatsoever between the uncreated and the created. Creation is neither a copy of immutable forms, nor is it grounded in the divine nature, which transcends the very category of Being. Creation is grounded rather in the divine will, which is not a form, idea, or universal. It is not to be equated with ontology, nor is it a static immutability in any predestinarian sense. God is both actuality and potentiality, and at the same time He is radically beyond both. Creation is therefore not a copy of something beyond itself, but rather it is unique in itself and not necessarily identical with itself at different stages of its history and development. It is impossible, therefore, to ground physical, social, and moral forms in supposedly eternal and immutable forms and laws, since forms belong only to the created realm of existence, whose very nature is determined by motion and change, not because of any fall from immutability, but because created so by God.

It is clear from such presuppositions that it is impossible to take analytical observations concerning nature and man as they are and project them into an imagined transcendental realm of changeless norms and thereby claim that the physical, moral, and social forms as they now exist, or once existed, or will exist, are the will of God because patterned according to immutable divine ideas. The will of God they might certainly be in a given situation, but not because copies of immutable realities. Also the will of God is not a static pattern, but encompasses history, evolution, and change.

The basis for the Orthodox approach is the revelation of God's glory to the patriarchs, prophets, apostles, and other saints of the church. It is through this revelatory experience that it becomes known that between God and creation there is and can be no similarity, that God is neither form, nor shape, nor chaotic being, that God can neither be conceived nor imagined by the human intellect and imagination. It is this revelation to the saints of both Old and New Testaments which breaks the back of the mythological and philosophical understandings of the gods of ancient and modern paganism and philosophies which approach the divine always in terms of man's needs and curiosities. Since this revelation of the saints of both the Old and New Testaments is transconceptual and supra-intellectual and supra-sentient, it is expressed by its recipients in symbols which are infallibly valid for those who have not seen God, and yet have in faith accepted the witness of those who have. But these symbols cannot be used as tools by those who have not received revelation for the attainment of a conceptual knowledge of God. God is radically beyond human categories and can be known undistortedly only by those to whom He reveals Himself. Yet in this very act of revelation God remains a hidden mystery to be witnessed to in human categories, but never defined.

The abyss between this understanding of revealed religion and natural religions generally is apparent. It becomes even more apparent when one takes seriously into consideration the fact that the relationship established between God and the prophets, apostles, and other saints is completely non-utilitarian, and therefore one of true friendship whereby one does not seek his own. Because of this relationship the saints have boldness towards God and can even argue and contend with God about the salvation of others (Gen. 18:22-32; Exod. 5:22-23; 8:8; 32:11-14; 32:30-32; 33:7-10; Rom. 9:3). God and the saints are involved in a relationship which transcends the categories of utilitarian, happiness-seeking love. This love which does not seek its own is known by revelatory experience and not by definition or analysis of the normal human situation. It is a mystery of union with the glory of God which transcends normal human relations based on sense, reason, and rational self-interested calculation. It is because of this revelation, made exceedingly clear in the Incarnation, that the Orthodox Fathers understood human destiny not in terms of the exhaustion or fulfillment of human potentiality by the attainment of actuality in a Platonic or Latin type of beatific vision, whereby immutability and changelessness and motionlessness and satisfaction of all intellectual desires are presented as perfection, but rather in terms of an historical process of perfection which will never end and in which motion and change toward ever higher reaches of glorification will become the norm.

Thus from the Orthodox doctrines of God and creation it is clear that natural religion, natural theology, and natural law are not completed by revelation or some supernatural theology, but rather are radically transformed. If St. Paul says that the Law of Moses had only a pedagogical significance, how much more must one say as much for what some call natural moral law.

Within the Orthodox tradition, however, one does not find any opposition between law and grace, or Old and New Testaments, or between an old period of enmity toward God and a new period of reconciliation. Grace, glorification, and reconciliation exist already in the Old Testament and were shared by the friends of God, the patriarchs and prophets (the glorification of Moses is the prime example). Now as then, not all baptized in the sea and in the cloud (I Cor. 10:1ff) are friends of God and partakers of the grace of glory. The friends of God in the Old Testament as well as those of the New Testament period by grace transcend the need of law. But now as then there are those who need the law by which to live because they are not friends of God. There are the *slaves* who do the will of God because of *fear* of eternal damnation and there are the workers or *hirelings* who do the will of God because of the profit of the *reward* of salvation. Their motivation is not that of a *friend*, because it is utilitarian.

In contrast to the legalism of the Latin tradition, the Orthodox never developed theories concerning merits, satisfaction, purgatory, and supererogatory works. The slave and the hireling work hard for their salvation, but their works are accepted by God, not because He deems them meritorious, but only because God is compassionate and wants the salvation of all. Actually, even the friend of God has neither merit nor extra merit, because he is only performing his duty as a human being when by grace he transcends the realm of utilitarian relations. Also in Orthodox theology there was never any question of works becoming meritorious because of any baptismal grace which makes man agreeable and acceptable to God. God already loves even the devil and all who are going to be eternally damned. Augustine's doctrines of original sin in terms of inherited guilt and of predestination in terms of God loving and dying for only those whom He has predestined for salvation were never known in the East. Salvation is not a satisfaction of a divine justice, but liberation from death, sin, and the devil.

Also the reward-and-punishment structures of Latin theology were unknown in the East. Salvation could not become a matter of God's moving the will to good works whose unmerited merit earns the beatific vision. Nor was damnation understood as a divine decision not to give irresistible grace so that man justly receives his real merit due to the inherited guilt of Adam. In the Greek Patristic tradition both damned and glorified will be saved. In other words both will have the vision of God in His uncreated glory, with the difference that for the unjust this same uncreated glory of God will be the eternal fires of hell. God is light for those who learn to love Him and a consuming fire for those who will not. The reason for this is not that God has any positive intent in punishing, but that for those who are not prepared properly, to see God is a cleansing experience, but one which does not lead to the eternal process of perfection. Being a Christian, therefore, is not to attain to the reward, which in a real sense will be common to all, but of being prepared so that the reward will not in fact lead to the perfect stagnation of an immutable bliss. In a certain sense the Platonic and Latin beatific vision is similar to the Orthodox understanding of hell.

It follows from all that has been said thus far that Orthodox Christians have been aware of God's love for those within and without the church. No one can claim to have a monopoly on God's love because of membership in any religious group or because of any special piety. The saints who are friends of God know this better than anyone else. Yet, on the other hand, no one can afford to be indifferent to the question of salvation because of confidence in the divine love.

This universal love of God together with the fact that true Christian faith is a free response to God's grace makes it imperative that Orthodox Christians not only tolerate other religious groups, but also recognize and guarantee their human rights to religious and civil liberties. It is a fact that *not one Father or saint of the Greek Patristic tradition ever proposed the death penalty for heretics*, as happened with the Roman Catholic and some Protestant traditions. Social and political disabilities, however, have been applied at various times in history by Orthodox governments against religious groups considered politically or socially dangerous.

The idea that religious liberty is necessary for the expression of the inner Christian freedom of faith is from an Orthodox point of view absolutely wrong. Religious liberty is no doubt a human right and a wonderful thing to have, if this be the will of God in any given situation, but martyrdom is after all one of the best and in many cases the highest expression of one's inner Christian freedom. To remain faithful in one's love of God in the face of persecution or any kind of suffering and to be willing to forego one's own salvation and well-being for that of others is an expression of non-utilitarian love or inner Christian freedom.

It remains to relate the general presuppositions thus far described to Orthodox presuppositions concerning the doctrine of the church in order to examine the church's relations and attitudes toward extra-church social and political realities. The leading idea in Orthodox ecclesiology is that the church is the New Israel, the New Jerusalem, and the New Zion, the people and nation of God. The patriarchs, prophets, apostles, and other saints are members of an identical group of elite witnesses to the glory of God, and the living leaders of the faithful. The very foundation of Orthodox ecclesiology is the fact that, in Christ, God has extended His kingdom or reign (*basileia*) to the dead so that the church is now composed of the saints of all ages. They are in a permanent way already sharing in the victory of Christ over death, or in what is called the first resurrection, and are awaiting the final consummation. That aspect of the church comprised of the saints of all ages has been established by the victory of Christ over the devil, death, and sin in such wise that "the gates of Hades (death) shall not prevail against it." The baptized this side of death are also sharing in this first resurrection, but not in any final and guaranteed manner, since they can still be defeated by sin and the devil through inattention that may quench the Spirit. The saints before and after the incarnation are in the lives of the Orthodox living guides and actual members of Orthodox society. The church, therefore, is the body of Christ, the Israelitic nation of God, composed of the saints of all ages and Christians of all places. Local congregations are not part of the church universal, but identical with the church universal. In Christ, the entire catholic church of saints of all ages and all places is present in and identical with each local congregation nourished by the life of love centered in Eucharistic worship. Therefore each worshipping congregation is related to other congregations not by a common participation in some superstructural organization higher than itself, but by an identity of existence in Christ. By baptism and faith an individual is born into the body of Christ which is at once the local congregation and the church universal, but he remains alive and increases in this body of Christ by participation in the community life of love centered in Eucharistic worship and communion. A person is born into the family of God and stays in it because he is fed by the corporate life of this same family of God, the body of Christ.

Thus a person does not become a member of the body of Christ, the church, once for all, just as a child does not continue to live simply because it is once born. There is no life in Christ apart from the corporate love within the local congregation, manifested in and formed by Eucharistic worship and communion. It is for this reason that the canons of the Church call for the excommunication of those who do not participate in Eucharistic worship and communion. Thus according to the canons of the period of the early Councils, baptism and the corporate Eucharistic worship and communion were, although certainly not guarantees, at least visible signs or indications of continuous participation in the body of Christ.

Therefore for Orthodox Christians every gathering of the local congregation for Eucharistic worship and communion is an anticipation of the final eschatological event. By their love for each other, they gather together and continue to participate in the victory of Christ over sin, death, and the devil, or by their lack of love and unworthy communion (St. Paul) put themselves under judgment.

It is obvious, so it seems, from the points thus far made that this primitive Christian universalism which still survives as the very essence of Orthodox ecclesiology has nothing in common with such understandings of unity as are based on local or universal centralization. Since the fullness of the body of Christ, the church of all ages and all places, is manifested in and one with the local congregation gathered in the same place, and since the local congregations are related to each other by an identity of existence in Christ, the church cannot be identified with the boundaries of nations, denominations, or the papacy. Even at the local level, the church is not simply the local society nominally connected by cultural background to the church. The gathered community *is* the church in process of becoming the church and those who gather unworthily and those who do not gather are not members of the church. In Orthodoxy neither baptism nor predestination can be guarantees of continuous participation in the body of Christ. Only Christ and the struggle to fulfill His commandment to love by the power of grace as expressed in corporate communion are such guarantees.

II

On the basis of the theological principles enumerated above, the following remarks which bear on the topic of church and state may be made.

The Orthodox Church is theologically not committed to any special form of political institution, culture, or society. Actually she is more oriented toward the desert (Abraham, Moses, Elijah, St. John the Baptist, Christ, St. Paul [Gal. 1:17-24; 2:1], the desert Fathers), but at the same time committed to do everything possible to sanctify, as much as possible, society, culture, political institutions, and nature.

At the same time Orthodox Christians are committed to a Eucharist-centered self-definition which is central to the doctrine that the church as the body of Christ is a *universal nation* which exists within many nations without being identified with any one or group of them. The church has a right to be legally recognized as such, and not merely as one private association among many.

The inner life of the church is not or is not supposed to be governed by the norms of society at large. What is natureal (e.g. utilitarian love) outside the church may be accepted as a legitimate principle for human life in general, but is transformed by grace within the lives of those who truly believe in Christ into a love which does not seek its own.

The happiness-seeking-love of so-called natural man is not satisfied but rather transformed by the grace of God.

The fact that Christian spirituality manifests itself in the lives of Christians at different levels, means that the immature spiritually are in need of the law. The Orthodox, therefore, accept the rule of law as something positively good both within the church and outside the church. It is not a necessary evil but a positive pedagogical means of fulfilling the will of God for society and the church at certain spiritual levels. The higher or lower degree of the law's approximation to perfection depends not on its conformity to immutable archetypes, but rather on its proximity to selfless love and the will of God for man in any given situation.

The Orthodox understanding of divine love means that one cannot believe that he has a special claim on God's love because of membership in any special church or society. There is a real equality between God's love for the saved and the damned, for the rich and the poor, for the healthy and the sick, and for the powerful nation and the weak nation. This means that one cannot pride himself over others because he is a member of any special church, class, society, race, or nation. One must, therefore, treat those outside his own group in realization of this.

In seeking to do the will of God rather than the will of men, an Orthodox Christian is not exchanging mutability and motion for an immutable and motionless happiness in a transcendental world of immutable truths. In other words, Christian love is not a love for the changeless in contrast to a love for the transient. Rather it is in its first stages a self-seeking love which by grace is being transformed into a love which does not seek its own and which in the end loves God, man, and nature equally.

This means that history is, in Orthodox thought, part of the eternal plan of God, and not just a stage for the accumulation of such divine favors as will lead beyond history into a timeless eternity. When this significance of history and eternal motion toward ever-higher reaches of perfection is coupled with the realization of God's equal love and concern for extra-ecclesiastical society, one can understand the attitudes of Orthodox Christians toward the world.

The Augustinian way of thinking in terms of the world and the church as two conflicting cities is an impossibility in Orthodox theology. An Orthodox Christian could go along to some degree in agreeing about the work of the devil in and out of the church, but to transport this into the realm of God's love for one and hatred for the other, or to inject the Augustinian dualistic contrast between mutability and immutability, and to allow this to influence the church's attitude toward the secular state, is out of the question. Even the worst barbarian state is loved no less than the church by God. This does not mean, however, that the church must passively condone an unjust state and simply tell its people to grin and bear it. The fact that God loves a murderer as much as He loves a saint does not mean that the murderer should be left alone and not punished. Although the church is not committed dogmatically to any form of government, she is committed to order, justice, and the general welfare of society. In most cases, the church can be expected to do no more than accept society as it is and to do everything possible to influence it for the better. The characteristic attitude of the Orthodox toward the state is willingness to cooperate without compromising dogma and inner spiritual freedom for the general good of society. In exceptional circumstances Orthodox leaders have supported revolutionary movements against injustice and have and are serving as political leaders when called upon to do so by the people.

According to the theological presuppositions enumerated above, religious freedom must be recognized as an inalienable factor of human existence and is so declared by the church. This is guaranteed not only by the fact that faith must be a free response to God's revelation, but even more so by the fact that those with faith have no special claim on the love of God. Church-state separation from an Orthodox viewpoint is theologically guaranteed by the above mentioned definition of the church as the gathered community.

However, the overwhelming majority of citizens of a state may at times become at least nominal members of the church even as a gathered community, and in such cases the temptation exists to be not so faithful to one's church's dogmatic principles, and to contribute to the privation of the full religious liberty of minority groups.

In this respect, Orthodox history has been greatly determined by the union of Christian sacramental universalism with the universalism of the Roman Empire. The church as the new Israelitic nation of God became identical with the citizens of Rome. In this situation, political ideologists became very much concerned with making Roman universalism and Christian sacramental universalism coterminous.

However, the Greek churches of the Roman Empire never confused Imperial universalism with church universalism. The elements of Roman administration were built into canon law, but never elevated to the status of dogma. In contrast to this, the Latin churches lent themselves to the expansionist designs of the Franco-Germanic Empire, and bishops became in practice feudal vassals of the kings and only in theory vassals of the pope. The pope theoretically claimed for himself the relation the emperor already had with his vassal bishops. The papal centralization which evolved out of this was justified on a convenient exegesis of scripture and elevated to dogma.

The Greek churches could never evolve a centralized church administration not only for dogmatic reasons, but also because the feudal political theories of medieval Latin Christianity never existed in the Eastern Roman Empire where Roman law and administrative forms prevailed till the final collapse of the Empire in the fifteenth century. Besides this, the basic structure of church administration was already established long before Constantine. The self-determination of bishops and congregations grouped into provincial synods was an established fact, and in one form or another has remained so throughout the history of the Orthodox churches.

It is impossible to try to apply the church-state categories arising out of the conflict between caesaropapism and papocaesarism with medieval Latin Christendom to the Greek churches of the Roman Empire. Those who do so usually fail to take into consideration the administrative structure of the Orthodox churches and interpret an East Roman emperor's interest in the election of the bishop of the capital city as a general interference in the election of bishops. There is no doubt that the emperors showed an interest in the election of bishops of the capital cities, but the provincial bishops were elected without state interference. Exactly the opposite was true in the Latin West.

Basically there are two types of episcopal groupings within the Orthodox Church, autocephalous ones and autonomous ones. An autocephalous grouping is one in which the presiding bishop and the bishops of the province or diocese are elected by the clergy (and laity) and ordained by the bishops of the same province or diocese. An autonomous grouping is one which elects and ordains its own provincial bishops and elects its presiding bishop, but does not ordain its presiding bishop whose ordination is supervised by the presiding bishop of the autocephalous church under whose surveillance the autonomous grouping exists. As a rule presiding bishops are bishops of the capital cities of provinces or nations, and as such have a primacy of honor and are the presidents of the local provincial or national synods. It is very important to note that the many autocephalous and autonomous provincial and diocesan synods of the Roman Empire existed within one political administrative complex, and when one takes seriously the fact that the emperors concerned themselves with the election of only bishops of capital cities (usually Rome and New Rome or Constantinople), the suggestion that there was a general caesaropapism becomes groundless.

The observations in this brief article have been offered as an outline guide to the theological foundations of Orthodox attitudes to church-state relations and religious liberty and are not intended to be taken as a systematic and definitive statement on the subject.

The Nemesis of Christian Antisemitism[1]

A. ROY ECKARDT

One could describe and celebrate Christian friendship and even love for Jews in past and present, but this would be wholly different from the subject at hand. I write as a committed Christian and churchman who is also concerned for objective historical scholarship.

The long history of evil treatment of the Jewish people at the hands of Christians means that a certain tension lurks beneath any meeting between Christians and Jews. Those who find psychological conflict unbearable may offer the following advice to speakers and leaders at such encounters: "Do not call attention to the guilt of the one side for what it has done to the other side. The guilty party will become self-defensive and the other party will be disconcerted. Both sides may very well take out their unhappiness on you." This advice is discarded in the presentation that follows. In genuine dialogue not only candor is needed, but, even more, there is need for truthfulness.

I

No concept is more relevent to the morphology and life of Christian antisemitism than "nemesis." "Nemesis" involves an act of retribution. Throughout Christian history the church has sought to justify its anti-Jewishness and anti-Judaism through association with some kind of meritorious punitiveness. But "nemesis" is also linked to fate; it implies a condition that cannot be conquered.

---

1. This article is dedicated to Dr. James Parkes, the noted British historian, Anglican clergyman, and pioneering scholar in Jewish-Christian understanding. Parkes rightly identifies the spelling "anti-Semitism" as "pseudo-scientific mumbo jumbo" that implies that the phenomenon in question is somehow a movement directed against an actual quality called "Semitism." The word "antisemitism" is "not a scientific word, and it is entitled to neither a hyphen nor a capital" (James Parkes, conversation with author).

Unlike "nemesis," the concept "antisemitism" is not ambiguous. The root of the English word does lack preciseness, but the meaning of the word is anything but imprecise. In *The Random House Dictionary* the sole definition of "antisemite" is "a persom who is hostile to Jews." I would only suggest adding the qualifying words, "because they are Jews." That Arabs are reputedly a Semitic people lessens in no way the potential power of antisemitism among them. A certain German word is not readily subject to semantic game-playing: *Judenfeindschaft*, enmity toward Jews. One favorite deception of antisemites is to claim that there is no such thing as antisemitism, or at least, that if anyone is guilty of it, *they* certainly are not. If some people try to get us to say that the disease is rare or dying out, or that the word is to be used sparingly or with great caution, lest name-calling afflict us, we must be very much on guard. We must not hesitate to apply the terms "antisemitism" and "antisemite" whenever and wherever the facts warrant.

Seymour M. Lipset points out that "when one draws on the age-old hostility to Jews to strengthen a political position, when one gives credence to the charge of a worldwide Jewish plot to rule, when one attacks those with whom one has political and economic differences as Jews, when one implies that Jews are guilty of some primal evil, then one is guilty of anti-Semitism . . . ."[2] It is here adjudged that hostility to Jews is actualized through the charge that Jews are themselves hostile people.

II

Christian enmity toward Jews generally concentrates on the hostilities that Jews reputedly manifest toward God or the church or the human race, or all these together. Defensive church spokesmen often protest that the term "Christian antisemitism" is self-contradictory. Idealists are usually mistaken, and here is one good case of this. In point of fact, the primary causal agent in Western antisemitism is the Christian message and the Christian church. Indeed, the causative influence of Christians and Christendom in the denigration and persecution of Jews, together with abiding Christian culpability for this crime, has become a truism of historical, psychological, and theological scholarship — so much so that those investigators who have researched

---

2. Seymour M. Lipset, " 'The Socialism of Fools;' The New Left Calls It 'Anti-Zionism,' But It's No Different from the Anti-Semitism of the Old Right," *The New York Times Magazine*, 3 January 1971, p. 6. Lipset indicates that in New Left and Black antisemitism the word "Zionist" is "simply a code word for Jew, just as it has become in Eastern Europe" (ibid., p. 26). Unlike some recent Arab hate-literature, current Soviet propaganda is too sophisticated to charge the existence of "an international Jewish conspiracy." It utilizes quite different terminology. It concentrates upon a "Zionist conspiracy," But the meaning and the purpose remain the same.

and documented the case need only be mentioned by name: Willehad P. Eckert, Ernst L. Ehrlich, Edward H. Flannery, Malcolm Hay, Jules Isaac, Fadiey Lovsky, James Parkes, Léon Poliakov, Karl Thieme, Joshua Trachtenberg, et al.[3]

Antisemitism is one constant that suffuses all Christian history. Partly by way of a simple reminder respecting the data, but also for the sake of later reference, attention needs to be called to the most important publication in English upon the subject in 1970, a volume entitled *God's First Love*, by Catholic scholar Friedrich Heer, a professor of the History of Ideas in the University of Vienna.[4] Dr. Heer recounts, in rather disorganized fashion but comprehensively, and in a poignant and compelling manner, the story of Christian antisemitism from its roots in the New Testament until our own day. Heer writes: "The Gospel of Jesus Christ, the 'Good News' of the Redeemer, became for millions of Jews the messenger of death. Millions of Christians have based their hatred of the Jews on it, have taken it as a call to destroy or at least enslave the Jews, 'the people who killed Christ.' "[5] In Christian Europe the "devilish, accursed race" of Jews was visited with one or more of three alternatives: death, banishment, or compulsory baptism. But we are confronted by more than ancient history. Behind the Christian world's callous indifference to the fate of Jews in the twentieth century lies an acquiescence and approval that Christians have sought "to conceal from their own conscience." It was this very indifference "that

---

3. Willehad P. Eckert and Ernest L. Ehrlich, *Judenhass—Schuld der Christen?!, Versuch eines Gesprächs* (Essen: Hans Driewer Verlag, 1964); Edward H. Flannery, *The Anguish of the Jews: Twenty-three Centuries of Anti-Semitism* (New York: The Macmillan Company, 1965); Malcolm Hay, *Europe and the Jews: The Pressure of Christendom on the People of Israel for 1900 years* (Boston: Beacon Press, 1960); Jules Isaac, *Genèse de l'Antisémitisme: Essai Historique* (Paris: Calmann Lévy, 1956), *Jésus et Israël*, 2d ed. (Paris: Fasquelle, 1959), *The Teaching of Contempt: Christian Roots of Anti-Semitism*, trans. Helen Weaver (New York: Holt, Rinehart and Winston, 1964); Fadiey Lovsky, *Antisémitisme et Mystère d'Israël* (Paris: Editions Albin Michael, 1955); James Parkes, *Antisemitism* (London: Vallentine Mitchell, 1963), *The Conflict of the Church and the Synagogue: A study in the origins of antisemitism* (Cleveland: World Publishing Company, 1961); Léon Poliakov, *The History of Anti-Semitism*, vol. 1 (New York: Vanguard Press, 1965); Karl Thieme, ed., *Judenfeindshaft, Darstellung und Analysen* (Frankfurt am Main: Fischer Bücherei, 1963); Joshua Trachtenberg, *The Devil and the Jews: The Medieval Conception of the Jew and its Relation to Modern Antisemitism* (Cleveland: World Publishing Company, 1961). See also Alan T. Davies, *Anti-Semitism and the Christian Mind: The Crisis of Conscience After Auschwitz* (New York: Herder and Herder, 1969); A. Roy Eckardt, *Elder and Younger Brothers: The Encounter of Jews and Christians* (New York: Charles Scribner's Sons, 1967); Charles Y. Glock and Rodney Stark, *Christian Beliefs and Anti-Semitism* (New York: Harper & Row, 1966); Rudolph M. Loewenstein, *Christians and Jews: A Psychoanalytic Study*, trans. Vera Dammann (New York: Dell Publishing Company, 1951); and Bernhard E. Olson, *Faith and Prejudice: Intergroup Problems in Protestant Curricula* (New Haven: Yale University Press, 1963).
4. Friedrich Heer, *God's First Love: Christians and Jews over two thousand years*, trans. Goeffrey Skelton (New York: Weybright and Talley, 1970). The original German version appeared in 1967. For a critical analysis of this work, see the review by A. Roy Eckardt in *Commentary* 51 (March 1971):91-98.
5. Heer, *God's First Love*, 22.

enabled Hitler to turn Europe into a graveyard of Jews."[6] Without centuries of Christian teaching and preaching against Jews, Nazism would never have been possible. The Nazi "final solution" was no more than a logical application of historic Christian attitudes and demands. Adolf Hitler could quite accurately testify that he was simply doing to the Jews what the church had counseled and acted upon for fifteen hundred years.[7] Right up to his death, Hitler "enjoyed the support of responsible leaders of both major Christian churches." He "was never excommunicated nor were his books ever placed on the Index."[8]

Some church spokesmen who are prepared to acknowledge the fact of Christian antisemitism in previous periods are not always as objective when it comes to the present. The temptation is to dismiss the evil as a thing of the past. A salient emphasis in Professor Heer's study is that the Nazi Holocaust by no means signified the end of Christian enmity to Jews. At this very moment Christian hostility to the Jewish people is manifesting itself in many and varied circles together with the propagation of teachings that perpetuate antisemitism. Since 1945, antisemitic acts and pronouncements have been legion in lands "whose way of life has been formed by Christian principles." Heer concludes that the Christian world now looks on either with indifference or approval, while a new Holocaust is planned in the Middle East.[9] The contemporaneity of Christian antisemitism will be noted later.

III

Because of the centrality of the New Testament in Christian faith, the question of the roots of antisemitism in those writings demands special attention. The Catholic theologian Rosemary Ruether asserts that the decree on the Jews of Vatican Council II was carefully framed so as to preclude "the raising of any questions" concerning antisemitic attitudes within the New Testament. She argues that antisemitism is deeply rooted in the Christian gospel of the New Testament.[10] The Catholic New Testament scholar Dominic M. Crossan is not as despairing as Dr. Ruether, but neither is he entirely happy with the biblical documents. Crossan concludes that the term "the Jews" as employed

---

6. Ibid., 341.
7. Ibid., 307.
8. Ibid., 296, 311.
9. Ibid., 3.
10. Rosemary Ruether, "Theological Anti-Semitism in the New Testament," *The Christian Century* 85 (14 February 1968): 191-96. Cf. Heer: It was "historically consistent that at the Second Vatican Council no fundamental declaration on the Jews was produced which might have led to real amends for Christian guilt towards that people" *(God's First Love*, 247). Subsequent events and trends within the Catholic Church have raised doubts of the complete validity of Heer's expectations.

by St. John is "a very dangerous symbolic term, and one cannot but wonder if it might be a root of anti-Semitism in the Christian subconscious."[11]

On the Protestant side, Alan T. Davies of the University of Toronto, in arguing in an important recent study *Anti-Semitism and the Christian Mind* that there is no anti-Judaism without some measure of hostility to Jews, attests that anti-Judaism inheres in any ideology that takes the New Testament to be sacrosanct, as in Protestant Biblicism. With specific reference to antisemitism, such as Biblicism is held to be quite as dangerous as the persisting, dogmatic traditionalism of historic Catholicism. Passages in the New Testament that are tainted with antisemitism have been put to exactly the same antisemitic use as patristic calumnies against Jews.[12] Another Protestant scholar, Robert E. Willis, is persuaded that until the Christian chruch performs acts of repentance for scriptural passages that convey anti-Judaic and antisemitic images, innuendos, and nuances, the church will continue to show that it has not been seriously affected by its continuing complicity "in the perpetuation of anti-Semitism and its nascent presence within the Christian community today. It is too much to hope that the church might begin now to acknowledge publicly the inconsistency between the truth given in Jesus of Nazareth and those passages in the New Testament that cast aspersion on his people?"[13]

What judgment are we to make? I have never proposed the absurd conclusion that the New Testament is an antisemitic book. The very opposite is the case. Nevertheless, that antisemitic proclivities are present in the New Testament is readily seen through references to such passages as John 5:16-18; 6:41, 7:1, 13; 10:31; 19:12, 15; Acts 13:50; 20:3; and I Thessalonians 2:14-16. The fateful consideration is that all these passages, and similar ones, resort to the indiscriminate phrase "the Jews." The judgment that these passages are not free of antisemitic bias is grounded in a principle of moral philosophy. Father Gregory Baum, after conceding that the Gospel of John has often served to justify contempt for the Jewish people, nevertheless insists that the historical and religious *context* of such seemingly hostile passages forbids us to apply the word "antisemitism" to John.[14] By contrast, the principle offered here is that while the context of any proposition is

---

11. Dominic M. Crossan, "Anti-Semitism and the Gospel," *Theological Studies* 26 (June 1965): 199. Crossan insists, however, that the only proper translation for John's special use of the phrase "the Jews" is "those among the authorities of the Jews who constantly opposed Jesus."
12. Davies, *Anti-Semitism and the Christian Mind*, 104, 110-111, 112.
13. Robert E. Willis, "A Perennial Outrage: Anti-Semitism in the New Testament," *The Christian Century* 87 (19 August 1970): 992.
14. Cf. Gregory Baum, *Is the New Testament Anti-Semitic?* (Glen Rock, N.J.: Paulist Press, 1965), 136. Baum maintains that there are no antisemitic elements in the New Testament.

relevant when discriminate or qualified judgments are tendered, the context becomes totally irrelevant when indiscriminate or unqualified judgments are being made. The truism, "some Americans are killers," is not an instance of anti-Americanism. But the indiscriminate proposition, "*the* Americans are killers," can never be redeemed through recourse to a context. The Gospel of John again and again makes indiscriminate, hostile judgments against "*the* Jews" as Jews, and this is what is meant by antisemitism. The article "the" is as decisive as the word "Jews," or more so.

The assertion "the Jews killed Jesus" (I Thess. 2:15) may be likened in structure to such a hypothetical sentence as "the Americans killed President Kennedy," containing as the latter sentence does a logical and psychological insinuation that Mr. Kennedy was not an American. So, too, the phrase "the Jews killed Jesus," which is hardly a hypothetical assertion from the standpoint of Christian detractors of Jews, insinuates that Jesus was not a Jew. It is not accidental that this very conclusion should have been eagerly drawn and perpetuated in Christian theology, a development that climaxed in the insistence of the "German Christian" movement in our century that Jesus was not Jewish but Aryan.

It need scarcely be added that as time went by during the New Testament period, the tendency was manifest to make less discriminate the category of Jewish blame respecting opposition to Jesus and the fate of Jesus.[15] How ironic it is that the more seriously the developing historical context of the New Testament is taken, the more indisputable are the evidences of *Judenfeindschaft*, indiscriminate hostility toward Jews.[16]

IV

Within Christendom antisemitism has been carried forward very largely by means of anti-Judaism and by denigration and persecution of Jews bereft of political protection. For some years these weapons have been supplemented and refined by means of anti-Zionism and/or anti-Israelism, the chief instrumentalities of contemporary Christian antisemitism.

---

15. As examples, when Jesus symbolically destroys the Temple he is challenged by "the Jews" in John 2:18 ff., whereas in the earlier narration of this symbolic act in Mark (11:27) the challenge comes only from "the high priests, the Scribes, and the elders." Again, the cripple whom Jesus cures on the Sabbath is reproached by "the Jews" in John 5:10, whereas in the Synoptic Gospels clashes over Sabbath cures involve only the authorities (cf. Mark 3:26; Luke 6:6-11; Matt. 12:9-10, 13-14; Crossan, "Anti-Semitism and the Gospel," p. 194). In Mark "the chief priests" and "the crowd" are involved in the shout "Crucify him!" (15:11-15); in John the shouters are "the Jews" (19:15).
16. Eckardt, *Elder and Younger Brothers*, pp. 124-125; cf., more generally, 122-129.

The question is hotly debated today: Is anti-Zionism necessarily a form of antisemitism? Perhaps the answer does not always have to be "yes." To Professor Lipset, "one may oppose Israeli policy, resist Zionism or criticize worldwide Jewish support of Israel without being anti-Semitic."[17] On the other side, the presence of the State of Israel as, allegedly, an aggravator of the world's woes, together with the permissiveness and even the favor accorded anti-Zionism, can certainly be used to excellent advantage by antisemites. Alan T. Davies contends that the most "fashionable contemporary guise" for antisemitism *is* anti-Zionism.[18] As Davies expresses it, antisemitic convictions "can be transposed without much difficulty into the new language of anti-Zionism, as meanwhile the reality of a Jewish nation-state offers a tangible scapegoat."[19] The antisemites often appear, therefore, to "have it made"; they can emphatically protest their complete innocence of any charge of hostility to Jews as Jews. A tried and true strategem of the devil is to convince as many as possible that he does not exist.

An analytical criterion for grappling with the relation of anti-Zionism to antisemitism has already been put forward. Insofar as anti-Zionists manifest hostility to Jews—and particularly, of course, to the Jews of Israel—there is no rational or scientific choice but to identify them as antisemites. Seymour Lipset reports that recent attacks in France upon Jews, Judaism, and Israel have diffused from the student New Left to different Catholic groups which "deny the historic claims of the Jews to Israel on the theological grounds that the church, rather than contemporary Jewry, is the true heir of ancient Israel."[20] Here is suggested a clue to the identification of anti-Israelism as a newer form of antisemitism. One measure of the presence or absence of antisemitism lies in the question: Is the integrity of the State of Israel being honored?

On 10 May 1970 a conference of Christians meeting in Beirut, Lebanon demanded the total "disappearance of Zionist structures," a euphemism for the destruction of Israel. Was this an instance of antisemitism? Well, before 1948 it may have been possible to question the practical wisdom, feasibility, or perhaps even the legitimacy of the reestablishment of a sovereign Jewish state in Palestine without being charged with antisemitism. We live almost a generation later. The assertion that Jewry has no right to Eretz Yisrael, and therefore, by implication, that the State of Israel ought to be abolished, is an instance

---

17. Lipset, " 'The Socialism of Fools,' " 6.
18. Davies, *Anti-Semitism and the Christian Mind*, 182.
19. Alan T. Davies, "Anti-Zionism, Anti-Semitism and the Christian Mind," *The Christian Century* 87 (19 August 1970): 989.
20. Lipset, " 'The Socialism of Fools'," 26.

of antisemitism. This conclusion is a perfectly objective one. There is simply no way to call for the destruction of Israel without support for a new Holocaust, the suffering and death of as many as two and one-half million Jews.[21]

V

In Christian circles, a dishonoring of the rightful integrity of Israel is not limited to categorical opposition to her continued existence. Implicit or explicit alliance with those who would harass Israel, or keep her in a threatened or insecure position, or ensure that Israel receives the short end of any political settlement, constitutes additional exemplification of hostility is hidden by a third party's protestations of devotion to justice for both sides. A formidable illustration here is the recent international Quaker statement of 35,000 words entitled *Search for Peace in the Middle East*.[22] The statement is indicative of the impossibility of separating anti-Israelism and anti-Zionism from antisemitism. The Friends' judgments are by no means atypical of what we have been getting from Christian quarters; their pronouncement has received considerable attention and acclaim beyond Quaker circles, and it is often described, revealingly, as "fairminded." The Friends are reputed to stand for peace; a close inspection of their pronouncement raises the question of the continuing accuracy of the reputation.[23]

Another contemporary Christian document, which comes from a quite different source and is directed to quite different purposes from the Quaker study, is a statement adopted by the General Synod of the Nederlandse Hervormde Kerk (Reformed Church of Holland) on 16 June 1970, and entitled *Israel: People, Land and State*.[24] This document is much more traditionalist than the Friends' pronouncement, in that it contains considerably more anti-Judaism than it does explicit anti-Zionism or anti-Israelism. The Dutch Synod lives at a different

---

21. Alice and Roy Eckardt, *Encounter With Israel: A Challenge to Conscience* (New York: Association Press, 1970), 217-218.
22. Two editions of the statement have been published, both under the title *Search for Peace in the Middle East*. The first was published in May 1970 by the American Friends Service Committee, Philadelphia. A slightly revised edition was published in November 1970 by the Fawcett World Library, New York, by arrangement with the American Friends Service Committee. In note 23 below, cited page references are from the revised edition.
23. A careful study of the document by the chairman of the Committee on Israel of American Jewish Congress, Judge Justine Wise Polier, shows that it contains deep-seated anti-Jewish bias (cf. Justine Wise Polier, "Open Letter to the 'Friends,'" *Congress bi-Weekly*).
24. The version of *Israel: People, Land and State* here referred to is a mimeographed English translation made available under date of October 1970 to the Department of Faith and Order, National Council of the Churches of Christ in the U.S.A. In the analysis that follows, all references are to paragraph numbers of the documents.

end of the theological spectrum from the Quakers, yet the Dutch statement reflects much of the same bias that permeates the Quaker statement and, together with the latter, its thrust is anti-Israel.[25]

In many places the Dutch pronouncement merely repeats the classical anti-Judaist sentiments of historic Christendom. We have instructed that Jesus "came into diametrical opposition to the 'pious' ones who tried to ensure and maintain the continued existence of the chosen people by faithful observance of the law." We are told that Jesus "repudiated those who wanted to restore national independence and who in this way strove for the self-preservation of their people" (par. 22). We are advised that "the Jewish people as a whole" rejected Jesus Christ, "their Messiah" (pars. 20, 28, 30, etc.). We are informed that "zeal for the law" was the reason for this rejection (par. 35). We are warned against "the moralism and legalism into which the observance of the law has often degenerated among the Jews" (par. 39).

Spokesmen within Jewry may succeed in propagating or opposing the doctrine of the election of Israel. That is their obligation. But whenever Christian representatives intervene in that doctrine, declaring, as does the Dutch Synod, that the Jews are "unlike" all other peoples, the specter of immorality is raised.

---

25. One can note also the Synod's refusal in one place to extend the integrity of the elected people's land to their right to an independent state and even to the city of Jerusalem (par. 13)—a refusal that reappears elsewhere in the effort to apply God's promise to "the lasting tie of people and land, but not in the same way to the tie of people and state" (par. 43). Despite their relative sanctioning of the Israeli state, the Dutch authors continue to "wonder" whether "the special place of the Jewish people" does not make questionable "the right of existence of the state of Israel" (par. 44). This curious disjunction between residency and sovereignty can only play into the hands of those who would have the Jews remain a (tolerated) minority devoid of independent political protection. Again, we are told that the land has been "allotted to this people in order that we might realize their vocation as God's people to form a holy society" (par. 11). The implication is all too evident that decisive Jewish irresponsibility respecting such a society may necessitate punitive expulsion from the land. The corruptness of such an outlook is attested by the fact that we never talk or act this way respecting Egypt, Syria, or Jordan. For Christians to expect from Jews, as does this pronouncement, more than is expected from other peoples (par. 52) is not only immoral, in light of the history of Christian treatment of Jews; the Synod's demand that the State of Israel be "exemplary" (par. 47) constitutes a wholly illicit intrusion of faith into the moral-political realm. This Dutch Reformed statement, together with the Quaker document, perpetuates a practice that runs all through Christian history and despoils the secular domain: the refusal to apply to the Jewish people the very same standards that are applied to all men simply because they are human beings. The Dutch pronouncement undertakes a politico-moral comparison between Israel and what it calls "Christian states," when in fact the only comparison that is legitimate is one between Israel and the states that now surround her. In the presence of foes committed to the obliteration of Israel, the Synod's expressed fear that the Jews will make their dwelling place "into a nationalistic state in which the only thing that counts is military power" (par. 48) is a moral outrage. If these churchmen are really so worried about Israeli militarism, they had better address themselves to the culprits: the Arab states, the terrorists, and the Soviet Union. The church really ought to stop lecturing Israel as though church spokesmen were Biblical prophets.

Even more reprehensibly, we are told again and again that the Jewish people are alienated from God (pars. 30, 31, etc.), and indeed that the very Jewish act of taking refuge from death through a return to Eretz Yisrael exemplifies this alienation (par. 36). I think that a special delight of the devil must be to mete out theological-moral chastisement as the appropriate, historical sequel to human agony. That in this day after Auschwitz a Christian body should dare to stress over and over the religious alienation of the Jews is more than an instance of human callousness. It is proof that the voice of the church is sometimes a satanic voice.

Often Christians today are simply powerless to deliver themselves from traditional Christian immorality respecting the Jewish people and Judaism. Why is this? The Dutch Synod's captivity to Biblicism provides part of the answer. Unconscious Biblicism is still regnant in much of the Christian world. Moral outrages against Jews will continue to occur as long as Christendom engages in the politics of Biblicist moralism. For the Biblicist theologization of politics is a guarantor of immorality. In the case under review, this consequence is particularly ironic because these Dutch churchmen are doubtless reacting, and commendably so, against the terrible divorce of theology from politics in the Europe, and especially the Germany, of the 1930s and 1940s.

Most horrendous of all is the truth that the very Christian world that has brought incalculable suffering to Jews should continue to spawn representatives who make the same old accusations against the Jewish people and the same old impossible demands upon them. Sadly, these representatives are often well-meaning Christians and humanitarians, committed to "the highest moral values." Of one thing we may be quite certain: The Quakers who wrote the one statement and the Dutch Christians who wrote the other would in all honesty resent the charge that they are antisemites.

VI

How are we to account for this horror, this antisemitism that has afflicted the Christian church throughout her history, and that endures to this day? How is the evil to be rooted out or at least reduced? Each of these two questions is as baffling as the other. A lifetime of study may uncover a few clues, though perhaps no demonstrable certainties.

At the outset, some necessarily personal references will perhaps be excused. For some time I have sought to till soil that is shared by depth psychology, theology, and ethics: antisemitism is the war we Christians wage against Jesus the Jew; the reenactment of the crucifixion of Christ, who confronts Christians with God; the rejection of the Jew Jesus

NEMESIS OF CHRISTIAN ANTISEMITISM

turned against his own people.[26] As Friedrich Heer puts it: The Jew Jesus is to blame; the Jew has to be repressed.[27] Through our persecution of Jews we Christians can try to manage our guilt for defaulting before gospel demands.

While this (somewhat eclectic) position is not to be discarded, one may come to wonder whether God and man are the only leading protagonists in the revolting drama, or whether the devil is not also at center stage. I think that I never really began to take the devil with seriousness until I had developed what some of my critics regard as an obsession with antisemitism. Even so, my reflections upon the devil were not initiated until fairly recently.

To put the matter as circumspectly as possible, one cannot come to grips with the reality of Christian antisemitism, and hence of Christian hostility to Israel, without acknowledging the reality of satanic forces. Opponents will perhaps identify this development as a predictable culmination of years of unjust and misguided warfare on my part: the last resort of the frantic is to charge that the other is consorting with the devil. The risk of this kind of interpretation is simply one that has to be taken. (I am sometimes sent to the edge of despair by the fear that my endless preaching upon the fact of Christian antisemitism may, devilishly, serve to compound the evil.)

When the devil enters, what happens to the concept and the reality of nemesis? Upon whom is retribution visited? What becomes of responsibility? What of the future? What is to be the fate of fate?

So far, I hypothesize that Satan's major field of operations is the collective unconscious. In Christian antisemitism certain eruptions of the collective unconscious are taken captive by pathology. The pathology assumes a unique form, since it is different from ordinary racial or ethnic prejudice. The utilization of the Christian pulpit to defame Blacks or Germans, or even Russians, has, indeed, become quite unfashionable. Yet we shall continue to read the "Word of God" in, for example, the Gospel of John – and no one had better summon the Anti-Defamation League. Who wishes to be accused of undermining "religious freedom"?

Further, even though Professor Lipset has been cited above in support of the judgment that antisemitic hospility is actualized through the claim that Jews are themselves hostile or evil people, this judgment must not obscure the truth that antisemitism has a profound life of its own quite independent of the presence or behavior of Jews. In its depths, antisemitism has little if anything to do with Jews. It lives in the mind of the devil, the antisemite. This is why it is that changes

---

26. Eckardt, *Elder and Younger Brothers*, 22-25.
27. Heer, *God's First Love*, 424.

in Jewish behavior are of no consequence in the presence of antisemitism. Only antisemitism demands that certain human beings be angels yet insists that they are devils. Just as the reality of the devil is to be unreal, so antisemitism is immured to reality. Anti-Israeli Christians need have little if any connection with Jews or with the real Israel. They fabricate their own Israel: militant, aggressive, inflexible, vengeful, irreligious, alienated.

Is antisemitism simply one among many of the devil's enterprises, or is it a special malignancy that works to destroy the whole divine-human creation? David Polish contends that "the truth of every cause is validated or found fraudulent in the way in which it confronts the Jewish people."[28] It is not impossible that the world will reach its end by courtesy of the Middle East.

The reign of the Lord extends to all men, yet he chooses his elect nation. The dominion of the devil is also universalistic — his kingdom is indiscriminate — yet he too has his chosen ones, the antisemites. He does not leave himself without special witnesses. Through the centuries and in all places his faithful persist. The universality transcends the particularity, yet it is realized *through* the particularity: Jews are hated without boundaries of time or place. The devil is universal yet very particular. As Friedrich Heer points out, the Christian theologians proved Jewish guilt a thousand times.[29]

The "two-eyes-for-an-eye" Christian psyche calls down retribution upon the allegedly evil Jew for rejecting the divine light — an "inner light," perhaps, to our friends the Friends. To them, the refusal of Jews to surrender themselves like good pacifists must be an unforgiveable sin against some kind of Holy Ghost. Yet upon whom is the final retribution falling?

Why is it incumbent upon us to identify Christian antisemites as specially chosen legions of the devil? Because Christianity long ago arranged a pact with the demonic forces. The devil can only be known by his fruits. The antisemites of Christian history and of this moment whisper their secret to us: The Jews are the devil, the devil is the Jews. "Psychologically and morally construed, the charge of Jewish devilishness demonstrates the satanic conquest of the Christian soul. The Christian is the 'Jew' he despises. I would even go so far as to say that the Jew is in fact the 'Christian': Jewish ideals and behavior are the polar opposite of the church's accusations. The Jewish world-conspiracy is the invention of demon-ridden Christian conspirators."[30]

---

28. David Polish, "The Tasks of Israel and Galut," *Judaism* 28 (Winter 1969): 10.
29. Heer. *God's First Love*, 324.
30. Eckardt, review of Heer, *God's First Love,* in *Commentary*, 94.

VII

Can there be, then, any real hope for the conquest of Christian antisemitism? A collective-pathological state such as the one under analysis cannot be separated from either the idealism that demands perfection or the cynicism that awaits nothing good. Idealism and cynicism are common flights from the real world. But the Jew is *here*. He is the world, he is reality. The only end to antisemitism is a revolutionary restoration of reality. Yet is there a chance for any such development? Someone may interject that the cynicism implied in this very question must itself be pathological. Perhaps so. If Elie Wiesel is right, ours is the time when only madmen may be sane. But I believe that we are not yet so far gone that we cannot distinguish between pathological cynicism and the cynicism that is an objective and reasonable response to the fatefulness of the pathology.

Christianity means antisemitism; this is the dreadful truth that overwhelms us once more as we close such a volume as Friedrich Heer's agonized chronicle. Yet, Professor Heer does not surrender hope. Christianity can yet redeem itself, he tells us — by surmounting its Augustianian concept for the world and returning home to its Jewish foundation, where men are responsible partners of God and earthly love is accepted and incarnated.

I should love to share this expectation. There are, however, formidable stumbling blocks. The affirmation that Christianity ought to be Jewish at its very roots may only make for a metastasizing of antisemitism — although I have often made that affirmation myself (sometimes out of desperation). Heer pleads that Christians accept their guilt, and then through a massive act of self-analysis purge themselves of their sins. One serious difficulty is that to suggest to Christians that they may be antisemitic can quite likely make them more antisemitic. Were it not for the Jew — they may secretly tell themselves — no one could ever go around making the charge of antisemitism against them. Indeed, the very raising of the issue of Christian guilt sometimes proves counterproductive. Professor Davies points out that even minor Christian guilt feelings over Auschwitz

> produce a curious rejection: one is tempted to conclude that it comes almost as a relief to [Christians] to discover that Jews, like Christians, are capable of wrongdoing. The frequent journalistic comparisons between Zionist militarism and nazi militarism are instructive at this point. To find Israel in a morally ambiguous situation releases the Christian from thinking too much about Auschwitz and his own vicarious participation in one of the darkest moments of Western history. It is as if the Christian conscience whispers: "See, we aren't that bad after all — look at what the Jews are doing now!" Such an attitude, conscious or unconscious, is doubly bad. It is bad because it makes the Christian psychologically vulnerable to anti-Semitism

as well as to anti-Zionism, and it is bad because it deflects the church from its own sins by concentrating on the sins of others.[31]

However, the real nemesis is that Friedrich Heer's program may have come too late. The church that collaborated in the Nazi "final solution" dealt itself mortal blows. From that Jewish crucifixion and Christian self-crucifixion there could and did come a Jewish resurrection — the State of Israel — but not a Christian resurrection. For the church has nowhere to go now. Christianity is Cain, a fugitive upon the face of the earth. The fateful and all-decisive consideration is that the church of the "final solution" was simply living out to an ultimate fulfillment its own historical fate. For Christian antisemitism was born at the moment of God's first death. How, then, is antisemitism to die unless there is a new resurrection, the birth of a fresh God?

VIII

We are confronted, finally, by a grave moral danger: a realization of the nemesis of amassing prophetic judgments against the Christian community may combine with our terrible knowledge of Christianity's demise to make us abandon the struggle against Christian antisemitism. Does the death of Christianity force the Christian to betray his Christian identity? It is a blessing that we know so little of the battles that rage in heaven. We are ignorant of just what intentions God has for the devil. Consequently, we can see ourselves as free. We are responsible men. We have to fight against our own nemesis, lest sin gain the one victory it yet must covet, our final consent.

One battle for today has waged against the maneuver by either hidden or unconscious antisemites — or perhaps by well-meaning "liberals" who wish to bury the past for the sake of mutual Jewish-Christian acceptance in the present — to bar the subject of past and present Christian antisemitism from primary study and analysis. This can only mean cutting off the possibility of penitence and corrective action. Harvey Cox writes: "Psychiatrists have long reminded us that the loss of the sense of time is a symptom of personal deterioration . . . . The same is true for a civilization. So long as it can absorb what has happened to it and move confidently toward what is yet to come, its vitality persists." But alienation from its past means decline and ultimately death.[32] The tacit pretense that history never happened does not, unfortunately, ever make history go away. It simply is not true that the Christian world as a whole has ever repented of its antisemitic actions and attitudes. Yet the church will hardly change her behavior effectively or enduringly until she faces up to her past and present sins.

---

31. Davies, "Anti-Zionism, Anti-Semitism and the Christian Mind," 989.
32. Harvey Cox, *Feast of Fools* (Cambridge: Harvard University Press, 1969), 12.

There appears no way to work through or with self-defensive Christians who resent or at least oppose any raising of the issue of continuing Christian responsibility for antisemitism. Are we left, then, with nothing to say to Christians today who honestly feel no guilt for antisemitism? Much depends upon whether they consider themselves an integral, and therefore in a sense a responsible, part of the total Christian community. In other words, it may be asked whether these Christians have any really deep sense of their own history. At the very least, Christians ought to ask themselves whether a denial of any genuine responsibility for antisemitism is a morally justified conclusion, or whether it is in fact a temptation not unrelated to the machinations of the devil.

Is there a path out of the cynicism that is the ineluctable outcome of our own history? Is there any way for the Christianity that killed itself to be raised from the dead? Perhaps one hope for the future lies with that remnant of Christians who do not directly bear guilt for Christian antisemitism but who may be called to wage war upon a past that remains as yet unmastered *(eine unbewältigte Vergangenheit)*. Youth of today are expending wonderful energy in behalf of many social causes. They seek to redeem the past, a past that carries many evils for which they are obviously not subject to blame. Christian students and other young people in this country may be challenged by such an enterprise as the German Reconciliation Movement *(Aktion Sühnezeichen)*. Teams of German youth give up paid employment for a year in order to engage in deeds of construction within various European and Middle Eastern countries, to the end of forgiveness for the crimes of their fellow-countrymen against Jews and other "enemies" of the Third Reich. The overwhelming moral fact here is that the great majority of the participants in *Aktion Sühnezeichen* were not even born when World War II started. No one can accuse them of perpetrating the Nazi program against Jews. The penitence of these young people is entirely vicarious; they have taken upon themselves the sins of the fathers. They would be the first to grant that their efforts are not free from a wish for national self-respect and even from an element of self-interest. The plain truth stands that they are actively engaged in the search for human reconciliation. Who in fact builds for the future—the man who desires to bury the past, refusing to allow any real link between his present behavior and that past, or the man who dedicates himself to redeeming the present consequences of the past?[33]

Beyond Christianity and the nemesis of the Christian's own condition stand God and his people. We are left with a choice between hope

---

33. A. Roy Eckardt, "Christian Guilt," *Christian News From Israel* (Jerusalem) 28 (July 1967): 47-48.

and despair. I wish, in the end, to testify on the side of hope. Why do I do this? Because the Jewish people do not give in to us, who have been the devil. They do not give in to hatred. At the last we may join with Friedrich Heer: Perhaps God will live once more, not so much because of us, but because he is "the coming God: a God of the present and of the future, in which he will submerge the brutal past."[34]

---

34. Heer, *God's First Love*, 444.

From Barmen (1934) to Stuttgart (1945): The Path of the Confessing Church in Germany

FRANKLIN HAMLIN LITTELL

The study of totalitarianism is attracting increasing attention in university circles, drawing the efforts of students and professors in many differing disciplines. In the last two years, to mention one point, several scholars have received foundation grants to study special phases of totalitarian history or practice in Europe. The number of basic books in the field increases steadily. Proposals have been made in several universities for the establishment of research archives and/or institutes to study totalitarianism and, although to date none has reached the precipitation point, it is predictable that one or more will be formalized in the near future.

The reasons why such an area of study is attractive are of great variety, for totalitarianism — by definition, so to speak — affects all aspects of organized society, from art and architecture to zoology. The study of it appeals to those united in little else, and in this respect it affords an unparalleled foundation for interdisciplinary effort. At the level of theology, too, the study of totalitarianism affords a worthy basis for dialogue with other disciplines; it is in effect a pathological study of Western Christendom. Just as the medical pathologist can assist us to a better understanding of physical health by a careful analysis of diseased bodies, so the study of totalitarianism can help to an understanding of the factors which make for health in the open society.

The centers of facism were severly reduced by World War II, although Peronisme in Argentina, Falangisme in Spain, and American nativism in certain organizations, held on for a time. But more important is the threat posed by communism, the most serious encounter since the rise of Islam a thousand years ago and perhaps the most serious since the beginning of the Christian movement. We must not let our revulsion against the style and activity of various adventurers—professional "anti-communists" who in fact imitate the totalitarian tactics of character assassination, guilt by association, insinuation and slander, anonymous letters and handbills, the attempt to polarize the body politic between reaction and revolution, etc.—blind us to the fact that communism is in truth a real threat to the democratic way of life. And the Christian professor, as an officer in the *militia Christi* and a senator in the republic of learning, is under special obligation to see to it that the real nature of the conflict with totalitarianism is so plainly defined that even the anxious and misguided cannot blur the battlelines.

There are reasons why the struggle of the Confessing Church *(Bekennende Kirche)* with Nazism in Germany, 1934-45, has a special message for Christians who are trying to find their way through the confusions of the American religious situation. This was pointed out by Professor Arthur Cochrane of Dubuque in his presidential address to the American Theological Society last April, reading on "The Theological Significance of the Barmen Declaration, May, 1934":

... the need for a clarification of the old Confessions definitely exists. What is the likelihood of something like Barmen happening in America? One would be foolish to prophesy. There are signs that it may not be too far off, and then there is much that augurs against it. Are we living 'between the times'? Were those twelve terrible and yet blessed years of the Church under Hitler a foreshadowing of the destiny of the Church in other lands in this atomic age? Were they prophetic of a return for us, too, to a pre-Constantinian, New Testament time of the Church? Are we on the threshold of a day when the Church's only weapon and defence will be her Confession of Faith? We do not know. But this much is certain: no Confession of Faith has ever arisen that was not preceded by long, arduous and intense theological activity.

... Meanwhile we are charged with that earnest theological activity without which no Confession is possible.[1]

The Barmen Declaration (May, 1934)

Among the forty-two special studies assigned by the Commission on the History of the Church Struggle in the National Socialist Period, 1933-45—an official commission created by the Evangelical Church of Germany in 1955 and financed by regular monies from the Ministry of the Interior and an occasional grant by an American foundation—two of those already published deal with the background to the Barmen Six Articles. There were, of course, many previous meetings and exchanges of proposals before Barmen; there have been variant drafts subsequently published which caused some dispute among participants. But the source problem is now laid to rest. The two volumes, published

---

1. Arthur C. Cochrane, "The Theological Significance of the Barmen Declaration, May 1934." Mimeographed in *Newsletter* §4: *The History of the German Church Struggle with Nazism* (August 1, 1960), 11.

by Dr. Gerhard Niemöller, head of the great archive of *BK* materials at Bielefeld—were published by Vandenhoeck & Ruprecht in Göttingen in 1959: "Die erste Bekenntnissynode der Deutschen Evangelischen Kirche zu Barmen. I: Geschichte, Kritik und Bedeutung der Synode aund ihrer Theologischen Erklärung. 269 pp. and *Die erste Bekenntnissynode der Deutschen Evangelischen Kirche zu Barmen, II: Text—Dokumente—Berichte.* 209 pp."

The statement was drawn up by three theologians; two of them, Karl Barth and Hans Asmuszen, are well known in America. After describing the threat to the faith posed by the political capture of much of the church machinery by means of the German Christians *(Deutsche Christen)*, some one hundred forty delegates from nineteen territorial churches (Lutheran, Reformed, and United) stated in the form of a classical Confession of Faith the matters at stake in the encounter of the Church with Nazi totalitarianism. Breaking with the harmonistic mind and spirit of the nineteenth century, they stressed the discontinuity between the church and the spirit of the times ("the world" of New Testament parlance). Each article is put forward on the basis of a key text of the Bible, re-stated in terms of the present crisis, and followed by the traditional *damnanus* against heresy.

Article One, based on John 14:6 and John 10:1, 9, reads:

Jesus Christ, as he is testified to us in the Holy Scriptures, is the one Word of God, whom we are to hear, whom we are to trust and obey in life and in death.

We repudiate the false teaching that the church can and must recognize yet other happenings and powers, images and truths as divine revelation alongside this one Word of God, as a source of her preaching.[2]

The position condemned was that of tribal religion, which saw in the resurgent national spirit and its leader manifestations of Divine providence and revelation. In October of 1933 the German bishops had celebrated the 450th anniversary of Luther's birth with a proclamation which included the phrase, "We German Protestant Christians accept the saving of our nation by our Leader Adolf Hitler as a gift from God's hand." And in January of 1934, shortly after Karl Barth had read his great appeal for resistance, the Lutheran bishops announced, after a conference with Hitler, their unqualified support:

Under the impress of the great hour in which the church leaders of the German Protestant Church were gathered with the Chancellor, they affirm unanimously their unlimited fealty to the Third Reich and its Leader. They sharply condemn all machinations of critique of the State, the Nation and the Movement, which may have the effect of endangering the Third Reich. Especially they condemn the situation when the

---

2. The Barmen Declaration (May 1934), the Stuttgart Declaration (October 1945), and The Platform of the German Christians (1932) may be found in translation in my book, *The German Phoenix* (New York: Doubleday & Co., 1960), Appendices B, c and A.

foreign press is used to portray falsely the debate in the church as a battle against the State. The assembled church leaders [*Kirchenführer*] place themselves openly in support of the National Bishop (*Reichsführer*) and are determined to carry through his measures and instructions in the way he wishes, to hinder the church-political opposition against them, and to strengthen the authority of the National Bishop with all means provided by the church constitution.[3]

In the light of this, Dietrich Bonhoeffer's bitter words about the orthodox Lutherans take their meaning: "It will yet come to the point when the Beast, before which the worshippers of idols bow down, presents a twisted face of Luther."[4]

The Platform of German Christians (1932) put the matter clearly in Article Ten: "We want an Evangelical Church with roots in the national character, and we repudiate the spirit of a Christian cosmopolitanism. We want to overcome the corrupt developments which have sprung from this spirit — such as pacifism, internationalism, Freemasonry, etc. — through faith in the national mission given us by God." And again in Article Four we find articulated that position against which the men of Barmen were taking their stand: "We take our stand on the platform of positive Christianity. We assert an affirmative style of Christian faith, as appropriate to the German spirit of Luther and heroic piety." A professor in Berlin, Cajus Fabricius, who was perhaps the preëminent champion of the power of positive thinking in those years, stated the position of hyphenated Christianity, of the homogenization of "the German way of life" and "heroic piety" — "spirituality," as it comes to our ears today! — clearly and unmistakably:

Germany has been raised from out of the depths of the direct need by an overwhelming act of Divine Providence. And in this great happening we look upon the fact that the *Führer*, Adolf Hitler, has been given to us as a very special mark of God's mercy toward us.

We as Germans of German type are at the same time Christians, and as Christians are at the same time Germans of the German type. Hence to us Christianity means no eradication of folk characteristics but rather an experiencing of the Supreme Divine Power behind the outward wrappings that go to make up our racial characteristics.[5]

The threat of reversion to tribal religion was not sudden, nor had it been unnoticed in some quarters. Dietrich Bonhoeffer's friend, Helmut Röszler, had outlined the problem very clearly in a letter under date of 22 February 1931:

The greatest tragedy of the church and of our people I see at the moment *en kairo* is that a purified, glowing national feeling in the powerful movement is tied up with a new heathenism — the exposure and opposition to which is more difficult for

---

3. Ibid., 9-10.
4. Dietrich Bonhoeffer, *Gesammelte, Schriften, I: Okumene . . . 1928-1942* (Munich: Chr. Kaiser Verlag, 1958), 47. Edited by Eberhard Bethge; hereafter *DB I*.
5. Cajus Fabricius, *Positive Christianity in the Third Reich* (Dresden: Puschel, 1937), 23, 46, 45.

psychological reasons than is the case with the religion of Free Thought, because it appears in Christian dress. The foundation of this neo-heathen religion is the claim of a demonstrated unity of Religion and Race, more precisely the Aryan (Nordic) race . . . . The church is approved only when it serves folk and race. Confessional contradictions are denied for the most part, for the sake of a popular syncretism with the slogan—"all who believe in God, who are of good will . . . ."[6]

The first article of Barmen was to halt the identification of Christian faith with a national or racial way of life and to assert the exclusive claims of the Word revealed in Christ Jesus, Lord of the world's peoples and of human history.

Article Two, based on I Corinthians 1:30, reads:

Just as Jesus Christ is the pledge of the forgiveness of our sins, just so—and with the same earnestness—is he also God's mighty claim on our whole life; in him we encounter a joyous liberation from the godless claims of this world to a free and thankful service to his creatures.

We repudiate the false teaching that there are areas of our life in which we belong not to Jesus Christ but another lord, areas in which we do not need justification and sanctification through him.

The Confessing Church was severely attacked for "meddling in politics." Because they would not accept the institutional changes made when the state laid violent hands on the church offices, because they refused to accept the Aryan paragraph in the church, because they were determinedly loyal to the ecumenical fellowship, they were attacked by German Christian pamphleteers as "the political church." One of the most widely circulated pamphlets asserting the Aryan origin and contribution of Jesus of Nazareth, along with the German racial genius in spiritual matters, was a tract entitled, *The Political Church and its So-called "Biblical Foundations."*[7] It is a revealing point that to this day—in Dallas and Atlanta, Budapest and Kiev (as then in Berlin and Essen)—the world's criticism of the church comes when the preachers "meddle in politics": Nativism, Nazism, and communism never attack a church as long as it concentrates on personal "spirituality" and purely familial piety.

The answer of Barmen was to assert the Lordship of Jesus Christ— the "Crown Rights" of the Lord—over all of life; there are no reservations where His claim does not reach. And in putting forward this dimension of the authority of the Lord of the Universal Church they clung with tenacious hands to the fellowship of the ecumenical movement. As early as 1931, the conservative Lutherans Emmanuel Hirsch and Paul Althaus had published a statement opposing German participation in ecumenical conferences.[8] The martyr Dietrich Bonhoef-

---

6. *DB I*, 57.
7. Friedrich Murawski, *Die politische Kirche und ihre biblischen 'Urkunden'* (Berlin: Theodor Fritsch Verlag, n. d.).
8. *DB I*, 18. See also Glenthj, Jorgen, "Dietrich Bonhoeffer und die Okumene," *Mundige Welt* (Munich: Chr. Kaiser Verlag, 1956), II, 116 ff.

fer, however, continued to serve as a courier for the Christian fellowship even after *Reichsbischof* Mueller had threatened to bring charges of high treason against any German churchmen who shared information with foreigners on the continuing struggle in the German church.

Article Three, based on Ephesians 4:15-16, reads:

> The Christian Church is the community of brethren . . . . We repudiate the false teaching that the Church can turn over the form of her message and ordinances at will or according to some dominant ideological and political convictions.

Here again the Aryan paragraph was, among other things, involved. Although the Barmen Articles do not explicitly deal with Anti-Semitism, it was the men of Barmen who protested the Nürnberg Laws (1935) and a tribal church. The German Christians' statements were explicit enough:

> 7. We see in race, national character and the nation orders of life given and entrusted to us by God, to maintain which is a law of God for us. Therefore racial mixing is to be opposed. On the basis of its experience the German foreign missions have for a long time called to the German nation: 'Keep yourself racially pure,' and told us that faith in Christ doesn't disturb race but rather deepens and sanctifies it.
>
> 9. In the mission to the Jews we see a grave danger to our national character. It is the entryway for foreign blood into our national body. It has no traditional justification side by side with foreign missions. We deny the validity of the mission to the Jews in Germany, as long as the Jews have the rights of citizenship and thereby there exists the danger of racial deterioration and bastardization . . . .

The Confessing Church already faced this issue and adopted an unequivocal Scriptural stand. In the very first issue of *Theologische Existenz heute*, the main magazine of the resistance, Karl Barth took the position that when a church introduced the Aryan paragraph it ceased to be the Christian Church. There followed, in the practical situation, a lively discussion of whether men could in conscience take a pastorate in a parish which had become an Aryan reservation.[9] Niemöller and Bonhoeffer released a declaration to the effect that in accepting the Aryan rule the Old Prussian Union Church had separated itself from the Church of Jesus Christ.

Many of the brethren were close to the position that those faithful to the confessions must set up a free church. Bonhoeffer's friend, Franz Hildebrandt (later a professor at Drew), drew up a series of ten propositions stating the case for a free church.[10] Just a month before Barmen, however, the Westphalian Church — where the resistance was strong — seceded from the union, and this strengthened the case for continued resistance within the territorial churches. Then the Barmen Declaration itself formed the basis for the continuing *BK* claim to be

---

9. Dietrich Bonhoeffer, *Gesammelte Schriften, II: Kirschenkampf und Finkenwalde . . . 1933-1943* (Munich: Chr. Kaiser Verlag, 1959), 126. Edited by Eberhard Bethge.
10. Ibid., 167-68.

representative of the only true Evangelical Church of the land.[11] Articles Five and Six define the proper mutual restraint of church and state if a true *Volkskirche* is to be maintained. This position was reasserted by Hermann Ehlers in his key address at the Confessing Synod in Augsburg (June 4-6, 1935): "We *will not abandon this our Church and become a 'free church'; we are the Church.*"[12]

The basic work at church law, which determined the status of the *BK* and the "caretaker church governments" until the *EKiD* was established after the war, was done at the Synod of Dahlem (1935). At this second synod of the Confessing Church the claim of legality, to being the true church of the land, was laid; thereafter the question of going the way of the free church receded. The report of Dahlem has been critically edited by D. Wilhelm Niemöller: *Die zweite Bekenntnissynode der deutschen Evangelischen Kirche zu Dahlem* (Göttingen: Vandenhoeck & Ruprecht, 1958), with 240 pages. But the whole foundation was really fixed in Article Four at Barmen, based on Mathew 26:25-26. "The various offices in the church establish no rule of one over the other but the exercise of the service entrusted and commanded to the whole congregation. We repudiate the false teaching that the church can and may, apart from this ministry, set up special leaders [*Führer*] equipped with powers to rule." The kind of leadership which the *BK* sought was the leadership of Christ the Head of the Church. The ministry it cultivated was the ministry of the whole church. It was to be a leadership of service—not like that of the Gentiles, who have lords over them. It was to be a ministry of the whole *laos tou Theou*—the kind which after the war produced the greatest contemporary movements to express "the apostolate of the laity": the Deutscher Evangelischer Kirchentag and the Evangelical Academies. These are the legitimate children of the resistance, more than the new church constitutions which were fixed in the post-war reorganizations.

The Stuttgart Declaration of Guilt (October, 1945)

The prevailing interpretation has been that the course of the Confessing Church leaders runs from Barmen to Dahlem—from illegality and expulsion to the assertion of the claim to represent the true line of the Evangelical (territorial) Church. The argument of this paper is that the course of the *BK* runs from Barmen to the Stuttgart Declaration of Guilt, 1945, and that this symbolizes what happened in Germany—and what it means to the Ecumene—better than the restate-

---

11. *DB I*, 201.
12. *Erik Wolf*, ed., *Im Reiche dieses König had man das Recht lieb* (Psalm 99:4) (Tübingen & Stuttgart: Furche-Verlag, 1946), 23.

ment of the confessional and juridical foundations of a *Volkskirche* which had salvaged a remnant from apostasy. For the apostasy of the German Christians was but part of the general problem of reversion to culture-religion in the West. And the most important service of redemptive witness which began at Barmen does not begin to be exhausted with the reëstablishment of (more or less) purified land-churches in Germany after the war. The most important contribution of Barmen is in pointing the way through repentence to the end of culture-religion, the culture-religion of the nineteenth century.

At Stuttgart there took place one of the most remarkable events in church history. In the presence of God and delegates from the sister churches, leaders of the Christian resistance identified themselves with the sin of the German people, expressed repentance, and begged forgiveness. The language bears close attention:

The Council of the Evangelical Church in Germany, at its session on 18-19 October 1945 in Stuttgart, welcomes the representatives of the World Council of Churches.

We are all the more thankful for this visit in that we are not only conscious of oneness with our nation in a great community of suffering, but also in a solitarity of guilt. With great pain we say: Unending suffering has been brought by us to many peoples and countries. That which we have often witnessed to our congregations we now proclaim in the name of the whole church: We have in fact fought for long years in the name of Jesus Christ against the spirit which found its terrible expression in National Socialist government by force; but we accuse ourselves that we didn't witness more courageously, pray more faithfully, believe more joyously, love more ardently.

Now a new beginning is to be made in our churches. Founded on the Holy Scripture, with all earnestness directed to the sole Lord of the church, they are going about to purge themselves of influences foreign to the faith and to put themselves in order. Our hope is in the God of grace and mercy, that He will use our church as his tool and give it authority, to proclaim His Word and to create obedience to His Will among ourselves and in our whole nation.

That in this new beginning we may know ourselves to be warmly tied to the other churches of the ecumenical fellowship fills us with deep rejoicing.

We hope in God that through the joint service of the churches the spirit of violence and revenge, that begins again today to become powerful, may be controlled, and the spirit of peace and love come to command, (the spirit) in which alone tortured humanity can find healing.

So we pray in a time when the whole world needs a new beginning: *Veni creator spiritus!*

(signed)	Stuttgart, 19 October 1945
Bishop Wurm	Pastor Niemöller
Bishop Meiser	*Landesoberkirchenrat* Lilje
Bishop Dibelius	Superintendent Held
Superintendent Hahn	Pastor Niesel
Pastor Asmuszen	Dr. Heinemann[13]

The shrewdly political interpreted this action as another German trick. Astonished newspapermen asked what men who had resisted Nazism

---

13. In German in Joachim Beckmann, ed., *Kirchliches Jahrbuch: 1945-48* (Gutersloh: C. Bertelsmann Verlag, 1950), 26-27.

for years and experienced jail and concentration camp had to repent of. They answered: "We accuse ourselves that we didn't witness more courageously, pray more faithfully, believe more joyously, love more ardently." They confessed not sins but sin, that *Erbsünde* or "blood guilt" which was theirs as members of the German folk. That act at Stuttgart, which was so unintelligible to the secular mind, drew a line across the pages of history and more than any other single thing opened the way for the spirit of reconciliation which has been at work in Germany and the rest of Europe since the war.

Epilogue

What do we Americans have to learn from such special studies and from the witness of the Christian resistance to Nazi totalitarianism? The dialogue with our recent past becomes, you see, a discussion of the terms of our present situation. What does the church struggle have to say to us about our preached word, our churches, our faith? Is it not to point out the bankruptcy of "positive Christianity," of "nonsectarian religion," of "spirituality" without objective norms, of religious individualism which ends in anarchy? Is it not to warn of the perils of culture-religion, of tribal religion? Is it not to lift up again the Person of Him who alone is the center of our history, "the one Word of God"—even Jesus Christ?

Catholic Opposition to Hitler: The Perils of Ambiguity

GORDON C. ZAHN

In their introduction to *Religion and Society in Tension*, Charles Y. Glock and Rodney Stark make the point that, at least in Judeo-Christian cultures, "religion is expected to be at odds with the world around it."[1] If this is a normal state of affairs, how much more intense the strain and antagonisms must be in a "world" dominated by a state authority openly dedicated to the objective of subverting organized religion to serve its own purposes or, if that is not possible, eliminating it and its influence altogether. Since the emergence of such states seems to be a recurring event in the history of man, a definite sociological problem presents itself as to how the religious community is to cope with them. Adolf Hitler's Third Reich is deserving of special mention only in that it is among the most recent and more successful of such attempts. One might be tempted to balk at the "Judeo-Christian culture" description in the context of the Nazi experience, but the fact is that throughout its aborted "thousand year" reign, the National Socialist regime continued to present itself to supporters, admirers, and opponents alike as "the defender of Western Civilization." Even its efforts to expunge the "Judeo" component of that Western heritage (and, in the process, exterminate its living representatives) were justified, assuming that word can be used in this connection, in terms of perfecting and purifying the culture stream Germany shared and still shares with the other nations of "the Christian West."

The problem of dealing with the Christian churches was somewhat more complicated. The ultimate goal may have been the same, the complete eradication of Christianity—though in fairness it is possible to question whether this was actually the goal for any but the more ex-

---

1. Charles Y. Glock and Rodney Stark, *Religion and Society in Tension* (Chicago: Rand McNally & Co., 1965), ix.

tremist Party ideologues. In any event, even for these, it had to be a dream deferred. This did not mean, of course, that the churches had to be tolerated until such time as the regime was ready and able to give them the full treatment; instead, there was a gradual acceleration and intensification of the struggle as the totalitarian power succeeded in consolidating itself. For many different reasons,[2] this particular struggle reached something of a peak in relations between the Nazi state and the Roman Catholic Church and its imposing network of auxiliary organizations. And it was a two-sided struggle, though a losing and finally hopeless one for the church. The only notable exception to the string of defeats that began with the liquidation of church-related organizations, the deconfessionalization of the schools, the formal restriction of religious services and activities, and, ultimately, the dissolution of convents and religious orders was the "victory" won by the Church on the euthanasia issue.

Historians of the Nazi era have provided us with a generously documented record of the struggle.[3] It shows that the principal explanation of why the battles ended in defeat lay, first, in the greater range of effective force available to the secular power and, secondly, in the failure of the leaders of the religious community to inspire the kind of resistance that might have brought Hitler to his Canossa. Hidden behind this explanation, however, is a more troubling suggestion that these religious leaders never really thought the outcome could be otherwise, that from the very beginning they operated on the prudential (and probably correct) assumption that if they were to risk issuing a call to spiritual arms against the state, their troops probably would not have rallied to the cause.

The implications of this for the sociologist of religion should be obvious. An assumption of a lack of commitment, which is really what this posture of prudent self-restraint reflected, must effectively under-

---

2. To suggest only the most obvious few, the Catholic Church represented an international body in what the Nazis intended to make a jealously nationalistic social order; its range of organizations and its wealth made it a potential competitor for the power they intended to make absolute; many of the prominent leaders of the Party had "turned away" from their own personal formation as members of the Catholic Church; there had been a long history of active and influential involvement by the Church and its leaders in national political affairs.

3. Some of the titles most directly related to the subject of this paper would be: J. S. Conway, *The Nazi Persecution of the Churches* (New York: Basic Books, 1968); Guenter Lewy, *The Catholic Church and Nazi Germany* (New York: McGraw-Hill, 1962); Benedicta Maria Kempner, *Priester vor Hitlers Tribunalen* (München: Rütten-Loening Verlag, 1966); Johannes Maria Lenz, *Christus in Dachau* (Vienna: Buchversand "Libri Catholici," 1957); Johannes Neuhäusler, *Kreuz und Hakenkreuz* (München: Verlag Katholische Kirche Bayerns, 1946); Max Bierbaum, *Nicht Lob, Nicht Furcht: Das Leben des Kardinals von Galen* (Münster: Verlag Regensberg, 1957); and Hans Müller, *Katholische Kirche und National Sozialismus* (München: Nymphenburger Verlagshandlung, 1963).

mine the essential viability of the church association as an institutional structure. At the very least it destroys the basis for any significantly prophetic function (the "sacred mission to denounce and resist matters of the flesh" as Glock and Stark have it). The thesis to be set forth and illustrated in this highly exploratory paper is that such was the case for the German Catholic Church under the Nazi tyranny. Lest this be misunderstood, it should be added at once that there is no intent to deny the truly heroic resistance mounted by individual spokesmen and members of the Catholic Church or to dishonor the sacrifices, even of life, they made for their religious faith.[4]

As indicated above this is an exploration and will probably seem to be lacking in scientific quality as that term has come to be defined. In a sense we are limited to such tentative and admittedly impressionistic efforts if only because of the fact that such data as are available are too spotty and much too inconclusive to support a more thorough and systematic analysis. Nor is it possible to test the validity of the reflective commentary to be offered here. Cogent though these observations may hopefully appear, we must not forget that a quite contrary and equally persuasive interpretation could be proposed by others.

Early in 1970 a priest in a small Bavarian village wrote to ask whether I might be interested in seeing the accumulation of diocesan instructions and notices his predecessor had saved during the Nazi years.[5] The eager anticipation with which I answered his inquiry faded considerably when the package finally arrived: most of the items were for the pre-war years, and virtually all of them had already been published in one documentary collection or another. Nevertheless, included among the almost 140 items were two which, treated as a unit, provide dramatic illustrations of the strength and the weakness of the Church's efforts to protest and oppose the repressive measures directed against it.

II

On 31 January 1937, the Reverend Johannes Kraus, rector of the Eichstätt Cathedral parish, mounted his pulpit and delivered a scathing denunciation of false and inaccurate reports in the local press which,

---

4. Neuhäusler and Bierbaum include many such instances, as does Kempner, of priests imprisoned and put to death by the Nazis. Other instances would be Gordon C. Zahn, *In Solitary Witness: The Life and Death of Franz Jägerstätter* (New York: Holt, Rinehart & Winston, 1964) Alfred Delp, S.J., *Prison Meditations* (New York: Herder & Herder, 1963), and Max Josef Metzger, *Gefangenschaftbriefe* (Meitingen: Kyrios Verlag, 1948).
5. These materials were sent with the understanding that the sender and his parish would not be identified. A more complete review of the documents was presented at an international convocation of scholars held at Wayne State University in March 1970. The text of the paper, entitled "Catholic Resistance? A Yes and a No," will be published in the proceedings of the convocation.

he felt, were aimed at discrediting and vilifying the Catholic priesthood. On 12 April of that same year, Bishop Michael Rackl of Eischstätt used the same forum to announce and denounce police orders that had been issued to Kraus giving him twenty-four hours to leave the diocese. Two sermons can not tell the whole story of the church-state struggle, not even in that single diocese,[6] but they give clear evidence of what proved to be an unquestionably effective and, at the same time, eminently self-defeating line of defense.

Dompfarrer Kraus was straightforward enough. Declaring that his sole objective was to counteract the smear campaign being waged against the priesthood and promising to speak not an uncharitable word, he quickly moved to a general statement in the abstract of the theme that he was to personalize in the body of his remarks. Catholics in Germany were compared with the "ancient Israelites" (in retrospect, perhaps not the happiest of identifications to use, but this was before the anti-Jewish campaign reached full momentum): "We returned from the Great War with our other fellow citizens; we all suffered alike the inflation and the years of crisis; we felt and saw the wounds from which our people were bleeding; we endured the effects of the lost war and we wanted to build, nothing more than to build." But time and again, Catholics found their efforts disrupted so that "it became necessary to leave the workplace and take up defense." In the single year he had served as their pastor, he had been obliged to rise to such defense on two previous occasions,[7] but these had brought him little notice or opposition until he dared to take public issue with the controlled press and its anti-Catholic propaganda. Three items in particular were to be reviewed: (1) an openly anti-Semitic letter to the notorious *Stürmer* by a writer who identified himself as a priest; (2) the great wave of publicity given the case of a seventeen-year-old "theology student" charged with sexual perversion; and (3) a journalistic account of a visit to Dachan in which the author described a "chance" meeting with an internee (also a sex deviant) identified as a priest who had formerly served in Rome as a secret negotiator between the Vatican and Moscow. Each item in turn was systematically and factually refuted in the Kraus sermon: no official directory carried a priest by the name signed to the *Stürmer* letter; the unfortunate young man was a high school student who, whatever his career aspirations might have been, could neither

---

6. The Neuhäusler book, *Kreuz und Hakenkreuz*, already cited provides the most complete record of the struggle as it developed in the Munich-Freising Archdiocese, at least for the period preceding World War II.
7. The first such instance had to do with the leaflets and placards distributed by the opponents of the confessional schools and the second was a public defense of Archbishop Gröber of Freiberg after that dignitary had been attacked at a gathering in the vicinity.

have been engaged in nor accepted for priestly studies; and, when pressed for more explicit facts, the journalist (apparently well-known for other anti-Catholic "feature" articles) came up with a quite different description of the man he had talked to at Dachau.[8]

It was the second item, however, that served as the vehicle for the Kraus protest. The identification of this young man as a theology student and, by this device, extending his personal misdeeds to reflect upon the priesthood itself was as illogical and unjust, in Kraus's eyes, as would have been an attempt to smear the officer caste with those misdeeds had the young man expressed an interest in a military career instead. It was an effective logical argument, of course, but Kraus did not intend to stop with that. As a former officer such an attempt would have been an affront to his honor, and he would be bound to protest.

> I am an old front-line officer and have given of my heart's blood for the Fatherland. At the Somme I earned Saxony's Friedrich August medal; at Verdun, the Iron Cross, second class; at Damenweg, the silver metal for bravery; in Aillywald, the Order of Bavaria with crown and swords; and in the battle of Amiens in 1918, the Iron Cross, first class. My left arm was wounded by a grenade splinter, my right upper arm bored by a machine gun bullet so that even today I do not have full strength it it; my right lung was pierced, and I have undergone three operations as an aftermath of this. Two of my ribs were broken. I have gone through the strongest crossfire without falling back. In the advances I scorned cover. When I went forward the soldiers followed me blindly because they considered me invulnerable — and all of my regimental comrades, with whom I am still bound in the true brotherhood of arms, would testify to this.

Having made his point in the context of the hypothetical case, he then drove the argument home in the actual case at hand. "And now I should forget honor, meekly accept the blows on my head which are raining down upon clergy who served in the war as much as upon the other priests and the Church herself — and from those who were still in swaddling clothes when we were shedding our blood for the Fatherland?"

The argument did not end with this, however. The litany of personal war sacrifices was also linked to his refusal to contribute to the various "voluntary" collections organized by the Nazi state. It was not, he assured his listeners, a matter of refusing help to those who needed it (he gave his contributions to the Catholic charities) but, rather, symbolic protest against violations of rights and privileges supposedly guaranteed by the Concordat between the Vatican and the Third Reich. He felt secure in taking such a position, he went on, because he need never "fear the charge that I do not love the Fatherland." As he put it, "I have proven my love for the Fatherland; I prove it every day as

---

8. An interesting point stressed in the rebuttal to the offending article was the assurances given by the Dachau camp commandant that there were no priests interned there. As Lenz and Kempner make quite clear, hundreds of priests spend some time in that camp; it is almost certain that some were already there in 1937. To give such emphasis to what may have been "cover-up" assurances could also be self-defeating in the context of this particular protest sermon.

one of Christ's officers when, in keeping with the words of the dying Field Marshall von Hindenburg, I see to it that Christ is preached in Germany."

The reference to the revered military leader and former President is reflected and expanded in the crescendo of patriotic fervor which brings the sermon to its end. "Everything for Germany, and Germany for Christ! And again: Everything for Germany, and Germany for Christ. And yet a third time, the pledge! Everything for Germany, and Germany for Christ!"

Surely a tough act to follow, but less than three months later Bishop Rackl proved more than equal to the task. Here we have the added benefit of parenthetical insertions at appropriate points in the mimeographed text describing the hearers' reactions to his remarks. These include no less than ten references to applause (ranging from "long" or "sustained" to "loud," "stormy," and in one instance "tumultuous") and two to jeers and whistles of derision directed against actions or statements attributed to the Church's opponents by the bishop.

He began by summarizing the situation: the suddenness of the order requiring their pastor to leave the diocese; the failure to provide specific charges or follow procedural formalities; the bishop's own response in the form of telegraphed protests and appeals for assistance to Hitler and all other concerned officials along with instructions to Kraus not to leave his assigned post (an announcement which brought the first outburst of "stormy" applause). He then addressed himself to the broader meaning of the action, prefacing his remarks on this subject with a disclaimer of any intent to stir passions which might not be fully compatible with the Christian ideal of love. That out of the way, he launched into a statement of his case couched in the most passionately nationalistic terms. He spoke of the cruelty of driving from his native province a dedicated priest who had "poured out his heart's blood" in the nation's battles, particularly at a time when the nation had "learned anew to understand the meaning of soldierly honor and officers' honor" — a "healthy" understanding, in his eyes, that was never completely lost to the German people, not even in "the dark days" of the 1918 Revolution. Referring with approval to the ceremonial honor paid to the Unknown Soldier, he reminded his audience that respect and memorials were due the "known" soldiers as well (wild applause). In what must have been a particularly telling thrust, he expressed his "deepest pain" that the authorities had chosen to treat this former officer in a manner usually reserved for dealing with a pimp.

A reference in that morning's newspaper to "circles in Eichstätt who think they can march against the State" is characterized by Rackl as

CATHOLIC OPPOSITION TO HITLER

"today's declaration of war" and used as the opportunity to move full steam ahead on the patriotism theme:

I take it this is supposed to mean in particular that the Dompfarrer belongs to those who march against the State. (stormy cries of "pfui") My friends! once again I say: anyone who has stood at the Front for four long years, at the very frontmost lines for Germany's honor and well being, has never marched against the State and can not march against the State. (loud applause) And once an officer of the Fatherland has become in addition an officer of the Catholic Church, an officer of Jesus Christ, and officer of God—then that Loyalty which is inscribed on his banner is a Loyalty toward State and Fatherland as well. No one loves his Fatherland more truly than the Catholic priest.

That rousing affirmation was extended at once to the full range of issues troubling church-state relations. The bishop mentioned his own experiences with threatening crowds outside his palace; the injustices and indignities suffered by the Church in all spheres of religious press, to answer and refute the scurrilous charges and rumors directed against the Church and her priests. As he saw it, a new *Kulturkampf* was underway, with the important difference being that where Bismarck had tried to win the people away from the Church, his Nazi successors were moving systematically to isolate the priests from people. It was, therefore, a time to renew one's loyalty to the Church and its priesthood and to pray for grace and strength from above:

I believe the State knows the Dompfarrer is no revolutionary! (applause) The struggle is between two ideologies which are as opposed to each other as fire is opposed to water. And in the struggle the Church now sees what a dangerous opponent she has in the State! We have always been loyal and wish to be obedient to the State unto death. (loud applause) But one thing we will never permit any power on earth to take from us: our holy Catholic faith! (never! never!)

Affirming once again that "in our love and in our loyalty to the German Fatherland and in our love and loyalty to the holy Catholic Church we will never allow others to surpass us," he concluded with a call for a "crusade of prayer" and dedicated the first prayer to "our German Fatherland... that the sun of peace may shine over the German provinces of our truly and deeply beloved German homeland."

III

What we have in these two sermons—and it is a pattern to be found in whatever formal and public Catholic opposition to Hitler did exist— is a combination of strong, explicit protest and equally strong affirmations of patriotism and national loyalty. In its historical context, the protest was truly heroic both in its clarity and its directness. The very fact that it led to official reprisals such as that taken against Kraus is testimony to its effectiveness. It might be noted in passing that while Bishop Rackl did not suffer the same consequences for this or his other pronouncements of similar content,[9] his colleague, Bishop Sproll of Rottenburg, was not so fortunate. Sproll, like Kraus, was formally exiled and, in fact, removed bodily from his diocese, the only German bishop to receive so serious a penalty from the Nazi regime. Whatever legitimate criticism one may make of the Christian churches for their failure to produce an adequate witness for that unhappy time, it must be said to their credit that, weak and unsuccessful though it may have been, they represented the only institutional source of open and public opposition to the tyranny.

The emphasis placed upon the other element, the patriotic motif, was equally open and public and at least as strong. At times, indeed, its superheated emotional tone boiled over into nothing less than rabble-rousing nationalism. The Kraus-Rackl sermons, as the audience reaction inserts make quite clear, reached several such peaks of enthusiasm. What we have, then, given the peculiarities of the situation, is a pairing of two not altogether compatible themes, an exercise in studied ambiguity. It was, needless to say, a tactical ambiguity in that it represented an attempt to set the protest in the form most likely to evoke the desired response from the listening faithful and still, if possible, avoid penalty or suppression. Since the German Catholic was just as much exposed and just as vulnerable to the ultra-nationalistic milieu created by the architects of the Third Reich as were their fellow citizens, the language of patriotic commitment may have been the only vehicle to assure any kind of hearing. This seems, at least, to have been the judgment of the official spokesmen of the Church.

To this extent the stress placed upon the battlefield sacrifices of a Kraus, together with the indignant rejection of any suggestion of disloyalty on his part, must be seen as a calculated rhetorical device. It would be much too simple, however — and probably an insult to the churchmen who used this device — to assume that this was all it was. The national pride, the patriotic fervor, and, it would even more certainly follow, the indignation voiced in these sermons were unquestionably real and sincere.[10] It scarcely bears noting that this would be equally true of the enthusiastic echo their words found in the heart of the listener in the pew.

---

9. An equally emotional sermon — once again protesting the exile of another of his priests — was preached by Rackl at Ohsenfurt some weeks later.

10. An inquiry addressed to the Eichstätt chancery requesting further information concerning Kraus brought a most interesting and informative response from a member of the faculty at the *Bischöfliche Hochschule*. It seems that Bishop Rackl's intervention was successful to the extent that Kraus was able to remain at his post until May 1942, at which time another outspoken sermon brought him a renewed order to leave the area. He returned from this exile and resumed his position as *Dompfarrer* in July 1950.

My correspondent took the occasion to warn against the impression one might take from these two sermons that their authors were "Hurrah-patriots," "militarists," or "nationalists," explain-

There is no way to determine the actual impact of these patriotic effusions. That they were singularly ineffective in convincing the Nazis is clear enough from the pattern of continued and intensified persecution. Of course, this in itself proves little: it is quite possible that without this fervent and public exploitation of heroic war exploits as evidence of Catholic loyalty, the pace of the persecution might have been speedier and the defeat of the church much more complete.

In our readiness to make this allowance, however, we must not disregard other equally important effects that appeals of this nature would almost certainly produce. In a situation of crisis in which the tension between church and state is heightened to the danger point, ambiguity, whatever tactical justification it may possess, has its perils as well. At the very least, it can operate to confuse and blur the very issues it is to the interest of the religious community to define as sharply as possible. In the present case, for instance, the Nazi authorities and their captive press had embarked upon a deliberate campaign to undercut the influence of the Catholic Church and its leadership by drastically restricting their sphere of permissible activities and attempting to destroy their public image. Kraus made specific reference to this: "Children point their fingers at us and their elders murmur among themselves, 'There's another one of those.' You all know what I mean." Then, when someone like Kraus did dare to respond to these attacks and speak out in defense of the priesthood, he was simply removed from the scene by arbitrary police action. This was the issue, but the rhetoric of the sermons converted it into something else. It now became a matter of denouncing these smears and unjust punitive actions *because they were directed against heroes who had fought and bled for Germany*, men who deserved better treatment from the nation and its rulers. The essential fact that priests *as priests* were being

---

ing that the emphasis given to Kraus's wartime service was intended to forestall reprisals that might otherwise be taken against him. Soldiers, he went on, were held in high regard, especially at the time the German re-armament program was getting under way. Even Jews who had won decorations in World War I were at first exempted from the restrictive legislation. As far as the Church was concerned, if one wanted to accomplish anything at all, it was necessary that these circumstances be exploited as cleverly as possible without, of course, acting in such a manner as to bind or appear to bind the Church to the regime. The same strategic stance, he noted further, applied to all newspapers and periodicals which might wish to register criticism of the Party and the regime: such criticism was necessarily hidden and indirect if it hoped to avoid immediate suppression.

Nothing in the present paper denies the validity of these concerns and considerations. However, one might take issue with the familiar assertion advanced by this correspondent that perhaps only those who have lived under a dictatorship will be able to interpret this material correctly. What is suggested here is the possibility that the other side of the coin may not have been given sufficient consideration by those who do look at the issue from the perspective of their personal experience under the dictatorship — that is, the very real possibility that by using these tactics they may have reinforced, however inadvertently, the hold the Nazis had upon the ordinary German citizen who also happened to be a member of the Catholic Church.

slandered — and that this was to be protested even if the victim had not so much as a day of military service to his credit — was simply smothered by this blanket of super-patriotic rhetoric.

Distortion of the real issues at stake is bad enough, but other more subtle effects must be recognized as perils too. That same flagwaving, bloody-shirt rhetoric which was intended to arouse the indignation of the hearers (and probably did) could not fail to reinforce the Nazis' own efforts to instill and exploit nationalistic pride and identification in the hearts of the general public. In this way the religious opposition actually helped the regime to secure the foundations for the totalitarian power which would later be turned against the Church. After listening to sermons like these, Catholics would emerge indignant; but it is at lest equally certain that they would also emerge "charged up" in their emotional attachment to German national traditions and the patriotic virtues. Once convinced that "no one loves his Fatherland more truly than the Catholic priest," the conclusions to be drawn by the Catholic faithful concerning their obligations to the nation's leaders should be obvious enough.

The contribution made by the patriotism component of the protest-and-patriotism tactic to the Nazi propaganda drive had still another effect that could only prove dysfunctional to the church and its interests. The vast majority of the faithful, even assuming they might not be in full sympathy with the regime, was not, as the old phrase has it, "thirsting after martyrdom" or, for that matter, looking for any avoidable trouble with the authorities. Even making due allowance for the effects of selective perception, the German Catholic citizen would have to be extremely obtuse not to realize that his church was under severe pressure and extremely insensitive not to be worried by that fact.

Sermons like the two discussed here not only put the situation in distressingly clear perspective, but they usually included passages specifically calling for the kind of spiritual heroism that might endanger the comfortable patterns of compromise and conformity that most of the Catholic faithful had been able to achieve in their individual lives. If this were all, the citizen who was also a believer would have been faced with an unpleasant but inescapable choice. But it was not all. How helpful it must have been to find these troubling details of persecution and injustice interwoven with sentiments exhorting the faithful to loyalty and obedience to the state. "Everything for Germany and Germany for Christ" may have carried all sorts of subtle overtones for *Dompfarrer* Kraus that his listeners did not catch or, in what may have been the majority of cases, *would not have wanted to catch*. As a result, those very same qualities of ambiguity that, it was hoped, would mollify the Nazi authorities actually opened the way for the man in the pew to avoid drawing the intended conclusions.

In summary, then, the failure of the Catholic Church to mount an effective opposition to Hitler's Third Reich was due, at lest in part, to this failure to "tell it like it was" and to insist that its members "stand up and be counted" against tyranny. How substantial a part this played in that failure is beyond our power at this point in time and space to determine. It may well be that a contrary course would have failed, too, with even more disastrous consequences.

This is admittedly an inconclusive note upon which to end this modest attempt to explore and interpret that record; but even if we are less than happy with the highly tentative answers we have suggested, at least there is some satisfaction in having focused attention upon questions that all too often have been ignored or overlooked in the literature dealing with the "struggle between Cross and Swastika." There may be some important lessons to be learned as well for churches and their leaders who may in other times and places find themselves confronted with governments, whether professedly democratic or authoritarian, whose policies or programs represent a threat to the religious practices and teachings it is their responsibility to uphold and spread. In any such future tests — that is, whenever the tension between church and state becomes acute — it might be instructive to reflect upon the German experience before preferring the wisdom of serpents, represented by the kind of tactical ambiguity described here, over the direct simplicity of authentic prophetic witness. And if, as the Berrigans (brother-priests charged with complicity in a bombing-and-kidnap plot) and others might insist, such a crisis is upon us here and now, the lesson is particularly timely.

The Formulation of Religious Policy in the Soviet Union

BOHDAN R. BOCIURKIW

According to an official 1984 exposition of Soviet religious policy by the recently retired government spokesman on the subject, Vladimir Alekseevich Kuroedov,[1] the Kremlin's treatment of religious groups and believers has been guided by the following eight "Marxist-Leninist" principles enshrined in the 1977 Constitution: (1) The right to profess any religion and to perform rites of religious cult (worship); (2) the right not to profess any religion and to conduct antireligious propaganda; (3) equal rights for all citizens regardless of their attitudes toward religion; (4) equality of all religions before the law; (5) the absence of any coercion with respect to profession or non profession of religion; (6) inadmissibility of utilizing religion to the detriment of society, the state, or individual citizens; (7) noninterference of the state with internal affairs of the church; (8) noninterference of the church with affairs of the state.[2] In fact, claimed Kuroedov in an earlier brochure written in English, "Far from oppressing the church or preventing believers from practicing their religion, Soviet legislation stipulates that any violation of law through infringement on the rights of believers is a criminal offense."[3]

Even a hasty examination of the Soviet Russian statute on religious

---

1. A former party *obkom* secretary, Kuroedov assumed in 1960 the chairmanship of the governmental Council for the Affairs of the Russian Orthodox Church and, after the former merged with the Council for the Affairs of [non-Orthodox] Religious Cults in the winter of 1965-66, he continued to head the unified Council for Religious Affairs (CRA) until his retirement in November 1984. He was replaced by another former party official and, more recently, diplomat, Konstantin Mikhailovich Kharchev. (*Izvestiia*, 4 January 1985).
2. V. A. Kuroedov, *Religiia i tserkov v Sovetskom obshchestve* (Moscow: Politizdat, 1984), 7.
3. V. Kuroedov, *Church and Religion in the USSR* (Moscow: Novosti, 1977), 3.

associations (1975)[4] and other enactments and instructions on religious activities,[5] the relevant sections of the Criminal Code,[6] and the party-state documents on religion and antireligious propaganda,[7]—let alone those classified governmental reports that found their way to the West over the last decade[8]—reveals Kuroedov's exposition to be the familiar mixture of truth, half-truth, fiction, and omission designed not to elucidate, but to conceal the actual operative principles of Soviet religious policy. Only two out of the eight "principles" listed above have been honored in practice—"the right not to profess any religion and to conduct antireligious propaganda"[9] and "noninterference of the church with the affairs of the state." Given the actively antireligious orientation of the Soviet state (and, in particular, of its "leading core"—the Communist party), "inadmissibility of utilizing religion to the detriment of . . . the state" places in question all rights of religious believers in the USSR.

A point-by-point refutation of Kuroedov's claims could well take up the remainder of this essay and, indeed, of many more studies, considering the volume of evidence to the contrary.[10] There is already considerable literature in English[11] and other Western languages

---

4. Formally, an amendment to the RSFSR decree, "On Religious Associations" of 8 April 1929, adopted by the Presidium of the RSFSR Supreme Soviet on 23 June 1975 [*O religii i tserkvi*. Sbornik vyskazyvanii klassikov marksizma-leninizma, documentov KPSS i Sovetskogo gosudarstva] (Moscow: Politizdat, 1981), 126-39.
5. Ibid., 142-43, 154-65.
6. Ibid., 161-65.
7. Ibid., 15-108.
8. V. A. Kuroedov and A. S. Pankratov, eds., *Zakonodatelstvo o religioznykh kultakh* [*Sbornik materialov i documentov*] (Moscow: Iuridicheskaia literatura, 1971). The volume, though published in a printing of twenty-one thousand, is designated "for official use" and is not listed in any Soviet publication guides for 1971. Another classified collection that was also smuggled to the West was published in the Ukranian SSR two years later: K. Z. Lytvyn and A. I. Pshenychnyi, eds., *Zakonodavstvo pro relihiini kulty* [*Zbirnyk dokumentiv i materialiv*] (Kiev: Politvydav Ukrainy, 1973).
9. Until 1929, the Soviet constitituon allowed for both "religious and antireligious propaganda." Subsequently, authoritative Soviet commentary on religious legislation in the USSR interpreted "freedom of worship" as excluding the right to religious propaganda, and prohibiting "the recruitment of new toilers, especially of children, into the ranks of supporters of religion." N. Orleanskii, *Zakon o religioznykh obedineniiakh RSFSR* (Moscow: Bezbozhnik, 1930), 47.
10. Including the two "classified" collections listed in footnote 8, which clearly contradict Kuroedov's public statements, as well as his deputy's, V. Furov's secret reports for 1970 and 1974 on the Russian Orthodox Church presented on behalf of the Council on Religious Affairs to the Party Central Committee, "Iz otcheta Soveta po delam religii TsK KPSS (za 1970 god)," *Vestnik Russkogo Khristianskogo Dvizheniia (VRKhD)*, no. 131, I-II (1980), 362-72 (excerpt); and "Iz otcheta Soveta po delam religii chlenam TsK KPSS," *VRKhD*, no. 130, IV (1970), 275-344
11. See in particular, W. Kolarz, *Religion in the Soviet Union* (London: Macmillan, 1961), and *Religion and the Soviet State: A Dilemma of Power* (New York: Praeger, 1969); N. Struve, *Christians in Contemporary Russia* (New York: Scribners, 1967); R. H. Marshall, Jr., ed., *Aspects of Religion in the Soviet Union* (Chicago: University of Chicago Press,

dealing with various aspects of church-state relations in the Union of Soviet Socialist Republics. The task here, however, is not polemics with the former chairman of the Council on Religious Affairs (CRA) in Moscow, but a much more complex one. What will be attempted here is, first, identification of the objectives of Soviet religious policy; second, clarification of the underlying perceptions and attitudes of the makers of this policy; third, a reconstruction of interdependent policy considerations that enter into the formulation of the regime's line on religion; and, fourth, an examination of the attitudes of religious groups to the Soviet system and the extent to which these groups could influence this policy. Finally, this essay shall attempt to place the religious policy-making process in its institutional framework and conclude by confronting Kuroedov's "principles" with the actual operational norms guiding this process as they can be inferred from actions of the Party and state officials.

The Objects and Objectives of Soviet Religious Policy

Religion, churches, and religious activities are not a private matter either to the ruling Communist party or to the Soviet state.[12] The moment it is openly professed, religion becomes a highly political matter in a system that claims monopoly of truth and power for the party committed to the ultimate eradication of all religion in communist society. Being ideologically incompatible with the official creed of "Marxism-Leninism," religious organizations cannot be absorbed, like all other structures, into a centralized system of social controls; by the very nature of their organization and activities, churches cannot be turned into institutional "conveyer belts" that the party employs to mobilize, indoctrinate, and manipulate the masses. They cannot but remain the sole institutional "islands of non-conformity" within the Soviet system, which grudgingly tolerates them for two principal reasons: they still command a significant following in society (officially estimated in 1983 at "20 to 30 percent of the adult population of the Soviet Union, or about 10 percent of the total number of citizens"[13]); and most religious faiths are closely

---

1971); B. R. Bociurkiw and J. W. Strong, eds., *Religion and Atheism in the USSR and Eastern Europe* (London: Macmillan, 1975); M. Bourdeaux, *Patriarch and Prophets: Persecution of the Russian Orthodox Church Today* (New York: Praeger, 1970; and D. J. Dunn, ed., *Religion and Modernization in the Soviet Union* (Boulder, Colo.: Westview, 1977). See also O. Luchterhandt, *Der Sowjetstaat und die Russisch-Orthodoxe Kirche* (Cologne: Wissenschaft u. Politik, 1976), and E. Voss, ed., *Die Religionsfreiheit in Osteuropa* (Zollikon: Glaube in der 2 Welt, 1984).
12. See N. S. Gordienko, ed., *Osnovy nauchnogo ateizma*, 3d rev. ed. (Moscow: Mysl, 1983), 156-73.
13. Ibid., 173.

linked with the ethnicity and culture of nations and national minorities encompassed by the Kremlin's vast Euro-Asian empire.[14]

Some forty-eight religious groups and movements exist in the Soviet Union, according to Kuroedov's deputy, V. G. Furov. In a confidential briefing he gave in May 1976 to the editorial staff of the *Greater Soviet Encyclopedia*,[15] Furov admitted that "at present, there are sixteen thousand congregations of all cults; however, in the press we cite the figure of twenty thousand so that anti-Soviet [elements] would not shout that 'religion is being destroyed'." The largest among the religious groups is the Russian Orthodox Church with fewer than seventy-five hundred "working" churches,[16] served by only fifty-nine hundred priests; next to the Orthodox are Roman Catholics with one thousand surviving churches (out of forty-two hundred in mid-1940); twenty-four thousand Islamic mosques before the Revolution, only three hundred are "registered," while seven hundred more are "semi-existing." Only three hundred Old Believers' churches are still operating (one-fifth of the prerevolutionary total), and of the five thousand synagogues once operating only two hundred remain, of which ninety-two are "registered" (of these, forty-two are active only intermittently). Some four thousand sectarian congregations comprise four hundred thousand believers, but only 60 percent of them can be considered loyal to the Soviet regime, observed Furov. Twelve hundred sectarian communities operate illegally and the majority of them have an "anti-Soviet orientation." This category apparently includes the dissident Council of Churches of Evangelical Christians-Baptists, unregistered Pentecostalist and Adventist congregations, the Jehovah's Witnesses, and some smaller banned sects. Significantly, Furov's account omits the largest outlawed religious group in the USSR, the Ukrainian Greek Catholic (Uniate) Church which, prior to its forcible "reunion" with the Russian Orthodox Church in the late 1940s, embraced some four million believers. The Church still retains its own clandestine hierarchy, the clergy and lay believers united with Rome.[17] Since 1977, states

---

14. See this writer's "Institutional Religion and Nationality in the Soviet Union," in E. Wimbush, ed., *Soviet Nationalities in Strategic Perspective* (London: Croom Helm, 1985).
15. As reported by *Khronika tekushchikh sobytii*, no. 41 (3 August 1976): 7.
16. Ibid., 8. However, according to Furov's secret CRA report for 1974, in some dioceses only two-thirds or fewer churches were operating on a regular basis due to the shortage of clergy. "Iz otcheta Soveta" (1974), 298-300.
17. See this writer's "The Uniate Church in the Soviet Ukraine: A Case Study in Soviet Church Policy," *Canadian Slavonic Papers* 7 (1965): 89-113; and O. Zinkevych and Taras Lonchyna, comps., *Martyrolohiia ukrainskykh tseerkov, Tom II: Ukrainska Katolytska Tserkva, Documenty, materiialy, khrystyianskyi samvydav Ukrainy* (Baltimore: Smoloskyp, 1985).

Kuroedov, a total of 810 "new" religious congregations were "registered," while 1,035 congregations were "deregistered" by the authorities. Thus, between 1977 and 1984, 225 religious communities were delegalized in the USSR.[18]

Together with many millions of believers, these religious groups are the primary object of Soviet religious policy; the more remote objects of this policy are their coreligionists abroad, international religious centers (in particular, the Vatican), ecumenical organizations, and those policy and opinion elites outside the Soviet bloc that may be swayed to support Soviet foreign policies or at least to desist from actions unfavorable to the USSR. Between these immediate and remote objectives of Soviet religious policy are nonbelievers in Soviet society, especially the party and state elites, the police and the military, and above all, the youth; they all must be "immunized" against religion and prevented from succumbing to the influence of the clergy and appeal of religious "cult." Nonbelievers are thus the second target of Soviet religious policy, courted in particular by the massive antireligious propaganda, indoctrination in the so-called scientific atheism, and socialization into the substitute civic rituals and ceremonies.[19]

As far as one can infer from Soviet official and unofficial accounts and an ever-growing body of religous *samizdat*, Soviet religious policy appears to pursue four major objectives. First, it strives to accelerate the "dying-away of religion" by minimizing legal possibilities for the propagation of religious beliefs by reducing the number of licenced houses of worship; by making it impossible for religious groups to replace all the clergy that have become disabled by sickness or old age, or who have died; by siphoning away from the churches much of their income from believers in the form of alleged "donations" to the Soviet Peace Fund; and by strictly enforcing a legal ban against any organized religious instruction for minors, while reserving for official atheism a monopoly in education and political socialization.

Second, Soviet religious policy has always aimed at maximizing state and police controls over religious organizations and their activities. The state accomplishes this not just through the growing legal and administrative restrictions on their external conduct, but increasingly through the CRA control of selection, transfer, promotion, and demotion of religious hierarchy and the clergy, as well as through preliminary screening of their decisions and records at all levels of ecclesiastical organization, including their local

---

18. Kuroedov, *Religiia i tserkov*, 144.
19. See David E. Powell, *Antireligious Propaganda in the Soviet Union* (Cambridge, Mass.: Harvard University Press, 1975).

congregations' executive and auditing committees.[20] Through their control of religious cadres and structures, the authorities have sought to police, monitor, restrain, and manipulate the rank-and-file believers and, if need be, impose additional constraints on religious activities under the guise of decisions allegedly reached by church leaders themselves.[21]

Third, to facilitate and perpetuate their control over the "recognized" religious leaders, Soviet authorities have, once such control has been established, actively protected these leaders from any effective competition or challenge from their flock by centralizing such religious organizations,[22] minimizing or suppressing any spontaneous grass-roots input from believers into ecclesiastical decision-making, and by persecuting internal dissent, opposition, and schism movements within the "loyal" churches.[23]

Fourth, the Kremlin has sought to exploit the so-called patriotic churches for its own political ends: at home, the churches have been used to combat and displace the so-called disloyal churches, such as the Ukrainian Autocephalous Orthodox Church and the Ukrainian Greek-Catholic Church,[24] as well as to integrate non-Russian Orthodox (Ukrainians, Belorussians, Moldavians) with the Russians in a single "imperial church." Abroad, the "patriotic" churchmen have been relied upon to project and rationalize the current Soviet foreign policy and propaganda line dressed up as "religiously" motivated ecumenical and peace-making initiatives.[25] (A reader of the *Journal of the Moscow Patriarchate* would be surprised to discover that these external activities occupy some nine-tenths of the business at the Holy Synod's meetings.)

THE UNDERLYING PERCEPTIONS AND ATTITUDES

Several factors have shaped Soviet religious policy since the Bolshevik seizure of power in 1917: the party's perception of religion;

---

20. See Furov, "Iz otcheta Soveta," (1974), esp. pp. 266-67, 297, 315, 317, 319, 321, 337-43.
21. Ibid. See also "Iz otcheta Soveta" (1970), 363.
22. The only religious groups that are denied central authority are those of doubtful political loyalty to the regime—the Roman Catholic Church, Judaic communities, and Adventists.
23. Note, e.g., the government's involvement in the struggle against the opposition to the AUC ECB, in particular against the Council of Churches of ECB.
24. Note this writer's *Ukrainian Churches Under the Soviet Rule: Two Case Studies* (Cambridge, Mass.: Harvard University Press, Ukrainian Studies Fund, 1984).
25. For an early and still relevant rationalization by the Moscow Patriarchate of its peace-making propaganda involvement on the side of the regime, see Moskovskaia Patriarkhiia, *Russkaia Pravoslavnaia Tserkov: Ustroistvo, polozhenie, deiatelnost* (Moscow: Moskovskaia Patriarkhiia, 1958), 244.

the "inner logic" or "systemic compulsion" of the political system that remains the closest approximation to a "totalitarian model"; pragmatic policy considerations; and the attitudes taken towards the regime by individual religious groups.

The Soviet notion of religion derives from a simplistic militant version of Marxist atheism developed in the writings of Vladimir Ilyich Lenin and his followers, who were strongly influenced by the anticlerical tradition of Russian radicalism. Leninism has "explained" religion not merely in terms of the masses' cultural backwardness and ignorance, but also as a product of a deliberate "fraud" perpetrated by the greedy and reactionary clergy, dispensing a "spiritual home brew" to the working masses in order to prevent them from developing a true class consciousness, to dull and distort their political instincts and paralyze their revolutionary potentialities. Unlike classical Marxism, Leninism does not trust the "objective" socio-economic processes to emancipate the masses from religious "illusion." Lenin's impatience with these slow-working processes combined with his distrust of the masses' rationality to reinforce the Bolshevik inclination to "accelerate" secularization processes by manipulation, agitation, and force. At the same time, the party's claim to a truly "scientific" theory and collective infallibility generated its intolerance of "false" teachings, making it incapable of any meaningful dialogue with religious believers.

Soviet communism, however, is not without ambiguities in its treatment of "religious survivals." While advocating a strategy of active antireligious struggle ultimately to "liberate" all society from religion, Leninism counsels tactical flexibility, including manipulation of religion whenever it will serve the party's political interests.[26] Hence the contradictory and yet complementary tendencies in the Bolshevik treatment of religion—"fundamentalism" and "pragmatism"—the two poles between which Soviet church policy has vacillated since 1917.[27]

Under Joseph Stalin, Russian nationalism increasingly affected the party's attitudes toward the individual churches and faiths. After he had nearly wiped out the Russian Orthodox Church by the end of the 1930s, Stalin turned to Russian Orthodoxy as a "patriotic," integrating force during the crisis of World War II and used it as a weapon against the Ukrainian Uniates and other "nationalistic" churches.

---

26. See this writer's "Lenin and Religion," in L. Schapiro and P. Reddaway, eds., *Lenin—The Man, the Theorist, the Leader: A Reappraisal* (London: Pall Mall, 1977), 107-34.
27. Cf. this writer's "The Shaping of Soviet Religious Policy," *Problems of Communism* 12, no. 3 (May-June 1973), 37-51.

Systemic Compulsion to Control

Perhaps even more important than ideology in motivating the party's policy on religion has been the compulsion inherent in all "totalitarian" regimes, to suppress or closely control all those social institutions and activities that cannot be fully assimiliated by the political system. Under Soviet conditions, religion remains the only formally tolerated and thus readily available alternative to the communist belief system, and the church (apart from the family), the regime's sole institutional rival in socialization of children and youth.

Alienation from the system, a sense of relative deprivation, the search for one's unfalsified cultural roots and for absolute moral values, as well as psychological and aesthetical wants continue to attract to religion not only the most exploited and neglected strata of Soviet society—the peasants, women, and elderly people—but also disillusioned intellectuals and youth. Moreover, in the absence of other relatively autonomous structures within Soviet society, institutional religions have assumed some important extrareligious functions, including the maintenance of national tradition and culture. What has been the source of perhaps the greatest anxiety to the Soviet authorities is the attraction that churches and sects have always had for the so-called anti-Soviet elements within the USSR who, deprived of any other legal channels for dissent, may seek to utilize religious structures as instruments of political opposition to the regime.

This is why religion has always been viewed by the Kremlin as an actual or potential threat to internal stability and security and why the day-to-day control over religious activities and the penetration of religious structures has been assigned to the secret police, from Cheka to the present KGB. This powerful institution has always overshadowed the formal government bodies—presently, the CRA—that are entrusted with the supervision of churches and sects and their relations with the state. At the same time, religious institutions and activities have been circumscribed by a maze of detailed laws, decrees, regulations, and instructions—some of them secret.[28] Secrecy has been employed to conceal blatant official violations of the constitutional "separation of church from the state," of published laws on "religious cults," and of solemnly signed international covenants on human rights. This secrecy has also been used to spare ideological embarrassment for the atheist regime whose

---

28. See Kuroedev and Pankratov, especially the 1961 and 1968 secret instructions of the Council.

involvement in the administration of internal church affairs has surpassed that of the old czarist regime.[29]

The contradictions inherent in the Soviet religious policy have caused some confusion, even for the CRA plenipotentiary for the city of Kiev, Rudenko, whose observations were quoted in the Council's secret report to the Party Central Committee:

> ... on the one hand their [the clergy's] numbers should be reduced due to their religious influence, [but] on the other hand, the numbers of believers do not decline and there is a growing need for them [the priests]; on the one hand, they ought to be compromised, on the other hand they are loyal, conduct their activities within law, know a lot and can influence many things, and, therefore, we are interested in carrying out with them certain work.... Particularly while [they] meet and accompany foreign tourists, religious and governmental organizations and delegations, the numbers of which grow every year.[30]

Pragmatic Considerations

Rudenko's musings point to the fact that, while continuing to combat religion, the Soviet regime has had no scruples in exploiting religion for immediate political gains at home and abroad.

In the USSR, the authorities have relied on the "loyal" clergy to pacify and educate the faithful in the spirit of "Soviet patriotism" and obedience to the "providentially established" regime. Behind this now obligatory function of the "registered" clergy, one finds the Kremlin's anxiety that the believers' sense of deprivation, engendered by a lifelong exposure to official ridicule and harassment, and the denial of access to positions of any importance may otherwise explode in an open dissent.

Even more useful have been "loyal" bishops and clergy—by virtue of greater credibility accorded to them abroad—in promoting Soviet foreign policy objectives through their involvement in international communist front organizations such as the Christian Peace Conference and in ecumenical organizations, particularly the World Council of Churches, as well as in their bilateral contacts with the Vatican and other religious centers in the West.

Historically, the Soviet treatment of religion has also been closely related to the regime's peasant and nationalities' policies, both because of the particularly strong hold of religion on the peasant masses as well as the traditional interdependence of religion and ethnicity within the multinational population of the USSR.

---

29. With the important difference, that the old Czarist regime represented a confessional Orthodox state in which the Church was established and fully integrated into the system.
30. Furov, "Iz otcheta Soveta" (1974), 304.

The Churches' Attitudes Toward the Regime

An important factor in shaping the regime's policy toward organized religions and affecting the treatment accorded to individual churches has been the churches' attitude toward the Soviet regime and the degree of their compatibility with the current domestic and foreign objectives of the governemnt. To the extent to which ideology or personality factors have not interfered with its "rationality," the Kremlin has pursued the policy of rewarding its friends and punishing its enemies among and within churches and sects. Clearly, from the Kremlin's point of view, the most "patriotic" and politically and culturally most compatible church has been the Russian Orthodox Church, historically most closely associated with Russian nationhood and the guardianship of Russia's imperial legacy. The index of "patriotism" has been the distance to which individual religious groups were willing to go in proving their unconditional loyalty to the atheist state by: keeping silent in the face of outright religious persecution (as, e.g., during Khrushchev's sweeping antireligious campaign of 1959-64); "covering-up" such persecution through purportedly "voluntary" self-imposed restrictions on the church's activities; closing down "with their own hands" 'redundant' churches, monasteries, convents, and theological schools; and "retiring" "superfluous" clergy. (Furov's CRA reports for 1970 acknowledged the "loyalty" and "realism" of the patriarch and a number, if not all, of the bishops in not refusing such collaboration with the state.)[31] The ultimate proof of "Soviet patriotism" required of religious leaders has been to "bear false witness for the sake of the Church," i.e., to falsify for the benefit of foreigners the true situation of the church and "indignantly deny" in public the actual cases of religious persecution,[32] or even to disown as "unchurchly trouble-makers" those courageous priests and laypersons who dared to speak out openly in defense of the faith.[33]

While the Russian Orthodox Church has been singled out among all religious groups for a special treatment as a kind of "patriotic vanguard," several other groups, such as the Armenian-Gregorian Church, the Georgian Orthodox Church, the All-Union Council of

---

31. Ibid., 278-83; as well as his 1970 report, 363.
32. The classic example, still cited in Soviet publications, was set in 1930 by Patriarchal deputy Metropolitan Sergii (Stragorodskii), who in the midst of violent antireligious campaign assured the domestic and foreign press that "there never was and there is no persecution of religion in the USSR" and that Soviet repressions against clergymen "are applied to them not for their religious convictions at all, but . . . for various antigovernmental activities" (cited in Kuroedov, *Religiia i tserkov*, 78-79).
33. Furov (1974), 312-13; and Bourdeaux, *Patriarch and Prophets*.

the Evangelical Christians-Baptists, and the four Islamic "Spiritual Administrations" (Muftiates), seem to have scored relatively highly on this "index of patriotism."

Other religious groups, especially the Roman Catholics, have ended up somewhere between complete submission to and defiance of the atheist state.[34] They have foresworn political opposition to the Soviet regime but would not silently assist the CRA and other regime agencies in "reducing the level of religiosity" in the country. Their relative standing with the authorities does reflect their limited political usefulness, if any, to the regime, caused in particular, in the case of Roman Catholics, by their subordination to an international religious center outside Soviet control.

Some churches and sects (as well as elements of the Russian Orthodox Church and other "recognized" groups) could not or would not pay this price for a limited and insecure legal status; they opted for or were driven into the religious underground, persecuted by but independent of the atheist state. The largest among these "catacomb" groups is the Ukrainian Catholic (Uniate) Church, while the most dynamic and resilient, despite severe Soviet persecution, is the Council of Churches of the Evangelical Christians-Baptists, which split away from the collaborationist All-Union Council in the mid-1960s.

According to Soviet law, no religious congregation is allowed to engage in collective worship or is permitted to use a nationalized house of worship until it has first been "registered," in fact, licensed, by the CRA, which may refuse to "register" certain congregations and faiths or terminate, without any mechanism of appeal, an earlier "registration" of a congregation or its minister. A secret 1961 instruction issued by the CRA's predecessors, stipulates that "not eligible for registration are religious associations and groups of believers who belong to sects the doctrines and activities of which have an anti-state and fanatical character: The Jehovah's Witnesses, True Orthodox Christians,[35] Adventists-Reformists, Murashkovites, etc."[36]

---

34. For the internal accounts of the Lithuanian Roman Catholic Church's situation in the USSR, see the samizdat *Chronicle of the Catholic Church in Lithuania*, which has appeared regularly since 1972.
35. An underground network of those Russian Orthodox, including some unregistered clergy, who have rejected Metropolitan Sergii's 1927 compromise with the Soviet regime and have since refused to recognize the canonicity of the official Church for its surrender to the "Satanic" power. See W. C. Fletcher, *The Russian Orthodox Church Underground, 1917-1970* (London: Oxford University Press, 1971).
36. Instruction of 16 March 1961, "O primeniiu zakonodatelstva o kultakh" in Kuroedov and Pankratov, eds., 157.

At least some believers have perceived the close collaboration between their subservient church leaders and the atheist state as an "unholy alliance of shepherds and wolves" at the expense of the flock. Such a perception, not entirely unfounded, could not help but generate a growing sense of frustration and alienation among sections of the clergy and believers. Since the mass closings of churches during 1959-64, these perceptions crystallized into the movements of religious dissent within several "registered" religious groups, most notably among the Evangelical Christians-Baptists, Pentecostalists, and Adventists, but also among the Russian and Georgian Orthodox. Another major movement of self-defense emerged within the Lithuanian Roman Catholic Church, its principal voice being, since 1972, the *samizdat Chronicle of the Catholic Church in Lithuania*. Intensified persecution of the Uniates in the Western Ukraine has more recently stimulated a similar clandestine publication, *The Chronicle of the Catholic Church in the Ukraine*.[37]

POLICY INPUTS FROM RELIGIOUS GROUPS

To be sure, the Moscow Patriarchate, the All-Union Council of the Evangelical Christians-Baptists, and some other "recognized" religious groups have tried to turn their services to the state, especially abroad, to their own advantage. They have employed these "patriotic works" as their bargaining tools with the regime in an attempt to cut their losses or to preserve their institutional strength from further inroads by state atheism. It is safe to assume, for example, that frequent meetings between most Orthodox bishops and the officials of the governmental Council on Religious Affairs—described in Furov's secret 1974 report—feature more than just a one-sided exchange of state directives and churchmen's reports to the state. Individual bishops have reportedly attempted to influence CRA commissioners by means ranging from flattery and bribes to threats and complaints to higher authorities.[38] It is exactly in terms of their determination to alter or at least to frustrate the implementation of Soviet religious policy, that Furov's report classified the episcopate into three categories.

In the first category are found the most "patriotic" but also the most indifferent bishops, including Patriarch Pimen, who "realistically acknowledge that our government is not interested in

---

37. See issues 1-9 (April to December 1984), reproduced in RFE/RL *Materialy samizdata*, from AS 5414 to AS 5444, during 1984 and 1985.
38. Furov (1974), 287, 289, 295-96; cf. "Zvernennia Iepyskopa Feodosiia do Brezhneva," *Suchasnist* 21, no. 7-8 (July-August 1981).

expanding the role of religion and the church in our society, and who . . . are not personally involved in spreading the influence of Orthodoxy among our population."[39]

The second category embraces otherwise "loyal" bishops, "who in their daily administrative and ideological work are trying to activate the clergy and the church body, who are trying to expand the role of the church in the private, family, and social life, and . . . who are recruiting for priesthood young zealots of Orthodox piety."[40] Among them, Furov listed the late Metropolitan Nikodim (Rotov) of Leningrad and the current Metropolitan Filaret (Denysenko) of Kiev. Other bishops include former Poltava bishop Feodosii (Dykun) who later, in 1977, wrote a long protest to Brezhnev against the local CRA plenipotentiary, in which Feodosii detailed his long struggle to preserve the remnants of his diocese from further reduction by the atheist officials.[41]

In the third category, Furov placed bishops, led by the now "retired" Metropolitan Nykolai (Iuryk) of Lviv, who attempt to "evade the laws on cults," "misrepresent" the situation in their dioceses, or attempt to "bribe" local CRA officials, or who accuse them before the higher state organs.[42]

While expanding their contacts with foreign religious and public organizations in the pursuit of Soviet policy objectives, Orthodox (and, to a lesser extent, other) churchmen have not only sought to make themselves indispensable to the regime, but also to bargain their propaganda achievements into concrete Soviet concessions, such as permission to ordain more young bishops or to admit more students to theological schools, and to expand or improve central facilities for the Moscow Patriarchate.

Indirectly, religious dissidents have also exercised some restraining influence on church-state relations in the USSR by publicizing in *samizdat* and through foreign mass media the grievances of the rank-and-file clergy and believers; by revealing clearly illegal acts of the atheist authorities, they have been undermining the credibility of the official disinformation about the alleged benevolence of the Soviet state toward religion. By compromising "patriotic" churchmen for concealing the truth about religion in the USSR, the dissidents have made it more difficult for these churchmen to carry on their propaganda functions abroad. This dissident role has been the prime reason behind continuing Soviet efforts to break down leading

---

39. Furov (1974), 278.
40. Ibid.
41. See footnote 38.
42. Ibid., 279. A number of bishops in this category have since been "retired."

religious protest figures and to force out of them self-incriminating testimonials confirming Soviet propaganda stereotypes of dissidents as nothing more than "religious extremists" who "fabricate slanders" for sale to "anti-Soviet propaganda and intelligence services abroad."[43]

The existence or at least a clear danger of dissent within their religious group has allowed "loyal" church leaders some protection against "excessive" Soviet demands for collaboration to the detriment of their own churches; similar benefit has been derived by the Russian Orthodox Church in the Western Ukraine from the continuing illegal existence of the popular Ukrainian Catholic Church. In the same way, continued vigorous but informed Western criticism of Soviet violations of religious freedom cannot but help those religious groups whose government-picked "spokesmen" would not or could not defend the rights of their flocks and who, on occasion, are called upon by the authorities to help conceal the plight of religious believers in the USSR.

THE INSTITUTIONAL FRAMEWORK

The formulation and application of Soviet religious policy—which affects millions of Soviet citizens—have been conducted in a secretive institutional framework of which the only visible part is the relatively low-ranking government agency attached to the federal Council of Ministers—the Council on Religious Affairs—with its republican and oblast branches and commissioners,[44] and local commissions to monitor the observance of the legislation on religious cults.[45] Behind the facade of the CRA and its predecessors,[46] responsibility for

---

43. Kuroedov, *Religiia i tserkov*, 153-90.
44. In two republics, the Ukraine and Armenia, subordinate republican Councils for Religious Affairs (in Armenia, for Affairs of the Armenian-Gregorian Church) have been established. In the Ukranian SSR, approximately four CRA officials are deployed per oblast, with their greatest concentration in Kiev and other major cities, as well as the western Ukraine. A rare insight into the operation of a Lithuanian republican CRA plenipotentiary, P. Anilionis, appears in an excerpt from his secret report on the Lithuanian Catholic Church for 1983, which has been in the samizdat *Chronicle of the Catholic Church in Lithuania*, no. 66, 1985. See summary of this report in S. Girnius, "Religious Societies in Lithuania," *RFE Baltic Area Situation Report*, SR/6 of 26 July 1985, 33-39.
45. Ibid., 35-37, where Anilionis lists among the commissions' activities, spying after the local clergy and religious activists; uncovering violations of laws, instructions, and directives (some of which are secret) on the part of the clergy; summarizing priests' sermons, etc., cf. Furov (1974), 337-44.
46. The first such agency—a Department for the Implementation of the Separation of Church from the State ("Liquidation Department") otherwise known as the Eighth and, later, Fifth Department of the Commissariat of Justice existed during 1918-24; in 1924, it was absorbed into NKVD as "section on cults" within its Administrative Department; simultaneously, a higher coordinating body was set in the form of the secretariat (since 1929, Permanent

religious affairs has been traditionally shared by two powerful and functional hierarchies: the central propaganda apparatus (*agitprop*) of the party[47] (with its Komsomol, military, and trade-union affiliates), on the one hand, and the secret police, from Cheka to the present KGB,[48] on the other hand. The latter dominates other "law and order" agencies involved in policing and disciplining religious groups, particularly the Ministry of Internal Affairs and the Procuracy.

These functional controls converge at the Party Central Committee level (to which the CRA reports) under a senior CC secretary and Politburo member,[49] assisted at times by an inter-departmental party-state commission.[50] During the interwar period, a mass antireligious organization—the League of Militant Godless[51]—was undoubtedly also involved in the religious policy process, with its leader, Emilian Iaroslavskyi, heading the so-called Antireligious Commission of the Party Central Committee during much of that period.[52]

Since the early 1960s, in view of the growing Kremlin deployment of the Moscow Patriarchate and some other "loyal" religious centers for foreign policy promotion and propaganda abroad, it is likely that the Ministry of Foreign Affairs and, on the Central Committee side, the International Information Department, have also been brought into the formulation, application, and feedback-monitoring of Soviet religious policy.

Commission) for the Affairs of Cults, attached to the Presidium of the All-Russian Central Executive Committee (and its equivalents at other republics), continuing in this form until the end of the 1930s. In 1943, Stalin's "New Deal" for the Russian Orthodox Church resulted in the establishment of a separate Council for the Affairs of the Russian Orthodox Church, followed in 1944 by the formation of a parallel agency for other groups—Council for the Affairs of Religious Cults. The two councils were merged in December 1965.

47. More specifically, Sector for Mass Work, within the party CC Secretariat's Department of Propaganda (the former, incidentally, was headed by K. Chernenko during the late 1950s).

48. In all earlier incarnations of the KGB—Cheka, GPU, OGPU, NKVD, NKGB, and MGB—secret subdivisions "for cults" or, simply, on "churchmen and sectarians" have been in existence, with most of the CRA personnel (as well as that of its predecessors) either being recruited from this police unit or coopted into it.

49. As, e.g., Mikhail Suslov, during the post-Krushchev era.

50. E.g., the so-called Ideological Commission of the CCCPSU under L. Il'ichev, which presided over Khrushchev's antireligious campaign.

51. Formed in 1925, the League was dissolved immediately after the Nazi invasion of the USSR. After the late 1940s its propaganda functions were assumed by what is now called Society "Knowledge" (*Znanie*).

52. Iaroslavskii, Stalin's follower, displaced L. Trotsky in 1922 as chairman of this commission, which was then known as a Standing Commission on the Implementation of the Decree on the Separation of Church from the State." See J. Delaney, "The Origins of Soviet Antireligious Organizations," in Marshall, ed., 103-10; and S. N. Savelev, "Emilian Iaroslavskii i preodolenie anarkhistskikh vliianii v antireligioznoi rabote v SSSR," *Ezhegodnik Muzeiia religii i ateizma*, vol. 7 (Leningrad, 1964), 37-49.

Conclusions

What are, then, the actual operative principles of Soviet religious policy? From the available internal evidence and from examination of the party and state activities in this realm, we may conclude that these operative principles comprise:

The right to profess religion which is restricted to the performance of religious cult. The Soviet authorities reserve unto themselves the exclusive right to determine what constitutes "freedom of religion," "performance of religious cult (worship)," and which religious groups may be allowed to worship legally and under what conditions.

Possessed of "false" religious consciousness, known believers cannot be given equal rights with those with a "scientific" communist consciousness. Election to political offices, admission to institutions of higher learning, and responsible, sensitive, or command positions in all spheres of life are reserved for the party and Komsomol members, who are required by their respective statutes to be atheists. The only exceptions in tolerating believers among university students and among the nonruling elite are made for exceptionally talented individuals, as long as their loyalty is not in question.

The Soviet authorities discriminate among religions and churches, as well as among the clergy, in terms of their political usefulness to the regime.

Coercion is applied, especially in school and during the obligatory military service to "convert" believers to atheism.

The regime perceives all religions as detrimental to the Soviet state and society, except whenever they can be utilized for the political ends of the regime at home or abroad, as in promoting among foreign churches and believers Soviet foreign propaganda.

In order to contain as much religious influence as possible in society, the state interferes with the internal affairs of each licensed religious group, seeking to preselect its leaders and predetermine their decisions, infiltrate the ranks of each group with informers, and manipulate it for the immediate benefit of the state.

While the state prohibits any group instruction of minors in religion, it encourages and supports, administratively and materially, the right to conduct antireligious propaganda. Religious propaganda is implicitly prohibited in the USSR, except when it may be directed against a politically less desirable religious group or projected abroad for the benefit of the regime.

The Status of Christianity in Albania

JANICE A. BROUN

Writing in the eighteenth century, Edward Gibbon described Albania as "a country within sight of Italy, which is less known than the interior of America." The same could be said today with even more justification. Probably no other country is more impenetrable in its self-imposed isolation, and more paranoid in its attitude toward the outside world. The difficulty of the language, the ban on foreign journalists, and the fact that the only sources of information are official newspapers and broadcasts, supplemented by odd scraps from the handful of people who manage to escape, and from a very few observant visitors on the strictly regulated tours, make it almost impossible to assess accurately the extent of religious survival a decade and a half since the late Party Secretary Enver Hoxha took the unprecedented step in 1967 of declaring Albania the world's first atheist state and making all religious practices illegal. This essay concentrates on the Christian churches, although there are references to Islam and paganism.

HISTORY

Without some knowledge of Albania's complex and little-known history, particularly its religious and cultural background, it is impossible to understand present-day Albania and Hoxha's attitude toward religion.

Albania is populated by the remnants of the fierce Illyrian tribes that occupied most of the Balkans in pre-Christian times. Under firm Roman Rule, Illyria was probably better governed, more prosperous, and more within the orbit of European culture than it has ever been since.[1] It seems probable that it was visited, independently of each other, by both the apostles Paul and Andrew.[2] There were seventy Christian families when Durrachium (the modern city of Durres) was established as a bishopric around 66 A.D.[3] Its

---
1. It lay astride a key road, the Via Egnatia, linking the Adriatic with Thessalonika, Constantinople, and the Black Sea.
2. Rom. 15:19.
3. Gjon Sinishta, *The Fulfilled Promise: Grave Violations of Human Rights in Albania* (Santa Clara, Calif.: published by author, 1976), 29 (hereinafter cited as *Fulfilled Promise*).

bishop, Astio, was one of the earliest Christian martyrs.[4] Albanian bishops attended early church councils. St. Jerome may have been a native of that land.[5]

Slav invasions between 600 and 800 A.D. destroyed all vestiges of Roman civilization and drove many Albanians into the mountains. Albanians were also split ecclesiastically; increasingly they came under the jurisdiction of the Patriarch of Constantinople, although Rome retained the North.[6] From 1385, the Ottoman conquerors imposed yet another system and propagated another religion, which eventually most Albanians came to profess. According to the 1938 census,[7] Albania, with 69 percent of its population professing Islam, was the only predominantly Muslim state left in Europe. Initially, conversion was slow, involving only the feudal landowners who wanted to retain their lands and positions. In the fifteenth century the Catholic Church in particular was well-organized and active, although it declined progressively thereafter, and in 1610 the bishop of Bar could report that only 10 percent of Albanians had become Muslims.

From the seventeenth century, with the Turkish authorities imposing higher taxation on Christians, conversion to Islam took place at a faster rate,[8] particularly in the cities and the narrow coastal plains. The mountainous northern region, centered on Shkodra, remained a stronghold of Catholicism. The Orthodox lived primarily in the districts of Korce and Gjirocaster in the South, adjacent to Greece and to some extent protected by the Greeks, and were never under such pressure to convert. Generally those who refused to convert were respected by those who did. Some, who became known as Laramani, conformed to Muslim practices but said Christian prayers at home. They occupied an uneasy position, unable to integrate fully with either Muslim or Christian communities.[9] The figures for 1938 show 10 percent Catholic and 21 percent Muslim.

Particularly after the death of Gjergje Kastrioti, or Scanderbeg, in 1468, thousands of Christians from the South fled to Sicily or southern Italy, where they still form a substantial community, the Arberesh, who maintain their Byzantine-rite Orthodox services under

---

4. Some time between 98 and 117 A.D. Francis Dvornik, *Les Slaves Byzance et Rome en IXme Siecle* (Paris:1926), 85-6.
5. D. Farlati, S.J., *Illyricum Sacrum* (Venice, 1751).
6. Anton Logoreci, *The Albanians: Europe's Forgotten Survivors* (London: Victor Gollanz, 1977), 16 (hereafter cited as *The Albanians*).
7. Bernard Tonnes, "Religious Persecution in Albania," *Religion in Communist Lands* 10 (1982):243 (hereafter cited as Tonnes).
8. Ibid., 242-3.
9. Logoreci, *The Albanians*, 33.

papal jurisdiction. Scanderbeg led a successful revolt against the Turks that helped to save Western Christendom from the onslaught of militant Islam.

Albanian Muslims were themselves split between Sunni (54 percent) and Shiite (15 percent). Most of the latter are Bektashis, a sect that originated as a syncretic religious secret society in Asia Minor in the thirteenth century, incorporating Muslim, Christian, and pagan beliefs.[10] Indeed, for many Albanians, Islam and even Christianity were only a veneer. They clung tenaciously to their pagan beliefs and superstitions and to their ancient Law of Lek with its exacting code of vengeance for the sake of honor, which took precedence over state laws in the more remote areas well into the twentieth century.[11]

To Enver Hoxha, the Paris-trained Marxist intellectual and former schoolteacher who shaped the destiny of Albania after the Communists seized power in 1944, religion was such a divisive factor that it was a prime target for attack. Ottoman rule, moreover, had, from the eighteenth century, entered a period of stagnation that left Albania the most backward country in Europe. Religion, too, seemed to tie Albania to other countries. Muslims had strong links with Turkey; the Orthodox had for centuries been under the jurisdiction of Constantinople and, though unwillingly, under Greek influence; Catholics looked to Italy and Rome, and worshipped in Latin; their clergy often completed their training in Italy, and some clergy and members of religious orders were Italians. Although political independence had been won in 1912, under Ahmet Zogu (King Zog), who seized power in 1924, Albania became virtually an Italian protectorate. When Mussolini invaded Albania in 1939, some Catholics did collaborate, although not as many as Hoxha claimed, but the fact that Catholic guerillas in the North held out longest against the Communists hardly endeared them to him. To brand all Catholics as Fascist traitors became a standard government procedure.

Despite elements of truth, this accusation is basically unfair, for the primary loyalty of most Albanians has been to Albania. Owing to historic conditions, they were not a particularly religious people. It was a leading Catholic intellectual, Vaso Pasha (1825-92), who actually coined the phrase: "The religion of Albania is Albanianism,"[12] since appropriated by Hoxha. As a proud and independent people

---

10. Tonnes, "Religious Persecution in Albania," 243.
11. Even in 1920, one quarter of male deaths were due to vendettas. See Mehat Biber, "Albania Alone Against the World," *National Geographic Magazine* (October 1980):
12. Tonnes, "Religious Persecution in Albania," 243.

they had resented Ottoman rule. Their independence, however, was delayed longer than that of other Balkan peoples because of their backwardness and isolation; many of their most able and enterprising people had left in search of careers in Ottoman administration or in Christian societies where they had more scope. As a result there are now far more Albanians living outside Albania than in the country.[13]

Most of the intelligentsia came from two groups, the Catholics and the Bektashis, and they spearheaded the struggle for independence. Their role, too, in cultural, social, and educational development was out of all proportion to their numbers. Hoxha's ruthless censorship and rewriting of history keeps those educated under communism in ignorance of all this and presents a purely negative and hostile picture of religion.[14]

THE CHURCHES DURING THE PERIOD OF INDEPENDENCE, 1912-39

Although most of Albania's acute internal problems were still unresolved when Italy invaded in 1939,[15] the Christian churches had made a positive contribution to the nation's life. The churches were neither privileged nor wealthy. Church and state were separate.[16] All communities were free to practice their religion and did so in a remarkable spirit of mutual trust.

The Orthodox Church had four dioceses, two hundred parishes, and twenty-nine monasteries, with a total membership of about 220,000. Its leaders and the town clergy were articulate, cultured, and well-educated. Outstanding were Archbishop Kristofori Kissi,

---

13. The relevant figures are: 1.3 million in Yugoslavia; 1 million in Turkey; 320,000 in the United States; 100,000 in Greece; with others elsewhere, approximately 3 million. See Gjon Sinishta," in *Le Droit*, (Ottawa), 25 March 1978. Among notable Albanians of the diaspora are Johan Francis Albani, Pope Clement XI (1649-1720); the late Ecumenical Patriarch of Constantinople, Athenagoras, and Agnes Gonzhe Bojaxkiu, better known as Mother Teresa, who was born in Skopje, Yugoslavia. Sinishta, *Fulfilled Promise*, 34-5, 222-4, 227-32.
14. E.g., Scanderbeg (see above), and the three Frasheri brothers who led the independence movement in the nineteenth century are correctly portrayed as national heroes, but no mention is made of the fact that Scanderbeg was a Christian and the Frasheris Bektashi. Nor is it mentioned that the first books in Albanian, such as a prayerbook in 1552, were produced by Catholics and that their missionary orders showed a modern awareness of the need to use the vernacular; nor that in the 1950s they pioneered Albanian education, opening the first schools, which educated the first leaders of an independent Albania, whatever their religion. See *Fulfilled Promise*, 35:41-2; Logoreci, *The Albanians*, 38-9, 42-3.
15. Illiteracy was about 80 percent, the highest in Europe; there was no university; nothing had been done to help the peasants, who were exploited by tax-collectors, money-lenders and landlords; tuberculosis and malaria were rife.
16. But Zog closed all Catholic schools between 1933 and 1936, an interesting precedent. Drita, *The Church and Its History* (Yugoslavia: Albanian Catholic Publishers); section on Albania, privately translated. (hereafter cited as Drita).

head of the Church, and Bishop Fan Noli, a moderate liberal who was Albania's first delegate to the League of Nations, and prime minister, briefly, in 1924.[17] Unlike Serbs, Bulgars, and Romanians, the Albanians had been too few and weak to become autonomous in the nineteenth century. It was at the National Congress at Berat in 1922 that they finally declared their independence, although it was not until 1937 that Constantinople recognized it. During this period, they removed Greek influence and introduced a newly translated Albanian liturgy in place of the Greek one.[18] They are generally respected as good Albanians who had kept their faith through years of persecution.

Unlike the Catholic clergy, however, the educational and spiritual level of their village priests was low; most were peasants with just enough primary education to conduct the services. Thus, they were not equipped to cope with the onslaught on religion under communism, and, indeed, a number actively supported communist partisans.[19]

The Catholic Church in 1939 had two archdioceses, three dioceses, and 123 parishes, with 124,000 members in all. They were served by forty-one indigenous and sixty-two foreign priests, some of them religious, thirty-two laymonks, and seventy-three indigenous and sixty foreign nuns.[20] They ran a seminary in Shkodra with about sixty-five students, as well as the fifteen secondary, trade, and primary schools (which were almost the only schools in the North) and thirteen orphanages. Much of what scholarship there was in the country came through Catholic education, and many priests were poets and writers. There was a lively and popular Catholic press.

Many priests and religious, mainly Jesuits and Franciscans, carried out a self-sacrificing and arduous ministry in primitive conditions among a proud and undisciplined people, particularly in the mountains where blood feuds were still rife. The few hospitals were staffed by nuns who also worked for women's emancipation in a society that even today, despite Communism's emphasis on the equality of the sexes, is still essentially male-dominated.

World War II

The war period was a time of chaos. In 1943, German occupation

---

17. Though even he had been educated in the U.S. whither he returned, living on till 1965. Noli was the instigator of this and pioneered the translations.
18. Drita, *The Church and Its History*.
19. Logoreci, *The Albanians*, 73.
20. Tonnes, *Religious Persecution in Albania*, 251.

succeeded Italian. Meanwhile a bitter civil war raged between the Balli Kombetar, comprised of nationalist resistance units aiming to free Albania from all foreign domination, and the communist partisans, the National Liberation Front, who had strong Yugoslav backing. By labeling their opponents as "Fascists," the more ruthless and efficient NLF deprived them of American and British support and emerged victorious in 1944.

Church-State Confrontation

Party Secretary Enver Hoxha was unique on several counts. He was, until his recent death on 11 April 1985, the only East European leader to rule uninterruptedly since World War II. Until 1948 he was dependent upon Yugoslavia, then on the Soviet Union, when Tito turned westward. By 1961 he felt secure enough to break with Nikita Khrushchev, largely because of his de-Stalinization, and instead maintained close ideological and economic ties with China, which was then seeking allies against Russian hegemony. This lasted until 1978 when China began to break away from Maoism. Despite temporary, forced concessions, Enver Hoxha's aim was consistent: to create a purely Marxist state in modern Albania, capable of resisting all invaders. To achieve this he imposed a totalitarian, militaristic regime with complete control, in theory, over the minds, wills, and beliefs of his subjects, isolating them from allegedly dangerous foreign influences. In addition, traditional religious beliefs of the more primitive kind had instilled a fatalistic attitude of passivity and submission in the face of injustice, and had kept women, as Hoxha described it in 1955, "in the miserable state of slavery." Religion, therefore, had to be totally eradicated, and Hoxha, thereby, became the first ruler to follow the Marxist approach to religion to its logical conclusion.

In establishing national independence, and in raising educational and economic standards, Hoxha achieved much, but at an immeasurable cost to the minds and spirits of his people. There is something almost terrifying when a fiercely independent, undisciplined, and divided nation votes 1,436,285 out of a population of 1,436,289 for its government, as it was reported to have done in the 1978 elections.

The anti-religious campaign can be divided into three stages.[21] Between 1944 and 1951 the government set itself to "nationalize" the churches and to terrorize believers by its treatment of all who opposed its policy. Next, between 1949 and 1967, when the state had gained complete control over the churches, persecution slackened,

CHRISTIANITY IN ALBANIA

but during the latter part of this period preparations were quietly made for the final attack. Finally, since 1967 all religion has been banned.

First Period: 1944-51

Until a series of five statutes were imposed between 1949 and 1951, believers were officially "guaranteed" free practice of their religion, and the separation of church and state was made official. However, the discrepancy between law and its practice was such that the guarantees were meaningless. The party practiced individual terrorism against clergy and active believers, using murder, torture, and fake trials. Concurrently, the state began to undermine and destroy church institutions while exploiting whatever formal power the churches had to support the aims of international communism. A massive campaign to discredit religion was started, at first directed in the form of slander against the more uncooperative religious leaders. The basic income of the churches was seriously reduced by the appropriation of property belonging to monasteries, religious orders, and religious institutions by the Agrarian Law of 29 August 1985. Monasteries, religious orders, and religious institutions were then banned.

Second Period: 1949-67

On 26 January 1949, Decree no. 743, "On Religious Communities" restricted religious activity to the place of worship only, and limited it to the holding of services. This was comparable with Soviet practice and at least allowed believers that minimum security. The state, however, kept a strict overall control. All pastoral letters and announcements required prior approval of the government. By subsidizing the clergy's stipends and pensions, the state was able to control the clergy. All education was in the hands of the state, and Hoxha's policy was to concentrate on the young, to make them literate and, at the same time, teach them a materialistic and atheistic world view. The decree also stipulated that each of the four major religious communities should present a draft statute within three months. Since none of them met this ridiculously short deadline the statutes were dictated by the Council of Ministers. In some respects, policies toward the different religious groups varied.

Islam

Hoxha's attitude toward Islam must have been colored by his

own Muslim origin; certainly he never regarded Islam as a serious obstacle to communism. Nevertheless, his initial tactic, in May 1945, was to emphasize the division between Muslims by recognizing the Sunni and Bektashi as two separate religious bodies. He felt that at first the party should not offend the feelings of the large number of Muslims who were closely bound to it.[22] The hierarchy was too weak and inexperienced to cause trouble; such leaders who did oppose communism were removed by long prison terms or by execution. Those who accepted the changes were used as propaganda tools to show the Muslim world how Muslims and Communists could coexist harmoniously.[23]

Religious instruction and attendance at mosques, however, were progressively discouraged and later severely restricted. By the sixties, many mosques had been closed, along with madrasshas where their clergy trained. In the final analysis, the softer line toward Islam was deceptive, and neither it nor the compromises by the hierarchy did anything to protect Islam from extinction in 1967.

ORTHODOXY

The regime tried to exploit the Orthodox Church, through appeals to nationalism, as an instrument for mobilizing its fifth of the population behind communist policies. Communist agents and sympathizers infiltrated churches and monasteries,[24] closed the seminary at Korce, and brought the entire church under state control. During the period of Soviet domination, Hoxha was put under pressure to subordinate the Albanian Church to the Moscow Patriarchate. Thus, Albanian Orthodox adherents were humiliated into conceding the autonomy they had struggled for so long to achieve. From 4 May 1950 they had to accept their new status and found themselves working alongside so-called sister churches (i.e., those within the communist camp) in promoting Soviet policy at "peace"

---

21. Most of the information in the following sections is from *Fulfilled Promise: Grave Violations of Human Rights in Albania*, also by Sinishta, hereafter cited as *Grave Violations*, and Tonnes. *Fulfilled Promise*, written from a Catholic point of view, is the only detailed, systematic account of the persecution. No Orthodox, Muslim, or Bektashi in the free world seems to have made any attempt to document it. It should be noted, however, that Catholics were the prime target and suffered most.
22. Enver Hoxha, *History of the Labour Party of Albania*, 622-24, as quoted in *Grave Violations*, 3-4.
23. Exploited in this way was the Ded, spiritual head of the world's seven million Bektashi, who had his seat in Tirana. There is evidence that some Bektashi, not surprisingly, considering their background and tolerant outlook, were deeply unhappy about Hoxha's policies. Even the leaders who had supported the communists, Baba Fajo and Baba Fejzo, died violent deaths in March 1947 in circumstances that are not clear.
24. A few Orthodox monasteries were, it seems, left open.

conferences. Hoxha's actions aroused considerable opposition, led at first by Archbishop Kissi.[25] He was deposed in August 1949 on the grounds that he had plotted to bring his Church under Vatican control, tortured to death, and replaced by a pro-communist militant, Pais Vodica, a married priest (and thus ineligible to be a bishop) who had no authority whatever in the eyes of devout believers. Nevertheless, churches continued to be well-filled, with flourishing choirs and traditional observances of Orthodox fasts and feasts.

CATHOLICISM

As Hoxha had foreseen, the Catholic Church, well-organized, with strong traditions and close links with the Vatican, proved a much tougher obstacle. His campaign was aimed at discrediting it, branding its leaders as Fascists and American or Vatican spies, and then at eliminating it entirely. This period is well-documented. In May 1945 Hoxha expelled the Apostolic Delegate, Archbishop Leone Nigris. He then summoned Gasper Thaci, Archbishop of Shkodra and Primate, and Vincent Prendushi,[26] Archbishop of Durres, and demanded that they separate from Rome, promising in return "a conciliatory attitude" and material help in maintaining church institutions. Both refused. Thaci died at the hands of the Sigurini (security police) in 1946 while under house arrest. After his death a similar demand was made of Bishop Fran Gjini,[27] acting Nuncio. He, too, refused, but had an open letter to Hoxha read out in all churches in which he urged Catholics to cooperate in the reconstruction of their ravaged country. Annoyed by this show of independence, Hoxha had him arrested on a charge of spreading anti-government propaganda. Meanwhile, Prendushi had been sentenced to twenty years of hard labor and probably died just over a year later after torture in February 1949. Bishop Nikol Dedi and the youngest bishop, Gjergj Volaz, also perished at this time.[28] Thus

---

25. The opposition included the whole hierarchy: Visarion Xhuvani, archbishop of Elbasan; Bishop Irine of Apollonia; Bishop Agathangjel Cance of Berat; and Bishop Irene, deputy metropolitan of Korce and Gjirocaster; as well as many priests and deacons, and Papas Josif Pamihaili, a promoter of a small Eastern Rite Church under Roman jurisdiction in Central Albania. (*Grave Violations*, 5)
26. He was a nationally famed poet and writer. See "In Memory of Archbishop Vincent Prendushi" by Professor Arshi Pipa, *Fulfilled Promise*, 79-87, for an account of his last days in prison.
27. Professor Jeh Vala, "Bishop Fran Gjini—Dignified Defender of His Flock," *Fulfilled Promise*, 91-4.
28. A very active person who had shown considerable bravery in defending Albanians from the Germans, the National Liberation Front, and the communists. Anton Gaspi, "A Testimony to Bishop Volaj of Sappa," *Fulfilled Promise*, 95-8.

by 1949 the only bishop left alive was seventy-five-year-old Bernadin Shllakau.

In January 1946 all foreign priests, monks, and nuns, numbering about a hundred and twenty, had been expelled.[29] Then it was the turn of native clergy to be attacked. Leading Jesuits, Franciscans, seminary lecturers, and students were accused of political crimes and imprisoned. Many were executed.[30] Nuns were publicly humiliated, religious orders banned, and the seminary closed. All church schools and other institutions were confiscated and nationalized. It is estimated that thirty Franciscans, thirteen Jesuits, sixty parish priests, ten seminarians and eight out of forty-three nuns sentenced to labor camp actually died by execution or during the course of their imprisonment: a heavy loss for such a small Church. At least one Muslim was executed with them, a young lawyer, Mustafa Pipa, who had undertaken the defense of the Franciscans.[31]

The expulsion of Yugoslavia from the Cominform in 1948 caused considerable problems, for in 1944, Tito had annexed a large inland area, Kossovo province, and thus took out of reach of Hoxha an area and population nearly as large as what was left as Albania. A reduction in the drive against the Catholic Church resulted as Hoxha worried over his border security.

Although the Catholic Church has been considerably weakened, it took two and a half years of lengthy negotiations involving deception, intimidation, and treachery on the part of the state before the statute on the Catholic Church was made law, on 30 July 1951, long after the other churches had accepted their statutes. The church leaders, under Shllaku, were forced to accept nationalization of religious communities, but remained adamant that, even if organizational and economic relations with Rome had to be cut, in no way would they renounce the spiritual sovereignty of the pope. When the government falsified the text and stated that all ties with Rome would be broken, the clergy courageously denounced this betrayal from their pulpits. The government also broke promises

---

29. The government was very angry when a great crowd of grateful Christians and Muslims turned out to bid them farewell.
30. These include: the Franciscan Father Anton Harapi, executed in 1945 for collaboration (during the Nazi occupation, he had been the Catholic representative on an inter-religion regency council); Father Jak Gardin and Professor Gjergi Vata, given long sentences after public ideological discussions in which they had discomforted the Communists; and a number of leading priests, seminarians, and laymen, executed in March 1946, ostensibly for printing leaflets criticizing the government on behalf of the Albanian Union, a broadly based legal political organization, prior to the first parliamentary elections. Several people executed in January 1947 after arms and ammunition, planted by the police, were "found" in a Franciscan church.
31. Michael Marku, "Profile of a Young Martyr," *Fulfilled Promise*, 138-40.

to reopen the seminary and some of the closed churches, and to allow children to receive religious instruction in church.

Catholics responded by filling churches to demonstrate their faith. They were aware, however, of the vulnerability of their position. Crude propaganda against religion was increasing, and the government expected the churches themselves to become channels for communist teaching. The four new titular bishops consecrated by Shllaku and the clergy resisted this pressure and, within the narrow confines laid down for church life, continued to preach the faith. One of the titular bishops, the late Ernest Coba, ensured that a basic church organization was continued by ordaining about a dozen ex-seminarians in secret.

As a result, there was renewed persecution, though on a reduced scale, between 1958 and 1965. More than a dozen priests and members of religious orders were shot, and many others were imprisoned or sent to labor camps. This was a time of crisis for Hoxha, as he opposed Khruschev's demand for a rapprochement with Yugoslavia, which would have meant the loss of party leadership and of his life. He needed complete discipline within Albania. At a show trial in April 1959, two priests, Fathers Ded Malaj and Donrad Gjalaj, and five laymen were condemned to death by a court consisting of Muslims, for allegedly betraying state secrets to Yugoslavia. Diocesan offices and parishes were harassed, services impeded, and titular bishops and their priests forced to clean streets and public conveniences and wear clown outfits and placards reading, "I have sinned against the People." In 1952, Hoxha purged the only Catholic in the Politburo, Tuk Jakova, previously one of his closest collaborators, on the grounds that he had befriended the clergy.

THE CAMPAIGN TO DESTROY ALL RELIGION

All these humiliations and harassments led to the final blow in 1967. The occasion was provided by Hoxha's new ally, Red China, and the Cultural Revolution initiated there by Mao Tse-Tung in 1966. In a speech on 6 February 1967, Hoxha set the stage for action by urging Albanian youths to fight "religious superstition." It was followed by a letter of 27 February providing guidelines for the district party committee, for "the struggle against religion, and religious preconceptions and customs." On 13 November, all decrees on religion were repealed. Religion was thus forced into illegality even though the practice of religious observances was not expressly declared illegal until 1976.

The events of 1967 were the culmination of a carefully planned campaign,[32] in which as early as 1965, students, "liberated" from reactionary beliefs through their education, took the initiative in ways similar to China's Red Guards months later. Meetings were organized in which the government's point of view was explained to the people. The arguments were that Albanians had never been a religious people, that religion was outdated now, being largely a matter of the performance of superstitious rites, and that these obstructed the development of Albania as a socialist state.

In these arguments, mosques and churches no longer served any useful purpose.[33] By May 1967, all 2,169 mosques and churches, including 327 Catholic churches, had been vandalized by youths, closed, or were in the process of being put to a secular use.[34] Muslim and Christian clergy were now obviously "superfluous." A considerable number of the clergy (significantly no Catholics among them) renounced their "parasitic" past.[35] Two hundred and seventeen who resisted were sentenced to prison or labor camps.[36] Others were sent to re-education camps or given mainly manual jobs.

Only a few managed to go into hiding. The campaign inevitably met with considerable opposition. Some clergy provided a focus for widespread discontent, particularly for that of the peasants against collectivization. Such clergy, including priests like father Shtjefen Jak Kurti, who was sentenced to a further fourteen years (he had already served eighteen), and Father Zef Bici, who was executed, were accused of sabotage, anti-government agitation, and spying for the Vatican. There was violence on both sides; Father Kurti fought off those who came to destroy his church with his bare fists.[37] Most of the violence, however, originated with hot-headed young

---

32. Dlava Sadikaj, "Revolutionary Movement Against Religion in the Sixties," *Studime Historik* (University of Tirana Quarterly Journal) 4 (1981), as translated in *Albanian Catholic Bulletin* 4, (1983):20-34 (hereafter cited as *Revolutionary Movement*).
33. Sadikaj's figures are 2,035 buildings, including 740 mosques, 608 Orthodox churches, and only 157 Catholic churches. ("Revolutionary Movement," p. 23). The figure 327 is from Catholic sources.
34. E.g., in Shkodra, the cathedral became a sports center complete with swimming pool; St. Nicholas's church became workers' flats; a former convent church, the Sigurini headquarters; others became clubs, cinemas, dance halls, barns, and latrines. Perhaps, because of their historical interest, and with an eye to tourism, more of the Orthodox churches were left relatively untouched and some are now museums.
35. *Zer I Populit*, the Party daily newspaper.
36. E.g., Bishop Ernest Coba, apostolic administrator of Shkodra, was seen pushing a dustcart. Former nuns were given cleaning or public toilet jobs, unless a party official's wife was ill and needed skilled nursing. Two elderly priests, Father Benedict Dema and, in 1973, Father Mark Harapi, were deprived of their ration books, and starved to death. Also in 1973 a Catholic priest who had secretly converted his room into a chapel was arrested for stealing corncobs.
37. For further information on Kurti, see *Fulfilled Promise*, 150-57.

communists. Four elderly Franciscans were burned to death when vandals set their church on fire. At the time, the government admitted that there had been mistakes through over-enthusiasm, and warned campaigners to respect the deeply held convictions of "honorable people," good Albanians of the older generation.[38] Its subsequent pronouncements and actions, however, indicate a much tougher line. Later, Albania vehemently attacked all other communist regimes, including the Soviet Union, and, since the death of Mao, China especially, for their lukewarm, "anti-revolutionary" attitude to religion.

Legislation Against Religion

Article 37 of the new Constitution of 1976 says: "The State does not recognize any religion at all, and supports and develops atheistic propaganda in order to implant in mankind the scientific-materialistic world-view." Article 55 reads: "The formation of any organization of a fascist, anti-democratic, religious or anti-socialist nature is forbidden. Fascist, religious, warmongerish, anti-socialist activity and propaganda are forbidden, as is the incitement to hatred between peoples and races."

This was followed by Clause 55 of the new Penal Code of June 1977 which states: "Religious propaganda and also the production, distribution or storage of literature of this kind" will be punished with imprisonment of between three and ten years. In time of war, or if they are deemed to have had particularly serious consequences, such activities carry a sentence of not less than ten years, and the death penalty can be imposed.[39]

This penal code merely systematized an already existing situation. Decree no. 5339, of 23 September 1975, announced that "all citizens whose names do not conform to the political, ideological and moral standards of the State are to change them as from 1976." Under this, parents cannot officially give their children the names of Christian saints.[40]

In June 1979, a decree was passed allowing internment in labor camps of anyone over fourteen years old without trial if suspected of being a danger to the system. Reports from refugees confirm that people have been sent to camp without trial[41] for possessing religious objects, e.g., Bibles, prayer books, crucifixes, icons, or for

---

38. "Revolutionary Movement," 26.
39. Tonnes, *Religious Persecution in Albania*, 250.
40. *Albanian Catholic Bulletin*, 2 (1981):32.
41. *Keston News Service*, 108:9.

taking part in religious services. In this respect, Albanian society is riddled with secret police and informers and, from the earliest age, schoolchildren are taught to denounce parents who pursue forbidden, reactionary practices. There is recent news of a new wave of arrests.[42]

The Application of the Laws

Reliable information on Albania is hard to come by and often leaks out after a considerable lapse of time. The following instances of persecution, however, are well-attested and indicate how draconically the laws are enforced. Five thousand Christians underwent a six-month brainwashing, using Mao's Little Red Book,[43] and carrying out degrading cleansing jobs, in a camp near Tirana in 1966. The Orthodox bishop Damian Kononessi, elected primate in 1966, died in 1973, aged eighty, after six years in prison. It is believed that by 1975 the entire hierarchy and most of the clergy had been imprisoned.

In 1972, news came of the execution of seventy-four-year-old Father Kurti in prison, for baptizing a fellow prisoner's baby at her request. When Vatican protests aroused considerable reaction in the free world, the government retorted that he had been executed for spying.

All three Catholic titular bishops, appointed with papal permission after the official break with Rome, were sentenced to labor camp for holding services in private. Monsignor Antonin Fishta died after much suffering, probably in 1973. Monsignor Ernesto Coba, apostolic administrator of Shkodra, a man held in great affection as a pastor for his work among the poor, the sick, and orphans, was arrested for the second time in 1974. At Easter in 1979, he conducted a secret mass at the request of fellow prisoners; they were betrayed and badly beaten up. Coba, then sixty-eight years old, frail and almost blind, died the next day. The only bishop presumed still to be alive is Nikolla Trosnani, sixty-nine, sentenced to twenty years in 1971.[44]

In 1977, Father Fran Mark Gjoni of Shkodra was sentenced to twelve years for having Bibles and religious literature in his attic. He admitted that he had found them in parks and at the seashore,

---

42. *Keston News Service*, 120:11.
43. David Bligh, "Red China in Europe," *America* vol. (1967):   (from Keston archives). A *London Daily Telegraph* report of the same year mentions that Father Marino Shkurti, who escaped with a group of parishioners to Yugoslavia, was handed back to the Albanian authorities and executed by firing squad in November 1968, in accordance with Albanian law.
44. *Albanian Catholic Bulletin*, 1 (1980):1-2; 2 (1981):10.

left by tourists or floated in by sea. He was keeping them in the hope that the ban on religious materials might be lifted eventually. Although his trial was not mentioned in the national media, people knew it was happening and took great interest in it.[45]

In May 1980, after much hesitation, the former director of Xavier College, Shkodra, Father Ndoc Luli, S.J., baptized his twin nephews on the agricultural commune where he was working as a laborer. His sister-in-law, who had persuaded him to do it, was sentenced to eight years, and Father Luli to "life until death."[46]

It is believed that there are thirty Catholic priests serving sentences in labor camps.[47] No information as to the number of Orthodox priests, laity of either church, or Muslims is available, but it is known that a considerable number of the estimated sixteen thousand political prisoners in Albania are serving religion-connected sentences.

Religious Activity Today

To what extent religion survives in Albania is nearly impossible to assess. The draconic sentences recorded above, however, suggest that it is still causing the government much concern. Official pronouncements in the media show that "liberating people's consciousness from unfounded religious faiths" is an uphill task.

Glimpses of the situation can be gleaned from the press. People are said to be lax in reporting what they consider to be harmless superstitious practices, and there are many calls to vigilance. In 1980, there was a complaint that although children were using suitable, i.e., secular, names at school, at home they were reverting to religious names.[48] The older generation is sometimes criticized for transmitting religious teaching to the young. References are found from time to time of people listening to foreign religious broadcasts, or of manufacturing religious objects, and of foreigners trying to smuggle religious literature into the country.[49]

There are many signs of silent protest. The chief fasts are still

---

45. *Keston News Service*, 161:2-3.
46. *Albanian Catholic Bulletin*, 3 (1982):10.
47. They include Father Gege Lumaj, sentenced to seven years imprisonment in 1967, subsequently extended by a further fifteen years; Father Zef Pllumbi (fifteen years) and Father Mark Hasi (twenty years) in 1968; Father Pjeter Meshkella, S.J., imprisoned from 1946-64 for "sabotage" (trying to get international relief for flood victims), given a further sentence of twenty years in 1971. (Various sources including *Fulfilled Promise*, 188). Others include Fathers Injaj Gjoka, Rrok Gjuraj, Anton Luli, S.J., Gjerj Vata, S.J., Simon Jubani, and his older brother Lazar; also two Franciscans. (Reported alive in camps along with Fathers Hasi and Meshkella, in *Grave Violations*, 13-14).
48. *Keston News Service*, 180:15.
49. "Vestiges of Religion in Albania," *Keston News Service*, 120:11.

observed, Ramadan by the Muslims and Lent by the Christians. In Orthodox areas the consumption of milk and meat products falls markedly during Lent. On important feast days, such as Easter, people sometimes refuse to work. Officially, of course, these feasts and fasts do not exist. Funeral rites, not surprisingly, survive; Muslims are still buried in graves facing Mecca; in Orthodox communities, prayers are recited on the third, ninth, and fortieth days after a death. Tourists report seeing people furtively crossing themselves and saying the rosary.[50]

Disguised pilgrimages to holy places continue, particularly to those where healings have taken place. A church building near Shkodra that once housed a miraculous icon was finally razed to the ground and the area cordoned off when the authorities discovered that relatives of party functionaries had been visiting it. It is reported that a former prominent Politburo member, notorious for his hostility to Christians, had his seriously ill child taken to a well-known holy place to have him prayed for, and that child was healed.[51] There have been rumors of demonstrations on the sites of churches and mosques in northern Albania by believers who want them reopened.[52]

Whether or not these are manifestations of deep faith or merely of innate superstition cannot be assessed, particularly since Albania is a country where primitive pagan superstitions have survived, despite the influence of centuries of Christianity and Islam. Years of intensive indoctrination have also had some effect; some young refugees from a Catholic family did not know what a priest was, for instance. Most have never heard of their fellow Albanian, Mother Theresa. On the other hand, there are still individuals and groups who have managed to maintain their faith. In 1967, before the complete clampdown on religion, farsighted clergy gave out religious literature to keen members, taught them services they could perform at home, and emphasized that a believer could do without a church and worship in secret, provided "he has religion in his heart."[53] We hear official complaints that there are still people with prayerbooks reciting the liturgy at home. Ex-seminarian and refugee Mark Ndocaj has emphasized how crucial has been the role of the family in preserving

---

50. Groups of women have been seen apparently gossiping, but actually saying the rosary together. The rosary may well be the chief and simplest method of keeping the faith alive, as it was under Ottoman rule.
51. "Albania—Some Comments," *Keston News Service*, 108:9. A recent editorial in the monthly *Ruga a Partise* mentions Catholics still going to pray at the "former holy places of Lac." Soldiers have been seen guarding derelict churches.
52. *Keston News Service*, 159:3.
53. "Revolutionary Movement,"

the faith;[54] despite the enforced absence of a priest, baptisms, weddings, and funerals are celebrated within closed family circles. Gardens, caves, forests, and even sometimes closed churches are the scene also of religious rites. It appears that there are still priests not under arrest, some of them actually administering the sacraments at mortal risk.[55] Of these, some are said to be former well-instructed laymen who have been secretly ordained. Two sisters from an educated family who managed to swim the seven miles to Corfu in 1984 attributed their survival to the "mercy of Allah."

All this adds up to what must be the most heartening message to come out of Albania in many years. After the Assemblies of God in Great Britain and Ireland had claimed that over the past three years thirty thousand gospels have been successfully sent into Albania, and that people are trying to find out how to get a copy instead of aiding the authorities, a letter was received saying, "Church of Jesus Christ is alive and growing in Albania. Thank you for the literature and please send more." Another message reaching the West said, "We pray not only for ourselves but for all who are suffering anywhere."[56]

There is a feeling of insecurity in Albania today. In December 1981, Prime Minister Mehmet Shehu officially committed suicide; it seems that he was killed. This was followed by a purge, revealing deep rifts within the apparently united leadership. Hoxha became ill and died on 11 April 1985. For some time now, even the well-indoctrinated younger generation has been showing signs of unrest. So far, his well-groomed successor, Ramiz Ajai (61), has followed Hoxha's religious policy, but has opened up marginally more normal relations with a wide range of countries.[57]

Some amazing official statistics came to light in 1980[58] that reveal the true role of religion as a determining social factor. In the past, intermarriage between people of the four major religious groups in Albania (Catholic, Orthodox, Bektashi, and Muslim) had been reasonably common. A sociologist recently complained that 96 percent of the population of this "atheist" country were choosing their partners from the same religious background as themselves.

---

54. *Albanian Catholic Bulletin*, 1 (1980):2.
55. *Keston News Service*, 120:11; 159:3.
56. *Keston News Service*, 159:7.
57. These do not yet include the USA or USSR. With a birth rate four times the average for Europe, and 37% of the population under 15, the economy is under pressure. The delicate area of relations is with Yugoslavia, where in the autonomous Kossovo region of Serbia there is a growing (and heavily repressed) movement among the province's 1.8 million Albanians for reunion with Albania.
58. Tonnes, *Religious Persecution in Albania*, 254-55.

The effect of all the might of Albanian religious policy has apparently been to produce an integrating effect on the religious communities, causing believers to consider it prudent to maintain the purity of their faiths by insulating themselves from outside influences. The defeat of Hoxha's policies could hardly have been greater.

Religion and the State in China: Winter Is Past

JAMES E. WOOD, JR.

Today there is evidence of a religious resurgence in China. In the words of a Chinese university professor on a recent visit to the United States, "Religions in China are reviving, not dying; they are alive, not dead." Nowhere is this more evident than with respect to Christianity, which presently has more than twice as many churches and believers as were to be found in China prior to the Communist Revolution in 1949. This new-found status of Christianity in China is dramatically celebrated and symbolized in a contemporary Chinese hymn, "Winter Is Past," which today has become for Chinese Christians one of their most beloved hymns. After almost two decades of trying to eliminate religion from the country, climaxed by a decade of the Cultural Revolution (1966-1976), during which time an intense effort was made to stamp out all vestiges of religion, since 1976 the government of China has been gradually liberalizing its policies toward religion. Indeed, during the past decade, particularly since 1980, great strides toward religious freedom have been made in China.

I

In China's more than four thousand years of history, religion has played a long and varied role. As in other civilizations and societies throughout the world, religion has been a molder and purveyor of much of Chinese culture. As elsewhere, religion in China was traditionally for the community as a whole and not for the individual. In addition, religion and the state were inextricably intertwined. Consequently, the emperors of China enjoyed a sacred status, in which political and religious authority were merged and this fusion of power formed the basis of unity for the empire.

Identification of Chinese emperors with divinity became a time-honored tradition. Because of their reputedly close relation to heaven, Chinese rulers were given the title *T'ien Tzu* (Son of Heaven), the human counterpart of *Shang Ti* (Sovereign Ruler). Also, only the emperor addressed *Shang Ti* or "sublime T'ien," in the ceremonies of the Altar of Heaven outside of the capital of the empire. The extensive imperial palace grounds situated in the center of the capital of Peking came to be known as the Forbidden City, since entrance was forbidden to all except members of the royal family and their retainers. This blending of religion with the state meant that to be a dissenter was to be guilty of heresy and sedition simultaneously.

Part of the uniqueness of China's religious heritage is that China's cultural identification was not with one but several religious traditions. Before the Communist Revolution, one could quite correctly speak of the religion rather than the religions of China. It was quite customary to speak of the religion of China as embodying all three religious traditions — Confucianism, Taoism, and Buddhism — all three of which are radically humanistic. Throughout China they were referred to as *San Chiao* or "Three Teachings" and symbolized an identity that virtually all Chinese felt toward these three religions, each of which was seen as complementary to the others.

The integration of religious and political institutions in China was accomplished by government supervision of religion. This is not to ignore, let alone infer, that conflict between religious and political institutions did not on occasions occur. The Legalists of ancient China, who sought strict legal control over all activities, provide ample evidence of occasions when antireligious attitudes periodically manifested themselves in Chinese society. Conflict between Legalism and Confucianism, for example, has a long history in China.

The traditional religion of China, with its concerns for social norms and moral values, held forth the concept of the ideal person and the ideal society. Through its teachings the religion of China held forth the model of a moral and harmonious society. As China's religious traditions came to permeate Chinese society and to enjoy a homogeneous relationship with one another, *San Chiano* came to embody the socially recognized values of Chinese society; although complete penetration of Chinese society by the *San Chiao* was, to be sure, never realized.

While China's three religious traditions were viewed harmoniously in principle, they largely operated at different levels in Chinese society. There was the religion of the masses and the religion of the enlightened, the literati. Confucianism became the official teaching of the state and was used for centuries as a tool of the ruling classes to perpetuate their privileged positions in society. By contrast, Taoism and Buddhism became primarily identified with the illiterate masses, although these class distinctions among their respective adherents should be understood as broad generalizations and should not be perceived as rigid class differences. In any event, by the beginning of the twentieth century, many Chinese had come to regard all three of China's religious traditions (*San Chiao*) as reactionary forces in Chinese society and incompatible with the emergence of a new China and the movement toward the first Chinese Revolution of 1911-1912. As such, the traditional religion of China stood in the way of progress and China's becoming a republic.

Attempts to bring Christianity to China span a period of over a thousand years. The first three separate attempts to do so met with failure. Nestorian missionaries, Syrian monks from Persia, first introduced Christianity to China in 635 during the T'ang Dynasty (618-907). After more than two centuries, Nestorianism, which was centered around monasteries and not congregations, disappeared after an edict was issued by Emperor Wuzong in 845 suppressing all religions. A second attempt, also by the Nestorians, came during the Yuan (Mongol) Dynasty (1271-1368), during which time Roman Catholic churches were established in various parts of the empire. When the Yuan Dynasty was overthrown by the Ming Dynasty (1368-1644) in 1368, Christianity disappeared a second time from China. During the latter part of the sixteenth century, a third attempt was made by Jesuit missionaries, headed by Matteo Ricci. Ricci's efforts to reconcile Christianity with Chinese culture resulted in the "Rites and Terms Controversy," the result of which was that Rome banned Ricci's accommodation to Confucian terms for God and the ancestral cult. In each instance, Christianity remained a foreign religion and, therefore, did not take root.

Protestant mission work began in China with the arrival of Robert Morrison in 1807, shortly before the Opium War. While largely independent of Western colonialism, Protestant missions flowered during the nineteenth century, a century marked by a wave of Western imperialism, during which almost all of Africa, most of the islands of the Pacific, and a large part of Asia were brought under the control of Western Europeans. Unfortunately, Christianity's ties with Western imperialism in China were manifest throughout most of the period from 1807 to 1949.

That there were ties of Christian missionaries in China with Western imperialism cannot be denied. With China's defeat in the infamous Opium War, both Catholic and Protestant missionaries benefited from a series of treaties forced upon China by Western powers. These treaties guaranteed extraterritorial protection to both missionaries and their converts, whereby they were assured protection and special privileges under the laws of sovereignty of Western powers. In some cases, as in the case of France, Christian missions (i.e., Roman Catholic) in China were used as a means of reenforcing French prestige in China. France insisted on and obtained the right of a protectorate over all Catholic missions in China, both their own and those of other nationalities. This association of Christianity with Western imperialism was but further compounded during the 1930s and 1940s when many American missionaries became closely associated with American national interests in China. Today, few China observers within Christianity would disagree with the following observation made by Ray Wylie: "Many of the missionaries became too closely identified with the imperialistic policies of their respective governments, and this compromised Christianity itself in the eyes of many Chinese."[1] As Hendrik Kraemer painfully reminded the churches in the West almost three decades ago, "The younger churches pay a heavy price for the fact that they originated mainly in the time of modern missions under colonial aegis."[2]

As in mission efforts in China centuries earlier, Christian missions from 1807 to 1949 remained far too missionary-dominated and mission-controlled to permit the emergence of truly indigenous churches, at least on any wide scale. In a centennial observance in 1907 held in commemoration of the beginning of Protestant missions in China, there was not a single Chinese Christian present. Christian leaders in China today continue to lament the dominance of mission boards and missionaries in the churches of China before 1949 and to celebrate the steps that have been taken since the Communist Revolution to make the churches of China authentically Chinese.

Before the Communist Revolution, the Chinese generally spoke of Christianity as a "foreign" religion. They did so as a way of stigmatizing Christianity as an instrument of foreign aggression. Interestingly enough, the Chinese did not similarly label Buddhism and Islam, although they, too, were religions brought to China from other countries. The reason for this was that, in the words of Jiang Wenhan, vice chairman of the National Three-Self Patriotic Movement Committee, Christianity in China was "an entirely mission-controlled enterprise up to the time of China's liberation of 1949, and was never truly in-

---

1. See Stephen Neill, *Colonialism and Missions* (New York: McGraw-Hill Book Co., 1966), especially chap. 4, "China and the West," 116-69; Kenneth Scott Latourette, "Colonialism and Missions: Progressive Separation," *Journal of Church and State* 7 (Autumn 1965):330-49; and James E. Wood, Jr., "Church, State, and Missions," *Journal of Church and State* 7 (Autumn 1965):317-29.
2. Hendrik Kraemer, "Missionary Implications of the End of Western Colonialism and the Collapse of Western Christendom," in *History's Lessons for Tomorrow's Missions: Milestones in the History of Missionary Thinking* (Geneva: World's Student Christian Federation, 1960), 205.

digenous on Chinese soil."³ Christianity was seen as having a denationalizing effect on Chinese converts. Hence, the oft-repeated saying prior to 1949, "The addition of a Christian to the church means the loss of a citizen to China." For many, conversion to Christianity meant not only the breaking with family and community traditions but also signified a betrayal of one's national heritage.

Notwithstanding its "foreign" associations, Christianity experienced substantial growth prior to 1949. Protestant adherents numbered approximately 100,000 in 1900. By 1920 they had quadrupled and by 1949 numbered more than 700,000. Even though Roman Catholic missions experienced even closer ties with Western powers and more foreign domination than Protestant missions, Catholic membership rose from 700,000 in 1900 to more than 3,250,000 by 1949. By the 1920s, China had become the largest center of Christian missionary activity on the part of the churches of North America and Europe. The number of Christian missionaries serving in China reached its zenith in 1926 with 8,325 missionaries. Subsequently, nationalist and revolutionary attacks on Christian missions brought a drop in missionary personnel to about 6,000, but this still represented a substantial number.[4]

Of even greater significance, as Kenneth Scott Latourette and Robert Bellah, among others, have observed, was the influence of Christianity and Christian institutions as catalysts for change, which was far out of proportion to the relatively small number of people involved.[5] Even with a very small percentage of the total population claimed as Christian, with never more than 1 percent, the thirteen Protestant and three Catholic colleges of China transmitted Western thought and contributed substantially to a newly emerging Western educated elite who were to come virtually to dominate the Who's Who of China. In introducing Western culture and science, Christian missionaries contributed substantially to international understanding and cultural exchange. Ironically, the impact of Western political domination, Western education, and Christianity—all indissolubly linked—also greatly contributed to the political and social revolution in China and ultimately to a resurgence of nationalism in China. As Western education took root, secular thought was often used to attack Christianity.

Although a balanced view of Christian missions in China during

---

3. Jiang Wenhan, "How 'Foreign' Was Christianity in China," in *Chinese Christians Speak Out: Addresses and Other Sermons*, ed. Bishop K. H. Ting et al. (Beijing: New World Press, 1984):22.
4. Kenneth Scott Latourette, *Advance Through Storm*, vol. 7 of *A History of the Expansion of Christianity* (New York: Harper and Brothers, 1945), 328-78; G. Thompson Brown, *Christianity in the People's Republic of China* (Atlanta: John Knox Press, 1983), 41-42.
5. Robert N. Bellah, ed., *Religion and Progress in Modern Asia* (New York: The Free Press, 1965) and Latourette, *Advance Through Storm*.

the nineteenth and twentieth centuries must give attention to the intimate association of Christian missionaries with Western imperialism and the widespread perception among the Chinese people of Christianity as a "foreign" religion, it would be a distortion not to take note of the personal integrity, genuine commitment to service, and unselfish devotion to the Chinese people on the part of countless missionaries who sought to contribute to the moral and social uplift of China and the Chinese people through an authentic Christian witness. Many missionaries were, in fact, openly critical of colonialism and imperialism and some sympathized with the revolutionary movement in which patriotic Chinese Christians, let it be noted, were among the participants.

Deeply felt suspicions toward Christianity and Christian missionaries in China, including periodic manifestations of hostility, as in the case of the Anti-Christian Movement of the 1920s, appeared for many decades before the Communist Revolution of 1949. By that time, however, a wave of reaction against Christianity was intensified and compounded by a variety of forces unleashed by the Revolution. While all religion in China came under attack for a variety of reasons readily identified with Marxist ideology, Christianity was particularly vulnerable. Out of a resurgent Chinese nationalism, allegations against Christianity as a "foreign" religion and an arm of Western imperialism reached a new intensity. Accusations against Christianity, as well as other religions, were further sustained by Marxist ideology, which argues that religion is an "opiate" of the people, a social aberration that has been used for centuries by the bourgeoisie to control and exploit the masses. Contributing still further to the hostility toward Christian missions, as well as to Christianity, was its association with the Kuomingtang and the Generalissimo Chiang Kai-shek, against whom the Revolution had for so long been waged.

II

Mao Tse-tung proclaimed the establishment of the People's Republic of China on 1 October 1949. When the Chinese Communists came to power, their intent with respect to religion was to monitor and regulate all religions and to cut them off, as in the case of Christianity, from all types of foreign control and support. Unlike the Soviet Union, Maoist China sought not to eliminate religion, but rather to control it. As Mao declared, "We cannot abolish religion . . . . In settling matters of an ideological nature . . . we can only use democratic methods of discussion, of criticism, of persuasion, and education." Land holdings of Buddhist and Taoist temples were confiscated in large numbers and redistributed in a land reform movement, with many temples designated for secular use. Buddhist monks and nuns were forced to find other ways of "filling the rice bowl." Freedom of street evangelism and overt acts of proselytizing were denied all religions, whether Buddhist, Christian, or Muslim. Religious educational institutions, generally including China's sixteen Christian colleges, were nationalized and became state institutions of learning and technology. Social programs under religious auspices were no longer permitted.

By 1950, with the outbreak of the Korean War, the work of Christian missionaries from overseas was brought to an end. The People's government sought to channel and direct all religious activity toward the furtherance of Communist objectives. As Chairman Mao had written in *New Democracy* almost a decade before the establishment of the People's government, "For the purpose of taking concerted political action against Imperialism, Chinese Communists may form a united front with certain classes of idealists and with members of certain religious faiths, but they certainly should not approve of such idealism or the religious doctrine concerned."[6]

Early after the establishment of the People's Republic of China, recognition was given to five officially designated religions—Buddhism, Taoism, Islam, Catholicism, and Protestantism, but at all times, even up to the present, the People's government has sought rigid control over them. Nevertheless, the government has not failed to recognize many of their cultural and social values to the nation and their enormous political value as a means of bringing about the united support of ethnic and religious minorities on behalf of a democratic socialist state and as an aid in diplomatic relations. To be sure, the price to be paid by the religions for this official recognition and protection has been their unequivocal support of the government's economic and political programs and their acceptance of the policy of no public criticism of the government.

Meanwhile, Buddhism, with its 40 million adherents, is recognized and respected for its place in Chinese artistic and cultural history. On the initiative of the Bureau of Religious Affairs, the Chinese Buddhist Association was formed in 1953, "to unite all the country's Buddhists so that they will participate, under the leadership of the People's Republic government, in movements for the welfare of the motherland, the defense of world peace . . . to link up Buddhists from different parts of the country; and to exemplify the best traditions of Buddhism." The purpose of the Chinese Budist Association was, as Holmes Welch, a leading authority on Buddhism in China, has observed, "pirmarily as an instrument for remolding Buddhism to suit the needs of the government."[7]

---

6. Mao Tse-tung, *New Democracy* (Shanghai: Chinese-American Publishing Co., 1949), 70.
7. Holmes Welch, *Buddhism under Mao* (Cambridge, Mass.: Harvard University Press, 1972), 25.

In a similar manner, the Chinese Islamic Association was organized the same year to serve as a liaison between the Muslim community and the government. With its 20 million adherents, Islam enjoys some measure of status as a cultural and ethnic entity, but is denied religious independence. Nevertheless, Islam has enjoyed some degree of tolerance, even during the Cultural Revolution, that has not been accorded China's other officially designated religions, primarily because of China's diplomatic relations with various Muslim countries.

The Bureau of Religious Affairs also led in the organization in 1954 of the Chinese Taoist Association "in order to unite all the Taoists of China in the protection of the fatherland, in the participation in socialist reconstruction, in the defense of peace; in order to cooperate with the government's policy of religious liberty." As one of China's two major indigenous religions, Taoism has experienced strong opposition from the beginning of the People's government since it is viewed largely as a superstitious, folk religion. While religious Taoism, as expressed in its practices through rites and rituals, has, for decades, been in serious decline and was virtually brought to an end by the Cultural Revolution, philosophical Taoism remains as a part of China's heritage. Never designated as one of the official religions of China by the People's government, Confucianism as a religion was condemned. Its shrines were secularized and its temples closed to religious practices. The worship of Confucious was forbidden.[8]

Christianity, also was enlisted to form a united front with the new People's government of China. In July 1950, forty prominent Protestant leaders of China issued a Christian Manifesto under the title: "Direction of Endeavor for Chinese Christianity in the Construction of New China." By September, the document had been signed by 1,527 Protestant church leaders and within a year or two over 400,000 had signed, more than half of the total Protestant membership in China. The obvious intent of the document was to foster reconciliation with the People's government and to assure the government of Protestantism's patriotic commitment to it. Portions of the document read as follows:

> Protestant Christianity has been introduced to China for more than one hundred and forty years. During this period, it has made a not unworthy contribution to Chinese society. Nevertheless, and this was most unfortunate, not long after Christianity's coming to China Imperialism started its activities here; and since the principal groups of missionaries who brought Christianity to China all came themselves from these imperialistic countries, Christianity consciously or unconsciously, directly or indirectly,

---

8. See Charles S. Braden, *War, Communism, and the Religions of China* (New York: Harper and Brothers, 1953); Richard Clarence Bush, Jr., *Religion in Communist China* (Nashville: Abingdon Press, 1970); and Donald McInnis, *Religious Policy and Practice in Communist China: A Documentary History* (New York: The Macmillan Company, 1972).

became related with Imperialism. Now that the Chinese revolution has achieved victory, these imperialistic countries will not rest passively content in the face of this unprecedented historical fact in China. They will certainly seek to contrive by every means the destruction of what has actually been achieved; they may also make use of Christianity to forward their plot of stirring up internal dissension, and creating reactionary forces in this country. It is our purpose in publishing the following statement to heighten our vigilance against Imperialism, to make known the clear political stand of Christians in New China, to hasten the building of a Chinese Church whose affairs are managed by the Chinese themselves, and to indicate the responsibilities that should be taken up by Christians throughout the whole country in national reconstruction in New China. We desire to call upon all Christians in the country to exert their best efforts in putting into effect the principles herein presented . . . .

Christian Churches and organizations in China should take effective measures to cultivate a patriotic and democratic spirit among their adherents in general, as well as a psychology of self-resepct and self-reliance. The movement for autonomy, self-support, and self propagation hitherto promoted in the Chinese Church has already attained a measure of success. This movement from now onwards should complete its tasks within the shortest possible period. At the same time, self-criticism should be advocated, all forms of Christian activity re-examined and readjusted, and thoroughgoing austerity measures adopted, so as to achieve the goals of a reformation in the Church.

All Christian Churches and organizations in China which are still relying upon foreign personnel and financial aid should work out concrete plans to realize within the shortest possible time their objective of self-reliance and rejuvenation.

From now onwards, as regards their religious work, Christian Churches and organizations should lay emphasis upon a deeper understanding of the nature of Christianity itself, closer fellowship and unity among the various denominations, the cultivation of better leadership personnel, and reform in the systems of Church organization. As regards their more general work, they should emphasize anti-imperialistic, anti-feudalistic, and anti-bureaucratic-capitalistic education, together with such forms of service to the people as productive labor, teaching them to understand the New Era, cultural and recreational activities, literacy education, medical and public health work, and care of children.[9]

While the Manifesto is based upon a distortion of the actual history of Christian missions in China, the document should be viewed as a corollary of Chinese Communist ideology at that time, arising out of a militant nationalism that was directed particularly against the United States, which was viewed as the prototype of evil and China's archenemy. No doubt, for many Chinese Christians the Manifesto served as a way of survival for the churches in Communist China at that time and as an expression of patriotism on the part of Chinese Christians in the "New" China.

By 1951, all Protestant churches in China had severed their relationships with the churches of the free world and virtually all missionaries had left the country. Protestantism in China not only denounced its

---

9. Frances P. Jones, ed., *Documents of the Three-Self Movement* (New York: Far Eastern Office of the Division of Foreign Missions, National Council of the Churches of Christ in the U.S.A., 1963), 19-20.

foreign ties from earlier years, it also eliminated all denominational divisions among Protestants and affirmed a policy of post-denominationalism for the Protestant churches in China. All Protestant churches were united in the Three-Self Patriotic Movement, which proved to be the instrument by which the churches were brought under the control of the state. Strongly advocated as early as 1950 by Wu Yao-tsung (Y. T. Wu), a national YMCA leader, the Movement was formally established in 1954. The Movement's name meant that churches were to be free from all foreign control and were to be characterized by "self-support, self-government, and self-propagation." In the words of its national president, Bishop Ding Guangxun (K. H. Ting), its "aim is limited to achieving a Chinese identity for the Churches in China."[10] As the Three-Self Patriotic Movement grew in influence, it provided the liaison with the government Religious Affairs Bureau, from which it has received a measure of financial support. Similarly, the Chinese Catholic Patriotic Association was formally established in 1957 and adopted a policy of independence from the Vatican. One year later, the Association declared its total separation from Rome. Thereafter, Catholic bishops in China have been named by the Association without appointment by the Holy See in Rome.

While the Chinese Communist party and the new People's government were openly atheistic, vigorously maintaining that religion is an "opiate of the people" and an obstacle to social progress, churches were allowed to function, though under strict supervision. Religious freedom was declared in Article 88 of the Draft Constitution of 1954, as it was adopted earlier by the First Plenary Session of the Chinese People's Political Consultative Conference in 1949: "The people of the People's Republic of China shall have freedom of thought, speech, publication, assembly, association, correspondence, person, domicile, change of domicile, religious belief, and the freedom of holding processions and demonstrations. Among the representatives at the 1949 conference were seven persons representing religious groups, two Buddhists and five Protestants. Muslims were also present, but their representatives came as members of an ethnic minority. Taoism was entirely ignored.

During the period from 1954 to 1957, there was a gradual lessening of tension between the churches and the People's government and some renewed contacts were established between the churches in China and churches in both Communist and non-Communist countries. By the middle of 1957, however, a period of antirightist repression, accompanied by waves of denunciation, began throughout China against fellow religionists, including many former missionaries, all of whom, by that time, had been removed from China. Six prominent church

---

10. See Ting et al., *Chinese Christians Speak Out: Addresses and Sermons*, 1-21.

leaders came in for severe denunciations for their rightist views and alliances with imperialism from years past. By the 1960s, Francis Price Jones, a veteran missionary to China from 1915 to 1951 and editor of the *China Bulletin* for the National Council of Churches in the U.S.A., could write as follows:

> Something of a modus vivendi has been arrived at between Protestant Christianity and the Chinese Communist party. The latter, so far, is willing to recognize the former, and guarantees a certain degree of freedom of religious belief, on the condition that Chinese Christians show themselves loyal citizens and co-operate in the establishment of a new economic order.
>
> These conditions of acceptance and co-operation are not in themselves necessarily subversive of the principles of Christian liberty . . . . It is therefore understandable that most Christians in China have accepted these conditions, and that the Christian church has in consequence received government recognition and been accorded a modest niche in Chinese society, so that it has not been compelled to go underground.[11]

Under Chairman Mao, freedom of religion came to mean freedom to hold religious views compatible with and in support of the goals and objectives of the People's government for social and political reform.

With the Cultural Revolution, which was to last for a decade from 1966 to 1976, a vigorous and violent campaign was waged against the "Four Olds"—old ideas, old culture, old customs, and old habits. Although religion was not specifically mentioned, it was regarded as the foundation of these "Four Olds." While it cannot be said that the Cultural Revolution was directed primarily against religion, nonetheless all religions in China came under unrelenting attack, along with much Chinese tradition and Western Culture, even art, literature, and music. Under the Gang of Four, rigid and repressive measures were undertaken against all religion, although somewhat less against Islam as a goodwill gesture to African Muslim countries. With rare exception, all places of worship were closed, Bibles and religious writings were confiscated and destroyed, and religious services, whether public or in private, were forbidden. The Three-Self Patriotic Movement and the Catholic Patriotic Association vanished and, thereby, ceased to exist. Thousands of clergy and many more church members were shipped to labor camps, churches, mosques, and temples closed, but many were vandalized, as the case of the main Catholic center in Peking, the South Cathedral; windows were broken and religious objects and pictures were mutilated. Conspicuously placed busts and statues of Mao Tse-tung were erected at the location of former religious centers and institutions.

---

11. Frances Price Jones, *The Church in Communist China: A Protestant Appraisal* (New York: Friendship Press, 1962), 162-63.

Reports of intense religious persecution were frequent throughout the decade.[12]

III

After the death of Mao Tse-tung in 1976, a new political regime seized political power in China. Within two years, Deng Xiaoping was brought back from disgrace and became the undisputed leader of China. While Deng does not hold China's highest political titles, he dominates the six-man standing committee that holds the Supreme Power of the Politburo and is chairman of the Central Military Commission. Under Deng, the program of the Cultural Revolution was repudiated and sweeping economic, political, and social reforms have been initiated. Two years after Deng's rise to power, the Gang of Four was tried, convicted, and sentenced to life imprisonment.

Beginning in the late 1970s, toleration of religion was gradually reinstituted. Perhaps not surprisingly in view of the role often played by religion during times of crisis, religion not only survived but also grew during the Cultural Revolution, which proved to be neither cultural nor a revolution. Millions of Chinese defied the ban on religious activity and engaged in religious services surreptitiously. In the case of Christianity, it grew underground in the house church movement, with which the vast majority of Protestants remain identified rather than with regular churches, which now enjoy a legal status but remain under the controls and regulations of the government. After being dormant for almost two decades, the Three-Self Patriotic Movement was revised in 1979 under the leadership of Bishop Ding Guangxun (K. H. Ting). A member of the Standing Committee of the National People's Congress, Bishop Ding also serves as president of the China Christian Council, an organization established in 1980 by the government to coordinate and oversee the activities of the churches.

With the new political leadership, many of the repressive restrictions on religion were gradually lifted. By 1978, reports from China were indicating that, because of modifications of government policy toward religion, public religious services were beginning to be held in major cities such as Peking and Nanking. That same year, Peking's new attitude toward religion officially manifested itself when a number of prominent Roman Catholic, Protestant, and Buddhist leaders reappeared for the first time since the early 1960s at the Chinese People's Political Consultative Conference. Within a few years, churches in in-

---

12. See Brown, *Christianity in the People's Republic of China*, chap. 7 "The Great Proletarian Cultural Revolution," 115-35 and Raymond Fung, comp. and trans., *Households of God on China's Soil* (Maryknoll, N.Y.: Orbis Books, 1983); a collection of firsthand experiences of fourteen Chinese Christian communities during the turbulent years of the Cultural Revolution.

creasing numbers were allowed to hold public services in various parts of the country. The reopening of churches was soon followed with the printing of Chinese Bibles, although at first in rather limited quantity.

Under Deng's leadership, a new state constitution, the fourth since 1954, was promulgated in December 1982. It marked a step toward the recognition of religious freedom in China. Prior to the new constitution, China's official position on religion read, "Citizens enjoy the freedom to believe in religion and the freedom not to believe in religion and to propagate atheism." Article 36 of the new constitution treats freedom of belief, as follows: "Citizens of the People's Republic of China enjoy freedom of religious belief. No State organ, social organization, or individual person may compel a citizen to believe in religion or not to believe in religion; nor may they discriminate against citizens who believe in religion or who do not believe in religion. The State guarantees normal religious activities. Nobody is allowed to use religion to carry out destructive activities against public order, harm the health of citizens, or impede the work of the State's educational system."

Significant gains may be found in the present constitution in its deletion of "freedom to propagate atheism" and in its prohibition of the state to exercise compulsion of or discrimination against citizens on the basis of their religion. The omission of the atheism clause has been primarily attributed to the organized efforts of the president of the Buddhist Association of China, Zhao Pu-chu, and the president of the Three-Self Patriotic Association, Bishop Ding. A final sentence on "freedom of belief," new to previous constitutions, states that "religious organizations and religious affairs must not tolerate interference from foreign powers," no doubt aimed at Christianity in general but Roman Catholicism in particular.

China's new policy on religion, however, must be interpreted not only by the State Constitution of 1982, but also as it is delineated in the Chinese Communist Party Central Committee's classified Document 19, "The Basic Viewpoint in Policy on the Religious Question During our Country's Socialist Period."[13] This document provides an "official" history of China's policy on religion since 1949. On visits to China, one can hear repeatedly this "official" history reviewed by religious leaders whenever responding to questions regarding China's policy toward religion since 1949.

The first period (1948-1956) is described as one of religious freedom and the elimination from the religions of China of those elements of

---

13. A photocopy of the original version of this important document appears in *Studies on Chinese Communism* 17 (15 March 1983):107-36; English translations may be found in *Issues and Studies* 19 (August 1983):72-90 and in a booklet published in 1984 by the Fao Fong Shen Ecumenical Center of Hong Kong, trans. Janice Wickeri. Document 19 was promulgated in March 1982 and transmitted throughout China to the provencial and local levels for implementation.

reactionary feudalism and imperialistic foreign domination. The second period (1957-1975) is referred to as one of an "ultra-leftist" deviation that denied religious freedom and sought by means of force to eradicate religion from Chinese life. This action is to be deplored as anti-Marxist, disruptive of Chinese unity, and a repudiation of the important contribution to be made by China's patriotic religious citizens. The third stage (1976-   ) marks the reestablishment of religious freedom for all Chinese citizens. Religious belief is "a private matter, one of individual free choice for citizens." Faithful to the Marxist view of religion, according to Document 19 religion will eventually fade away but only "after many generations have passed, and after the combined struggle of the broad masses of both believers and non-believers."

While Document 19 emphasizes that all Chinese—Marxists, believers and non-believers—are to enjoy certain religious rights, there are limitations and restrictions that are to be maintained on religious activity. Christian worship services are to be restricted to officially designated meeting places, outside of which no religious propagation is to be permitted. House churches are prohibited but this prohibition should not be "harshly" enforced. Unless approved by the Three-Self Patriotic Movement or the Catholic Patriotic Association, however, house churches are to be regarded as illegitimate activities. Finally, and most important, all religious organizations must accept the leadership of the Communist party and the state and all religious activities must be conducted and managed by these religious organizations under the directions of the Religious Affairs Bureau. All religious affairs must be conducted "only under or through patriotic associations" to which each religious group must belong. All "patriotic religious organizations" are charged with the responsibility of helping the religious masses and religious leaders to heighten their patriotic and socialist consciousness.

While religion in China remains clearly under the control of the government, more liberal attitudes toward religion on the part of the political leadership are widely evident throughout the country. Just last year in 1985, a senior Chinese academician and a member of the Chinese People's Political Consultation Conference, Zhao Fusan, publicly disputed the classical Marxist view that religion is an "opiate of the people" in a session held in Beijing. Deputy Chief of the Religious Research Division of the Chinese Academy of Social Sciences, Zhao declared, "Religion is a part of every nation's spiritual civilization whose influence is reflected in varying degrees in its art, literature, architecture, philosophy, morals, customs, and way of life." He continued, "The view that religion is entirely spiritual opium is unscientific and incomplete."[14]

---

14. *China News and Church Report* (*CNCR*), 12 April 1985; subsequently widely reported in the Western press.

There is also evidence of a religious resurgence in China, certainly there is an upturn in religious activity and religious identity on a scale unprecedented since the establishment of the People's Republic of China in 1949. Reports of increasing religious freedom and religious activity are readily confirmed today even by those who have made only brief visits to China. Chinese Muslims are once again making the pilgrimage to Mecca, and almost fourteen thousand mosques have been reopened in recent years. Many Buddhist temples, monasteries, and nunneries have been reopened and Buddhist membership is increasing. Even some Taoists temples have been reopened.

The greatest gains have been noted in Christianity. In 1980, only thirteen churches were open in all of China. By 1986 there were more than four thousand Protestant churches with at least one new congregation being added each day. Today, it is conservatively estimated that there are more than 3 million Protestants and more than 3 million Catholics to be found in China. These statistics, however, include only the membership of regular churches and do not include the more than 20 to 50 million Christians estimated to be found meeting in house churches throughout China. In 1983 a new hymnal of more than four hundred hymns, 102 composed by Chinese, was published. Recently, 2.1 million Bibles in modern Chinese were printed in China and distributed throughout the country. Since 1979, the government has allowed the restoration of numerous churches, including the Pehtang Catherdral, Peking's largest Catholic church.[15]

Christian seminaries, monasteries, and nunneries have been reestablished, including the fully accredited Nanking Union Theological Seminary that is academically related to the University of Nanking and serves also as the University's Center of Religious Studies. This seminary presently has more than two hundred students, representing only a small percentage of the students who applied for admission. Twelve regional theological seminaries also serve the churches in the training of pastoral leadership. In recent years, one out of six pastors ordained is a woman. In addition to the University of Nanking, academic recognition of the importance given to religion in China may also be found in the work of the Institute of World Religions of the Chinese Academy of Social Sciences in Peking, the department of religion of Peking University, and the religious studies institutes and/or religion courses that are now to be found in nearly all of the major universities in China.

---

15. See Brown, *Christianity in the People's Republic of China*, pp. 137-213; David H. Adeney, *China: The Church's Long March* (Ventura, Cal.: Regal Books, 1985); and Britt Towery, *The Churches of China: Taking Root Downward, Bearing Fruit Upward*, 2nd ed. (Hong Kong: Long Dragon Books, 1987).

The future course of religion in Communist China necessarily remains uncertain and unpredictable, made all the more so by the advanced age of China's present leader, Deng Xiaoping, but Chinese believers may rightly affirm, at least for now, "Winter is past."

Religion and the State in Japan

NOBUHIKO TAKIZAWA

On 15 August 1985, a national controversy of thirty year's standing concerning the question of religion and the state in Japan reached its peak; on that day Prime Minister Yasuhiro Nakasone performed the one postwar official act of worship at the Yasukuni (Shinto) Shrine, where the Japanese war dead are enshrined.

The date, 15 August 1945, marks the termination of the Pacific War. For Japan, the date is symbolic of release from fear and oppression and an earnest desire for peace. Also, the date serves as the memorial day for the war dead. Almost all of the war dead were enshrined in the Yasukuni-jinja (Shrine) as fallen heroes fighting for the emperor and the empire. It might appear natural, therefore, for prime ministers to visit the Yasukuni Shrine on that day. However, if they do so officially their visits constitute a religious act, which is prohibited by the Constitution of Japan. If the visit is made on the memorial day it may well suggest a possible union of religion and the state—the rebirth of State Shinto and militarism—since the Yasukuni Shrine is a Shinto shrine that once played a leading role in glorifying fallen soldiers and whipping up war sentiment of the people for the purpose of expansionistic military activities as a constituent of the State Shinto regime.

From the year of Japan's independence in 1952 to 1984, successive prime ministers from time to time visited the Yasukuni Shrine as private individuals or without official declaration of the nature of the act. In 1975, 1978, and 1980-1984, they visited the Yasukuni Shrine on 15 August, but did so as private individuals. On 15 August 1985, for the first time after the war, Prime Minister Nakasone and cabinet members performed the act declaring that they did so as public officials. They also paid ¥ 30,000 from public funds for a floral offering. This meant an apparent change of the government's view, as published in 1978 and 1980, that the constitutionality of official worship at the Shrine can still be doubted.

In the latter half of the 1950s, the Japan Association for the

Bereaved Families of the War Dead (*Nihon Izoku Kai*) initiated a campaign calling for some form of state patronage of the Yasukuni Shrine, including financial aid. After the Yasukuni Shrine State Patronage Bill (*Yasukuni Jinja Hoan*) passed the House of Representatives in 1974 but was killed in the House of Councilors, the same Association started and led a new campaign for official worship at the Yasukuni Shrine by the prime minister and cabinet members. Thorough going in making preparations for an opportunity to respond to such a demand, the Nakasone government took two strategic positions. First, in April 1984, the government party affirmed the constitutionality of official worship as a party decision on the basis of the Supreme Court's decision in 1977.[1] Second, in August 1984, the government itself established the Research Council for the Question of Official Worship at the Yasukuni Shrine by Cabinet Members (*Kakuryo no Yasukuni Jinja Sampai Mondai nikansuru Kondankai*), composed of men of learning and experience, as a private advisory organ for the chief cabinet secretary. Its aim was to arrive at the conclusion, couched as popular opinion, that official worship at the Yasukuni Shrine was a "generally accepted social idea." In fact, six days before the prime minister and cabinet members officially visited the Yasukuni Shrine, the Research Council concluded that such official worship was socially accepted and could be performed in such a way as not to be contrary to the principle of separation of religion and the state as defined in the above-mentioned decision of the Supreme Court.

As a matter of course, the official act of shrine worship drew strong protests from within and without Japan. All nongovernment parties, all leading newspapers, influential organizations of the new Buddhist religions and of Protestant churches, the Catholic Church, and organizations for peace and the Constitution's protection concertedly condemned the act of official shrine worship.[2] The common arguments voiced against it were as follows: (1) the Yasukuni Shrine is a symbolic institution to arouse and exalt a militant spirit; (2) official shrine worship is not only an unconstitutional practice, but also one step toward the rebirth of State Shinto, a tool for whipping up self-centered patriotism and militarism; and (3) official shrine worship ignores the sentiment of and Japanese responsibility

---

1. *Kakunaga* v. *Sekiguchi*, 31 Minshu 533 (Supreme Court, 13 July 1977).
2. In August 1985, suit for the return of the expense of the floral offering to the National Treasury was filed in the Tokyo District Court against Prime Minister Nakasone. Again, in November 1985, suit demanding compensation equivalent to that expense was filed in Kobe District Court against the government. Also, soon thereafter, the same actions were brought in the Osaka District Court and Fukuoka District Court.

to Asian peoples who suffered from Japan's armed aggression. As a matter of fact, voices were raised in protest from the People's Republic of China, the Democratic People's Republic of Korea, the Republic of Korea, Hong Kong, and Singapore. Above all, the government of the People's Republic of China protested vigorously against official shrine worship by the Japanese prime minister. The Chinese protest developed into a diplomatic controversy.

The Japanese government placed its main defense on the Report of the Research Council in implementing an official worship at the Yasukuni Shrine. The Report urged governmental action relying primarily upon the Supreme Court decision and the use of the terms "sentiment of the nation and the war bereaved families," namely the indigenous religious sentiment of the Japanese people. This essay examines the background or context of the official worship in its religious, constitutional, and political dimensions: the original or traditional function of the Yasukuni Shrine and the indigenous religious sentiment of the Japanese which constituted the soil that gave birth to the function and which has sustained it; the Supreme Court's relativism in regard to the relation of religion and the state and tests, which are based on religious uniqueness of the people; finally, the political context of the official worship and why Prime Minister Nakasone had to risk his political life in carrying out this official act of worship.

The Yasukuni Shrine and Japanese Popular Religion

The Traditional function of the Yasukuni Shrine. From 1869 to 1907, the Meiji government established shrines (Yasukuni Shrine in Tokyo and its branches, Gokoku shrines, in each perfecture) sacred to the memory of those killed serving the emperor or the state under the *Tenno* system.[3]

During the period ranging from the arrival of Commodore M. C. Perry at Uraga, Japan (1853) to the Boshin Civil War (1868), bloody political strife continued between the royalist-exclusionist party and the shogunate party. For the first time, a memorial service for the dead of the royalist-exclusionist party was performed by order of the Emperor Komei in Kyoto in 1862. After that time, such services were often performed in various places. The memorial service, which

---

3. Shigeyoshi Murakami, *Kokka Shinto* (State Shintoism) (Tokyo: Iwanamishoten, 1970), 182-195 and "Yasukuni Jinja no Rekishi-teki Yakuwari to Koshiki Sampai no Mondaiten" (The Historical Role of the Yasukuni Shrine and the Point at Issue of the Official Worship), *Jurisuto* 848 (November 1985):60-66, are very helpful in understanding the traditional or original function of the Yasukuni Shrine.

invoked the souls of the dead, had the effect of exalting the morale of the members of the royalist-exclusionist party and soldiers of the Imperial Army and strengthening their sense of solidarity. In such services they propitiated the souls of those of their own party who laid down their lives for the emperor and the country and swore to follow them.[4]

The Shinto shrines dedicated to such souls were established first in Shimonoseki by the Choshu clan in 1865, then in Kyoto in 1868, in Tokyo in 1869 by the government, and later in various feudal domains by each clan. Originally, the Tokyo Shinto Shrine was dedicated exclusively to those who died after 1853 in the Imperial Army during the civil war. In 1875, those who were enshrined in feudal domains of the Royalist Party, were enshrined together in the "Tokyo Shinto Shrine Dedicated to the Souls of the War Dead" (*Tokyo Shokon Sha*). Thus, a central Shinto shrine dedicated to the souls of the dead of the Imperial Army was established. The formation of the State Shinto regime and the need to establish a unified and strong national army, after the heavy death toll suffered by the government army's soldiers in the Southwest Civil War beginning with the Satsuma Rebellion (1877), provided the opportunity in 1879 for the renaming of the *Tokyo Shokon Sha* to the "Yasukuni Shrine." The Yasukuni Shrine then was assigned a very important position in the State Shinto hierarchy; its function changed from that of invoking and appeasing the individual souls of the war dead to that of enshrining the souls of fallen heroes fighting for the country as guardian deities of the state. It was believed that these guardian deities defended the empire and protected the emperor and the Imperial Palace. At the same time, the Yasukuni Shrine was made a special government shrine.[5] It fell under the jurisdiction of the Ministry of Home Affairs and the army (the Ministry of War) and the navy. After 1887, it also fell under the army and the navy.[6]

After the Sino-Japanese War, casualties from diseases contracted at the front were enshrined in the Yasukuni Shrine. After that, the emperor, who was Manifest Deity, came to worship at the Yasukuni Shrine. In 1907, after the Russo-Japanese War, the Ministry of Home Affairs started to integrate into the Yasukuni Shrine the many Shinto shrines in each prefecture dedicated to the souls of the war dead. After this, the Shinto shrines, as branches of the Yasukuni Shrine,

---

4. Murakami, "Yasukuni Jinja no Rekishi-teki Yakuwari," 60-61.
5. *Bekkaku Kampei Sha* (special government shrines) were sacred to deities who originally were mere men and subjects as distinguished from the emperors, who were made the Manifest Deities, and the Imperial family. Ibid., 64.
6. Ibid., 61-64.

had to enshrine only the war dead enshrined in the Yasukuni Shrine according to a standard being classified as "in the service of the Emperor." Moreover, thereafter monuments to the loyal dead were established in cities, towns, and villages and the people were forced to worship at those shrines and monuments. All these military Shinto shrines, capped by the Yasukuni Shrine, played an influential role in glorifying fallen heroes, whipping up the war sentiment of the people, and consoling the war bereaved.[7]

In September 1946, the Yasukuni Shrine and its branches were made nonpublic religious institutions. The Yasukuni Shrine, as a religious corporation, continued to enshrine the war dead that numbered 2,464,151 as of the end of July 1985. The Shrine kept its founding purpose and basic nature as expressed in the "Regulations of Religious Corporation, the Yasukuni Shrine": "This corporation has the purpose of enshrining those who sacrificed themselves for the country on the basis of the Imperial Will, the 'peaceful country' that Emperor Meiji spoke of . . ." (Article 3).[8] In 1879, when the Yasukuni Shrine was given its name and status as a special government shrine, its true motive was stated officially as follows: the words "peaceful country" are fulfilled by the distinguished services of those who gave their lives to defeat and punish internal and external enemies of the country.[9] In including casualties resulting from aggressive, expansionistic military activities, the use of the word "peaceful" is clearly contradictory.

Japanese popular religion. In 1953 the government began to refer to people who met their death from war crimes as "persons killed by judicial action" and to treat them equally with the war dead identified in general.[10] The Yasukuni Shrine enshrined the A-class "war criminals" in 1978 as "martyrs in the Showa era" (*showa junnansha*).[11] In relation to the enshrinement of the A-class "war criminals," the Research Council in its report stated that "the Yasukuni Shrine may at its discretion decide who should be enshrined."[12]

For the first time, on 20 September 1985, the government of the People's Republic of China stated that the official worship at the

---

7. Ibid., 64-65.
8. Shukyohojin Yasukuni Jinja Kisoku (The Regulation of Religious Corporation, the Yasukuni Shrine), *Jurisuto* 848 (November 1985):155.
9. Murakami, *Kokka Shinto*, 186.
10. *Yasukuni*, 1 May 1986.
11. *Yomiuri Shimbun*, 6 January 1986.
12. "Kakuryo no Yasukuni Jinja Sampai Mondai nikansuru Kondankai Hokokusho" (The Report by the Research Council for the Question of Official Worship at the Yasukuni Shrine by the Cabinet Members) (hereafter cited as "Report"), *Jurisuto* 848 (November 1985):112.

Yasukuni Shrine dedicated to the A-class "war criminals" offended the feelings of the Chinese people.[13] In mid-October 1985, the Japanese Minister of Foreign Affairs visited Peking and talked with the Chinese political leaders concerning the topic of official worship. The latter put the official worship at the Yasukuni Shrine dedicated to the A-class "war criminals" as the crux of the question, while the former appealed to them to understand the "popular sentiment" in Japan in favor of the official worship.[14] Also, relying upon the words "popular sentiment," the Research Council urged implementation of the official worship.[15]

On 2 May 1952, just after the effectuation of the Japanese Peace Treaty with the United States (28 April 1952), the Japanese government performed for the first time a national ceremony consisting of mourning and honoring the war dead in the Shinjuku Imperial Gardens. Since then, the government has held this ceremony in secular form in various places;[16] the prime ministers and cabinet members have also participated in those ceremonies. However, the Report by the Research Council pointed out that "the majority of the people and the bereaved families still regard the Yasukuni Shrine as a central institution for mourning and honoring the war dead and therefore desire . . . official worship at the Shrine by the prime minister and cabinet members."[17] Some members of the Research Council proposed that the government should establish a religiously neutral mausoleum in which memorial services would be performed

---

13. *Asahi Shimbun*, 10 September 1985.
14. *Mainichi Shimbun*, 12 October 1985. In early December 1985, a former Japanese Minister of Foreign Affairs, a man of influence of the Nakasone faction, talked with the Chinese Minister of Foreign Affairs on the question and, just after that, expressed his doubt regarding the relationship of A-class war criminals enshrined at the Yasukuni Shrine to the Japanese Peace Treaty (1951): in Article 11 of that Treaty, Japan should warrant the punishment of the war criminals; also he demanded conversations between the Yasukuni Shrine and the bereaved families of the war criminals regarding withdrawal of their enshrinement. *Mainichi Shimbun*, 5 December 1985. The Yasukuni Shrine rejected the withdrawal on the basis of freedom of religion. *Yomiuri Shimbun*, 6 January 1986. The bereaved families did likewise asserting that the victims, who were condemned in the Tokyo War Crime's Trial, should not be regarded as criminals. *Jinja Shimpo*, 20 January 1986. Also the persons concerned with Shrine Shinto condemned the Tokyo Tribunal as illegal, authorized only by the power of the victors from the viewpoint of the principle of *"nulla poena sine lege"* and asserted that souls of the dead should not be related to the Japanese Peace Treaty, Article 11, but should be exempted, due to the illegality of the acts of the victors. *Jinja Shimpo*, 20 January 1986. Such responses may be taken as an expression of the Japanese indigenous sentiment of souls of the dead.
15. "Report," 112.
16. The Chidorigafuchi National Tomb Garden for the War Dead (3 March 1959 and every spring from 1965 on) to which all the war dead (including the unknown soldiers) were dedicated; the precincts of the Yasukuni Shrine (15 August 1964); the Japan Martial Arts Hall (Nihon Budo Kan) every 15 August from 1965 on, as held for the bombed dead as well.
17. "Report," 111.

for the war dead as well as others dying in line of official duty in various forms. Against the proposal, "even if such an institution will be established," stated the Report, "the Yasukuni Shrine will not be able to be replaced with that, in consideration of the sentiment of the nation and the war bereaved families."[18]

In the view of this author, the terms "the sentiment of the nation," "popular sentiment," or "national ethos" should refer to the indigenous or unique religious sentiment that constitutes the popular religion of the Japanese. Originally, the Yasukuni Shrine was established as *Tokyo Shokon Sha*, a Shinto shrine dedicated to the souls of the war dead. "*Shokon*" means that the living invoke and appease the souls of those who died in unusual ways, especially in war or accident, to keep them out of harm's way and receive protection from the latter.[19] Indigenous religious sentiment could be found in such a religious act. The Japanese word "*kami*," deity or deities, refers to deities coexistent in the myths or dwelling in all nature as well as in the soul of a dead person. On the one hand, the Shinto gods are not divine but human. On the other hand, "*hito*," a man (or men), may be transformed into a deity according to merit or virtue although he may fall into a brutal existence because of his vice. A feature intrinsic to Japanese religious sentiment is that "*kami*" and "*hito*" fuse into one concept.[20] In such a religious sentiment, in which a mixture of ideas of Shintoism and Buddhism can be found, interchange between living souls and dead persons is possible. Besides, it must be pointed out that the above-mentioned religious sentiment has had an intrinsic connection with another indigenous religious or ethical idea: the deepest and strongest desire of the Japanese to be pure. To be pure, negatively, means for a man to be purged of impurities. Positively, it means for him to be innocent and noble, rising above self-interest. The dead, then, become "*hotoke*," i.e., benevolent, semi-deities.

Thus, for the Japanese, there is no severance of this life from the other world and no sharp distinction between the sacred and the secular. Their religious sentiment is still polytheistic or syncretic and pantheistic or animistic. It explains the reason why most Japanese are both Shintoists and Buddhists.[21] Japanese popular religion is

---

18. Ibid., 113.
19. Murakami, "Yasukuni Jinja no Rekishi-teki Yakuwari," 62.
20. Yoshio Toda, "Jinja Shinto" (Shrine Shintoism), *Gendai Shukyo Shiso no Essensu* (The Essence of Modern Religious Thoughts) (Tokyo: Perikan-sha, 1969), 35-36.
21. Interestingly, according to statistics of the 1985 *Religion Year Book (Shukyo Nenkan)*, the Agency for Cultural Affairs of Japan (Tokyo: Gyosei, 1986), Shintoists are 112,106,000; Buddhists are 87,470,000; Christians are 1,656,000; others are 14,377,000. The total is about 217 million. The population of Japan is about 120 million.

neither Shrine Shinto itself nor Buddhism itself. The popular religion gave birth to and has developed Shintoism and has given Japanese Buddhism its unique nature.

It is interesting to note that in the process of modernization from the Meiji Restoration to today that indigenous sentiment remained in its intrinsic world of static sensation. The Japanese in general have been regarded as irreligious people because they do not like total affiliation with a particular religious group.[22] However, they are very religious in the depths of their minds; their indigenous religious sentiment keeps them from a rigid personal commitment to a particular deity or religious dogma and sect.[23]

Ironically, whether leftists or pacifists, Buddhists or Christians, journalists or union leaders or scholars, opponents to official worship at the Yasukuni Shrine all at least subconsciously recognize the indigenous religious sentiment. This is why such grandiose words as "the rebirth of State Shinto and militarism" and "a breach of the Constitution," which the opponents hurl against official shrine worship, do not awake a responsive chord in the hearts of the public.[24]

However, it is true that such a religious sentiment was the soil in which military Shinto shrines functioned as the core of the State Shinto regime. Indigenous religious sentiment, the substance of the popular religion, was an essential base for establishment of the dogma and regime of State Shinto in which the emperor was a divine figure who descended in direct and unbroken line from the founding sun-goddess (*Amaterasu Omikami*). The emperor system might have an intrinsic connection with such a Shinto ideology as well as grassroots support in a popular religious sense. This, at the same time, might explain the fact that the majority of the Japanese did not resist the State Shinto regime during and before World War II or criticize recent official worship by Prime Minister Nakasone at the Yasukuni Shrine (central to such shrines all over the nation), which has been

---

22. According to the *World Christian Encyclopedia* (London & New York: Oxford University Press, 1982), the numbers of persons who profess Shinto or Buddhism as their first or major religion and profess Christian faith are as follows: Shintoists 3,520,000; Buddhists 16,450,000; Christians 3,000,000; and new religionists including Sect Shinto and new denominations of Buddhism are 26,330,000. The total is about 42 percent of the population of Japan. However, the numbers of people who profess active affiliation or the number of total affiliated followers seem to be less than the above-mentioned numbers.

23. According to polls of Japan Broadcasting Corporation and Mainichi Shimbun Sha, a prestigious daily press, more than 85 percent of the Japanese have indigenous and basic religious sentiment. The Public-opinion Poll Department of the NHK, ed., *Nihon-jin no Shukyo Ishiki* (Religious Consciousness of the Japanese) (Tokyo: Japan Broadcasting and Publishing Corporation, 1984); *Mainichi Shimbun*, 4 January 1986.

24. Tadao Adachi, "Yasukuni Jinja Mondai to Shimin" (The Question of the Yasukuni Shrine and Citizenry), *Ho to Seiji* (*Journal of Law and Politics*, Kanseigakuin University), 26 (December 1975):193.

sacred to the memory of those killed serving the emperor and the empire.

The Official Worship and the Principle of Separation of Religion and the State

Scarcely referring to the above-mentioned original role and fundamental nature of the Yasukuni Shrine, the Report by the Research Council regards the Shrine as a central institution in which the war dead have been enshrined, mourned, and honored through prewar and postwar days.[25] It points out that official mourning and honoring of the war dead, as an opportunity to pray for peace and appease the bereaved, has also been performed in many countries other than Japan.[26] However, needless to say, such an official ceremony at the Yasukuni Shrine must be related to the principle of separation of religion and the state in the Constitution because the Shrine is a religious institution. To justify constitutionally such an official worship, the governmental act at the Yasukuni Shrine depended heavily on the Supreme Court's interpretation of "religious activity" from which the state and its organs shall refrain as stated in the Constitution, Article 20, Section 3.

In the "Site Purifying Ceremony" case the Supreme Court, for the first and only time (as of this writing), interpreted the articles on separation of religion and the state in the Constitution.[27] The Court first distinguished provisions of the principle of separation of religion and the state as follows:

The Constitution makes the following provisions guaranteeing religious liberty in a narrow sense: "Freedom of religion is guaranteed to all" (Article 20, Section 1); "No person shall be compelled to take part in any religious act, celebration, rite or practice" (Article 20, Section 2), while it makes provisions based on the

---

25. "Report," 111.
26. Ibid.
27. *Kakunaga* v. *Sekiguchi*, 31 Minshu 533 (1977). The ceremony of purifying a building site (*jichin-sai*) for a gymnasium of Tsu City was held in Shinto rites with Shinto priests presiding and under the auspices of the city, under the direction of a member of the city staff, at the building site on 14 January 1965, and 7.663 yen, the expense of the ceremony, was defrayed by public funds by the Mayor of the city, the defendant [*Kakunaga*]. The plaintiff [*Sekiguchi*], a resident of Tsu City, filed an action in Tsu District Court against the Mayor alleging that the official Shinto ceremony dedicated to a municipal gymnasium and the expenditure from public funds for that purpose are against the Constitution, Article 20, Section 3, prohibiting religious activity, and Article 89, prohibiting the payment to any religious institution from public funds. The Tsu District Court held for the defendant on the ground that it realistically is a customary folk function and not a religious activity with the purpose of propagating and propagandizing Shinto religion. *Sekiguchi* v. *Kakunaga*, 18 Gyosaireishu 246 (Tsu District Court, 16 March 1967). Nagoya High Court reversed it. However, the Supreme Court upheld the District Court's decision.

"principle of separation of religion and state" as follows: "No religious organization shall receive any privilege from the State nor exercise any political authority" (Article 20, Section 1); "The State and its organ shall refrain from religious education or any other religious activity" (Article 20, Section 3); "No public money or other property shall be expended or appropriated for the use, benefit or maintenance of any religious institution or association . . ." (Article 89).

The Court then stated the meaning of separation of religion and state and emphasized the impossibility of complete separation:

In the light of various evils in the past resulting from a close connection between the State and Shintoism after the Meiji Restoration, the Constitution, promulgated on 3 November 1946, provides the unconditional guarantee of freedom of religion and stipulates the provision for separation of religion and state to ensure the guarantee all the more. In our country, unlike Christian and Muslim countries, various religions have pluralistically and syncreticly developed and coexisted. In such a religious situation, to give practical effect to the guarantee of freedom of religion not only needs the unconditional guarantee, but also the provision for separation of religion and state in order to eliminate the connection between the State and any religion. From all these considerations, it should be so interpreted that under the Separation Clauses of the Constitution complete separation of religion and the State shall be ideal and secularity or religious neutrality of the State ensured.

However . . . the State cannot avoid involvement with religion in the actual enforcement of regulations respecting social life and policies of assistance or aid for education, welfare, culture, and so forth. Therefore, it is hardly possible that complete separation of religion and state is realized in implementing the principle of the separation as a system of government in practice. The principle of separation of religion and state is to be given concrete expression in a system of government in consideration of the case and degree in which governmental involvement with religion cannot be permitted in relation to fundamental purpose, such as guarantee of freedom of religion, in the light of social and cultural conditions in individual nations and on the assumption that such involvement is unavoidable to some extent. From such point of view, the principle of separation of religion and state, on the basis of which the Separation Clauses in the Constitution as mentioned above are established and which should be a guiding principle in interpreting them, demands of the State religious neutrality, while it should not be interpreted as absolutely prohibiting governmental involvement with religion, but as prohibiting that involvement only when it cannot be deemed proper in the light of such conditions, considering the purpose and effect of the action that is to give birth to the involvement.

And the Court set forth tests by which to recognize "religious activity" impermissible to government.

The Constitution, Article 20, Section 3, provides that "the State and its organs shall refrain from religious education or any other religious activity." The said "religious activity," in the light of the aforesaid significance of the principle of separation of religion and state, should not mean all actions of "the State and its organ" that have involvement with religion, but only involvement that has gone beyond the proper limits: action the purpose of which is religious and that the effect of which is the assistance, promotion, and advancement of or the oppression of or the interference in religion. Such "religious activity" should be the typical propagation, preaching, and propaganda of religion, such as "religious education" exemplified in Article 20, Section 3 and should include religious ceremony, rite, and practice the purpose and effect of which are stated above. A judgment, whether or not an act comes under "religious activity," should be objectively made according to the generally accepted social idea and after consideration of all circumstances concerning the concerned act: the place where the act is performed, the general public's judgment whether or not it is religious, intent or purpose of and existence or degree of religious consciousness of the performers, and the effect or influence on the general public.

According to such interpretation, the Report concluded that there may be religious activities from which the state and its organs are not prohibited by the Constitution, Article 20, Section 3. The majority of the Research Council relied greatly upon the Supreme Court's "narrow" interpretation of "religious activity" and its tests of "purpose" and "effect" in judgment whether or not a state action constitutes "religious activity."[28] The minority of the Council opposed the official worship on the basis of "broad" interpretation of "religious activity" as declared in the High Court's decision:"[29] Under the principle of complete separation of religion and state in the Constitution, 'religious activity' in Article 20, Section 3 should be interpreted not only as overt activities to propagate, preach, and propagandize a particular religion, but also as all activities, the expression of religious faith including religious acts, celebrations, rites, functions, and so on."

Interestingly, the Supreme Court concluded, "It is not admitted that the site purifying ceremony greatly promotes the interest in religion of attendants and the general public, nor is an effect in its performance of assistance, promotion or advancement of Shintoism," which is based upon the following: (1) "many people have syncretic religious sentiment and not always much real interest in religion"; and (2) "Shrine Shinto devoted itself to rites or observance and is hardly engaged in external activities, propagating, or preaching of religion."[30] The Supreme Court regarded the religious sentiment of the general public and the specific character of Shrine Shinto as factors lessening the effect, advancement of religion.

Chief Justice Ekizo Fujibayashi, in his dissenting opinion, very properly pointed out that the syncretic religious sentiment and simplicity of Shrine Shinto made it easy for the people to accept State Shinto and enforcement of worship at Shinto shrines.[31] Cleverly, the Research Council relied upon such two factors as lessening the effect of advancement of religious activities to urge the official worship

---

28. "Report," 111-112.
29. *Sekiguchi* v. *Kakunaga*, 22 Gyosairei-shu 680 (Nagoya High Court Judgment, 14 May 1971).
30. *Kakunaga* v. *Sekiguchi*, 31 Minshu 533 (1977).
31. Ibid.

upon the government. The indigenous religious sentiment of the Japanese is intrinsically "syncretic" and substantially constitutes "popular sentiment" which, as stated in the Report, demands the official worship and regards the Yasukuni Shrine as a central institution for mourning of the war dead.[32] Also, the "popular sentiment" constitutes a substantive part of a "generally accepted social idea" on which the Supreme Court relied greatly and which the Research Council used effectively to support the conclusion that the prime minister and cabinet members, without causing any public controversy, may "attend funerals or memorial services in the form of any particular religion for persons of distinguished services to the country . . . as well as mourning services for the war dead."[33]

The minority of the Research Council asserted that the official worship at the Yasukuni Shrine must be distinguished from the "site purifying ceremony" which the Supreme Court held constitutional.[34] It is unfortunate that the Liberal Democratic party, the Research Council, and the Nakasone administration relied on this Supreme Court's decision, since the purpose of the provisions of separation of religion and the state is to prohibit the government from making religion a means to political ends, which should be the guiding principle in the Court's interpretation.

THE OFFICIAL WORSHIP AS A "FINAL CLOSING OF THE ACCOUNT OF POSTWAR POLITICS"

Questions of state patronage of and official worship at the Yasukuni Shrine have provoked or revived an unending controversy among various groups and have caused serious political and social dispute and divisiveness.

The Liberal Democratic Party introduced the Yasukuni Shrine State Patronage Bill five times in five years beginning in 1969. The bill passed the House of Representatives for the first time in 1974, only to be killed in the House of Councilors by expiration of the session of the Diet. The bill has not been introduced since then for the following reasons: (1) in the House of Councilors' election, just after the bill died, the Liberal Democratic Party won by a very slim majority; (2) the bill presupposed that the Yasukuni Shrine had changed from a religious corporation to a sort of public service corporation (Article 2) and was not permitted to perform traditional

---

32. "Report," 111-113.
33. Ibid., 111-112.
34. Ibid., 112.

religious rites intrinsic to Shinto religion (Article 5);[35] (3) both the Yasukuni Shrine and Central Office of Shinto Shrines (*Jinja Honcho*) opposed the bill and divisive disputes occurred not only among citizenry but also among members of the Liberal Democratic Party;[36] and (4) the religious world, especially Christian churches and new Buddhist religious organizations, also conducted an energetic campaign against the bill.

Following all this, a drive took place for official worship at the Yasukuni Shrine. Meanwhile, from 1952 to 1984, prime ministers visited the Yasukuni Shrine privately, without official declaration of the nature of the act. However, their unofficial visits on the memorial day of the war dead, aroused a great deal of controversy. After receiving a report from the Research Council on 9 August 1985, the chief cabinet secretary stated on 14 August that "the Prime Minister will worship in the capacity of the Prime Minister at the Yasukuni Shrine on 15 August." On that day, the official worship was performed in an informal way so that it would not be condemned as a religious activity prohibited by the Constitution, but in order to make it "official," public funds were expended for a floral offering.[37]

Such governmental performance was on the basis of the Report of the Research Council, a "private advisory organ" (*shiteki shimon kikan*), which urged the official worship and furnished advice about its implementation. The Council played a decisive role in this venture of Prime Minister Nakasone. The full use of "private advisory organs" constitutes a central feature of his political technique for handling controversial or long-pending questions.[38] However, it is natural that the use of such an organ for implementing the official worship invited

---

35. Yasukuni Jinja Hoan (The Yasukuni Shrine State Patronage Bill), *Jurisuto* 848 (November 1985):150.
36. Kenji Saito, "Sengo no Yasukuni Jinja Mondai no Suii" (The Postwar Progress of the Question of the Yasukuni Shrine), *Jurisuto* 848 (November 1985):86.
37. *Asahi Shimbun*, 15 August 1985.
38. Such organs established by Prime Minister Nakasone number as many as 22: matters of privatization of public corporations or enterprises, advancement of public undertakings by private capital, avoidance of wasting subsidy, or matters of culture and education, Japan's trade disputes with the United States, Japanese-American and Japanese-Chinese relations, exceeding the ceiling on national defense cost (1 percent of gross national income at present) official worship at the Yasukuni Shrine, and so forth. In general, the will of Prime Minister Nakasone can be reflected strongly in the establishment of "private advisory organs" and their selection of members, contents of reports or their conclusions, and time of reporting. Yutaka Tsujinaka, "Shiteki Shimon Kikan no Yakuwari to Yasukunikon" (The Role of Private Advisory Organs and the Research Council for Question of Official Worship at the Yasukuni Shrine by the Cabinet Members), *Jurisuto* 848 (November 1985):68-70. The advisory organs he has used are composed of intellectuals regarded as representatives of various publics. For instance, the Research Council includes a well-known commentator on political affairs, a very famous female novelist, a popular philosopher, and scholars of law, religion, history, and so on. In an attempt to portray the Council as "impartial," Prime Minister Nakasone

strong criticism. Whereas a "formal" advisory organ is established on the basis of laws or cabinet orders, a "private" advisory organ is not based on such, but on the decision or consent of the cabinet, or ministerial ordinance, or the decision of the director of a bureau, but it does not have a legal basis. Therefore, it is only a place for the discussion of problems. The government has explained that "a private advisory organ shall not express its own opinion."[39] Nevertheless, Prime Minister Nakasone in effect used advice of a mere "private advisory organ" as an official decision of a governmental organ.

It seems that Prime Minister Nakasone tried to put an end to the long pending controversy by relying mainly upon the Report by the Research Council as a last resort, although it was clearly expected that the official worship would give rise to violent domestic political and social reaction and Asian countries, especially the People's Republic of China, would take a strong, negative attitude toward it. The following facts or context may constitute reasons why Prime Minister Nakasone risked his political life and crossed this Rubicon.

Military merit. According to a literal interpretation of the constitution, Article 9, the state cannot be permitted to have an army. There has been much national divisiveness and controversy over the meaning of the article in regard to rearmament. The Constitution stipulates that "land, sea, and air forces, as well as other war potential, will never be maintained" (Article 9, Section 2). An army should exist for a state and be authorized by patriotism. Soldiers should serve their country and their fellow men. However, it is not too much to say that the Japanese army does not have the constitutional basis for existence because of the extremely idealistic pacifism of the Constitution.

In the "Imperial Instructions for Soldiers and Sailors" (*Rikukai Gunjin nikudashitamaeru Chokuyu,* 1882), the Emperor Meiji said that "the army has been under the command of the emperors" and "I assume supreme military power." The Meiji Constitution gave the Emperor the power to command the armed forces (Article 11). The "Imperial Instructions" emphasized that the basic duty of soldiers is to protect and serve their country. In the past, the Yasukuni Shrine

---

appointed some people who appeared to be dissenters. However, it seems that the majority of the members have been selected according to the Prime Minister's will. Yoshio Hijikata, *Yasukuni Jinja* (Yasukuni Shrine) (Tokyo: Shakaihyoron-sha, 1985), 146-149. His political strategy as such served to dodge or soften opposition of nongovernment parties, interference by other factions, and national reaction and divisiveness.
39. Tsujinaka, "Shiteki Shimon Kikan no Yakuwari," 67.

played a great role as a national institution which encouraged soldiers to throw themselves into the jaws of death. It was most honorable for a soldier to give his life for his country and the emperor and then be enshrined as a deity in the Yasukuni Shrine. The government and the Liberal Democratic Party may intend to make the Yasukuni Shrine fulfill such traditional functions as[40] establishing the object of loyalty of the army, raising soldiers' morale, and creating patriotism among the people. For these reasons, it would be natural for the Liberal Democratic Party to plan an amendment to the provisions of the Constitution as follows: (1) the emperor shall be not only "the symbol of the State and of the unity of the people" (Article 1), but also the head of the state; (2) recognition should be made of maintenance of war potential in Article 9; and (3) revision should be made of Article 20 and 89 to make the state patronage of the Yasukuni Shrine permissible.[41]

Reactive nationalism. The Report by the Research Council on official worship at the Yasukuni Shrine emphasized that strict separation of religion and the state was enforced and governmental support, preservation, supervision, and propagation of State Shinto and Shrine Shinto were prohibited on the basis of the "Order of Shinto" (*Shinto Shirei*) issued by the general Headquarters of the Allied Powers on 15 December 1945.[42] From that viewpoint, the principle of separation of religion and the state and the guarantee of religious liberty in the Constitution, Articles 20 and 89, are an extension of the "Order of Shintoism" as a part of the occupation policy; strict separation of religion and the state in Japan was forced by the occupation authorities. Therefore, according to the Report, it is natural that a movement for nationalizing or state patronage of the Yasukuni Shrine would start after the state of occupation by the Allied Powers was terminated and the "Order of Shinto" nullified with the effectuation of the "Japanese Peace Treaty" of 28 April 1952.[43] After all, the whole tone of the Report is that there is no constitutional requirement which makes impermissible government respect for the traditional role of the Yasukuni Shrine based on the spiritual needs of the majority of the people.

Prime Minsiter Nakasone held up a political objective: "a final closing of the account of postwar politics" (*sengo seiji no sokessan*). He emphasized that any argument over or reconsideration of the

---

40. Hijikata, *Yasukuni Jinja*, 44-45.
41. Shigeyoshi Murakami, *Shukyo no Showashi* (The Religious History in Showa Era) (Tokyo: Mitsumine-shobo, 1985), 161.
42. "Report," 110.
43. Ibid.

existing fundamental systems and institutions should not be tabooed in a democratic society.[44] His view appears to imply that Japan should be free from being spellbound, particularly by the "MacArthur Constitution" established under the Occupation. This might mean a declaration for returning to the past and a recovery of Japanese uniqueness in the political dimension which can be found to be established on the basis of the following:[45]

1. Prime ministers and the emperor have worshipped at the Yasukuni Shrine since 1952, the year of Japan's independence.

2. The government has continued to enshrine the war dead in the Yasukuni Shrine, giving rise to the demand of the national administration for official patronage of the Yasukuni Shrine.

3. In 1966, the Diet passed the Bill of Amendment of the National Holidays Act (*Shukujitsu Ho Kaiseian*) which established National Foundation Day (*Kenkoku Kinenbi*) on 11 February. This day corresponds to the anniversary of Emperor Jimmu's accession as based on legendary stories of old Japan (*Kojiki*) and Chronicles of Japan (*Nihonshoki*) compiled in the early eighth century A.D. for the purpose of justifying the authority of the emperor and making it absolute. The story of Emperor Jimmu's accession was used for the same purpose by the Meiji government. Since 1978, the government has sponsored the ceremony celebrating National Foundation Day[46]; Prime Minister Nakasone attended that ceremony in 1985 for the first time.[47]

4. On the memorial day of 15 August in 1975, 1978, and 1980 and annually thereafter, prime ministers have visited at the Yasukuni Shrine.

5. In 1977, the government recognized "*Kimigayo*," which refers to the Imperial reign, as the national anthem of Japan in the officially approved course of study for public elementary schools: the purpose of this was to plant patriotism in children's minds.[48]

6. In 1977, the Supreme Court held that the Shrine Shinto ceremony of purifying a public building site is constitutional.

7. In 1978, the fourteen A-class "war criminals" of World War II were enshrined in the Yasukuni Shrine in profound secrecy.

---

44. Saito, "Sengo no Yasukuni Jinja Mondai," 89.
45. Yasukuni Jinja Mondai Kankei Nempyo (Chronological Table of Question of the Yasukuni Shrine), *Jurisuto* 848 (November 1985):169-186.
46. Prime Minister's Office from 1978 on; Ministry of Education from 1981 on; Ministry of Home Affairs from 1983 on. Ibid., 180-183.
47. Many political and economic leaders and a union leader participated in the ceremony with the Prime Minister. Hijikata, *Yasukuni Jinja*, 163-164.
48. Masato Miyachi, *Tenno Sei no Seijishi-teki Kenkyu* (A Study of the *Tenno* System: from the Viewpoint of Political History) (Tokyo: Azekura-shobo, 1981), 213.

8. In 1979, the Diet passed the bill on "Using the Japanese Era" (*Gengo Hoan*), which actually forces the people to use the Japanese system of accounting years by era which represented each emperor's reign.

9. In 1982, the People's Republic of China and the Republic of Korea condemned textbook wording changes of the word "*shinryaku*" (aggression) to the word "*shinshutsu*" (entry into) in description of military occupation in these countries.

10. In 1982, the cabinet established the Day for Mourning and Honoring the War Dead and Offering a Prayer for Peace (*Sembotsusha wo Tsuito shi Heiwa wo Kinen suru Hi*) on 15 August, which may also represent the day for honoring the fallen "heroes."

11. In 1984, the Liberal Democratic party held the opinion that the official worship at the Yasukuni Shrine by the prime minister and cabinet members is constitutional based on the Supreme Court decision of 1977.

12. On 15 August 1985, the first official worship at the Yasukuni Shrine was performed.

13. By 5 September 1985, the Ministry of Education had issued an order to the superintendent of education in the metropolis and districts that the national flag (*Hinomaru*) should be raised and the national anthem (*Kimigayo*) be sung in every public elementary and high school.[49]

National Identity. Some explanation is needed for understanding the historical and political context of the official worship cited above. Prime Minister Nakasone persisted in his view of the necessity of establishing the national identity and emphasized the "uniqueness of Japanese thought."[50] In the postwar era, the Japanese people generally have maintained that rebirth of the nation should demand denial of the past and traditional values. The first experience of suffering defeat in World War II resulted in great psychological shock, depriving them of ethnic self-confidence. However, the people began to regain a sense of their self-esteem in the 1960s, which was a period of rapid economic growth.[51] Moreover, they began to recover their self-confidence in the 1970s when Japan became one of the economic powers of the world, overcoming the oil shock crisis, economic recession, and the Japan-U.S. trade conflict. In the latter half of

---

49. *Mainichi Shimbun*, 6 September 1985. The government actions and programs will be tried and arranged to instill nationalist feeling of the people, although Prime Minister Nakasone abstained from visiting the Yasukuni Shrine in 1986 and 1987.
50. Masumi Ishikawa, *Nihon Seiji no Toshi-zu* (A Perspective View of Politics in Japan) (Tokyo: Gendainoriso-sha, 1985), 19.
51. *Nihon-jin no Shukyo Ishiki*, 109.

the 1970s, foreign writers began to affirm and set a high value on Japanese uniqueness, from business management to religious sentiment. The Japanese have gradually been able to reaffirm their way of life and thinking as well as traditional culture.[52]

However, in spite of and simultaneous with their attaining economic affluence and material prosperity, a high degree of competitiveness, urbanization, pollution, a decreasing rate of economic growth, and so on have made the people lose sight of their sense of true values in human life, resulting in a spiritual imbalance and a sense of collapse, potential crisis, unease, dissatisfaction, and so on.[53] As a matter of course, various social and moral problems burst forth. At the same time that the Japanese began to recover ethnic self-confidence, they began to be aware of having lost their spiritual identity.

The conservative leaders of the political and economic worlds have posed doubts regarding values of democratic education and human rights which, they think, partly have been responsible for these serious social problems. In other words, they think that the Japanese must keep their traditional sense of values and discipline in their social life, their family relationships, and the relationship of capital and labor, so that Japan may survive in an increasingly competitive international economic race, maintain the present political and economic regime, and defend the country against any external menace. The most useful, ideological tool with which to cope with such problems is "*Tennosim.*" Conservative leaders, as either victims or beneficiaries of the imperial education (*kokoku kyoiku*) according to State Shinto ideology,[54] have no other spiritual home. This may best explain the fact that, in historical background and political context, *Tenno*, still holds supreme religio-political authority and remains the foundation of the official worship at the Yasukuni Shrine.

---

52. Ibid., 111.
53. See, ibid., 112-114.
54. The Imperial Rescript on Education (*Kyoiku Chokugo*) (1890), as a declaration of national morality, was granted public schools in the name of Emperor Meiji. It regarded the Imperial Ancestors as an exclusive source of national morality or ethos on assumption of an unbroken line of emperors to be the offspring of gods. It is the organic mixture of a theocratic idea formed in ancient times and feudalistic morality: filial devotion to parents or family's obedience to paternity; subjects' loyalty to the feudal lord or sovereignty. Moreover, the traditional sense of ancestor worship was connected with emperor worship. Thus, the Rescript's central intention was a possession of people's minds by the state: to implant in them the idea of "family nation" where the emperor is parent and people are his children or babies, the sense of absolute authority of the emperor, and the spirit of self-annihilation for the sake of the country, the empire or the emperor. Murakami, *Kokka Shinto*, 135-138.

Conclusion

After the Liberal Democratic Party abandoned a sixth presentation of the Yasukuni Shrine State Patronage Bill to the Diet in 1975, the Party and the Japan Association for the Bereaved Families of the War Dead started a national movement for the official worship. For that purpose, in 1976, the Association for Memory and Glorification of the Souls of the Fallen Heroes (*Eirei ni Kotaeru Kai*) was established. It initiated a signature-collecting campaign and demanded that local assemblies petition the government to acknowledge the official worship at the Yasukuni Shrine.[55] Besides the movement's contribution to implementation of the official worship in 1985, it led to the passing of the Law on "Using the Japanese Era" (*Gengo Ho*) in the Diet in 1979, and to the decision by the cabinet in 1982 to make every 15 August the day for mourning and honoring the war dead (*Sembotsusha Tsuito no Hi*).[56]

In the first paragraph of its prospectus, the Association stated its purpose as follows: "Peace and prosperity of our country have been established on the honorable foundation of the souls of the two million five hundred thousand departed war heroes."[57] As mentioned in that prospectus, it may be proper that "the state and the people should heartily show their respect and gratitude for the devotion and self-sacrifice of many fellow countrymen who rose to meet the national crisis and gave their lives for their country."[58] But, were the war dead truly heroes? In general, the majority of soldiers, especially nonprofessional, might have died holding a grudge against the state which sent them into battle and forced them to murder and destroy cities and the peace of foreign countries. Might not they never have been heroes but victims who were forced to participate in national crimes and to die? Moreover, it seems that the war-bereaved families may entertain the following doubt: Did the war in which their flesh and blood participated and died need to be? Did they need to die? The bereaved families do not want to recognize that their fathers, or husbands, or sons, or brothers were mere victims and that their deaths were useless. This may be the true reason why they demand of the government public mourning

---

55. Eirei ni Kotaeru Kai no Yoseisho (The Memorial for Official Worship of the Association), *Jurisuto* 848 (November 1985):132. By 1984, the Association collected the signatures of more than ten million, and thirty-seven prefectural assemblies and 1,548 assemblies of cities, towns, and villages officially demanded the official worship. Hijikata, *Yasukuni Jinja*, 28. Saito, "Sengo no Yasukuni Mondai," 88.
56. Ibid.
57. Eirei ni Kotaeru Kai no Kesseishuisho (The Prospectus of the Association), *Jurisuto* 848 (November 1985):130.
58. Ibid.

and honoring of their blood relatives, the war dead.[59] For this reason, the government must apologize every 15 August to the bereaved families in Japan, and to people in other countries, for death caused by war. However, in the view of this author, the government has taken advantage of the sentiment of the war-bereaved families and the indigenous sentiment of the general public and has used the Yasukuni Shrine, which was a spiritual propellant of war and a symbolic institution of the State Shinto regime, to advance its nationalistic policy.

This process resulting in the official worship is a dangerous sign; a turning back to *Tennoism* can be found in the political use of popular religion and the *Tenno* system. This might be a return to an early and indigenous ethos, in itself giving rise again to a narrow nationalism.

---

59. Adachi, "Yasukuni Jinja Mondai," 45-46 analyzes such a psychical problem of the war bereaved families.

The Ideal Social Order in the Arab World, 1800 - 1968

ISMA'IL R. AL FARUQI

When Napoleon's army marched on Egypt, on the eve of the nineteenth century, the Mamluk ruler and commander of the Egyptian defense forces picked from his loyal troops the most courageous soldier and ordered him to march forward to the enemy lines and challenge Napoleon, the enemy commander, to a duel. With sword drawn, fanfare blowing, and drums beating, the Egyptian hero mounted his decorated horse and advanced. As soon as the French forces knew what he was about, they answered with one rifle shot, and the Egyptian hero fell bleeding from a mortal wound. This is a real story, and it expresses clearly the gap that existed between Western society and Arab society at the close of the eighteenth century. For Egypt and the Arabs, the time was still the Middle Ages. For the West, it was modern times.

Napoleon's expedition to Egypt served as an alarm bell to awaken Arab society to modern times. Though at first the French were regarded as infidels and their military equipment as the devil's artifact, as soon as their success was ascertained, they became in Muslim eyes worthy of emulation and their science worthy of learning.[1] Envisaging, not a military confrontation with Egypt, but a grand alliance with the whole East against Britain, Napoleon had brought with him the first Arabic press, whole libraries, science-laboratories, and the cream of French intellectuals to help him in the task of awakening and rejuvenating the new allies he was seeking. Some Arab enthusiasts rejected outright both Napoleon and all that he brought. These suffered the destruction of their claims regarding the witchcraft of modern science as it succeeded demonstrably in their very midst. The others—and they were the majority as well as the religious leadership—quickly learned to desire

---

1. The Witness is that of a native Egyptian contemporary historian, al Jabarti. See his *'Aja'ib al Athar fi al Tarajim wa al Akhbar* (3 vols.; Cairo: Bulaq, 1910).

science and modernity in good Islamic conscience. Al Jabarti, the on-the-spot historian of the period, described the visit which Shaykh Hasan al 'Attar, Rector of al Azhar, and his staff of 'Ulama' paid to the French factories, workshops, and laboratories at the invitation of Napoleon and reported the Rector as saying, in conclusion, of the visit: "Our country must needs change; many branches of knowledge must be renovated." Only five years later, the same Rector wrote:

> Many of the books of the French have been translated in our time, in which we read many of their works and came to know of their accomplishments in engineering and natural science. These books tell of the military industries and the instruments of fire. They elaborate their principles and laws and systematize them into an autonomous science with many branches. Whoever is anxious enough to read these strange compositions will learn many precise and scientific truths.[2]

The Napoleonic Expedition to Egypt not only awakened the Arabs as far as military strategy and science and the natural sciences are concerned, it also rang an alarm bell in other fields, notably, the social order. Unlike the field of natural science, however, the French did not here furnish any new ideas; and if they had, their ideas could not have been grafted into the Islamic system. The role the Expedition played was to shake the Arabs into turning their gaze at their social order, to diagnose its ills, and to prescribe and begin the implementation of the cure.

Fortunately, a conflict made-to-order, with all the necessary details presented itself to Arab society at the turn of the nineteenth century. This conflict was utterly unrelated to the outside world, whether Muslim or non-Muslim. It was born within and enacted on a purely Arab theatre, a stage untouched by an alien influence. That is Najd or the desert of Central Arabia. The movement, known by its founder's name, was al Wahhabiyyah.[3] This movement both furnished Arab society with the diagnosis and prescribed the cure. The century and a half which has elapsed since is its continuous unfolding.

The society which Muhammad ibn 'Abd al Wahhab[4] lived in and looked into in the second half of the eighteenth century was a sick society. The disease was *Tasawwuf*, otherwise known as Sufism or

---

2. Ibid., III, 35-37. See also the bibliography of the Rector of al Azhar at the time by 'Ali Mubarak, entitled, *Al Khitat al Tawfiqiyyah fi Tarjumat al Shaykh Hasan al'Attar* (Cairo: Burlaq, 1924), IV, 38.

3. Unfortunately, there is as yet no English work devoted to the Wahhabiyyah movement. Only the travel works of H. St. John Philby and Bertram Thomas are available, and these deal only cursorily with the subject. Still more cursory than these is the brief mention that the movement gets in English books dealing with the modern history of Islam and the Near East.

4. Born at 'Uyaynah in Najd in 1115 AH/1703 AC, the son of a jurist and judge. In 1158 AH he launched his movement from his adopted base of al Dar'iyyah, and died after seeing it successfully spread throughout central and East Arabia in 1206 AH/1791 AC. Besides a great number of letters and *fatawa* (judgments establishing jurisprudential precedents) he wrote three main books: *Al Tawhid, Kashf al Shubuhat* and *Al Kaba'ir wa al Masa'il.*

Islamic mysticism. That *Tasawwuf* had succeeded in keeping personal faith and piety at such a high level of intensity that it had converted countless millions of people in South Asia, Southeast Asia, Central Asia, and Black Africa—educating, Islamizing, Arabizing, and integrating them into the *Ummah* (or the organized world-community of Islam) over the centuries—is certain. Equally certain is the sublime beauty of the countless volumes of poetry *Tasawwuf* has produced. But it is no less certain that it presented the following deadly symptoms:

1. *Kashf*, "gnostic illumination," was substituted for knowledge. Under *Tasawwuf*, the Arab World abandoned its commitment to and pursuit of rational, scientific knowledge for the vision of mystical experience. It forsook the critical weighing and verification of alternatives for the esoteric, oracular, and authoritarian pronouncements of the Sufi *shaykh* or leader.

2. *Karamat*, "little miracles," "granted by God to the Sufi as favor," destroyed the Arab's respect for natural causation and taught him to seek results by the methods of spiritualistic conduction. In his mind, the natural relation of cause to effect, of means to objective, was a shamble.

3. *Tawakul*, the total reliance upon the spiritual factor to produce the empirical results, replaced *tawakkul* or conviction of the certain efficacy of God's inexorable laws in nature and, hence, of the absolute necessity of human intervention into the causal nexus of nature, if the projected ends are to be realized.

4. *Qismat*, the passive acquiescence to what happens as being the action of arbitrary supernatural forces, replaced *taklif*, or man's obligation to reknead, recut, and remould space-time so as to realize therein the divine pattern. Rather than *amanah*, or man's assumption of this divine purpose for space-time as his own personal *raison d'etre*, *Tasawwuf* taught a shortcut through *dhikr* or repeated prayers and cultivated the hope for manipulation of the arbitrary supernatural force through *Karamat*.

5. *'Adam*, the unreality, ephemerality, and non-importance of the world, replaced *wujud*, the seriousness of man's existence, his *khilafah* or "vice-gerency" of God on earth—in short, his cosmic status as the sole bridge through which God's will as moral value can be realized in space and time. Sufism taught that life on earth is but a brief journey to the beyond. Against the Islamic principle that the final realization of the absolute in space-time is not only a distinct possibility, but the supreme human duty, *Tasawwuf* taught that the world is no such a theatre after all, that such realization belongs to the beyond. Following al Ghazzali, it denigrated the world beyond reason or common sense.

6. *Ta'abbud*, the deliberate giving up of social, political, and economic activity for the sake of total (i.e., all day and all night) wor-

ship and the commitment of all energies to *dhikr* or pious devotion, were substituted for *'ibadah*, which demanded (a) performance of the institutionalized five pillars of Islam and (b) fulfillment, in every field of endeavor, of man's *khilafah* or "vice-gerency" and of *amanah*, "the divine trust."

7. *To'ah*, absolute, i.e., unquestionable, unreasoned, and totalistic obedience to the *shaykh* of one's Sufi fraternity replaced *tawhid*, or unization of God, i.e., the recognition of no lord as Lord but He. Cultivation of the mystical union and the *hal* or mystical trance came to replace the *shari'ah* or fulfilment of the daily duties and lifelong obligations. This, together with *Tasawwuf*'s pantheistic metaphysics, blurred all of Islam's ethical notions.

These symptoms ruined the health of Arab society during half a millennium, from the fall of Baghdad to the Tatars in 1257 to the rise of the Wahhabiyyah movement in 1747.[5] Under the Sufi spell, the Arab became a-political, a-social, a-military, a-ethical, and hence, non-productive, unconcerned for the *Ummah* (i.e., for the world brotherhood under the moral law), an individualist, and in the last resort an egotist whose prime objective is for himself to be saved, i.e., to be absorbed into the consuming majesty of divine being. He was shaken neither by the misery, poverty, disease, and subjection of his own society as a whole, nor by the cause of mankind in history. The ideal manhood *Tasawwuf* had provided for his imagination was that of the *dervish*, clad in his rags of blue wool, either sitting as absolute passivity at the foot of his *shaykh* or whirling in the mystic trance where total nonentity, or *fana'*, is achieved.

The Wahhabiyyah movement hurled its heaviest weapons upon the whole system and did so furiously. It conceived its action as a reassertion of pristine Islam. It overleaped the medieval synthesis and reached the fountainhead, the Qur'an, Muhammad's commonwealth of Madinah, and the social order of the Rashidun Califs the first thirty years after the Prophet. These have always been normative; but their normativeness had suffered eclipse at the hands of Sufism which reinterpreted them all, by means of allegorical, eisegetical acrobatics *(bi-al-batin)* so as to confirm its own insights. With the epistemological ground exploded and discarded, the Arab could, after the Wahhabiyyah movement, look objectively and critically upon his own early history. Al Wahhabiyyah took the Arabian Peninsula by storm and began its conquest of the Fertile Crescent in Iraq. An unfortunate system of circumstances (Wahhabi extremism in the purge of Sufi practices, Ot-

---

5. Al Mukhtar, Salahuddin, *Tarikh al Mamlakah al 'Arabiyyah al Su'udiyyah fi Madiha wa Hadiriha* (2 vols.; Beirut: Dar Maktabat al Hayah, 1957), I, 35 ff.

toman involvement with Russia in the Balkans, Muhammad 'Ali's personal ambition to found a separate kingdom in Egypt, the Western powers' connivance at Egyptian separation from the Ottoman Empire, etc.) caused the reorganized, refurbished, and modern-equipped armies of Egypt to stand in the face of the Wahhabi desert fighters. The pair was unmatched and the Wahhabis were defeated. The Egyptians, on the other hand, became immediately entangled in world power contests (then in Suez Canal politics) and eventually lost their political independence to Britain.

Three daughter-movements, all seeking to achieve the same objectives as the Wahhabiyyah movement, emerged in the process in different parts of the Arab World. In every case the diagnosis was the same. The means varied but only slightly. The *Sanusiyyah* movement, founded by Muhammad Ali al Sanusi in 1837 AC, spread in North Africa absorbing the earlier movement of *Tijaniyyah* and built an empire which, in the third quarter of the nineteenth century, spread over the whole of Muslim Africa except the Nile Valley and counted hundreds of *zawaya* or regional headquarters, some 30,000 troops, and over 3 million members. Not before putting up the toughest resistance, the movement was knocked out in 1914 by the completion of Western conquest of Africa. The French and Italians were bloodied enormously in the struggle, and the Sanusis still rule in Libya.[6] Secondly, *al Mahdiyyah* movement, founded by al Sayyid al Mahdi in 1881, sought after the same ideals and objectives but restricted its operation to the Sudan and East Africa.[7] Thirdly, a revivalist movement in Yaman was founded by Imam Muhammad ibn Ali al Shawkani, following the earlier reforms of his teacher, ibn al Murtada.[8] The movement entertained the same ideals and sought to realize them by the same means, allowing for slight variation consonant with local situations. Later on, Jamal al Din al Afghani, Muhammad Abduh and Rashid Rida,[9] the towering figures of Arab modernism in the last one hundred years,

---

6. Octave Depont and X. Cappolani, *Les Confréries religieuses Musulmames* (Algiers, 1897). H. Duveyrie, *La Confrérie Musulmane de Sidi Mohammad ben 'Ali es. Senous* (Paris: Societé de Géogrphie, 1886). E. E. Evans-Pritchard, *The Senusi of Cyrenaica* (Oxford: Clarendon Press, 1949). N. A. Ziadeh, *Sanusiyyah: A Study of a Revivalist Movement in Islam* (Leiden: E. J. Brill, 1958)
7. A. B. Theobald, *The Mahdiya: A History of The Anglo-Egyptian Sudan, 1881-1899* (New York, 1951). J. S. Trimingham, *Islam in the Sudan* (London 1949). *'Abbas, Makki, The Sudan Questions, 1884-1951* (London, 1952) A. J. Arkell, *History of the Sudan* (London: Athlone Press, 1954). Ministry of Foreign Affairs, *Egypt-Sudan: Collection of Documents* (Cairo: Government Press, 1947). Mahmud Brelvi, *Islam in Africa* (Lahore: Institute of Islamic Culture, 1964).
8. Fadlur Rahman, *Islam* (New York: Holt, Rinehart and Winston, 1966), 196 ff.
9. Besides the works of the three reformers, consult C. C. Adams, *Islam and Modernism in Egypt* (London: Oxford University Press, 1933), Henri Laoust, *Le Califat dans la doctrine de Rashid Rida* (Berkeley: University of California Press). Kedouri, Elie.

again built their thinking entirely upon the theological and social thought of Muhammad ibn Abd al Wahhab, if not deliberately, then by perfect coincidence of their individual Islamic consciousness. The content of Arab social thought during the last two centuries has remained *essentially* the same. Political and military events have always helped the Arabs to sharpen and clarify, to make precise and to validate critically, but not to change radically their thought. What are the categories of Arab social thought, which are so universally shared by all major Arab thinkers and leaders in modern times?

Categories of modern Arab social thought have been amply argued by most thinkers of the nineteenth and twentieth centuries, as they have been by Muhammad ibn Abd al Wahhab as well as by Taqiyyuddin Ahmad ibn Taymiyah (died 728 AH/1350 AC) who witnessed the Tatar invasion of Syria and who anticipated not only every item in the later diagnosis of Arab thinkers, but even every cure they were to prescribe down to the present day.[10] Before we list these categories, let us ask the question, why is all this singleness of purpose and uniformity of thought-content through the centuries? The answer is simple: Because of Islam. Islam, al Qur'an, its scripture, and al Sunnah, the exemplification of the ideal by the Prophet, have determined and still determine Arab consciousness. It is this Islam, concrete, specific, and founded on an uncorrupted, complete and untranslated historic book, that constitutes the base, the presupposition, and the ultimate *prius* determining Arab thought. Let us now return to the categories.

1. The Ideal is to be understood in the Qur'an which is the prime source of truth and value. But its claim, though authoritative is not authoritarian. It must be validated and understood by, set at peace with, the critical reason. *A fortiori*, no Muslim's word is valid until evidence has fully justified it. Away, therefore, thought the modernist, with all the legacy of tradition until it has established its points anew and critically! The speculations, Israelitisms, Christianisms, Persianisms, historical materials of the fathers — all the legacy of the past must be purged clean. Only *al Sunnah al Sahihah*, or the verified *Sunnah*, those traditions of the Prophet, of his immediate companions and of their children, which pass the critical tests of a most fastidious consciousness and can truly be said to explicate and instantiate the abstract ideal of the Qur'an constitute the normative *Sunnah*. Ijma', or concensus, is only *their* ijma', that of the sick society constitutes none. No eisegetic interpretation *(bi al batin)* but with reference to the

---

10. Muhammad Adu Zahrah, *Ibn Taymiyah: Hayatuh wa 'Asrh, Ara' uh wa Fikruh* (2nd ed.; Cairo: Dar al Fikr al 'Arabi, 1958). H. Laoust, *Contribution á une étude de la méthodologie canonique de Taki-d-Din Ahmad B. Taimaya* and *Essai sur les doctrines sociales et politiques de Taki-d-Din Ahmad B. Taimiya* (Cairo: Institut Francais d' Archéologie Orientale, 1939).

Qur'an itself and "the verified *Sunnah*." Hence too, no pantheism, no miracles—not even by Muhammad—and no knowledge by esoteric illumination.

2. The gates of *ijtihad*, or creative interpretation of the Islamic imperative and of its application, are to be reopened (after their closure in the thirteenth century) and kept open. Since Islam has no church *magisterium* and rejects the idea of one, and since its scripture is open, public, and makes rational claims upon men, every man is duty bound to seek a first-hand understanding of its message. Every thinker of the modern period, from Ibn Taymiyyah down, has repeated the Prophet's *hadith*, "Whoever does *ijtihad* and errs deserves one measure of reward; whoever does *ijtihad* and falls not into error deserves two." Moreover, since the law, in the sense of *fiqh* or prescriptive law, is human through and through (Muhammad's final prophethood implying the maturity of man henceforth to create his own "how" to the eternal, divine "what," the crystallizations of the past are not authoritative though they have immense didactic value, a value which becomes authoritative if and only if it is proved beyond question that it is associated through prophethood with the divine Source. Even then and so, there is a distinction as to whether it has to do with worship and is hence a sunnah *fi'liyyah* (i.e., an actional, as opposed to verbal tradition, the former being always demonstrably universal, with *ghayb* (the beyond), or pertains to the affairs of this world. In the latter cases, the Qur'anic verses, "I (Muhammad) am but human, like you (My fellow men!)"[11] "I never claim to possess the treasures of heaven, nor to know the beyond, nor that I am angel,"[12] and the verified *hadith*," "You, Men, know better the affairs of your world," determine the Muslim's attitude *a priori*. *Ijtihad* is a source of Islamic law built-in within, and hence inseparable from, the system of jurisprudence.[13] The Muslim, all these leaders and thinkers asserted, is free to visit all schools of thought, all sects, all realms of knowledge and, to pick out, to create and recreate what in his best judgment fulfills the imperative of Islam.[14]

3. Existence is a serious affair, for God has endowed us with a trust which we must fulfill, and may or may not fulfill at the risk of damnation and peril.[15] This trust is to be realized in the rough and tumble

---

11. Qur'an, 18:111.
12. Ibid., 11:32; 7:189.
13. Kemal Faruki *Muslim Jurisprudence* (Karachi: Pakistan Publishing House, 1962), pp. 75 ff. Imam Muhammad Idris al Shafi'i, *Al Risalah*, translated by Majid Khadduri under the title *Islamic Jurisprudence* (Baltimore: The Johns Hopkins Press, 1961), 68. Abu al Husayn Muhammad ibn 'Ali ibn al Tayyib, *Kitab al Mu'tamad fi Usul al Fiqh*, eds. Muhammad Hamidullah et al. (Damascus: Institut Francais de Damas, 1964), 8-12.
14. A. A. A. Fyzee, *Outlines of Muhammadan Law* (Oxford: The Clarendon Press, 1949), 27.
15. Qur'an, 33:72; 47:38, 9:40.

of space-time, as Muhammad himself has done in the market places and battlefields of Makkah and Madinah. It is to be realized *yoqzatan, la hilman* (in clear wakefulness and not in dreamlike reality) as ibn Taymiyyah and Muhammad ibn 'Abd al Wahhab said.[16] His realization implies the operating of the casual threads of nature, the positive construction of history. Al Ghazzali's claim that causality is not real because *al husul 'indahu* ("occurance at") does not necessarily imply *al husul bihi* ("occurance by"), is false by what it omits, namely, that all the efficient, material, and final causation of God, does not exclude the responsibility of man's deflection of natural causation as God's built-in-law to ends which natural causation alone would not have realized without human intervention; that divine causation does not rule out human *Kasb* or responsibility.[17]

4. The poverty and misery of Arab society is, therefore, the work of Arab society and its responsibility, within the scheme of the all-encompassing *Sunnah* or pattern of God. Nobody will change their situation unless they change it themselves, for "God does not change the condition of a people unless they change themselves."[18] To call upon Muhammad to bring about supernatural change, or *shafa'ah*, is to ask him to break the pattern of God, to violate cosmic justice—in short, it is to fall into *shirk* (association of other beings with God) of the Meccan variety.[19]

5. *Al Imamah'* or the formation of the Muslim community into an organized whole, what some contemporary thinkers call "societism," is necessary.[20] For, the soteriology of Islam conceives of no personal salvation in dissociation from mankind. Even a prophet cannot be contented with his personal harmony, or mystical union with the divine. He has to reach his fellow men, to contend with them, to concert and lead them in the cause or perish at their hand. A successful prophet is better than an unsuccessful one. Where the case of a prophet must turn out to be a tragedy, his historic advent may yet serve a higher societistic purpose, thus confirming the general principle that God does not act in vain. God neither acts exclusively for one man nor wishes that man act exclusively for himself. *Al Imamah*, in the sense of leader-

---

16. Abbas Muhmud al 'Aqqad, *Al Islam fi al Qarn al 'Ishrin: Hadiruh wa Mustaqbaluh* (Cairo: Dar al Kutub al Hadithah, 1954), 102 ff.
17. T. A. ibn Taymiyah, "Risalat al Iradah wa al Amr" in *Majmu'at al Rasa'il al Kubra* (Cairo: Muhammad 'Ali Subayh, 1966), I, 32 ff. For Sanusiyyah, see N. A. Ziadeh, p. 88.
18. Qur'an, 13:12; 8:54. Muhammad 'Abduh, *Risalat al Tawhid* (Cairo: Matba'at Nahdat Misr, 1956), 164.
19. Ibid., 39:3. Ibn Taymiyah devoted a whole work to this subject, viz. *Qa'idah Jalilah fi al Tawassul wa al Wasilah* (Cairo: Al Matba'ah al Muniriyyah, 1373 AH/1952 AC). Muhammad 'Abduh, *Risalat al Tawhid* (Cairo: Matba'at Nahdat Misr, 1956), 57-62.
20. Ibid., 4:63. T. A. ibn Taymiyah, *Al Siyasah al Shar'iyyah fi Islah al Ra'i wa al Ra'iyyah* (Cairo: Dar al Kitab al'Arabi, 1951), 172-180. M. Adu Zahrah, 343-349.

ship of the community, is a contractual relation between ruler and ruled. Its basis is the law and it is a two-way affair, i.e. giving rise to rights and obligations for both ruler and ruled. Modern Islamic thought has rejected the idea of a unique *imam* for the whole community, and recognized the community's division into geographic and cultural groups as legitimate grounds for a multiplicity of *imams*, but not of laws.[21] Even the rule of the ruler is not unilateral in Islam; for the law demands of the ruled to give the ruler their advice and assistance.[22] Modern thinkers chastize those who blame their rulers for society's ills with the Prophet's *hadith*: "As you are in yourselves, so will be the men brought forth to rule over you."[23]

6. The ideal state is a replica of the cosmic state in that it embodies a perfect realization of justice.[24] Just as God never punishes without warning, His laws are inexorable and know no distinction, so should the worldly state honor the *Shari'ah* always, regardless of advantage to anyone. Rightly, it is a nomocracy. In it, responsibility is absolutely personal. Reward and punishment are never meted out vicariously, and no "atom's weight of good or evil" as the Qur'an says, is ever lost or overlooked. Everything must and will have to bear the consequences which properly belong to it. Besides governing itself, the Islamic state is obliged to extend its "peace" to its neighbors and enter with them into relations fulfilling the ideal of justice, of the freedom to listen and to be convinced of the truth. Unlike any international law before or after it, the Islamic law of nations has, significantly enough, granted *aman* (or safety) and jurisdiction to enter into contract not only to states as such, but to individuals, whether its own or those of another state.[25]

7. Within Arab society as conceived by the thinkers of the nineteenth and twentieth centuries, the citizen is free to earn his living singly and amass all the fortune he can. There is therefore no restraint upon his initiative and ambition. Capitalism is of the essence and private property is as "sacrosanct as the Day of Pilgrimage."[26] But, fortune may

---

21. Ibn Taymiyyah, *Al Siyasah al Shar'iyyah* 16-19.
22. Ibid., 169 ff.
23. Jamaluddin al Afghani, *Al 'Urwah al Wuthqa* (Beirut: Matba'at al Tawfiq, Reprint, 1328 AH), 190 ff; 215 ff; 233 ff; ibid., 2nd part, 188-196, where the *hadith* in question constitutes the title of the article.
24. Abbas M. al 'Aqqad, *Al Dimuqratiyyah fi al Islam* (Cairo: Dar al Ma'arif, 1952), 48-54.
25. Muhammad Hamiddalah, *Muslim Conduct of State* (Lahore: Sh. Muhammad Ashraf, 1961), 14-16. Khadduri, Majid, *War and Peace in the Law of Islam* (Baltimore: Johns Hopkins Press, 1955), 162 ff; 202 ff.
26. Ibn Hisham, *The Life of Muhammad*, Tr. by Alfred Guillaume (London: Oxford University Press, 1955), 651-52, Ibn Taymiyyah, *Al Siyasah al Shar'iyyah*, 28-29. Sayyid Qutb, *Social Justice in Islam*, tr. by John B. Hardie (Washington: American Council of Learned Societies, 1953), 102 ff.

not be amassed through injustice, by immoral or deceitful ways. The capital acquired may not be hoarded, but must be spent to the benefit of all, directly as in *zakat* (or the sharing of one's wealth with others at the rate of 2½% per year) and indirectly by reinvesting it in productive enterprises. Here too, exploitation, of whatever color or shape, is prohibited by law.[27] Although Arab thinkers until the turn of the century stood for the abolition of all interests as implying a measure of exploitation, many voices have arisen since to qualify this prohibition by limiting it to usury, i.e. to uncontrolled interest obeying the laws of supply and demand, the whim of the leader, and the helplessness of the borrower.[28]

Other citizens who are not fortunate enough to be capitalists, are to unite together in co-operative societies with limited or unlimited liability. The cooperative society provides for the citizen as well as administers his productive energies. It also owns the land, as in the Wahhabi experiments of Arabia (Dar'iyyah, etc.) and of the Sanusi experiments of North Africa (Jaghbub, etc.). It also owns the factory, be it a factory of clothes or of armaments. It distributes water for irrigation and drinking and operates all the wells. And it could also be a cooperative of small holders whom it serves and to whom its profits are distributed on patronage basis, with no disparity of share ownership among the members. Finally and most important, as if a revival of *tourneface* of the Sufi fraternity, the cooperative society is invested with the supreme duty of carrying the ideological mission of Islam within and without its borders. Thus, in the two examples mentioned by name, Dar'iyyah and Jaghbub, the Mosque was the center of the cooperative.[29] It was the school, the seat of the administration, the fortress, as well as the locus of the "holy fire." The *imam* of the Mosque was not only the leader of group prayers, but the chief administrator and supreme commander.

8. The ideal social order in modern Arab social thought may be characterized as comprehensive, enveloping this world and the next in full accord with classical Islam which conceived itself as leading to the two happinesses: Here and beyond. No Arab thought, to my knowledge, is secular in the sense of compartmentalizing human life

---

27. Muhammad 'Abduh, "Fatwa: Fi Mas' alat al 'Ummal wa Ashab al A 'mal' " in 'Uthman Amin, *Al Imam Muhammad 'Abduh* (Cairo: Maktabat al Anglo al Misriyyah, 1965), 284-289. Al 'Aqqad, 'Abbas M., 85-94.
28. Sayyid Qutb, 120-124. Ibid., *Ma 'rakat al Islam wa al Ra' smaliyyah* (Cairo: Dar al Kitab al 'Arabi, 1952), 486. Al 'Aqqad, 'Abbas M., *Haqa iq al Islam wa Abatil Khusumih* (Cairo: Matba' at Misr, 1957), 199 ff. Anwar al Khatib, *Al Naz'ah al Ishtirakiyyah fi al Islam* (Beirut: Dar al 'Ilm lil Malayin, 1956), 192 ff. Anwar Iqbal Qureshi, *Islam and the Theory of Interest* (Lahore: Sh. Muhammad Ashraf), 44 ff.
29. N. Ziadeh, 99 ff.

THE ARAB WORLD, 1800-1968

in two autonomous spheres. Every thinker has regarded the relation of happiness here and happiness beyond in Islamic manner, i.e. as organic and necessary, both areas falling and doing so *de jure*—within the jurisdiction of the community as a group, within that of the state or administration, indeed, as their prime responsibility.[30] There have of course been a few lonely voices who pleaded for secularism. But these, as I have shown elsewhere,[31] are either convinced and non-Islamic, or if Muslim then either ambivalent, or simpletonian and confused.

9. The ideal social order in modern Arab thought is populistic and free of class struggle. For over a century, the appeal of reform has been directed towards the masses. This appeal was so strong that it sometimes colored itself with provincialism, for the particular socioeconomic problems of the Arab masses in Iraq, Algeria, Egypt, and Palestine were not always identical. But inasmuch as it invoked Islamic values, the appeal was universal. Likewise, the classlessness of classic Muslim society inspired and guided Arab reformers to seek to wipe out the class differences which vitiate Arab society by peaceful means. Again here, it was the Islamic ideal which stood as guard against the outbreak of class warfare *a la Russe*. Neither *pasha* nor *fallah* could resist the appeal of Islamic brotherhood and equality, taught and nurtured by centuries of intermarriage, of prayer-in-one-straight-row, of pilgrimage in identical pieces of unsewn linen, of creaturely submission to the One Almighty God.[32]

10. Lastly, the ideal social order in modern Arab thought has always been open to influence by modern events, by experimentation and failure. Apparently, the absence of *ex-cathedra* definitions of Islam, the maintenance of the doctrinal prerequisites of Islamicity to the bare minimum of the *shahadah (i.e.* the profession that there is no God but God and that Muhammad is His Prophet) and the general Islamic refinement implied in the expression *"wa-Allahu a'lam"* (". . . And God knows better"), stood guard against the presentation of social thought as socio-political dogmatique. Neither are the rulers hesitant to give newer and newer versions of Arab social vision, nor do the ruled reject these versions as departures from any *dogmatique*. A dialectic with events has been the rule ever since Mohammad ibn 'Abd al Wahhab. Though he himself could not profit from the events which ruined his movements, other Arabs picked up the banner, under different names. Likewise, the series of Arab socialisms which we have witnessed since World War II will baffle any observer. But one must concentrate on

---

30. 'Abbas M. al 'Aqqad, *Haqa' iq al Islam*, 255 ff. Ibid., *Al Islam fi al Qarn al 'Ishrin*, 105-106.
31. Isma 'il R. al Faruqi, *On Arabism, Vol. I, 'Urubah and Religion: A Study of the Fundamental Ideas of Arabism and of Islam as Its Highest Moment of Consciousness* (Amsterdam: Djambatan, 1962), 121-132.
32. A. M. al 'Aqqad, *Haqa' iq al Islam, 199 ff.*

the commonness of their common points and the novelty, if any, of their new points rather than their advent as socio-political systems, if he is to discern the *logique* of Arab Society.

This is what *Al Mithaq* (the Covenant), the ideological statement of 1962 which the Egyptian Revolution proclaimed to the Arab world, has to say on the subject of religion and society:

The freedom of religious conviction must be a capital foundation of our new life . . . . The eternal spiritual values which spring from the religions of the world are worthy of leading man, and capable of illuminating his life with the power of goodness, truth, justice and love. . . . All the messages of heaven accord in essence with human revolutions aimed at realizing human honor, dignity and happiness. The greatest duty of religious thinkers is the safeguarding of this essence of religion. . . . This essence does not run counter to the facts of life. Conflicts do arise at times, but only from the attempt on the part of the forces of reaction to exploit religion contrary to its very nature and spirit for the purpose of obstructing human progress. They do this by exegetical interpretations which fly in the face of the divine wisdom. All the "message-religions" are progressivist. The reactionary forces, on the other hand, anxious as they are to exploit and monopolize the goods of the earth, perpetrated the crime of camouflaging their objectives with religion, converting it against its nature in order to stop the march of progress. The essence of each of the religions confirms the right of man to life and freedom. Indeed, the very system of religious reward and punishment is based upon equal opportunity for all men. Every man begins his life in front of the Almighty Creator with a clean slate on which he himself freely and responsibly enters his deeds. No religion accepts a classness which imposes upon the majority of men the inheritance of poverty, ignorance, and disease by reserving the good inheritance to the few. It was God Himself — May His Majesty be glorified — Who built equality of opportunity into the very system of human endeavor on earth, of reward and punishment in the beyond.[33]

The astounding enthusiasm on the part of all Arabs which this document has evoked is due, without a doubt, to its consonance with their Islamic conscience.

---

33. *Jamal 'Abdul Nasir, Al Mithaq* (Cairo: Al Dar al Qawmiyyah li al Tiba 'ah wa al Nashr, 1962), 78-80.

State and Religion: Religious Conflict Among Jews in Israel

EPHRAIM TABORY

The organization of religion in modern, industrialized, Western countries, where state and religion are structurally separate, has led to an increase in tolerance for religious pluralism and to the mitigation of conflict not only between different religions, but also between different denominations within the same religious grouping. The reason for this, according to Peter Berger, is that religion's plausibility structure is becoming less relevant to the entire societal plausibility structure, although retaining significance for individuals in society.[1] An example of this is the three main denominations of Judaism in the United States. There, Reform, Conservative, and Orthodox Judaism (in ascending order of adherence to traditional Jewish doctrine) are very much tolerant of one another, despite the basic differences in their belief structures. While Marshall Sklare notes that this is partially due to the cohesive, ethnic aspects of Judaism, especially in confrontation with non-Jews in the United States, this can only be so in society not governed by religious adherence.[2]

Societies in which religion plays a relatively important part in determining societal behavior, as the case of Iran demonstrates, carry with it the seeds of severe conflict and turmoil. Religious conflict, based as it is on an ideological plane, makes compromise much more difficult to achieve, for the very act of compromise (or the self-perception that one is compromising) can undermine the religious doctrine. The problem of tension between religious groups is exacerbated when religion and state are intertwined, and it is in this context that the case at hand—the religious situation in Israel—is discussed.

---

1. Peter L. Berger, *The Sacred Canopy: Elements of a Sociological Theory of Religion* (Garden City, N.Y.: Anchor Books, 1967), 128-35.
2. Marshall Sklare, "Jewish Religion and Ethnicity at the Bicentennial," *Midstream* 21 (November 1975):21.

In its Declaration of Independence, Israel guarantees freedom of religion and religious practice to all persons. About 80 percent of Israel's population is Jewish, with the rest belonging to Christian or Muslim communities. While there is no formal state religion, there is a Ministry of Religious Affairs which deals with all religious groupings in the country and provides them with some financial support. Despite formal freedom of religion, each religious community is empowered by secular law to establish autonomous, religious courts in matters of personal status (marriage and divorce) which are then binding on all members of the community, whether or not they personally are religious. To some degree, then, there is no freedom from religion. Thus, for example, civil marriages and divorces may not be performed in Israel, although such ceremonies performed outside of Israel are administratively recognized in that country.[3]

On a macro-societal level, Jewish religiously based law has a very pervasive influence, and, in some spheres, is binding upon religious and nonreligious Jews alike. This has led to charges of "religious coercion" and to antagonism between religious and nonreligious Jews.[4] In fact, the potential conflict between religious and nonreligious Jews is seen by some Israeli sociologists as constituting one of Israel's greatest social problems.[5] The purpose of this essay is to analyze the extent to which the intertwining of state and religion in Israel affects the conflict between religious and nonreligious Jews.

Religious Involvement on a State Level

The extensive involvement of religious Judaism in Israel may be analyzed on two levels. First, there is the ideological question of the legitimation of the state and the definition of the nature and traditions of society. This basically revolves around how the question of "who is a Jew" is to be answered. Religious adherents argue that *Halacha* (religious doctrine and precepts) must be the supreme source for setting standards in matters of marriage, divorce, and conversion. Nonreligious persons are willing to accept more liberal

---

3. For a survey of the impact of religion on state law in Israel, see Amnon Rubinstein, "Law and Religion in Israel," *Israel Law Review* 2 (1967):380-414.
4. Ibid.; see also Rubinstein, "State and Religion in Israel." *Journal of Contemporary History* 2 (October 1967):107-21.
5. Leonard Weller, *Sociology in Israel* (Westport, Conn.: Greenwood Press, 1974), p. 210. The relationship between Israeli Jews and Israeli Arabs is also colored by religious differences constituting one source of a social problem in itself. Obviously, living in a dominant Jewish culture does have some impact on non-Jewish Israelis, but this is beyond the scope of this paper.

rules governing the definition of who is a Jew. The issue is important because of the guiding principle behind Israel as a Jewish state—that it is open to the immediate immigration and granting of citizenship to any Jew throughout the world.

Individuals who do not meet the strict religious requirements (e.g., those persons who may have converted to Judaism under guidelines unacceptable to Israeli religious authorities) have occasionally brought their cases before the civil courts. This process has opened to question the relationship between the secular and the theoretically autonomous religious court systems. The entire issue has been the subject of some very severe political controversies as some persons, persecuted abroad as Jews, have immigrated to Israel only to find that they are not considered Jewish in their newly adopted country. Another critical aspect relates to certain religious requirements concerning marriage procedures, especially with regard to Israeli war widows whose husbands' bodies were not located after the 1973 War. Religious law requires substantial proof that death had indeed occurred before permitting widows to remarry, and this was not always easily available. Another example is the requirement in religious law that childless widows receive permission from a bachelor brother-in-law, if there is one, before they can remarry. In some instances families took nefarious advantage of the widows by demanding money in return for the permission.

The second level on which Judaism impinges relates to the general character of the Jewish state, and how religious laws are experienced on a daily basis. Exemplary of this on a national level is the requirement that all public institutions observe the Jewish dietary laws, or *Kashrut*. This means that the nation's airline and shipping companies serve only ritually acceptable food. This has led, in the past, to controversy when it was sought to have the Israeli flagship carry a nonkosher kitchen in order to attract non-Jewish passengers. Likewise, the attempt to raise pigs, an animal considered ritually impure, was also forbidden, and the source of controversy. Many places of employment and entertainment, in the Jewish sector, are closed on the Sabbath. Neither is there public bus transportation on that day in most Israeli cities. This is quite an inconvenience for those persons without cars and who cannot afford more expensive taxi service. It is especially so because many Israelis work a six-day week, and the time they have for leisure travel and family visits is basically limited to the Sabbath.

Another emerging issue of conflict is the relationship between the religious establishment in Israel with the Reform and Conservative Jewish denominations. Until now, the term "religious" has been used in this article as coterminous with "Orthodox" Judaism. This essentially reflects the situation in Israel where a majority of Jews who identify themselves as "religious" actually are "Orthodox." Reform and Conservative Judaism have not had much impact in Israel, and to be a "religious" Reform or Conservative Jew in Israel is almost a contradiction in terms. Orthodox authorities consider Reform and Conservative Judaism an abuse of the Jewish tradition. The non-Orthodox religious movements have been subjected to derogation and discrimination by the Orthodox-controlled religious establishment. Non-Orthodox rabbis are not recognized as such by the state, and they cannot perform marriages in Israel. Divorces granted by such rabbis abroad have, at times, been challenged. In some locations in Israel pressure has been exerted on public institutions to refuse to rent space to the movements for holding prayer services. Only two to three thousand families in Israel belong to the movements, and thus far the movements have chosen to work quietly to seek official government recognition.

Public Reaction to Religiously Based Laws

Protests over incursion of religious practices have been severe at times, but rarely long lasting. Antireligious movements, such as the Israel Secular Movement and the now defunct League Against Religious Coercion, have never gathered large-scale support. This is despite the fact that only a minority of Israel's Jews (between 20 and 30 percent) are Orthodox,[6] and that secularization has made great inroads in Jewish-Israeli society.[7] It is submitted that there are two basic reasons why protest has not been more forceful: the first is on the political level, and the second regards basic cultural patterns of Israeli Jews.

THE POLITICAL LEVEL

First, Israel's Parliament is based upon a coalition government. With the formation of the state, various Zionist organizations that originated in the prestate period became full-fledged political parties. These included the religious Zionists, who had developed their own movement in the past because of the basically secularistic trends of early Socialistic Zionists. Since the creation of the state, religious parties, with but brief interludes, have been part of the

---

6. Sammy Smooha, *Israel: Pluralism and Conflict* (London: Routledge & Kegan Paul, 1978), pp. 73-75.
7. Elihu Katz and Michael Gurevitch, *The Secularization of Leisure: Culture and Communication in Israel* (Cambridge, Mass: Harvard University Press, 1976).

coalition government. There are those who hold that Labor, the dominant political party until the rise of the Likud government, basically had to rely on the religious parties for support in order to stay in power.[8] Others hold that the ruling party wanted the religious parties to be part of the ruling faction in order to prevent a Kulturkampf threatening the unity of the people.[9] The fear was that the large Orthodox minority would create its own separate institutions, thus undermining the state. Yet another possibility is that secular leaders were affected by their own traditional background, and that they sought to ensure the presence of a Jewish character in the state by having the representatives of the religion that they themselves rejected participate in the government. Whatever the reason, the presence of the religious parties in the various governments has served to direct the demands of the religious and the nonreligious groups to political channels. This has led to moderations and compromise. In a sense, the religious and nonreligious parties have coopted one another, although the main benefit has accrued to the former. Generally they have been able to exert considerable influence on the religious sphere above and beyond the 15 percent of the Parliament seats which they generally hold.

Also, on the political level, the working relationships between religious and nonreligious elements in the prestate period were carried over to the statehood period. This status quo means that in certain fields religious provisions already in effect are to remain as they were. Any attempt to alter current religious arrangements is considered an abrogation of that status quo and not to be condoned.[10] While interpretations regarding the status quo have themselves led to controversy (such as whether television broadcasts begun only in the late 1960s are considered something new, and therefore to be forbidden, or whether they are merely an extension of radio broadcasts and therefore to be permitted), the principle of the status quo has generally forestalled greater religious controversy than it has generated.

JEWISH CULTURE IN ISRAEL

Throughout history, Judaism has been embued with religious

---

8. Ervin Birnbaum, *The Politics of Compromise: State and Religion in Israel* (Rutherford, N.J.: Fairleigh Dickinson University Press, 1970), p. 24.
9. Eliezer Don-Yehiya, "Religion and Coalition: The National Religious Party and Coalition Formation in Israel," in *The Elections in Israel—1973*, ed. Asher Arian (Jerusalem: Jerusalem Academic Press, 1975), pp. 255-84.
10. Shulamit Aloni, *Hahesder* (The Arrangement) (Tel-Aviv: Otpaz, 1971) pp. 91-92 (in Hebrew).

meaning carried over even into the sanctification of the secular and the provision of religious significance to everyday life. While early Zionists were secularly oriented, it appears that the question of the legitimacy of the Jewish state is being raised by a new generation of Israelis for whom the answers are not self-evident, as they were for their founding fathers. Israelis are asked to give a great deal to their state, not the least of which is a long period of initial military service and annual reserve duty. Additionally burdened by a problematic economy, an increasing number of those youth raised to believe their country is a "normal" state like all the others are asking what is the special significance of Israel as a Jewish state. They are, in a sense, searching for their Jewish roots. The temptation is great to cite this phenomenon in terms of Hansen's third generation theory of return to their grandparents' culture.[11] It is quite significant that a search for Jewish roots is taking place even in what has long been considered a "hotbed" of antireligious ideology, the kibbutz.[12]

The answers that are being provided, even if they are on an unconscious level, are of a historical-religious nature and relate to Israel's civil religion. Nationalistic elements and traditional religious practices are very much intertwined in Israeli Jewish culture.[13] This is so with regard to such symbols as the state flag, which is based on a Jewish prayer shawl, or more emotion-laden experiences such as the religious rituals which are an integral part of civil ceremonies like on Memorial Day. This intertwining of religious and nationalistic symbols leads to a basic acceptance of the role of religion in society as an integrative force.

Empirical evidence for these claims is only indirect. Various studies have found a substantial correlation between the experiencing of Jewish and Israeli identities.[14] Perhaps more significant for religious tolerance is that Judaism is a religion of behavior and rituals, to be performed according to a repeating cycle. Even nonre-

---

11. Marcus L. Hansen, "The Third Generation in America," *Commentary* 14 (November 1952):492-500.
12. Zvi Yaron, "Religion in Israel," in *American Jewish Year Book 1976*, ed. Morris Fine and Milton Himmelfarb (New York: American Jewish Committee, 1976), pp. 61-65; Shalom Lilker, "Kibbutz Judaism: A New Tradition in the Making" (Ph.D. diss., Hebrew Union College, Jewish Institute of Religion, 1972), pp. 88-116.
13. Charles S. Liebman, "Religion and Political Integration in Israel," *The Jewish Journal of Sociology* 17 (June 1975): 17-27; Charles (Yeshayahu) Liebman, "Towards the Study of Popular Religion in Israel," *Megamot* 23 (1977): 95-109 (in Hebrew); Charles S. Liebman and Eliezer Don-Yehiya, *Civil Religion and Traditional Judaism in Israel* (working title, forthcoming).
14. Simon N. Herman, *Israelis and Jews: The Continuity of an Identity* (Philadelphia: Jewish Publication Society of America, 1971), pp. 139-40; Katz and Gurevitch, *The Secularization of Leisure*, p. 274.

ligious Israelis perform many of these rituals to such a degree[15] that the nonreligious sector of Israel is quite similar in its religious behavior to Reform Jewry in the United States.[16] The observance of even a minimal amount of tradition by large numbers of Israelis may, therefore, contribute to the acceptance of religious practices on a state level.

Finally, there is the question of which interest groups are most affected by religious legislation. The most widespread encroachment of religious norms on the personal behavior of Israel's Jews is probably the lack of adequate bus transportation on the Sabbath. This limitation, however, is only partially felt by the relatively affluent middle class. Many of these persons have access to cars or can afford the private taxi service that continues to operate on that day. Sabbath practices thus most adversely affect the lower classes, but these classes tend to be the most religiously traditional sectors in Israeli society.[17] Furthermore, those persons affected by this might very well not have the leadership qualities requisite to the mobilization of large-scale protest. The evidence for this is the recurring failure of lower class groups to effectively organize for better housing and other social benefits.

Future Trends

There is one further religious issue which threatens the basic relationship between religious and nonreligious Jews in Israel. Traditionally, the religious political parties have dealt with internal religious issues and have not been prominent in external affairs.[18] Now, the question of the price to be paid for peace with Israel's Arab neighbors is increasingly becoming a political issue. Some of the modern Orthodox youth have organized themselves into a *Gush Emunim*, or Bloc of the Faithful, and argue that it is Israel's duty to annex the area west of the Jordan River and that the right to do this is based on religious grounds. These persons are even forcing the traditionally moderate religious parties to become increasingly intransigent on this matter, and questions of secular legality and

---

15. Yehuda Ben Meir and Peri Kedem, "Measure of Religiosity for the Jewish Population of Israel," *Megamot* 24 (1979): 359 (in Hebrew).
16. Ephraim Tabory and Bernard Lazerwitz, "Ideological Migration and Religious Affiliation: American Reform and Conservative Jews in Israel" (forthcoming).
17. Alan Arian, *The Choosing People: Voting Behavior in Israel* (Cleveland: Press of Case Western Reserve University, 1973), p. 67.
18. Michael Brecher, *The Foreign Policy System of Israel: Settings, Images, Process* (Oxford: Oxford University Press, 1972), p. 179.

human rights are secondary to them. To a considerable extent, *Gush Emunim* perceives itself as a new Messianic movement.[19] On the other hand, there is the Peace Now Movement, which was formed to counter *Gush Emunim* and which is apparently viewed by many as an organization of nonreligious persons, although it does have some religious supporters. The influence of the young religious idealists on the moderate religious parties on the question of foreign policy may extend to increasing resistance to religious compromises on the local level. Should the religious parties be unable to moderate the religious demands, as they have done until now, the ruling political parties might be forced to align with other parties, less sympathetic to traditional Jewish practices. Should such a situation produce a relaxation of religious law on the state level, the results would be the alienation of the religious camp, and their withdrawal and formation of their own subcommunity.

The above conclusion may give the impression that the ideal solution for the Israeli situation would be a capitulation to the demands of the religious in order to preserve Jewish unity. The situation is more complex than that, because although outright conflict over religious legislation has not been widespread, it is always latently present. There may be a limit to the extent nonreligious persons are willing to tolerate increased religious demands. It should be noted that the status quo discussed above has more often been used by the Orthodox to prevent the erosion of accepted religious practices, but it has not prevented them from seeking to expand those practices. The more attempts to codify religious law as state law, the more the religious practices will affect powerful groups that are unwilling to passively accept the changed situation. A religiously based law severely limiting autopsies passed in December 1980 has aroused the ire of the medical community and the open declaration by some doctors that they will not abide by the law. Likewise there may be a limit to the patience of Reform and Conservative leaders, both in Israel and abroad, to the amount of discrimination they are willing to tolerate.

A liberal political party has already attempted, in late 1980, to initiate a basic law guaranteeing these movements equal rights and governmental assistance. While the passage of such a proposal is not likely at this time, radicalization on the part of religious parties may lead to a form of psychological reactance on the part of the

---

19. Janet O'Dea, "Gush Emunim: Roots and Ambiguities," *Forum on the Jewish People, Zionism and Israel* 25 (1976):39-50.

non-Orthodox.[20]

The manner in which tradition and change can be balanced so as to maintain an equilibrium between the two has been described as the "perpetual dilemma" of the Jewish people.[21] Israel is still a young society composed of immigrants from a multitude of countries. Both ethnic and religious barriers threaten the overall national unity. While religious legislation is channeled through the government, the religious and nonreligious groups' attitudes toward the state and religious law affect the relationship between religious and nonreligious persons directly. While a Kulturkampf has not occurred, neither has there developed one united society in which religious differences are unimportant. Preliminary analysis of data concerning strictly religious and nonreligious middle class Israelis indicates very little social interaction between the two groups.[22] This finding supports earlier survey data indicating that religious and nonreligious Jews in Israel do not feel very close to one another.[23] It would appear that a resolution of the religious question is necessary to ensure the unity and social identity of Israel, given its position as an independent state—a status which the Jewish community has not experienced in modern history prior to 1948.

---

20. Jack W. Brehm, *A Theory of Psychological Reactance* (New York: Academic Press, 1966).
21. S. Zalman Abramov, *Perpetual Dilemma: Jewish Religion in the Jewish State* (Jerusalem: World Union for Progressive Judaism, 1976), pp. 400-2.
22. Ephraim Tabory, "Civil Religion in Israel" (research project in progress, Institute for the Study of Ethnic Groups, Bar Ilan University, Israel).
23. Herman, *Israelis and Jews*, p. 106.

Revolution and the Church in Nicaragua and El Salvador

BAHMAN BAKHTIARI

The political crisis and economic chaos that prevail in Central America have long provided necessary conditions for revolt. Were these also sufficient conditions, however, every nation of the region, or for that matter of the Third World, would have long ago been engulfed by the fires of revolution. Clearly, there are additional factors that have contributed to the political turmoil currently sweeping through the isthmus. The principal catalyst has been the emergence of liberation theology in the Catholic Church and, in the case of Nicaragua, the various Protestant churches. The theology of liberation in Central America has received relatively little attention in the relevant literature as a philosophical and political force.

This article represents an attempt to compare the impact of liberation theology on the church and its relationship to the revolutionary process in two countries: Nicaragua and El Salvador. The periods examined are not exactly identical. In Nicaragua, an examination is made of the churches before the overthrow of Anastasio Somoza in July 1979, with some discussion in the conclusion of what has caused the recent conflict between the Sandinistas and the Catholic Church. In El Salvador, the focus is on the recent events in this country's ongoing struggle, especially after the death of Archbishop Oscar Romero. First, however, it is necessary to outline and describe the origins of liberation theology in Latin America, especially its meaning and message for those who have embraced this revolutionary doctrine.

Over the last decade, religion has had a surprisingly powerful political impact, but the relation between religion and politics remains confused and unexamined. Conventional wisdom still holds on to the discredited notion that religion is primarily a pre-modern residue doomed to fade away along with other superstitions and myths. How can this residue thesis be seriously argued today, however, when almost every major political conflict exhibits extensive religious underpinnings? Any cursory list of current hot spots on the world map points to religion as a decisive feature in case after case: Islamic revolution in Iran; Catholic nationalism in Poland; the Jewish and Palestinian questions in the Middle East; the Catholic-Protestant clash in Northern Ireland; and liberation theology in Latin America.

In Latin America, the emergence of liberation theology has introduced an alternative perspective by attempting to redefine the meaning of religious symbols and redirect the social and political thrust of the church. The intense concern for politics, which lies at the heart of this perspective, has in fact brought religion and politics into a more dynamic, revolutionary relation than ever before. Liberation theology has identified two levels of crisis, quantitative and qualitative. On the quantitative level, liberation theology has stressed the failure of liberal capitalism to supply everyone with its products and, indeed, its tendency to contribute to the progressive impoverishment of the masses. On the qualitative level, it has drawn attention to the values of the capitalist ethos, which are held to be incompatible with Latin America's best traditions. Because of its secular nature, capitalism fosters individualism, competition, materialism, and greed. A "Christian" socialism offers an alternative set of values that which stresses the virtues of participation, community, equality, and sacrifice.[1] In this way, the methodology of liberation theology begins with a look at concrete social problems, drawing themes and imperatives for action from this analysis. The central problem for religion is, thus, no longer atheism, indifference, or even hostility to religion per se, but rather social and political transformation. Gustavo Gutierrez, a leading Peruvian theologian, states this sharply:

Much contemporary theology seems to start from the challenge of the *non-believer*. He questions our *religious world* and faces it with a demand for profound purification and renewal .... This challenge in a continent like Latin America does not come primarily from the man who does not believe, but from the *man who is not a man*, who is not recognized as such by the existing social order: he is in the ranks of the poor, the exploited; he is the man who is systematically and legally despoiled of his being as a man, who scarcely knows that he *is* a man. His challenge is not aimed at our religious world, but at our *economic, social, political and cultural world*.[2]

The two levels of crisis are analyzed within a framework that exposes the impact of a community's being peripheral, dominated, and exploited. José Míguez-Bonino captures the essence of the new point of view with the question: "Is there an understanding of

---

1. R. W. Berki, *Socialism* (New York: St. Martin's Press, 1973), 31.
2. Gustavo Gutierrez, *A Theology of Liberation* (Maryknoll, New York: Orbis Books, 1973), 69. (Emphasis added)

Christianity the correlate of which is not dependence but liberation?"[3] Liberation thus means overcoming dependence and transforming Latin American society through socialism. This is a Christian project of socialism that attempts to blend Latin America's perennial quest for a historical identity with its own vision of the Christian eschatology, linking other-worldly salvation to a this-worldly transformation of society. Gutierrez combines these themes as follows: liberation means "seeing the history of mankind as a process of the emancipation of man all through history, a process which aims at a society in which man will be free from all forms of servitude and in which he will determine his own destiny."[4]

To priests holding such views, Catholicism and the role of the Church must be reexamined in order to achieve a different meaning for the faith, ministry, and social mission of the Church. Their identification with the poor, combined with their growing awareness of the social roots of poverty, led to the emergence of a revolutionary doctrine called liberation theology. With the guidelines set by Vatican II and the Medellins' Conference, the identification and awareness have impelled the Church into an increasing commitment to the poor in deed as well as word. In the cases of Nicaragua and El Salvador, liberation theology has thrust the Catholic Church into politics and confrontation with state authority.

Revolution and the Church in Nicaragua

When the Sandinistas entered Managua on 19 July 1979, one of the first public events to celebrate victory was a mass presided over by Archbishop Miguel Obando y Bravo and attended by thousands. Dozens of similar masses occurred in parishes throughout the country. These masses were symbolic of the role played by Nicaraguan churches, both Catholic and Evangelical, in the Revolution. How and why the Nicaraguan churches came to support revolution was due to the efforts of many Catholics who subscribe to liberation theology.

The first signs of change in the Nicaraguan Catholic Church appeared in the late 1960s, stimulated by the historic Latin American Bishops Conference at Medellin. The bishops sought to apply the reforms of Vatican II to Latin America and precipitated a dynamic process of reflection within the Church. Encouraged and inspired

---

3. José M. Bonino, *Doing Theology in a Revolutionary Situation*, (Philadelphia: Fortress Press, 1976), 18.
4. Gutierrez, *A Theology of Liberation*, 167.

by a group of activist Catholics working in the poverty-stricken areas of the country, the bishops initiated programs to identify the Church with the poor.[5]

Important segments of the Catholic and Evangelical churches in Nicaragua sought to create organizations such as Communidades Eclesiales de Base (CEB-Christian Base Communities) in order to implement the guidelines of the Medellin Conference. Through these organizations, the churches came to identify the Christian liberation of their people with the armed struggle led by the Sandinista Front of National Liberation (FSLN). From this vantage point, the post-Medellin evolution of the Nicaraguan churches differs in significant ways from experiences of other Latin American countries, where post-Medellin activism took the form of organized clerical movements committed to peaceful structural change in society.[6] These movements typically consisted of an avant-garde nucleus of priests whose wish to change the Church and society often led to bitter struggles with the Church hierarchy as well as with political authorities.

An important area in which liberation theology and its proponents played a crucial role was education. Education constituted one of the prerequisites for revolutionary action. In Nicaragua, the educational process was directed by activist priests in the Christian Base Communities. Following the guidelines of Paolo Freire, the CEBs drew their objectives according to the perceived "need of turning the option of the poor into concrete actions." The CEBs are concentrated mainly in Brazil, where they originated in the 1960s, with about fifty thousand communities and 1.2 million members today.[7] In Nicaragua, the first CEB was formed by Father Ernesto Cardenal (current minister of culture) in 1965. About the time of the Bishops' Conference at Medellin, a group led by José de la Jara, a Spanish priest, began to work with families in the 14 September *barrio* of Managua to develop CEBs.

Christian base communities were formed in Nicaragua, but not in a systematic manner. The Church hierarchy was somewhat uncomfortable with the growth of the CEBs. Although they frequently were started to relieve overworked parish priests of some of their duties, and for this received the blessing of the official Church, some began without the sponsorship or even the knowledge of the official Church.[8]

---

5. For a more comprehensive description of the events at Medellin see *The Church in the Present Day Transformation of Latin America in the Light of the Council* (Washington D.C.: United States Catholic Conference (USCC), 1973).
6. Ibid., 80-2.
7. Ronald T. Libby, "Listen to the Bishops," *Foreign Policy*, 52 (Fall 1983):79
8. Michael Dodson and Tommie S. Montgomery, "The Churches in the Nicaraguan

THE CHURCH IN NICARAGUA AND EL SALVADOR

Much of the work of forming the CEBs and leading them in an overtly political direction was left to lay persons called Delegates of the Word. Originally a response to the chronic shortage of priests in rural areas of the country, they specialized in developing the "Christian formation of peasants, focusing on literacy, concientization, and health."[9] Opportunities for turning these communities into centers of political opposition to Somoza were numerous. As early as 1972 such a development took place in the northern department of Metagalpa, where Father Miguel Vasquez started CEBs "which soon produced enough political organizations to lead to conflict between parishioners and government."[10]

Even though the CEBs are primarily religious groups, the case of Father Vasquez illustrates that they have obvious socio-political implications. First, due to the authoritarian regime of Somoza, the CEBs offered an opportunity to participate in a society that had never encouraged participation and had failed to provide channels for this process. In Nicaragua, the politicization and radicalization of the CEBs was primarily due to the rigidity and dictatorial nature of Somoza's regime. Second, the increase in the numbers of CEBs following the 1972 earthquake was indicative of the increasing corruption and mismanagement of funds and aid given to Nicaragua. The various reports on the formation of the CEBs indicated that they were usually founded on concrete issues ranging from the problems associated with the earthquake to land tenure and lack of essential services and resources.[11] In other words, there emerged a clear correlation between the development of the CEBs, the political radicalization of the people, and the appearance of political organizations. This also increased the pressure on the Catholic Church.

In December 1973, on the first anniversary of the earthquake, the Church hierarchy held a commemorative mass in the central plaza of Managua. Somoza, who had intended to hold a government-sponsored event, cancelled his plans and invited himself to the Church celebration. Meanwhile, the CEBs of Managua resolved to make their own presence felt at the celebration and to attend with the explicit purpose of expressing a "theological position different from that of the bishops." The hierarchy conceived the event as a commemoration of the dead. The CEBs wanted to focus on the needs of the living. As a former priest who provided live radio

Revolution," in Thomas W. Walker, (ed.), *Nicaragua in Revolution*, (New York: Praeger Press, 1981), 179.
9. Ibid., 170.
10. Ibid., 172.
11. Ibid., 171.

commentary said, "the people of God had one set of theological concerns and the bishops had another."[12]

By January 1978, the churches consisted of three identifiable elements. A small group remained loyal to Somoza. A large, nonviolent opposition typified by Catholic Archbishop Obando y Bravo sought a mediator role, believing strongly that Somoza must go, but refrained from giving support to the Sandinistas. The third group, centered mainly in the Christian base communities, was now actively worked to bring about a Sandinista victory. Even the moderate, center position of the archbishop seemed to further the isolation of the regime and to help set the stage for the insurrection. For example, the bishops' pastoral letter of January 1977 described the atmosphere in the countryside as a "state of terror," pointing to the dispossession of peasant landholders and to direct repression of the Church, "particularly the Delegates of the Word."[13]

In May 1977, Somoza's newspaper *Novedades* called upon the archbishop to clarify the Church's position with respect to the government and to take a stand against subversive elements. In response, the advisory council of the archdiocese defended the archbishop and described the national scene as one of "institutionalized violence." The continuous repression by Somoza's National Guard culminated in the burning and rampaging of Solentiname in November, the arrest of some of its members (including Fr. Ernesto Cardenal, current minister of culture) and the exile of others. Thus, by the end of 1977, Somoza's regime had been isolated and found it difficult to get legitimacy for its actions from the official Church. At the same time, having repulsed the overtures of the Sandinistas a few years before because their Marxist, anti-religious arguments had little appeal, the Church hierarchy began to look for possibilities of dialogue, if not collaboration, with the FSLN. After all, there had been a precedent for this dialogue when Archbishop Obando had mediated a conflict between the government of Somoza and the FSLN in December 1974. In that event, members of FSLN captured Somocista officials at a Christmas party and the Archbishop presented himself as a neutral go-between. Intentionally or not, the Church gained some credibility with the FSLN during those negotiations. Perhaps even more important was the effect of the FSLN's success (its ransom demands, including the broadcast and publication of a lengthy FSLN position paper, were met by the

---

12. Ibid., 168.
13. The best example of this dialogue and the eventual victory by the liberationists appears in Ernesto Cardenal's *The Gospel in Solentinume*, vols 1 and 2, (Maryknoll, New York: Orbis Books, 1978).

government, and several political prisoners, such as Daniel Ortega, were freed) on people in the Christian Communities. In short, while the breach between regime and church was increasing by early 1978, the surface picture of regime-church conflict obscured a still deeper division within the Church between a moderate hierarchy and the followers of liberation theology.

The Church in the Insurrection

The assassination of Pedro Joaquin Chamorro, editor of *La Prensa*, on 10 January 1978, was the turning point for the opposition to Somoza's regime. He was the unofficial leader of the moderate opposition to Somoza and a member of the Broad Opposition Front (FAO), which was the most potent non-Sandinista opposition group in Nicaragua. It was widely believed that Somoza was involved. The death of Chamorro resulted in the call by the Nicaraguan Chamber of Commerce for a general strike in Managua. Violence in the countryside also increased. In the Christian communities, many people felt that they were now called upon to live out the values of the gospel in a revolutionary situation. They concluded that "the Church was the only place people could speak the truth in Nicaragua."[14]

The efforts to radicalize the opposition and the Church were also directed at the farmers and peasants of the Nicaraguan countryside. The instrument of Catholic/FSLN cooperation here was the Association of Rural Workers. This was created in March 1978, and was useful in the struggle against Somoza by changing the homes of peasant members into places of refuge, storehouses for arms, and supply depots for the guerrilla army.[15]

The Association of Rural Workers was an outgrowth of the Committees of Agricultural Workers, which were formed in 1976 by the FSLN and Catholic activists. These committees were developed out of the Evangelical Committee for Agrarian Advancement (CEPA), which was created by the Jesuit Order in 1969 with the express purpose of training peasants leaders to organize politically their communities. Among the prominent Nicaraguans active in CEPA was Fernando Cardenal.[16] In the beginning this organization encouraged collective action by the peasants and emphasized the

---

14. Dodson and Montgomery, "The Churches in the Nicaraguan Revolution," 173.
15. Luis Serra, "The Sandinist Mass Organization," in Walker's *Nicaragua in Revolution*, 107.
16. U.S. Congress House, Subcommittee on International Organizations, 91st Congress, 2nd sess., 1976.

biblical justification for the ownership of property.

In time, because of increased suppression by Somoza, the liberationists in CEPA convinced most of the members that peasants could not improve their conditions without organized, collective political action. When this awareness took hold, it raised the level of theological reflection among people in the Church. In this manner, a number of Christians working in CEPA became sharply politicized and militantly anti-Somocista. Some members even became armed combatants with the FSLN. This type of activity led to a split between CEPA and the Church's hierarchy, and the former cut all its ties and becoming an independent Christian organization. The falling out also had to do with CEPA's active promotion of a Christian-Marxist dialogue. The effect of this particular suggestion was to place the important agricultural sector of Nicaragua in a position of radical opposition and rejection of moderate solutions to its problems.

Most of the liberationists' activity took place on a behind-the-scenes organizational level and did not surface until the actual shooting started. According to one observer, most of the clergy, especially at lower levels, had opted to support actively the Revolution. Whether or not the Revolution's supporters actually constituted a majority of the clergy is debatable, but certainly elements of the Church were active in providing aid and comfort to the guerrillas. Food and medicine, for example, were available in many churches across the country.[17] In at least one case, a small rural church was used as a drop-off and pick-up point for mail to the Sandinistas.[18]

Liberationists were also involved in the actual fighting. Two priests led troops in combat, one of them Father Gasper Garcia, a Jesuit from Spain, who was an active practitioner of liberation theology.[19] In churches and in church schools in such cities as Managua, Masaya, Esteli, and Jinotega, students, priests, pastors, and religious began to assume specific revolutionary tasks in preparation for the general uprising. They made bombs and stored arms; they accumulated supplies and taught courses in first aid; they cleaned and filled baptismal fonts in the Evangelical Churches with drinking water;

---

17. Wayne H. Cowen, "Nicaragua, the Revolution Takes Hold," *Christianity and Crisis*, 12 May 1980, 140.
18. U.S. Congress, House, Subcommittee in Foreign Operations of the Committee on Appropriations, *Foreign Assistance and Related Agencies' Appropriations for 1978*, 95th Congress, 1st. Sess. 1977, 518.
19. Cowen, "Nicaragua, the Revolution Takes Hold," 140.

they published news and organized a communications link for and with the Sandinistas.[20]

The effect of this extensive participation in the Sandinista Revolution, most of which was carried out by the proponents of liberation theology, was twofold. First, the appearance of priests and nuns at the side of, or even among the ranks of guerrilla fighters legitimized the Sandinistas to an extent unthinkable without their participation. Certainly the leadership of the FSLN recognized how helpful this collaboration would be. A Sandinista communique released from San Jose, Costa Rica, in October 1978 stated: "Our Catholic religion will be the cornerstone of our nationality."[21] Catholic participation in the Revolution was actively encouraged by the FSLN and there is a definite chronological coincidence between the increasing radicalization of the Church and the growth of the Sandinista movement.[22]

Even authors who sympathize with the aims of the Sandinista Revolution admit that it did not have much popular support until quite near the end of Somoza's reign. Richard Millet wrote as late as 1977 that the guerrillas "have continuing problems in gaining effective local support in their areas of operation."[23] Penny Lernoux added in congressional testimony that the guerrillas "have never enjoyed widespread support."[24] Given these observations and the coincidence mentioned above, it is reasonable to assume that Catholic collaboration was pivotal in broadening support for the FSLN.

The second effect of Catholic participation was to create enormous

---

20. Ibid., 141.
21. U.S. Congress, Senate, Subcommittee on Western Hemisphere Affairs of the Committee on Foreign Relations, *Latin America*, 95th Congress, 2nd sess. 1978, 34.
22. Dodson and Montgomery, "The Churches in the Nicaraguan Revolution," 163. An examination of the role of the Protestant Churches in the revolutionary process in Nicaragua reveals an extensive operation by these churches in support of FSLN. In the first place, ten to twelve percent of Nicaraguans are Protestant, an unusually high proportion for a Latin American country. In El Salvador, for example, Protestants make up less than four percent of the population. The December 1972 earthquake proved to be the turning point for the Protestant churches of Nicaragua. Four days after the earthquake, a Protestant doctor, Gustavo Parajon, issued a radio appeal for a meeting of Protestant pastors. Within three weeks, twenty denominations were participating in five different aid programs. All these programs were organized under the recently created Comite Evangelico Pro-Ayuda a los Damnificados (CEPAD—Protestant Committee for Assistance to the Dispossessed.) Three months after the earthquake CEPAD changed the last word of its name to "Development." By 1977, these Protestants were moving in a direction that would culminate less than two years later in strong support for the revolutionary process. Similar to the liberationists who used the churches for political purposes, on 8 September 1978, CEPAD decided to provide broad support to the FSLN both by turning their churches into refuge centers and through the clandestine provision of food and medicine to combatants.
23. Richard Millet, *Guardians of the Dynasty*, Maryknoll (New York: Orbis Books 1977), 163.
24. House Subcommittee on Foreign Operations, 551.

difficulties for Somoza. To the extent that members of the clergy were connected to the revolutionaries, to counter them forcibly was to appear to persecute the Church itself. Miguel D'Escoto, Maryknoll priest and current foreign minister, told a United States congressional panel in early 1977 that vicious National Guard reprisals had taken place against the churches of Zelaya. Twenty-six churches in this department were allegedly used as barracks and torture chambers by the Guard. In addition, the words "Christian community," used to describe CEBs, were banned as communist propaganda.[25] D'Escoto was careful to portray these activities as persecution. Bishop Obando also complained of heavy-handedness in a May 1976 letter to Somoza outlining incidents of censorship of church publications.[26]

An insurrection with the approval of the lower level clergy, as serious as this was, might have been manageable if ecclesiastic support had been limited to the lower levels. As it was, however, Somoza also had to deal with the opposition of the Catholic hierarchy. The connection between the bishops and the government was always uneasy, but it took a decidedly unfriendly turn in 1968 with the arrival of Obando y Bravo. Besides refusing to endorse the 1972 constituent assembly elections, he also refused to attend the ceremony transfering power to the interim triumvirate. The episcopate was by this point already displeased with Somoza for extending his term earlier in the decade.[27]

The split widened with the earthquake in 1972. Somoza invited Obando to join an emergency committee to oversee relief operations, but Obando refused. The hierarchy also complained that relief supplies were distributed through voting precincts rather than through parish churches. These tensions were exacerbated when Obando y Bravo worked out the release of Somoza officials captured at a Christmas party in December 1974 by the Sandinistas.

It is clear, therefore, that the bishops had long-standing grievances against Somoza before they helped make the FSLN "important." As Chomorro said in his last interview, "Somoza lost the Church a long time ago."[28] The effect of liberation theology, once again, was to make this opposition progress from moderate to radical. The complaints about corruption and misuse of earthquake relief could have been made by any Catholic bishop. Only one that subscribed to liberation theology, however, could justify a revolutionary uprising,

---

25. Ibid., 554-546.
26. U.S. Congress House, Subcommittee on International Organizations, 91st. Congress, 2nd sess., 1976
27. Millet, *Guardians of the Dynasty*, 236.
28. *New York Times*, 13 January 1978.

as endorsed in a later pastoral letter.

The effect of this and similar hierarchical pronouncements was to legitimize even further the radical opposition to Somoza. When the Bishops called for Somoza's resignation and "a completely new socio-economic order" in August 1978, their letter got the support of major business associations and effectively undermined any moderate solution to the conflict. In other words, while the Church continuously criticized Somoza, it did not take a political position different from the liberationists who were calling for the support of FSLN. Despite this, as events have recently indicated, Archbishop Obando never felt supportive of the FSLN's radical ideology and participation by the priests in government.[29]

It is impossible to underestimate the importance of the church in Nicaragua. In fact, one of the few areas in which Somoza and the Sandinistas are in total agreement is the importance of a radicalized church to the success of the revolution. Daniel Ortega has said that "the best arguments the Sandinistas had in urging people to take up revolutionary struggle were Christian arguments."[30] Miguel D'Escoto described the Catholic Church as one of four pillars of support on which Somoza rested, the other three being the local oligarchy, the United States, and the National Guard.[31] By June 1979, a month before the takeover, Somoza was left with only the seventy-five hundred man National Guard, his last pillar.

The Church After Victory

The presence of representatives of the Roman Catholic Church in the Sandinista Revolution made this revolution seem more moderate and legitimate in the eyes of not just Nicaraguans and Latin Americans but also the United States. The hope among many people was that the Church would serve to restrain the more radical revolutionaries. The Sandinista government itself took a keen interest in the role of the Church and invited church support in a variety of ways. However, below the surface there were deep seated fears and divisions within the Church over how and to what degree Christians should participate in the Sandinista Revolution. There

---

29. "In post-revolutionary Nicaragua the Church still faces the issue of survival. The differences put aside in the face of the common enemy have surfaced and there are divisions between the government and the Church, and between the two churches, "iglesia popular," and the traditional church." Eric Selbin, "The Changing Church in Latin America: Nicaragua's Christian Revolution," a paper presented at the 1984 Southwest Social Science Association Meetings, Fort Worth, Texas, 24-27 March, 1984, 18.
30. Dodson and Montgomery, "The Churches in the Nicaraguan Revolution," 170.
31. Ibid., 171.

appeared to be two pervasive fears among church people who did not wholeheartedly support the revolution. First, they recalled the example of Cuba, where the Church had refused to accept the revolution, became anti-revolutionary, and, as a result, suffered a decline of influence and persecution. The traditionalists in Nicaragua did not want to "blow the opportunity" in this sense and be pushed to the sidelines in the Nicaraguan revolution. On the other hand, they did not want to politicize the Church to such a degree that it would begin to lose its own spiritual identity and independence. There were also those democratic elements who supported the revolution, but who were profoundly anti-communist and concerned that Nicaragua would become a second Cuba. Therefore, the Church's position seemed even more complicated and sensitive than before the revolution.

One of the more notable features of the Sandinistas' government has been the presence of a large number of liberationists in government positions (Ernesto Cardenal, minister of culture, and Miguel D'Escoto, a Maryknoll missionary and current foreign minister). Numerous priests and nuns have also been working in social welfare ministries and the agrarian reform institute. There are several areas in which their influence has been quite visible. The most important of these has been the nationwide literacy campaign. This effort has been headed by Fernando Cardenal, whose experience in indoctrinating school children has been going on for years. As was mentioned earlier, he was one of the first liberationists to have formed the CEBs in Nicaragua.[32]

However, a major controversy that has split the Nicaraguan Church is the presence of five Catholic priests in the highest levels of the Sandinistas' government. D'Escoto, the Cardenal brothers, Edgar Paralles (minister of social welfare), and Alvaro Arguello, S.J. (council of state), have all been ordered to resign their political posts by the Bishops' conference.[33] The Episcopate has the full support of the pope in asserting its authority. A pastoral letter from the pope in August 1982 told priests that "it is not through a political role, but through the priestly ministry that the people wish to have them near."[34] Finally, during his visit to Nicaragua, the pope explicitly ordered Cardenal to "straighten out" his relation with the Church. Yet, in spite of orders from the pope and from the bishops, the

---

32. In the beginning, the official Catholic Church and the popular organizations connected to it provided much of the logistical support for the Sandinista's literary campaign. But the insistence on de-emphasizing the spiritual aspect of education was perceived as harmful to the Church's interests.
33. *New York Times*, 10 December 1980.
34. Ibid., 21 August 1983.

five have, as of this writing, refused to step down. In fact, in mid-June 1981, four of the five (Arguello excluded) declared an "unbreakable commitment to the popular Sandinista revolution . . . . We will continue in whatever place our presence and service might be necessary."[35]

If and how these dissidents will be disciplined remains to be seen. They may be forbidden from functioning as priests. This will no doubt hurt their credibility with many Catholics, but they will also attract significant personal followings. The grave danger this would pose to Nicaraguan Catholicism may explain the Church's caution in meting out a punishment. How such a ban would affect their political role really depends on how one views what that role has been so far. These priests in the government have so far failed to demonstrate any significant role that is clearly related to their priestly function. Consequently, it is difficult to foresee much of a change, especially in the light of this statement by Fernando Cardenal: "There will be no criticism of the revolution in the name of Christianity."[36]

Two other incidents in the second and third years of the revolution strained relations to the breaking point. These took place in August 1982. The 9 August edition of *La Prensa* planned to run a story about a pastoral letter sent by the pope to the Nicaraguan Bishops. The letter, which condemned involvement of the Church in the politics of radicalization and class struggle and called for unity and cohesion within the Church, was read to cheering congregations at a mass on 8 August. When the editors of *La Prensa* attempted to publish the letter and an article about the reaction to it, both were forbidden by the government censors. After an angry call by the archbishop, the letter (but not the article) was published a few days later.[37]

The second incident involved Rev. Bismark Carballo, spokesman for Archbishop Obando. He was interrupted by government troops while paying a pastoral call on a parishioner, forced at gunpoint to undress, and chased into the street, where photographers for government newspapers were waiting. Pictures of the nude priest appeared along with the suggestion that he had been caught in an intimate encounter.[38] Catholic students in Nicaragua reacted violently to what they called "systematic criticism and lack of respect for the Catholic Church leadership such as our priests," by taking over Catholic schools in Managua, Leon, Matagalpa, and Masaya. In Masaya, three people were killed in clashes with police.[39]

35. "No Nicaragua," *Time*, 22 June 1981, 68.
36. Senate Foreign Relations Committee. Document #32012, 1979, 93.
37. *Philadelphia Inquirer*, 11 August 1982.
38. *New York Times*, 21 August 1982.
39. *Philadelphia Inquirer*, 18 August 1982.

Having lost the support of the Catholic Church, the Sandinistas have increasingly emphasized and supported a "parallel" church called *iglesia popular* (People's Church). It is largely comprised of liberationists who have made a total commitment to support Sandinista policies. In his 29 June 1982 letter to Nicaraguan bishops, the pope charged that the *iglesia popular* pretends to the role of "parallel church," which by definition challenges the authority of the Nicaraguan hierarchy and of Rome itself. In response to this letter, the Sandinistas, along with their liberationist allies, arranged a sort of "welcome" for the pope during his visit to Nicaragua in March 1983.[40]

To summarize the involvement of the Catholic Church in Nicaraguan politics, it can be said that church-state relations have centered around four themes:

First, the emergence of liberation theology in the mid 1960s coincided in Nicaragua with the deepening of anti-Somoza sentiment, especially after the 1972 earthquake. The liberationists' objective of radicalizing the Church coincided with the growing strength and popular acceptance of the FSLN.

Second, while some of its key leaders were Marxist, the FSLN's ideology was not, on the whole, opposed to liberation theology; indeed, it accepted and even encouraged Christian participation in the Revolution.

Third, even though the Catholic Church hierarchy became anti-Somocista, or at least was perceived that way by the people, it was never pro-Sandinista. It played its traditional role of a mediator between the FSLN and Somoza, thus gaining credibility in the eyes of the people. After the revolution, the Church has maintained its traditional role of not becoming involved in Sandinistas' politics and has criticized the liberation theologians for their involvement in the government.

Finally, since politics is a crucial field of action, the political forces have impinged powerfully on the Catholic Church, shaping the challenges the Church faces and the constraints and opportunities within which the Church must work. Thus, the problems and possibilities of the Catholic Church in Nicaragua now differ sharply from those of earlier years.

Revolution and the Church in El Salvador

In Nicaragua, the divisions in the Catholic Church were more

---

40. In that visit, the supporters of the "People's Church" interrupted his mass by chanting pro-Sandinista slogans.

political than theological, without underestimating the significance of the latter. There were three factions in the Catholic Church: one supported Somoza until the end; one was anti-Somoza but not pro-FSLN; and the third was pro-FSLN. In El Salvador, there are also roughly three divisions in the Church. The first group emphasizes a traditionalistic, preconciliar theology that considers the values of tradition, the institutional and sacral aspect of the Church and hierarchical authority, important. The second group emphasizes a more democratic, popular theology concerned with a liberation process that is closer to the Christian Democrats' vision of a system that is neither capitalism nor Marxism. The third group emphasizes the liberation theology perception of incorporating Marxist categories and methodology. This orientation is very similar to the pro-FSLN faction in the Nicaraguan Catholic Church.

According to Jose Victor Guillen, a liberation theologian, the Church's political role began around 1964 when some priests, according to Vatican II's instructions, formed the first CEBs in El Salvador. They would meet monthly to share "experiences" and establish pastoral objectives. Guillen goes on to say that these activities had complete support from the then archbishop of San Salvador, Luis Chaves y Gonzalez.[41] Another priest, who was murdered in 1977, emphasized the importance of CEBs in transforming existing socio-political conditions. In a homily before his death, he stated that "much of our traditional faith must be purified by a new reading of the Gospel .... It is a process that celebrates life, the life we live out daily in our villages, at work, in the defense of human rights and in the struggle to organize."[42]

Three of the four members of the present Salvadoran hierarchy and a minority of priests generally adhere to a traditionalistic view of the Church's role in society. This traditionalist view is in accordance with the Catholic social doctrine dating generally from Pope Leo XIII's encyclical, *Rerum Novarum* in 1891. Included in this group are Bishops Jose Eduardo Alvarez (San Miguel Province), Pedro Arnauldo Aparicio (San Vicente), and Marco Ren Revello (Santa Ana).

The remaining bishop, Monsignor Arturo Rivera Damas, who was named archbishop of San Salvador in March 1983, accepted and promoted the positions of Vatican II and Medellin from the beginning. After all, Rivera had been the first choice of the progressive sector to succeed the aged Luis Chaves back in 1977. As it turned out, however, Rivera's political understanding of the situation in

---

41. *Latin American Press*, 15 (March 1983)
42. Ibid., 15 (20 October 1983)

El Salvador, along with his cooperation with the Vatican, could not accommodate those subscribing to liberation theology. Archbishop Rivera's position will be discussed more comprehensively later.

The second group in the Salvadoran Catholic Church emphasizes a form of popular theology that is more in line with the Christian Democrats' perception of "evolutionary" change. Liberation, it is emphasized, can only be achieved through non-violent, gradual change in the socio-political structure. They support such initiatives as land reform, elections, demilitarization of the political system, and negotiations with the leftist forces. Within this group, however, there are variations of center, center-left, and left positions. Archbishop Romero represented the latter position, whereas Rivera Damas and the previous archbishop of San Salvador, Gregorio Rosa Chavez, are more supportive of a center-left position.

Finally, the third group is supportive of liberation theology and has been operating within the CEBs. While Rivera Damas has been trying to maintain a coherent and principled position in the midst of the chaotic Salvadoran politics, this group has been working directly with the FDR (Democratic Revolutionary Front) and the FMLN (Farabundi Marti Front for National Liberation). The Jesuit Father, Rutilio Grande was once a major figure in this group. He, along with his associates, was convinced of the need for a revolution through the process of *"concientization."* Father Grande taught the peasants that they should not accept "their lot on earth because their reward will come in the hereafter," rather, they must begin to relate the gospel message to their own "situation of misery and injustice."

The Traditionalist Perspective

Of all the members of the present Salvadoran hierarchy that generally adhere to an institutional, sacramental view of the Church's role in society, Monsignor Pedro Arnauldo Aparicio from San Vicento has been the most prominent. His views regarding an appropriate role for the Church have often been misunderstood since he has denounced government repression on many occasions, but has not sided with either of the two groups mentioned above. Thus, for one scholar, Aparicio appeared to be "edging toward a centrist position, but the illusion was shortlived."[43] However, Aparicio's

---

43. Tommie S. Montgomery, "The Church in the Salvadoran Revolution," *Latin American Perspective*, 10 (Winter 1983):68.

traditionalistic perception must be seen within the framework of Pope John Paul's perception of the crisis in El Salvador.

Monsignor Pedro A. Aparicio represents a Salvadoran brand of traditionalism within the Church. He is the founder and organizer of a nationwide fraternity of *Caballero de Cristo Rey* (Knights of Christ the King), in which, as in similar *Cristero* movements in other countries, *campesionos* and poorly-educated men from small towns are brought together in militant allegiance to the traditional Church and opposition to communism. As early as 1963, its monthly publication had a circulation of ten thousand. However, as the situation in El Salvador deteriorated and repression of the Church increased, the traditionalists began to sense the deepening of divisions within the Church.[44] The political atmosphere in El Salvador put the traditionalists in an awkward position. Either they had to compromise their "neutral" stance and declare total support for the regime's policies or they had to identify with the opponents of the regime in the Church.

The collective documents issued by the Church, and pastoral letters of Luis Chavez Gonzales, the archbishop of San Salvador before Romero, indicate that the traditionalists placed during the 1970s a greater stress on deploring the situation of injustice in El Salvador. Monsignor Aparicio was the leader in encouraging a change in the traditionalists' attitude. In a pastoral letter signed by Aparicio, Romero, Auxiliary Bishop Rene Revello, and the secretary general of CEDES, the following demands were made:

1. "Let every type of violence cease, on the part of social groups, paramilitary organizations, Security Police and Army.

2. Let there be security guarantee for life and property for all citizens, including those who are imprisoned for political reasons or hiding for fear of reprisal, so that all may be reincorporated into public life.

3. Let there be a stop to every kind of torture to obtain extrajudicial confessions.

4. Let there be an end to persecution and arbitrary explusions of citizens, foreign or national priests. In the case of priests there should be dialogue between military and ecclesiastical authorities.

5. In the exceptional circumstances of a state of siege, there must be strict adherence to legality with no abuse of power.

6. Let there be no further transgression of basic human rights as mentioned above."[45]

Such a position, taken by Monsignor Aparicio, underlies two important factors. First, it is indicative of the division within the traditionalists themselves who differ on interpreting Catholic social

---

44. Alaster White, *El Salvador* (Washington, D.C.: Praeger Publishers, 1973), 210.
45. The letter was translated and published in *LADOC: Bi-monthly Publication of Latin American Documentation*, 7 (July-August 1977):29-30.

doctrine. However, Aparicio's interpretation has been reinforced by Pope John Paul II. Upon his visit to El Salvador, in addressing the clergy, the pope said: "Remember my dear brothers that, as I already told priests and other religious personnel in Mexico, you are not social or political leaders or officials of a temporal power ... The priest must be a man of dialogue. In his position as a mediator, he must bravely run the risks of making himself a bridge between groups of different persuasions, (promoting) concord and seeking fair solutions in difficult situations."[46] Obviously, other traditionalists like Jose Eduardo Alvarez, bishop of San Miguel, have opted for a conservative position. He is a military bishop with the rank of colonel in the Salvadoran army. In response to a letter sent by a group of sixteen priests who work in Panama, asking him to "resign" from his rank of colonel and "make a deep examination of conscience in the light of the gospel, and the Second Vatican Council," Bishop Alvarez rejected their assertion that he is not acting according to the orders and wishes of Pope John Paul II.[47] However, it is clear from the pope's statement to the clergy in El Salvador that, as much as he disagrees with the liberationists, he does not approve of those traditionalists who act as "social and political leaders, or officials of a temporal power."

The second factor in understanding the traditionalists in El Salvador is related to the polarization of Salvadoran society as a whole, specifically, the impact of the October 1979 coup by reformist junior officers, and the civilian government established by the Christian Democrats. Scholars such as T. S. Montgomery are puzzled by the fact that a traditionalist like Aparicio can be a signatory to the document mentioned above, and yet be supportive of the existing Christian Democratic regime. It is the perception of the traditionalists as supporters of the status quo (perpetuated by people like Bishop Alvarez), and the reluctance of the liberationists to accept anything less than a complete politicization of theology, that has made those traditionalists like Aparicio subject to misunderstanding. Furthermore, the emergence of charismatic figures like Romero has complicated the traditionalists' task of achieving a gradual transformation of their image. Following the assassination of Romero, Archbishop Rivera Damas has been aware of the difficulties faced by the traditionalists. Nevertheless, the ghost of Romero's "popular theology" continues to reemerge amid the increasing polarization of the country.

---

46. *Foreign Broadcasting Information Service* (FBIS), Latin America, 7 March 1983.
47. *LADOC* 11 (September-October 1980):53-4.

"Popular Theology" Perspective

"It is alarming to see how the country's political and economic crisis has rapidly worsened. A conflict is going on between the government and the popular organizations that has affected every sector of the population and even some foreign diplomats. It has cost many people their lives."[48] In his last days, Archbishop Romero had developed a reputation for "standing up to the authorities." As the quotation indicates, this statement is not far from the truth. Before being appointed archbishop of San Salvador, Monsignor Oscar Romero was the bishop of Santiage de Maria. When the papal nuncio, Archbishop Emmanuele Gerada, asked various church and state officials whom they preferred, the choice was Romero. However, the old archbishop, priests, religious, and laity hoped that Arturo Rivera Damas, the auxiliary bishop since 1960, would be chosen. But Rivera had too many enemies going back to the mid-sixties when the traditionalists accused him (erroneously) of ghosting Archbishop Chavez' pastoral letters. In 1970, Rivera had confronted Defense Minister Torres over the abduction of José Alas. On the other hand, Romero was considered to be quiet and noncontroversial. Leftist guerrillas, along with the liberationists, considered him a "priest of the oligarchy" and were extremely worried that he would halt or even try to reverse the process of liberation theology. A series of developments radicalized Romero to the point of advocating liberation theology but refraining from an open justification for violence.

The day before Romero was installed as archbishop, a liberationist by the name of Father Rafael Barahona was arrested and tortured. The day after his installation Romero went to the Casa Presidencial and requested the release of the priest. President Molina's response was: "I will release Barahona but you cannot ask us to treat them any differently until they go back to their basic business which is religion. These priests of yours," Molina continued, "have become politicians, and I hold you responsible for their behavior." Romero looked Molina straight in the eye and said, "With all due respect Mr. President, we take orders from someone higher."[49]

Three weeks later Father Rutilio Grande was assassinated, an act that outraged Romero. In an interview three months before his death, Romero rejected the notion that he had been "converted."

I have always tried to be faithful to my vocation, my priesthood. My fidelity to the Church's orientations has always been the rule of my priesthood . . . Many

---

48. Ibid., 10 (September-October 1979):8.
49. Quoted in T. S. Montgomery, "The Church in the Salvadoran Revolution" 76.

had the idea that I was conservative, that I would maintain relations with the government, with the rich, and that I would ignore the people's problems, the repression, the poverty. I found here many committed clergy and communities that thought a lot about the situation in the country . . . . Father Grande's death and the death of other priests after his impelled me to take an energetic attitude before the government . . . .[50]

At the same time, Romero found it difficult to ignore the traditionalists' influence within the Church. His support for CEBs and other revolutionary organizations such as the Christian Federation of Salvadoran Peasants did not have the support of the traditionalists. In an article in *El Mundo*, Aparicio, Revelo, Alvarez, and Freddy Delgado (secretary general of the Episcopal Conference) attacked Christian Federation of Salvadoran Peasants and CEBs as "Marxist oriented" and aligned with the guerrilla organizations. They stated their position quite clearly: "Does the Church accept class struggle and bloody revolution? Does she accept historical materialism and the consequent atheism? Can we live our faith in a Marxist praxis?"[51]

Sensing the buildup of a potential confrontation between the liberationists and the traditionalists, Archbishop Romero and Bishop Rivera Damas issued a communique intended to reduce tensions and declare an alternative position. In a communique issued from the Social Communications Secretariat of San Salvador, Romero and Rivera outlined a compromise by acknowledging the importance of pastoral activities (for the traditionalists) along with the need for a new religio-political direction. But Romero's bias toward the liberationists was clear in point seven of the communique: "Faith and politics, while maintaining their own identification, must be united in the Christian who has a political vocation. Faith should inspire the political action of the Christian but without substituting what is typical of faith and Christian justice."[52]

During Oscar Romero's three years and one month as archbishop, the role of the Church in the political life of the country expanded with each succeeding crisis. At the same time, Romero's own ideology, reacting to various crisis, was evolving toward a more radical, leftist orientation. The first phase of this radicalization occurred after the Aguilars incident (Rutilio Grande's murder) in which two Jesuit priests were killed by a right-wing death squad. The second period started after 13 August 1979, when the Bishops appointed by Romero withdrew from national dialogue with the military regime. Two weeks

---

50. Ibid., 77.
51. *LADOC*, 9 (May-June 1979):2.
52. Ibid., 10.

later, Archbishop Romero denounced the government and called on its officials to resign. The government responded by labeling Romero as a "leftist." The escalation of tensions between Archbishop Romero and the military regime no doubt had a profound impact on the decision of junior officers to overthrow the government in October 1979.

Following the October 1979 coup, it seemed that Romero was optimistic regarding the intentions of the junta. In a speech on 17 October 1979, he encouraged the junta to undertake revolutionary initiatives to alleviate El Salvador's problems, and called their military insurrection "legitimate."[53] Furthermore, Romero went on to criticize both leftist and rightist factions. The guerrillas, fearing a change in the attitude of the Church, mounted an attack on Monsignor Aparicio's church, holding him hostage. Archbishop Romero reacted by excommunicating those responsible for the attack.

Romero's optimism was short-lived. Divisions, indecisiveness, and conflict within the junta, coupled with an increase in the activities of right wing groups, convinced Romero that the new government was unable to carry through with its promises. "Is there no longer any hope? What will happen to Agrarian Reform process already begun? Will the new Cabinet continue to carry it out? Will the new Minister of Agriculture make it his primary objective? Or will he be frightened by the threats as when they machine-gunned the home of Dom Enrique Alvarez, the ex-minister?"[54]

The radicalization of Romero is confirmed by his supporters, who, on the third anniversary of his assassination, issued a communique from Mexico. In their statement, they pointed to "many conversions" in Romero's lifetime, but his conversion to the gospel's "preferential option for the poor," and to the belief that "the Church can not simplistically declare that it condemns all forms of violence," is emphasized as the most important development in Romero's ideology.[55] Therefore, it is clear that Archbishop Romero has had a great impact and was the first figure in El Salvador's (and for that matter in Latin America's) Roman Catholic Church to steer the traditionalist, conservative hierarchy of the Church toward a leftist "popular theology." He had said that his "death, if acceptable to God, will be for the liberation of my people," and a "testimony of hope in the future."[56]

The assassination of Archbishop Romero during a mass on 24

---

53. *FBIS*, Latin America, October 17, 23, 1979.
54. *LADOC* 10 (May-June 1980).
55. Ibid., 13 (May-June 1983):40.
56. Ibid.

March 1980 was shocking, but not the end of "popular theology." The nomination of Arturo Rivera Damas as apostolic administrator following the murder of Romero was greeted with joy and relief throughout progressive sectors of the Catholic Church. Rivera, after all, had been the first choice of this sector to succeed the aged Luis Chavez in 1977. Rivera began with a pledge to continue in the pastoral line of Romero and for a time it appeared that he would indeed do so. Just as everyone had thought Archbishop Romero to be a noncontroversial, neutral man, the prevailing perceptions of Rivera (advocated by Romero's supporters) had portrayed him as a revolutionary committed to radical "popular theology."

Rivera, a Salesian priest, was born in the farm town of San Esteban Catarina, and was the bishop of a tranquil parish in Santiago de Maria. Romero had called Rivera Damas "my best friend" a week before he was assassinated. Indeed, Rivera was the only supporter the archbishop had among the five bishops. But Rivera inherited a Church in chaos, decisively influential among the masses but suspected by government and deeply divided between the traditionalists, "popular theology" supporters, and the liberationists who were actively siding with the guerrilla forces. At the same time, the same elements within the Church insisted that El Salvador had a moderate, reformist government different from the one Romero had to face, and wanted Rivera to modify the increasingly radical position undertaken by the Church under Romero.

In early 1980, it was clear from listening to Romero's homilies Sunday after Sunday that he was moving toward a position of ultimately supporting the cause of violent uprising. As previously noted, this was the position of the archbishop of Managua, Miguel Obando y Bravo, who came to the support of the FSLN prior to the takeover. The reasoning in both cases (although with Romero's line, the change in position was much more radical) was that there was a general consensus among the people that the existing government no longer had the confidence and faith of the population, and that the evil confronting the people was greater than the evil of insurrection and war.

As the months passed, it became clear that the public pronouncements of Archbishop Rivera between April 1980 and March 1983 regarding the character of a resolution of the political conflict in El Salvador mirrored his reluctance to take sides with any of the forces in the country. Neither the government nor the guerrilla forces seem to have had extensive support. "In those years that Romero lived, there was hope in the liberation movements. There was a great sympathy on the part of the people. Later these movements were losing credibility and popular support. I do not think they lost it only because of government repression. They've lost this support because the people saw that they tended toward the conquest of power for its own sake and not toward satisfying the hopes of the people."[57]

The subject of elections reflected yet another change in the position of the Church under Rivera. After the failure of the January 1981 offensive by the guerrillas, the government proposed elections for early 1982. The Salvadoran Episcopal Conference issued an appeal to Salvadorans asking them "to participate in force during the 28 March elections in search of peace and social harmony . . . We urge those who are responsible for creating the necessary conditions for elections to allow the participation of all Salvadorans in the electoral campaign."[58] At the same time, however, Rivera warned that elections would be meaningless if the government continued to escalate the military conflict in the country.

By declaring support for the elections, Archbishop Rivera did not abandon his quest of seeking a political solution. As a matter of fact, by stating his support for the elections, he managed to enhance the Church's credibility and its determination to achieve a peaceful solution for El Salvador. Furthermore, he brought about a consensus among the traditionalists in the Church by pressuring both the guerrilla forces and the government to de-escalate the military confrontation. He also managed to gain confidence from the Vatican by showing that the Church was actively involved in attempting to mediate between the warring factions. He outlined the objectives of the Church quite clearly:

1) "That a cease fire be declared, along with an end to mutual harassment and threats. 2) That both sides respect the civilian population, giving them the free choice to remain in the area or to leave, 3) That the repression on the part of the paramilitary forces be stopped; in a state governed by law, which is what we all desire and which is what the high command of the Armed Forces itself wishes to constitute, all military forces and smiliar groups must be under control, 4) That in its 'mopping up' operations, the armed forces proceed with professionalism, using only necessary means, 5) That the International Red Cross and other institutions be given permission, with duly authorized safe conduct passes, to rescue many of the people and to bring them necessary food and medicine."[59]

By early 1983, it had become clear that Rivera's "popular theology" was different from Romero's. First, Rivera seems to have been more concerned about the divisions in the Church and the tremendous decrease in the number of priests, religious, and catechists. Many

---

57. Quoted in T. S. Montgomery, "The Church in the Salvadoran Revolution" 83.
58. *FBIS*, 2 March 1983.
59. *LADOC* 13 (January-February 1982):30

members of the lower clergy opted for political functions at the cost of abandoning the pastoral line. Rivera wanted to bring about a synthesis that gave equal concern to both pastoral and political functions. Romero, on the other hand, leaned more toward strengthening the liberationists' argument about the "legitimate right to insurrectional violence." Archbishop Rivera's position was more cautious, and he had the mental clarity to see with objectivity the present situation in the country. Second, Rivera's relation with the Vatican and his pragmatic approach helped to bring about a different, more conscious attitude by the traditionalists.

The Liberationists' Perspective

While Bishop Rivera Damas has sought to maintain a coherent and principled position in the morass of Salvadoran politics, many priests and nuns have worked directly with the FDR/FMLN forces. They are the supporters of liberation theology, a new doctrine that challenges the Church's traditional position. The price that liberationists have paid for their efforts to politicize Catholicism in El Salvador has been very high. Father Nicolas Rodriguez, a liberationist, was kidnapped on 2 January 1972 while attempting to form CEBs in El Salvador. His dismembered body was found several days later. Bishop Rivera has said that at that time the Church accepted the government explanation that Rodriguez's death was the work of unknown assailants. By mid-1975, the liberationists operating in Aguilares were being called "subversive" by various pro-government groups. In late December 1975, President Molina made public statements against what he termed "liberationist clerics."[60] In the meantime, Father Rafael Barahona, diocesan priest from San Vicente, was taken into custody for the first time. There, he was beaten as his assailants, according to Father Barahona, "used profanity to insult me as a priest." Barahona's bishop, Monsignor Aparicio, was outraged. "The torturer who clamored for excommunication now has it," Aparicio wrote the national government. In one of his defenses of the pastoral work of his priests, Aparicio inquired if "the constitution of El Salvador has two interpretations; one for the authorities and the other for the people? We would like a response, if it would not annoy you, Honorable Authorities, so as not to teach our students a mistaken lesson."[61] In 1976, five priests, along with eighteen others, including two Jesuits from the Central

---

60. Penny Lernoux, *Cry of the People* (New York: Doubleday Press, 1980), 68.
61. Ibid., *Cry of the People* 73.

American University, were expelled for "inciting the people to revolt." Finally, the climate was such that by May 1977, flyers urging Salvadorans to eliminate liberationist priests were circulated in San Salvador.

Certain elements in Salvadoran society took the call seriously. Father Rutilio Grande was assassinated along with his companions. Three other Jesuits who were working with him were expelled. These murders have continued and many are perplexed as to the reasons for murdering priests. One reason that is accepted by both proponents and opponents of liberation theology centers on the nature of political involvement by these priests. Similar to their comrades in Nicaragua, the liberationists in El Salvador believe in the implementation of doctrines that emerged from the Second Vatican Council and from the Medellin Conference.

The liberationists believe that pastoral activity in Latin America cannot be discussed without mentioning the CEBs. The liberationists believe that the CEBs are the church itself, that universal sacrament of salvation that carries on the mission of Christ. They derive their concepts from the Medellin Conference's publication, *The Conclusions*. In response to charges that CEBs are attempting to create a revolutionary atmosphere, the Salvadoran liberationists reply that they do not see any incompatibility in advocating revolutionary uprisings and the desire to be faithful to the kingdom of God. Accordingly, they proclaim the plan of salvation "as it is expressed in the words of God: Misery, hunger and injustice *do not come from God*, but from men of *ill will*, who go against God's plan." The Salvadoran liberationists called on the archbishop of San Salvador on 11 December 1976, to raise "the consciousness of the church in order to defend the people who are struggling for their liberation."[62]

In order to expand their activities and influence within the Church, more than three hundred liberationist priests and religious sent a letter on 7 March 1978, to Archbishop Emmanuele Gerada, the papal nuncio to El Salvador and Guatemala, rebuking him for "support of the repressive Carlos Humberto Romero government and powerful business." They also accused him of siding with Cardinal Casariego (Guatemala) and Bishop Alvarez, against Archbishop Romero. "We ask God that the blood of our martyrs may enlighten you so that you do not go on fighting against light and truth like Herod and Pilate."[63]

---

62. Clergy Coordinating Commission, "Salvadoran Priests Defend Ministry Among Peasants," text in *LADOC*. 7 (March-April 1977):24.
63. Ibid., 9 (November-December 1978):48.

In response to these statements by the liberationists, Archbishop Romero attempted to reduce tensions by acknowledging the legitimacy of the liberationists demands, but he did not go so far as to criticize them for their attack on the papal nuncio. Romero only questioned their reasoning for the need of violence. "As long as there is no social and political climate which permits the peasants to present their urgent needs and just demands, disturbing outbreaks will unfortunately increase . . . . But the Church believes in peace."[64]

According to the liberationists, the root of the problem is that the Church in El Salvador is not demanding change in the socio-economic structure of the country. There are persons who do not wish these nor any changes; others who tolerate changes but do not arrive at the root causes of the situation. The liberationists maintain that they have been frustrated and continuously ignored by the heirarchy because the latter refuses to follow or abide by the principles of the Vatican II and Medellin. One of the most outspoken supporters of liberation theology, Father Rutilio Grande, stated that "the real issue facing us today is how to be authentic Christians in our country."

The Sandinistas' victory in Nicaragua has both strengthened and weakened the liberationists' argument that to be an authentic Christian means to fight against oppression and tyranny by whatever means available. Institutionalized violence can not be challenged peacefully. The Nicaraguan Committee of Solidarity with El Salvador states that they "recognize that the struggle of the Salvadoran people represents a legitimate defense against power that has killed the poor, the peasants, and those who do not have nor have ever had either homes or bread . . . As Christians, we cannot be indifferent and must realize the necessity of violent uprising when all peaceful means have been exhausted."[65] As far as post-revolutionary Nicaragua is concerned, however, many Salvadorans fear the same treatment of their Catholic Church if the guerrilla forces take power in El Salvador.

Conclusions

While a more extensive study of the role of the churches in the Nicaraguan and Salvadoran revolutions must await a definitive resolution of the conflict in El Salvador, there are several observations that may be made based on the above discussion. The points may be summarized as follows:

---

64. Ibid., 48.
65. Ibid., 12 (November-December 1981):53.

THE CHURCH IN NICARAGUA AND EL SALVADOR

1. The Catholic Churches in Nicaragua and El Salvador have been an extremely important variable in the revolutionary struggle. For Nicaragua, it represents the first time in Latin American history that a significant part of the Catholic Church has been involved in support of a revolutionary process. The Salvadoran Church, especially during Archbishop Romero's time, became extensively involved in supporting a Nicaraguan-type revolution in El Salvador.

2. The rapid growth of the left in El Salvador cannot be explained without taking into account the role of the liberationists who are organizing and "concienticizing" the people in the CEBs.

3. The liberationists in Nicaragua have managed to influence the political process by placing leaders in top levels, four priests serving as ministers of state since the triumph. In El Salvador, however, (even though a different situation) the liberationists have not been able to penetrate the church's hierarchy.

4. The role of the traditionalists has been different in the two countries. In Nicaragua, Archbishop Miguel Obando y Bravo played a mediating role between FSLN and Somoza. It is clear that the masses the archbishop held after the Sandinistas' victory were not to celebrate the victory of the Sandinistas, but the victory of the people, and more emphatically, the fall of Somoza. In El Salvador, the traditionalists (with the exception of Monsignor Aparicio) have not been conciliatory and are not willing to compromise.

5. With the death of Archbishop Romero, the divisions that were a virtual rupture within the Church began to heal. His successor, Archbishop Rivera, has taken a moderate position, and thus has increased the credibility of the Church as a non-partisan institution.

6. Given the involvement of liberationists in the revolutionary process of each country, it is reasonable to assume that in El Salvador, there cannot be a Nicaraguan-type revolution unless the official Church under the leadership of Archbishop Rivera would support the guerrillas' coalition.

7. In both countries (more in the case of Nicaragua), popular alienation sprang from a perception of suffering not only at the hands of domestic rulers, but also of a foreign power (the United States), popularly perceived to sustain a despised regime in power as a means of dominating the whole society. Churches in both Nicaragua and El Salvador have been extremely critical of the United States.

8. Finally, this examination of the Church and the socio-political change in these two Central American countries suggests one more observation. Historically, the Catholic Church in Latin America has either tried to set itself above politics or found itself in alliance with

the state to preserve order. As can be seen in the case of El Salvador, due to the polarization of the society at large, the Church has taken a position of commitment to bringing about a peaceful resolution of the conflict, and to a peaceful change in the political and social order.

Human Rights:
The Role of the State and the Church

KENNETH W. THOMPSON

The role of state and church in foreign policy has become blurred in part because some religious figures on both extremes of the political spectrum have claimed for themselves semi-official standing in politics. In an era of crusading politics and ideological polarization, religious leaders have — more recently on the far right and somewhat earlier on the far left — asserted that they speak for a definable body of religious opinion. In making this claim and defending it as religious spokesmen, they have preempted for their followers free and open discussion of complex issues, including relations with the Soviet Union, American policy toward South Africa, and human rights.

Ironically, their claim to speak for the religious right or the religious left, and by implication for the whole of the right-minded religious community, has come at a time when more detached observers and thinkers are inspiring a search for great clarity of thought on certain outstanding issues of foreign policy. For example, successive administrations in Washington, D.C. have redirected the focus on human rights from an essentially skeptical view (Richard Nixon-Henry Kissinger) to a public campaign for human rights (Jimmy Carter) to a pulling back from too great an emphasis on human rights (Ronald Reagan). Thus, objective observers can point to a body of historical experience and public policy that illustrates how perplexing the molding of a human rights policy can be.

Moreover, human rights are a manifestation of a larger issue with which the nation has struggled since its founding — the issue of morality and foreign policy. It is often asked why it is that the United States returns to the writings of the Founding Fathers preserved in *The Federalist Papers* and other early political writings. One answer is that Thomas Jefferson, Alexander Hamilton, James Madison, John

Jay, and John Adams grappled with the most fundamental issues of the purpose and process of the nation's policies. Their discussion centered on timeless issues of power, authority, and the national interest. They discussed what was enduring and basic, not what was transient and of concern only for the moment.

Moreover, the authors of *The Federalist Papers* sought to test propositions about politics and foreign policy in the crucible of experience. They examined the rights of man, not alone in philosophy and thought, but as they emerged in the policies and practices of men and nation. Thus, they considered ideology and national interest not as disembodied concepts, but as they applied to the issue of American intervention in support of the French Revolution. In short, the nation's founders examined principles of politics and foreign policy in action. They wrote and spoke as responsible officials.

It is the problem of responsibility that intrudes itself most directly when one considers the role of the churches in politics and foreign policy. Churchmen, like intellectuals and scientists, have no constitutional responsibility for public policy. They are not elected officials. No one has chosen them as responsible officials. They have not taken an oath of office to defend the Constitution and the nation. They are not custodians of the national interest. For the most part, they are far removed from the sources of information about a problem. Even when they have information, they tend to be believers for whom facts are less important than faith. Few are disposed to seek compromise and accommodation on an issue. Their tendency is to want to prevail. As one turns to a problem such as human rights, the contribution of churchmen is sometimes less helpful than their supporters would imagine. The rights of churchmen to speak are unquestioned, however. This fact makes vital their study of the issues and the problems that surround human rights in international affairs.

The past two decades in America have witnessed an increasing consciousness of the issues of morality and politics in foreign policy. Some of the consciousness raising has been the result of the writings and speeches of important thinkers. Part of the impetus has come from the nature of the world crisis, especially the aftermath of two world wars. Another factor is doubtless the ebb and flow or the cyclical nature of the concerns of American leaders and of the public, which is inspired and mobilized by their leaders. The renewal of historic traditions must also be seen as having played a part, especially as such traditions are juxtaposed with political and international practice.

For observers in every nation, the temptation to describe their nation's own approaches and writings as altogether unique is strong. An opposite tendency, from which internationalists are not immune, is to assume that all nations and cultures are essentially the same in their perspectives on ethics and foreign policy. Thus, it would be difficult to equate the writings of Jefferson with those of Adolf Hitler, who, in 1923, defended himself at his own trial when accused of seeking to take over the state government of Bavaria by force in the Beer Hall Putsch, saying: "In political life there is no such thing as principles of foreign policy. The programmatic principles of my party are its doctrine on the racial problem and its fight against pacifism and internationalism. But foreign policy, in itself, is merely a means to an end. In questions of foreign policy, I shall never admit that I am tied by anything." His blatant cynicism in invoking the Wilsonian principle of national self-determination to justify German actions in Austria and Czechoslovakia rested on the proposition that "war is life. Any struggle is war.... What is war but cunning, deception, delusion, attack, and surprise?" As Herman Rauschning recounted in *The Voice of Destruction*, Hitler told his close associates that neither arguments nor international law would prevent him from using any advantage or instrument to achieve his ends.

Whatever the limits of law or principle in world politics, an important distinction is worth making. There is a significant difference between saying that foreign policy is subject to no restraints and saying that moral restraints are relative rather than absolute and are influenced by time and place. The difference between no restraints and those that are determined by interests and traditions is crucial. A dialogue on human rights between the late Hans J. Morgenthau and some of his critics helps illustrate this point:

HANS J. MORGENTHAU: One point I wanted to make concerned the relativity of moral judgment. In my view there is one moral code, filtered through cultural and moral particularities. In other words, you cannot say that this statement or that action is immoral per se. You have to put it into context and adapt your judgment to particular circumstances.

QUESTION: May I ask a clarification? You say there is one moral code. I would just like to ask what you have in mind by a moral code?

MORGENTHAU: I personally believe that it is impossible to postulate a plausible moral code without a theological foundation. But how you formulate that foundation is a difficult theological question. I do not believe that you can postulate, for instance, the dignity of human life or the sacredness of human life without a theological foundation.

QUESTION: What I was after was whether you saw the moral code as being there to be discovered, or whether it was emergent.

MORGENTHAU: I would say that it is something objective which is to be discovered. It is not a product of history.

QUESTION: Professor Morgenthau, you say there is a universal moral code. What would you consider to be some of the central principles or rules that are applicable to international politics today? How does that universal moral code relate to cultural relativism? How does one distinguish between a universal moral code and cultural particularism?

MORGENTHAU: Let me discuss a concrete example from my own recent experience—the question of lying. I once was deceived consistently by a close friend. I resented it to the point that I severed our relationship. On the other hand, I was lied to by Henry Kissinger time and again in his capacity as Secretary of State, and it amused me. I stick to the fundamental principle that lying is immoral. But I realize that when you are dealing in the context of foreign policy, lying is inevitable. In private affairs, however, you do not deceive others, especially friends.

Foreign policy operates in an entirely different social contest. Deception becomes a necessary remedy against the dangers to which the nation is exposed. For if you do not deceive others, if you do not accept the principle that is *homo homini lupus* (one man is to another like a wolf), then you will not survive. In other words, the principle of self-preservation forces you to deceive your companion, who is also your opponent. Different existential situations require actions, which, if you were doing for yourself, would be immoral. As Count Cavour put it succinctly, if we had done for ourselves what we had done for Italy, what scoundrels we would have been.

COMMENT: Don't you think, Hans, that diplomats have to distinguish situations? Bad diplomats lie to allies and colleagues. As long as we are speaking of specific personalities, this was a weakness of John Foster Dulles as Secretary of State. On the other hand, in war, deception of the enemy is appropriate. In warfare, lying is proper in any moral code. When you say that lying is inevitable, I hope you mean to confine it to war-time and not necessarily to dealing with allies. As you have pointed out, lying to your friends, to your colleagues in the domestic sphere is another breach of morals.

MORGENTHAU: I do not erect lying to be a positive pillar of statecraft.

QUESTION: Is it possible that lying, even in international affairs, would have a destructive effect?

MORGENTHAU: Yes, surely, I am far from saying to diplomats, go and lie. But look at the famous statement of Sir Henry Wooton in the sixteenth century, that an "ambassador is an honest man, sent to lie abroad for the good of his country." Again, this is an exaggeration of the basic truth that what is morally condemned in individual relations isn't necessarily morally condemned in relations of states.

COMMENT: Lying is not good politics either to your friends or to your enemies. It is better not to say anything than to lie. I learned what I know about international politics from Professor Morgenthau twenty-five years ago. I am also a long-time student of the most successful political machine in American politics and the principles on which it operates in Chicago. I do not think that politicians in Chicago are different from politicians in Peking or Moscow or anywhere else. One of the things they do not do—they almost never lie. They will not promise to do anything unless they can deliver it. They would rather do nothing.

A precinct captain will not tell a constituent he will do something unless he can get it done. A ward committeeman will try not to promise a job to a precinct captain unless he can deliver. The late Mayor of Chicago, Richard Daley, would not promise anybody anything unless he could get it done. They operated on the principle that it is better not to lie to your friends because they will never trust you again.

HUMAN RIGHTS: THE ROLE OF STATE AND CHURCH

And it is also better not to lie to your enemies either because that is very dangerous. They need to be able to rely on your word. So, while people may lie, it is not good politics.

MORGENTHAU: You certainly have a very important point. The ability of the machine to govern is based upon the confidence people have in its word.

COMMENT: And even its enemies have to be able to trust that. There is a qualification even with Sir Henry Wooton's principle of lying for, as Harold Nicolson wrote, while it is sometimes true a diplomat was a man sent abroad to deceive in the interests of his country, a diplomat must also return to negotiate another day. For a diplomat to negotiate effectively, a nexus of confidence and trust has to develop.

MORGENTHAU: Surely. The only point I was trying to make is the difference in moral principles which apply to the private citizen in his relations with other private citizens and to the public figure in dealing with other public figures. I agree with everything you just said.[1]

While truth-telling may be a principle that is not always and everywhere applicable in international politics, it is a factor of consequence, though subject to a process of intellectual and moral discrimination. Morgenthau offered one example of that process. Another is illustrated in the tension between two conflicting principles in the Trans-World Airlines (TWA) hijacking in the summer of 1985. Justice Oliver Wendell Holmes wrote: "People are always extolling the man of principle; but I think the superior man is one who knows he must find his way in a maze of principles." President Reagan's response to the hijacking was to announce that the United States would not negotiate or make concessions to the terrorists. To do otherwise would be to invite future hijacking. This was the public position of the government of the United States. Privately, the government sought to explore every available channel for contacts with those who might assist in freeing the hostages: the Red Cross, the Israelis, the Lebanese Minister of Justice, and the Syrians. It would be difficult to assign truth-telling to one and not the other endeavor. The fact they coexist in such circumstances testifies to the complexity of international politics.

If one turns to the subject of human rights against this background, it can be said that from the beginning, the American political tradition has recognized such rights. Moreover, Americans did not confine the writ for human rights within one nation's territorial boundaries. Benjamin Franklin wrote, "Establishing the liberties of America will not only make the people happy, but will . . . [diminish] the misery of those who in other parts of the world groan under despotism." Abraham Lincoln considered that the Civil War was a trial not only

---

1. Hans J. Morgenthau, *Human Rights and Foreign Policy,* First Distinguished CRIA Lecture on Morality and Foreign Policy (New York: CRIA, 1979), 10-13.

for Americans, but for the world. Until then, as he declared in a speech on 10 November 1864: "It . . . [had] long been a grave question whether any government, not *too strong* for the liberties of its people, can be strong *enough* to maintain its own existence, in great emergencies." The Civil War, he said on 13 May 1862, "involves, in my judgment, not only the civil and religious liberties of our own dear land, but in a large degree the civil and religious liberties of mankind in many countries and through many ages."

Lincoln was also conscious of the limits of his knowledge and his nation's virtue, however. On 15 November 1861, the renowned historian George Bancroft wrote Lincoln, declaring that the "Civil War is the instrument of divine Providence to root out social slavery; posterity will not be satisfied . . . unless . . . the war shall effect an increase of free states." Lincoln replied in the most guarded language saying, "The main thought in . . . your letter is one which does not escape my attention, and with which I must deal in all due caution and the best judgment I can bring to it." It was the American example of a society worthy of emulation that Lincoln stressed, not the existence of a model that could be exported or imposed on other societies.[2]

In every major European revolution against monarchy or aristocracy in the eighteenth and nineteenth centuries, certain Americans demanded that America underwrite the cause of humanity. Men like Noah Webster and Henry Clay were in the forefront of those who sought to induce others "to govern with a lighter hand." Almost always, such leaders spoke for those who had no power.

For another group, these cherished values, while vital, were not the primary determinants of policy. For leaders such as Alexander Hamilton and George Washington, the United States had a world mission, but it was one that had to be filtered through the requirements of separate national interests. Hamilton expressed this view in the Pacificus and Americanus papers. President Washington explained that "it is a maxim, founded on the universal experience of mankind, that no nation is to be trusted further than it is bound by its interest; and no prudent statesman or politician will venture to depart from it."[3] Some of the nation's most idealistic statesmen, including Jefferson, Madison, Lincoln, and John Quincy Adams, urged not American involvement in revolutions for human rights abroad, but the creation of an exemplary society at home. When President

---

2. Kenneth W. Thompson, ed., *Essays on Lincoln's Faith and Politics* (Lanham, Md.: University Press of America, 1983), 99, 100.
3. John C. Fitzpatrick, ed., *The Writings of George Washington* (Washington, D.C.: United States Printing Office, 1931-44), 10:363.

James K. Polk in 1845 urged that the United States' interest in the Western Hemisphere be universalized in the global Monroe Doctrine, John C. Calhoun rose to oppose him on the floor of the Senate, declaring: "No wise man . . . could pledge himself, by declaration, to do that which was beyond the power of execution, and without mature reflections on the consequences. There would be no dignity in it. True dignity consists in making no declaration which we are not prepared to maintain. If we make the declaration, we ought to be prepared to carry it into effect against all opposition."

None of the nineteenth-century revolutions in Europe or Asia succeeded because of what the United States did or failed to do. All reflected a worldwide trend toward self-determination and democracy. They apparently drew strength from the American example, not from political or military intervention.

The change in the American perspective came at the turn of the century. President William McKinley defended the Spanish-American War and the acquisition of the Philippines in humanitarian terms. Intervention was justified primarily by moral sentiment, not national interest. This trend reached its height with President Woodrow Wilson who, following Immanuel Kant, dreamed of a League made up of peaceful and democratic states. The post-World War I international order was to internationalize democratic values and the status quo. Leon Trotsky, who was Wilson's intellectual and political antipode, looked to communism as the route to international peace and justice. The two ideological spokesmen faced one another: each committed to opposing values and goals.

It is this constellation of political and moral forces that has inspired important thinkers who have generated more thoughtful discussions of human rights. Historian Arnold J. Toynbee chose to see the two competing political ideologies as gadflies to one another. The competition between Soviet communism and American democracy, Toynbee felt, would stimulate each side to outreach itself in striving to attain socially worthwhile goals. Cambridge historian Herbert Butterfield was less sanguine about such an outcome and feared the clash of two self-contained systems of national self-righteousness. Reinhold Niebuhr wrote that "the ordinary affairs of the community, the structure of politics and economics, must be governed by the spirit of justice."

In the national and international realms, however, love is practically impossible because it fails to consider the sinfulness of man and the power and persistence of self-interests. Justice is at best an "approximation of brotherhood under conditions of sin." Those who ignore the relativity of justice cannot make proximate moral judgments; they forever seek to absolutize one ideal or principle. Diplomacy and politics, however, "require a shrewd admixture of principle and expediency, of loyalty to general standards of justice and adjustment to actual power." Justice requires discriminate judgments between competing and often contradictory principles and goals. Writing in 1963, Niebuhr explained that "society . . . merely cumulates the egoism of individuals and transmutes their individual altruism into collective egoism so that egoism of the group has a double force. For this reason, no group acts from purely unselfish . . . interest, and politics is therefore bound to be a contest of power."[4]

Alongside the human rights proposals advanced by rival states in the Cold War, these views of contemporary thinkers help to provide a context for human rights debates and to concentrate attention on the nature of international politics as they affect the attainment of moral purpose. The various postwar thinkers in international morality have kept the discussion within more realistic bounds, undoubtedly inspiring leaders such as Secretary of State Cyrus Vance to warn against "stridency" in the human rights debate.

Another force that has given impetus to human rights is the nature of the world crisis. The struggle between the Union of Soviet Socialist Republics and the United States has been joined on two levels: power and ideology. The two have been mutually reenforcing, as the latter has fueled and added an internal dynamic to the power struggle, while the former has set boundaries within which the competition between communism and democracy has been waged. It is not accidental that the emphasis on human rights has come in the late 1970s and 1980s. Collectivism, viewed as the hope of mankind in the 1930s and 1940s, is now seen as posing contradictions and conflicts. Neither national socialism nor Stalinism has brought the millennium. Tyranny has accompanied authoritarian approaches to social justice, and even the most moral liberal experiments in social planning have created as many problems as they have solved. Collectivist political orders have stifled individual initiatives and trampled individual rights in the dust.

James Reston has written, "A generation or so ago it was the Western nations and their institutions that were defending the status quo while the Communist nations were demanding change. But now all this is quite different." The West, he points out, has taken the initiative diplomatically and ideologically, and while it has not yet found a way to harness its two-tiered program in some more coherent

---

4. See Reinhold Niebuhr, *Structure of Nations and Empires* (New York: Scribner, 1959).

grand design, it has begun to throw off the shackles of self-doubt and intellectual and spiritual malaise. Proponents of internationalism and the national interest have hardly reconciled their differences or even begun to listen to one another's valid points, and no one in any of the leading Western governments has grappled convincingly with the tensions between human rights and national sovereignty.

Diplomats and lawyers pass one another in their arguments at every intellectual and political crossroad, yet the beginnings of a valid exchange can be found in some of their more perceptive statements. The sense of longing for a different future world was evident in the selection of a Polish pope, the first non-Italian elected in more than four hundred years. Symbolically, the new pope appeals to the world because he is both a foe of communist authoritarianism and a social liberal on questions of justice. Reston concludes,

It is not Moscow or Peking but Washington that is trying to bring about a reconciliation between the Arabs and the Israelis in the Middle East or between the blacks and whites in sub-Saharan Africa. It is not Moscow or Peking but Washington, London, Paris, Bonn and the other Western capitals that are worrying about the control of population, nuclear weapons and nuclear wastes, industrial pollution and international anarchy in the airways of the world.

Perhaps significantly, Reston, in his column entitled "The West Is Ready to Embrace Change," made no mention of human rights, but the significance may result not from his rejecting the issue of human rights, but in placing it in the broader context of national and international politics. The subject of human rights, it would appear, is too important and too many-sided to be left exclusively to the protagonists of civil rights. Human rights are one facet of worldwide change, but not the totality.

The ebb and flow and the cyclical nature of the concerns of leaders and the public may be seen in the Carter human rights campaign and the changes wrought by President Ronald Reagan. As a presidential candidate, Jimmy Carter, having raised the issue of human rights late in the presidential campaign of 1976, pressed his views, at first rather tentatively in a Democratic issues forum in Louisville in late 1975, then in a speech the following March in Chicago, and finally in a more general statement in October 1976 at the University of Notre Dame in the second debate with President Ford. The issue, according to his pollster, Patrick Caddell, was "a very strong issue across the board," appealing to the followers of Senator Henry Jackson, to Jews concerned with the Soviet treatment of Jews, and to liberals concerned with Korea and Chile.

The politics of campaigning are often far removed from the politics of governance, and once in office the task confronting the Carter administration was to fashion viable human rights policies. In the words of the brilliant Washington journalist, Elizabeth Drew, "Having arrived, through a variety of circumstances, at a policy idea, the Administration's next problems were to define it, to find methods of implementing, and to reconcile it with various conflicting goals."[5] The issue had moved from the realm of ends to one of means.

The sequence of early administration effort is well known: the letter to President Carter from Andrei Sakharov, the Soviet nuclear physicist and dissident leader, on 28 January 1977; President Carter's personal reply made public by Sakharov on 17 February; the State Department's charge against Czechoslovakia for arresting and harassing signees of Charter 77 (a petition to the Czech government for protection of rights outlined in the Helsinki agreement); and President Carter's messages in February to Leonid Brezhnev and Ambassador Anatoly Dobrynin, as well as several public statements making his intention clear to speak out when human rights were threatened. In March, the president declared in a speech at the United Nations, "No member of the United Nations can claim that mistreatment of its citizens is solely its own business."

Not long thereafter, following the breakdown of talks on arms control in Moscow, Secretary Cyrus Vance on 30 April 1977, in a speech at the University of Georgia Law School, sought to define more precisely the main elements of American policy. Vance distinguished among governmental violations of the integrity of person (torture, arbitrary arrest, denial of a fair trial); fulfillment of vital human needs such as food, shelter, health care, and education; and the right to civil and political liberties such as freedom of speech, press, religion, assembly, movement, and participation in government.

Developmental loan assistance by multinational organizations—the World Bank, for example—through which the United States channels about one-third of its aid to developing countries, presented a special problem. Linkage of human rights with Strategic Arms Limitation Treaty (SALT) talks between the Americans and the Soviets and efforts to control nuclear proliferation in countries like Brazil and Korea also presented a problem. There, American policymakers found it necessary to make trade-offs on conventional arms assistance with economic incentives, such as status within the International Monetary Fund and similar agencies.

Human rights became a part of the overall policy-planning process called Presidential Review Memoranda (PRM) under the chairman-

---

5. Elizabeth Drew, "Human Rights," *The New Yorker*, 18 July 1977, 41.

ship of Undersecretary of State Warren Christopher. Private groups were enlisted. A struggle went on within and outside the government between spokesmen of contending viewpoints on human rights policies. References to human rights by President Carter and other administration officials continued to be made but, following the urgings of Secretary Vance and others, with less stridency. The administration was criticized alternately for doing too much or too little. Such criticism would appear to reflect more the difficult tasks of policy formulation then the abandonment of human rights. If universalizing human rights exceeded the limits of American foreign policy, a selective response brought charges of hypocrisy. The administration trimmed its sails on human rights in South Korea and the Philippines because of common security interests in Southeast and Northeast Asia. Criticisms of repression in Iran were muted because of Iranian oil and investments and Iran's strategic role in relationship to the Middle East and the Soviet Union.

In February 1977, Secretary Vance reminded the Senate Foreign Operations Committee, "In each case we must balance a political concern for human rights against economic and security goals." Statements of key administration leaders suggested a line of policy in which prudence replaced idealism. Marshall Shulman warned in 1974 in testimony before a Senate committee that any United States effort to improve human rights in the USSR would "pose conditions which the present Soviet regime cannot but regard as terms of surrender and of self-liquidation." Even National Security Advisor Zbigniew Brezinskii admitted that "a limited democratization of the Soviet society . . . would threaten the present political leadership."

If the Carter administration in its early days claimed too much for human rights, the Reagan administration claimed too little. Its first nominee for the human rights position was rejected for confirmation after protracted hearings. The successful nominee proved considerably more attentive to the importance of human rights. In El Salvador and elsewhere, prompted by Congress and joining forces with more enlightened national leadership, the administration shifted from a passive to a more active policy.

Historic traditions persist, however. The tension between human rights and national sovereign rights appears at one level to be the classic tension existent in all politics between general and particular or universal and national goals. The Universal Declaration of Human Rights proclaims the rights of mankind; the Bill of Rights declares that individual Americans enjoy certain inalienable rights under the Constitution. The observer striving to relate mankind's human rights and the rights of Americans or Russians or Nigerians may apply the concepts Crane Brinton employed when he wrote of the one and the many, the worldwide in contrast with particular local or regionally defined groups. Between the one and the many or the universal and the particular, tension almost inescapably will exist if only because full attainment of universality by definition means the undermining of what is separate, unique, and particular. Philosophically, universalism and particularism are in tension in any given political order, especially with reference to the exercise of sovereign authority within that order.

It is in this context that the church has a contribution to make. It speaks out of a tradition that is fundamental to the rights and responsibilities of the individual. Churchmen who have a hope that transcends human existence have the grounds for patience in practical politics. Christian realism, as theologians such as Reinhold Niebuhr defined it, knows that anything worth preserving cannot be achieved in a lifetime. What is strange is that this long view of time and eternity should have been driven from the contemporary religious and political scene by forces difficult to fathom. In part, such forces are technological and commercial: the linkage of television and religious fund raising. They may also stem from the emergence of a few charismatic and combative television preachers.

Whatever the cause of the demise of a more profound perspective on religion and politics, the role of the church persists. Churchmen speak out of a tradition that understands human nature. Church fathers and theologians like Reinhold Niebuhr and Paul Tillich understand the relationship of prophesy and politics. It is right that individual churchmen speak out on moral issues, including those on which statesmen may have to remain silent. As Robert Kennedy once told a group of church leaders, "Keep the pressure on us and help us to transcend a narrow view of the national interest." Churchmen can press for actions and policies that may be impossible for leaders who must balance competing national policies.

In summary, there is a role for churchmen on human rights provided they guard against the self-righteousness of the zealot. They must never forget that their political leaders and not they, themselves, carry the heavy burdens of responsibility from the sidelines. Therefore, churchmen should be true to their faith, but humble and forgiving in what they demand of their leaders.

CONTRIBUTORS

HENRY J. ABRAHAM is James Hart Professor of Government and Foreign Affairs, University of Virginia, Charlottesville. His publications include *Freedom and the Court* (1982), *American Democracy* (1986), and *The Judicial Process* (1986).

ISMA'IL R. AL FARUQI was Professor of Islamics, Temple University, Philadelphia, Pennsylvania. His publications include *'Urubah and Religion* (1962), *The Great Asian Religions* (1969), and *Historical Atlas of the Religions of the World* (1974).

BAHMAN BAKHTIARI is Assistant Professor of International Relations, Department of Political Science, University of Maine Orono, Maine. His articles have appeared in *Comparative Strategy* and *Journal of Church and State*. He is author of the forthcoming volume, *Religion and World Politics*.

R. PIERCE BEAVER was Professor of Missions and Ecumenics the Divinity School, University of Chicago. His publications include *Ecumenical Beginnings in Protestant World Mission* (1962), *Envoys of Peace* (1964), and *Church, State, and the American Indian* (1966), several chapters of which originally appeared in *Journal of Church and State*.

ERNST BENZ was Professor of Church and Dogmatic History at Philip University, Marburg on the Lahn, West Germany and a member of the Akademie der Wissenschaften und der Literatur of Mainz. His publications include *The Eastern Orthodox Church* (1963) and *Buddhism or Communism: Which Holds the Future of Asia?* (1965).

BOHDAN R. BOCIURKIW is Professor of Political Science, Carleton University, Ottawa, Ontario, Canada. His publications include *Religion and Atheism in the USSR and Eastern Europe* (1975) and numerous articles in scholarly books and periodicals.

HENRY WARNER BOWDEN is Professor and Chair, Department of Religion, Douglass College, Rutgers University, New Brunswick, New Jersey. His publications include *Church History in the Age of Science* (1971), *Dictionary of American Religious Biography* (1977), and *American Indians and Christian Missions: Studies in Cultural Conflict* (1981).

JANICE A. BROUN is a British free-lance journalist whose articles have also appeared in *The Christian Century, Commonweal*, and *Liberty*.

CONRAD CHERRY is Director of Scholars Press and formerly Professor of Religious Studies, Pennsylvania State University, University Park. His publications include *The Theology of Jonathan Edwards* (1966), *God's New Israel: Religious Interpretations of American Destiny* (1971), and *Horace Bushnell* (1985).

A. F. CARRILLO DE ALBORNOZ was Secretary of the Secretariat on Religious Liberty, World Council of Churches, Geneva, Switzerland. His publications include *Roman Catholicism and Religious Liberty* (1959), and *The Basis of Religious Liberty* (1963), and *Religious Liberty* (1967).

A. ROY ECKARDT is Professor Emeritus of Religious Studies, Lehigh University, Bethlehem, Pennsylvania. His publications include *Elder and Younger Brothers* (1973), *Long Night's Journey into Day* (1982), and *Jews and Christians: The Contemporary Meeting* (1986).

JAMES LEO GARRETT, JR. is Professor of Theology, Southwestern Baptist Theological Seminary, Fort Worth, Texas. His publications include *The Concept of the Believers' Church* (1969), *Baptist Relations with Other Christians* (1974), and *Calvin and the Reformed Tradition* (1980).

EDWIN SCOTT GAUSTAD is Professor of History, University of California, Riverside. His publications include *A Religious History of America* (1966; rev. ed. 1989), *Documentary History of Religion in America*, 2 vols. (1982, 1983), and *Faith of Our Fathers: Religion and the New Nation* (1987).

WINTHROP S. HUDSON is Adjunct Professor of Religion, University of North Carolina, Chapel Hill. His publications include *The Great Tradition of the American Churches* (1953), Religion in America (1965;

NOTES ON CONTRIBUTORS

4th rev. ed., 1987), and *The Cambridge Connection and the Elizabethan Settlement* (1980).

DEAN M. KELLEY is Director of Civil and Religious Liberty, National Council of Churches of Christ in the U.S.A., New York City. His publications include *Why Conservative Churches Are Growing: A Study in Sociology of Religion* (1972, 1984), *Why Churches Should Not Pay Taxes* (1977), and *Government Intervention in Religious Affairs, I and II* (1982, 1986).

KENNETH SCOTT LATOURETTE was Sterling Professor of Missions and Oriental History, Yale University, New Haven, Connecticut. His numerous publications include *A History of the Expansion of Christianity*, 7 vols. (1937-1945), *Christianity in a Revolutionary Age*, 5 vols. (1958-1972), and *A History of Christianity* (1953).

FRANKLIN HAMLIN LITTELL is Professor Emeritus of Religion Studies, Temple University, Philadelphia, Pennsylvania. His publications include *From State Church to Pluralism: A Protestant Interpretation of Religion in American History* (1962; rev. ed., 1971), *The Crucifixion of the Jews* (1975), and *The Macmillan Atlas History of Christianity* (1976).

MARTIN E. MARTY is Fairfax M. Cone Professor of Modern Christianity, Divinity School, University of Chicago. His numerous publications include *Righteous Empire: The Protestant Experience in America* (1975), *Pilgrims in Their Own Land* (1984), and *Modern American Religion*, Vol. 1: *The Irony of It all, 1893-1919* (1986).

SIDNEY E. MEAD is Professor Emeritus of Religion in American History, School of Religion and the Department of History, University of Iowa, Iowa City. His publications include *The Lively Experiment* (1963), *The Nation with the Soul of a Church* (1975), and *The Old Religion in the Brave New World: Reflections on the Relation Between Christendom and the Republic* (1977).

ROBERT T. MILLER is Professor and Chair, Department of Political Science, Baylor University, Waco, Texas. His publications include (coauthor) *Church and State in Scripture, History and Constitutional Law* (1958) and *Toward Benevolent Neutrality: Church, State, and the Supreme Court* (1977; 3rd ed., 1987).

WILLIAM LEE MILLER is Professor of Ethics and Institutions and Chair of Department of Rhetoric and Communication Studies, University of Virginia, Charlottesville. His publications include *Piety Along the Potomac* (1964), *Of Thee, Nevertheless I Sing: An Essay on American Political Values* (1975), and *The First Liberty: Religion and the American Republic* (1986).

JOHN J. MITCHELL, JR. is Associate Professor of Religious Studies, Seton Hall University, South Orange, New Jersey. He is coauthor of *Peace Making* (1985) and author of *Critical Voices in American Catholic Economic Thought* (1989) and various articles in scholarly periodicals.

NIELS C. NIELSEN, JR. is a J. Newton Rayzor Professor of Philosophy and Religious Thought and Chair of Religious Studies, Rice University, Houston, Texas. His publications include *God in Education* (1966), *Solzhenitsyn's Religion* (1976), and *The Crisis of Human Rights* (1978).

LEO PFEFFER is Adjunct Professor of Political Science, Long Island University, Long Island, New York. His publications include *Church, State and Freedom* (1953; rev. ed., 1967), *God, Caesar, and the Constitution* (1975), and *Religion, State, and the Burger Court* (1984).

JOHN S. ROMANIDES is formerly Professor of Dogmatics and History of Theology of Holy Cross Greek Theological School, Brookline, Massachusetts and formerly Editor of the *Greek Orthodox Theological Review*. He currently resides in Thessaloniki, Greece.

EPHRAIM TABORY is Chair and Senior Lecturer, Department of Sociology and Anthropology, Bar Ilan University, Ramat Gan, Israel. His articles have appeared in *Ethnicity, Journal of Higher Education*, and *Journal of Peace Research*. He is coauthor of the forthcoming volume, *Americans Abroad: A Comparative Study of Emigrants from the United States*.

NOBUHIKO TAKIZAWA is Professor of Law, Kitakyushu City University, Tokuyama City, Japan. He is author of *Separation of Religion and the State: The Development of Judicial Doctrines in the United States* (1985), in Japanese, and has published articles in *Journal of Law and Political Science* (Japan).

KENNETH W. THOMPSON is J. Wilson Newman Professor of Government and Foreign Affairs and Director of the White Burkett Miller Center of Public Affairs, University of Virginia, Charlottesville. His publications include *Christian Ethics and the Dilemmas of Foreign*

Policy (1959), *Understanding World Politics* (1975), and *Morality and Foreign Policy* (1980).

JAMES E. WOOD, JR. is Ethel and Simon Bunn Professor of Church-State Studies and Director of the J. M. Dawson Institute of Church-State Studies, Baylor University, Waco, Texas. Founding Editor of *Journal of Church and State*, his publications include *Nationhood and the Kingdom* (1977), *Religion and the State: Essays in Honor of Leo Pfeffer* (1985), and *Ecumenical Perspectives on Church and State: Protestant, Catholic, and Jewish* (1988).

GORDON C. ZAHN is Professor Emeritus of Sociology, University of Massachusetts, Boston, and National Director of the Center on Conscience and War. His publications include *German Catholics and Hitler's Wars* (1962), *In Solitary Witness: The Life and Death of Franz Jaegerstaetter* (1964), and *War, Conscience, and Dissent* (1964).